Monetary Economics

D1522312

From the same authors:

Wynne Godley

Industrial Pricing in the United Kingdom (with Ken Coutts and William D. Nordhaus) (Cambridge: Cambridge University Press) 1978.

Macroeconomics (with Francis Cripps) (Oxford: Oxford University Press) 1983.

Marc Lavoie

Macroéconomie: Théories et controverses postkeynésiennes (Paris: Dunod) 1987.

Foundations of Post-Keynesian Economic Analysis (Aldershot: Edward Elgar) 1992.

Milton Friedman et son œuvre, (co-edited with Mario Seccareccia) (Montréal: Presses de l'Université de Montréal) 1993.

Avantage numérique, l'argent et la Ligue nationale de hockey (Hull: Vents d'Ouest) 1997.

Désavantage numérique, les francophones dans la LNH (Hull: Vents d'Ouest) 1998.

Central Banking in the Modern World: Alternative Perspectives (co-edited with Mario Seccareccia) (Cheltenham: Edward Elgar) 2004.

Introduction to Post-Keynesian Economics (London: Palgrave/Macmillan) 2006.

Microeconomics: Principles and Policy, First Canadian Edition (with William J. Baumol, Alan S. Blinder and Mario Seccareccia) (Toronto: Nelson Education) 2009.

Macroeconomics: Principles and Policy, First Canadian Edition (with William J. Baumol, Alan S. Blinder and Mario Seccareccia) (Toronto: Nelson Education) 2009.

Money and Macroeconomic Issues: Alfred Eichner and Post Keynesian Economics (co-edited with Louis-Philippe Rochon and Mario Seccareccia) (Armonk: M.E. Sharpe) 2010.

Monetary Economics

An Integrated Approach to Credit, Money, Income, Production and Wealth

Second Edition by

Wynne Godley
Late Emeritus Professor, King's College, Cambridge University, Cambridge, United Kingdom

and

Marc Lavoie
Professor, Department of Economics, University of Ottawa, Canada

First edition published 2006
This edition published 2012 by
PALGRAVE MACMILLAN

Palgrave Macmillan in the UK is an imprint of Macmillan Publishers Limited, registered in England, company number 785998, of Houndmills, Basingstoke, Hampshire RG21 6XS.

Palgrave Macmillan in the US is a division of St Martin's Press LLC, 175 Fifth Avenue, New York, NY 10010.

Palgrave Macmillan is the global academic imprint of the above companies and has companies and representatives throughout the world.

Palgrave® and Macmillan® are registered trademarks in the United States, the United Kingdom, Europe and other countries.

ISBN 978–0–230–30184–9 paperback

This book is printed on paper suitable for recycling and made from fully managed and sustained forest sources. Logging, pulping and manufacturing processes are expected to conform to the environmental regulations of the country of origin.

A catalogue record for this book is available from the British Library.

A catalog record for this book is available from the Library of Congress.

Contents

Notations Used in the Book

A_d	Advances demanded by private banks
A, A_s	Central bank advances made to private banks
add	Random change in liquidity preference
add_{bL}	Spread of bond rate over the bill rate
add_1	Spread of bill rate over the deposit rate
add_2	Random change in government expenditures
AF	Amortization funds
$B_£^\$$	Bills held by £ households but issued by the $ country
$B_\$^£$	Bills held by $ households but issued by the £ country
$B_{cb£}^\$$	Bills held by the £ central bank but issued by the $ country (foreign reserves of country £)
$B_{cb\$}^\$$	Bills held by $ central bank and issued by the $ country
$B_{cb£}^£$	Bills held by the £ central bank and issued by the £ country
B_d, B_{hd}	Bills demanded by households (ex ante)
B_b, B_{bd}	Bills actually demanded by banks
B_{bdN}	Bills notionally demanded by banks
B_{cb}	Bills held by the central bank
B_h, B_{hh}	Bills held by households
B_s	Treasury bills supplied by government
$bandB, bandT$	Lower and upper range of the flat Phillips curve
BL_d	Long-term bonds demanded by households
BL_h	Long-term bonds held by households
BL_s	Long-term bonds issued by government
BLR	Bank liquidity ratio, actual or gross value
BLR_N	Bank liquidity ratio, net of advances
$BLPR$	Banks liquidity pressure ratio
bot	Bottom of an acceptable range
$botpm$	Bottom of the acceptable range of the profitability margin of banks

BP	Balance of payments
BPM	Bank profit margin
BUR	Relative burden of interest payments on loans taken by households
c, c_d	Consumption goods demand by households, in real terms
C_d	Consumption goods demand by households, in nominal terms
C, C_s	Consumption goods supply by firms, in nominal terms
CAB	Current account balance
CAR	Realized capital adequacy ratio of banks
CF	Cash flow of firms
CG	Capital gains
CG^e	Expected capital gains of the current period
DA	Depreciation allowance
DEF	Government deficit
DS	Nominal domestic sales
ds	Real domestic sales
dxr_e	Expected change in the exchange rate
E, E_f, E_b	Value of equities, issued by firms, issued by banks
e_b	Number of equities supplied by banks
e_d	Number of firms' equities demanded by households
e_s, e_f	Number of equities supplied by firms
ER	Employment rate (the complement of the unemployment rate)
ERr_{bL}	Expected rate of return on long-term bonds
F	Sum of bank and firm profits
F, F_f	Realized entrepreneurial profits of production firms
F_b	Realized profits of banks
F_b^T	Target profits of banks
F_{cb}	Profits of central bank
F^e	Expected entrepreneurial profits of firms
F_f	Realized entrepreneurial profits of production firms
F_f^e	Expected profits of firms
F_f^T	Target entrepreneurial profits of production firms
F_T	Total profits of firms, inclusive of interest payments on inventories
F_{nipa}	Profits, as measured by national accountants
FD	Business dividends

FD_b	Dividends of banks
FD_f	Realized dividends of production firms
FU	Business retained earnings
FU_b	Retained earnings of banks
FU_b^T	Target retained earnings of banks
FU_f	Realized retained earnings of production firms
FU_f^T	Target retained earnings of production firms
fs	Real fiscal stance
g	Pure government expenditures in real terms
g'	Real total government expenditures (inflation accounted)
G	Pure government expenditures in nominal terms
G_s, G_d	Services supplied to and demanded by government
G_{NT}	Total government expenditures, including interest payments net of taxes
gd	Real government debt
G_T	Total government expenditures, inclusive of interest payments on debt
G_{TD}	Total *domestic* government expenditures
GD	Government debt (public debt), in nominal terms
GL	Gross flow of new loans made to the household sector
gr	Steady-state growth rate of the economy
gr_k	Growth rate of net capital accumulation
gr_g	Growth rate of real pure government expenditures
gr_{pr}	Growth rate of trend labour productivity
H_{bd}	Reserves demanded by banks
H_b, H_{bs}	Reserves supplied to banks by the central bank
H_d, H_{hd}	Cash money demanded by households
H_d, H_h, H_{hh}	Cash money held by households
H_g	Cash money held by government
H_{hs}	Cash money supplied to households by the central bank
H, H_s	High-powered money, or cash money, supplied by the central bank
HC	Historic costs
HC^e	Expected historic costs
HUC	Historic unit cost
HUC^e	Expected historic unit cost
HWC	Historic wage cost

i_d	New fixed capital goods demanded by firms (investment flow), in real terms
I_d	New fixed capital goods demanded by firms (investment flow), in nominal terms
I_h	Residential investment of households
I_s, I, I_f	New fixed capital goods supplied by firms, in nominal terms
in	Realized stock of inventories, in real terms
in^e	Short-run target level (expected level) of inventories, in real terms
in^T	Long-run target level of inventories, in real terms
IN	Realized stock of inventories, at current unit costs
im	Real imports
IM	Imports, in nominal terms
IM_T	Total imports, inclusive of interest payments made abroad
INT_b	Interest payments paid by banks
INT_f	Interest payments paid by firms
INT_h	Interest payments received by households
k, k_f, k_b	Fixed capital stock, in real terms (number of machines), of firms, of banks
K, K_f, K_b, K_h	Value of fixed capital stock, in nominal terms, of firms, of banks, of households
K^T	Targeted capital stock
$KABOSA$	Capital account balance, inclusive of the official settlements account
KAB	Capital account balance, excluding official transactions
L_d, L_{fd}	Loans demanded by firms from banks
L, L_s, L_{fs}, L_f	Loans supplied by banks to firms
L_g	Loans to government sector
L_{hd}	Loans demanded by households from banks
L_{hs}, L_h	Loans supplied by banks to households
M, M_h, M_{hh}	Money deposits actually held by households
$M1, M1_h$	Checking account money deposits held by households

$M1_d$	Checking account money deposits demanded
$M1_s$	Checking account money deposits supplied
$M2, M2_h$	Time or term money deposits held by households
$M2_d$	Time or term money deposits demanded
$M2_s$	Time or term money deposits supplied
$M1_{hN}$	The notional amount of bank checking account deposits that households would hold
M_d, M_{hd}	Money deposits demanded by households
M_f	Financial assets of firms
M_g	Bank deposits of government
m_h	Real money balances held by households
M_s	Money supplied by the government (ch. 3) or the banks
ML	Mean lag
N, N_d	Demand for labour
N_{fe}	The full-employment labour force
N_s^e	Expected supply of labour
N_s	Supply of labour
N^T	Target level of employment by firms
$NAFA$	Net accumulation of financial assets by the household sector (financial saving)
$NCAR$	Normal capital adequacy ratio of banks (Cooke ratio)
$NHUC$	Normal historic unit cost
NL	Net flow of new loans made to the household sector
nl	Real amount of new personal loans
npl	Proportion of non-performing loans
npl^e	Expected proportion of non-performing loans
NPL	Amount of non-performing loans (defaulting loans of firms)
NUC	Normal unit costs
$NW, NW_h, NW_f,$ NW_g, NW_b	Net worth (of households, firms, government, banks)
or	Gold units
OF_b	Own funds (equity capital) of banks
OF_b^e	Short-run own funds target of banks
OF_b^T	Long-run own funds target of banks

p	Price level
p_{bL}	Price of long-term bonds (perpetuities)
p_{bL}^e	Expected price of long-term bonds in the next period
p_{ds}	Price index of domestic sales
p_e, p_{ef}	Price of firms' equities
p_{eb}	Price of banks' equities
p_g	Price of gold
p_k	Price of fixed capital goods
p_m	Price index of imports
p_s	Price index of sales
p_x	Price index of exports
p_y	GDP deflator
PE	Price-earnings ratio
PER_{bL}	Pure expected rate of return on long-term bonds
pr	Labour productivity, or trend labour productivity
$PSBR$	Public sector borrowing requirement (government deficit)
q	The valuation ratio of firms (Tobin's q ratio)
REP	Repayment by household borrowers (payment on principal)
r, r_b	Rate of interest on bills
r, r^e	Actual and expected yield on perpetuities (Appendix 5.2)
r_a	Rate of interest on central bank advances
r_{bL}	Yield on long-term bonds
r_k	Dividend yield
r_l	Rate of interest on bank loans
r_{lN}	Normal rate of interest on bank loans that firms use to set the markup
r_m	Rate of interest on deposits
rr_b	Real rate of interest on bills
rr_b^T	Target real bill rate
Rr_{bl}	Rate of return on bonds
rr_{bL}	Real yield on long-term bonds
rr_c	Real rate of interest on bank loans, deflated by the cost of inventories index
rr_l	Real rate of interest on bank loans
rr_m	Real rate of interest on term deposits

$\check{r}$	Average rate of interest payable on overall government debt
Ra	Random number modifying expectations
s	Realized real sales (in widgets)
s^e	Expected real sales
S	Sales in nominal terms
S^e	Expected sales in nominal terms
SA	Stock appreciation (inventory valuation adjustment IVA)
SAV_h, SAV_f, SAV_g, SAV	Household, business, government, and overall saving
T	Taxes
T_h	Income taxes of households
T_f	Indirect taxes on firms
T_d	Taxes demanded by government
T_s, T_s^e	Taxes supplied or expected to be supplied
top	Top of a target range
$toppm$	Top of a target range of bank profitability
TP	Target proportion of bonds in national debt held by households
UC	Unit cost of production
v	Wealth of households in real terms
V, V_h	Wealth of households, in nominal terms
V^T	Target level of household wealth
V^e	Expected wealth of households, in nominal terms
V_f	Wealth of firms, in nominal terms
V_{fma}	Wealth of households devoted to financial market assets
V_g	Wealth of government, in nominal terms
V_{nc}	Wealth of households, net of cash
V_{nc}^e	Expected wealth of households, net of cash
W	Nominal wage rate
WB	The wage bill, in nominal terms
wb	Real wage bill
x	Real exports
X	Exports in nominal terms
X_T	Total exports, inclusive of interest payments received from abroad

xr	Exchange rate
$xr^\$$	Dollar exchange rate: value of one dollar expressed in pounds
$xr^£$	Sterling exchange rate: value of one pound sterling expressed in dollars
xr_e	Expected level of the future exchange rate
Y	National income, in nominal terms
Y_{fc}	Full-capacity output
Y_T	National income plus government debt service
YD	Disposable income of households
YD^e	Expected disposable income
YD_{hs}	Haig–Simons nominal disposable income (including all capital gains)
YD_r	Regular disposable income
YD_r^e	Expected regular disposable income
YP	Nominal personal income
y	Real output
yd	Deflated regular income
yd_{hs}	Haig–Simons realised real disposable income
yd^e	Expected real disposable income
yd_{hse}	Haig–Simons expected real disposable income
yd_r	Realized real regular disposable income
yd_r^e	Expected real regular disposable income
z	Dichotomic variable or some numerical parameter
zm	Proportional response of the money deposit rate following a change in the bill rate

Greek Letters

α	(alpha)	Consumption parameters
α_0		Autonomous consumption
α_1		Propensity to consume out of regular income
α_2		Propensity to consume out of past wealth
α_3		Implicit target wealth to disposable income ratio of households
α_4		Long-run government debt to GDP ratio
β	(beta)	Reaction parameter related to expectations
γ	(gamma)	Partial adjustment function that applies to inventories and fixed capital
δ	(delta)	Rate of depreciation on fixed capital
δ_{rep}		Rate of amortization on personal loans
ε	(epsilon)	Another reaction parameter related to expectations Export parameter of a country

ζ	(zeta)	Reaction parameter related to changes in interest rates
η	(eta)	New loans to personal income ratio
θ	(theta)	Personal income tax rate
θ'		Taxes to GDP ratio
ι	(iota)	Parameter tied to the impact of interest rates on the propensity to consume
κ	(kappa)	Target fixed capital to output ratio
λ	(lambda)	Reaction parameters in the portfolio choice of households
λ_C		Cash to consumption ratio
μ	(mu)	Import propensity or parameter
v	(nu)	Parameter tied to import prices
ξ	(xi)	Reaction parameter tied to changes in interest rates
o	(omicron)	
π	(pi)	Price inflation rate
π_C		Inflation rate of unit costs
ρ	(ro)	Compulsory reserve ratios on bank deposits
σ	(sigma)	Various measures of inventories to output (or sales) ratio
σ_S		Realized (past period) inventories to sales ratio
σ_{se}		Expected (past period) inventories to sales ratio
σ^N		Normal (past period) inventories to sales ratio
σ^T		Target (current) inventories to sales ratio
τ	(tau)	Sales tax rate
υ	(upsilon)	Parameter tied to export prices
φ	(phi)	Costing margin in pricing
φ^T		Ideal costing margin
$\varphi'/(1 + \varphi')$		Realized share of entrepreneurial profits in sales
χ	(chi)	Weight of conviction in expected bond prices
ψ	(psi)	Target retained earnings to lagged investment ratio
ω	(omega)	Real wage rate
ω^T		Real wage target
Ω	(OMEGA)	Reaction parameters related to real wage targeting
ת	(hebrew letter)	$ת = \Delta p/p$ (nearly price inflation, but not quite)
$\$$		dollar
£		pound sterling

List of Tables

List of Figures

Preface

The premises underlying this book are, first, that modern industrial economies have a complex institutional structure comprising production firms, banks, governments and households and, second, that the evolution of economies through time is dependent on the way in which these institutions take decisions and interact with one another. Our aspiration is to introduce a new way in which an understanding can be gained as to how these very complicated systems work *as a whole*.

Our method is rooted in the fact that every transaction by one sector implies an equivalent transaction by another sector (every purchase implies a sale), while every financial balance (the difference between a sector's income and its outlays) must give rise to an equivalent change in the sum of its balance-sheet (or stock) variables, with every financial asset owned by one sector having a counterpart liability owed by some other. Provided all the sectoral transactions are fully articulated so that 'everything comes from somewhere and everything goes somewhere' such an arrangement of concepts will describe the activities and evolution of the whole economic system, with all financial transactions (including changes in the money supply) fully integrated, at the level of accounting, into the processes which generate factor income, expenditure and production.

As any model which includes the whole range of economic activities described in the national income and flow-of-funds accounts must be extremely complicated, we start off by imagining economies which have unrealistically simplified institutions, and explore how these would work. Then, in stages, we add more and more realistic features until, by the end, the economies we describe bear a fair resemblance to the modern economies we know. In the text we shall employ the narrative method of exposition which Keynes and his followers used, trying to infuse with intuition our conclusions about how particular mechanisms (say the consumption or asset demand functions) work, one at a time, and how they relate to other parts of the economic system. But our underlying method is completely different. Each of our models, before we started to write it up, was set up with its own stock and flow transactions so comprehensively articulated that, however large or small the model, the nth equation was always logically implied by the other $n - 1$ equations. The way in which the system worked as a whole was then explored via computer simulation, by first solving the model in question for its steady state and then discovering its properties by changing assumptions about exogenous variables and parameters.

The text which follows can do no more than provide a narrative supplemented with equations, but we believe that readers' understanding will be enhanced, if not transformed, if they reproduce the simulations for themselves and put each model through its paces as we go along. It should be easy to download each model complete with data and solution routine.[1]

In Chapters 3–5 we present very elementary models, with drastically simplified institutional structures, which will illustrate some basic principles regarding the functioning of dynamic stock-flow consistent (SFC) models, and which incorporate the creation of 'outside' money into the income–expenditure process.

Chapter 6 introduces the open economy, which is developed seamlessly out of a model describing the evolution of two regions within a single country.

Chapters 7–9 present models with progressively more realistic features which, in particular, introduce commercial banks and discuss the role of credit and 'inside' money.

The material in Chapters 10–11 constitutes a break, in terms of complexity and reality, with everything that has gone before. We first present models which describe how inside money and outside money interact, how firms' pricing decisions determine the distribution of the national income and how the financial sector makes it possible for firms and households to operate under conditions of uncertainty. The Chapter 11 model includes a representation of growth, investment, equity finance and inflation.

Finally, in Chapter 12, we return to the open economy (always conceived as a closed system comprising two economies trading merchandise and assets with one another) and flesh-out the Chapter 6 model with additional realistic features.

It has taken many years to generate the material presented here. But we are painfully aware that this is only a beginning which leaves everything to play for.

W.G. and M.L.

Background memories (by W.G.)

My first significant memory as an economist was the moment in 1944 when P.W.S Andrews, my brilliant teacher at Oxford, got me to extrude a question from my mind: Is output determined by the intersection of marginal revenue with marginal cost curves or is it determined by aggregate demand? Thus I was vouchsafed a precocious vision of the great divide which was to obsess me for years.

---

[1] At http://gennaro.zezza.it/software/eviews/gl2006.php.

My apprenticeship was served in the British Treasury, where, from 1956 to 1970, I mainly worked on the conjuncture[2] and short-term forecasting. This was the heyday of 'stop–go' policies, when we tried to forecast what would happen during the following 18 months and then design a budget which would rectify anything likely to go wrong. Forecasting consisted of scratching together estimates of the component parts of real GDP and adding them up using, so far as we could, a crude version of the Keynesian multiplier. I now think the theoretical and operational principles we used were seriously defective, but the whole experience was instructive and extremely exciting. The main thing I derived from this work was an expertise with statistical concepts and sources while gathering a considerable knowledge of stylized facts – for instance concerning the (non) response of prices to fluctuations in demand (Godley 1959; Godley and Gillion 1965) and the response of unemployment to fluctuations in output (Godley and Shepherd 1964). I also got a lot of contemporary history burned into my mind – what kind of year 1962 was and so on – and, always waiting for the next figure to come out, I learned to think of the economy as an organism which evolves through time, with each period having similarities as well as differences from previous periods. I came to believe that advances in macro-economic theory could usefully take place only in tandem with an improved knowledge of what was actually happening in the real world – an endless process of iteration between algebra and statistics. My perspective was very much enlarged by my close friendship with Nicholas Kaldor, who worked in the Treasury from the mid-sixties. Kaldor was touched by genius and, contrary to what one might suppose, he had an open mind, being prepared to argue any question through with anyone at any time on its merits and even, very occasionally, to admit that he was wrong.

In 1970 I moved to Cambridge, where, with Francis Cripps, I founded the Cambridge Economic Policy Group (CEPG). I remember a damascene moment when, in early 1974 (after playing round with concepts devised in conversation with Nicky Kaldor and Robert Neild), I first apprehended the strategic importance of the accounting identity which says that, *measured at current prices*, the government's budget deficit less the current account deficit is equal, by definition, to private saving net of investment. Having always thought of the balance of trade as something which could only be analysed in terms of income and price elasticities together with real output movements at

---

[2] I believe myself, perhaps wrongly, to have coined this word and its variants in 1967 when I was working on devaluation. Bryan Hopkin had given me a cutting from a French newspaper describing the work of a 'conjoncturiste', adding 'This is what you are.'

home and abroad, it came as a shock to discover that if only one knows what the budget deficit and private net saving are, it follows from that information alone, without any qualification whatever, exactly what the balance of payments must be. Francis Cripps and I set out the significance of this identity as a logical framework both for modelling the economy and for the formulation of policy in the *London and Cambridge Economic Bulletin* in January 1974 (Godley and Cripps 1974). We correctly predicted that the Heath Barber boom would go bust later in the year at a time when the National Institute was in full support of government policy and the London Business School (i.e. Jim Ball and Terry Burns) were conditionally recommending further reflation! We also predicted that inflation could exceed 20% if the unfortunate threshold (wage indexation) scheme really got going interactively. This was important because it was later claimed that inflation (which eventually reached 26%) was the consequence of the previous rise in the 'money supply', while others put it down to the rising pressure of demand the previous year.

However, far more important than any predictions we then made was our suggestion that an altogether different set of principles for managing the economy should be adopted, which did not rely nearly so much on short-term forecasting. Our system of thought, dubbed 'New Cambridge' by Richard Kahn and Michael Posner (1974), turned on our view that in the medium term there were limits to the extent to which private net saving would fluctuate and hence that there was a medium-term functional relationship between private disposable income and private expenditure. Although this view encountered a storm of protest at the time it has gradually gained some acceptance and is treated as axiomatic in, for example, Garratt *et al.* (2003).

We had a bad time in the mid-1970s because we did not then understand inflation accounting, so when inflation took off in 1975, we underestimated the extent to which stocks of financial assets would rise in nominal terms. We made some bad projections which led people to conclude that New Cambridge had been confuted empirically and decisively. But this was neither correct nor fair because nobody else at that time seems to have understood inflation accounting. Our most articulate critic, perhaps, was John Bispham (1975), then editor of the *National Institute Economic Review*, who wrote an article claiming that the New Cambridge equation had 'broken down massively'. Yet the National Institute's own consumption function under-forecast the personal saving rate in 1975 by 6 percentage points of disposable income! And no lesser authority than Richard Stone (1973) made the same mistake because in his definition of real income he did not deduct the erosion, due to inflation, of the real value of household wealth. But no one concluded that the consumption function had 'broken down' terminally if at all.

It was some time before we finally got the accounting quite right. We got part of the way with Cripps and Godley (1976), which described the CEPG's empirical model and derived analytic expressions which characterized its main properties, and which included an early version of the conflictual, 'target real wage' theory of inflation. Eventually our theoretical model was enlarged to incorporate inflation accounting and stocks as well as flows and the results were published in Godley and Cripps (1983)[3] with some further refinements regarding inflation accounting in Coutts, Godley and Gudgin (1985). Through the 1970s we gave active consideration to the use of import controls to reverse the adverse trends in trade in accordance with principles set out in Godley and Cripps (1978). And around 1984 James Tobin spent a pleasant week in Cambridge (finding time to play squash and go to the opera) during which he instructed us in the theory of asset allocation, particularly Backus *et al.* (1980), which thenceforth was incorporated in our work.

In 1979 Mrs Thatcher came to power largely on the grounds that, with unemployment above one million, 'Labour [wasn't] working', and Britain was subjected to the monetarist experiment. We contested the policies and the theory underlying them with all the rhetoric we could muster, predicting that there would be an extremely severe recession with unprecedented unemployment. The full story of the Thatcher economic policies (taking the period 1979–92) has yet to be told. Certainly the average growth rate was by far the lowest and least stable of the post-war period while unemployment rose to at least four million, once the industrial workers in Wales and the North who moved from unemployment to invalidity benefit are counted in.

In 1983 the CEPG and several years of work were destroyed, and discredited in the minds of many people, by the ESRC decision to decimate our funding, which they did without paying us a site visit or engaging in any significant consultation.

Still, 'sweet are the uses of adversity', and deprived of Francis Cripps (perhaps the cleverest economist I have so far encountered) and never having touched a computer before, I was forced to spend the hours (and hours) necessary to acquire the modelling skills with which I invented prototypes of many of the models in this book.

In 1992, I was invited to join the Treasury's panel of Independent Forecasters (the 'Six Wise Men'). In my contributions I wrongly supposed that the devaluation of 1992 would be insufficient to generate export-led growth for a time. But I did steadfastly support the policies pursued by Kenneth Clarke (the UK Chancellor of the Exchequer) between 1993 and 1997 – perhaps the best time for macro-economic management during the post-war period. Unfortunately a decision was made not to make any attempt to explain,

---

[3] A rhetorically adverse and unfair review of this book, by Maurice Peston (1983), appeared in the *Times* simultaneously with its publication.

let alone reconcile, the divergent views of the Wise Men, with the result that their reports, drafted by the Treasury, were cacophonous and entirely without value.

Through most of the 1990s I worked at the Levy Economics Institute of Bard College, in the United States, where I spent about half my time building a simple 'stock-flow consistent' model of the United States – with a great deal of help from Gennaro Zezza – and writing a number of papers on the strategic problems facing the United States and the world economies. We correctly argued (Godley and McCarthy 1998; Godley 1999c), slap contrary to the view held almost universally at the time, that US fiscal policy would have to be relaxed to the tune of several hundred billion dollars if a major recession was to be avoided. And in Godley and Izurieta (2001), as well as in subsequent papers, we forecast correctly that if US output were to rise enough to recover full employment, there would be, viewed *ex ante*, a balance of payments deficit of about 6% of GDP in 2006 – and that this would pose huge strategic problems both for the US government and for the world. The other half of my time was spent developing the material contained in this book. In 2002 I returned to the United Kingdom where I continued doing similar work, initially under the benign auspices of the Cambridge Endowment for Research in Finance, and more recently with the financial support of Warren Mosler, who has also made penetrating comments on drafts of this book.

My friendship with Marc Lavoie started with an email which he sent me out of the blue saying that he could not penetrate one of the equations in a paper I had written called 'Money and Credit in a Keynesian Model of Income Determination' which was published by the *Cambridge Journal of Economics* in 1999. The reason, I could immediately explain, was that the equation contained a lethal error! And so our collaboration began. Marc brought to the enterprise a superior knowledge of how the monetary system works, together with scholarship and a knowledge of the literature which I did not possess and without which this book would never have been written. Unfortunately, we have not been able to spend more than about two weeks physically in one another's presence during the past five years – and this is one of the reasons it has taken so long to bring the enterprise to fruition.

Joint authorship background (by M.L.)

The present book is the culminating point of a long collaboration that started in December 1999, when Wynne Godley made a presentation of his 1999 *Cambridge Journal of Economics* paper at the University of Ottawa, following my invitation. I had been an avid reader of Godley and Cripps's innovative book, *Macroeconomics*, when it came out in 1983, but had been put off somewhat by some of its very difficult inflation accounting sections, as well as by my relative lack of familiarity with stock-flow issues. Nonetheless, the book clearly stood out in my mind as being written in the post-Keynesian tradition, being based on effective demand, normal-cost pricing, endogenous money, interest rate targeting by the monetary authorities and bank finance of production and inventories. I could also see ties with the French circuit theory, as I soon pointed out (Lavoie 1987: 77). Indeed, I was later to discover that Wynne Godley himself felt very much in sync with the theory of the monetary circuit and its understanding of Keynes's finance motive, as propounded by Augusto Graziani (1990, 2003). A great regret of mine is that during my three-week stint at the University of Cambridge in 1985, under the tutelage of Geoff Harcourt, I did not take up the opportunity to meet Wynne Godley then. This led to a long span during which I more or less forgot about Wynne's work, although it is cited and even quoted in my post-Keynesian textbook (Lavoie 1992).

As an aside, it should be pointed out that Wynne Godley himself has always seen his work as being part of the Cambridge school of Keynesian economics. This was not always very clear to some of his readers, especially in the 1970s or 1980s.[4] For instance, Robert Dixon (1982–83: 291) argued that the ideas defended by the New Cambridge School, of which Godley was a leading figure, were virtually tantamount to a monetarist vision of income distribution, concluding that 'Doctrines associated with the New Cambridge School represent a dramatic break with the ideas of Keynes. New Cambridge theory seems to be more pertinent to long-run equilibrium than the world in which we have our being' (1982–83: 294). In addition, during a discussion of Godley (1983), two different conference participants claimed that Godley's model 'had a real whiff of monetarism about it' (in Worswick and Trevithick, 1983: 174), so that Francis Cripps, Godley's co-author, felt obliged to state that 'what they were doing was Keynesian monetary economics; it was not neoclassical let alone general equilibrium monetary economics' (in Worswick and Trevithick, 1983: 176). In retrospect, the confusion arose, so it seems, as a result of the insistence of New Cambridge School members upon stock-flow consistency and the long-run relationships or medium-run consequences that this required coherence possibly entailed. It is this focus on possible long-run results that led some readers to see some parallels with monetarism. But as is clearly explained by Keith Cuthbertson (1979), New

[4] And even more recently, as Godley is virtually omitted from King's (2003) history of post-Keynesianism. By contrast, Hamouda and Harcourt (1988: 23–4) do devote a full page to his work.

Cambridge authors were opposed to monetarists on just about every policy issue, and the underlying structure of their model was clearly of Keynesian pedigree. Godley himself, more than once, made very clear that he associated himself with the post-Keynesian school. For instance, in a paper that can be considered to be the first draft of Chapter 10 of the present book, Godley (1997: 48) claimed 'to have made, so far as I know for the first time, a rigorous synthesis of the theory of credit and money creation with that of income determination in the (Cambridge) Keynesian tradition. My belief is that nothing the paper contains would have been surprising or new to, say Kaldor, Hicks, Joan Robinson or Kahn'.[5]

In the late 1990s Anwar Shaikh, who had been working at the Levy Institute, brought my attention to a working paper that had been written there by Wynne Godley (1996), saying that this was innovative work that was of utmost importance, although hard to follow. I did get a copy of the working paper, and remember discussing it with my long-time friend and colleague at the University of Ottawa – Mario Seccareccia – and arguing that this was the kind of work that we ought to be doing if we wanted to move ahead with circuit theory and post-Keynesian monetary economics, which at the time seemed to me to be in a sort of an impasse with its endless and inconclusive debates. When a substantially revised version of the working paper came out in June 1999 in the *Cambridge Journal of Economics*, I was now ready to dig into it and put it on the programme of the four-person monthly seminar that we had set up in the autumn of that year, with Mario Seccareccia, Tom Rymes (TK), Colin Rogers (visiting from Adelaide), and myself. From this came out the invitation for Wynne to give a formal presentation at the end of 1999.

Wynne himself looked quite excited that some younger scholars would once more pay attention to his work. What I found stimulating was that Wynne's working paper and published article had managed to successfully integrate the flow aspects of production and bank credit with the stock features of portfolio choice and money balances – an integration that had always evaded my own efforts – while offering a definite post-Keynesian model, which I felt was in the spirit of one of my favourite authors – Nicholas Kaldor. Indeed, in contrast to other readers of the 1999 article, I thought that Godley's model gave substantial (but indirect) support to the so-called Kaldor–Moore accommodationist or horizontalist position, of which I was one of the few supporters at the time, as I have tried to explain in great detail recently (Lavoie 2006a).

---

[5] Elsewhere, in Godley (1993: 63), when presenting what I believe to be a preliminary version of his 1999 *Cambridge Journal of Economics* article, Wynne mentions that his new work is based on his 'eclectic understanding' of Sylos Labini, Graziani, Hicks, Keynes, Kaldor, Pasinetti, Tobin and Adrian Wood.

Around that time I was working on improving Kaldor's (1966) well-known neo-Pasinetti growth model, in which corporate firms keep retained earnings and issue stock market shares. I had successfully managed to incorporate explicit endogenous rates of capacity utilization (Lavoie 1998), but was experiencing difficulties in introducing money balances into the model, while taking care adequately of capital gains on the stock market. These accounting intricacies were child's play for Wynne, who offered to help out and build a model that would provide simulations of this modified Kaldorian model. This became our first published joint effort – the Lavoie and Godley (2001–2) paper in the *Journal of Post Keynesian Economics*. This gave rise to a very neat analytical formalization, with a variety of possible regimes, provided by Lance Taylor (2004b: 272–8, 303–5), another keen admirer of the methodology propounded by Wynne Godley. In my view, these two papers taken together, along with the extension by Claudio Dos Santos and Gennaro Zezza (2005), offer a very solid basis for those who wish to introduce debt and stock market questions in demand-led models, allowing them, for instance to tackle the issues brought up by Hyman Minsky with his financial fragility hypothesis.

At the time of our first meeting Wynne himself was trying to put together a small book that would summarize his main methodological and economic ideas, by lining up a string of elementary models that would emphasize the key relationships between producers, banks and households, as well as the government and the external sectors. The first draft of this book was sent to a number of friends and researchers in February 2000. The models of Chapters 3–6 in the present book very closely resemble the models of the draft. Towards the end of 2000, as our collaboration on the Kaldorian model seemed to be going very well, Wynne asked me to embark on his book project and to become a co-author. In particular, I was to provide the links with the existing post-Keynesian literature.

A substantial portion of the book was written during 2001–03, but progress got bogged down by other commitments, the difficulties of communicating from a distance, some disagreements on contents, a slowdown due to illness and some unexpected problems encountered when trying to model and simulate what seemed at first sight like simple and obvious concepts (for instance the model of Chapter 11 had to be completely revamped). In the end both of us had to recognize that we would never achieve a perfect product, and that it was better to publish a book with some imperfections than no book at all. The completion of the book was also both helped and slowed down by the fact that after 2003 we worked very hard at writing together three papers on stock-flow consistent open-economy models.

I would like to take the opportunity to acknowledge, both in my name and in that of Wynne, the support and keen interest of a variety of colleagues (such as Ken Coutts, Adrian Wood, Anwar Shaikh, Tom Palley, Duncan Foley, Mario Seccareccia) who induced us to move forward and achieve our task. By giving us the opportunity to present our work and/or by asking us regularly whether we had completed the manuscript, many colleagues helped us realize that it was important that we did so. Alex Izurieta provided encouragement and a lot of very helpful technical advice, without which in particular we could not have imported the charts; Claudio Dos Santos made a lot of suggestions and provided references to previous related literature of which we were unaware; Gennaro Zezza organized a conference on stock-flow-consistent modelling, and gave his time to translate our models into Eviews; Fernando Pellerano and Juan Carlos Moreno-Brid provided an everlasting dose of enthusiasm about the importance and relevance of our work for economists in semi-industrialized or less developed countries; Jacques Mazier, thanks to his student Mickaël Clévenot, provided both of us with generous opportunities to present our work on several occasions to a large number of seminar participants. And finally, Geoffrey Harcourt offered his support and gave us a *coup de pouce*, inducing us to submit a book proposal and complete the project, while two PhD students of mine, Jung-Hoon Kim and Jun Zhao, made sure that no reference and no notation were omitted and that the bibliography was in proper form.

To close this preface, it should be pointed out that all the models were run and figures charted with the MODLER software, which was provided to us free of charge by Charles G. Renfro. MODLER is a wonderful tool to do econometrics, simulations and charts.

Summary[1]

Ever since the death of Keynes there have existed two fundamentally different paradigms for research into macroeconomics. One, which I shall call 'neo-classical', basically sees the economy as a market place where individual agents sell their labour which, via an aggregate production function, can get translated into the things they want to buy. Some kind of auction, unless thwarted by rigidities, then finds prices which bring all supplies into equivalence with all demands, incidentally maximizing profits and rendering involuntary unemployment impossible.

According to the other 'Keynesian' paradigm, the economy's driving force resides in the decisions of entrepreneurs to invest, employ labour and produce goods and services, initially (perforce) using borrowed funds to carry out their plans in an environment of fundamental uncertainty. Their aspiration is to achieve sales, at prices they set, such as to generate a surplus sufficient to pay back their initial borrowings and fund continuing investment while rewarding themselves with unearned income, perhaps in the form of capital gains. According to this vision there is no presumption that there will be full employment unless governments sustain aggregate demand by fiscal and monetary policies.

It is as well to emphasize the profoundly different political programmes implied by these two paradigms because each is habitually taught as though it were as value-free as physics. The neo-classical story rejects virtually all state activity, except that it encourages the removal of 'rigidities' which may impede the efficient functioning of markets. The Keynesian story insists that a correct setting for fiscal and monetary policy is essential if full employment is to be maintained, while interventions in fields such as regional disparities, the distribution of income and the provision of social services are at the discretion of governments.

Notwithstanding that the neo-classical paradigm dominates the field at the moment, and notwithstanding that it spawned 'monetarism' in all its forms, there is a paradoxical and embarrassing lacuna in the theoretical structure which is supposed to underpin it. Since the neo-classical equilibrium is achieved via some kind of auction process, in which the right prices and quantities must be found if exchange and production are to proceed, there is no need and therefore no essential place in the system for money, debt or, more generally, for banks and other financial institutions. Many Keynesians

---

[1] Wynne Godley passed away in May 2010. However, in May 2007 he wrote this summary of our book, which readers may find helpful. M.L.

(for instance Nicholas Kaldor and Augusto Graziani) have written percep-
tively about monetary production economies. Yet their aspirations have not,
in our view, quite provided a full integration of money and finance into the
characteristic Keynesian income/expenditure model. It is a fuller integration
that our book is designed to characterize.

The models we deploy are all grounded in double entry systems of accounts
(pioneered by James Meade, Richard Stone and James Tobin, among others)
in which every entry describing an income or expenditure is invariably seen
as a transaction between two sectors, with every outlay by one sector (say
on personal consumption) having an identical counterpart in the form of a
receipt by another (say a sale by a firm). However, to complete such a system
of accounts, so that 'everything comes from somewhere and everything goes
somewhere', it is essential to additionally include all those flows of funds
which show how each sector's financial balance (the gap between its total
income and expenditure) is disposed of. It will then be found that it is impossible to complete the implied matrix of all transactions in such a way that
every column and every row sums to zero without calling into existence a
banking sector which provides the funds which firms need in order to finance
investment, thereby simultaneously creating the credit money which households need to finance transactions and to store wealth. Money and credit
are thus fully incorporated into the system of concepts right from the start.
And as all flow-of-funds entries describe changes in stock variables, every
complete transactions matrix implies that there exists a consistent system of
balance sheets comprising stock variables which link each transaction in one
period to its counterpart in the following period.

It is a vitally important feature of such an accounting structure, since every
column and every row of the transactions matrix sums to zero, that the nth
variable is logically implied by the other n−1 variables. Accordingly, when
it comes to solving the whole model, replete with behavioural relationships,
there will always be one equation which must be dropped, according to quasi-
Walrasian principles, to avoid over-determination. For instance, while there
will always be a demand for, and a supply of, money there may be no need
and no place for an equation to bring the two into equivalence because such
equivalence is automatically implied by the logical structure of the accounts
as a whole.

Coming to behaviour, the relationships we postulate are for the most part
quite conventional. For instance, consumption is determined by expected
real (inflation accounted) disposable income and wealth inherited from
the past, while expected wealth is allocated between assets according to
Tobinesque principles. Business output depends on expected sales. And so
on.

As all the key decisions are based on expected values, each sector must have
a 'buffer' which reconciles expected with realized outcomes. For households
the buffer is taken to be credit (or 'inside') money, for firms it is inventories,

for banks and the government it is stocks of government securities. So outside certain financial markets (e.g. the market for equities), there is no need for equilibrium conditions to bring supplies into equivalence with demands. It will almost always be quantities rather than prices which give the signals which keep the economy on track, the role of prices being to distribute the national income between wages and profits rather than to allocate resources.

Starting with extremely simple stock-flow consistent models, our book describes a succession of increasingly complex models using a conventional narrative style backed up by equations which bring precision to individual propositions. Then comprehensive solutions of these models are used to illustrate, with figures, ways in which whole monetary economies evolve through time when shocked in various ways.[2]

---

[2] There is now a website devoted to people interested in stock-flow consistent modelling in economics: http://sfc-models.net/.

1
Introduction

I have found out what economics is; it is the science of confusing
stocks with flows.

A verbal statement by Michal Kalecki,
circa 1936, as cited by Joan Robinson, in
'Shedding darkness', *Cambridge Journal of
Economics*, 6(3), September 1982, 295–6.

1.1 Two paradigms

During the 60-odd years since the death of Keynes there have existed two,
fundamentally different, paradigms for macroeconomic research, each with
its own fundamentally different interpretation of Keynes's work.[1] On the one
hand there is the mainstream, or neo-classical, paradigm, which is based on
the premise that economic activity is exclusively motivated by the aspirations
of individual agents. At its heart this paradigm requires a neo-classical production function, which postulates that output is the result of combining labour
with capital in such a way that, provided all markets clear, there will be no
involuntary unemployment while the national income is distributed opti-
mally and automatically between wages and profits. If markets do not clear
because wages or prices are 'sticky', the same structure will generate determinate, if sub-optimal, disequilibrium outcomes and, for many economists, it is
the possibility of such stickiness that defines Keynesian economics. The key
assumption that individual welfare maximization is the universal mainspring
is not consistent with the view that firms have an independent existence
with distinct motivations, because optimum prices, output and employment
are all decided for them by the location of aggregate demand and supply

---

[1] For a masterly survey of the entire field see Lance Taylor (2004b).

schedules. And as production is instantaneous, while supply is brought into equivalence with demand through the market-clearing process, there is no systemic need and therefore no essential place for loans, credit money or banks. The concept of 'money' is indispensable, yet money is an asset to which there is not, in general, a counterpart liability and which often has no accounting relationship to other variables. Mainstream macroeconomic theory is a deductive system which needs no recourse to facts (though it may be 'calibrated' with numbers) and lends itself to analytic solutions.

The alternative paradigm, which has come to be called 'post-Keynesian' or 'structuralist', derives originally from those economists who were more or less closely associated personally with Keynes such as Joan Robinson, Richard Kahn, Nicholas Kaldor, and James Meade, as well as Michal Kalecki who derived most of his ideas independently. So, far from being a deductive system, the post-Keynesian vision is underpinned by 'stylised facts' recognizing the manifest existence of institutions, together with regularities and magnitudes in the economic data which can be checked out empirically. Central to this system of ideas is that, in a modern industrial economy, firms have a separate existence with a distinct set of objectives, for example, to make enough profits to pay for growth-maximizing investment. Rejecting as chimerical the concept of the neo-classical production function,[2] post-Keynesians hold that, in an uncertain world, firms, operating under conditions of imperfect competition and increasing returns, must decide how much to produce and how many workers to employ, what prices to charge, how much to invest, and how to obtain finance. It will be the pricing decision which, in general, determines the distribution of the national income between wages and profits. And as production and investment take time while expectations are in general falsified, there is a systemic need for loans from outside the production sector which generates acceptable credit money endogenously – in other words (in accordance with common observation) there must exist a banking sector. According to post-Keynesian ideas, there is no natural tendency for economies to generate full employment, and for this and other reasons growth and stability require the active participation of governments in the form of fiscal, monetary and incomes policy. And it will probably be impossible to derive analytic solutions which describe how economies as a whole evolve, particularly as institutions and behavioural patterns change drastically through historic time.

Luigi Pasinetti (2005) laments the fact that post-Keynesians have progressively failed to establish 'a permanent winning paradigm'. And indeed, while pockets of stubborn resistance remain, the post-Keynesian tradition has now been virtually written out of the literature; it has lost out to the mainstream in terms of how the subject is taught, what the 'top' learned journals will accept, where research money is allocated, how appointments

---

[2] Appendix 1.1 provides compelling reasons for this rejection.

are made and how empirical models are built. Pasinetti attributes this collapse in large part to the personal characters of the formidable economists who directly succeeded Keynes, maintaining (correctly in our opinion), that they did not admit outsiders to their circle or sponsor their work. But Pasinetti also points to 'a lack of theoretical cohesion in the various pieces which emerged from the Keynesian School', which 'paid scant attention to the fundamentals on which an alternative, but coherent, paradigm could be built'. He suggests that 'a satisfactory blueprint that could house, beneath one single roof, the development of the existing ideas along the Keynesian lines ... is still lacking' ... and that there is a need for 'an account of what happens – as Keynes put it – in a "monetary production economy", which is more complex than a pure exchange stationary economy, because it is intrinsically dynamic, continually affected by history subject to changes both in scale and structure'. This is an admission that post-Keynesian economics up to the present time simply does not cover the ground.

Geoffrey Harcourt (2001: 277) in similar vein observes that post-Keynesians have been following the Marshallian/Keynesian method which 'consists at looking at parts of the economy in sequence, holding constant or abstracting from what is going on, or at least the *effects* of what is going on elsewhere, for the moment', in the hope that it would be possible eventually 'to bring all our results together to give a full, overall picture'. Harcourt thinks that 'this may be one of the reasons why ultimately both Marshall and Joan Robinson thought that they had failed – not from realizing that by following the procedure they were attempting the impossible, but because the *procedure* itself was at fault'. While neo-classical economists have general equilibrium theory and computable general equilibrium models that helped capture the overall implications of their vision and the interdependence between markets and sectors, post-Keynesian economics could only offer the Sraffian model as a formal tool to tackle production interdependencies and relative prices, but which, ironically, did not and could not deal with the crucial Keynesian issues of output, unemployment, inflation, financial flows and debts. Post-Keynesian models that dealt with these topics lay in spreadout pieces, with no account of how the system as a whole worked. There is no statement which characterizes how post-Keynesian theory can underlie the way in which an industrial capitalist economy works *as an organic whole*. Despite valiant efforts, such as the book by Eichner (1987), there is no post-Keynesian textbook which covers all of the monetary macro ground as a coherent whole.[3]

---

[3] This was already pointed out in Godley (1993: 63), where the author deplored the absence of a Kaldorian textbook, stating that 'Kaldorian ideas in their positive mode have not been put together in a way which covers the syllabus'. In a footnote to this, the author added that an exception to this generalization was the 1987 (unfortunately unfinished) Eichner book (Godley 1993: 80).

1.2 Aspiration

In writing this book it has been our aspiration to lay the foundations for a methodology which will make it possible to start exploring rigorously how real economic systems, replete with realistic institutions, function as a whole. Our starting point, though a little intricate for an introduction, is yet so simple that we propose to plunge straightaway *in medias res*.[4]

The standard textbook introduces macroeconomic concepts via the national income identity. Thus total production, or gross domestic product (GDP), is defined as the sum of all expenditures on goods and services or, alternatively, as the sum of all incomes paid for production of goods and services. More precisely, the GDP (assuming the economy to be closed) is made up of personal consumption, investment and government expenditure on goods and services; looked at from the income side, it is made up of income from employment and profits. All these concepts are introduced as 'real' variables, the GDP being an economy's total volume of production. Writing these identities formally we have:

$$C + I + G = Y = WB + F \tag{1.1}$$

where C is consumption, I is investment, G is government expenditure, Y is GDP, WB is the wage bill and F is profits.

And that is about it, so far as accounting goes, though when it comes to studying the consumption function the student will quickly have to learn that personal disposable income is given by:

$$YD = Y - T \tag{1.2}$$

where YD is personal disposable income and T describes all taxes and transfers received or paid by the government. Equation (1.2) builds in the implicit (but counterfactual) assumption that all profits are instantaneously distributed to households.

Decomposing the wage bill into a quantity of employment times a wage rate and postulating the existence of a rate of interest, a stock of money, a price of real product and a stock of fixed capital equipment, we have enough concepts to erect the 'core' model of the so-called neo-classical synthesis, which constituted mainstream macroeconomics at least until the 1980s and from which more recent schools of thought (e.g. Rational Expectations, Real Business Cycles, New Keynesian) are directly descended. By this model, in its most basic manifestation, the demand for output is determined by consumption and investment functions, the profit-maximizing

---

[4] Latin for 'into the middle of things'.

Table 1.1 Standard textbook simplified national income matrix

	Households	Business Current	Business Capital	Government	Σ
Consumption	−C	+C			0
Govt. expenditure		+G		−G	0
Investment		+I	−I		0
[GDP (memo)]		[Y]			
Wages	+WB	−WB			0
Profits	+F	−F			0
Tax net of transfers	−T			+T	0
Σ	SAVING	0	INVESTMENT (−)	GOVT SURPLUS	0

supply of output is determined by the marginal product of labour and the real wage. The demand and supply for labour are both determined by the real wage. The demand for real money balances is determined by income and the rate of interest, while the supply of money is exogenous and given. The entire system is in market-clearing equilibrium when all three demands are in equivalence with all three supplies, yielding determinate values for all the components of the national income as well as for employment and for each 'price'.

Although every author will have his or her own gloss on how exactly this model works, and what happens if in various ways it doesn't work, we have no doubt whatever that this account does fairly summarize the core model which dominated the scene for so long.[5] The purpose of reproducing it here is not to criticize it, but rather to set up a clear reference point in terms of which we can clearly deploy a radically different way of viewing the world and setting up a research agenda to explore it.

The difference between the world to be deployed in the following chapters and that introduced in most textbooks is well introduced by first fitting the variables described in equation (1.1) into a matrix such as that shown in Table 1.1, which brings out the fact that each variable is a transaction between two sectors which takes place in some given period of time.

[5] The classic expositions are to be found in Patinkin (1965) and Modigliani (1944, 1963). The basic model is not changed when markets fail to clear. It is, for instance, commonly argued that 'Keynesian economics' – using this model – is encapsulated by assuming that the nominal wage is exogenously determined, in which case the supply of labour can exceed the demand, causing, and suggesting a cure for, unemployment – in advance of any empirical investigation whatever.

The second column of Table 1.1 does nothing more than reproduce equation (1.1) in a vertical arrangement. The other columns show the transactions implied by the component parts of equations (1.1) and (1.2). Thus, for instance, consumption is a receipt by the business sector and a payment by the household sector. The only thing which might be unfamiliar to a student is the third column, which describes the capital account of the business sector. But there should be no difficulty about the meaning and significance of this; sales of investment goods give rise to receipts by the business sector like any other sales. But these receipts will all have to come (at this level of abstraction) from payments by the business sector itself, which is assumed to do all the investing.

But now it is easy to see that this system of concepts is seriously incomplete. Consideration of the matrix immediately poses the following questions. What form does personal saving take? Where does any excess of sectoral income over expenditure actually go to – for it must all go somewhere? Which sector provides the counterparty to every transaction in assets? Where does the finance for investment come from? And how are budget deficits financed?

There is an obvious answer to these questions, which follows from an elementary knowledge of the way the real world works and which can be quickly verified by inspecting the Flow-of-Funds tables published by the Federal Reserve in the United States, which provide data relating to every quarter since 1952.

Table 1.2 completes and rectifies the story adumbrated in Table 1.1, showing a relatively simple comprehensive system of accounts which describes all the intersectoral transactions implied by the Table 1.1 concepts but not shown there.

The upper, national income, part of the table reproduces Table 1.1, with the important difference that the usual assumption that all profits are distributed has been dropped. Instead some proportion of profits is transferred to firms' capital account, where it may be used to finance investment.[6] The lower, flow of funds, part of the table could have been completed in various different ways depending on the degree of detail and the simplifications deemed appropriate. However, it will be a cardinal principle applying here and to every array of concepts we shall deploy in the future that all rows and all columns sum to zero,[7] thus ensuring, in the catch-phrase, that 'everything comes from somewhere and everything goes somewhere'.

---

[6] Table 1.2, although an improvement over Table 1.1, still omits several relevant features, such as interest payments, and it assumes that the central bank is amalgamated with the government. A more complete matrix will be introduced in Chapter 2.

[7] For this reason the closed economy described above could not be 'opened' by adding a column describing exports and imports since this will not normally sum to zero. The solution will be to include all trading partners in the matrix, as will be shown

Table 1.2 Transactions flow matrix

	Households (1)	Production firms Current (2)	Capital (3)	Banks (4)	Government (5)	Σ
Consumption	$-C$	$+C$				0
Investment		$+I$	$-I$			0
Govt. expenditures		$+G$			$-G$	0
Wages	$+WB$	$-WB$				0
Profits	$+FD_f$	$-F_f$	$+FU_f$			0
Taxes-transfers	$-T$				$+T$	0
Change in loans			$+\Delta L_f$	$-\Delta L$		0
Change in cash	$-\Delta H_h$			$-\Delta H_b$	$+\Delta H$	0
Change in deposits	$-\Delta M$			$+\Delta M$		0
Change in bills	$-\Delta B_h$			$-\Delta B_b$	$+\Delta B$	0
Change in equities	$-\Delta e \cdot p_e$		$+\Delta e \cdot p_e$			0
Σ	0	0	0	0	0	0

However, no sooner does one contemplate filling in the assets which are acquired by households than a second important inadequacy of Table 1.1 immediately becomes manifest. Households may (for instance) acquire credit money as an asset, but where is the counterpart acquisition of liabilities to be found? And firms may require loans to finance investment in excess of retained profits, but from where are these to come? The answers are obvious as soon as the questions are asked. The matrix cannot be completed unless a whole new sector – a banking sector – is introduced into the elementary system of concepts.

In column 1 the saving of the personal sector is assumed to go entirely into cash, credit money, government securities and newly issued equities. There are no entries in column 2 because profits are defined as the residual between current inflows and outflows. In line 5 profits are in part distributed and in part – in practice by far the greater part – undistributed. In column 3 the funds in excess of retained profits required for investment are assumed to come in part from the issue of equities, with the balance coming from loans. In column 5 the government is assumed to finance any deficit by the issue of securities and cash. Finally in column 4 we have the banks' transactions in assets which comprise the genesis of loans and credit money and which bring

in Chapters 6 and 12, making a larger closed system in which there is no place for a balance of payments column.

Table 1.3   Balance-sheet matrix

	Households	Production firms	Banks	Government	Σ
Loans		$-L$	$+L$		0
Cash	$+H_h$		$+H_b$	$-H$	0
Deposits	$+M$		$-M$		0
Bills	$+B_h$		$+B_b$	$-B$	0
Equities	$+e \cdot p_e$	$-e_f \cdot p_e$	$-e_b \cdot p_e$		0
Tangible capital	$+K_h$	$+K_f$			$+K$
Sum (net worth)	NW_h	NW_f	NW_b	NW_g	K

these concepts firmly into the most basic accounting structure, and they also say, non-trivially, that any gap between these two supplies must always be matched exactly by net accumulation by banks of cash and government bills – for the balance of banks' transactions in assets must sum to zero if only because every other row and column in the table sums to zero.

All entries in the flow-of-funds sections of Table 1.2 describe changes in stock variables between the beginning and end of the period being described.[8] Thus the evolution of historic time is introduced into the basic system of concepts. The transactions in asset stocks in Table 1.2 imply the existence of an interlocking system of balance sheets, described in Table 1.3. These balance sheets measure the levels of all stock variables at some given point of time. And it is the configuration of stock variables which is providing the link between each period of time and that which follows it.

The evolution of the entire system may be characterized (at the level of accounting) by saying that at the beginning of each period, the configuration of stock variables (i.e. all physical stocks together with the interlocking system of financial assets and liabilities) is a summary description of (relevant[9]) past history. Then the transactions described in Table 1.2 heave the stock variables from their state at the beginning of each period to their state at the end,[10] to which capital gains will have to be added.

For this system of accounting identities to hold, all variables must be measured at current prices, since they describe the sums of money that actually change hands each period – otherwise, unless there is no change in any price,

[8] The variables are defined in the matrix. The term e in the final line describes the number of equity titles and p_e describes their price.

[9] A more comprehensive definition would comprehend human capital, natural resources and many other items.

[10] Capital gains and losses, which are not transactions, will have to be accounted for when we come to examine the relationship between the two matrices.

the columns would not add up to zero.[11] Yet a number of key decisions regarding, in particular, production, consumption, investment and many kinds of government expenditure are taken in terms of real, physical quantities. So we shall at some stage have to describe, at the level of accounting (i.e. before considering behaviour) how prices translate nominal into real variables, thereby determining the distribution of the national income.

1.3 Endeavour

We can now disclose in a nutshell the nature of the task we have set for ourselves. We are going to define a series of evolutionary models, each of which describes an economy moving forward non-ergodically in historic time, as Paul Davidson (1988) would put it. We start with truly primitive models containing a mere handful of equations and end up with relatively elaborate models containing one hundred or more equations. Each model must account for every single one of the variables contained in the relevant transactions and balance sheet matrices. So in sharp contrast with the Marshallian method, we shall always be exploring the properties of complete systems, never assuming that we can consider one topic at a time in the hope that the rest of the world stays in place while we do so.

The method will be to write down systems of equations and accounting identities, attribute initial values to all stocks and all flows as well as to behavioural parameters, using stylized facts so well as we can to get appropriate ratios (e.g. for the proportion of the national income taken by government expenditure). We then use numerical simulation to check the accounting and obtain a steady state for the economy in question. Finally we shock the system with a variety of alternative assumptions about exogenous variables and parameters and explore the consequences. It will be our contention that via the experience of simulating increasingly complex models it becomes possible to build up knowledge, or 'informed intuition',[12] as to the way monetary economies must and do function.

The use of logically complete accounts (with every row and every column in the transactions matrix summing to zero) has strong implications for the dynamics of the system as a whole. This completeness carries the implication that once $n-1$ equations are satisfied then the nth equation will be found to be satisfied as well and for this reason must always be dropped from the computer model to avoid overdetermination. If the accounting is less than complete in the sense we use, the system dynamics will be

---

[11] Put another way, conventional real disposable income less real consumption does not equal the change in the real stock of wealth – a major contention in inflation accounting to be discussed in Chapter 9.

[12] An expression of James Tobin to describe the IS/LM model!

subverted – rather as though we were trying to operate a hydraulic machine which had leaky pipes.

Yet what we offer is no more than a beginning. We are not writing as experts with special knowledge concerning, say, the investment or consumption functions. Our accounting will always be solid and comprehensive – and this by itself will carry us a considerable distance, particularly when it comes to characterizing the interactions between the real and financial parts of the more elaborate models. But we leave every functional relationship in a primitive state yelling to be more thoroughly explored. For instance, we make the assumption that some small fixed proportion of investment is financed by the issue of equity in accordance, very broadly, with the facts as revealed in the flow-of-funds accounts. But industry finance, as it changes radically in the course of time, is a major subject worth deep and ongoing analysis though always, we argue, in the context of how the system as a whole must be behaving. It is an implication of our method that, by virtue of its comprehensive nature, it will ultimately enforce empirical study of the entire range of macroeconomic relationships, both accounting and functional, all dancing together as one.

Although we shall be writing down postulated 'parameters' for all functional relationships in the service of grinding out numerical simulations, we doubt whether these have, in the real world, anything remotely like the stability we have perforce attributed to them. We take the view, on the contrary, that all behavioural relationships are contingent in the technical sense that they 'may or may not happen'. The elementary models presented in Chapters 3–6 of this book achieve steady states and use stable 'parameters' in order to obtain comprehensible simulation results, but we have not yet had time to explore alternative possibilities thoroughly. Steady states are theoretical constructs which would be achieved '*if all parameters and functions of the model are taken as given*. Since in reality they are not given, the real-world counterparts of such constructs do not imply that the economy is at a position of rest' (Dutt 1997: 450). The steady state is just an analytical device never in practice reached, because parameters and exogenous variables are actually changing all the time. This implies that steady states should be treated as a reference point (Turnovsky 1977: 7). With the simulations advocated here, one ends up knowing something about the initial effects of some change (in the early periods of the dynamic response) as well as the terminal effects (in the steady state). These terminal effects will eventually arise as long as the structure of the model is left unchanged, although we know that this is unlikely. However, the far more complex later models, described, for example, in Chapter 11, do not spontaneously achieve steady states in any useful way, because sensible solutions to them require one to make assumptions about how the government reacts – for instance to an increase in inflation.

The only thing about which we are really certain at this stage is that the various items must always and everywhere add up appropriately. For instance in those models where households have a choice as to how their wealth is to be allocated, we have followed the procedure suggested by Tobin whereby the proportion of wealth held in any particular form is determined in a regular way by the rate of return on that asset compared with the return on all other assets. However, we do not for a moment suppose that the coefficients determining the relevant proportions are fixed through time and do not, therefore, believe that the theory is confuted because econometricians have so far failed to discover coefficients which are stable. All we can be sure of at this stage is that all (exactly all) wealth must go somewhere and that expected rates of return have something to do with this allocation. We should, however, be able to think coherently about the nature of the difference made to the outcome if the proportions change in various ways. Similarly we are certain that the finance for investment comes in some proportion from undistributed profits, issues of securities and bank loans, and the changing proportions merit empirical study. But for the time being we may, through simulation, develop a sense of the difference which alternative financing methods may make to the solutions obtained. And so on.

Our method guarantees that we will always be learning to live in a logically coherent world. And we are prepared to conjecture that, given that there are limits to the extent to which stock-flow ratios can change, the system dynamics of whole economies will pin down their overall behaviour in a way that can override the findings of econometrics as to the putative behaviour of bits and pieces.

A final *obiter dictum*. We have no compunction whatever about aspiring to describe the behaviour of whole sectors, in defiance of the putative maximization of utility by individual agents.

1.4 Provenance

Over the past few years, centred along the axis of the New School University and the Levy Economics Institute, both located in New York State, there has been a revival of interest in the stock-flow consistent approach to macroeconomic modelling, or what we could call a sectoral monetary stock-flow consistent approach.[13] The purpose of the present book is to feed this revival, in the hope that an accessible introduction to stock-flow consistent

[13] This revival is exemplified by the works of Godley (1996, 1997, 1999a,b) and Godley and Shaikh (2002), but also those of Dos Santos (2002a,b, 2005, 2006), Izurieta (2003), Lavoie and Godley (2001–2), Lavoie (2003), Moudud (2007), Taylor (2004a,b), Foley and Taylor (2004), Zezza and Dos Santos (2004), who all explicitly refer to a social accounting matrix (SAM) approach or to stock-flow consistency (SFC). One may also include as part of this revival the works of Willi Semmler, also partly located at the New School, and his associates (Flaschel, Franke and Semmler 1997; Chiarella and Flaschel 2000; Flaschel, Gong and Semmler 2001). In addition one can note the

macroeconomic modelling will induce more students and more colleagues to adopt and develop such an approach. Our belief is that, if such an adoption occurs, macroeconomics in general and heterodox economics in particular should become sounder and more transparent.

A relatively small group of authors in the past have suggested that such a coherent financial stock-flow accounting framework be part of macroeconomic theory. In broad terms, one can identify two schools of thought which actively developed a series of models based on the stock-flow consistent approach to macroeconomic modelling, one located at Yale University and led by the Nobel Prize winner James Tobin, and the other located at the Department of Applied Economics at Cambridge University and led by one of the present authors (Wynne Godley). To a large extent, both groups worked independently, at least until a conference on Keynes that was organized in Cambridge (UK) in 1983, most of their papers and articles having been written in the 1970s and early 1980s. The Yale group, also known as the 'pitfalls approach' or the New Haven school, focused its attention on portfolio and asset choice; its inspiration was essentially neo-classical and based on a practical variant of general equilibrium theory. The Cambridge UK group, which was known as the Cambridge Economic Policy Group (CEPG) or the New Cambridge school, used the stock-flow consistent framework mainly for forecasting whether an expansion was *sustainable*, as Godley (1999c) still does today, and to discuss the balance of payments problems that were then plaguing the United Kingdom.

Both research groups faded in the middle of the 1980s, as their funding was cut off, and their ideas, whatever their importance or their relevance, were put on the back-burner, and overtaken by research based on the representative agent, as in New Classical and New Keynesian economics.[14] But these new models are devoid of the comprehensive outlook that characterizes the approach advocated by the Yale school and the CEPG, as could be seen from a reading of Tobin (1982a) and Godley and Cripps (1983) respectively, or by the reading of other outstanding individual contributions to the stock-flow consistent approach, such as that of Turnovsky (1977) or Fair (1984).

The more recent work of Godley (1996, 1997, 1999a), which has led to the creation of the present book, owes a substantial debt to Tobin, most particularly the work of Tobin as it appears in Backus, Brainard, Smith and Tobin (1980), which presented the most explicit and most empirically-oriented version of

work of students and colleagues from various countries, such as Lequain (2003), Kim (2006a,b), Mouakil (2005), Le Héron (2006), Tymoigne (2006), Clévenot and Mazier (2005), Firmin (2006), Zhao (2006) and Charpe (2006).

[14] It is true that mainstream economists have retained the intertemporal budget constraints of the representative agent, which is a form of stock-flow consistency internal to a single sector, but the stock-flow consistency required throughout the various sectors of the economy has been left in the void.

the research programme that was being pursued at Yale University on the stock-flow consistent approach to macroeconomic modelling.[15] Indeed, because the paper was empirically oriented, it contains many heterodox features which are not present in the other Tobin papers. The present book, in some directions, goes further than those previously enlightened authors, or so we believe, and it also treks along paths that were not suggested by these precursors – paths that generally have a post-Keynesian flavour.[16]

1.5 Some links with the 'old' Yale school[17]

In his Nobel lecture, Tobin (1982a: 172–3) identified the main features that distinguished his work. Four features stood out, and they certainly apply to the present book.

1. Tracking of stocks and precision regarding time;
2. Several assets and rates of return;
3. Modelling of financial and monetary policy operations;
4. The budget constraint and the adding-up constraint.

We have already extensively discussed feature (1). It is simply the idea that one should adopt a stock-flow coherent approach to modelling. This implies, as was pointed out by Turnovsky (1977: 3), that there are *intrinsic dynamics*, that reflect 'the dynamic behaviour stemming from certain logical relationships which constrain the system; specifically the relationships between stocks and flows', and which cause the modelled system to evolve over time. The short-run determination of macroeconomic variables is one among several steps of a dynamic sequence. These intrinsic dynamics must be distinguished from the *lag dynamics*, which are involved with the passage of time. These lags insure that causes precede effects, so that we keep the time-sequence right and understand the processes at work. Lags, even small ones, are required to avoid telescoping time (Hicks 1965: 66–7), and they will be extensively used in our models – more so than in Tobin's own models. As well, we shall often be appealing to the existence of stock-flow *norms*, both for firms and for households. These norms are well known in the case of governments, where political discussions often centre around sustainable public debt to GDP ratios.

[15] 'The paper could not have been written without Tobin's monumental contribution to the subject' (Godley 1997: 48).
[16] See Chapter 13 for a more detailed assessment of the specific behavioural equations and closures used in our models, compared with those of Tobin.
[17] This section has strongly benefited from the assessment provided by Dos Santos (2002a,b).

Feature (2) says that a comprehensive model should have several assets and several rates of return. Tobin objected to the standard representation of the IS/LM model, which has only one explicit rate of return, the bill rate, and one explicit asset, money. Since financial relations are so important in a modern economy, a sophisticated financial framework must be developed to understand the various interactions between borrowers and lenders, as well as the role of the banking system. In our book, we shall experiment with various numbers of assets, and various kinds of assets. In some models, where we wish to emphasize other blocks of the economy, we shall stick to a single monetary asset. However, in most chapters, there will be indeed a multiplicity of assets and liabilities, each with their own rate of return. The portfolio choice of households will follow the tracks laid out by Brainard and Tobin (1968) in their famous 'pitfalls' article. This hypothesis has been abandoned by the profession (on the grounds that its econometric performance, due to collinearity problems, was 'a mixed success at best' (Buiter 2003: 7), but, as we have already argued, there is no theoretical reason to assume that Tobin's asset demands are (stable enough to be) amenable to econometric treatment in the first place.

Feature (3), the modelling of financial and monetary policy, will be a key part of our book. How the stocks of the various assets are supplied, in particular by the monetary authorities and the government, will be described in detail. Whatever financial or monetary rule must be followed will be modelled precisely. Indeed, how the banking and financial systems are precisely being modelled constitutes one of the major differences between the Yale approach on the one hand and the New Cambridge approach which is being advocated here.

Finally, there is feature (4), which says that agents must respect their budget constraint, both in regard to their expectations and when they assess realized results. In the case of expected results, this is sometimes referred to as Walras' Law, as does Tobin in his Nobel lecture, but we would rather refer to a budget constraint or to a system-wide consistency requirement. In a water-tight accounting framework, the transaction flows of the ultimate sector are entirely determined by the transaction flows of the other sectors. Indeed, we shall see that this consistency requirement always implies a *redundant* equality. Feature (4) means that there cannot be any *black hole*. In the words of Godley and Cripps (1983: 18), 'the fact that money stocks and flows must satisfy accounting identities in individual budgets and in an economy as a whole provides a fundamental law of macroeconomics analogous to the principle of conservation of energy in physics'. While consistency is required at the accounting level, it is also required at the behavioural level. This consistency requirement is particularly important and useful in the case of portfolio choice with several assets, where any change in the demand for an asset, for a given amount of expected or end-of-period wealth, must be reflected in an overall change in the value of the remaining assets which is of equal size but opposite sign.

The above four features distinguish the work of Tobin and that of the New Haven school, along with the work of individuals such as Turnovsky (1977), compared with that of standard mainstream macroeconomics.[18] The same features apply to the work and the approach being presented in this book. Thus, on the method – consistent accounting, consistent stock-flow analysis and consistent adding-up constraints on behavioural relationships – the New Haven school and the New Cambridge school are in agreement.[19] In addition, as already pointed out, the modelling of portfolio behaviour by households in the present book is essentially being inspired by the method propounded by Brainard and Tobin (1968).

However, agreement on the method does not preclude disagreement on the model. While it is crucial to have coherent accounting and stock-flow consistency, the behaviour of the model and its results depend as well on the *closure* and the *causality* of the model, that is, on the behavioural equations that will be associated with the accounting equations. More precisely, as defined by Lance Taylor (1991: 41): 'Formally, prescribing closure boils down to stating which variables are endogenous or exogenous in an equation system largely based upon macroeconomic accounting identities, and figuring out how they influence one another.... A sense of institutions and history necessarily enters into any serious discussion of macro causality'. It is at this stage of modelling that the work that we pursue can be best distinguished from that of the New Haven school. As we shall see our book is essentially post-Keynesian or heterodox, rather than neo-classical Keynesian as is the case of Tobin's work. Still, as was advocated by Thomas Palley (1996: 2), to

---

[18] For instance, in Hicks's (1937) famous IS/LM model of Keynes's *General Theory* (1936), investment is carried on, and saving occurs, while the supply of money is assumed to be exogenous to the model. What happens to wealth or debt at the end of the period is never discussed. Whereas the money stock ought to be an endogenous variable, determined by the system, it is assumed to be exogenous and controlled by the monetary authorities. As pointed out by Tobin (1982a: 187), 'the conventional strategy is to model the determination of asset prices and interest rates as a temporary stock equilibrium independent of flows of new saving'. The stock-flow consistent approach to macroeconomic modelling, advocated here and advocated by Tobin, precisely goes beyond this temporary equilibrium, where time seems to be frozen and the flows of investment and household saving have no impact on fixed capital, debt, wealth, and money stocks. The IS/LM model is only one slice of time (Tobin 1982a: 172), and a bad one at that.

[19] We thus disagree with a statement by Victoria Chick (1992: 81), who said that 'economics is not about the logical consistency of models – mercifully, as very few models are logically consistent and those which are, are sterile'. However we do agree with the rest of her paragraph, when she writes that 'models involve compromise, and the trick [is] to find the right compromise for the problem at hand'. All sorts of simplifications must be introduced, and different simplifications will be needed depending on the problem at hand. However, compromise cannot involve a lack of stock-flow consistency.

add some aspects of Yale Keynesianism to heterodox post-Keynesian theory may yield a good mix.

1.6   Links with the post-Keynesian school

In contrast to neo-classical economics, the adjustment processes towards the steady state will be based on simple reaction functions to disequilibria. There will be no need to assume that firms maximize profit or that agents optimize some utility function, nor will there be any need to assume that agents have perfect information or know perfectly how the macroeconomic system behaves. In other words, there is no need nor no room for the rational expectations hypothesis. Still agents in our models are rational: they display a kind of *procedural rationality*, sometimes misleadingly called *weak rationality* or *bounded rationality*, or more appropriately named *reasonable rationality*.[20] They set themselves norms and targets, and act in line with these and the expectations that they may hold about the future. These norms, held by agents, produce a kind of autopilot. Mistakes, or mistaken expectations, bring about piled-up (or depleted) stocks – real inventories, money balances, or wealth – that signal a required change in behaviour. With stock-flow norms, the exact way in which expectations are formed generally is not crucial. In addition, except in the simplest models, agents will be assumed to know only the values taken by the various key variables of the previous period, and not those of the current period. This information about the past will allow them to make predictions about future values, but in a world of uncertainty. The required behavioural assumptions are not very strong. What is needed is an appropriate knowledge of the structure of the economy and the functioning of its main institutions.[21]

This kind of epistemology, that is, this theory of available knowledge, is quite in line with a brand of economics which has become known as post-Keynesian or Post Keynesian economics. Post-Keynesian economics is associated with a fundamentalist reading of John Maynard Keynes's *General Theory* but it is also associated with the work of the Polish economist Michal

---

[20] Several psychologists now argue that people take their decisions on the basis of satisficing, that is when thresholds have been met as Herbert Simon (1959) would put it, and on the basis of fast and frugal heuristics, and that these heuristics give rise to decisions which are as valid if not better than decisions that would be based on compensatory criteria or linear regressions. See Gigerenzer and Todd (1999).

[21] As shown in Lavoie (2006b), our views on this are very close to those of Duménil and Lévy (1993: ch. 10), who advocate the *principle of adjustment* to observed disequilibria by decentralized agents or institutions, in opposition to the optimization principle used by neo-classical authors , and in opposition to the centralized tâtonnement of the Walrasian commissaire-priseur. As Duménil and Lévy (1995: 372) point out, 'adjustment concerns all behaviour. ... It can serve to describe the behaviour of an individual ... it applies to an institution, like a firm. We can also apply it to the banking system and the entire system that governs monetary policy.'

Kalecki, who is said to have discovered Keynes's principle of effective demand on his own. The other features of Kalecki's models – imperfect competition, imperfect information, mark-up pricing, fixed technical coefficients, the relevance of income distribution, the role of capacity utilization and corporate retained profits, the importance of lags and time, long-run trends being conceived as 'a slowly changing component of a chain of short period situations' (1971: 165) – are all characteristics that have been taken over by the better-known Cambridge economists, in particular Joan Robinson and Nicholas Kaldor. Most of these features are incorporated into the present book, and they have been discussed at length in the past by both authors (Godley and Cripps 1983; Lavoie 1992).

It should be pointed out that Kaleckian mark-up pricing is a specific variant of the more generic *cost-plus* pricing (Lee 1998; Lavoie 2001a). Cost-plus pricing asserts that prices are determined by unit costs, somehow measured, to which is added a costing margin. For a long time, heterodox Cambridge economists denied that Kaleckian mark-up pricing had anything to do with full-cost pricing or normal-cost pricing as developed by members of the Oxford Economists' Research Group, such as Hall and Hitch (1939), P.W.S. Andrews (1949) and Andrews and Brunner (1975). It is now generally acknowledged that Kaleckian markup pricing and Andrewsian normal cost pricing are based on the same general conceptual cost-plus framework. One of us studied under Andrews and worked under Hall, and has done a substantial amount of empirical work vindicating their theories (Coutts, Godley and Nordhaus 1978), which may help to explain why full-cost pricing or normal pricing is such an integral part of the more realistic models to be deployed in the latter chapters. Because cost-plus pricing ties together labour costs, interest costs and normal profits, it is also crucial in determining income distribution, which is of such importance in heterodox economics.

Our book also has links with post-Keynesian theory because of its emphasis on *monetary* macroeconomics. Post-Keynesians attribute great importance to the fact that Keynes wished to deal with a monetized economy of production, an *entrepreneur* economy in the words of Keynes. This means that production is made possible by bank advances, while firms go into debt before attempting to recover monetary proceeds. It also means that households hold financial assets, as well as real ones, and that this feature has to be taken into consideration when dealing with their behaviour. In particular, it should be clear, as was already pointed out by Davidson (1968a), that although households hold property rights to corporations, in the form of equities which carry a certain rate of return, they do not directly hold the physical capital goods used in the production process, and hence do not make their portfolio decisions on the basis of the profit rate generated by these capital goods.

This focus on the monetary side of production, debt and portfolio behaviour requires a serious examination of the banking system and of the financial system more generally. Banks and their balance sheets have to be fully integrated to the production process, and interest flows have to be taken into account explicitly. Our accounting framework will allow us to do just that. In addition, this framework will allow us to describe and understand the monetary circuit, that is, the monetary creation, circulation and destruction that accompanies production and wealth creation. The role of government expenditures, and their link with monetary creation and interest rates prevailing on government securities will also be understood through the use of the same rigorous accounting framework. In particular, that the money stock is *endogenous*, as post-Keynesians such as Kaldor (1970a, 1982) and Robinson (1956, ch. 23) have long asserted, will be a crucial element of our models.

Another feature of post-Keynesian models, which can be associated with the *principle of effective demand*, is that market clearing through prices does not usually occur except in financial markets. The real markets, those for products and labour, are assumed to be demand-led. Full employment of labour is not assumed, nor is full employment of capacity, although, in the later chapters, where the possibility of inflation is introduced, high levels of employment or capacity will be assumed to generate inflationary pressures. In that sense, one can say that our later models will be demand-led but eventually supply constrained. Post-Keynesians believe that if market forces based on price clearing were to act on the labour market, they would generate instability. As to product markets, when dealing with the simplest models it will be assumed that supply adjusts to demand – the reverse of Say's law – while when dealing with more realistic models there will be another sort of quantity adjustment, a partial one, through inventories. It follows that the models to be described are typically *Keynesian*: product markets clear through quantity adjustments, and the models are *demand-led*. The lack of production capacity, brought about by insufficient past investments will not be discussed here although it may provide a possible explanation of current unemployment.

Our claim is thus that the present modelling approach is an integral part of the post-Keynesian school.[22] Indeed, as emphasized by Dos Santos (2005), there is a long tradition among post-Keynesian authors in attempting to analyse flows and financial stocks together, as can be seen from the works of Davidson (1968a,b), Minsky (1975, 1986) and Eichner (1987), just to mention a few well-known authors, and more recently from Dalziel (2001).[23] The purpose of our book is to make this concern more explicit.

1.7   A sketch of the book

1.7.1   How the book was written

Our approach is to present a series of models, starting from very simple ones so that the reader can fully comprehend the methodology which is being

---

[22] See Harcourt (2006) for a recent review of post-Keynesian thought.

[23] See appendix 1.2 for more details on the links with previous post-Keynesian authors.

advocated here, as well as its implications. Gradually, various complications will be added to the basic model, and these complications will make the model richer and more realistic, enabling us to understand more features of the real world surrounding us. Initially, some of the added complications will be removed, leaving room for yet other realistic complications, which will allow us to deal with new facets of reality. To give two instances, price inflation, and its adequate accounting, will not be considered in the initial stages of the book; similarly, open economies will only be considered at first within a highly simplified setting. As a result, we shall present first a series of highly simplified models, the behaviour of which shall be simple enough to be understood intuitively. Only towards the end of the book shall we consider some of these complications all at the same time.

All the descriptions of models in the text were preceded by the construction of a numerical simulation model which the computer solved successfully and displayed. This procedure guaranteed that each model was complete and that the accounting was correct, that is to say that the model endogenized all the relevant variables, that it yielded a stable solution and that the missing equation was satisfied. We found the simulation experiments, some of which will be illustrated later on, to be extremely instructive. It has to be admitted that the text does not always do justice to the insights we obtained.

1.7.2   And how it should be used

As most of our models do not lend themselves to analytic solution, we strongly recommend readers to carry out simulations for themselves (Table 1.4). It will be via the experience of trying out alternative values for exogenous variables and parameters – and, indeed, by changing the models themselves – that major intuitions will be achieved. It will be found that key results will be far less arbitrary (less open to the 'garbage in garbage out' gibe) than one might suppose. The reader will be able quite easily to verify our results and conduct his or her own experiments because our colleague Gennaro Zezza has set up every one of our models (complete with data and solution routine) in a form that can be readily accessed.[24]

The material to be covered in Chapter 2, is undoubtedly difficult for under-graduates. But this material is also of the utmost importance, because it will clearly illustrate why the method and the approach advocated in this book is different from that to be found in standard macroeconomics. There is thus some dilemma here. As a strategic move, undergrads may prefer to skip Chapter 2, and jump right away into Chapter 3, where a very simple model – the simplest we could imagine – illustrates some of the principles which have been evoked in this introductory chapter. After having worked out the models presented in the next three chapters, where these principles appear time and time again, in various simplified economies, usually with several assets, the

---

[24] At http://gennaro.zezza.it/software/eviews/gl2006.php.

Table 1.4   Suggested reading sequence

Undergraduate students	Graduate students and professors
Chapter 1	Chapter 1
Chapter 3	Chapter 2
Chapter 4	Chapter 4
Chapter 5	Chapter 5
Chapter 6	Chapter 6
Chapter 2	Chapter 7
	Chapter 8
	Chapter 9
	Chapter 10
	Appendices 3.3 and 3.4
	Chapter 11
	Chapter 12
	Chapter 13

reader should become drilled enough to understand the material presented in Chapter 2. It would then be quite advisable to track back to that chapter, where the reader will find the answers to some of the queries that could have arisen while dealing with the formal models see (Table 1.4).

Appendix 1.1:   Compelling empirical failings of the neo-classical production function

Felipe and McCombie (2006) have brilliantly demonstrated that the neo-classical production function is an *artefact*. They start off from a world with mark-up pricing procedures, made up of firms producing a unique good under the laws of identical Cobb-Douglas production functions (so there is no problem of *aggregation* as such). Regressions run on physical data confirm that the output elasticity of capital is equal to 0.75, as assumed in the production functions. However, when regressions are run on deflated monetary values, as they must be since macroeconomists do not have direct access to physical data, the coefficient representing the apparent output elasticity of capital turns out to be equal to 0.25, a value that corresponds to the 25% share of profit income embedded in the assumed costing margin. Thus Felipe and McCombie show that regressions on production functions assessed in deflated values yield coefficients that measure the share of profits in national income, instead of the output elasticity of capital as neoclassical authors maintain. Such econometric estimates of the production function simply reproduce the national account identities, as Shaikh (1974) had shown earlier.

Thus, whereas neo-classical authors believe that the estimates of the output elasticities of capital and labour turn out to be nearly equal to the shares of profit and wages in national income because neoclassical theory predicts that this will be so in a competitive economy with diminishing returns and constant returns to scale where production factors are paid at the value of their marginal product, the reality is that estimates of the production function based on deflated values simply reproduce the identities of the national accounts and that the *pseudo* estimates of the output elasticity of capital are really approximations of the profit share. Even when diminishing returns do rule, the true output elasticities are most likely to be completely unrelated to their pseudo econometric estimates. Indeed, Shaikh (2005) shows that even when the economy has a fixed-coefficient technology with mark-up pricing and Harrod-neutral technical progress, so that neither marginal productivity nor marginal cost pricing exist, regressions will yield econometric estimates that seem to support the existence of a neo-classical production function with factors of production being paid at marginal productivity, provided technical progress is specified appropriately.

These critiques have serious consequences for nearly all of neo-classical applied aggregate work, since most of it relies on constant price monetary estimates of 'well-behaved' production functions. Even when setting aside problems of aggregation, these estimates are either completely off target (if the world is made up of neo-classical production functions) or imaginary (if economies are run on fixed technical coefficients, as we believe they are essentially).

Appendix 1.2:   Stock-flow relations and the post-Keynesians

In her survey of post-Keynesian economics, Chick (1995) considers that stock-flow analysis is among its achievements. Chick refers to the works of Hyman Minsky, who she says was always concerned by the gap between flow analysis and its stock implications. The influence of Minsky can also be felt in Wray (1990: ch. 9), where a balance sheet approach including firms, banks and households is being proposed to explain the appearance of endogenous money. Chick (1995) also refers to the balance-sheet approach of Godley and Cripps (1983), which elsewhere, in Chick (1992: 81), she called 'a very successful integration of stocks and flows'. In an article originally published in 1973, Chick (1992) challenged the separation of IS from LM and said that the IS/LM model only made sense in a stationary equilibrium, arguing that if one could ignore the impact of investment on output capacity, one could not ignore the immediate financial consequences of investment financing. In this article, Chick also directs the reader towards two articles of Paul Davidson. In the first one, Davidson (1968a) criticizes Kaldor (1966) for omitting money balances in his famous neo-Pasinetti growth model with stock equities, which is at the origin of an important and successful attempt at integrating growth of output flows and portfolio analysis, that of Peter Skott (1989). In his second paper, Davidson (1968b) provides an excellent critique of Tobin's growth model and portfolio analysis. Davidson underlines the fact that that Tobin does not introduce an independent investment function, which is the hallmark of Keynesian analysis, so as to avoid Say's law, thus assuming that households choose between money balances and real capital, whereas their choice ought to be between money balances and placements, that is, securities or equities. While putting forward his own q-theory of investment, before Tobin, while not attaching much faith in it, Davidson points out that more household saving would lead to higher valuation ratios, and hence, lower long-term yields or dividend yields, but that this will not in general lead to faster investment. Both of these Davidson papers show a substantial concern for stock-flow consistency.

Another post-Keynesian author who is clearly concerned with stock-flow consistency is Alfred Eichner (1987), in his synthesis of post-Keynesian economics. Eichner (1987: ch. 12) also presents the endogeneity of money, the creation of loans, as well as clearinghouse and central bank operations through a balance-sheet approach, where he makes a distinction between the financial sector and two non-financial sectors. Eichner explicitly ties this approach to the flow-of-funds approach of Jacob Cohen (1986) and to the work of Godley and Cripps (1983). The post-Keynesian theory and the flow-of-funds approach also intersect in a paper by Alan Roe (1973), who also worked with Richard Stone in the early 1970s to establish flow-of-funds measures of financial interdependence, in a way which closely resembles the coefficients of Leontief's input-output analysis, as recently advocated by Lawrence Klein (2003). Roe (1973) believes that individuals and institutions generally follow stock-flow norms related to their assets, liabilities, income or sales, but that during expansion, because of improved expectations, they may agree to let standards deteriorate. Roe is particularly concerned with brisk attempts at changing the composition of portfolios, when cash flows or expectations return to normal values. This sounds very much like Minskyan economics, and indeed it is, as Roe explicitly refers to the work of Minsky on financial fragility, showing that a stock-flow consistent framework is certainly an ideal method to analyse the merits and the possible consequences of Minsky's financial fragility hypothesis.[25]

Minsky himself certainly paid attention to stock-flow consistency. This is not surprising since he underlined the fact that stocks of assets and debts led to cash flows and debt payments through time. Minsky, just like Eichner, had a clear understanding of the relationships between the various sectoral balance sheets. As the following quote demonstrates, he was fully aware of the all-important *quadruple entry* principle, which we will discuss in Chapter 2.[26]

> The structure of an economic model that is relevant to a capitalist economy needs to include the interrelated balance sheets and income statements of the units of the economy. The principle of double entry bookkeeping, where financial assets and liabilities on another balance sheet and where every entry on a balance sheet has a dual in another entry on the same balance sheet, means that every transaction in assets requires four entries (Minsky 1996: 77).

The ties between flow-of-funds analysis and post-Keynesian economics are reinforced by the fact that most proponents of financial flows analysis were heterodox economists, associated more or less closely with (old) Institutionalism. For instance, in the preface to his handbook on flow-of-funds analysis, Dawson (1996: xx) says that 'the book will reveal me as an institutionalist, practical in orientation, and skeptical of economic doctrine'. Dawson (1996: 5) points out that 'the acceptance of ... flow-of-funds accounting by academic economists has been an uphill battle because its implications run counter to a number of doctrines deeply embedded in the minds of economists', and he adds that Morris A. Copeland, who is considered to be the inventor of flow-of-funds accounts, 'himself was at pains to show the incompatibility of the quantity theory of money with flow-of-funds accounting'. Indeed, James Millar (1996: 85) claims that 'Copeland always proudly proclaimed his commitment to institutionalism' even though he is not 'fully recognized today as an institutionalist'. He can surely be recognized as some early radical post-Keynesian author, since Copeland argued that 'the changes Keynes introduced represented modifications of neoclassicism, not its rejection', adding, as early as the late 1950s that 'Keynes was being brought back into the neoclassical church' – an assessment which looks quite similar to those that Cambridge Keynesians such as Robinson and Kaldor were also making at that time.

---

[25] On this specific issue, see the recent efforts of Dos Santos (2005) and Tymoigne (2006).
[26] Tarik Mouakil brought our attention to this quote.

2
Balance Sheets, Transaction Matrices and the Monetary Circuit

2.1 Coherent stock-flow accounting

Contemporary mainstream macroeconomics, as it can be ascertained from intermediate textbooks, is based on the system of national accounts that was put in place by the United Nations in 1953 – the so-called Stone accounts. At that time, some macroeconomists were already searching for some alternative accounting foundations for macroeconomics. In the United States, Morris A. Copeland (1949), an institutionalist in the quantitative Mitchell tradition of the NBER, designed the first version of what became the flow-of-funds accounts now provided by the Federal Reserve since 1952 – the Z.1 accounts. Copeland wanted to have a framework that would allow him to answer simple but important questions such as: 'When total purchases of our national product increase, where does the money come from to finance them? When purchases of our national product decline, what becomes of the money that is not spent?' (Copeland 1949 (1996: 7)).

In a macroeconomic textbook that was well-known in France, Jean Denizet (1969) also complained about the fact that standard macroeconomic accounting, designed upon Richard Stone's social accounting, as eventually laid out in the 1953 United Nations System of National Accounts, left monetary and financial phenomena in the dark, in contrast to the approach that was advocated from the very beginning by some accountants (among which Denizet) in the Netherlands and in France. In the initial standard national accounting – as was shown in its most elementary form with the help of Table 1.1 – little room was left for banks and financial intermediaries and the accounts were closed on the basis of the famous Keynesian equality, that saving must equal investment. This initial system of accounts is a system that presents 'the sector surpluses that ultimately finance real investment', but it does not present 'any information about the flows in financial assets and liabilities by which the saving moves through the financial system into investment. These flows in effect have been consolidated out' (Dawson 1991 (1996: 315)). In standard national accounting, as represented by the National Income and Product Accounts (NIPA), there is no room to discuss the questions that Copeland was keen to tackle, such as the changes in financial stocks of assets and of debts, and their relation with the transactions occurring in the current or the capital accounts of the various agents of the economy. In addition, in the standard macroeconomics textbook, households and firms are often amalgamated within a single private sector, and hence, since financial assets or debts are netted out, it is rather difficult to introduce discussions about such financial issues, except for public debt.

The lack of integration between the flows of the real economy and its financial side greatly annoyed a few economists, such as Denizet and Copeland. For Denizet, J.M. Keynes's major contribution was his questioning of the classical dichotomy between the real and the monetary sides of the economy. The post-Keynesian approach, which prolongs Keynes's contribution on this, underlines the need for integration between financial and income accounting, and thus constitutes a radical departure from the mainstream.[1] Denizet found paradoxical that standard national accounting, as was initially developed by Richard Stone, reproduced the very dichotomy that Keynes had himself attempted to destroy. This was surprising because Stone was a good friend of Keynes, having provided him with the national accounts data that Keynes needed to make his forecasts and recommendations to the British Treasury during the Second World War, but of course it reflected the initial difficulties in gathering enough good financial data, as Stone himself later got involved in setting up a proper framework for financial flows and balance sheet data (Stone 1966).[2]

By 1968 a new *System of National Accounts* (SNA) was published by the national accountants of the UN. This new system provided a theoretical scheme that stressed the integration of the national income accounts with financial transactions, capital stocks and balance sheet (as well as input-output accounts), and hence answered the concerns of economists such as Copeland and Denizet. The new accounting system was cast in the form of a matrix, which started with opening assets, adding or subtracting production, consumption, accumulation and taking into account reevaluations, to obtain, at the bottom of the matrix, closing assets. This new integrated accounting system has been confirmed with the revised 1993 SNA.

---

[1] Such an integration of financial transactions with real transactions, within an appropriate set of sectors, was also advocated by Gurley and Shaw (1960: ch. 2) in their well-known book, as it was by a number of other authors, inspired by the work of Copeland, Alan Roe (1973) for instance, whose article was appropriately titled 'the case for flow of funds and national balance sheet accounts'.

[2] Various important surveys of flow-of-funds analysis and a stock-flow-consistent approach to macroeconomics can be found, among others in Bain (1973), Davis (1987), Patterson and Stephenson (1988), Dawson (1996).

Several countries now have complete flow-of-funds accounts or financial flows accounts, as well as national balance sheet accounts, so that by combining the flow-of-funds account and the national income and product account, and making a few adjustments, linked in particular to consumer durable good, it is possible to devise a matrix that accomplishes such an integration, as has been demonstrated by Backus *et al.* (1980: 270–1). The problem now is not so much the lack of appropriate data, as shown by Ruggles (1987), but rather the unwillingness of most mainstream macroeconomists to incorporate these financial flows and capital stocks into their models, obsessed as they are with the representative optimizing microeconomic agent. The construction of this integrated matrix, which we shall call the *transactions flow matrix*, will be explained in a later section. But before we do so, let us examine a simpler financial matrix, one that is better known, the *balance sheet matrix* or the *stock matrix*.

2.2 Balance sheets or stock matrices

2.2.1 The balance sheet of households

Constructing the balance sheet matrix, which deals with asset and liability stocks, will help us understand the typical financial structure of a modern economy. It will also give clues as to the elements that ought to be found in the transaction flow matrix.

Let us consider a simple closed economy. Open economies will not be examined at this stage because, for the model to be fully coherent, one would need to consider the whole world, that is, in the simplest open-economy model, one would need to consider at least two countries.

Our simple closed economy contains the following four sectors: the household sector, the production sector (made up of firms), the financial sector (essentially banks) and the government sector. The government sector can itself be split into two subsectors: the pure government sector and the central bank. The central bank is a small portion of the government sector, but because it plays such a decisive role with respect to monetary policy, and because its impact on monetary aggregates is usually identified on its own, it may be preferable to identify it separately.

Before we describe the balance sheet matrix of all these sectors, that is, the *sectoral* balance sheet matrix, it may be enlightening, in the first stage, to look at the balance sheet of individual sectors. Let us deal for instance with the balance sheet of households and that of production firms. First it should be mentioned that this is an essential distinction. In many accounts of macroeconomics, households and firms are amalgamated into a single sector, that is, the private sector. But doing so would lead to a loss in comprehending the functioning of the economy, for households and production firms take entirely different decisions. In addition, their balance sheets show substantial differences of structure, which reflect the different roles that each sector plays. For the same reasons, it will be important to make a distinction between production firms (non-financial businesses) and financial firms (banks and the so-called non-banking financial intermediaries).

We start with the balance sheet of households, since it is the most intuitive as shown in Table 2.1. Households hold tangible assets (their tangible capital K_h). This tangible capital mainly consists of the dwellings that households own – real estate – but it also includes consumer durable goods, such as cars, dishwashing machines or ovens. An individual may also consider that the jewellery (gold, diamonds) being kept at home or in a safe is part of tangible assets. But in financial flow accounts, jewellery is not included among the tangible assets. Households also hold several kinds of financial assets, for instance bills B_h, money deposits M_h, cash H_h and a number e of equities, the market price of which is p_e. Households also hold liabilities: they take loans L_h to finance some of their purchases. For instance households would take mortgages to purchase their house, and hence the remaining balance of the mortgage would appear as a liability.

The difference between the assets and the liabilities of households constitutes their *net worth*, that is, their *net wealth* NW_h. The net worth of households is a residual, which is usually positive and relatively substantial. This is because households usually spend much less than they receive as income, and as a result they accumulate net financial assets and tangible (or real) assets. Note, however, that if equity prices (or housing prices) were to fall below the value at which they were purchased with the help of loans taken for pure speculative purposes – as would happen during a stock market crash that would have followed a stock market boom – the net worth of households taken overall could become negative. This is because household

Table 2.1   Household balance sheet

Assets	64,000	Liabilities	64,000
Tangible capital K_h	25,500	Loans L_h	11,900
Equities $e \cdot p_e$		Net Worth NW_h	52,100
Bills B_h			
Money deposits M_h	5,900		
Cash H_h			

Source: Z.1 statistics of the Federal Reserve, www.federalreserve.gov/releases/z1, Table B.100, 'Balance sheet of households and nonprofit organizations', March 2006 release; units are billions of dollars.

assets, in particular real estate and shares on the stock market, are valued at their market value in the balance sheet accounts.[3] In the case of American households, this is not likely to happen, based on the figures presented in Table 2.1, which arise from the balance sheet of households and nonprofit organizations, as assessed by the Z.1 statistics of the Federal Reserve for the last quarter of 2005. Loans represent less than 20% of net worth. Tangible assets – real estate and consumer durable goods – plus deposits account for nearly 50% of total assets. The other financial assets are not so easy to assign, since a substantial portion of these other assets, including equities and securities, are held indirectly, by pension funds, trust funds and mutual funds.

In general net worth turns out to be positive. A general accounting principle is that balance sheets ought to *balance*, that is, the sums of all the items on each side of the balance sheet ought to equal each other. It is obvious that for the balance sheet of households to balance, the item *net worth* must be *added* to the *liability side* of the household balance sheet, since net worth is positive and the asset value of households is larger than their liability value.

In the overall balance sheet matrix, all the elements on the asset side will be entered with a plus sign, since they constitute additions to the net worth of the sector. The elements of the liability side will be entered with a negative sign. This implies that net worth will be entered with a negative sign in the balance sheet matrix, since it is to be found on the liability side. These conventions will insure that all the rows and all the columns of the balance sheet matrix sum to zero, thus providing consistency and coherence in our stock accounting.

2.2.2 The balance sheet of production firms

It could be sufficient to deal with the household sector, since the balance sheets of all sectors respond to the same principles. The balance sheet of firms, however, suffers from one additional complication, which is worth looking at. The complication arises from the existence of corporate equities. In some sense, the value of these shares is something which the firm owes to itself, but since the owners consider the value of these shares to be part of their assets, it will have to enter the liability side of some other sector, since we wish to be fully consistent. Equities pose a problem 'because they are financial assets to whoever holds them, but they are not, legally, liabilities of the issuing corporation' (Ritter 1963 (1996: 123)), in contrast to corporate paper or corporate bonds issued by the firm. This implies that interest payments

---

[3] This is how it should be; but some statistical agencies still register real estate or stock market shares at their acquisition value.

are a contractual obligation, whereas the payment of dividends is not – it is at the discretion of the board of directors.

However, in practice, as pointed out by Joan Robinson (1956: 247–8), this distinction becomes fuzzy since directors are reluctant to cut off dividends (because of the negative signal that it sends to the markets) and because creditors often will accept to forego interest payments temporarily to avoid the bankruptcy of their debtor. As a result, as suggested by Ritter (1963 (1996: 123)), 'for most purposes the simplest way to handle this is to assume that corporate stocks and bonds are roughly the same thing, despite their legal differences and treat them both as liabilities of the corporation'.

This is precisely what we shall do. The current stock market value of the stock of equities which have been issued in the past shall be assessed as being part of the liabilities of the firms. By doing so, as will be clear in the next subsection, we make sure that a financial claim is equally valued whether it appears among the assets of the households or whether it appears on the liability side of the balance sheet of firms. This will insure that the row of equities in the overall sectoral balance sheet sums to zero, as all other rows of the matrix. The balance sheet of production firms in our framework, will thus appear as shown in Table 2.2.

It must be noted that all the items on this balance sheet (except inventories) are evaluated *at market prices*. This distinction is important, because the items on balance sheets of firms, or at least some items, are often evaluated *at historical cost*, that is, evaluated at the price of acquisition of the assets and liabilities (the price paid *at the time that the assets and liabilities were purchased*). In the present book, balance sheets at *market prices* will be the rule. This means that every tangible asset is evaluated at its replacement value, that is, the price that it would cost to produce this real asset now; and every financial asset is evaluated at its current value on the financial markets. For instance, a \$100 bond issued by a corporation or a government may see its price rise temporarily to \$120. With balance sheets evaluated at market prices, the bond will be entered as a \$120 claim in the balance sheets of both the holder

Table 2.2 Balance sheet of production firms at market prices, *with* equities as a liability

Assets	2001	2005	Liabilities	2001	2005
Total	17,500	22,725	Total	17,500	22,725
Tangible capital K_f	9,200	11,750	Loans L_f	9,100	10,125
Financial assets M_f	8,300	11,975	Equities issued $e_f \cdot p_{ef}$	10,900	10,925
			Net Worth NW_f	−2,500	+1,675

Source: Z.1 statistics of the Federal Reserve, www.federalreserve.gov/releases/z1, Table B.102, 'Balance sheet of nonfarm nonfinancial corporate business', March 2002 and 2006 releases, last quarter data; units are billions of dollars.

and the issuer of the bond, although the corporation or the government still look upon the bond as a $100 liability.

However, in the case of firms, the combination of equities treated as a debt of firms with market-price balance sheets yields counter-intuitive results. This is why it becomes important to study in detail the balance sheets of firms. Balance sheets computed at market prices and treating equities issued by firms as a liability of the firm are the only ones that will be utilized in the book because they are the only balance sheets which can be made coherent within the matrix approach which is advocated here.

In the example given by Table 2.2, firms have an array of tangible capital – fixed capital, real estate, equipment and software, and inventories, which, evaluated at *production prices* or *current replacement cost*, that is, at the price that it would cost to have them replaced at current prices, are worth K_f.[4] The numbers being provided are in billions of dollars and are those of the United States economy at the end of the fourth quarters of 2001 and 2005, as they can be found in the flow-of-funds Z.1 statistics of the Federal Reserve. In 2005, tangible assets thus held by nonfinancial corporate business amounted to $11,750 billions. Financial assets of various sorts amounted to $11,975 billions, and hence total assets were worth $22,725 billions.

On the liability side, liabilities are split into two kinds of liabilities. First there are liabilities to 'third parties', which we have summarized under the generic term loans L_f, but which, beyond bank loans, comprises notably corporate paper, corporate bonds and all other credit market instruments. Second, there are liabilities to 'second parties', that is, the owners of the equity of firms. In our table, all these liabilities are valued at market prices. In the case of equities, an amount of e_f shares have been issued over the years, and the current price of each share on the stock market is p_{ef}. The market value of shares is thus $E_f = e_f \cdot p_{ef}$. In 2005, 'loans' L_f amounted to $10,125 billions, while equities E_f were worth $10,925 billions, for an apparent total liability amount of $21,050 billions. Compare this to the total asset amount of $22,725 billions. This implies, to insure that the value of total liabilities is indeed equal to the value of total assets, that in 2005 the net worth of the firm, NW_f as shown in Table 2.2, is positive and equal to +$1675 billions.

But the situation could be quite different and net worth as measured here could be negative, as we can observe from the 2001 data, where we see that net worth then was negative and equal to $2500 billions. Such a negative

---

[4] Real estate, as in the case of residential dwelling, is evaluated at market prices, but it will enter none of our models. Capital goods are valued at their replacement price. *Inventories* are valued at their *current cost of production*. All these assets are valued neither at their historical cost of acquisition, nor at the price which firms expect to fetch when these goods will be sold. This will be explained in greater detail in Chapter 8.

net worth value will arise whenever the net financial value of the firm is larger than the replacement value of its tangible capital. The ratio of these two expressions is the so-called q-ratio, as defined by Tobin (1969). Thus whenever the q-ratio is larger than unity, the net worth is negative.[5] A similar kind of macroeconomic negative net worth could plague the financial firms, the banks, if banks issue shares as they are assumed to do in the stock matrix below. This will happen when the agents operating on the stock market are fairly optimistic and the shares of the firm carry a high price on the stock market. The negative net worth of the firm is a rather counter-intuitive result, because one would expect that the firm does well when it is being praised by the stock market.

This counter-intuitive phenomenon could be avoided either if accounting at historical cost was being used or if equities were not considered to be part of the liabilities for which firms are responsible. Obviously, accounting at historical cost in the case of the producing firms would make the whole macroeconomic accounting exercise incoherent. In particular the macroeconomic balance sheet matrix, to be developed below, would not balance out. Also, such accounting at cost would omit price appreciation in assets and products.[6] Another way out, which national accountants seem to support, is to exclude the market value of issued shares from the liabilities of the firms. This is the approach taken by the statisticians at the Federal Reserve. As Ruggles (1987: 43) points out, this implies that 'the main break, on the liability side, is no longer between liabilities and net worth, but rather between liabilities to "third parties", on the one hand, and the sum of liabilities to "second parties", that is, owners of the enterprise's equity and net worth, on the other'. This kind of accounting, which can be found in the works of economists of all allegiances (Malinvaud 1982; Dalziel 2001), is illustrated with Table 2.3. Under this definition, the net worth, or stockholders'equity, of American nonfinancial businesses is positive and quite large ($8400 billions in 2001), as one would intuitively expect. But again, such accounting would not be fully coherent from a macroeconomic standpoint, as is readily conceded by an uneasy Malinvaud (1982: 20), unless the q-ratio were equal to unity at all times. As a result, we shall stick to balance sheets inspired by Table 2.2, which include equities as part of the liabilities of firms, keeping in mind that the measured net worth of firms is of no practical significance. Indeed, in the book, no behavioural relationship draws on its definition.

---

[5] This q-ratio will also be discussed in Chapter 11.

[6] At the microeconomic level, such a situation gives rise to the appearance of a 'goodwill' asset, which takes into account the fact that some tangible asset may have been bought at a price apparently exceeding its value, because it is expected to yield superior profits in the future.

Table 2.3 Balance sheet of production firms at market prices, *without* equities as a liability

Assets	2001	2005	Liabilities	2001	2005
Total	17,500	22,725	Total	17,500	22,725
Tangible capital K_f	9,200	11,750	Loans L_f	9,100	10,125
Financial assets M_f	8,300	11,975	Net Worth NW_f	8,400	12,600

Source: Z.1 statistics of the Federal Reserve, www.federalreserve.gov/releases/z1, Table B.102, 'Balance sheet of nonfarm nonfinancial corporate business', March 2002 and 2006 releases, last quarter data; units are billions of dollars.

2.2.3 The overall balance sheet matrix

We are now ready to consider the composition of the overall balance sheet matrix, to be found in Table 2.4. We could assume the existence of an almost infinite amount of different assets; we could also assume that all sectors own a share of all assets, as is true to some extent, but we shall start by assuming a most simple outfit. The assets and liabilities of households and production firms have already been described, and we shall further simplify them by assuming away the financial assets of firms. Government issues short-term securities B (Treasury bills). These securities are purchased by the central bank, the banks, and households. Production firms and financial firms (banks) issue equities (shares), and these are assumed to be purchased by households only. We suppose that production firms (and households, as already pointed out) need loans, and that these are being provided by the banks. The major counterpart to these loans are the money deposits held by households, who also hold cash banknotes H, which are provided by the central bank. This special kind of money issued by the central bank is often called *high-powered money*, hence the H notation being used. This high-powered money is also usually being held by banks as reserves, either in the form of vault cash or as deposits at the central bank.

In models that will be developed in the later chapters, it will generally be assumed that households take no loans and the value of their dwellings will not be taken into consideration, but here we shall do otherwise for expository purposes. Finally, it will be assumed that the real capital accumulated by financial firms or by government is too small to be worth mentioning.

As already mentioned, all assets appear with a plus sign in the balance sheet matrix while liabilities, including net worth, are assigned a negative sign. The matrix of our balance sheet must follow essentially one single rule: all the columns and all the rows that deal with financial assets or liabilities must sum to zero. The only row that may not sum to zero is the row dealing with

Table 2.4 A simplified sectoral balance sheet matrix

	Households	Production firms	Banks	Government	Central bank	Σ
Tangible capital	$+K_h$	$+K_f$				$+K$
Bills	$+B_h$		$+B_b$	$-B$	$+B_{cb}$	0
Cash	$+H_h$		$+H_b$		$-H$	0
Deposits	$+M_h$		$-M$			0
Loans	$-L_h$	$-L_f$	$+L$			0
Equities	$+E_f$	$-E_f$				0
Equities	$+E_b$		$-E_b$			0
Net worth	$-NW_h$	$-NW_f$	$-NW_b$	$-NW_g$	0	$-K$
Σ	0	0	0	0	0	0

tangible capital – the actual stock of machines and inventories accumulated by the firms in the production sector and the dwellings of households. A tangible asset – a real asset – only appears in a single entry of the sectoral balance sheet, that of its owner. This is in contrast to financial assets and all liabilities, which are a claim of someone against someone else.

Reading now the column of each sector, the sum of all the components of a column represents the net worth of that sector. Thus adding the net worth, with a negative sign, to all the other elements of the column must by necessity yield a zero result. This guarantees the coherence of the balance sheet matrix. It should be noted that the net worth of the economy, as shown in the last entry of the penultimate row, is equal to the value of tangible capital assets K (Coutts, Godley and Gudgin 1985: 97; Patterson and Stephenson 1988: 792). If there were only financial assets in an economy, the macroeconomic net worth would be nil.

A few additional remarks may be in order. As already mentioned, financial firms, that is, the banks, will also experience some net worth, NW_b, unless we assume by construction that they issue no shares and make no profits, as we shall sometimes do to simplify our earlier models. On the other hand, the government sector usually runs a large negative net worth (therefore, in Table 2.4, $-NW_g$ is a positive entry). This negative net worth NW_g is better known as the *public debt*, which arises as a result of past deficits. It may be noticed that the government public debt is the same whether or not we include the central bank in the government sector. This is because the profits of the central bank are always returned to the general revenues of government, so that the net worth of the central bank is zero (provided the central bank does not hold long-term bonds, the value of which can change through time, as we shall see later, and provided the central bank started to be run with no capital of its own).

2.3 The conventional income and expenditure matrix

2.3.1 The NIPA matrix

While the balance sheet matrix has its importance, the really interesting construct is the transactions flow matrix. This matrix records all the monetary transactions that are occurring in an economy. The matrix provides an accounting framework that will be highly useful when defining behavioural equations and setting up formal models of the economy. The transactions matrix is the major step in fully integrating income accounting and financial accounting. This full integration will become possible only when capital gains are added to the transactions matrix. When this is done, it will be possible to move from the opening stocks of assets, those being held at the beginning of the production period, to the closing stocks of assets, those being held at the end of the production period.

But before we do so, let us consider the conventional income and expenditure matrix, that is, the matrix that does not incorporate financial assets. This matrix arises from the consideration of the standard National Income and Product Accounts, the NIPA. We have already observed a very similar matrix, when we examined the national accounts seen from the perspective of the standard mainstream macroeconomics textbook. Consider Table 2.5. Compared with the previous balance sheet matrix, the financial sector has been scotched, amalgamated to the business sector, while the central bank has been reunited with the government sector. We still have the double entry constraint that the sum of the entries in each row ought to equal zero. This is a characteristic of all social accounting matrices.

It should be pointed out that all the complications that arise as a result of price inflation, for instance the fact that the value of inventories must be adjusted to take into account changes in the price level of these inventories, have been assumed away. In other words, product prices are deemed

Table 2.5 Conventional Income and expenditure matrix

	Households	Business Current	Business Capital	Government	Σ
Consumption	$-C$	$+C$			0
Govt expenditure		$+G$		$-G$	0
Investment		$+I_f$	$-I_f$		0
[GDP (memo)]		$[Y]$			
Wages	$+WB$	$-WB$			0
Net Profits	$+FD$	$-F$	$+FU$		0
Tax net of transfers	$-T_h$	$-T_f$		$+T$	0
Interest payments	$+INT_h$	$-INT_f$		$-INT_g$	0
Σ	SAV_h	0	$FU - I_f$	$-DEF$	0

to remain constant. Unless we make this assumption we shall have to face up, at far too early a stage, to various questions concerning the valuation of capital, both fixed and working, as well as price index problems. These complications will be dealt with starting with Chapter 8.

Before we start discussing the definition of gross domestic product, the perceptive reader may have noted that capital accumulation by households seems to have entirely disappeared from Table 2.5. It was already the case in Table 1.1, but then such an omission was tied to the highly simplified nature of the standard mainstream model, where only investment by firms was considered. Why would investment in residential housing be omitted from a more complete NIPA? What happens is that, in the standard NIPA, automobiles or household appliances purchased by individuals are not part of gross capital formation; rather they are considered as part of current expenditures. In addition, to put home-owners and home-renters on an identical footing, 'home ownership is treated as a fictional enterprise providing housing services to consumer-occupants' (Ruggles and Ruggles 1992 (1996: 284)). As a result, purchases of new houses or apartments by individuals are assigned to fixed capital investment by the real estate industry; and expenditures associated with home ownership, such as maintenance costs, imputed depreciation, property taxes and mortgage interest, 'are considered to be expenses of the fictional enterprise', and 'are excluded from the personal outlays of households'. In their place, there is an imputed expenditure to the fictional real estate enterprise. This is why there is no I_h entry in Table 2.5 that would represent investment into housing.

2.3.2 GDP

In this matrix, the expenditure and income components of gross domestic product (GDP), appear in the second column. The positive and negative signs have a clear meaning. The positive items are receipts by businesses as a result of the sales they make – they are the value of production –, while the negative items describe where these receipts 'went to': they are the product of the economy. It has been assumed that every expenditure in the definition of GDP (consumption C, investment I, and government expenditures on goods and services G) is a sale by businesses, although in reality this is not quite true, government employment – which is a form of expenditure which is not a receipt by firms – being the major exception. And as a counterpart, every payment of factor income included in the income definition of GDP is a disbursement by businesses in the form of wages WB, distributed profits FD and undistributed profits FU, interest payments INT_f, and indirect taxes T_f. From the second column, we thus recover the two standard definitions of income:

$$Y = C + I + G = WB + F + INT_f + T_f \tag{2.1}$$

We must now confront the fact that firms' receipts from sales of investment goods, which from the sellers' point of view are no different from any other kind of sales, do not arise from outside the business sector itself.[7] So the double entry principle that regulates the use of accounting matrices requires us to postulate a new sector – the capital account of businesses – which makes these purchases. As we work down the capital account column, we shall eventually discover where all the funds needed for investment expenditure come from.

There is no need to assume that all profits are distributed to households as is *invariably* assumed, without question, in mainstream macroeconomics. In the transactions matrix shown above, part of the net profits earned by business are distributed to households (*FD*) while the rest is undistributed (*FU*) and (considered to be) paid into their capital accounts to be used as a source of funds – as it happens, the principal source of funds – for investment. Figure 2.1 shows that in the United States total internal funds of non-financial businesses exceeds their gross investment expenditures in nearly every year

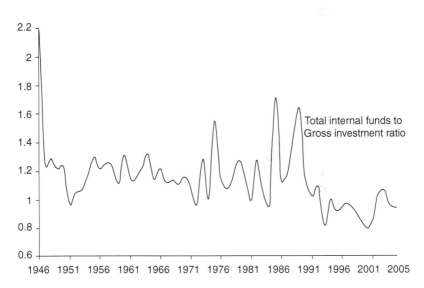

Figure 2.1 Total internal funds (including IVA) to gross investment ratio, USA, 1946–2005.

Source: Z.1 statistics of the Federal Reserve, www.federalreserve.gov/releases/z1, table F102, Non-farm non-financial corporate business. The curve plots the ratio of lines 9 and 10.

---

[7] As pointed out above, households' investment in housing is imputed to the real estate industry.

since 1946. In fact, it would seem that in many instances retained earnings are even used to finance the acquisition of financial assets.

To complete the picture, we include transfer payments between the various sectors. These are divided into two categories, payments of interest (*INT* with a lower case suffix to denote the sector in question) that are made on assets and liabilities which were outstanding at the beginning of the period and therefore largely predetermined by past history; and other 'unilateral' transfers (*T*), of which the most important are government receipts in the form of taxes and government outlays in the form of pensions and other transfers like social insurance and unemployment benefits.

All this allows us to compute the disposable income of households – personal disposable income – which is of course different from GDP. It can be read off the first column. Wages, distributed dividends, interest payments (from both the business and the government sector, minus interest paid on personal loans), minus income taxes, constitute this disposable income *YD*.[8]

$$YD = WB + FD + INT_\mathrm{h} - T_\mathrm{h} \tag{2.2}$$

2.3.3   The saving = investment identity

Matrix 2.5 has now become a neat record of all the income, expenditure and transfer payments which make up the national income accounts, showing how the sectoral accounts are intertwined. The first column shows all current receipts and payments by the household sector, including purchases of durable goods, hence the balance at the bottom is equal to household saving (SAV_h) as defined in NIPA. The second column shows current receipts and payments by firms which defines business profits as the excess of receipts from sales over outlays. The third column shows firms' investment and the undistributed profits (*FU*) which are available to finance it, the balance at the bottom showing the firms' residual financing requirement – what they must find over and above what they have generated internally. The entries in the fourth column give all the outlays and receipts of the general government, and the balance between these gives the government's budget surplus or deficit. The fact that every row until the bottom row, which describes financial balances, sums to zero guarantees that the balances' row sums to zero as well. It is this last row which has attracted the undivided attention of national accountants and of Keynesian economists. This last line says that:

$$SAV_\mathrm{h} + (FU - I_\mathrm{f}) - DEF = 0 \tag{2.3}$$

Considering that the retained earnings of firms constitute the savings of the firm's sector, we can write $FU = SAV_\mathrm{f}$; similarly, the surplus of the government

---

[8] Note that interest payments from government are not included in GDP.

sector is equivalent to its saving, so that $SAV_g = -DEF$. From these new definitions, and from the definition implicit to the investment row, we can rewrite equation (2.3) in its more familiar form:

* $$I = SAV_h + SAV_f + SAV_g = SAV \qquad (2.4)$$

Equation (2.4) is nothing else than the famous Keynesian equality between investment and saving. This is the closest that most mainstream accounts of macroeconomics will get from financial issues.[9] What happens to these savings, how they arise, what is their composition, how they link up the surplus sectors to the deficit sectors, is usually not discussed nor modelled. In Matrix 2.5, until the final row, the nature of the transactions is pretty clear: households buy goods and firms sell them, etc.[10] However, the transfer of funds 'below the (bold) line' requires a whole new set of concepts, which are not part of the conventional income and expenditures national accounts. The answers to the questions that were put to the reader in section 1.2 of the previous section are to be found quite straight forwardly, using concepts which are familiar and easy to piece together so long as the double entry principle continues to be observed and so long as we always live up to our motto that everything must go somewhere and come from somewhere. In other words, we need to bring in the transactions flow matrix.

2.4 The transactions flow matrix

2.4.1 Rules governing the transactions flow matrix

We shall require the reintroduction of the financial sector, the banks that had been introduced in the balance sheet matrix but that had been amalgamated

---

[9] Note that neo-classical economists don't even get close to this equation, for otherwise, through equation (2.4), they would have been able to rediscover Kalecki's (1971: 82–3) famous equation which says that profits are the sum of capitalist investment, capitalist consumption expenditures and government deficit, minus workers' saving. Rewriting equation (2.3), we obtain:

$$FU = I_f + DEF - SAV_h$$

which says that the retained earnings of firms are equal to the investment of firms plus the government deficit minus household saving. Thus, in contrast to neo-liberal thinking, the above equation implies that the larger the government deficit, the larger the retained earnings of firms; also the larger the saving of households, the smaller the retained earnings of firms, provided the left-out terms are kept constant. Of course the given equation also features the well-known relationship between investment and profits, whereby actual investment expenditures determine the realized level of retained earnings.

[10] The nature of these transactions is not, in reality, so simple as this. In many, perhaps most cases, the contract to purchase and sell something is separated from the transfer of money one way and the goods themselves going the other.

to the business sector in the conventional income and expenditure matrix. Similarly, the operations of the central bank will reappear explicitly in the new transactions flow matrix which is the corner stone of our approach. These additions to the conventional income and expenditure matrix will allow us to assess all transactions, be they in goods and services or in the form of financial transactions, with additions to assets or liabilities.

As in the balance sheet matrix, the coherence of the transactions flow matrix is built on the rule that each row and each column must sum to zero. The rule enforcing that all rows must sum to zero is rather straightforward: each row represent the flows of transactions for each asset or for each kind of flow; there is nothing new here. The top part of the matrix, as described in Table 2.6 resembles the income and expenditure matrix, with a few additions and new notations. In particular, the flow of interest payments, which was noted *INT* in Table 2.5, is now explicit. The flow of interest on an asset or a liability now depends on the relevant rate of interest and on the stock of asset at the opening of the production period, that is, the stock accumulated at the end of the previous period, at time $t - 1$. The lagged variable r_m stands for the rate of interest prevailing on money deposits. Similarly r_l and r_b stand for the rates of interest prevailing on loans and Treasury bills.

The bottom part of the matrix is the flow equivalent of the balance sheet matrix. When we describe purchases and sales of assets of which the nominal value never changes, there is no problem of notation. We simply write ΔH or ΔM (for instance) to describe the increase in the stock of cash, or money deposits, between the beginning and end of the period being characterized. When the capital value of the asset can change – that is, when capital gains and losses can occur, as is the case with long-term bonds and equities – we keep the convention that the assets are pieces of paper, say e for equities, which have a price, p_e. The value of the piece of paper is then $e \cdot p_e$ at a point of time, and the value of transactions in equities – new issues or buy-backs – is given by the change in the number of pieces of paper which are issued (or withdrawn) times their price, $\Delta e \cdot p_e$.

The rule enforcing that all columns, each representing a sector, must sum to zero as well is particularly interesting because it has a well-defined economic meaning. The zero-sum rule for each column represents the budget constraint of each sector. The budget constraint for each sector describes how the balance between flows of expenditure, factor income and transfers generate counterpart changes in stocks of assets and liabilities. The accounts of the transactions flow matrix, as shown by Table 2.6, are comprehensive in the sense that everything comes from somewhere and everything goes somewhere. Without this armature, accounting errors may pass unnoticed and unacceptable implications may be ignored. With this framework, 'there are no black holes' (Godley 1996: 7).

There is no substitute for careful perusal of the matrix at this stage. It is a representation, not easily come by, of a complete system of macroeconomic

Table 2.6 Transactions flow matrix

	Households (1)	Production firms — Current (2)	Production firms — Capital (3)	Banks — Current (4)	Banks — Capital (5)	Government (6)	Central Bank — Current (7)	Central Bank — Capital (8)	Σ
Consumption	$-C$	$+C$							0
Investment	$-I_h$	$+I$	$-I_f$						0
Govt. exp.		$+G$				$-G$			0
Wages	$+WB$	$-WB$							0
Profits, firms	$+FD_f$	$-F_f$	$+FU_f$						0
Profits, banks	$+FD_b$			$-F_b$	$+FU_b$				0
Profit, central Bk						$+F_{cb}$	$-F_{cb}$		0
Loan interests	$-r_{l(-1)} \cdot L_{h(-1)}$	$-r_{l(-1)} \cdot L_{f(-1)}$		$+r_{l(-1)} \cdot L_{(-1)}$					0
Deposit interests	$+r_{m(-1)} \cdot M_{h(-1)}$			$-r_{m(-1)} \cdot M_{(-1)}$					0
Bill interests	$+r_{b(-1)} \cdot B_{h(-1)}$			$+r_{b(-1)} \cdot B_{b(-1)}$		$-r_{b(-1)} \cdot B_{(-1)}$	$+r_{b(-1)} \cdot B_{cb(-1)}$		0
Taxes – transfers	$-T_h$	$-T_f$		$-T_b$		$+T$			0
Change in loans	$+\Delta L_h$		$+\Delta L_f$		$-\Delta L$				0
Change in cash	$-\Delta H_h$				$-\Delta H_b$			$+\Delta H$	0
Change, deposits	$-\Delta M_h$				$+\Delta M$				0
Change in bills	$-\Delta B_h$				$-\Delta B_h$	$+\Delta B$		$-\Delta B_{cb}$	0
Change, equities	$-(\Delta e_f \cdot p_{ef} + \Delta e_b \cdot p_{eb})$		$+\Delta e_f \cdot p_{ef}$		$+\Delta e_b \cdot p_{eb}$				0
Σ	0	0	0	0	0	0	0	0	0

transactions. The best way to take it in is by first running down each column to ascertain that it is a comprehensive account of the sources and uses of all flows to and from the sector and then reading across each row to find the counterpart of each transaction by one sector in that of another. Note that all *sources* of funds in a sectoral account take a *plus* sign, while the *uses* of these funds take a *minus* sign. Any transaction involving an incoming flow, the proceeds of a sale or the receipts of some monetary flow, thus takes a positive sign; a transaction involving an outgoing flow must take a negative sign. Uses of funds, outlays, can be either the purchase of consumption goods or the purchase (or acquisition) of a financial asset. The signs attached to the 'flow of funds' entries which appear below the horizontal bold line are strongly counter-intuitive since the *acquisition* of a financial asset that would *add* to the existing stock of asset, say, money, by the household sector, is described with a *negative* sign. But all is made clear so soon as one recalls that this acquisition of money balances constitutes an *outgoing* transaction flow, that is, a *use* of funds.

2.4.2   The elements of the transactions flow matrix

Let us first deal with column 1 of Table 2.6, that of the household sector. That column represents the budget constraint of the households. In contrast to the standard NIPA, investment in housing is taken into account. Households can consume goods $(-C)$ or purchase new residential dwellings $(-I_h)$, but only as long as they receive various flows of income or provided they take in new loans $(+\Delta L_h)$ – consumer loans or home mortgages – or reduce their holdings of assets, for instance by dishoarding money balances $(+\Delta H_h$ or $+\Delta M_h)$. At the aggregate scale, at least as a stylized fact, households add to their net wealth, through their saving. The excess of household income over consumption will take the form of real purchases of dwellings (I_h), and the form of financial acquisitions: cash (ΔH_h), bank money (ΔM_h), fixed interest securities (ΔB_h), and equities $(\Delta e \cdot p_e)$, less the net acquisition of liabilities, in the form of loans (ΔL_h) from banks. The change in the net financial position of the household sector, which will require counterpart changes in the net financial position of the other sectors, appears in the rows below the bold line. The categories shown are simplified: there are other important ways in which people save – for example, through life insurance, mutual funds and compulsory pension funds; but for the time being these acquisitions will be treated as though they were direct holdings, perhaps subject to advice from a manager.[11]

---

[11] It has been shown by Ruggles and Ruggles (1992 (1996)) that once the fictitious real estate enterprises of NIPA that take care of households new purchases of residential units have been taken out, and once pension fund schemes are considered as saving by firms rather than that of their employees, then the change in the net financial position of the household sector is virtually nil, and even negative on the average in the United States since 1947.

Column 2 is no different from the one discussed in Table 2.5: it shows the receipts and the outlays of production firms on their current account. Column 3 now shows how production firms ultimately end up financing their capital expenditures, fixed capital and inventories. These capital expenditures, at the end of the period, appear to be financed by retained profits, new issues of securities (here assumed to be only equities, but which could be bonds or commercial paper) and bank loans.

Columns 4 and 5 describe a relatively sophisticated banking sector. Once more, the accounts are split into a current and a capital account. The current account describes the flows of revenues and disbursements that the banks get and make. Banks rake in interest payments from their previous stocks of loans and securities, and they must make interest payments to those holding bank deposits. The residual between their receipts and their outlays, net of taxes, is their profit F_b. This profit, as is the case for production firms, is split between distributed dividends and retained earnings. These retained earnings, along with the newly acquired money deposits, are the counterparts of the assets that are being acquired by banks: new granted loans, newly purchased bills, or additional vault cash. Column 5 shows how the balance sheets of banks must always balance in the sense that the change in their assets (loans, securities and vault cash) will always have a counterpart in a change in their liabilities.

Finally, the last columns deal with the government sector and its central bank. The latter is split from the government sector, as it allows for a more realistic picture of the money creation process, although it adds one slight complication. Let us first deal with Column 7, the current account of the central bank. From the balance sheet of Table 2.4, we recall that central banks hold government bills while their typical liabilities are in the form of banknotes, that is, cash, which carries no interest payment. As a result, central banks make a profit, F_{cb}, which, we will assume, is entirely returned to government. This explains the new entry in column 6 of the government sector, $+F_{cb}$, compared with that of Table 2.5. The fact that the central bank returns all of its profits to government implies that the while the government gross interest disbursements on its debt are equal to $r_{b(-1)} \cdot B_{(-1)}$, its net disbursements are only $r_{b(-1)} \cdot [B_{(-1)} - B_{cb(-1)}]$.

Column 6 is the budget constraint of government. It shows that any government expenditure which is not financed by taxes (or the central bank dividend), must be financed by an issue of bills. These newly issued bills are purchased by households, banks and the central bank, directly or indirectly. Column 8 shows the highly publicized accounting requirement that any addition to the bond portfolio of the central bank must be accompanied by an equivalent increase in the amount of high-powered money, $+\Delta H$. This relationship, which is at the heart of the monetarist explanation of inflation – also endorsed by most neo-classical economists – as proposed by authors such as Milton Friedman, has been given considerable attention in the recent past, since it seems to imply that government deficits are necessarily associated with high-powered money increases, and hence through some money multiplier story, as told in all elementary textbooks, to an excess creation of money. A quite different analysis and interpretation of these accounting requirements will be offered in the next chapters.

2.4.3 Key features of the transactions flow matrix

It is emphasized that so far there has been no characterization of behaviour beyond what is implied by logical constraints (e.g. that every buyer must have a seller) or by the functions that have been allocated to the various sectors (e.g. that firms are responsible for all production, banks for making all loans) or by the conventional structure and significance of asset portfolios (e.g. that money is accepted as a means of payment).

Reconsider now the system as a whole. We open each period with stocks of tangible assets and a tangle of interlocking financial assets and liabilities. The whole configuration of assets and liabilities is the legacy of all transactions in stocks and flows and real asset creation during earlier periods which constitute the link between past, present and future. Opening stocks interact with the transactions which occur within each period so as to generate a new configuration of stocks at the end of each period; these will constitute past history for the succeeding period. At the aggregate level, whatever is produced and not consumed will turn up as an addition to the real capital stock. At the sectoral level, the sum of all receipts less the sum of all outlays must have an exact counterpart in the sum of all transactions (by that sector) in financial assets less financial liabilities.

The only elements missing for a full integration are the capital gains that ought to be added to the increases in assets and liabilities that were assessed from the transactions matrix. Thus what is missing is the *revaluation* account, or what is also known as the *reconciliation* account. When this is done, it becomes possible to move from the opening stocks of assets, those being held at the beginning of the production period, to the closing stocks of assets, those being held at the end of the production period. This will be done in the next section.

The system as a whole is now closed in the sense that every flow and every stock variable is logically integrated into the accounting to such a degree that the value of any one item is implied by the values of all the others taken together; this follows from the fact that every row and every column sums to zero. This last feature will prove very useful when we come to model behaviour; for however large and complex the model, it must always be the case that one equation is redundant in the sense that it is implied by all the other equations taken together.

As pointed out in the first part of this chapter, other authors have previously underlined the importance of the transactions flow matrix. In his book, Jean Denizet (1969: 19) proposed a transactions flow matrix that has *implicitly* all the features of the matrix that has been presented here. Malinvaud (1982: 21) also presents a nearly similar transactions flow matrix. The article written by Tobin and his collaborators (Backus *et al*. 1980), has a theoretical transaction flow matrix, nearly identical to the one advocated here, with rows and columns summing to zero; they also have presented the empirical version of such a matrix, including capital gains, with actual numbers attached to each cell of our transaction flow matrix, derived from the national income and product accounts and the flow-of-funds accounts, thus demonstrating the practical usefulness of this approach. The transactions flow matrix has been utilized *systematically* and amalgamated to behavioural equations by Godley in his more recent work (1996, 1999a). It was not present in Godley's earlier work (Godley and Cripps 1983).

2.5 Full integration of the balance sheet and the transactions flow matrices

We are now in a position to integrate fully the transactions flow matrix to the balance sheet. Table 2.7 illustrates this integration (Stone 1986: 16). As before, we consider five sectors: households, production firms, banks, government, and the central bank. The first row represents the initial net worth of each sector, as they appear in the penultimate row of Table 2.6. We assume again that the net worth of the central bank is equal to nil, as a result of the hypothesis that any profit of the central bank is returned to government. We shall also see that a central bank zero net worth requires that the central bank holds no bonds, only bills, the price of which does not change. We may also note, as was mentioned earlier, that the aggregate net worth of the economy, its macroeconomic net worth, is equal to the value of tangible capital, K. Finally, it should be pointed out once more that the net worth of any sector, *at the end of the previous period*, is considered to be the same thing as the net worth of that sector *at the beginning of the current period*, and in what follows we shall make use of the (-1) time subscript whenever beginning-of-period wealth is referred to.

The *change* in the net worth of any sector is made up of two components, as is clearly indicated in the first column of Table 2.7: the change in net assets arising from transactions, and the change arising from revaluations, that is, changes in the prices of assets or liabilities. These two components of change, added to the net worth of the previous period, yield the new net worth of each sector. This new net worth – the net worth at the end of the current period – appears in the last row of Table 2.7.

The first component of the change in net worth arises from the transactions flow matrix. The first five rows of these changes are the exact equivalent of the last five rows (the last row of zeros having been set aside) of the transactions flow matrix 2.6. They reflect the financial transactions that occurred during

Table 2.7 Full-integration matrix

	Households (1)	Production firms (2)	Banks (3)	Government (4)	Central bank (5)	Σ
Net worth, end of previous period	NW_{h-1}	NW_{f-1}	NW_{b-1}	NW_{g-1}	0	K_{-1}
Change in net assets arising from transactions						
Change in loans	$-\Delta L_h$	$-\Delta L_f$	$+\Delta L$			0
Change in cash	$+\Delta H_h$		$+\Delta H_b$		$-\Delta H$	0
Change in deposits	$+\Delta M_h$		$-\Delta M$			0
Change in bills	$+\Delta B_h$		$+\Delta B_h$	$-\Delta B$	$+\Delta B_{cb}$	0
Change in equities	$+\Delta e_f \cdot p_{ef} + \Delta e_b \cdot p_{eb}$	$-\Delta e_f \cdot p_{ef}$	$-\Delta e_b \cdot p_{eb}$			0
Change in tangible capital	$+\Delta k_h \cdot pk$	$+\Delta k_f \cdot pk$				$+\Delta k \cdot pk$
Change in net assets arising from revaluations						
Capital gains in equities	$+\Delta p_{ef} \cdot e_{f-1} + \Delta p_{eb} \cdot e_{b-1}$	$-\Delta p_{ef} \cdot e_{f-1}$	$-\Delta p_{eb} \cdot e_{b-1}$			0
Capital gains in tangible capital	$+\Delta pk \cdot k_{h-1}$	$+\Delta pk \cdot k_{f-1}$				$\Delta pk \cdot (k_{h-1} + k_{f-1})$
Net worth, end of period	NW_h	NW_f	NW_b	NW_g	0	K

the period. The only difference between these five rows as they appear in Table 2.7 compared to those of Table 2.6 is their sign. All minus signs in Table 2.6 are replaced by a plus sign in Table 2.7, and vice versa. In the transactions flow matrix of Table 2.6, the acquisition of a financial asset, say cash money ΔH_h by households, is part of the *use* of funds, and hence carries a minus sign. However, in Table 2.7, the acquisition of this cash money adds something to household wealth, and hence it must carry a plus sign, in order to add it to the net worth of the previous period. Similarly, when households or firms take loans, these new loans provide additions to their *sources* of funds, and hence carry a plus sign in the transactions flow matrix of Table 2.6. By contrast, in the integration matrix of Table 2.7, loans taken by households or firms, all other things equal, reduce the net worth of these sectors, and hence must carry a minus sign.

The last element of the first block of six rows arising from the transactions flow matrix, as shown in Table 2.7, is the row called 'change in tangible capital'. The counterpart of this row can be found in the 'investment' row of Table 2.6. Households, for instance, can augment their net wealth by acquiring financial or tangible capital. In their case, tangible capital is essentially made up of residential dwellings (since, in contrast to financial flows accountants, we do not consider purchases of durable goods as capital accumulation). This was classified as investment in the transactions flow matrix, and called I_h, whereas in the full-integration matrix, it is called $\Delta k_h \cdot pk$, where pk is the price of tangible capital, while Δk_h is the flow of new residential capital being added to the existing stock, in real terms. In other words, Δk_h is the number of new residential units which have been purchased by households. It follows that we have the equivalence, $I_h = \Delta k_h \cdot pk$. Similarly, for firms, their investment in tangible capital (essentially machines, plants, and additions to inventories) was called I_f in the transactions matrix of Table 2.6. *Setting aside changes in inventories,*[12] the value of new investment in tangible capital is now called $\Delta k_f \cdot pk$ in Table 2.7, so that we have the other equivalence, $I_f = \Delta k_f \cdot pk$. Note that for simplification, we have assumed that the price of residential tangible capital and the price of production capital is the same and moves in tandem.

The second major component of the change in net worth arises from capital gains. For exposition purposes, we assume that only two elements of wealth can have changing prices, and hence could give rise to capital gains or capital losses. We assume that the prices of equities can change, those issued by production firms and those issued by banks; and we also assume that the

---

[12] This is an important restriction, because, as already pointed out, inventories are valued at current replacement *cost*, while fixed capital is valued at current replacement *price*, and hence they cannot carry the same price variable. See Chapter 11 for an in-depth study of this issue, which is briefly dealt with in section 2.6.2.

price of tangible capital, relative to consumer prices, can change. We assume away changes in the price of securities. The implicit assumption here is that all securities are made up of bills – short-term securities that mature within the period length considered here. In the case of bonds – long-term securities the prices of which change from period to period, before they mature and come up for redemption – capital gains or losses would have to be taken into account. Capital gains on bonds will be explicitly taken into consideration in Chapter 5.

The study of capital gains underlines an important principle: any change in the value of an asset may be made up of two components: a component associated with a transaction, for instance when new equities are issued and bought up for instance, thus involving additional units of the asset in question; and a component associated with a change in the price of the asset, when for instance, existing (and newly issued) equities carry a higher price. In the case of equities issued by production firms, as shown in Table 2.7, the change in the value of equities arising from transactions is $\Delta e_\mathrm{f} \cdot p_\mathrm{ef}$ while the change in the value of equities arising from capital gains is $\Delta p_\mathrm{ef} \cdot e_{\mathrm{f}-1}$. In Chapter 5, we shall provide a precise proof of this result in discrete time (with time subscripts, as done here). In the meantime, it is sufficient to remember first-year university calculus, deal with continuous time, and recall that, given two functions, u and v, the derivative of the product of these functions is such that $\mathrm{d}(u \cdot v) = \mathrm{d}u \cdot v + u \cdot \mathrm{d}v$. In the present case, with e and pe acting as the two functions u and v, we have:

$$\mathrm{d}(e \cdot p_\mathrm{e}) = \mathrm{d}e \cdot p_\mathrm{e} + e \cdot \mathrm{d}(p_\mathrm{e}) \qquad (2.5)$$

The first term represents the change arising from transactions, while the second term represents capital gains due to the change in prices. The same rules apply to the changes in the value of tangible capital, where a real term component and a price component can be identified.

Thus, adding the capital gains component so defined and the transactions component to the net worth of the previous period, we obtain the net worth at the end of the current period, as shown in the last row of Table 2.7. The integration of the flow of funds financial transactions and the sector balance sheets with the national income accounts is thus complete. It should be pointed out however that it is no easy matter to produce an empirical version of Tables 2.6 or 2.7. While the flow of funds published by the Federal Reserve in the United States, or by other statistical agencies in other countries, contain a vast amount of information about transactions in financial assets, the sectoral classification and to some extent the concepts employed in NIPA are sufficiently different to make any simple junction of the two data sets. Although the Z.1 accounts themselves provide some reconciliation (in tables F.100 and higher), relatively large discrepancies remain.

2.6 Applications of the transactions flow matrix: the monetary circuit

2.6.1 The quadruple-entry principle and production with private money

It has already been claimed that the transactions flow matrix serves an important purpose in guaranteeing the coherence of the accounting when macroeconomic models are built. But the transactions flow matrix can also be shown to serve a further purpose. The transactions flow matrix can really help us to understand how production is being financed at the initial finance state, that is at the beginning of the production period, before households have decided on what they will do with their newly acquired income or their newly acquired savings. The transactions flow matrix sets the monetary circuit – about which so much has been said by French and Italian post-Keynesian school, the so-called circuitistes – within a comprehensive accounting framework, which will help to justify the story told and the claims made by these post-Keynesians (Graziani 1990). In other words, the transactions flow matrix, which ties together real decisions and monetary and financial consequences, is the backbone of the monetary production economy that Keynes and his followers, the post-Keynesians, wish to describe and to model. To get a feel for how the system works we may follow through a few transactions as though they were sequences. We will examine two of these transactions. First, we shall look at how the production of firms is being financed; then we shall see how government expenditures enter the economy.

Suppose, as we assumed in the transactions flow matrix, that firms distribute wages in line with production, that dividends are distributed according to past profits, and that interest payments, as shown here, depends on the past stock of deposits and on a rate of interest administered by the banking system. Suppose further that firms borrow, at the beginning of the production period as the circuitistes would have it, the amount needed to pay the wages of the current period. This is, as the circuitistes say, the first step of the monetary circuit (Lavoie 1992: 153). Thus in the first step of the circuit, both the loans and the deposits newly created by the banking system belong to the production sector. This initial step of the monetary circuit with private money is shown in Table 2.8A, which is a subset of the transactions matrix of Table 2.6.

A clear feature of Table 2.8A. is that it contains four entries. This is an illustration of the famous *quadruple-entry* system of Copeland (1949 (1996: 8)). Copeland pointed out that, 'because moneyflows transactions involve two transactors, the social accounting approach to moneyflows rests not on a double-entry system but on a quadruple-entry system'. Knowing that each of the columns and each of the rows must sum to zero at all times, it follows that any alteration in one cell of the matrix must imply a modification to at least three other cells. The transactions matrix used here provides us with

Table 2.8A   First step of the monetary circuit with private money

	Households	Production firms Current	Production firms Capital	Banks Capital	Σ
Consumption					
Investment					
Wages					
Δ loans			$+\Delta L_f$	$-\Delta L$	0
Δ deposits			$-\Delta M_f$	$+\Delta M$	0
Σ			0	0	0

an exhibit which allows to report each financial flow both as an inflow to a given sector and as an outflow to the other sector involved in the transaction. In the current instance, the production and the banking sectors are the two parties to the financial transaction, and each sector must have two modified entries, since all columns must balance.

A peculiar feature of the quadruple-entry system is that it corrects a prevalent misconception regarding the creation and the role of money. In the mainstream framework, money is sometimes said to fall from the sky, thrown out of an helicopter, as in the famous parable by Milton Friedman. In that mainstream framework, which is highly popular in mainstream intermediate macroeconomic textbooks, money is a given stock, which seems to appear from nowhere, and which has no counterpart in the rest of the economy. Despite changes in the real economy, and presumably in financial flows, the stock of money is assumed to remain at all time constant. The quadruple-entry system shows that such a conception of money is meaningless.

Coming back to Table 2.8A, a very important point, related to the dangers of confusing semantics, must be made. Recall that a minus sign in the transaction matrix is associated with the use of funds, while a positive sign implies the source of funds. In Table 2.8A, in the column of banks, the addition to money deposits is associated with a plus sign, while the addition to bank loans is associated to a minus sign. From a flow-of-funds standpoint, increased deposits are thus a source of funds while increased loans are a use of funds for the banks. For some, this terminology seems to reinforce the mainstream belief, associated with the loanable funds approach, that banks provide loans only insofar as they have the financial resources to do so; in other words, banks make loans only when they have prior access to deposits. The source of the funds to be lent, in Table 2.8A, is the money deposits, as the minus sign would show.

Needless to say, this loanable funds interpretation is not being defended here. On the contrary, a key feature of the banking system is its ability to create deposits *ex nihilo*. More precisely, when agents in the economy are willing to increase their liabilities, banks can increase the size of both sides of their balance sheet, by granting loans and simultaneously creating deposits. As neatly summarized by Earley, Parsons and Thomson (1976, 1996: 159), 'to encapsulate, we see fluctuations in borrowing as the primary cause of changes in spending'. It may be that, in flow-of-funds terminology, money deposits is the source of funds allowing the use of bank loans. But the *cause* of this increase in deposits and loans is the willingness to contract an additional liability and the desire of the borrower, here the production firm, to expand its expenditures.

2.6.2 Initial finance versus final finance

This situation as shown in Table 2.8A, however, can only last for a split second. Firms only draw on their lines of credit when they are required to make payments. In the second step of the circuit, the deposits of the firms are transferred by cheques or electronic payment to the workers who provided their labour to the firms. The moment these funds are transferred, they constitute households' income. Before a single unit is spent on consumer goods, the entire amount of the bank deposits constitutes savings by households, and these are equal to the new loans granted to production firms.

This is all shown in Table 2.8B. The matrix requirement that all rows and columns must sum to zero makes clear the exigencies of the second step of this monetary circuit. Because of these zero-sum requirements, the following three equations must hold:

$$I - WB = 0 \tag{2.6}$$
$$I - \Delta L_f = 0 \tag{2.7}$$
$$\Delta M_h - \Delta L_f = 0 \tag{2.8}$$

At that stage of the circuit, output has been produced but not yet sold. The unsold production constitutes an increase in inventories (which will later be

Table 2.8B The second step of the monetary circuit with private money

| | Households | Production firms | | Banks | |
		Current	Capital	Capital	Σ
Consumption					
Investment		$+I$	$-I$		0
Wages	$+WB$	$-WB$			0
Δ loans			$+\Delta L_f$	$-\Delta L$	0
Δ deposits	$-\Delta M_h$			$+\Delta M$	0
Σ	0	0	0	0	0

associated with the symbol *IN*). This increase in inventories is accounted as investment in working capital. Staying faithful to our requirement that all rows and all columns must sum to zero, inventories must necessarily rise by an amount exactly equal to the production costs, the wages paid *WB*, as in equation (2.6).[13] The zero-sum column requirement, as applied to the current account of firms makes it so. This demonstrates a very important point: that inventories of unsold goods should be valued at cost, and not according to the price that the firm believes it can get for its goods in the near future.

On the side of the capital account, it is clear that the value of this investment in inventories must be financed by the new loans initially obtained, as in equation (2.7). Table 2.8B, contrasted with Table 2.6, helps us understand the distinction between *initial* and *final* finance which has been underlined by the circuitistes (Graziani 1990). Initial finance, or what Davidson (1982: 49) calls *construction finance*, appears in Tables 2.8A: it is the bank loans that firms usually ask to finance the initial stages of production and hence to finance inventories. Final finance, or Davidson's *investment funding*, is to be found in the last rows of Table 2.6. Final finance are the various means by which investment expenditures are being ultimately financed by the end of the production period; the retained earnings of corporations constitute the greatest part of gross investment funding.

The transition from Tables 2.8A and 2.8B, which represent the first and second steps of the monetary circuit, to Table 2.6, which represents the third and last step of the monetary circuit, is accomplished by households getting rid of the money balances acquired through wages, and eventually the additional money balances received on account on their dividend and interest payments. As the households get rid of their money balances, firms gradually recover theirs, allowing them to reimburse the additional loans that had been initially granted to them, at the beginning of the period.

The key factor is that, as households increase their consumption, their money balances fall and so do the outstanding amount of loans owed by the firms. Similarly, as households get rid of their money balances to purchase newly issued equities by firms, the latter are again able to reduce their outstanding loans. In other words, at the start of the circuit, the new loans required by the firms are exactly equal to the new deposits obtained by households. Then, as households decide to get rid of their money balances, the outstanding loans of firms diminish *pari passu*, as long as firms use the proceeds to pay back loans instead of using the proceeds to beef up their money balances or their other liquid financial assets. Although determined by apparently independent mechanisms, the supply of loans to firms and

---

[13] Note that it is assumed as well that the new fixed investment goods have not yet been sold to the corporations which ordered them.

the holdings of deposits by households (and firms) cannot but be equal, as they are at the beginning of the circuit, as in equation (2.8). This mechanism will be observed time and time again in the next chapters, when behavioural relations are examined and formalized. The primary act is best thought of as a decision to produce something. This induces firms to take up a loan to start up the production process. The build up of initial inventories, when production begins, is the result of such a production decision, made with the agreement of a bank. It is this act which brings a bank loan into existence and simultaneously brings a bank balance of equal size into existence (that of the firm asking for a loan). As soon as households are paid for their services, the money deposits are transferred to the bank accounts of the newly employed labour force.[14] We can already see how it is that the household sector comes to 'lend' its surplus to the production sector, as mainstream economists would say. In the example just given, the mere holding of the money paid out as wages has a loan as its exact counterpart. When the household sector buys something from the production sector, this destroys money and loans by an exactly equal amount. While the loan-granting activity created an efflux of money into the economy, the purchase of goods by households creates a reflux – the destruction of money. Thus, any series of transactions can be conceived as the creation, circulation and destruction of money.

2.6.3 Production with central bank money

The steps of the monetary circuit can once again be used to help us understand how money creation and government deficits are related to each other. Suppose that, at the beginning of the circuit, the government sector orders the production of some goods to the private production sector. Once these goods have been produced, they must be purchased by government. The simplest course of action would be for government to draw on its line of credit at the central bank: the government sector would get high-powered money as the central bank would grant a loan to its government. But such credit facilities are now regarded as inflationary by mainstream economists and politicians, and as a result, these direct credit facilities are often forbidden by law. The alternative is for government to issue new bills, which can either be purchased by the central bank or by a private bank. Direct government bond sales to the central bank are also feared by mainstream economists, and as a result, in some countries, they are either forbidden or highly restricted. But let us assume that such a sale occurs anyway. The counterpart of the newly purchased bills, in the books of the central bank, is the amount of high-powered money credited to the government account. This is, once

---

[14] There is some resemblance with Moore's (1997: 426) point that 'depositors can only "supply" banks with deposits if they have somehow previously acquired them'.

more the first step of the monetary circuit, and it is shown with the help of Table 2.9A. This money will circulate, first to pay the producing firms. These firms get cheques, drawn on the account of the government sector at the central bank. Once cashed at the private banks, these cheques give rise to bank deposits. This is shown in Table 2.9B. The firms then use these bank deposits to pay their workers and remunerate their owners. Here for simplification, the income so created is to be found on a single row, as Y.[15] The money balances so created will thus wind up in the deposit accounts of households. This is illustrated with the help of Table 2.9C.

Table 2.9A   The first step of government expenditures financed by central bank money

	Households	Production firms		Banks	Central bank	
	Households	Current	Capital	Government	Capital	Σ
Govt. exp.						
Income [GDP]						
Change in cash				$-\Delta H_g$	$+\Delta H$	0
Change in deposits						0
Change in bills				$+\Delta B$	$-\Delta B_{cb}$	0
Σ				0	0	0

Table 2.9B   The second step of government expenditures financed by central bank money

	Households	Production firms		Banks	Central bank	
	Households	Current	Capital	Government	Capital	Σ
Govt. exp.		$+G$		$-G$		0
Income [GDP]						
Change in cash			$-\Delta H_b$		$+\Delta H$	0
Change in deposits		$-\Delta M_f$	$+\Delta M$			0
Change in bills				$+\Delta B$	$-\Delta B_{cb}$	0
Σ		0	0	0	0	0

[15] Here we have slightly cheated, assuming that all profits are distributed to households.

Table 2.9C The third step of government expenditures financed by central bank money

	Households	Production firms Current	Banks Capital	Government	Central bank Capital	Σ
Govt. exp.		$+G$		$-G$		0
Income [GDP]	$+Y$	$-Y$				0
Change in cash			$-\Delta H_b$		$+\Delta H$	0
Change in deposits	$-\Delta M_h$		$+\Delta M$			0
Change in bills				$+\Delta B$	$-\Delta B_{cb}$	0
Σ	0	0	0	0	0	0

Once again, all rows and columns must sum to zero. Before households decide what to do with their newly acquired money balances, spending them on consumption or acquiring interest-earning assets – including government bills – all accounts must balance. As a consequence, the deficit cannot but be 'monetized' initially, in line with what neo-chartalist post-Keynesians have been recently arguing (Wray 1998: ch. 4–5; Mosler and Forstater 1999). The matrices of Tables 2.9B and 2.9C also show the standard result, so often underlined in mainstream textbooks, that private banks now wind up with additional reserves, the ΔH_b entry in the capital account of banks. These extra reserves do not mean however that a multiple amount of money deposits will be created, as the standard money multiplier has it. If banks do not find any credit-worthy borrower – and the fact that they now have additional reserves implies in no way that additional credit-worthy borrowers will be forthcoming – they always have the choice to purchase government bills.[16] As we shall see more formally in Chapter 4, if the central bank is to keep the interest rate at its target level, the central bank must sell to the banks (and to households) the bills that they look for, and by so doing, the central bank will absorb the money balances that neither the banks nor the households wish to hold.

We said before that the government sector, to finance its expenditures, could also have sold its bills to private banks. The transactions matrix that corresponds to such a transaction, with the ensuing deposits ending up in the hands of workers and stockholders is even simpler, as illustrated with the help of Tables 2.10A and 2.10B. Private banks buy the bills and grant a bank deposit to the government, as shown in Table 2.10A. This deposit then moves on to the household sector, after having transited through the

[16] There is another possibility that will be examined in the next subsection.

Table 2.10A   The first step of government expenditures financed by private money

	Households	Production firms Current	Banks Capital	Government	Central bank Capital	Σ
Govt. exp.						
Income [GDP]						
Change in cash						
Change in deposits			$+\Delta M$	$-\Delta M_g$		0
Change in bills			$-\Delta B_b$	$+\Delta B$		0
Σ			0	0		0

Table 2.10B   The third step of government expenditures financed by private money

	Households	Production firms Current	Banks Capital	Government	Central bank Capital	Σ
Govt. exp.		$+G$		$-G$		0
Income [GDP]	$+Y$	$-Y$				0
Change in cash						
Change in deposits	$-\Delta M_h$		$+\Delta M$			0
Change in bills			$-\Delta B_b$	$+\Delta B$		0
Σ	0	0	0	0	0	0

production sector, when the public goods are paid for. This is shown with the help of Table 2.10B. It would seem this time that there is no inflationary danger, since banks hold no additional high-powered money, in contrast to the case where bills were being purchased directly by the central bank. But this is all an illusion. Whether the bills are initially purchased by banks or by the central bank makes no difference whatsoever. If banks or households are in need of additional cash, as a consequence of the increased activity generated by the public expenditures, the central bank will need to intervene in the second-hand market, purchasing some of the bills initially bought by the private banks, as long as it wishes to maintain its interest rate target. In the end, the only money or high-powered money left in the economy will be held voluntarily, and this amount in no way depends on the exact financial scheme used to finance government expenditures.

2.6.4 The case of the overdraft economy

Up to now, we have assumed that government expenditures were financed either by selling securities to the private banks, or by selling securities to the central bank. This corresponds however to a particular institutional set-up, that Hicks (1974: 51) has called the *pure auto-economy*. It turns out however that the pure auto-economy, or what Lavoie (2001b: 216) has called the *asset-based economy*, is only one of the possible institutional set-ups. While the asset-based economies have been described in great detail in mainstream textbooks, specially in Anglo-saxon textbooks, the other institutional set-ups have been usually ignored. It turns out, however, that most financial systems in the world are not of the asset-based type, but rather can be described as

Table 2.11A First step of government expenditures in overdraft system

| | | Production firms | | | | Central bank | |
	Households	Current	Capital	Banks	Government	Capital	Σ
Govt. exp.							
Income [GDP]							
Change in cash							
Change in deposits				$+\Delta M$	$-\Delta M_g$		0
Change in bank loans				$-\Delta L$	$+\Delta L_g$		0
Change in central bank advances							
Σ				0	0		0

Table 2.11B Second step of government expenditures in overdraft system

| | | Production firms | | | | Central bank | |
	Households	Current	Capital	Banks	Government	Capital	Σ
Govt. exp.		$+G$			$-G$		0
Income [GDP]	$+Y$	$-Y$					0
Change in cash	$-\Delta H_h$					$+\Delta H$	0
Change in deposits	$-\Delta M_h$			$+\Delta M$			0
Change in bank loans				$-\Delta L$	$+\Delta L_g$		0
Change in central bank advances				$+\Delta A$		$-\Delta A$	0
Σ	0	0		0	0	0	0

overdraft economies, making use once more of the terminology proposed by Hicks (1974: 53).

In the pure overdraft economy, as defined by Hicks, firms hold no financial assets, and are thus 'wholly dependent, for their liquidity, on the banks'. The notion of a pure overdraft economy can however be extended to the relations between the private banks and the central bank, as is done in Lavoie (2001b). In pure overdraft financial systems, private banks hold little or no government securities. On the contrary, private banks in such overdraft economies are permanently in debt *vis-á-vis* the central bank, having borrowed funds from the central bank to acquire the reserves that they are legally required to hold, and to obtain the central bank banknotes that their customers have been asking for.

The impact of new government expenditures on the transactions flow matrix, or at least a part of it, is shown in Tables 2.11A and 2.11B. As before, we assume new government expenditures of an amount G. This is now financed by a loan from the private banks to the government. This is shown in Table 2.11A, which is very similar to Table 2.8A. These government expenditures generate an income of Y, which we assume as before to be kept initially in the form of money balances by households. A new assumption, compared with Tables 2.9 or 2.10, is that households wish to hold a certain portion of their new money balances in the form of cash money. In the pure overdraft economy, private banks must borrow all cash money from the central bank. Private banks obtain advances A from the central bank, to cover the needs in cash money of the public, as shown in Table 2.11B. Within such a system without government securities, the determination of interest rates is quite straightforward. The central bank simply needs to set the rate of interest on the advances made to private banks. This rate of interest on advances is then the base rate of interest, that sets the standard for all other rates of interest in the financial system. The study of overdraft financial systems thus helps to pierce through the veil of the asset-based financial systems, showing with obvious simplicity that central banks do have the ability to set short-term interest rates.

3
The Simplest Model with Government Money

3.1 Government money versus private money

Money is created in two fundamentally different ways. On the one hand there is *outside* money, which is created whenever a government pays for something by making a draft on its central bank or by paying for something with banknotes, and which is extinguished when a payment is made by a member of the public to the government, typically in the form of taxes. This kind of money we may call *government* money, since it is issued by public institutions, namely the central bank or the Treasury department of central government. Government money is usually called *central bank* money or *high-powered* money in the literature. On the other hand there is *inside* money, which is created by commercial banks when they make loans, and which ceases to exist when loans are repaid. This second kind of money will be called *private* money, since it is issued by private institutions, namely private banks.

We shall eventually cover both types of money creation and destruction. But we have reluctantly come to the conclusion that it is impossible to deploy a really simple model of a complete monetary economy in which inside and outside money both make their appearance at the outset. We have therefore decided to start by constructing and studying a hypothetical economy in which there is no private money at all, that is, a world where there are no banks, where producers need not borrow to produce, and hence a world where there are no interest payments. We have done this while fully recognising that money generated by loans from private banks (e.g. to finance inventories when production takes time) is of the utmost importance in the real world of monetized economies. This detour will enable the student to master the main principles inherent in fully coherent stock-flow macroeconomics, including the principles of portfolio behaviour within a simple but yet complete stock-flow framework. Very strong simplifying assumptions will have to be made initially and the reader is asked to suspend disbelief until more realistic systems are introduced.

In the chapters which follow, we shall present a series of increasingly complex models. Each model will be complete in its own terms, with its whole set of equations. And for each model, we shall present the balance sheet and the transactions matrix which belong to it. Each model will then be subjected to experiments, that is, parameters or exogenous variables will be modified, and we shall observe the consequences of these changes for the relevant endogenous variables.

3.2 The service economy with government money and no portfolio choice

3.2.1 Assumptions

Let us start with the simplest meaningful model that can be built – *Model SIM*, for *simplest*. The economy is closed to the outside world: there are neither exports nor imports, nor foreign capital flows. We postulate a monetary economy in which economic agents, beyond the institution of government, can be divided conceptually into their business activities on the one hand, selling services and paying out wages and, on the other, receiving income, consuming and accumulating assets when they act as households. All production is undertaken by providers of services, who have no capital equipment and no intermediate costs of production. Production of services is assumed to be instantaneous, so that inventories do not exist. Finance for inventory accumulation is thus unnecessary *a fortiori*. There are no private banks, no firms and no profits whatsoever. We are in a *pure labour economy*, *à la* Adam Smith, where production is carried out by labour alone.[1]

The government buys services and pays for them with money, which consists of pieces of paper which it prints. Money is made acceptable as a means of payment because there is a law which makes it legal tender, which means that creditors are legally obliged to accept money in settlement of debts. The government also levies taxes and ordains that these be paid in money, which people therefore have to obtain by selling their services for it.[2] In other words, all transactions occur in *government* money, that is, banknotes issued by government. This government money is the vehicle via which people receive income, settle their debts, pay their taxes, and store their wealth.

It will further be assumed that the government fixes the price for an hour's labour and that there is an unlimited quantity of labour which is potentially available. In other words, it will be assumed initially that the supply of labour never constitutes a constraint on production. The economy is not

---

[1] See the book by Pasinetti (1993), for the formal description of a multi-sector economy, with pure labour processes.

[2] This is sometimes called the cartalist or chartalist view (Wray 1998). Some may regard it as an artificial assumption, others as an important and realistic principle.

Table 3.1 Balance sheet of Model *SIM*

	1. Households	2. Production	3. Government	Σ
Money stock	+H	0	−H	0

supply-constrained; it is demand-led. Production responds immediately to demand. Whatever is demanded will be produced.

3.2.2 Balance sheet and transactions matrix

Model *SIM* (and every subsequent model) will be introduced with a balance sheet matrix which describes each sector's stocks of assets and liabilities and their logical inter-relationship with those of other sectors – each financial asset owned by one sector always having a counterpart financial liability in one or more other sectors. The balance sheet matrix for Model *SIM*, given by Table 3.1, is extremely simple as there is only one item – money (*H*) – which is a liability of the government and an asset of households. This money is printed by government: we can assume it consists of banknotes, that is, what is usually called *cash* money. Because economists often call this *high-powered* money, we shall let the letter *H* stand for it.

Here, as everywhere else, stocks of assets will be entered with a plus sign and stocks of liabilities with a minus sign. Since the stock of money is an asset for households – it constitutes their accumulated wealth at a point of time – it appears with a plus sign (+) in the column allotted to households. On the other hand, the outstanding stock of money constitutes a liability for government. It is the public debt, the debt of government. Thus it is entered with a minus sign (−) in the government column.

In this elementary model, people in their capacity as producers and payers of income (shown in column 2) have been treated distinctly from the same people in their capacity as consumers, receivers of income and savers (shown as 'households' in column 1). People as producers are assumed to hold no cash at all, while they do hold cash when they act as consumers; at a later stage this will become a straightforward distinction between firms and households.

The second matrix, given in Table 3.2, describes all the transactions which take place between the sectors in any given period of time.

As pointed out in Chapter 2, it is impossible to overestimate the usefulness, when deploying a macroeconomic model, however simple, of using a system of accounts like that of Table 3.2. The system is comprehensive, in the sense that 'everything comes from somewhere and everything goes somewhere'. Or, to put it more formally, all flows can be fitted into a matrix in which columns and rows all sum to zero. Without this armature,

Table 3.2   Accounting (transactions) matrix for Model *SIM*

	1. Households	2. Production	3. Government	Σ
1. Consumption	$-C$	$+C$		0
2. Govt. expenditures		$+G$	$-G$	0
3. [Output]		$[Y]$		
4. Factor income (wages)	$+WB$	$-WB$		0
5. Taxes	$-T$		$+T$	
6. Change in the stock of money	$-\Delta H$		$+\Delta H$	0
Σ	0	0	0	0

accounting errors may pass unnoticed and unacceptable implications may be ignored.

The first five lines of the transactions matrix describe the variables which correspond, in principle, to the components of the National Income and Product Accounts (NIPA) arranged as transactions between sectors and which take place in some defined unit of time, such as a quarter or a year. These are the transactions which are usually to be found in standard macroeconomic textbooks. The sixth line, row 6, describes the changes in stocks of financial assets and liabilities which correspond, in principle, to the Flow-of-Funds Accounts and which are necessary to complete the system of accounts as a whole. The inclusion of stock variables (as in Table 3.1) and transactions in stock variables (the last line of Table 3.2) in the basic system of concepts is an important distinguishing feature of our approach. It will lead us to conclusions about motivation and the 'equilibrium' (or steady state) to which economic systems tend which are fundamentally at odds with those postulated in conventional textbooks.

Reading horizontally, the matrix shows that every component of the transaction-flow matrix must have an equivalent component, or a sum of equivalent components, elsewhere. For instance, reading row 5, we see that the tax revenues collected by the government sector must, by logical necessity, be equal to the sum of the taxes paid by the other sectors of the economy.

Reading vertically, the matrix shows how any sector's financial balance – that is, the difference between inflows of income and outflows of expenditure – must be exactly matched by the sum of its transactions in stocks of financial assets. Note that the first difference symbol (Δ) describes changes in a stock variable between the beginning and end of the period, that is $\Delta H = H - H_{-1}$ where the time subscript refers to the end of the previous period. It is assumed that the stock of an asset, at the end of a period, is identical to the stock of that asset at the beginning of the next period. The stock that you end up with is the same as the stock that you next start with.[3] As was the case in Chapter 2, the reader should recall that all *sources* of funds appear with a plus sign – these are incoming flows of money; on the other hand, all *uses* of funds appear with a minus sign. Take for instance the household column. In this simple model, households have only one source of funds, namely wages (the wage bill WB), which arise from sales of their work.[4] They have three ways in which they can use their funds: they pay taxes (T), they purchase consumer services (C) and they accumulate additional financial assets (ΔH). Thus the acquisition of new financial assets takes a minus sign, because the purchase or the acquisition of a financial asset is part of the *use* of the income they have received.

The matrix shows one item in square brackets which will prove crucial, namely total production (Y), which is not a transaction between two sectors and hence only appears once, in the production Column 2. Total production is here defined in the standard way used in all national accounts, either as the sum of all expenditures on goods and services or as the sum of all payments of factor income.

$$Y = C + G = WB \tag{3.10A}$$

3.3 Formalizing Model *SIM*

3.3.1 The behavioural transactions matrix

As with all the models which will follow, the coherent system of accounts arising from the balance sheet and the transactions-flow matrices provides the backbone of the model now to be developed. Although the model is extremely simple, it will enable us to lay down some fundamental principles and theorems which will remain useful later on.

The accounting matrices shown in Tables 3.1 and 3.2, since every row and every column sum to zero, describe the identities that must be satisfied in every solution to the model. However, beyond displaying the universe to be

---

[3] Some authors prefer to call H_t the stock of money being held at the beginning of the period, but the convention that we adopt is more akin to the use of computer simulations.

[4] It has been assumed that the government sector only purchases services from producing agents. There are no state employees and hence no civil servants. If this simplification is too hard to swallow, the reader may imagine that all civil servants have taken early retirement and have been replaced by contractuals. These contractuals, many of them previously forced into early retirement, have organized themselves as self-employed workers, setting up companies specialized in providing government services, and as a result the individuals hired to provide government services are part of the production sector.

Table 3.3 Behavioural (transactions) matrix for Model SIM

	1. Households	2. Production	3. Government	Σ
1. Consumption	$-C_d$	$+C_s$		0
2. Govt. expenditures		$+G_s$	$-G_d$	0
3. [Output]		$[Y]$		
4. Factor income (wages)	$+W \cdot N_s$	$-W \cdot N_d$		0
5. Taxes	$-T_s$		$+T_d$	0
6. Change in the stock of money	$-\Delta H_h$		$+\Delta H_s$	0
Σ	0	0	0	0

considered, these matrices do no more than show how all columns and rows must in the end 'add up'. By themselves they can say nothing at all about how the system is motivated or how it works. To understand the behaviour of the system as a whole we first have to make sure that every entry individually makes behavioural sense in the place where it appears. The agent buying a service is engaged in a completely different activity from that performed by the seller of that service and the motivation behind the two types of activity is completely different. The vertical columns must necessarily sum to zero, because the change in the amount of money held must always be equal to the difference between households' receipts and payments, however these are determined. Similarly the change in the amount of money created must always, by the laws of logic, be equal to the difference between the government receipts and outlays. And, as they are assumed to hold no cash, producers receipts from sales must equal their outlays on wages. But it may not be assumed in advance that the horizontal entries sum to zero; we have to specify the mechanisms by which these equalities come about. These mechanisms will be extremely simple ones in our first models, but the principle is theoretically fundamental; and as we advance to more complex models the equalizing mechanisms will be far more complex.

In Table 3.3 we show a modified version of Table 3.2 in which each transaction now has a suffix, s, d and h. The suffixes s and d, denote what, in a broad sense, may be called 'supply' and 'demand' while the suffix h attached to H, describes households' end period holdings of cash. The 'wage bill' has been modified so that it reads $W \cdot N$, that is, a wage rate (W) times employment (N). The production sector supplies services to the household sector and the government, and it 'demands' a certain volume of employment at a wage rate assumed to be exogenously determined – from outside the model. The household sector 'demands' consumption services, supplies labour and pays taxes. The government 'demands' services and taxes. It ought to be emphasized that Table 3.3 is a 'behavioural' transactions matrix, and not an 'ex ante' matrix. The behavioural matrix does not describe what is *expected* by the various agents before the period opens. Rather it describes the behaviour of agents at the time of the transactions. This distinction will become clearer in a later section.

3.3.2 Mechanisms adjusting supply and demand

The equations that describe Model *SIM* are to be found in Appendix 3.1. Because it is so very much simplified, only eleven equations are required to complete it and make it work.
We start with the equations which equalize demands and supplies.

$$C_s = C_d \tag{3.1}$$

$$G_s = G_d \tag{3.2}$$

$$T_s = T_d \tag{3.3}$$

$$N_s = N_d \tag{3.4}$$

These four equations imply that whatever is demanded (services, taxes and labour) is always supplied within the period. These (apart possibly from (3.3)) are strong assumptions implying, obviously enough, that we are describing an economy that has no supply constraints of any kind. In particular, equation (3.4) implies that there is a reserve army of unemployed workers, all eager to work at the going wage, whenever their labour services are being demanded.[5] The equalities of equations (3.1) and (3.2) require more attention, as some delicate points need to be emphasized. The rest of this subsection is devoted to the product and service markets.

First, it needs to be emphasized that, from the transactions matrix point of view, C_s and G_s represent the *sales* of consumption and government services. C_s and G_s both carry a positive sign in the production column of the behavioural transactions matrix. C_s and G_s thus represent sources of income – revenues that are collected by the production sector. Similarly, C_d and G_d represent the purchases of consumption goods and government services. Of course, we know that the sales have to equal purchases; this is nearly a tautology. But starting from a situation where production could be different from supply, and where supply could be different from demand, how do we arrive at the equality between sales and purchases?

There are several mechanisms that could lead to such a result, thus ensuring that the first two rows of the behavioural matrix sum to zero. The

[5] Thus equation (3.4) must certainly not be interpreted as implying that there is full employment. On the opposite, it is the amount of *supplied* labour that adjusts to labour demand.

first mechanism is mainly associated with mainstream theory, that is, neo-classical theory: variations in prices clear the market. Excess demand leads to higher prices, which is assumed to reduce excess demand.[6] This mechanism is put into effect within the period, before transactions are made. When transactions occur, as reflected in the transactions-flow matrix, supply and demand have already been equated through the price clearing mechanism. We believe that such a market clearing mechanism, based on price variations, is only appropriate in the case of financial markets. In the case of goods and services markets, and in the case of the so-called labour market, we believe that the hypothesis of market-clearing equilibrium prices is wholly counterfactual, inappropriate and misleading.

The second mechanism is associated with the so-called rationing theory, also called constrained equilibrium theory.[7] Despite being based on an essentially neo-classical view of markets, this approach eschews market clearing prices, by imposing some rigid prices. It says that whenever supply and demand are different, because of these rigid prices, the adjustment is done on the short side of the market. For instance, if demand is less than supply, sales will equate demand; if supply is less than demand, sales (and purchases) will equate supply. In this approach however, it is still the case that prices and nominal wages give the signals and what happens to unsold commodities is waived aside. For these reasons, we shall not pursue this line of thought.

The third mechanism is linked to the existence of inventories. Firms hold a buffer of finished goods, which can be called upon whenever demand exceeds production. Sales are always equal to demand because it is assumed that inventories are always large enough to absorb any discrepancy between production and demand. In this approach it is necessary to track the evolution of inventories from period to period, and to pay meticulous attention to the way in which they are measured, in particular to how they are valued. It has been advocated by authors of various heterodox traditions, in particular Godley and Cripps (1983) and Duménil and Lévy (1993: 95), who call it the

---

[6] Although elementary and intermediate textbooks often claim that excess demand is always eliminated by rising prices, things are not so simple in a world with several commodities: demand curves may not be downward sloping; they may not be 'well-behaved'. In the world of produced commodities, this problem is included among what are known as the Cambridge capital controversies (Harcourt 1972; Garegnani 1990). In general equilibrium theory, it is known as the Impossibility theorem, or the Sonnenschein-Debreu-Mantel theorem (Kirman 1989); despite starting with all the conditions associated with rational consumers, it is impossible to demonstrate that the market excess demand curve of every good is downward sloping. In other words, the equilibrium may not be stable, and there might be a multiplicity of them.

[7] The names of Clower, Barro and Grossman, Bénassy, Malinvaud are usually associated with this particular school of neoclassical Keynesians.

'general disequilibrium approach'. This mechanism – which we consider to be the most realistic one – will be described in detail, but only when we deal with private money, for reasons that will become obvious.

Finally, there is a fourth mechanism, the so-called Keynesian, or Kaleckian, quantity adjustment mechanism. This is the mechanism that is being called upon in the present model. With the previous three adjustment mechanisms, production was assumed to be given, set at some constant level at the beginning of the period. In the Keynesian and Kaleckian approach, production is the flexible element of the model. Producers produce exactly what is demanded. In this approach, there are no inventories. In the national accounts, variations in inventories adjust national expenditures to national output whenever sales differ from production. Here there is no such accounting adjustment mechanism, since inventories cannot change by assumption. Sales *are* equal to production. The equality between demand and supply, the latter being here defined as production, is achieved by an instantaneous quantity adjustment process, as is always the case in standard Kaleckian and Keynesian models. In the words of the mainstream, equations (3.1) and (3.2) embody the equilibrium between aggregate supply and aggregate demand, that is, between produced output and sales, being understood that the equality is achieved by a quantity process, and not by variations in prices. This mechanism is more likely to be appropriate in a service industry, where the service often is being provided right away, as soon as it is demanded. In the case of manufacturing, where production takes time, such an instantaneous quantity adjustment process is unlikely; the third mechanism, that based on inventory adjustments, is much more realistic.

In Model *SIM*, we are thus making two behavioural assumptions: first, that firms *sell* whatever is demanded (there is no rationing) – an assumption that we shall make throughout the book; and second, that there are no inventories, which implies that sales are equal to *output* – an assumption that will be abandoned in Chapters 8–11, where production will be equal to sales *plus* changes in inventories. It is best not to confuse these two assumptions.

3.3.3 Other equations of Model *SIM*

We next define disposable income (*YD*) as the wage bill earned by households less paid taxes:

$$YD = W \cdot N_S - T_S \tag{3.5}$$

We may now enter two behavioural equations. First, taxes are levied as some fixed proportion of money income, θ, which the government decides. The tax rate on (taxable) income is thus θ. This yields equation (3.6):

$$T_d = \theta \cdot W \cdot N_S \quad \theta < 1 \tag{3.6}$$

Second, we must specify the consumption function. At what rate do households spend on consumption? We know that they open each period with a stock of wealth inherited from the previous period (H_{-1}) and during the period they receive post tax income equal to YD. There are many ways to portray consumption behaviour. We suggest that households consume on the basis of two influences: their current disposable income YD, which we must assume is accurately known to households when they make their decisions, and the wealth they have accumulated over the past, H_{-1}. This yields equation (3.7), which says that consumption is determined as some proportion, α_1, of the flow of disposable income and some smaller proportion, α_2, of the opening stock of money. Consumption functions have been subjected to intense debates, and more will be said about the relative merits and the implicit features of the one chosen here.

$$C_d = \alpha_1 \cdot YD + \alpha_2 \cdot H_{h-1} \quad 0 < \alpha_2 < \alpha_1 < 1 \tag{3.7}$$

The next two equations arise once more from the transaction-flow matrix. Equation (3.8) is an identity, taken from column 3 of either of the transaction matrices. It says that the change in the stock of money issued by the government in each period, that is, the change in the supply of money H_s, is given by the difference between government receipts and outlays in that period. Both the change in the stock of money and the government deficit are endogenous; once the government has determined its own expenditure and the tax rate, the actual tax take will be determined as part of the solution of the model. When government expenditures exceed government revenues (taxes), the government issues debt to cover the difference. The debt, in our simplified economy, is simply cash money, which carries no interest payment. Thus equation (3.8) represents the budget constraint of government. The government expenditures that are not covered by taxes must be covered by the issue of a debt. Cash money is that debt.

$$\Delta H_s = H_s - H_{s-1} = G_d - T_d \tag{3.8}$$

Next, there is the third equation arising from the transactions-flow matrix, that given by equation (3.9). It corresponds to column 1 of the transactions-flow matrices. This identity describes the budget constraint of households. The accumulation of households' wealth is determined by their financial balance – the excess of disposable income over expenditure. Because there is only a single financial asset, and because there are no tangible assets in this economy, *additions* to cash holdings constitute the *saving* of households.

It follows that H_h stands for the cash held by households and also for the level of wealth which they possess. The h subscript is there to indicate that the cash is being held by households.

$$\Delta H_h = H_h - H_{h-1} = YD - C_d \tag{3.9}$$

Finally, we need the expressions which describe the determination of output and the determination of employment. This is the national income identity:

$$Y = C_s + G_s \qquad (3.10)$$

which, seen from the point of view of income, is rewritten as:

$$Y = W \cdot N_d \qquad (3.11\text{A})$$

or rather as:

$$N_d = \frac{Y}{W} \qquad (3.11)$$

The elementary model is now complete. We have 11 equations and 11 unknowns, Y, YD, T_d, T_s, H_s, H_h, G_s, C_s, C_d, N_s and N_d. Each of the eleven unknowns has been set on the left-hand side of an equation. There are three exogenous variables, G_d, θ, and W, the first two of which are set by the autonomous decisions of government – fiscal policy in other words. Wages will be determined largely by conditions in the labour market but are assumed at this stage to be fully exogenous.[8] All these, together with initial (stock) conditions and the parameters of the consumption function, make it possible to solve the model as a sequence proceeding through time. In sharp contrast with the conventional treatment, the solution for each period will depend crucially on stock variables created the previous period; and it will create the stock variables necessary for the solution of the model in the following period.

It should finally be noted that two separate equations (3.8) and (3.9) describe respectively the issue of money by the government and the additional amount of money which people decide to hold as two distinct processes; *yet the model contains no equilibrium condition which makes the two equal to one another.* The two (changes in H_h and H_s) must however turn out to be the same once the model is solved, as can be inferred from the behavioural matrix (Table 3.3). The vertical columns all sum to zero by the rules of logic, and we have described behaviour which will guarantee that all the rows except the bottom row (which contains H_h and H_s) also sum to zero. By virtue of the watertight accounting of the model, combined with behavioural assumptions which guarantee the equality between demand and supply for services and labour, we have stumbled on the Walrasian principle, which is not to be gainsaid, that any properly constructed model must contain one equation which is redundant, in the sense that it is logically implied

---

[8] In this highly simplified model, as written, it would be meaningless to change the wage rate W.

by all the others and which can – indeed must – be 'dropped' out of the model if a solution of the model is not to be over-determined. The computer could not solve the model if this additional equation were to be included in the program. We shall encounter time and time again this quasi-Walrasian principle. Here, the redundant equation is:

$$\Delta H_h = \Delta H_s \tag{3.12}$$

We draw attention here to a fundamental difference between the model which we are beginning to set forth compared with that which sees clearing (or non clearing) markets as the determinants of macro phenomena. In this, our elementary model, the equality between the demand and supply of money is the logically inevitable consequence of using a comprehensive system of accounts. By contrast, the identical equation in the neo-classical model is an equilibrium condition which somehow brings the demand for money into equivalence with the 'money supply' determined exogenously.

The equality expressed by equation (3.12) contains nothing surprising from a Keynesian point of view. It simply expresses the well-known Keynesian identity that says that investment must be equal to saving. In Model *SIM*, there is no investment. This implies that social saving, the saving of the overall economy, must sum to zero. Here the term ΔH_h represents household saving; the term ΔH_s stands for the government fiscal deficit, and hence government dissaving. For overall saving to be zero, the two terms must equal each other.

3.4 A numerical example and the standard Keynesian multiplier

3.4.1 A numerical example

It may help to give a numerical example of how this whole model evolves through time, starting with the beginning of the world.

Assume the tax rate is 20%, while the parameters of the consumption function, α_1 and α_2, are 0.6 and 0.4, respectively. We start from a situation where there is no economic activity whatsoever, and where none has ever existed. Households have no income, and they never accumulated any wealth. The causal chain is set off by a stream of payments by the government. These government expenditures generate income, a tax yield, a money supply and a consumption stream. The government has suddenly come in, and decides to order $20 worth of services from the production sector. These services are paid for by the creation of 20 units of cash money, that is $20. The money created is then circulated within the system in the following way.

First, producers will pay households with these 20 units of cash. Households will then be forced to pay taxes on 20% of that, that is, they will have to pay 4 units in taxes. These 4 units of money are thus destroyed, as soon

Table 3.4 The impact of $20 of government expenditures, with perfect foresight

Period	1	2	3	∞
G	0	20	20	20
$Y = G + C$	0	38.5	47.9	100
$T = \theta \cdot Y$	0	7.7	9.6	20
$YD = Y - T$	0	30.8	38.3	80
$C = \alpha_1 \cdot YD + \alpha_2 \cdot H_{-1}$	0	18.5	27.9	80
$\Delta H_s = G - T$	0	12.3	10.4	0
$\Delta H_h = YD - C$	0	12.3	10.4	0
$H = \Delta H + H_{-1}$	0	12.3	22.7	80

as the taxes are paid back to government. Households then purchase consumer services from one another, using 60% of the remaining 16 units of cash money, that is, 9.6 units, while the rest, 40% of the 16 units, will be put aside to accumulate wealth, in the form of cash balances. But the 9.6 units of consumption now generate production and an income equal to 9.6 units. Out of this income, more taxes will be paid, more cash will be accumulated, and more consumer expenditures will be carried out. But these expenditures will lead to more production and more income being distributed, all this within the very same period.

The initial $20 government injection thus has ripple effects throughout the economy. The government injection has a multiple effect on income. This is the well-known Keynesian multiplier process, to be found in all elementary macroeconomics textbooks. Because perfect foresight has been assumed, households must know precisely how much will be produced and how much income the initial injection of government expenditures is able to generate. They must also know with certainty the various parameters of the overall economy (the average tax rate and the average propensity to consume out of disposable income) and they must know the initial injection. Here, all these multiplier effects are assumed to take place within the single period. Starting with no economic activity at all in period 1, the government expenditures taking place at the beginning of period 2 along with the standard multiplier process will bring about the numbers given at the end of period 2, as shown in Table 3.4.

Since mechanisms equating the various supply and demand variables have been provided, the suffixes s and d have been omitted.

3.4.2 The standard Keynesian multiplier

How did the economy achieve the numbers of period 2? The standard Keynesian analysis – precisely the analysis beyond which we wish to go – provides the explanation.

Since there is no past accumulated wealth at the beginning of period 2, the consumption function given by equation (3.7) comes down to the standard textbook consumption function (with no autonomous term):

$$C_d = \alpha_1 \cdot YD \tag{3.13}$$

The national expenditures equation (3.10), given equations (3.1) to (3.4), and equations (3.5) and (3.6), omitting the subscripts becomes:

$$Y = C + G = \alpha_1 \cdot \{Y \cdot (1 - \theta)\} + G$$

With perfect foresight national income in the consumption function must be identical to national income defined as production. Solving for Y, we obtain the equilibrium value of Y at the end of period 2:

$$Y^* = \frac{G}{1 - \alpha_1 \cdot (1 - \theta)} \tag{3.14}$$

For the assumed parameter values, the multiplier $1/\{1 - \alpha_1 \cdot (1 - \theta)\}$ is equal to 1.92, and hence, for $G = 20$, $Y^* = 38.5$, as shown in period 2 of Table 3.4.

In the standard story, for instance that told by the well-known IS/LM model, the expression of Y^* given by equation (3.14) would be the end of the story. The reader of the standard textbook would be told that Y^* is the equilibrium national income. The textbook would then consider whether the multiplier should be interpreted as a logical relationship, occurring within the period, as has been done here, or as a dynamic relationship, occurring over several periods, possibly using trial and error. The reader would then be told that provided government expenditures are kept at the same level (here 20) in the following periods, national income would remain forever at its Y^* value (here 38.5).

3.4.3   The drawbacks of the standard multiplier analysis

This view of the multiplier process lacks coherence however. The equilibrium value of Y^* is only a *short-run* equilibrium. It is not a *long-run* equilibrium, that is, it is not a *steady state* in the sense that it is a solution that can repeat itself for a large number of periods. Once we think of it, the fact that equation (3.14) cannot be a steady-state is quite obvious. If the expression of Y^* provided by equation (3.14) and the numbers provided in period 2 of Table 3.4 were to be the algebraic and numerical long-run solutions of our model, then there would be absurd consequences. In particular, in period 2, the government is running a deficit: government expenditures G minus taxes T are equal to $20 - 7.7 = 12.3$. Since the level of national income is deemed to be constant at Y^*, the constant deficit of every period would add to one another, so that government debt would rise forever. The public debt to income ratio would rise to infinity. This, of course, is impossible. The solution of equation (3.14) and the numbers of period 2 can only provide us with a *temporary* solution, a short-run one.

The problem with the standard textbook story is that it deals with flows, while not taking into account the impact of flows on stocks – and the subsequent impact of stocks on flows. Until a steady state has been reached, short-run flows will generate changes in stocks. In the case of Model *SIM* the short-run solution reached in period 2 gives rise to a government deficit and to a flow of saving on the part of households. The government deficit each period adds to the stock of debt owed by government. Similarly the saving of households adds cash money to their existing stock of cash balances. Unless everything else grows at the same rate, this cannot go on forever. The way out of this puzzle is offered by the formulation of the consumption function given by equation (3.7). As households accumulate wealth – as they accumulate more and more cash balances – they become richer, and consume part of their accumulated wealth. This gives rise to the second term of the consumption function (3.7), the $\alpha_2 \cdot H_{h-1}$ term, which says that households consume a proportion α_2 of the wealth H_{h-1} which they have accumulated in the past. This is why the level of income in period 3, and in successive periods is now higher than what it was in period 2, despite the fact that the autonomous government expenditures remain fixed at 20. Consumers spend out of their current income but also out of the money balances which they have accumulated in previous periods.

3.5 Steady-state solutions

We may now explore the steady-state solutions of Model *SIM*, those given by the last column of Table 3.4. First we define what we mean by a steady-state. It is a state where the key variables remain in a constant relationship to each other. This must include *both* flows and stocks, and not flows only as with *short-run* (temporary) equilibria . When, in addition, the *levels* of the variables are constant, the steady state is a *stationary* state. In general, the steady state will be a *growing* economy, where *ratios* of variables remain constant. Whether we are in a stationary state or a steady state with growth, we may then speak of the *long-run* solutions. But most of our models will omit growth, and hence will deal with *stationary* states, as is the case with Model *SIM*. In the stationary steady state of the model, in which neither stocks nor flows change, government expenditure must be equal to tax receipts, that is, there is neither a government deficit nor a government surplus. This is the condition for a zero change in the stock of money (i.e. government debt). Formally, still omitting subscripts, we have:

$$G = T^* = \theta \cdot W \cdot N^* = \theta \cdot Y^*$$

Hence the stationary state flow of aggregate income must be:

$$Y^* = \frac{G}{\theta} \tag{3.15}$$

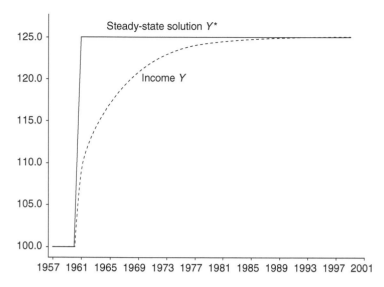

Figure 3.1 Impact on national income Y and the steady state solution Y^*, following a permanent increase in government expenditures ($\Delta G = 5$)

where stars now denote a steady state solution.[9] In the numerical example, the stationary level of income is 100, as can be seen in the last column of Table 3.4, since $G = 20$, while $\theta = 0.2$.

The G/θ ratio we call the *fiscal stance*. This is the 'ratio of government expenditure to its income share' (Godley and Cripps 1983: 111). It plays a fundamental role in all of our models with a government sector, since it determines GDP in the steady state.

This fundamental property of the model is also illustrated in Figure 3.1 which shows how the stationary solution G/θ is modified following a permanent step addition of $5 to the flow of government expenditure. As the average tax rate is assumed to be 20%, the addition to the stationary state aggregate flow, by (3.10), is $25. As Figure 3.1 shows, the addition to aggregate income does actually converge to this number. Income Y gradually increases from its $100 steady state value until it finally reaches $125, which is the new value of G/θ – the new stationary value.[10]

---

[9] This result was first achieved by Ott and Ott (1965). See also Christ (1968) and Godley and Cripps (1983: 111).

[10] Not too much attention should be paid to the numerical years which are shown on the x-axis of the chart. These really represent periods: they could be years, quarters, months.

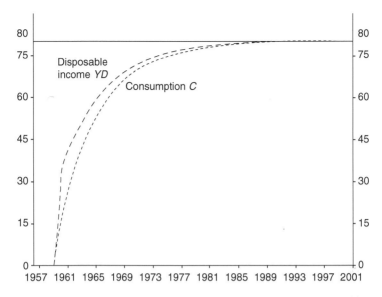

Figure 3.2 Disposable income and consumption starting from scratch (Table 3.4)

Another property of the *stationary* state is that consumption must be equal to disposable income. In other words, in a model without growth, the *average* propensity to consume must be equal to unity. This property of fully coherent stock-flow models – which is often forgotten – can be easily derived, because in the stationary state there is no change in financial stocks, that is, there is no saving. Thus, by virtue of equation (3.9), we have:

$$\Delta H_h^* \equiv YD^* - C^* = 0$$

where the stars once more denote steady state values. This implies that:

$$YD^* = C^*$$

and hence, given equations (3.5)–(3.7), (3.11A) and (3.15):

$$YD^* = C^* = \frac{G \cdot (1 - \theta)}{\theta} \tag{3.16}$$

In the numerical example of Table 3.4, we can see in the last column that disposable income and consumption are equal to each other in the stationary state only, when they reach 80. Figure 3.2 also illustrates how the change in disposable income responds to the addition to government expenditure; and how consumption responds to disposable income, eventually converging onto it, as implied by equation (3.16).

Finally, we may compute the stationary value of the stock of household wealth, that is the stationary value of cash money balances which is also the stationary value of the stock of government debt. In the consumption function (3.7), we substitute the equality $YD^* = C^*$. Knowing that in the steady state, $H = H_{-1}$, we obtain:

$$H^* = \left\{ \frac{(1-\alpha_1)}{\alpha_2} \right\} \cdot YD^* = \alpha_3 \cdot YD^* = \alpha_3 \cdot G \cdot \frac{(1-\theta)}{\theta} \tag{3.17}$$

where $\alpha_3 = (1 - \alpha_1)/\alpha_2$.

With numerical values attributed to the various parameters, we note that $\alpha_3 = 0.4/0.4 = 1$. Thus, in the numerical simulation given by Table 3.4, the stationary value of the stock of money balances is identical to the value taken by *disposable* income, and equal to 80. Figure 3.3 also shows how, consistent with equation (3.17), wealth – here the stock of money – converges onto its steady state value. The chart also shows that household saving – here additions to money balances – converges to zero, as it should in a model that converges to a stationary state.[11]

3.6 The consumption function as a stock-flow norm

The definition of the steady-state solution for household wealth is the occasion to discuss further the meaning of the consumption function (3.7), and to reach a very important result. When first presented, the consumption function was viewed as a consumption decision based on both the flow of income and the stock of past accumulated wealth. Another interpretation of this relationship can now be offered, in terms of a *wealth accumulation function*, thus showing that consumers' behaviour can be represented in either of two, logically equivalent, ways. First note that equation (3.9) can be rewritten as:

$$C = YD - \Delta H_h \tag{3.9A}$$

This simply says that consumption is disposable income minus changes in cash money (i.e. minus the household saving of the period). This identity may be substituted back into (3.7), which, after rearrangement, turns the consumption function into a saving function or a wealth accumulation function. We have:

$$C = YD - \Delta H_h = \alpha_1 \cdot YD + \alpha_2 \cdot H_{h-1}$$

---

[11] From the identities of the balance sheet and of the transactions matrix, we know that the two curves of Figure 3.3 also trace out the evolution of government deficit and government debt.

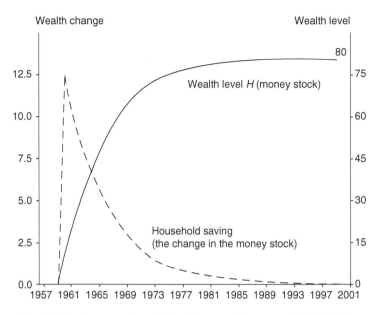

Figure 3.3 Wealth change and wealth level, starting from scratch (Table 3.4)

and hence:

$$\Delta H_h = (1 - \alpha_1) \cdot YD - \alpha_2 \cdot H_{h-1}$$

from which we obtain:

$$\Delta H_h = \alpha_2 \cdot (\alpha_3 \cdot YD - H_{h-1}) \tag{3.7A}$$

where once again $\alpha_3 = (1 - \alpha_1)/\alpha_2$.

Equation (3.7A) is a partial adjustment function. It says that wealth is being accumulated at a certain rate, determined by the partial adjustment parameter α_2, towards some desired proportion α_3 of disposable income. Thus households are saving, wishing, we may suppose, to end the period with some well defined quantity of accumulated wealth. In other words, the existing wealth of households, when any period begins, is equal to H_{-1}, and given the disposable income of the period, households now have a target level of wealth, given by $V^T = \alpha_3 \cdot YD$. The α_3 coefficient is the *stock-flow norm* of households. It is the assumed wealth to income target ratio which is implicitly embedded into the so-called Modigliani consumption function proposed with equation (3.7). Thus whenever the target level of wealth is higher than the realized level, households save, in an attempt to reach their target.

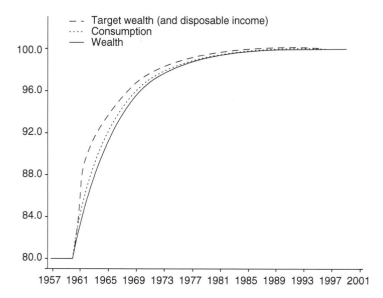

Figure 3.4   Evolution of wealth, target wealth, consumption and disposable income following an increase in government expenditures ($\Delta G = 5$) – Model *SIM*.

This is illustrated with the help of Figure 3.4, which starts off from the stationary state identified in the previous graphs, which is shocked by a step increase in government expenditures. We see that target wealth (here also equal to disposable income since $\alpha_3 = 1$) remains higher than realized wealth, so that households save in their attempt to adjust their historically given level of wealth to their target wealth. As a result, consumption is systematically below disposable income, until the new stationary state is reached, at which point $H_h = V^T = YD = C$.

The fact that the wealth accumulation function (3.7A) can be directly obtained from consumption function (3.7), by the simple addition of equation (3.9A) which identically defines consumption, is very important. It shows that the assumption of stock-flow norms in the case of households is not far-fetched, at least within a Keynesian research programme, for the existence of the stock-flow norm is equivalent to the existence of a well-accepted Keynesian consumption function with lagged wealth, that of equation (3.7). In Godley and Cripps (1983: 41), it was argued that the proposed theory, which is roughly similar to the one advocated in the present book, was 'a conditional theory as to how *whole* economic systems function'. Godley and Cripps argued that 'the main results are conditional on the behavioural axiom that stock variables will not change indefinitely as ratios to related flow variables'. In other words, the theory presented was conditional on the existence of stock-flow norms. But equations (3.7) and (3.7A) show that these stock-flow norms can be extracted directly from (nearly) standard Keynesian consumption functions. All that needs to be assumed, as did Modigliani (1986), is that consumption depends on lagged wealth besides current disposable income. If one believes in the relative stability of consumption functions, that is if one agrees that the α coefficients are fairly stable, then one accepts the relative stability of stock-flow norms in the case of households.

For instance, in period 3 of Table 3.4, since $\alpha_3 = 1$, the target level of wealth is $V^T = 38.3$, whereas the previously achieved level of wealth is $H_{-1} = 12.3$. Rather obviously households do not attempt to reach their wealth target at once as this might leave them consuming nothing at all for a time. Only a proportion α_2 of the discrepancy will be remedied within a single period. The adjustment to the target level is partial. Again, in the case of period 3 of Table 3.4, with $\alpha_2 = 0.4$, and with a discrepancy between the target and the achieved wealth of 26, the saving of period 3, ΔH_h, equals 10.4. Only 40% of the discrepancy is remedied at once.

In general, dissaving will occur when the wealth target has been surpassed. Also, as is clear from equation (3.7A), once the target has been reached, that is, when $H^* = V^T = \alpha_3 \cdot YD^*$, no more saving will occur and the stationary state defined by equations (3.14–3.17) is reached.

It may finally be useful to add something about what, in a properly articulated stock-flow system, the consumption function *is not and cannot possibly be*. It cannot be:

$$C = \alpha_1 \cdot YD \quad 0 < \alpha_1 < 1 \tag{3.13}$$

The reason why this version of the consumption function must be categorically rejected is that, *in models without growth*, its use renders the model unstable.[12] Why? Because, as shown in section 3.4, if α_1 is less than unity the equation implies that if ever a flow stationary state were reached, there would have to be a stock disequilibrium; with C and YD constant, the money stock and government debt must be rising for ever (by an amount equal in each period to $YD - C$).

There is however another consumption function, very similar to equation (3.13), which is admissible, although it does not have all the nice

---

[12] In models with growth, the standard consumption function, without a wealth term, does not lead to formal instability. Thus there is nothing wrong, from a purely logical viewpoint, with all the Cambridge growth models (à la Kaldor, Robinson, Pasinetti, and even Lavoie and Godley (2001–2)), that exclude a wealth term, being based on specific propensities to save out of profits and out of wages. Such models achieve a determinate wealth to income ratio, although there is no explicit wealth to income target ratio.

properties of equation (3.7). It is:

$$C = \alpha_0 + \alpha_1 \cdot YD \tag{3.13A}$$

with α_0 a positive constant, which represents autonomous consumption, independent of current income.

This is, of course, the consumption function to be found in Samuelson's elementary 45 degree-line model – the workhorse of principles of macroeconomics – and in the IS-LM model – the workhorse of most intermediate macro textbooks. Consumption function (3.13A) is also often to be found in the work of various post-Keynesians. For instance, it can be found in the textbook of Paul Davidson (1994: 39), who, in the footsteps of Keynes himself, deals with short-run equilibria, without growth. With consumption function (3.13A), it is possible to achieve a coherent stationary state. The *average* propensity to consume can be unity, that is we can have $C = YD$ in the stationary state, even though the marginal propensity to consume out of disposable income, given by α_1, is below one. What happens is that the constant term in equation (3.13A) plays a role similar to that of the consumption out of wealth. When we deal with private money, in Chapter 8, we shall introduce a mixture of these two coherent consumption functions, those given by equations (3.7) and (3.13A).

3.7 Expectations mistakes in a simple stock-flow model

3.7.1 Introducing expectations into the model

In this section we introduce uncertainty into the model by making consumption depend on *expected* income – not actual income, which households can only guess. In the process we shall discover a new and extremely important function for money – that it acts as a 'buffer' whenever expectations turn out to be incorrect.

Model *SIM* used the strong assumption that consumers have perfect foresight with regard to their income – something which is inconceivable in a world dominated by uncertainty, where the future states of nature are themselves uncertain, and where agents have unreliable knowledge and limited capacity in processing information.[13] Yet if consumers do not know precisely what their income is going to be, the only change which has to be made to the model is to substitute expected for actual disposable income in the consumption function. But we must then have some way of describing how expectations are formed.

---

[13] Those two aspects of uncertainty are respectively called *ontological* and *epistemological* uncertainty.

The new consumption function is:

$$C_d = \alpha_1 \cdot YD^e + \alpha_2 \cdot H_{h-1} \qquad (3.7E)$$

where the superscript e denotes an expected value.

It is assumed that households make some estimate of the income they will receive during the period, and that they base their consumption over the current period on this estimate. Since agents decide what to spend on the basis of their expected income, this implies that households correctly estimate the money stock they will end up with only when they have correctly anticipated their disposable income. In general, households can only make an estimate of the amount of money which they desire to hold. This conditional demand for money, the amount of money desired by households conditional on their expectations regarding disposable income, we shall call H_d. At the beginning of the period, households decide on the amount of additional money which they desire to hold by the end of the period. The new stock of money which they wish to hold is their demand for money. We thus add one variable to the model, H_d, the demand for money at the beginning of the period (based on expectations), and one extra equation:

$$\Delta H_d = H_d - H_{h-1} = YD^e - C_d \qquad (3.18)$$

To the extent that expectations about disposable income are falsified, the end period stock of money must differ to an equal extent from what was initially demanded. Subtracting equation (3.18) from (3.9), we obtain:

$$H_h - H_d = YD - YD^e \qquad (3.19)$$

The above equation shows that if realized income is above expected income, households will hold the difference in the form of larger than expected cash money balances. The reason for this is that households have already decided on the amount they would consume. Any additional income, additional to what was expected, will thus be saved and added to cash balances. The stock of cash people find themselves holding at the end of each period is not the outcome of a plan which they have made. We have reached a point here where our model of money holding differs fundamentally from that in conventional macroeconomics; we could hardly be further from a situation in which there is a difference between the supply and demand for money which must be resolved via an equilibrating mechanism. The quantity of cash households end up with will bear *some* relationship to what they planned but this will be modified by any error in their expectations. Thus money provides a function which is sometimes called 'buffering' – apart from being the form in which wealth is held, money provides an essential *flexible* element which enables people to transact although they never quite know what their income or their expenditure is going to be. This is one reason why

Table 3.5 Behavioural (transactions) matrix for Model *SIM*, with mistaken expectations

	1. Households	2. Production	3. Government	Σ
1. Consumption	$-C_d$	$+C_s$		0
2. Govt. expenditures		$+G_s$	$-G_d$	0
3. [Output]		$[Y]$		
4. Factor income (wages)	$+W \cdot N_s^e$	$-W \cdot N_d$		$W \cdot N_s^e - W \cdot N_d$
5. Taxes	$-T_s^e$		$+T_d$	$T_d - T_s^e$
6. Change in the stock of money	$-\Delta H_d$		$+\Delta H_s$	$\Delta H_s - \Delta H_d$
Σ	0	0	0	0

the term 'demand' for money is so misleading and why we have given it the subscript h from the very beginning to mean 'holding' rather than the usual d subscript.

The appearance of mistaken expectations on the part of households can be described within the framework of another behavioural transactions matrix, shown here in Table 3.5. Let us include, however, within this matrix, the adjustment processes of equations (3.1–3.4), that guarantee that the sums of some rows are equal to zero. Then the new behavioural transactions matrix appears as in Table 3.5.

Because only households are assumed to have mistaken expectations, only the column of households and that of summations are changed compared to Table 3.3. However, as before, the column of households must sum to zero, for otherwise the plans and the expectations of households would be incompatible with their budget constraint. The budget constraint of households as it appears in the first column of Table 3.5 is reflected in equation (3.18). Similarly, equation (3.19) can be extracted from the last column, by recalling the definition of disposable income and by recalling equation (3.12) – the redundant equation – which says that $\Delta H_s = \Delta H_h$.

3.7.2 A more recursive system

The inclusion of expected income, rather than realized income, in the consumption function yields a more recursive picture of the system. Recall the difficulties that we had in identifying income in the very first stage of our numerical example in Table 3.4, what we called then the second period of the model. Because all was simultaneously happening at once, we required the short-term solutions of the multiplier process to achieve the required computations. In other words we had to assume that households knew what the

Table 3.6 The impact of $20 of government
expenditures, with mistaken expectations

Period	1	2	3	∞
G	0	20	20	20
$Y = C + G$	0	29.6	39.9	100
$T = \theta \cdot Y$	0	5.9	8.0	20
$YD = Y - T$	0	23.7	31.9	80
$YD^e = YD_{-1}$	0	16.0	23.7	80
$C = \alpha_1 \cdot YD^e + \alpha_2 \cdot H_{-1}$	0	9.6	19.9	80
$\Delta H_s = G - T$	0	14.1	12.0	0
$\Delta H_h = YD - C$	0	14.1	12.0	0
$H = H_s = H_h = \Delta H + H_{-1}$	0	14.1	26.1	80
$\Delta H_d = YD^e - C$	0	6.4	3.8	0
$H_d = \Delta H_d + H_{-1}$	0	6.4	17.9	80

equilibrium level of income was, hence assuming that they had knowledge of the multiplier process and of the various parameters of the economy.

Here things are much simpler. For instance, starting again from scratch, as we did with the numerical example of Table 3.4, we can suppose that, in the second period, households only expect as income the services purchased by government. In the following periods, let us for the time being assume that expected income is equal to the realized income of the previous period, that is, we have:

$$YD^e = YD_{-1} \tag{3.20}$$

The four new equations now help to define model SIMEX. From it, we can build a numerical example, as shown in Table 3.6. In period 2, households assume an income level of 20, and hence expected disposable income is equal to 16. Since there is a marginal propensity to consume of 0.6, this implies that actual consumption is 9.6 and hence income is 29.6(= $G+C$ = 20+9.6). The reader can verify that equation (3.19) is satisfied: the discrepancy between desired and realized holdings of money is equal to the discrepancy between expected and realized disposable income. Also, one can see that the expected disposable income at period 3 is the same as realized disposable income at period 2. Despite the mistakes in expectations, as time goes on, the same stationary state as that of Table 3.4 will be achieved, as shown in the last column of Table 3.6. The evolution of disposable income YD and expected disposable income YD^e are specifically charted in Figure 3.5, where it is shown that both series eventually converge to 80, as they did without the mistaken expectations.

As period succeeds period, people amend their consumption decisions as they find their wealth stocks unexpectedly excessive (or depleted), and as

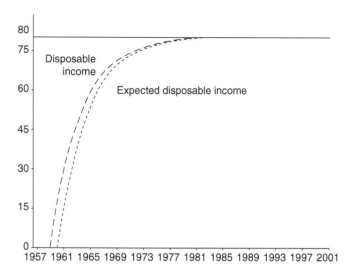

Figure 3.5   Disposable income and expected disposable income starting from scratch with delayed expectations (Table 3.6) – Model *SIMEX*

their expectations about future income get revised. In sequences, the realized stock of money links each period to the period which comes after. We thus have some kind of autopilot.

3.7.3   An extreme illustration of mistaken expectations: inert expectations

Mistaken expectations concerning income are relatively unimportant in a stock-flow model, that is, in a model where changes in stocks are taken into consideration and where some flows depend on the values taken by the stocks, as is the case here with the consumption function. This is well illustrated by the following numerical simulation with extreme assumptions regarding income expectations. We assume the same step addition to government expenditure takes place, but expectations about future disposable income are inert: they remain obstinately and permanently unchanged at the level which existed before the shock (YD^e is a constant). Even using these rather exotic assumptions, the new steady state GDP will be exactly what it was under the assumption of perfect foresight. So long as a stationary state is reached at all it must be one in which government liabilities are constant and hence where $Y^* = G/\theta$.

What has happened is that, because income turns out to be continually higher than expected, the accumulation of wealth also continues to be larger than expected and it is this which makes consumption grow. Growth ceases when wealth has risen to the level at which additional consumption out of wealth is exactly equal to consumption which is lost because of mistaken expectations about income.

Although the fact that expectations are invariably falsified has great importance for the theoretical and practical role of money, this doesn't make a huge difference to how the model actually solves. It doesn't matter much if expectations are falsified, because we have a sequential system with a built in mechanism for correcting mistakes.

The consequence of making extreme assumptions about persistently wrong expectations is illustrated in the next two charts. Assume that the economy has achieved a stationary state where $Y^* = 100$, and where $YD^* = C^* = 80$. Assume now a permanent step increase in government expenditures ($\Delta G = 5$, $G = 25$), as was done to obtain Figures 3.1 and 3.4, but this time with the assumption that the expected disposable income remains fixed at the old stationary equilibrium ($YD^e = 80$). Figure 3.6 shows that despite the completely fixed expectations about future disposable income, the actual national income Y converges towards the steady state level of income, given by $Y^* = G/\theta = 125$, as in the case of perfect foresight. Comparing Figure 3.6 with Figure 3.1, what we observe is that this convergence is much slower than in the perfect foresight case, as it takes many more periods to approach the steady state solution. In other words, the traverse is different but the stationary equilibrium is no different from what it had been in the previous experiment.

Figure 3.7 helps to explain why this is so. Because people act on wrong expectations – underestimating disposable income – saving is higher than expected and hence the stock of wealth grows faster than in the perfect foresight case. Consumption eventually reaches the same steady state value ($C^* = 100$) that it would have reached in a perfect foresight model. Expectations about income never adapt at all to the new circumstances – so consumption out of (expected) income never changes. However wealth does rise – faster than it would otherwise have done – and it is this which causes consumption to rise. The rise only tails off as consumption reaches its new steady state. This happens at the point when the budget is once again balanced. Indeed, actual wealth in the new steady state is much higher than it would have been in a perfect foresight model (or in the adaptive expectations model), as we can see by comparing the evolution of wealth in Figures 3.4 and 3.7. Thus in an economy where agents systematically underestimate their incomes, public debt would be larger than that of an economy where forecasts are correct.

3.8 Out of the steady state

3.8.1 Difference equations

To finish the chapter, let us come back to the model with perfect foresight. The discussion of the properties of the model has so far concentrated entirely

84

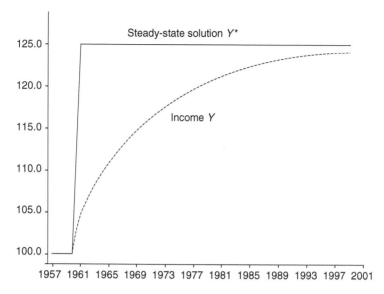

Figure 3.6 Impact on national income *Y* and the steady state solution *Y**, following an increase in government expenditures ($\Delta G = 5$), when expected disposable income remains fixed

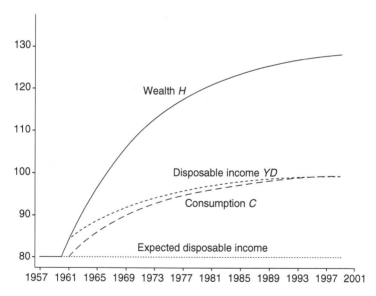

Figure 3.7 Evolution of wealth, consumption and disposable income following an increase in government expenditures ($\Delta G = 5$), when expected disposable income remains fully fixed

on steady states. The solution for Y in all intermediate situations can be obtained by putting the consumption function back into the national income identity to obtain the difference equation:

$$Y = \frac{G + \alpha_2 \cdot H_{-1}}{1 - \alpha_1 \cdot (1 - \theta)} \qquad (3.21)$$

The fact that current income is determined by the stock of money that was held in the previous period gives some credence to Keynes's claim that money is the link between each period and the next, between the past and the future.

The analogue solution for the stock of money in every intermediate situation (in this perfect foresight model) – a rearrangement of (3.9A) – is:

$$H_h = (1 - \alpha_1) \cdot (1 - \theta) \cdot Y + (1 - \alpha_2) \cdot H_{-1} \qquad (3.22)$$

Substituting Y for its value taken in equation (3.21), the current value of wealth, H, can be fully assessed in terms of the parameters of the system, the past values of the variables, and the policy decisions regarding the level of government expenditures and the tax rate. The stocks of financial assets at the beginning of each period constitute the legacy from past history. Given that history, and with appropriate knowledge of the parameters, we can follow through future flows and future increments in financial stocks. The numerical example of Table 3.4 can be built sequentially from these two out-of-equilibrium equations.

Note that from our point of view, the solutions given by equations (3.21) and (3.22) are out-of-equilibrium values. But many economists would say that these intermediate solutions are short-run equilibria, or temporary equilibria. They are short-run or temporary equilibria, because, given the parameters and past values of wealth, these are the values that would be achieved in each period.

It should also be noted that while the propensities to save (out of income or accumulated wealth) have no impact on the stationary solutions of the model, they do have a temporary or short-run impact. As can be ascertained from equation (3.21), it is clear that, all else equal, an increase in the propensity to consume out of current income – the α_1 parameter – leads to an initial rise in national income, due to the increase in consumption expenditure. This initial rise, however, will be cancelled eventually by the accompanying decline in accumulated money balances, and hence the decline in consumption expenditures out of wealth. The evolution of aggregate income, consumption and wealth, following the increase in the propensity to consume, is shown in Figure 3.8. Wealth falls off, since consumption is above

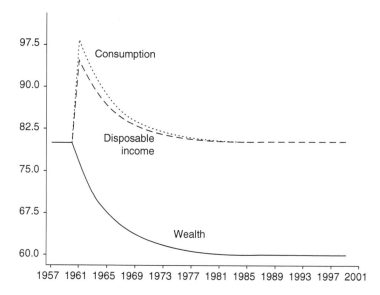

Figure 3.8 Evolution of consumption, disposable income and wealth following an increase in the propensity to consume out of current income (α_1 moves from 0.6 to 0.7).

disposable income during the transition, and the latter two variables eventually revert to their previous steady state levels.[14] More on this peculiar effect of the propensities to consume over the long run will be discussed in the next chapter.

3.8.2   Stability analysis

One important question in economics, although it is a question that is too often ignored, is whether the model is stable. More often than not, textbooks show that there exists an equilibrium solution to the model, then proceed with some comparative statics – by taking the partial derivative of the equilibrium solution, but omit any stability analysis. In other words, textbooks often 'make the arbitrary assumption that the process of economic adjustment inevitably leads to an equilibrium' (Chiang 1984: 435). Stability analysis checks whether the equilibrium can be attained. It checks whether there is some path leading, say from the old to the new equilibrium.

Stability analysis is closely linked to economic dynamics, as understood here. Our models are dynamic, because they take time into consideration.

---

[14] The wealth to disposable income ratio falls down since the α_1 consumption parameter moves up while the α_2 parameter stays put, thus driving down the α_3 parameter which defines this wealth to disposable income ratio.

For instance, as shown in the previous subsection, current income depends on the stock of money that was held in the previous period. Our simulations trace out the time paths of the various key variables. These simulations allow us to verify whether the model converges to a definite solution, at least for some parameter values.

In the present case, however, the model is so simple that it is an easy task to verify that the model converges to its equilibrium solution for all (economically meaningful) parameter values. Take the value of H given by equation (3.22), and replace Y by its value in equation (3.21). We obtain a simple difference equation in H and H_{-1}:

$$H = \frac{G \cdot (1 - \alpha_1) \cdot (1 - \theta)}{1 - \alpha_1 \cdot (1 - \theta)} + H_{-1} \cdot \left\{ \frac{1 - \alpha_1 \cdot (1 - \theta) - \alpha_2 \cdot \theta}{1 - \alpha_1 \cdot (1 - \theta)} \right\} \tag{3.23}$$

Equation (3.23) is of the form $H = A + BH_{-1}$. This difference equation yields a non-oscillatory convergent path whenever B takes a positive value which is less than one, that is, whenever $0 < B < 1$. In the present case, by comparing the numerator to the denominator of the coefficient tied to the H_{-1} variable (the B coefficient), we see that this coefficient is necessarily smaller than one. The coefficient is also larger than zero. This can be seen by noting that the numerator can be rewritten in the following manner:

$$1 - \alpha_1 \cdot (1 - \theta) - \alpha_2 \cdot \theta = (1 - \alpha_1) + (\alpha_1 - \alpha_2) \cdot \theta$$

The first term on the left-hand side is the propensity to save out of current income, which is always assumed to be positive, while the sign of the second term depends on the difference between the propensity to consume out of current income and the propensity to consume out of past wealth. Thus, provided we have:

$$(1 - \alpha_1) > 0 \tag{3.24}$$

and

$$\alpha_1 > \alpha_2 \tag{3.25}$$

– two inequalities that are considered to be met in all economically significant models – the B coefficient tied to the H_{-1} variable is always positive. This means that, when out-of-equilibrium, the model takes a non-oscillatory convergent path towards its stationary solution.

Thus knowing that the B coefficient tied to H_{-1} is positive and smaller than unity, we can draw Figure 3.9, which represents the phase diagram of our little model, for the money variable. Equation (3.23) is represented by the upward-sloping line, called the *h* curve, which originates from point A. The stationary solution of the model, H^*, as given by equation (3.17), is to be

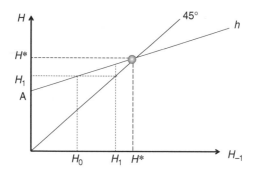

Figure 3.9   The stability of the dynamic process

found at the intersection of this line and the 45-degree line. It is the stationary state, since at that point we have $H = H_{-1}$. At all other points on the h curve, the current and the past money balances are different. Starting from an out-of-equilibrium amount of money balances H_0, the figure illustrates the evolution of money balances through time, as it increases in step until it reaches its stationary value. For instance, if in the initial period the amount of money balances is H_0, in the next period it will be H_1, and so on.

3.9   A graphical illustration of Model *SIM*

Because Model *SIM* is so simple, it is possible to provide a further, more conventional, graphical representation of it. But despite its simplicity, the model still requires four quadrants to be fully closed.

Let us consider the first quadrant of Figure 3.10, the north-east quadrant. This is nearly similar to the standard 45° graph, which can be found in most introductory texts in economics. The horizontal axis represents disposable income YD, while the vertical axis features national income Y. Since we know that $Y = YD/(1 - \theta)$, we trace out the $YD/(1 - \theta)$ line. This line is the equivalent of the 45° line in the Keynesian model of the introductory textbooks. Along this line, a production level of Y is equivalent to a disposable income level of $YD = (1 - \theta)Y$. The question now is the following: given the various household consumption parameters and the fiscal policy parameters set by government, what is the level of production compatible with aggregate demand? In other words, for what level of income is the equality of equation (3.1) verified?

We already know that there are two answers to this question. There is a short-run answer and there is a long-run answer. In the short-run, we take the level of wealth as a parameter, given by the amount of cash money balances that have been accumulated by the end of the previous period. In

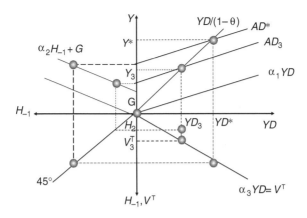

Figure 3.10 Temporary versus stationary equilibria

the long-run, the level of wealth is itself an endogenous variable, such that household saving and government deficit are both nil.

Let us consider the short-run solution first. Consumption demand, out of current income, is given by the line $\alpha_1 \cdot YD$. The AD_3 line represents aggregate demand (say at period 3), which is the sum of induced consumption demand, $\alpha_1 \cdot YD$, and of autonomous demand. In other words, aggregate demand $AD = C_d + G_d$. There are two components of autonomous demand in Model *SIM*: autonomous consumption demand, which arises from consumption out of previously accumulated wealth, $\alpha_2 \cdot H_{-1}$; and government expenditures, G. The amount of government expenditures is shown explicitly on the vertical axis. The sum of these two autonomous demand components is shown by the intersection of the AD_3 curve with the Y vertical axis. This implies that consumption out of wealth is given by the difference between this intercept and the G level. Consumption out of wealth, and the intercept of the AD_3 curve, will be explained when we deal with the fourth quadrant.

For the moment, note that the aggregate demand curve, the AD line, only cuts the production line $YD/(1 - \theta)$ once. The point of intersection of these two lines is the short-run equilibrium of the model. At that level of income, called here Y_3 and corresponding to a level of disposable income YD_3, whatever is being produced is being sold. The level of income Y_3 arising from the point of intersection is the temporary equilibrium obtained from equation (3.14). It could be, for instance, the level of income achieved in period 3 of Table 3.4, on the basis of wealth that had been accumulated in period 2.

Let us now come back to the graphical depiction of autonomous demand. Autonomous expenditures are explained in the fourth quadrant, the north-west quadrant, where the horizontal axis represents the previously accumulated amount of wealth H_{-1}. The line arising from the origin represents consumption demand out of accumulated wealth, $\alpha_2 \cdot H_{-1}$. The line above it, and parallel to it, represents total autonomous demand. It has been shifted up by the autonomous component of demand arising from government expenditures, G. Here, since we wish to know the short-run equilibrium in period 3, the relevant wealth is H_2, the wealth accumulated at the end of period 2. With wealth H_2, and government expenditures G, autonomous demand is given by the intercept of the aggregate demand curve AD_3.

The second quadrant, the south-east quadrant, now allows us to figure whether the equilibrium found is a temporary or a steady-state one. The second quadrant illustrates equation (3.7A), the wealth accumulation function. The horizontal axis is disposable income, while the vertical axis represents wealth. The curve appearing in the quadrant represents the targeted level of wealth, $V^T = \alpha_3 \cdot YD$, while previously accumulated wealth H_{-1} is obtained by a straightforward translation of its value in the fourth quadrant, through the 45° line of the third quadrant.

In the case corresponding to income and disposable income Y_3 and YD_3, we see that the previously accumulated wealth H_2 is smaller than the target wealth level V_3^T corresponding to the realized disposable income YD_3 of period 3. As a result, households will be saving in this period, and hence we know that the equilibrium given by Y_3 and YD_3 is a temporary one.

Because households have saved part of their current income, their accumulated wealth at the beginning of the next period will now be higher. As a result, consumption demand arising out of accumulated wealth will be higher in the next period, and this will lead to an upward shift of the aggregate demand curve AD, and hence to an increase in income and disposable income. The AD curve thus drifts upwards, period by period, pushed up by consumption demand out of a growing accumulated wealth. Eventually, the new aggregate demand curve will be AD^*, and the economy will reach the income levels Y^* and YD^*. This will be the steady-state of the model – the long-run equilibrium. This can be seen by checking the second quadrant: at a level of disposable income YD^*, the achieved level of wealth H^* and the target level of wealth V^{T*} are identical. There is no need to save anymore. The stationary state has been reached.

The reader can also figure out what would happen if government expenditures G were to rise. The AD curve would shift up, and this would induce a higher temporary income level. However, at the new higher disposable income, the new target level of wealth would exceed the previously achieved stationary wealth level. This discrepancy would induce wealth accumulation, the effect of which would be to further reinforce the impact of government expenditures over national income, until a new, higher, stationary income level would be reached.

3.10 Preliminary conclusion

There is a stupendous difference between the world which we are now setting out to explore and the neo-classical world. In one way our models will all be super-rigorous, in another they will be super-contingent. With no need to make the strange assumption that there is a given, fixed, exogenous stock of money in order to obtain a solution for any kind of general equilibrium (market clearing or otherwise), we can freely restore to money its natural attributes. We have a plausible story about how money enters and leaves the system. And money is the vehicle via which people receive income, settle their debts, pay their taxes and store their wealth, thus linking each period to the next. In a world of uncertainty, money permits glitches and mistakes. So far from being fixed, money is as volatile as Tinker Bell – as any book of monetary statistics will immediately reveal. Add finally that money in the stock-flow model, unlike 'money' in the mainstream model, is an asset which does, and always, must have a counterpart liability.

In what follows, we shall eventually be describing the role and operation of financial markets in some detail. Paradoxically it is with regard to the role of financial markets in macroeconomic systems that neo-classical economics has very little to say, because, if labour and product markets worked the way neo-classical economics would like them to work, there would be no need and even no place for finance.

Appendix 3.1: Equation list of Model *SIM*

$$C_s = C_d \tag{3.1}$$

$$G_s = G_d \tag{3.2}$$

$$T_s = T_d \tag{3.3}$$

$$N_s = N_d \tag{3.4}$$

$$YD = W \cdot N_s - T_s \tag{3.5}$$

$$T_d = \theta \cdot W \cdot N_s \quad \theta < 1 \tag{3.6}$$

$$C_d = \alpha_1 \cdot YD + \alpha_2 \cdot H_{h-1} \quad 0 < \alpha_2 < \alpha_1 < 1 \tag{3.7}$$

$$\Delta H_s = H_s - H_{s-1} = G_d - T_d \tag{3.8}$$

$$\Delta H_h = H_h - H_{h-1} = YD - C_d \tag{3.9}$$

$$Y = C_s + G_s \tag{3.10}$$

$$N_d = \frac{Y}{W} \tag{3.11}$$

The redundant, or hidden, equation is:

$$\Delta H_h = \Delta H_s \tag{3.12}$$

$$G = 20$$
$$\alpha_1 = 0.6$$
$$\alpha_2 = 0.4$$
$$\theta = 0.2$$
$$W = 1$$

Appendix 3.2: Equation list of Model *SIM* with expectations

SIMEX Model

$$C_s = C_d \tag{3.1}$$

$$G_s = G_d \tag{3.2}$$

$$T_s = T_d \tag{3.3}$$

$$N_s = N_d \tag{3.4}$$

$$YD = W \cdot N_s - T_s \tag{3.5}$$

$$T_d = \theta \cdot W \cdot N_s \quad \theta < 1 \tag{3.6}$$

$$C_d = \alpha_1 \cdot YD^e + \alpha_2 \cdot H_{h-1} \quad 0 < \alpha_2 < \alpha_1 < 1 \tag{3.7E}$$

$$\Delta H_s = H_s - H_{s-1} = G_d - T_d \tag{3.8}$$

$$\Delta H_h = H_h - H_{h-1} = YD - C_d \tag{3.9}$$

$$Y = C_s + G_s \tag{3.10}$$

$$N_d = \frac{Y}{W} \tag{3.11}$$

$$\Delta H_d = H_d - H_{h-1} = YD^e - C_d \tag{3.18}$$

$$YD^e = YD_{-1} \tag{3.20}$$

The hidden equation is still:

$$\Delta H_h = \Delta H_s \tag{3.12}$$

SIMEXF model

Replace equation (3.20) by equation (3.20F)

$$YD^e = \overline{YD^e} \tag{3.20F}$$

Appendix 3.3: The mean lag theorem

The system dynamics of a fully consistent stock-flow model are largely pinned down by stock-flow norms, if these exist and if they are reasonably small. The intuition here is perhaps best conveyed by a water analogy. Imagine a cistern containing a certain quantity of water into which and out of which there is a steady inflow and a steady outflow of equal size. The question now arises: suppose the rate of inflow is raised by x units so that after a certain period of time the rate of outflow is raised to the same extent. How long does it take before the outflow rises? It will hopefully be obvious that the time taken will be longer, for any given change in the inflow, the larger is the initial quantity of water. If this is not intuitive to the reader, consider the relationship between the stock of people queuing to buy tickets and the flows of people joining and leaving the queue. If the stock of people in the queue is long the time taken for a new arrival to actually buy a ticket will be longer than if it is short (given the time it takes for the ticket to actually be bought at the box office).

The systematic inclusion of stock variables, with steady-state stock to flow ratios, imposes certain constraints on the speed at which the system as a whole will respond to shocks. In this very simple model there is a precise answer to the question of how rapidly the system responds to shocks which, though it must be modified as things proceed, will resonate through much of what follows. We are able to assess the time it takes *on average* for the effects of a change in government expenditures to take place. This is the *mean lag*.

To illustrate the relationship between stock/flow norms and the system dynamics of Model *SIM*, consider Figure A3.1.[15] Up until period A is reached, the system is assumed to be in a stationary steady state where $Y^* = G_1/\theta$ and the stock of wealth (that is, government debt) is $V = \alpha_3 \cdot (1 - \theta)Y^*$. Now suppose that government expenditure is raised to G_2 in a step from A to B. A new steady state is eventually found at C, where $Y^{**} = G_2/\theta$. The curve AC describes the flow of additional tax payments on the way between the two steady states and also acts as a proxy for the flow of additional output since $Y = T/\theta$. There is no way of telling, from this information, how long is the distance between B and C, that is, the total length of time taken by the entire adjustment process. It could be two minutes or 100 years. However the average length of time for a unit of additional inflow to re-emerge as outflow is exactly pinned down.

The average lag between inputs and output is equal to the average of the *horizontal* distances between the vertical straight line AB and the AC curve. In other words the mean lag is given by the area ABC divided by the vertical line AB – a quotient which is easy to calculate.

The area ABC, whatever the shape of the response of the tax flow, is equal to the addition to government debt during the whole period between the two steady states (during each of which debt is not changing and therefore $G = T = \theta \cdot Y$). The change in debt between the steady-states, by (3.17) is $\alpha_3 \cdot \Delta YD = \alpha_3 \cdot (1 - \theta)\Delta Y$. But ΔY, by (3.15), is equal to $\Delta G/\theta$. Therefore the area ABC is given by: $ABC = \alpha_3 \cdot \Delta G \cdot (1 - \theta)/\theta$. And the mean lag, the area ABC divided by the line AB (which describes the step in government expenditure), is:

$$ML = \alpha_3 \cdot \Delta G \cdot \frac{\left\{ \dfrac{(1-\theta)}{\theta} \right\}}{\Delta G} = \alpha_3 \cdot \frac{(1-\theta)}{\theta}$$

where ML is the mean lag.

With the parameters which we have used up to now, this implies that on average the effects of the increase of government expenditures on tax revenues and national

---

[15] What follows is an illustration. For a more extensive discussion, see Godley and Cripps (1983, ch. 3).

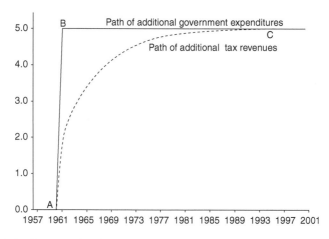

Figure A3.1   The mean lag theorem: speed at which the economy adjusts

income would occur within four periods (four quarters for instance).[16] Thus if the stock-flow norm is small, as is normally the case with government debt, the theorem has a powerful implication for the system response to changes in fiscal policy.

The equation defining the mean lag may appear as a slightly surprising result, because it is entirely independent of the lag profile and a fortiori of the total lag. It is saying that the lag in the response of the economy to a shock in the form of increased government expenditure is determined solely by the long-run aspiration to acquire government debt quite irrespective of the short-run parameters of the consumption function, specifically the α_1 parameter.[17] In the case of government expenditures, the stock-flow ratio that determines the mean lag is given by the government debt to government revenues ratio.[18]

The invariance of the mean lag to the size of the short-term marginal propensity to consume is illustrated in Figure A3.2 where the identical shock from government expenditure is applied in two different situations. While by construction the wealth aspiration (α_3) is the same in each case, the short-run propensities to consume are wildly different; the propensity to consume out of current income, given by α_1, is 0.6 in one case and 0.9 in the other. When the propensity to consume out of current income is high, tax revenues initially increase much faster, so that the government deficit is initially smaller than when the propensity to consume out of current income is low; however, as time passes on, the reverse occurs, so that in the end the increase in government debt is the same whatever the propensities to consume (provided α_3 remains the same).

---

[16] $\alpha_3 = 1$, $\theta = 0.2$, and $(1-\theta) = 0.8$, so that the mean lag is equal to $1(0.8)/(0.2) = 4$. With the tax rate at 40%, the mean lag would only be 1.5 periods.

[17] It should be noted however, that, for a given propensity to consume out of past wealth, that is, for a given α_2, a higher propensity to consume out of current income – the α_1 parameter – implies a lower wealth to income ratio, and hence a shorter mean lag.

[18] With our parameter values, the initial steady state government debt is 80, while taxes are 20, so that the ratio is indeed 4, as pointed out in footnote 16.

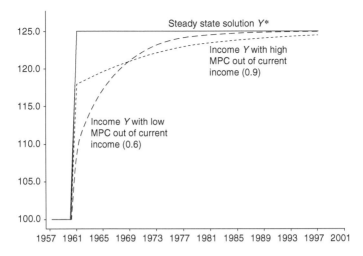

Figure A3.2 Adjustment of national income on different assumptions about the marginal propensity to consume out of current income (MPC), for a given target wealth to disposable income ratio

The full significance of the mean lag theorem will only become clear when we have some empirical numbers to look at. The point to remember at this stage is that in a properly specified stock-flow model, the dynamics of the system as a whole will to some extent be pinned down by stock-flow norms, that is, the wealth to disposable income target ratio, α_3. The smaller the stock-flow norms the shorter the time lags will be.[19]

A word of warning should be added. The mean lag theorem is valid as long as the income path converges monotonically to its new equilibrium. In the case of the *SIM* model, as was seen in section 3.8, the section that dealt with stability analysis, this condition is always fulfilled as long as the propensity to consume out of regular income is larger than the propensity to consume out of wealth. In more complex models with cyclical or oscillatory variations, the mean lag theorem would lose its usefulness (Godley and Cripps 1983: 124; cf. Malinvaud 1983: 159 , and Solow 1983: 165).

Appendix 3.4: Government deficits in a growing economy

Model *SIM* was built under the assumption of a stationary steady state. We saw that in such a steady state, the government budget had to balance. What happens if the steady state happens to be an economy growing at a constant rate?

In a growing system the private sector will be accumulating wealth, here cash money. The rate of accumulation of wealth will be equal to the rate of growth of GDP. This implies that, in the steady state, the government budget position must be such that cash money is continuously being issued by government. In a growing steady state, *in*

---

[19] We add the observation, which at this stage readers may take or leave, that the normal scale of government liabilities is so small that we shall be able to infer that in the real world these processes work themselves out quite rapidly.

a model such as ours, the government *has to be* in deficit. Combining equations (3.9) and (3.7), and knowing that $H_s = H_h = H$, we need to have:

$$\Delta H = YD - C = YD - (\alpha_1 \cdot YD + \alpha_2 \cdot H_{-1})$$

Making use of the definitions of T and YD, this yields:

$$\Delta H = Y \cdot (1 - \theta) \cdot (1 - \alpha_1) - \alpha_2 \cdot H_{-1} \qquad (A3.3.1)$$

Divide now the whole equation by ΔH. One obtains:

$$\frac{\Delta H}{\Delta H} = \left(\frac{Y}{\Delta H} \right) \cdot (1 - \theta)(1 - \alpha_1) - \alpha_2 \cdot \left(\frac{H_{-1}}{\Delta H} \right)$$

Note that the expression $\Delta H / H_{-1}$ is the rate of growth of the government deficit and the rate of growth of cash money, that is the rate of accumulation of wealth. Let us call *gr* this rate of growth. The equation above may then be rewritten as:

$$1 = \left(\frac{Y}{\Delta H} \right) \cdot (1 - \theta) \cdot (1 - \alpha_1) - \frac{\alpha_2}{gr}$$

Rearranging we get:

$$\frac{\Delta H^*}{Y^*} = \frac{gr \cdot (1 - \theta) \cdot (1 - \alpha_1)}{gr + \alpha_2} \qquad (A3.3.2)$$

Equation (A3.3.2) tells us that the government deficit to national income ratio has to be positive in a growing steady state. It is obvious that in the particular case where $gr = 0$, the deficit to income ratio must be zero, that is in the stationary state the government budget must be balanced. It can also easily be verified, by taking the derivative of expression (A3.3.2) with respect to *gr*, that the higher the growth rate of the economy *gr*, the higher the permanent deficit to income ratio $\Delta H^*/Y^*$. Similarly, it is easily seen that an increase in either α_1 or α_2, the propensities to consume out of current income and lagged wealth, would lead to a fall in the required steady-state deficit to income ratio. Since higher propensities to consume are associated with a lower target wealth to income ratio, this implies that a higher target wealth to income ratio $\dot{\alpha}_3$ is associated with a higher steady state deficit to income ratio.

Thus, to sum up, 'if nominal income is growing, the appropriate equilibrium condition calls not for a balanced budget but for a deficit big enough to keep the debt growing in proportion to income, the proportion being determined by portfolio considerations' (Solow in Worswick and Trevithick 1983: 165). The larger the growth rate or the target wealth to income ratio, the larger the required deficit to income ratio.

Similarly, we may wish to compute the steady-state public debt to income ratio, H/Y. This of course is no different from the wealth to income ratio of households. Take equation (A3.3.1) and divide through by H_{-1}, to obtain:

$$\frac{\Delta H}{H_{-1}} = \left(\frac{Y}{H_{-1}} \right) \cdot (1 - \theta) \cdot (1 - \alpha_1) - \alpha_2 \cdot \left(\frac{H_{-1}}{H_{-1}} \right)$$

The term on the left-hand side is *gr*, the steady rate of growth of the economy. By recalling that $H = (1 + gr)H_{-1}$ and rearranging the above equation, we obtain:

$$\frac{H^*}{Y^*} = \frac{(1 + gr) \cdot (1 - \theta) \cdot (1 - \alpha_1)}{gr + \alpha_2} \qquad (A3.3.3)$$

This is the steady-state government debt to national income ratio. By taking the derivative of expression (A3.3) with respect to gr we can verify that a faster growth rate is associated with a lower steady state debt to income ratio. When $gr = 0$, we get the special case of the stationary state, as exemplified by the ratios of equations (3.16) and (3.14).

Notwithstanding the extreme simplicity of this model we are already able to reach a supremely important policy conclusion which will survive throughout this book. Given the level of activity, the quantity of private wealth and the rate at which it accumulates are determined entirely by the propensities of the private sector, which the government cannot change. But this is to imply (again given the level of activity) that government deficits and debts (being identically equal to, respectively, private saving and wealth) are endogenous variables which cannot be controlled by governments. This conclusion totally contradicts many influential, or even statutory, proposals regarding the regulation of fiscal policy which are made in abstraction from any consideration of how economies actually work – for instance the European Maastricht rules, Gordon Brown's Golden Rule in the United Kingdom and, most important, the view widely held by ignorant politicians and members of the public that government budgets should be balanced.

Figure A3.3 illustrates what happens when the economy moves from a stationary equilibrium, with no growth, to a steady state with growth, led by an exogenously imposed growth rate of 3% in government expenditures. The government debt to national income ratio decreases until it reaches its new steady state value, below the old stationary ratio, somewhere below 80% in our example. By contrast, the government deficit to national income ratio, which was zero in the initial stationary state, gradually moves up in a growing economy, until it reaches a new steady state ratio, somewhere above 2%.

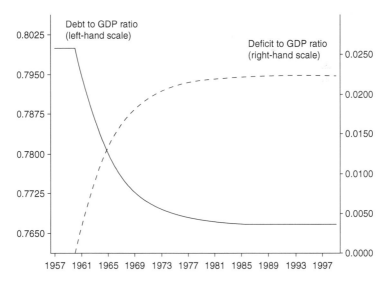

Figure A3.3 The transition from a stationary to a growing economy: impact on the government debt to GDP ratio (continuous curve) and on the government deficit to GDP ratio (dotted curve)

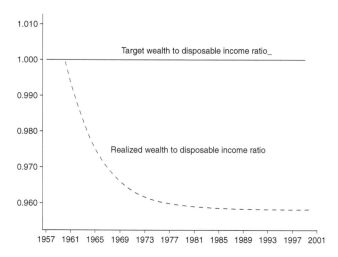

Figure A3.4 Discrepancy between the target wealth to income ratio and the realized wealth to income ratio with economic growth

What about the wealth to *disposable* income ratio? In the stationary state, as seen in section 3.5, the target ratio is the realized ratio, and it is equal to:

$$\frac{V^T}{YD^*} = \frac{H^*}{YD^*} = \alpha_3 = \frac{(1-\alpha_1)}{\alpha_2} \tag{A3.3.4}$$

where V^T is the target level of wealth.

In a growing steady state, the realized wealth to disposable income ratio would be:

$$\frac{H^*}{YD^*} = \frac{(1+gr) \cdot (1-\alpha_1)}{gr + \alpha_2} \tag{A3.3.5}$$

and hence the target wealth to disposable income ratio α_3 would never be achieved.

This is illustrated with the help of Figure A3.4. Once again it is assumed that the economy starts from a stationary equilibrium, where the target wealth to disposable income ratio is achieved. However, once government expenditures and then the rest of the economy grow at a 3% rate, it can be seen that the realized wealth to disposable income ratio diverges from its target ratio, finally stabilizing at a lower than targeted value in the steady state.

A word of warning is perhaps required concerning the relationships just established. We are not claiming that economic growth invariably requires continuously growing government deficits. There may be long periods of economic growth during which the government budget is balanced or even experiencing large surpluses, as in the United States at the end of the 1990s. But such periods of growth cannot be approximations of 'balanced growth' or steady-state growth. When there is economic growth without government deficits, this implies that the balance sheets of the private agents are getting modified, as more private claims are being accumulated, while the private sector is holding less claims over government liabilities. In other words, private debt must grow faster than the rate of growth of the flow of output.

4
Government Money with Portfolio Choice

4.1 Introduction

The present chapter combines the circular flow approach to money (featured in the last chapter) with the stock approach. In the circular flow approach, money is a device allowing transactions between agents to take place and illustrates Keynes's famous 'transactions' motive for holding money. In the stock approach, money is seen as a financial asset which agents hold for investment purposes, or more precisely, as a *placement* as French scholars and Joan Robinson (1956: 8) say. The quantity of money held depends, in particular, on the rate of interest that can be obtained on other assets – an approach associated with Keynes's 'speculative' and 'precautionary' motives. Agents make a portfolio choice between money and other possible financial assets. For this reason, the model developed in Chapter 4 is called Model *PC*, for portfolio choice.

4.2 The matrices of Model *PC*

Model *PC* introduces government bills and interest payments into Model *SIM*. It also takes a major step in the direction of realism by introducing a central bank. Bills (*B*) are short-term government securities which pay interest at a rate *r*. These bills are often called Treasury bills, since they are usually issued by the Treasury Department of central governments. It is assumed that each bill has a price of one unit, and that its price does not change during the duration of its life.[1] As a result, we need not worry about possible capital

---

[1] The assumption could be, for instance, that Treasury bills are three-month assets, and that each period lasts three months (one quarter) or more. Provided bills are issued once every three months, interest rates are not changed within the period, so there cannot be any change in the price of bills.

Table 4.1 Balance sheet of Model *PC*

	Households	Production	Government	Central Bank	Σ
Money	$+H$			$-H$	0
Bills	$+B_h$		$-B$	$+B_{cb}$	0
Balance (net worth)	$-V$		$+V$		0
Σ	0		0	0	0

gains that could arise from price changes in financial assets. This assumption will be relaxed when we introduce long-term government liabilities, that is, when we introduce bonds in the next chapter. We can imagine that economic agents purchase government bills at that unit price, and then, one month or three months later, when the bills reach maturity, households receive back the principal plus the interest. In the real world, things usually go the other way around. Treasury bills are discount bonds, which state that a given amount of money will be paid, say three months later: this is the face value of the bond. The price which the market determines, that is, the price which agents are willing to pay for such a promise, which will be lower than the face value (at a discount), implies a yield to maturity – the interest rate.

We start, as always, with a pair of matrices which describe the whole system of stocks and flows. Table 4.1 shows the new balance sheet matrix. Here we have added, in the lowest row, balance items that ensure that all columns, as well as all rows, sum to zero. Column 1 shows the assets of households: they may hold either money H or bills B_h. The sum of the two is private wealth (V).

The production sector has no entry in the balance sheet. This is because, as in Model *SIM*, we assume the existence of a pure service economy, with neither circulating nor fixed capital. As a result, the net worth of the household sector is also the net worth of the private sector.

The counterpart of the net worth of the private sector is public debt. It follows that private wealth, in Model *PC*, is equal to the sum of cash money and bills held by households. Also, as can be read from column 3, public debt is equal to the amount of outstanding bills B issued by government to households and the central bank combined.

Column 4 introduces the central bank. The central bank is sometimes amalgamated with the government sector, and indeed, this is what was done implicitly in Model *SIM*. Here, the central bank is considered as an institution in its own right. The central bank purchases bills from government, thereby adding to its stock of assets (B_{cb}). On its liability side, the central bank provides money to households. This money can take the form of either

Table 4.2 Transactions-flow matrix of Model *PC*

	Households	Production	Government	Central bank Current	Central bank Capital	Σ
Consumption	$-C$	$+C$				0
Government expenditures		$+G$	$-G$			0
Income = GDP	$+Y$	$-Y$				0
Interest payments	$+r_{-1} \cdot B_{h-1}$		$-r_{-1} \cdot B_{-1}$	$+r_{-1} \cdot B_{cb-1}$		0
Central bank profits			$+r_{-1} \cdot B_{cb-1}$	$-r_{-1} \cdot B_{cb-1}$		0
Taxes	$-T$		$+T$			0
Change in money	$-\Delta H$				$+\Delta H$	0
Change in bills	$-\Delta B_h$		$+\Delta B$		$-\Delta B_{cb}$	0
Σ	0	0	0	0	0	0

cash or deposits at the central bank. In either case, it would be high powered money. It is assumed that central banks have zero net worth.

The flow matrix in Table 4.2 is similar to that in Table 3.2 – most importantly all rows and columns once more sum to zero to ensure that all transactions are taken into account – but there are two important differences. First, the flow-of-funds accounts – the two rows inserted between the two lines at the bottom of the table – now comprise two financial assets. Second, there are now interest payments arising from government debt. These interest payments, made by the government sector, are paid both to households and to the central bank. Interest payments each period are generated by stocks of assets in existence at the end of the previous period. Because of this time lag, the rate of interest on bills relevant in period t is the rate of interest that was set at the end of the previous period, at time t_{-1}.[2]

Interest payments on government debt are not part of national income Y, as can be checked by looking at column 2. National income consists solely of income derived from the sales to households and to the government. Interest payments on government debt, though part of government outlays, are transfer payments, not part of GDP.[3]

Finally, there is the new central bank sector. Note that this sector has two components – a current account and a capital account. The distinction

[2] Several authors write, in our view mistakenly, that interest payments at time t are equal to $r \cdot B_{(-1)}$. Some other writers recognize however that the time lag must apply as well to the interest rate on bills. See Turnovsky (1977: 74), and Flaschel, Gong and Semmler (2001: 111).

[3] This is now universal practice in national accounting, although this was not always the case.

between the current and the capital account will become more important and more interesting when we deal with industrial firms, which undertake investment and have to find finance to pay for it. But let us see here how the distinction applies to the central bank sector. The current account describes the inflows and the outflows that form the current operations of the central bank, for instance interest payments on existing assets or liabilities, and salaries paid to the employees of the central bank (in our simplified account, the latter have been omitted). The capital account describes changes in the balance sheet of the central bank, for instance when it purchases new bills.

We have taken the central bank's net worth to be zero, which implies that any profit it makes is always distributed. Here, the central bank obviously does make profits since it owns bills which yield interest payments, whereas its liabilities – cash money H – pay no interest.[4] In line with the current practice of most central banks of the world, we have assumed that profits are all paid to the government. This is shown in the row called 'central bank profits'. The consequence of this rule, as a moment's reflection makes obvious, is that, once central bank profit is taken into account, the public sector as a whole does not pay interest on its overall debt B; rather net interest payments are made only on the part of the debt B_h which is being held by the private sector, that is, the household sector.

In order to slim down the exposition, we shall not use a 'behavioural' transactions flow matrix but we again assume that firms sell whatever goods or services are demanded by the consumers and by government, and that households supply the labour that is demanded by firms.

4.3 The equations of Model *PC*

4.3.1 Old wine and new bottles

Although there are strong similarities between models *SIM* and *PC*, the structure of the two models is not identical. All the equations of Model *PC* are to be found separately, in Appendix 4.1, so that we can count equations and unknowns more easily. The first model in this chapter, as in the last, is built on the assumption of perfect foresight, that is, it is assumed that producers sell whatever is demanded, no more and no less, and that households have correct expectations regarding their incomes.

---

[4] In the case where H would represent households deposits at the central bank (in some countries, individuals are allowed to hold deposits at the central bank), these deposits would carry no interest.

We start with three equations that are closely related to those of Model *SIM*.

$$Y = C + G \tag{4.1}$$

$$YD = Y - T + r_{-1} \cdot B_{h-1} \tag{4.2}$$

$$T = \theta \cdot (Y + r_{-1} \cdot B_{h-1}) \tag{4.3}$$

The national income identity, which equates production to sales, is unchanged, as shown in equation (4.1): production is equal to consumption plus government expenditure on services.

Equation (4.2) defines disposable income. As pointed out in our discussion of matrix 4.2, the definition of households' disposable income is enlarged by adding interest payments on government debt. As a result, as can be seen from equation (4.3), taxable income is also enlarged by adding interest payments on bills held by households. The state takes back with one hand part of what it has paid out with the other.

4.3.2 The portfolio decision

We now move to the household sector. A key behavioural assumption made here, as well as in the chapters to follow, is that households make a two-stage decision (Keynes 1936: 166). In the first step, households decide how much they will save out of their income. In the second step, households decide how they will allocate their wealth, including their newly acquired wealth. The two decisions are made within the same time frame in the model. However, the two decisions are distinct and of a hierarchical form. The consumption decision determines the *size* of the (expected) end-of-period stock of wealth; the portfolio decision determines the *allocation* of the (expected) stock of wealth. This behavioural hypothesis makes it easier to understand the sequential pattern of household decisions.[5]

Equation (4.4) below simply says that the difference between disposable income and consumption is equal to the change in total wealth – not just money as was the case of equation (3.4) of Model *SIM*. Similarly, as shown in equation (4.5) below, the new consumption function now has total wealth,

[5] In his simulation work, but not in his theoretical work, Tobin endorsed the sequential decision that has been proposed here: 'In the current version of the model households have been depicted as first allocating income between consumption and savings and then making an independent allocation of the saving among the several assets' (Backus *et al.* 1980: 273). Skott (1989: 57) is a concrete example where such a sequential process is not followed in a model that incorporates a Keynesian multiplier and portfolio choice.

instead of money, as its second argument.

$$V = V_{-1} + (YD - C) \tag{4.4}$$

$$C = \alpha_1 \cdot YD + \alpha_2 \cdot V_{-1} \quad 0 < \alpha_2 < \alpha_1 < 1 \tag{4.5}$$

How is wealth to be allocated between money and bonds? This is a question that has elicited several answers over the years. As was pointed out in the introduction, two traditions have prevailed, one, related to the Quantity theory of money, links money balances to the flow of income, and the other, of more recent vintage, makes money balances some proportion of total wealth. The latter idea was given some early empirical support by H.F. Lydall (1958) and is related to the Keynesian notion of liquidity preference. The lower is liquidity preference, the lower is the money to wealth ratio (Boulding 1944). The transactions demand for money and the liquidity preference story may both be comprised within a single model, as was shown by Brainard and Tobin (1968) and Tobin (1969) in two famous articles. The two equations below, (4.6A) and (4.7), embody the Brainard-Tobin formula, slightly amended.

$$\frac{H_h}{V} = (1 - \lambda_0) - \lambda_1 \cdot r + \lambda_2 \cdot \left(\frac{YD}{V}\right) \tag{4.6A}$$

$$\frac{B_h}{V} = \lambda_0 + \lambda_1 \cdot r - \lambda_2 \cdot \left(\frac{YD}{V}\right) \tag{4.7}$$

The main point is that households wish to hold a certain proportion λ_0 of their wealth in the form of bills, and hence, because there is no third asset, a proportion equal to $(1 - \lambda_0)$ in the form of money. This proportion, however, is modulated by two elements: the rate of return r on Treasury bills and the level of disposable income YD relative to wealth. For instance, equation (4.6A) says that the share of wealth which people wish to hold in the form of money is negatively related to the interest rate;[6] and that it will be positively related to disposable income because of the transactions demand for money to which this gives rise. Equation (4.7) shows what has to be the share that people wish to hold in the form of bills – given equation (4.6A) and given that there is no third asset available. Because portfolio decisions are forward-looking, the relevant rate of interest for these portfolio decisions is the rate of interest r – the rate of interest that equalizes the supply of and the demand for bills at the end of the current period. In the current period, in period t, the interest payments depend on the stock of bills of the previous period and on the rate of interest r_{-1} that was promised in the previous period, as shown

---

[6] Remember that money is assumed to carry no interest, either because it is made up of cash or because the central bank does not pay any interest on its deposits.

in equation (4.2). On the other hand, the rate of interest r arrived at or set in the current period will generate interest payments equal to $r \cdot B_h$ in the next period, in period $t + 1$. The coefficients in (4.6A) and (4.7) follow from the assumption that people make consistent plans with regard to the allocation of their wealth. Thus the sum of the 'constants' $((1 - \lambda_0)$ and $\lambda_0)$ must be unity because the decision to hold some proportion of wealth in the form of cash implies a decision to hold the rest in the form of bills. And the sum of the coefficients with respect to each of the arguments of the portfolio equations must be zero for an analogous reason; if a change in interest rates (or incomes) causes people to wish to hold a higher proportion of their wealth in the form of money, they must simultaneously be wishing to hold an equivalently lower proportion in the form of bills. This is why the same λ_1 and λ_2 coefficients are respectively attached (with opposite signs) to the interest rate and income in both the money demand and the bill demand functions. This is the all-important *wealth constraint* or *adding-up constraint*, emphasized by Tobin (1969), which will be discussed in more detail in the next chapter. The two fractions identified with equations (4.6A) and (4.7) must sum to unity, whatever the values taken by the variables.

Note that income – the last term in each equation – must be scaled by wealth if the share going to cash is not to rise without limit in a growing system. As written, since in a steady state wealth will always revert to some given relationship to disposable income, equation (4.6A) guarantees that the stock of cash does the same thing; so the transactions demand for cash ultimately 'wears off' as the ratio of consumption to income becomes normal.[7] Indeed, as we saw in the previous chapter, the target V/YD ratio constitutes a key stock-flow norm, and hence in the steady state we should expect the target ratio to be realized.

When we come to solve the model, equations (4.6A) and (4.7) cannot both be included because either one of them is obviously a logical implication of the other. It has been decided to model cash holdings as the residual equation because when there is imperfect foresight the amount of cash held will, in a very real sense, be a residual. With the demand for cash a residual, equation (4.6A) is dropped, and we use equation (4.6) instead. This equation, as shown below, simply says that money holdings are the discrepancy between total

---

[7] The failure to scale income by wealth was a slip in the original Brainard and Tobin (1968) article. This was remedied in Tobin (1969), but not in many subsequent formulations. Other slips appear in some suggested portfolio equations, as in B. Friedman (1978) and Karacaoglu (1984). These slips can give rise to artificial results, for instance that as income rises households wish to hold a larger proportion of their wealth in the form of money balances, thus setting up the stage for rising interest rates even when money grows in line with income.

household wealth and the demand for bills by households. We shall need to verify, in the simulations, that equation (4.6A) is indeed always found to be satisfied.

$$H_h = V - B_h \tag{4.6}$$

4.3.3 The endogeneity of the money supply and the closure of the model

We now consider equations which deal with the government sector and the central bank.

$$\Delta B_s = B_s - B_{s-1} = (G + r_{-1} \cdot B_{s-1}) - (T + r_{-1} \cdot B_{cb-1}) \tag{4.8}$$

$$\Delta H_s = H_s - H_{s-1} = \Delta B_{cb} \tag{4.9}$$

$$B_{cb} = B_s - B_h \tag{4.10}$$

$$r = \bar{r} \tag{4.11}$$

Equation (4.8) describes the government budget constraint, which is an identity illustrated by column 3 of the transactions matrix. The equation simply says that the government deficit is financed by bills newly issued by the Treasury department (over and above bills which are renewed as they mature). The first term in parentheses on the right-hand side of equation (4.8) represents the total outlays of the government: expenditures on services, purchased from the production sector and interest payments that must be made on the overall outstanding debt. The second term in parenthesis on the right-hand side represents the revenues of the government: its income tax revenue, and the profits which it receives from the central bank.

Equation (4.9) describes the capital account of the central bank, as given in column 4 of the transactions matrix. It says that additions to the stock of high-powered money ΔH_s, by accounting logic, are equal to the additions in the demand for bills by the central bank, ΔB_{cb}. Equation (4.10) must be understood in tandem with equation (4.11). It explains how the demand for bills by the central bank is determined. The central bank is the residual purchaser of bills: it purchases all the bills issued by the government that households are not willing to hold *given the interest rate*. Equations (4.8) to (4.10) are three crucial equations within the post-Keynesian framework. They imply that, when the central bank acts as a residual purchaser, it provides cash money on demand. By reason of equation (4.6), the fact that households fail to purchase outstanding bills implies that households wish to hold part of their wealth in the form of cash money. Equation (4.10), as is more obvious when combined with equation (4.9), thus means that the central bank is providing cash money to those who demand it. The amount of cash money in the system is endogenous and demand-led, while the rate of interest on bills is the exogenous variable, as shown explicitly through equation (4.11).[8]

If we treat as exogenous the rate of interest, r, and also the two fiscal policy variables G and θ, we now have, with the parameters describing private sector responses (the α's and λ's), an equation in every variable, that is, we have 10 independent equations and 10 unknowns. The unknowns are Y, YD, T, C, V, H_h, B_h, H_s, B_{cb} and B_s. The rate of interest represents monetary policy, and is a given of that policy.[9]

Whether it is the interest rate or the demand for bills by the central bank which is treated as exogenous, we are again left with H_s and H_h on the left-hand-side of two different equations. As in Model *SIM*, Model *PC* contains no equilibrium condition that makes H_s and H_h equal to each other. But there will always be equivalence between these two variables by virtue of the watertight accounting of the system as a whole, namely by virtue of the first row of the balance sheet of Table 4.1. This is again an illustration of the Walrasian principle, according to which any properly constructed model contains one equation that is redundant, in the sense that it is logically implied by the others. Here, the redundant equation, which cannot be included in the computer program, for otherwise the model would not solve, is the following:

$$H_h = H_s \tag{4.12}$$

Given the other equations of the model, the amount of cash money that households hold is always found to be equal to the amount of cash money supplied by the central bank.

4.4 Expectations in Model *PC*

4.4.1 Expectations and portfolio choice

In the following section we introduce, as we did in the previous chapter, the idea that consumption will depend on expected income, and that expectations will in general turn out to be wrong. As in Model *SIM*, the consumption function is now

$$C = \alpha_1 \cdot YD^e + \alpha_2 \cdot V_{-1} \tag{4.5E}$$

where YD^e is the expected disposable income.

---

[8] More on this can be found in Appendix 4.3.

[9] An exogenous interest rate is also a feature of the so-called *New Consensus* macroeconomic models (see Fontana 2002; Lavoie and Seccareccia 2004). However, most other mainstream models have assumed an exogenous stock of money or an exogenous amount of central bank assets, in which case there is one less degree of freedom, and one constant has to give way. In mainstream models, it is the rate of interest that becomes an endogenous variable. The rate of interest becomes a price equilibrium market mechanism. See Appendix 4.4 for more details.

The portfolio equations must also be changed because, as households do not know exactly what their income will be, they cannot know what their end-period wealth will be. We must thus rewrite equations (4.7) and (4.6A) in terms of expectations. With these hypotheses, consumption and portfolio decisions carry a truly hierarchical relationship. Consumption decisions are irreversible (the decided amount of consumption will be the actual amount) while portfolio decisions are tentative (the desired proportions need not be the actual ones). Now, because the amounts of financial assets that households will end up with might not be the same as those that they initially demanded, one has to be careful to distinguish between assets that are demanded, at the beginning of the period, from those that will be held by the end of the period. Once again, we use the subscript d for the assets that are demanded at the beginning of the period, and the subscript h for the assets that are effectively held at the end of the period. We thus have:

$$\frac{B_d}{V^e} = \lambda_0 + \lambda_1 \cdot r - \lambda_2 \cdot \left(\frac{YD^e}{V^e}\right) \tag{4.7E}$$

$$\frac{H_d}{V^e} = (1 - \lambda_0) - \lambda_1 \cdot r + \lambda_2 \cdot \left(\frac{YD^e}{V^e}\right) \tag{4.6E}$$

where V^e is the level of wealth that is expected to be accumulated by the end of the period.

This means that, in addition to equation (4.6), which tells us how actual assets will be distributed at the end of the period, we need an additional equation that constitutes an adding-up constraint when households make their portfolio plans at the beginning of the period. This additional equation, which takes the place of equation (4.6E), is:

$$H_d = V^e - B_d \tag{4.13}$$

And to be internally consistent, household expectations with regard to the amount of wealth to be accumulated by the end of the period must be such that:

$$V^e = V_{-1} + \left(YD^e - C\right) \tag{4.14}$$

What happens when expectations regarding current income and hence the amount of wealth accumulated by the end of the period are incorrect? The *crucial* assumption which is made here, and which will be used time and time again, is that *money balances are the element of flexibility in a monetary system of production*. Money balances are the *buffer* that *absorbs unexpected flows of funds*.

Suppose for instance that realized disposable income is higher than expected. According to the consumption function (4.5E), the additional disposable income will not be spent within the period. That unexpected portion of disposable income will be entirely saved. But how will this affect the structure of the household portfolio? The assumption we make is that the entire amount of unexpected saving will be kept in the form of additional cash money balances. Errors in expectations are entirely absorbed by unexpected fluctuations in money balances. Money balances act as a buffer against mistakes in expectations. Any mistake regarding expected disposable income is entirely absorbed by an equivalent unexpected change in money balances. This implies that, regardless of whether they are realized or not, households actually invest in bills on the basis of their expectations with respect to disposable income that were made at the beginning of the period. This means that the amount of bills held by households at the end of the period is exactly equal to the amount of bills that were demanded by households at the beginning of the period. We have:

$$B_h = B_d \tag{4.15}$$

With the added expectations, excluding the rate of interest which can be considered as an exogenous policy parameter, Model *PC* thus consists of 13 equations and 14 variables. We have equations (4.1) to (4.4), (4.5E), (4.6), (4.7E), (4.8) to (4.10), and (4.13 to 4.15).We also have the original 10 unknowns, which are Y, YD, T, C, V, H_h, B_h, H_{cb}, B_{cb}, B_s, to which we now add YD^e, V^e, H_d and B_d. We thus have 13 equations and 14 unknowns. All that is lacking is an equation defining expected disposable income YD^e. The simplest such equation would be one of the adaptative type, where expected disposable income would simply depend on the realized level of disposable income achieved in the previous period:

$$YD^e = YD_{-1} \tag{4.16A}$$

But the model will easily accommodate any other scheme of expectations-formation so long as it is not systematically perverse as would be the case if an error in one period were to be larger and in the same direction in the subsequent period. In Figures 4.1 and 4.2 we show the effect of assuming that expectations are subject to a random process, such as the one described by the following equation.

$$YD^e = YD \cdot (1 + Ra) \tag{4.16}$$

where Ra is a random series normally distributed with a mean equal to zero.[10]

The model with expectations (*PCEX*) is thus complete (and is to be found in compact form in Appendix 4.2). Once again, as in equation (3.19), the differential between the amount of money held by households H_h and the

---

[10] Once again, as pointed out in Chapter 3, readers should not pay any attention to the precise numbering of the periods as indicated on the horizontal axis of the charts. These periods could be years, quarters or months.

110

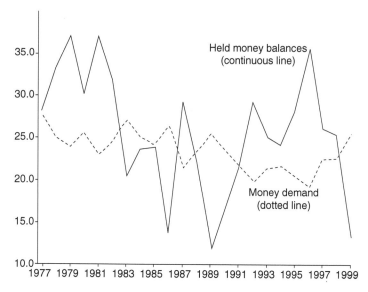

Figure 4.1 Money demand and held money balances, when the economy is subjected to random shocks

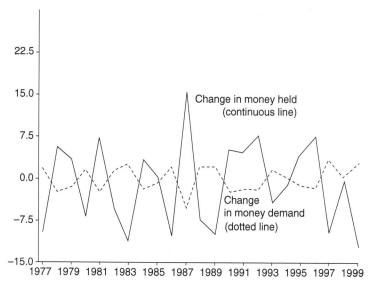

Figure 4.2 Changes in money demand and in money balances held (first differences), when the economy is subjected to random shocks

amount of money demanded by households at the beginning of the period H_d, conditional on their expectations regarding their income of the current period, is equal to the difference between realized and expected income. We have once again:

$$H_h - H_d = YD - YD^e \qquad (4.17)$$

This equality arises from equation (4.15) and the fact that, from equations (4.13) and (4.14) we know that:

$$H_d = V_{-1} + (YD^e - C) - B_d$$

while from equations (4.4) and (4.6) we also know that:

$$H_h = V_{-1} + (YD - C) - B_h$$

Once more we have shown, through equation (4.17), that the amount of money households will hold at the end of each period differs from what they were expecting to hold by the size of their mistake about what their income will be. Money plays a buffering role.

Once again, also, there is a left-out equation, equation (4.12), such that: $H_h = H_s$. Whether households make mistakes or not, the central bank will always be found to provide the amount of cash money that the public finds itself holding at the end of the period, without any need for an additional equilibrating mechanism.

The buffering role of money is illustrated with the help of Figures 4.1 and 4.2. These two charts show how the mistakes about what disposable income will be show up as fluctuations in the demand for cash money. The reader will notice that the fluctuations of the actual stock of money – the money balances held at the end of each period by households – are greater than the fluctuations in money demand, which have regular components. Held money balances do act as a buffer, absorbing the consequences of mistaken expectations. But it should be remembered that the stock of cash which households end up with at the end of each period will provide a corrective signal telling them how to modify their consumption next period.

4.5 The steady-state solutions of the model

4.5.1 The puzzling impact of interest rates

It is now time to examine some properties of Model *PC* by simulating it numerically. The main difference with Model *SIM*, as one can easily imagine, is that the interest rate set by the central bank will play a substantial role. This can be seen immediately, by experimenting with Model *PC*. The next two charts illustrate the effects of adding 100 basis points to the interest rate (moving it from 2.5% to 3.5%), starting from a full stationary state and assuming no change in other exogenous variables.

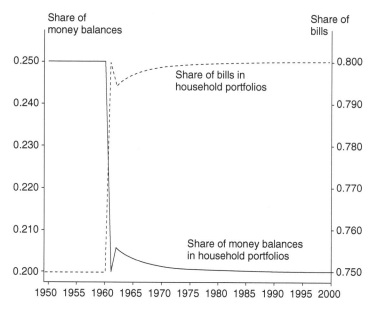

Figure 4.3 Evolution of the shares of bills and money balances in the portfolio of households, following an increase of 100 points in the rate of interest on bills

Figure 4.3 shows how the allocation of wealth between cash and bills changes when the interest rate goes up. As such, there is nothing surprising here. The model is built in such a way that higher interest rates induce households to hold more interest paying bills, following the well-known principle that households tend to hold more of an asset when its rate of return is higher (at a constant risk level). Figure 4.4 is more surprising: it shows that a higher rate of interest induces a rise in disposable income and consumption, both in the short run and in the new stationary state. How is that possible?

Once again, it is easy to ascertain the steady-state solutions of the model, by noting that in the stationary state the government budget must be in balance. This time, however, government balance means that state revenues *plus* the profits of the central bank must be equal to pure government expenditures on goods and services *plus* the cost of servicing the government debt. We have:

$$T^* + r_{-1} \cdot B^*_{cb} = G + r_{-1} \cdot B^*_s$$

and hence by virtue of equations (4.3) and (4.10),

$$\theta \cdot \left(Y^* + r_{-1} \cdot B^*_h\right) = G + r_{-1} \cdot B^*_h$$

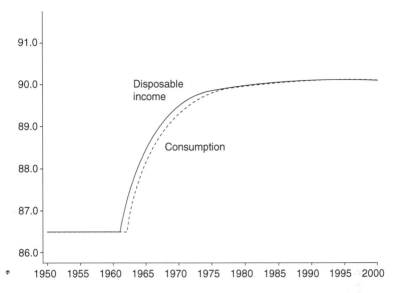

Figure 4.4 Evolution of disposable income and household consumption following an increase of 100 points in the rate of interest on bills

Solving for the steady-state value of national income, we get:

$$Y^* = \frac{G + r \cdot B_h^* \cdot (1 - \theta)}{\theta} = \frac{G_{NT}}{\theta} \tag{4.18}$$

where, as before, the asterisk indicates a long-run steady-state solution, and assuming that in the steady state $r_{-1} = r$. The term G_{NT} stands for total government expenditures, including interest payments *net* of taxes.[11] The expression G_{NT}/θ is the *fiscal stance*, first introduced in Chapter 3, when interest payments on government debt are taken into consideration.

The steady-state solution for disposable income can likewise be obtained. Recall that in the stationary state households make no saving. This implies that consumption is equal to disposable income. In formal terms:

$$C^* = YD^* = Y^* + r \cdot B_h^* - T^* = Y^* + r \cdot B_h^* - \theta \cdot \left(Y^* + r \cdot B_h^* \right)$$

---

[11] As far as we know, the addition of interest payments in the multiplicand was first pointed out by Blinder and Solow (1973).

Substituting Y^* by its value in equation (4.18), and with some manipulations, we obtain:

$$C^* = YD^* = \left(G + r \cdot B_h^*\right) \cdot \frac{(1-\theta)}{\theta} \tag{4.19}$$

Equations (4.18) and (4.19) have the counterintuitive property that in the full stationary state, the aggregate income flow and the disposable income flow are an *increasing* function of the interest rate. This explains why, in Figure 4.4, the higher interest rate is associated with a higher steady-state national income. As higher interest payments on government debt builds up, disposable income rises and so do consumption and national income. As disposable income rises, this induces households to hold ever greater wealth, and hence a larger *absolute* amount of bills, provided the α_3 ratio, redefined below, does not drop. In addition, with higher interest rates, households are encouraged to hold a larger *proportion* of their wealth in the form of bills, as we saw with Figure 4.3. All this leads to ever larger interest payments on debt.

It follows, in contrast to what most students of principles of economics are taught, that higher interest rates generate more economic activity, not less, unless high interest rates have a detrimental impact on some components of aggregate demand.

4.5.2 Fully developed steady-state solutions

Though interesting, the stationary solutions in (4.18) and (4.19) are not entirely satisfying because one of the components of the solutions, B_h^* is itself an endogenous variable. Thus, although we can presume, by intuitive reasoning, that an increase in the rate of interest will lead to an increase in the amount of bills held by households, and hence to an increase in the overall interest payments received by households, this still needs to be formally demonstrated. In other words, we need to find the value of B_h^* in terms of the various parameters, and then substitute this value in equations (4.18) and (4.19) to get the fully-developed stationary solutions of Model *PC*.

This is not too hard a task, although it involves some tedious algebra. First, recall that we can turn the consumption function (4.5) into a wealth accumulation function. We pulled a similar trick with the consumption function (3.7) via equation (3.7A). Here, combining equations (4.4) and (4.5), we obtain the wealth accumulation function:

$$\Delta V = \alpha_2 \cdot \left(\alpha_3 \cdot YD - V_{-1}\right) \tag{4.20}$$

where $\alpha_3 = (1 - \alpha_1)/\alpha_2$.

Once again, we know that in the stationary steady state (with no growth), households accumulate no additional wealth, and hence $\Delta V = 0$. Thus in the stationary state, the target level of wealth is achieved, and wealth and disposable income are in a constant ratio given by:

$$\frac{V^*}{YD^*} = \alpha_3 \tag{4.21}$$

Combining equations (4.21) and (4.7) – the equation that defines the portfolio decision of the households – and after some manipulation, we thus have:

$$B_h^* = \{(\lambda_0 + \lambda_1 \cdot r) \cdot \alpha_3 - \lambda_2\} \cdot YD^* \tag{4.22}$$

We may now replace in equation (4.19) the value of B_h^* given by (4.22). Solving for YD^*, we obtain its fully determined solution in terms of the various parameters and constants. We obtain:

$$YD^* = \frac{G}{\left[\dfrac{\theta}{(1-\theta)}\right] - r \cdot [(\lambda_0 + \lambda_1 \cdot r) \cdot \alpha_3 - \lambda_2]} \tag{4.23}$$

This can be reinterpreted in a slightly different way. Recall that the last term in square brackets is equal to:

$$[(\lambda_0 + \lambda_1 \cdot r) \cdot \alpha_3 - \lambda_2] = \frac{\alpha_3 \cdot B_h^*}{V^*}$$

Recall also that V is the total debt of the government sector, and that B_h^* is the portion of the debt upon which the state has to pay a rate of interest r. It follows that $\check{r}$, where,

$$\check{r} = \frac{r \cdot B_h^*}{V^*}$$

is the *average* rate of interest payable on the *overall* amount of government liabilities.

With that interpretation, the steady-state disposable income may also be rewritten as:

$$YD^* = \frac{G}{\left[\dfrac{\theta}{(1-\theta)}\right] - \alpha_3 \cdot \check{r}} \tag{4.24}$$

Then, since in the steady state $T^* = G + r \cdot B_h^*$, we have $Y^* = YD^* + G$, and hence:

$$Y^* = \frac{G \cdot (1 - \alpha_3 \cdot (1 - \theta) \cdot \check{r})}{(\theta - \alpha_3 \cdot (1 - \theta) \cdot \check{r})} \tag{4.25}$$

Obviously, in the special case where $\check{r} = 0$, we are back to the simple case described by Model *SIM* and equation (3.15):

$$Y^* = \frac{G}{\theta} \tag{3.15}$$

Equation (4.25) can also be rewritten in a form that is reminiscent of equation (3.15), and which highlights the fact that the steady-state level of GDP depends on the fiscal stance, which, whatever the target wealth to disposable income ratio and the *average* rate of interest payable on the *overall* amount of government liabilities, depends on the G/θ ratio. After some manipulations, we get:

$$Y^* = \left(\frac{G}{\theta}\right) \left\{ \frac{\theta - \alpha_3 \cdot \theta(1 - \theta) \cdot \check{r}}{\theta - \alpha_3 \cdot (1 - \theta) \cdot \check{r}} \right\} \tag{4.26}$$

4.6 Implications of changes in parameter values for temporary and steady-state income

4.6.1 Some puzzling results

We can now see what are the implications of various changes in the values of the parameters. Some of these effects are intuitive, others are not. To start with the former, obviously an increase in the permanent level of government expenditures G will lead to an increase in the stationary level of income and disposable income: $dY^*/dG > 0$. Similarly, any permanent decrease in the overall tax rate θ leads to an increase in the stationary level of income and disposable income: $dY^*/d\theta < 0$.

On the other hand, an *increase* in the rate of interest r, or in the *average* rate of interest $\check{r}$ payable on the *overall* amount of government liabilities, leads to an *increase* in the steady-state level of disposable income (and income). This can be seen by computing the derivative $dY^*/dr > 0$, from equation (4.23), or the derivative $dY^*/d\check{r} > 0$ from equation (4.24). What happens is that higher rates of interest on government debt increase the flow of payments that arise from the government sector, and this leads to more consumer spending on the part of households. In addition, the higher rate of return on bills induces households to hold more interest-paying government debt. In the present model, national income is the result of a multiplier effect over a multiplicand. This multiplicand is government expenditures, and these include pure expenditures on goods and services as well as the expenditures needed for servicing the debt.[12] Because the multiplicand includes interest payments on the debt, the puzzling positive long-run effect of higher interest rates on

---

[12] This positive impact of higher interest rates on economic activity was noted in Italy during the 1980s. The effect noted in the model was noticeable in Italy, because its debt to GDP ratio exceeded 100% while the entire debt was being held by Italians. As a result, an increase in interest rates led to Italians being flooded with additional interest revenues arising from their government's efforts to service the public debt.

national income still arises in more sophisticated models where interest rates do have strong negative short-run effects, as we shall see later in the chapter and in other chapters.

It should also be noted that an increase in the desire to hold bills, that is, an increase in the parameter λ_0 of the portfolio equations, would increase the proportion of government debt taking the form of bills, and hence it would raise $\check{r}$, thus leading to an increase in the steady-state value of national income. Thus, in this model, a reduction in liquidity preference leads to an increase in national income.

There is another surprising feature of Model *PC*. We can see that any increase in the α_3 parameter – the wealth to disposable income ratio – also eventually leads to an increase in stationary income or disposable income. For instance, from both equations (4.18) and (4.19), we obtain the derivative $dY^*/d\alpha_3 > 0$. Remember however that α_3 is defined as: $\alpha_3 = (1 - \alpha_1)/\alpha_2$, where α_1 and α_2 are respectively the propensities to consume out of current income and out of accumulated wealth. The smaller these two propensities to consume, the larger the α_3 parameter. Thus the smaller the propensities to consume, the larger the steady-state levels of income and disposable income. In other words, if households are more thrifty – if they decide to save a larger proportion of their income and of their wealth – the steady-state income will be higher.

Although this puzzling result is in line with what many mainstream economists would claim today, it contradicts the well-known *paradox of thrift*, that had been advanced by Keynes (1936) and emphasized over the last sixty years or so by Keynesians and post-Keynesians alike. Once again, the reason for which higher thrift leads to a higher stationary level of income is that a larger α_3 parameter implies that households are aiming at a higher wealth target, for a given income ratio. But a higher wealth target, all else being equal, implies larger interest payments on government debt held by households, and hence, ultimately, higher absolute consumption and income levels once the steady-state has been achieved.

4.6.2 A graphical analysis

The effects of an increase in the rate of interest have already been shown in Figures 4.3 and 4.4. The effect of an increase in the propensity to consume out of disposable income (α_1) are shown in the next two figures, built with the help of model *PCEX*, under the assumption that expectations about current disposable income are based on actual disposable income in the previous period (equation 4.16A, $YD^e = YD_{-1}$). Recall that an increase in any of the propensities to consume implies a decrease in the target wealth to disposable income ratio. Figure 4.5 shows that the effect of a higher propensity to consume out of expected disposable income is positive in the short run, with GDP rising; however, in the long run GDP converges to a new steady-state value which is lower than the initial steady state.

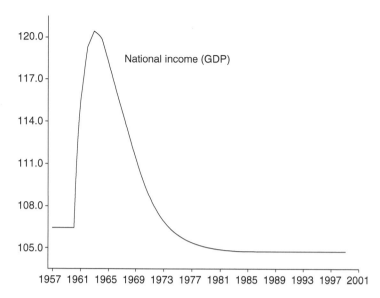

Figure 4.5 Rise and fall of national income (GDP) following an increase in the propensity to consume out of expected disposable income (α_1)

Figure 4.6 helps us to understand this behaviour of national income. The chart traces the evolution of household consumption, along with the two arguments of the consumption function – expected disposable income and lagged wealth. National income first rises in the short run, because, for a given amount of accumulated wealth, the increase in consumption expenditures out of current income leads to an increase in aggregate demand; however this effect is only temporary. The lower propensity to save leads to a gradual reduction in the stock of wealth, as consumption exceeds disposable income. Eventually, the reduced consumption out of this shrinking wealth fully compensates for the higher consumption out of current income. Then, as wealth continues to drop, consumption keeps falling, along with the reduced interest income on government debt (the counterpart of household wealth), so that, as shown with the derivatives of the steady-state solutions, national income keeps falling – until it reaches a new stationary state the level of which is ultimately lower than what existed in the previous steady state.

Readers may wonder why, with a higher propensity to consume, both the wealth of households and the debt of government decrease. Remember that we start from a situation where the economy is in a stationary state, which implies that the private sector is neither saving nor dissaving, while the government budget is balanced, neither in deficit nor in surplus. As households decide to consume more, targeting a lower wealth to disposable income ratio, this means that households are now dissaving, which explains why their

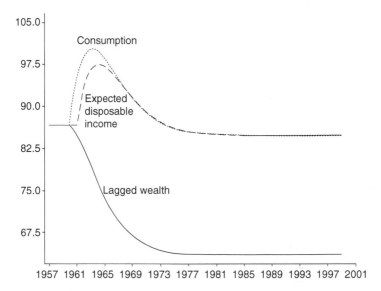

Figure 4.6 Evolution of consumption, expected disposable income and lagged wealth, following an increase in the propensity to consume out of expected disposable income (α_1)

wealth would be falling. In addition, as the households are spending more, there is a boost in economic activity, which generates more tax revenue for the government; as a result, the government budget goes into a surplus which allows the government sector to reduce its debt. Thus both household wealth and government debt decrease together, by exactly the same amount, as they must (in this simplified model).

The short-run effects shown in the previous figures can also be illustrated using a modified version of Figure 3.10 from Chapter 3. Figure 4.7 illustrates the case of an increase in the rate of interest set by the central bank. Figure 4.7 keeps the first two quadrants of Figure 3.10. The Y line illustrates the relationship between disposable income *YD*, on the horizontal axis, and national income *Y* on the vertical axis. The relationship is more complicated than it was with Model *SIM*, because, beyond taxes, we must also take into account interest payments on debt. Given these, from equations (4.2) and (4.3), we may write:

$$YD = Y(1 - \theta) + r_{-1} \cdot B_{h-1}(1 - \theta)$$

Rearranging this equation, we obtain the relationship between national income and disposable income that we need to equate production to aggregate demand, arising out of disposable income and government expenditures. We have:

$$Y = -r_{-1} \cdot B_{h-1} + \frac{YD}{(1 - \theta)} \tag{4.27}$$

This is the line that arises from below the origin. Aggregate demand *AD*, as shown in the first quadrant of Figure 4.7, is the sum of consumption expenditures and government expenditures, and is given by equations (4.1) and (4.5). We may write it as:

$$Y^{AD} = \alpha_1 \cdot YD + \alpha_2 \cdot V_{-1} + G \tag{4.28}$$

The short-run, or temporary, solution of Model *PC* is given at the intersection of these two curves. In other words, the out-of-equilibrium level of disposable income is given by the following difference equation, obtained by putting together equations (4.27) and (4.28):

$$YD = \frac{(1 - \theta) \cdot (\alpha_2 \cdot V_{-1} + r_{-1} \cdot B_{h-1} + G)}{1 - \alpha_1 \cdot (1 - \theta)} \tag{4.29}$$

The same short-run, or temporary, solution, for aggregate income can be obtained from (4.27) and (4.29). We get another difference equation:

$$Y = \frac{G + \alpha_2 \cdot V_{-1} + \alpha_1 \cdot (1 - \theta) \cdot r_{-1} \cdot B_{h-1}}{1 - \alpha_1 \cdot (1 - \theta)} \tag{4.30}$$

These equations show clearly that any increase in the rate of interest or in the propensities to consume lead to a temporary increase in disposable income and national income. In Figure 4.7, the increase in the rate of interest is

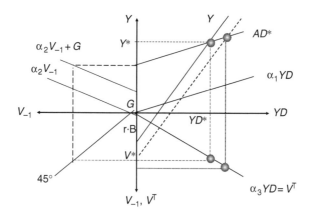

Figure 4.7   Short-run effect of an increase in the interest rate

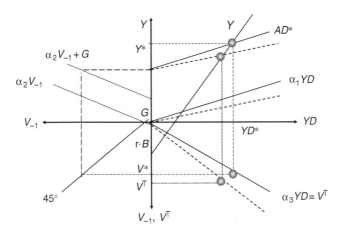

Figure 4.8   Short-run effect of a fall in the propensity to consume

represented by a shift downwards of the Y curve, thus leading to a higher temporary national income and disposable income. Assuming we had started from a stationary position, where accumulated wealth is the targeted level of wealth, we can see in the bottom quadrant of the graph that the new target level of wealth is now higher than the level previously achieved. This implies that within the period households will be saving, accumulating larger amounts of wealth and larger amounts of bills. As a result, in the next periods, consumption will be rising and so will income, until the new, higher, stationary level of income is reached.[13]

A similar analysis is provided with Figure 4.8, in the case where the propensity to consume out of current income would fall, and hence when the target wealth to income ratio would rise. The decrease in the propensity to consume is illustrated by the downward rotations of the aggregate demand curve and of the target wealth curve. The figure shows that this reduction in the propensity to consume would initially lead to a fall in national income, but that this would be accompanied by a discrepancy between the new target level of wealth and the current level of wealth, thus inducing households to accumulate new wealth and hence purchase bills. The increase in interest payments would push down the Y curve, eventually pushing its point of intersection with the new AD curve beyond the initial stationary levels of income and disposable income.

[13] Similarly, a difference equation can also be obtained for wealth. Given equations (4.4) and (4.5), it turns out that: $V = (1 - \alpha_2) \cdot V_{-1} + (1 - \alpha_1)YD$. Also, from equation (4.7), we can deduce B_h as a function of V and YD.

4.6.3 The puzzling impact of interest rates reconsidered

The purpose of this subsection is to reconsider the puzzling impact of interest rates on national income. We saw previously that higher interest rates have a positive impact both on the temporary and the steady-state values of national income. Is this a necessary result? What if propensities to save were positive functions of the interest rate, as is often assumed in mainstream textbooks? Let us suppose then that the propensity to save is not constant anymore, but rather assumes a value which depends negatively on the rate of interest on bills, with the Greek letter ι being the reaction parameter. Formally, this implies that:

$$\alpha_1 = \alpha_{10} - \iota \cdot r_{-1} \tag{4.31}$$

Since we know that $\alpha_3 = (1-\alpha_1)/\alpha_2$, this implies that a higher rate of interest will generate a higher target wealth to income ratio. In other words, with equation (4.31) and a constant propensity to consume out of the opening stock of wealth, α_2, it follows that:

$$\alpha_3 = \frac{(1 - \alpha_{10} + \iota \cdot r_{-1})}{\alpha_2} \tag{4.32}$$

With the addition of equation (4.31), an increase in the rate of interest r can once more be simulated with Model *PC* (here *PCEX2*). This experiment is illustrated with the help of Figure 4.9. The initial impact of the increase in interest rate on economic activity is negative, as central banks claim. There is a fall in consumption, disposable income and national income, as standard short-run macro models would claim (based on some negative interest elasticity of investment). However, our model goes beyond flows and takes stocks into account. The reduction in the propensity to consume and hence the associated increase in the target wealth to income ratio leads to a gradual increase in the stock of wealth, through the partial wealth adjustment function, as households now spend less than they earn. Figure 4.9 shows that consumption demand is lower than disposable income as long as household wealth keeps increasing.

Figure 4.9 shows that, *when comparing steady states*, the aggregate income flow is still an *increasing* function of the interest rate, even though the short-run impact of higher interest rates is to reduce consumption and hence income as we would expect. Thus, even when the temporary solutions are subjected to the standard Keynesian effects, that is, when the paradox of thrift is being observed in the short run, stationary income is an increasing function of the rate of interest. Of course, we already knew this from the observation of equation (4.24), since the term $\alpha_3 \cdot \check{r}$ which appears with a negative sign in the denominator, is now larger.

The increase in the wealth of households has, as a counterpart, an increase in the debt of government. Figure 4.10 shows why this is so. The short-run

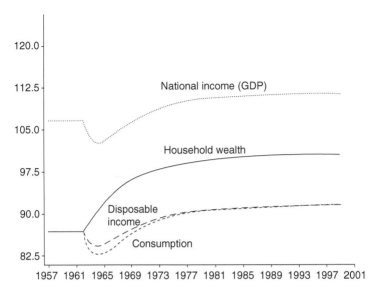

Figure 4.9 Evolution of GDP, disposable income, consumption and wealth, following an increase of 100 points in the rate of interest on bills, in Model *PCEX2* where the propensity to consume reacts negatively to higher interest rates

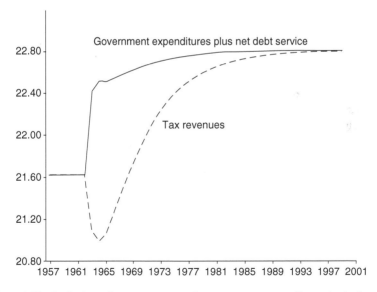

Figure 4.10 Evolution of tax revenues and government expenditures including net debt servicing, following an increase of 100 points in the rate of interest on bills, in Model *PCEX2* where the propensity to consume reacts negatively to higher interest rates

recession caused by the negative impact of higher interest rates on consumption demand drives down government tax revenues. This negative effect on the government budget position is reinforced by the brisk increase in overall government expenditures, caused by the higher cost in debt servicing arising from the higher interest rates. This immediately creates a government deficit. This deficit gets shrunk gradually, while both government expenditures and taxes rise, until they reach a stationary level, at which point the government budget is balanced. The deficit flow is eventually wiped out as a result of the rising consumption expenditures induced by rising household wealth, as we saw in Figure 4.9. Our model thus shows clearly the short-run perverse effects of higher interest rates on the government budget position.

4.7 A government target for the debt to income ratio

In the 1980s and 1990s, governments became concerned about the relative amount of public debt which they had piled up in their attempt to save their countries from the oil supply shocks and the slowdown of the economy. The relative amount of public debt was usually measured as a ratio, the public debt to GDP ratio. In terms of our notation, this is measured by the expression V/Y, where V is the wealth of households, which corresponds to the debt owed by government to the private sector, while Y is national income or GDP. Can governments do anything about this debt to income ratio in the long run?[14]

First it should be pointed out the steady-state wealth to disposable income ratio – the V/YD ratio – is determined by the behaviour of households. As stated in equation (4.21), this wealth to disposable income ratio, which also turns out to be equal to the public debt to disposable income ratio, is precisely equal to the α_3 ratio which arises from the saving behaviour of households. It follows that governments can do nothing, in the present model, to modify the public debt to disposable income ratio. If governments were to reduce government expenditures, in an attempt to produce a budgetary surplus and induce a fall in the public debt to disposable income, they would be unsuccessful, since this would only lead to a reduction in income and disposable income, but no change in the targeted ratio, unless the reduction in disposable income led households to reduce their saving propensities, and hence led them to reduce their targeted wealth to disposable income ratio.

Governments, and securities grading agencies, however, are not really concerned with public debt as a ratio of disposable income, but rather with public

---

[14] A question put by Creel and Sterdyniak (1999: 138), among others.

debt as a ratio of GDP. Is it possible for governments to modify the steady-state level of the public debt to GDP ratio – the V/Y ratio – although they would be hopeless in their attempts to modify the public debt to disposable income ratio? To answer this question, we can compute the steady-state public debt to GDP ratio. Making use of the property that in the stationary state, $Y^* = YD^* + G$, and using equation (4.23), we obtain the steady-state ratio:

$$\frac{V^*}{Y^*} = \frac{\alpha_3}{1 + \left[\dfrac{\theta}{(1-\theta)}\right] - r \cdot [(\lambda_0 + \lambda_1 \cdot r) \cdot \alpha_3 - \lambda_2]} \tag{4.33}$$

It follows that if households are targeting too high a wealth ratio, one that is higher than the maximum debt to GDP ratio that government officials judge to be bearable, it is possible for government to reduce its stationary debt to GDP ratio by acting on two parameters that are under its control. By inspection of equation (4.33), it can be easily seen that an increase in the tax rate θ leads to a reduction in the stationary V^*/Y^* ratio. Similarly, equation (4.33) also reveals that a reduction in the rate of interest on bills will lead to a reduction in the public debt to GDP ratio.[15] This reduction will even be achieved if the propensities to save of households react positively to changes in interest rates, for an autonomous or induced reduction in the α_3 coefficient – a proxy for an overall saving propensity – will also reduce the V^*/Y^* ratio. In other words, equation (4.31) may apply. To summarize, government officials that would like to induce a reduction in the public debt to GDP ratio would need to increase tax rates or reduce interest rates. However both of these actions will lead to a reduced level of stationary income. Thus if governments wish to sustain full-employment income, they have to disregard the debt to income ratio, which, as we saw, is essentially determined by the target wealth to disposable income ratio set by the households.

In the next chapter, more will be said about the dire consequences of government obsession with public deficit reduction and the reduction of the size of the public sector, the effect of which has been to encourage reductions in pure government expenditures.

---

[15] This can also be seen, in reverse gear, by inspecting Figure 4.9. The increase in interest rates led to a large increase in household wealth, and hence net government debt, while GDP decreased only later to rise slightly. As a result, one can say that increases in interest rates lead to an increase in the debt to GDP ratio.

Appendix 4.1: Equation list of Model *PC*

$$Y = C + G \tag{4.1}$$

$$YD = Y - T + r_{-1} \cdot B_{h-1} \tag{4.2}$$

$$T = \theta \cdot (Y + r_{-1} \cdot B_{h-1}) \quad \theta < 1 \tag{4.3}$$

$$V = V_{-1} + (YD - C) \tag{4.4}$$

$$C = \alpha_1 \cdot YD + \alpha_2 \cdot V_{-1} \quad 0 < \alpha_2 < \alpha_1 < 1 \tag{4.5}$$

$$H_h = V - B_h \tag{4.6}$$

$$\frac{B_h}{V} = \lambda_0 + \lambda_1 \cdot r - \lambda_2 \cdot \left(\frac{YD}{V} \right) \tag{4.7}$$

$$\frac{H_h}{V} = (1 - \lambda_0) - \lambda_1 \cdot r + \lambda_2 \cdot \left(\frac{YD}{V} \right) \tag{4.6A}$$

$$\Delta B_s = B_s - B_{s-1} = (G + r_{-1} \cdot B_{s-1}) - (T + r_{-1} \cdot B_{cb-1}) \tag{4.8}$$

$$\Delta H_s = H_s - H_{s-1} = \Delta B_{cb} \tag{4.9}$$

$$B_{cb} = B_s - B_h \tag{4.10}$$

$$r = \bar{r} \tag{4.11}$$

The redundant, or hidden, equation is:

$$H_h = H_s \tag{4.12}$$

Appendix 4.2: Equation list of Model *PC* with expectations (*PCEX*)

$$Y = C + G \tag{4.1}$$

$$YD = Y - T + r_{-1} \cdot B_{h-1} \tag{4.2}$$

$$T = \theta \cdot (Y + r_{-1} \cdot B_{h-1}) \quad \theta < 1 \tag{4.3}$$

$$V = V_{-1} + (YD - C) \tag{4.4}$$

$$C = \alpha_1 \cdot YD^e + \alpha_2 \cdot V_{-1} \tag{4.5E}$$

$$\frac{B_d}{V^e} = \lambda_0 + \lambda_1 \cdot r - \lambda_2 \cdot \left(\frac{YD^e}{V^e} \right) \tag{4.7E}$$

$$\frac{H_d}{V^e} = (1 - \lambda_0) - \lambda_1 \cdot r + \lambda_2 \cdot \left(\frac{YD^e}{V^e} \right) \tag{4.6E}$$

$$H_d = V^e - B_d \tag{4.13}$$

$$V^e = V_{-1} + (YD^e - C) \tag{4.14}$$

$$H_h = V - B_h \tag{4.6}$$

$$B_h = B_d \tag{4.15}$$

$$\Delta B_s = B_s - B_{s-1} = (G + r_{-1} \cdot B_{s-1}) - (T + r_{-1} \cdot B_{cb-1}) \tag{4.8}$$

$$\Delta H_s = H_s - H_{s-1} = \Delta B_{cb} \tag{4.9}$$

$$B_{cb} = B_s - B_h \tag{4.10}$$

$$r = \bar{r} \tag{4.11}$$

$$YD^e = YD \cdot (1 + Ra) \tag{4.16}$$

The redundant equation is still:

$$H_h = H_s \tag{4.12}$$

Model *PCEX1*

Replace equation (4.16) with:

$$YD^e = YD_{-1} \tag{4.16A}$$

Model *PCEX2*

Transform the parameter α_1 into a variable, and add to Model *PCEX1*:

$$\alpha_1 = \alpha_{10} - \iota \cdot r_{-1} \tag{4.31}$$

Appendix 4.3: Endogenous money

There is a school of thought that has long been arguing in favour of endogenous money. This line of thought goes back to the writings of Thomas Tooke and the Banking School, and has been present in the history of economic thought ever since. It can be associated with the Swedish economist Knut Wicksell as well as several economists of the Austrian tradition, such as von Mises and Friedrich Hayek in the 1920s and 1930s. The endogenous money tradition was eclipsed for a long time by the Quantity theory of money, which was defended by David Ricardo and the Currency School in the 1830s, and then later by the marginalists who needed an exogenous stock of money to make sense of their models. While Keynes and Keynesianism brought back momentarily the idea that monetary policy was essentially based on an interest rate decision, the Quantity theory of money regained momentum with the arrival of Milton Friedman and his 'Monetarism', who claimed that the central bank only needed to, and could, control the rate of growth of the money supply. The response of heterodox economists to this far-fetched claim was that the money supply has no stable relationship with output or prices – the *unstable velocity* argument, and that, in any case, the money supply is endogenous – the so-called *reverse-causation* argument.

The equations presented here endorse the reverse-causation argument. It is argued that central banks cannot control the money supply directly. What central banks can do is set the rate of interest, and hope that high interest rates will slow down the economy and abate inflation in the long run. This view of the monetary process, in particular the reverse-causation argument, was put forward in very clear terms by the French economist Jacques Le Bourva (1992), in two articles published in 1959 and 1962. The well-known British economist Nicholas Kaldor (1964) first endorsed the unstable velocity argument in his 1958 memorandum to the Radcliffe Committee, only to support twelve years later the much more powerful reverse-causation argument (1970a), when it became clear that the views of Friedman and of monetarism were sweeping the profession. In the 1970s and the 1980s, heterodox economists (post-Keynesian ones in particular), were the only academic economists defending the view that central banks were essentially setting short-term interest rates, letting the supply of money find its level determined by portfolio demand (Moore 1988). Only practitioners – some economists working at central banks such as Goodhart (1984) – seemed to realize that high powered money and money were endogenous variables, not under the direct control of the central bank.

For a long time mainstream textbooks have faithfully reflected the Quantity theory of money and its modern incarnation, Monetarism. Even today, this is still the case. There is however a clear schizophrenia in the mainstream economics profession. On the one hand, textbook writers claim that monetary policy acts through changes in the money supply. On the other hand, all press releases relative to the actions of central banks speak of rates of interest being set or targeted by the central bank. The financial press is full of reports about the possible changes in rates of interest under the control of the central bank. There is hardly ever any indication about the supply of money or its rate of growth. In addition, the working papers issued by central banks to explain the procedures followed by central bankers very explicitly show that central banks set a 'discount rate' and a 'deposit rate' – which constitutes the intervention band. The same central bank papers show that the overnight rate – the one-day rate that banks charge to each other – is usually right in the middle of that band.

Some mainstream economists are starting to recognize that fact, and build models that explicitly rely on real interest targeting rather than money supply targeting (Romer 2000). Indeed, such models are now part of what some call the *New Consensus* in macroeconomics (J.B. Taylor 2000; Meyer 2001). This change of mind among academic economists seems to have arisen out of the more transparent operating procedures adopted by a number of central banks throughout the world, in particular in Australia, Canada, Sweden and the United States (Lavoie 2005; Fullwiler 2006). Whereas, at least according to our view, central banks always operated monetary policy by relying on changes in the short-term interest rates under their control, the interest rate targets are now explicit and publicly announced at regular intervals. Many, perhaps most central banks, with the important exception of the European Central Bank, have completely abandoned any reference to monetary targets. This is usually justified on the grounds that money demand is too unstable for monetary targets, whatever they are, high powered money or wider monetary aggregates, to be of any help. Although the money supply seems to play no useful role in these new consensus models, it is not yet clear, however, whether these mainstream authors clearly see the money supply as being endogenous and demand determined. One could argue that New Consensus authors perceive the money supply to be endogenous by default, whereas post-Keynesians believe that the money supply is endogenous because it cannot be otherwise in a well-functioning monetary system.

Appendix 4.4: Alternative mainstream closures

An exogenous stock of money

An alternative way to close Model *PC* would be to consider the demand for securities by the central bank to be the exogenous policy variable, in which case the rate of interest becomes endogenous. This corresponds to what we believe to be a standard neo-classical closure, and it has been incorporated into Model *PCNEO*. This new closure can be obtained from Model *PC* by first writing an additional equation:

$$B_{cb} = \overline{B}_{cb} \qquad (A4.3.1)$$

By reason of equation (4.9), which says that $\Delta H_s = \Delta B_{cb}$, the above equation implies that the supply of cash money is also an exogenous variable. In other words, we have:

$$\overline{H}_s = \overline{B}_{cb} \qquad (A4.3.2)$$

The choice of equation (A4.3.1), instead of (4.11), should be taken to mean that the demand for bills by households is forced to adjust to the exogenously determined supply of bills, net of the demand for bills by the central bank. This means that equation (4.10), is rewritten in the following way:

$$B_h = B_s - \overline{B}_{cb} \qquad (A4.3.3)$$

There are now two equations, instead of one, that determine the holdings of bills by households (the other one is equation (4.7)). This implies the need for an *equilibrium condition*. The net supply of bills and the demand by households are brought into equivalence by a market clearing price – the rate of interest. The rate of interest that clears the bill market is given by equation (4.7), which could be rewritten as $r = r(B_h/V,$

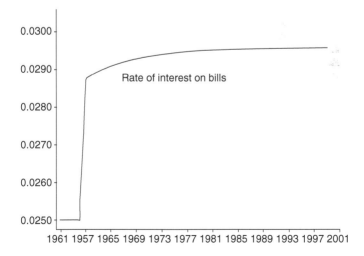

Figure A4.1 Evolution of the rate of interest on bills, following a step decrease in the amount of Treasury bills held by the central bank (Model *PCNEO*)

YD/V, λ_0, λ_1, λ_2). This market-clearing rate of interest r, determined at the end of period t, is the rate that will be used to define the interest payments $r \cdot B_h$ received by households in period $t + 1$.

According to Walras' Law, if the securities market clears so does the money market (or if the money market clears so does the securities market), so that equation (4.12) is still fulfilled: $H_h = H_s$. The difference with the post-Keynesian closure advocated in Chapter 4, is that the money market clears thanks to a price-equilibrating mechanism, whereas no such equilibrating mechanism was required in the post-Keynesian closure of Model *PC*.

Figure A4.1 shows what happens when the central bank decides to reduce the amount of bills it is holding within such a setup. The interest rate briskly increases in the period where the reduction occurs, so that households voluntarily take up the bills that the central bank does not want to hold any more. As the chart shows, there is some further adjustment down the line, since the higher interest rates generate slightly more economic activity, thus requiring larger money balances for transaction purposes, balances that the central bank refuses to provide. As a result, there are some further increases in the level of interest rates, until the stationary state is reached.

It should be pointed out however that in a model with expectations and additional realistic features, the introduction of a fixed money supply rule would create havoc in the system, as interest rates would sharply rise or fall. An exogenous stock of money is not really an alternative.

An exogenous share of government deficit

Some authors assume that the government, in cooperation with the monetary authorities, decides that a fixed proportion of the government deficit is being financed by issuing cash money, while the rest gets financed by issuing bonds or bills. Tobin (1982a: 182) makes such an assumption. He supposes that 'the budget deficit in dollars ... is financed in fraction γ_B by selling bonds ... and in fraction γ_H by printing high-powered money ($\gamma_H + \gamma_B = 1$)' (Backus *et al.* 1980: 267). Such an assumption, which can also be found in Ott and Ott (1965), is just a variant of the previous assumption of an exogenous stock of money or bills. Here, for a given budget deficit, what is exogenous is the change in the stock of money. Clearly, this closure again requires endogenous rates of interest and is consistent with an exogenous money view.

This Backus *et al.* assumption is inconsistent with the post-Keynesian view of endogenous money. This must be pointed out, because some authors such as Moudud (1999: 22–3) and Franke and Semmler (1991: 340) claim to be working within an endogenous money framework, whereas in reality they are not, since they are assuming that a predetermined percentage of the government deficit is being financed by the issue of cash money. The same remark applies to Dalziel (2001: 104), who claims that 'the government must decide what portion of the deficit will be funded by the central bank, and what portion will be funded by selling government securities to savers in the economy', and who then assumes that a constant proportion m 'is funded with central bank liabilities'. This assumption allows these authors to reintroduce the conventional notion of an excess supply of money, with its monetarist inflationary consequences.

5
Long-term Bonds, Capital Gains and Liquidity Preference

5.1 New features of Model *LP*

The definition of wealth in Model *PC* in Chapter 4 comprised only two assets, money and bills. In this chapter a third asset, long-term government bonds, is introduced and this will provide an opportunity to discuss the notion of *l*iquidity *p*reference – hence the name Model *LP* – and also to introduce capital gains and losses into the system of accounts. An important feature of the new model will be that an increase in long-term interest rates will have a short-run negative effect on demand.

5.2 The value of a perpetuity

Long bonds are here defined as consols, also called perpetuities because they are never redeemed. It is assumed that each consol is a piece of paper which pays the owner one dollar after one period has elapsed, this one dollar payment being the coupon of the perpetuity. If there are BL such pieces of paper in existence at the end of the previous period, it follows that the total flow of interest payments on these assets in the current period is simply BL_{-1}, since each piece of paper provides an interest revenue of one dollar. The value of a bond is the piece of paper times its price (p_{bL}) – that is, $BL \cdot p_{bL}$ and the long rate of interest r_{bL} is simply the reciprocal of the bond price. To obtain that answer formally, we can look at it the other way: how much would you pay for an asset that would guarantee a payment of one dollar, from next period into eternity, if you discount these future payments at the rate r_{bL}? Mathematically, we have:

$$p_{bL} = \sum \frac{1}{(1 + r_{bL})^t}$$

where the sum is from period one to infinity, and where the price p_{bL} is the price at period zero. It turns out that the sum of this geometric series is simply

$1/r_{bL}$, so that:

$$p_{bL} = \sum \frac{1}{(1 + r_{bL})^t} = \frac{1}{r_{bL}}$$

or:

$$r_{bL} = \frac{1}{p_{bL}}$$

In common parlance, r_{bL} is the long-term rate of interest, when the price p_{bL} has been determined by financial markets. But r_{bL}, among financial market operators, is better known as the yield (to maturity) of long-term bonds. In our models, which use discrete time, bonds that give rise to an interest income in the current period must have been owned and valued in the previous period. For instance, in the geometric sum, the price of bonds p_{bL} is the price of bonds this period, given the interest payments of the future. This implies that the rate of interest on long-term bonds that applies to the current period is given by the yield of the previous period, based on the price paid for bonds in the previous period.

That this relationship is the correct one can be verified by recalling that the interest income of the perpetuity is just one dollar, and hence that the overall interest income on long-term bonds must be equal to the number of long-term bonds at the end of the previous period, BL_{-1}. As is the case for any asset, this overall interest income must be equal to the product of the rate of interest times the value of the overall stock of long-term bonds, but here both elements are computed at the end of the previous period. In other words, we must have the equality:

$$BL_{-1} = r_{bL-1} \cdot p_{bL-1} \cdot BL_{-1}$$

This implies, once more, that: $r_{bL-1} = 1/p_{bL-1}$. In other words, the long-term bond rate relevant to the present period is the bond yield r_{bL-1} of the previous period. This is symmetrical with the statement made in Chapter 4, according to which the rate of interest on bills r_{-1}, determined at the end of the previous period, was the rate of interest that determined the amount of interest payments on bills $r_{-1} \cdot B_{-1}$ that was made in the current period.

5.3 The expected rate of return on long-term bonds

This long rate of interest is not the same thing as the *rate of return* on long-term bonds. In contrast to bills, the price of which was assumed to remain constant until it was redeemed, the price of a long-term bond can change. The overall rate of return thus consists of two components: the interest revenue, represented by the yield r_{bL-1}; and the capital gain, represented by the change in the value of the bond between the last period and the current period. The rate of return Rr_{bL} on a bond that was purchased (or owned) in the previous period is thus equal to:

$$Rr_{bL} = r_{bL-1} + \frac{\Delta p_{bL}}{p_{bL-1}} = \frac{1}{p_{bL-1}} + \frac{\Delta p_{bL}}{p_{bL-1}}$$

$$= \frac{1 + \Delta p_{bL}}{p_{bL-1}} = \frac{1 + p_{bL} - p_{bL-1}}{p_{bL-1}}$$

This rate of return can only be known at the end of the current period, when the current price of long-term bonds has settled to its final value. Whether the individual who bought the bond in the previous period decides to sell or to keep the bond in the current period will not change the rate of return. When the bond is sold, the capital gain is realized. When the bond is kept in the portfolio, the capital gain is only a 'paper' gain. The capital gain is not realized; it only accrues to the owner of the asset.

When households make their portfolio choice, three features matter. First financial investors are concerned with the price that the long-term bond fetches in the current period, for this defines the yield of the asset which will arise in the next period. Second, what also matters is the expected price of the bond in the next period, when it will be possible to sell the bond. These two prices help define what we shall call the *pure expected rate of return* on bonds purchased or held in the current period. This *pure* expected rate of return on bonds purchased now is equal to:

$$PERr_{bL} = \frac{1 + p_{bL}^e - p_{bL}}{p_{bL}}$$

or

$$PERr_{bL} = r_{bL} + \frac{(p_{bL}^e - p_{bL})}{p_{bL}}$$

where $PERr_{bL}$ is the rate of return which is expected on long-term bonds purchased this period at the price p_{bL}, while p_{bL}^e is the price of bonds that is expected to arise by the end of the *next* period, an expectation which is made in the *current* period, as households make their portfolio decisions.

However there is an additional factor, a third factor, that plays a role in such portfolio decisions. This third factor is the confidence with which households hold their expectations about future bond prices. It is a measure of the degree of confidence of financial investors, or a measure of the weight that household investors attribute to the validity of their expectations. In other words, households may believe that bond prices will be p_{bL}^e in the next period, but they may attribute little weight or conviction to this belief. We shall call χ (chi) this weight. It reflects the fact that although households expect the future bond price p_{bL}^e to be somewhat different from the present price p_{bL}, their portfolio decisions will only partly reflect their belief in this discrepancy. In standard terms, one could say that they assign a probability χ that such a change in bond prices will actually occur. We shall call ERr_{bL} the expected rate of return that takes into account either such probabilities or the conviction with which future bond price changes are being held. Hence we have:

$$ERr_{bL} = r_{bL} + \chi \cdot \frac{(p_{bL}^e - p_{bL})}{p_{bL}}$$

In a world where there is a multiplicity of opinions, one could assume that χ reflects the proportion of agents who believe *a priori* that bond prices will change towards p_{bL}^e, while $(1 - \chi)$ reflects the proportions of agents who believe *a priori* that bond prices will remain where they are at p_{bL}. *A posteriori*, in a Bayesian world, agents should expect the price change to be $\chi \cdot (p_{bL}^e - p_{bL})$.

If agents expect no future change in the price of bonds, the expected rate of return ERr_{bL} on bonds is simply the current yield r_{bL} on bonds. In general the expected rate of return on bonds, rather than the pure expected rate of return, will be the relevant concept when comparing the profitability of various assets within portfolio choice.

5.4   Assessing capital gains algebraically and geometrically

The introduction of capital gains brings to the fore a distinction that we shall have to make time and time again, with all sorts of assets the value of which can change while they are being held.

The value of the stock of bonds at the beginning of the period is given by the stock of bonds held at the end of the previous period, say $p_{bL-1} \cdot BL_{-1}$, while the value of the stock of bonds held at the end of the current period is $p_{bL} \cdot BL$. Hence the overall change in the value of the stock of bonds, that is, the increase in the amount of wealth held in this form is given by: $(p_{bL} \cdot BL - p_{bL-1} \cdot BL_{-1})$. This difference is made up of two components. Part of the increase in the value of wealth held in the form of bonds is due to the fact that more bonds have been purchased in the current period; this is described by the number of bonds which change hands times their price (that is, $(\Delta BL) \cdot p_{bL}$). These will appear in the transactions flow matrix. But there will also be capital gains or losses on existing holdings when the price of bonds changes, which are described by $(\Delta p_{bL}) \cdot BL_{-1}$. This capital gain is equal to the change in price times the opening number of bonds, to which no transaction between

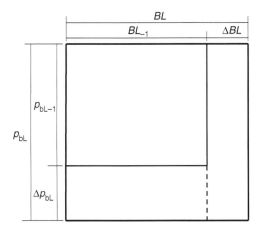

Figure 5.1 The Ostergaard diagram

agents of different sectors corresponds. Hence capital gains are included in the transactions matrix below as a memorandum item only.

It is worth stopping for a moment to demonstrate that changes in the value of stock variables are indeed made up in this way. The breakdown of changes in the value of stock variables is going to turn up again and again, and the formula will greatly assist the understanding of some tiresome concepts which will simply have to be mastered at some stage, for example, stock appreciation and, more generally, inflation accounting.

The simplest proof is a geometrical one, as can be found in Figure 5.1, which we shall call the Ostergaard figure.[1] The end-period value of a stock of bonds is given by the area of the large rectangle in bold, that is $p_{bL} \cdot BL$. The end-of-previous-period stock is given by the area of the small rectangle in bold, $p_{bL-1} \cdot BL_{-1}$; hence the *change* in the value of the stock is given by the sum of the two remaining rectangles. Algebraically, we have:

$$\Delta(p_{bL} \cdot BL) = (p_{bL} \cdot BL - p_{bL-1} \cdot BL_{-1}) = (\Delta BL) \cdot p_{bL} + (\Delta p_{bL}) \cdot BL_{-1}$$

[1] In 1987, one of us (WG) was berated by an undergraduate class at Aalborg University in Denmark for fudging the proof of this expression so he offered a bottle of whisky to anyone who could do it better. After less than 24 hours this geometric proof was produced by Jorgn Ostergaard who was, of course, appropriately rewarded. The proof, which has a straightforward three dimensional counterpart for use when there are two sources of capital gain (Godley 1999b: 18), has proved extraordinarily useful.

where the two terms on the right-hand side correspond to the two remaining rectangles of the Ostergaard figure. The first term on the right-hand side describes transactions in bonds during the current period, while the second describes the capital gain.

The above can also be proved algebraically. By definition, the difference between the new value of the stock of bonds and the old value that was held is equal to:

$$(p_{bL} \cdot BL - p_{bL-1} \cdot BL_{-1})$$

$$= (p_{bL-1} + \Delta p_{bL}) \cdot (BL_{-1} + \Delta BL) - (p_{bL-1} \cdot BL_{-1})$$

$$= (p_{bL-1} \cdot BL_{-1}) + (\Delta p_{bL}) \cdot BL_{-1} + (p_{bL-1} \cdot \Delta BL)$$

$$\quad + (\Delta p_{bL} \cdot \Delta BL) - (p_{bL-1} \cdot BL_{-1})$$

$$= (p_{bL-1} \cdot \Delta BL) + (\Delta p_{bL} \cdot \Delta BL) + (\Delta p_{bL}) \cdot BL_{-1}$$

$$= (p_{bL-1} + \Delta p_{bL}) \cdot \Delta BL + (\Delta p_{bL}) \cdot BL_{-1}$$

$$= (\Delta BL) \cdot p_{bL} + (\Delta p_{bL}) \cdot BL_{-1}$$

The algebraic and the geometric proofs have here been conducted in terms of bonds. But these proofs apply to any asset stock, tangible or financial, subject to appreciation or depreciation, and the breakdown will be used time and time again.

5.5 Matrices with long-term bonds

To obtain the balance sheet of Model *LP*, shown in Table 5.1, the balance sheet matrix of Model *PC* in Chapter 4 has been amended simply by including the various stocks of long-term bonds as an additional asset for the household sector and as a liability for the government sector. We have assumed that central banks do not deal in long-term bonds (to avoid being concerned with capital losses).[2]

---

[2] It has been assumed that the central bank does not hold long-term bonds, presumably on the basis that central banks would dislike taking the risk of making capital losses when interest rates rise; but this is a simplification, as central banks do have long-term securities on the asset side of their balance sheet, although they generally deny any attempt to influence long-term rates. For instance, in early 2005, nearly 75% of the domestic assets held by the Bank of Canada were bonds rather than bills, while nearly half of the domestic securities held had maturity dates going over three years (data drawn from the Bank's Weekly Financial Statistics).

Table 5.1 Balance sheet of Model *LP*

	Households	Production	Government	Central bank	Σ
Money	$+H$			$-H$	0
Bills	$+B_h$		$-B$	$+B_{cb}$	0
Bonds	$+BL \cdot p_{bL}$		$-BL \cdot p_{bL}$		0
Balance (net worth)	$-V$		$+V$	0	0
Σ	0		0	0	0

Similarly, to obtain Table 5.2 and the transactions-flow matrix of Model *LP*, the flow matrix of Model *PC* is amended by including interest payments on bonds to the household sector. Since each long-term bond pays a single dollar to its owner, the total amount of interest payments made on long-term bonds is exactly equal to BL_{-1} ($= r_{bL-1} \cdot p_{bL-1} \cdot BL_{-1}$), as shown in Table 5.2. The rate of interest on bills is now called r_b, to make sure it is distinguishable from the rate of interest on long-term bonds r_{bL}. Finally, capital gains have been added to the current transactions matrix, but only as a memo item. The matrices of Model *LP* thus read as follows.

Table 5.3 below fully integrates the household sector's flow accounts with its stock accounts, thus achieving full consistency between the two accounts.

5.6 Equations of Model *LP*

5.6.1 Regular income versus Haig–Simons income

The equations of Model *LP* are all to be found in Appendix 5.1. Equation (5.1) is the same as equation (4.1), which states that all goods and services demanded are provided.

$$Y \equiv C + G \tag{5.1}$$

The next two equations deal with household income and taxation.

$$YD_r \equiv Y - T + r_{b-1} \cdot B_{h-1} + BL_{h-1} \tag{5.2}$$

$$T = \theta \cdot (Y + r_{b-1} \cdot B_{h-1} + BL_{h-1}) \quad \theta < 1 \tag{5.3}$$

Equations (5.2) and (5.3) incorporate the fact that current disposable income now includes interest payments on both bills and long-term bonds. It should be noted that capital gains have not been included within the definition of disposable income, but this of course is a matter of convention. Disposable income YD_r as defined here only incorporates the flow of *regular* income, and

Table 5.2 Transactions flow matrix of Model *LP*

	Households	Production	Government	Central bank Current	Central bank Capital	Σ
Consumption	$-C$	$+C$				0
Government expenditures		$+G$	$-G$			0
Income = GDP	$+Y$	$-Y$				0
Interest payments on bills	$+r_{b-1} \cdot B_{h-1}$		$-r_{b-1} \cdot B_{-1}$	$+r_{b-1} \cdot B_{cb-1}$		0
Interest payments on bonds	$+BL_{-1}$		$-BL_{-1}$			0
Central bank profits			$+r_{b-1} \cdot B_{cb-1}$	$-r_{b-1} \cdot B_{cb-1}$		0
Taxes	$-T$		$+T$			0
Change in money	$-\Delta H$				$+\Delta H$	0
Change in bills	$-\Delta B_h$		$+\Delta B$		$-\Delta B_{cb}$	0
Change in bonds	$-\Delta BL \cdot p_{bL}$		$+\Delta BL \cdot p_{bL}$			0
Σ	0	0	0	0	0	0
Memo: Capital gains	$-\Delta p_{bL} \cdot BL_{-1}$		$+\Delta p_{bL} \cdot BL_{-1}$			0

Table 5.3 Integration of household flow and stock accounts, within Model *LP*

		Money	Bills	Bonds	Σ assets
Initial assets (end of previous period)		H_{h-1}	B_{h-1}	$p_{bL-1} \cdot BL_{h-1}$	V_{-1}
Consumption	$-C$				0
Income = GDP	$+Y$				0
Interest payments on bills	$+r_{b-1} \cdot B_{h-1}$				0
Interest payments on bonds	$+BL_{h-1}$				0
Taxes	$-T$				0
Change in money	$-\Delta H_h$	$+\Delta H_h$			0
Change in bills	$-\Delta B_h$		$+\Delta B_h$		0
Change in bonds	$-\Delta BL_h \cdot p_{bL}$			$+\Delta BL_h \cdot p_{bL}$	0
Σ	0	H_h	B_h	$p_{bL-1} \cdot BL_{h-1} + \Delta BL_h \cdot p_{bL}$	$H_h + B_h + \Delta BL_h \cdot p_{bL} + p_{bL-1} \cdot BL_{h-1}$
Capital gains				$+\Delta p_{bL} \cdot BL_{h-1}$	$+\Delta p_{bL} \cdot BL_{h-1}$
Final assets (end of period)		H_h	B_h	$p_{bL} \cdot BL_h$	V

this is why it carries the subscript r. To make it consistent with the convention we have adopted, capital gains have not been included in taxable income either, as can be read from (5.3). Only income arising from business activity and the interest payments received from held assets are assumed to be taxed. It is indeed the case that, for reasons of convenience, capital gains are not taxed in several countries, or they are taxed at a lower rate. Even in countries where capital gains are taxed, they are usually taxed only if they have been realized, that is, if the asset which has benefitted from price appreciation has been sold (a transaction has occurred). Here it is implicitly assumed that the capital gains that have accrued in favour of the household sector have not been realized.

We now move to household wealth accumulation, as given by equation (5.4).

$$V = V_{-1} + (YD_r - C) + CG \tag{5.4}$$

with:

$$CG = \Delta p_{bL} \cdot BL_{h-1} \tag{5.5}$$

Equation (5.4) is an important equation reproducing the results exhibited in Table 5.3. It tells us that the increase in household wealth is equal to the difference between regular disposable income and consumption, plus the capital gains of households, as assessed in section 4 in the case of bonds and as assessed here in equation (5.5). Equation (5.4) generates an alternative definition of income, that of Haig (1921) and Simons (1938), who define income as consumption plus the change in wealth. This is a very crucial definition of income which we shall often use in models with capital gains and price inflation. Denoting this Haig–Simons disposable income as YD_{hs}, equation (5.4) can be rewritten as:

$$YD_{hs} = \Delta V + C = YD_r + CG \tag{5.4a}$$

This implies that the Haig–Simons definition of income is equal to regular disposable income plus capital gains. Equation (5.4a) is not part of Model *LP* – the Haig–Simons income plays no role in Model *LP*. But it is important to understand the link between disposable income based on regular flows and the Haig–Simons definition of income, which incorporates capital gains.

Equation (5.6), which describes the consumption function, again assumes that consumption depends on expected (regular) disposable income and on past accumulated wealth,

$$C = \alpha_1 \cdot YD_r^e + \alpha_2 \cdot V_{-1} \quad 0 < \alpha_2 < \alpha_1 < 1 \tag{5.6}$$

But what about capital gains then? Here we implicitly assume that capital gains in the current period have no impact on consumption. Capital gains only have an impact in the next period, since they then appear in the wealth accumulated in previous periods. Thus, capital gains or losses feed into the consumption function with a lag, via the term in wealth (V_{-1}). This is not the only way to incorporate capital gains into the consumption function. They could have been included as part of disposable income or given a separate entrance all their own. Empirical research alone can determine the appropriate specification. But empirical studies seem to show that only lagged measures of capital gains have a significant impact on consumption (Baker 1997: 65), which justifies partially our treatment of capital gains in the consumption function (equation 5.6).

Finally we introduce another equation, which is the exact equivalent in the realm of expectations of equation (5.4). This latter equation described the evolution of *realized* wealth. Equation (5.7) below describes the *expected* evolution of wealth. We have:

$$V^e = V_{-1} + (YD_r^e - C) + CG^e \tag{5.7}$$

The wealth that households *expect* to acquire by the end of the period, in excess of their wealth of the previous period, is equal to the difference between expected regular disposable income and consumption expenditures, plus the capital gains of the current period.

5.6.2 Portfolio behaviour in matrix form

We now come to the equations defining the portfolio behaviour of households. But before we deal with the behavioural equations, let us lay out two identities related to the stocks of assets held by households. Just as we defined two equations dealing with the realized and the expected accumulation of wealth, we again write out two equations that define the various components of wealth – actual (at the end of the period) and expected (at the start of the period). We have:

$$H_h = V - B_h - p_{bL} \cdot BL_h \tag{5.8}$$

$$H_d = V^e - B_d - p_{bL} \cdot BL_d \tag{5.9}$$

Equation (5.8) says that household wealth at the end of the current period is made up of the money balances H_h actually held by households, the bills B_h they hold, and the value $p_{bL} \cdot BL_h$ of the bonds that they have. Note that these actual values carry the subscript h to indicate that they are indeed being *held* by households at the end of the period. By contrast equation (5.9) outlines the various components of *expected* wealth, and carries subscripts 'e' or 'd'.

Money balances, bills and the volume of bonds in equation (5.9) all carry the subscript d for they represent the traditional meaning of the demand for assets – the demand for assets at the beginning of the period, based on expectations. These expectations are made up of the expected total amount of wealth V^e, as defined in equation (5.7).

The behavioural equations of the portfolio choice model, in line with the model first proposed by Tobin (1969) are similar to those in Model *PC* except that they comprise three different assets, cash money, bills and long-term bonds. With so many assets, it becomes neater to present portfolio behaviour in the form of matrix algebra, and the notations of the parameters, accompanied by plus signs only, reflect this possibility. In matrix form, equations (5.9A), (5.10), and (5.11) – which are found in their usual form in Appendix 5.1 – could be rewritten as:

$$\begin{bmatrix} H_d \\ B_d \\ BL_d \cdot p_{bL} \end{bmatrix} = \begin{bmatrix} \lambda_{10} \\ \lambda_{20} \\ \lambda_{30} \end{bmatrix} V^e + \begin{bmatrix} \lambda_{11}\lambda_{12}\lambda_{13} \\ \lambda_{21}\lambda_{22}\lambda_{23} \\ \lambda_{31}\lambda_{32}\lambda_{33} \end{bmatrix} \begin{bmatrix} 0 \\ r_b \\ ERr_{bL} \end{bmatrix} V^e$$

$$+ \begin{bmatrix} \lambda_{14} \\ \lambda_{24} \\ \lambda_{34} \end{bmatrix} YD_r^e$$

Once again, households are assumed to hold a certain proportion λ_{i0} of their expected wealth in the form of asset i but this proportion is modified by the (expected) rates of return on these assets and by the level of expected regular disposable income. The reader may notice that one of the elements of the rate of return vector has a 0 element in it. The zero corresponds to the rate of return on cash money. It reflects the fact that cash money H provides no interest payment, and as a consequence, the rate of return is zero.[3] As with model *SIM*, when households make their portfolio decision, they are concerned about r_b, the rate of interest on bills to be determined at the end of the current period, but which will generate the interest payments in the following period. We have further assumed that it is the expected rate of return on bonds, ERr_{bL}, rather than the yield on bonds, r_{bL}, that enters into the determination of portfolio choice. More will be said about this ERr_{bL} rate a bit further. But in the meantime, we note that indeed portfolio decisions of households are forward-looking.

---

[3] If we were to take price inflation into account, the rate of return on cash would be negative and its absolute value would be approximately equal to the rate of inflation. See Chapter 10.

As was the case before, we cannot keep all three of equations (5.9A), (5.10) and (5.11) as given in the above matrix form, otherwise we would run into a problem of over-identification. Equation (5.9A) is thus replaced, in the computer model, by equation (5.9), which simply says that the share of expected wealth which households do not wish to have in bills and bonds must be held in the form of cash money.

Before we examine the various parameters of the asset demand function, one problem must be dealt with right away. The asset demand functions determine the value of money balances, bills and bonds that households would like to hold, given their expectations about income and end-of-period wealth. Following Turnovsky (1977: 134), we assume, in contrast to Brainard and Tobin (1968), that households are able to achieve within the period the shares of assets that they desire, provided they make no forecasting mistakes.[4] The intuitive assumption is that financial markets carry low transaction costs, and hence agents can quickly recover the asset distribution that they want. But what happens when their expectations turn out to be mistaken?

As in Chapter 4, we shall assume that any mistakes in expectations are fully absorbed by fluctuations in money balances. That this assumption seems to be the best one, given the limitations of modelling, seems to be recognized by Backus *et al.* (1980: 288) when they write that 'in the case of demand deposits and currency, which serve as buffers or "temporary abodes of purchasing power", the partial adjustment mechanism seems particularly inappropriate.' Hence, it is best to assume that any unexpected income flows into the money balances of households, as happens here. This is why the money balances *actually* held by households at the end of the period, given by H_h, appear as a residual in equation (5.8). The implications of such an assumption is that households end up holding other assets on the scale that they expected. Thus:

$$B_h = B_d \qquad (5.12)$$

$$BL_h = BL_d \qquad (5.13)$$

5.6.3 The adding-up constraints of portfolio behaviour

As before the adding-up constraints, underlined by Tobin (1969), must hold. This implies the following five *vertical* conditions:

$$\lambda_{10} + \lambda_{20} + \lambda_{30} = 1 \qquad (ADUP.1)$$

---

[4] Brainard and Tobin (1968) as well as Backus *et al.* (1980) focus their attention on the dynamics of adjustment from an arbitrary distribution of assets to the one desired by agents. They are rather silent about the macroeconomic implications developed here.

$$\lambda_{11} + \lambda_{21} + \lambda_{31} = 0 \qquad\qquad \text{(ADUP.2)}$$

$$\lambda_{12} + \lambda_{22} + \lambda_{32} = 0 \qquad\qquad \text{(ADUP.3)}$$

$$\lambda_{13} + \lambda_{23} + \lambda_{33} = 0 \qquad\qquad \text{(ADUP.4)}$$

$$\lambda_{14} + \lambda_{24} + \lambda_{34} = 0 \qquad\qquad \text{(ADUP.5)}$$

Equation (ADUP.1) simply says that the total of the shares of each asset must sum to unity, whatever the actual values taken by the rates of return and disposable income. Thus the sum of the exogenous components must sum to unity. The rule is that in a completely coherent system, people can only have more of one thing by having less of another. The same rule applies to the other vertical constraints. In reality, the λ parameters will be shifting around like mad, as people change opinions on what is appropriate, but they are always subject to the adding-up constraints.

Given the first condition ADUP.1, the next three ADUP equations imply that the *vertical* sum of the coefficients in the rates of return matrix must be zero. These equations ensure that the sum over all assets of responses to a change in any of the rates of return is zero. Similarly, the ADUP.5 equation implies that the response of assets in total to a change in disposable income is zero. These vertical conditions imply that if the change in one of the relevant variables of the portfolio matrix induces an increase in the share devoted to one asset, the shares of the other two assets must decrease. The adding-up requirements thus imply, of course, that some coefficients of the (3×3) matrix above need to be negative. Indeed, here, only λ_{11}, λ_{22}, λ_{33} and λ_{14} are positive.[5] The first three positive coefficients imply that an increase in the 'own' rate of return has a positive impact on the share of wealth held in that form. For instance, a higher rate of interest on bills induces households to hold more bills, while a higher expected rate of return on bonds induces them to hold more bonds. Finally, greater disposable income push households to hold more cash money, by reason of the transactions demand for money.

There is another constraint which, surprisingly, is explicitly present neither in Tobin (1969) nor in the following literature (as far as we know). This additional constraint, which is proposed by Godley (1996: 18), is that the sum of all the coefficients on rates of return, reading *horizontally*, should also sum to zero; more precisely, the coefficient on each positive 'own' rate of return should equal the (negative of) the sum of all the other coefficients in the row. The grounds for introducing this constraint are that the effect on demand for the asset in question of an increase in the own rate of interest,

---

[5] Here λ_{11} is an irrelevant parameter since the return on money is zero. But in a model with deposit money instead of cash money, where deposit money would bring in interest income, the coefficient λ_{11} would also be positive.

with all the other rates remaining constant, should not be any different from that of a fall, of the same size, in all the other rates, with the own rate staying put. We thus have the following *horizontal* constraints:

$$\lambda_{11} = -(\lambda_{12} + \lambda_{13}) \tag{ADUP.6}$$

$$\lambda_{22} = -(\lambda_{21} + \lambda_{23}) \tag{ADUP.7}$$

$$\lambda_{33} = -(\lambda_{31} + \lambda_{32}) \tag{ADUP.8}$$

Some authors, such as Benjamin Friedman (1978) and Karacaoglu (1984), impose instead what they call *symmetry* constraints on the asset demand functions, in addition to Tobin's vertical constraints. These symmetry conditions are of the kind $\lambda_{ij} = \lambda_{ji}$, for all $i \neq j$. In our case, since the rate of return on cash money is nought, only one of these symmetry constraints remains: $\lambda_{23} = \lambda_{32}$. This equality implies that an increase in the expected rate of return on bonds will generate a drop in the holdings of bills that will be of the same amplitude as the drop in the holdings of bonds generated by a similar increase in the rate of interest on bills. In the general case of a three-asset portfolio choice, the symmetry conditions would imply that:

$$\lambda_{12} = \lambda_{21} \tag{ADUP.9}$$

$$\lambda_{13} = \lambda_{31} \tag{ADUP.10}$$

$$\lambda_{23} = \lambda_{32} \tag{ADUP.11}$$

In such a three-asset model, starting from the above symmetry conditions, assigning a value to each of the above three equations (to the six parameters involved), and taking the vertical adding-up constraints into account, will insure that the horizontal conditions are also respected. Thus, the authors who add the symmetry conditions (ADUP.9 to ADUP.11) to the vertical adding-up conditions of the rate-of-return matrix (ADUP.2 to ADUP.4) implicitly fulfil the requirements of the horizontal adding-up conditions (ADUP.6 to ADUP.8).

On the other hand, incorporating the horizontal and the vertical adding-up conditions does not necessarily lead to the symmetric conditions. With three arbitrarily given parameters, and both the vertical and horizontal conditions, there is an infinity of possible sets of parameters, one of which is a set responding to the symmetric conditions. By contrast, starting with three arbitrary parameters, and either vertical or horizontal conditions associated to the symmetry conditions, there is a single set of possible parameters. Making use of the symmetry conditions thus allows one to easily build up a set of rates of return parameters that are consistent with the horizontal and the vertical adding-up constraints.

As an instance take the following numerical values for the symmetric conditions:

$$\lambda_{12} = \lambda_{21} = -0.3$$

$$\lambda_{13} = \lambda_{31} = -0.2$$

$$\lambda_{23} = \lambda_{32} = -0.1$$

Making use in this case of the horizontal sum constraints, we obtain:

$$\lambda_{11} = -(\lambda_{12} + \lambda_{13}) = (0.3 + 0.2) = 0.5$$

$$\lambda_{22} = -(\lambda_{21} + \lambda_{23}) = (0.3 + 0.1) = 0.4$$

$$\lambda_{33} = -(\lambda_{31} + \lambda_{32}) = (0.2 + 0.1) = 0.3$$

and hence the rate of return matrix would look like:

$$\begin{bmatrix} 0.5 & -0.3 & -0.2 \\ -0.3 & 0.4 & -0.1 \\ -0.2 & -0.1 & 0.3 \end{bmatrix}$$

The reader can verify that both the horizontal (by construction) and the vertical adding-up conditions are fulfilled.

5.6.4 The closure of Model *LP*

We now present equations describing the behaviour of the central bank and the government. Equation (5.14) is none other than the government budget constraint.

$$\Delta B_s \equiv B_s - B_{s-1} = (G + r_{b-1} \cdot B_{s-1} + BL_{s-1})$$

$$- (T + r_{b-1} \cdot B_{cb-1}) - \Delta BL_s \cdot p_{bL} \tag{5.14}$$

This constraint is expressed in terms of the additional Treasury bills that are issued within the period. The bills that need to be newly issued are equal to government expenditures, including its interest payments, minus the government revenues – taxes and central bank profits – plus the value of the newly issued long-term bonds. Needless to say, when there is a government surplus, or when the government deficit is financed by new issues of long-term bonds, the change in Treasury bills will be negative and bills will be redeemed.

$$\Delta H_s \equiv H_s - H_{s-1} = \Delta B_{cb} \tag{5.15}$$

$$B_{cb} = B_s - B_h \tag{5.16}$$

$$BL_s = BL_h \tag{5.17}$$

Equation (5.15) above reflects the capital account constraint of the central bank. As pointed out earlier, we assume that central banks only purchase bills, and not bonds. The amount of cash money supplied by central banks is simply equal to the amount of bills purchased by the central bank. In turn, as shown by equation (5.16), the amount of bills purchased by the central bank is equal to the difference between the outstanding amount of bills supplied by government and the amount of bills that households end up holding. Finally, equation (5.17) says that the amount of bonds supplied by government is equal to the amount of bonds demanded by households. These last two equations are thus saying that the (net) supply of bills and the supply of bonds are provided passively, in response to demand.

One way to interpret equations (5.15)–(5.17) is to rely on the following story. Suppose that households do not want to hold so many bonds, either because of a change in their liquidity preference (the parameter λ_{30} goes up while parameter λ_{20} goes down), or because they expect a fall in the price of bonds. Households will thus offer part of their holdings of bonds for sale. We can assume that the central bank purchases the offered bonds at the previously set price, and immediately turns around, asking the Treasury to redeem the bonds so obtained, exchanging them for new issues of bills of an equivalent amount. This story is compatible with equation (5.14), which says that the government issues new bills as a response to a government deficit and as a response to changes in the value of newly issued or newly retired bonds. With this story, the quantity of bonds outstanding depends on the demand for bonds, so that we do have $BL_s = BL_h$, while the central bank still only hold bills.

We now come to various definitions or relations which relate to variables that have been used in previous equations, but without our having defined what they were equal to. We start with the definitions that were explained at the beginning of the chapter, in sections 5.2 and 5.3. Equation (5.18) defines the expected rate of return on bonds, while equation (5.19) defines the yield on bonds, as a function of the price that the bond carries at the end of the current period.[6]

$$ERr_{bL} = r_{bL} + \chi \cdot \frac{(p^e_{bL} - p_{bL})}{p_{bL}} \tag{5.18}$$

$$r_{bL} = \frac{1}{p_{bL}} \tag{5.19}$$

We need also to define some expected values. First, it should again be stated that p^e_{bL} represents the price of bonds which, with some given conviction χ, is expected to occur in the future (in the next period, at time $t+1$). The expectation is entertained during the current period (at time t), and this is why it carries no time subscript. Second, we could assume that expectations regarding the price of bonds in the next period is a given in the model, a parameter that we do not try to explain, something that depends on a convention firmly established among households, and which may not be moved or modified easily by the monetary authorities. That would be equation (5.20A).

$$p^e_{bL} = \bar{p}^e_{bL} \tag{5.20A}$$

However, as a means of freezing the implications of bond price expectations, we shall initially assume that households expect the current bond price to remain the same in the next period. This implies the following equality:

$$p^e_{bL} = p_{bL} \tag{5.20}$$

In general, if bond price expectations differ from current prices, expectations regarding capital gains to be realized or accrued *in the next period* are assumed to be based on the calculations made in the current period to assess the expected rate of return on bonds. The expected capital gains CG^e are thus given by the χ weighted product of the expected change in bond prices (relative to the bond price of the current period) and the acquired number of bonds. Naturally, if equation (5.20) rather than (5.20A) applies, expected capital gains or losses are nil, and equation (5.21) plays no role.

$$CG^e = \chi \cdot (p^e_{bL} - p_{bL}) \cdot BL_h \tag{5.21}$$

Finally, there remains the expected level of regular disposable income YD^e_r. One assumption we make, as in Chapter 4, is that expected regular income is simply the regular income of the previous period:

$$YD^e_r = YD_{r-1} \tag{5.22}$$

---

[6] See Appendix 5.2 for some implications about the so-called liquidity trap.

Another assumption we have made in simulations is that expectations are governed by a random process. Alternative assumptions will give yet other results, but it is a property of all these models that errors in expectations have counterparts in end-period stock variables which will correct matters in succeeding periods.[7]

We now have 22 equations and 24 possible variables: Y, YD_r, YD_r^e, T, V, V^e, C, H_h, H_d, B_h, B_d, BL_h, BL_d, H_s, B_s, B_{cb}, BL_s, p_{bL}, p_{bL}^e, CG, CG^e, ERr_{bL}, r_{bL} and r_b. There are thus two equations that are needed to complete the model. The remaining two equations, equations (5.23) and (5.24) indicate that in such a world, it is possible in this preliminary exposition for the government sector to fix both the rate of interest on bills and the rate of interest on bonds, the latter by fixing the price of government bonds (in the simulations, the bill rate and the price of bonds are treated as parameters).

$$r_b = \bar{r}_b \tag{5.23}$$

$$p_{bL} = \bar{p}_{bL} \tag{5.24}$$

The equivalence between the supply of cash and holdings of cash, that is, the equality $H_s = H_h$ which arises from the balance sheet matrix of Table 5.1, will again be treated as the missing or redundant equation.

The assumption that both the short and the long rates of interest may be set exogenously contradicts the usual presumption that central banks or central governments are only able to influence short-term rates, such as the Treasury bill rate, while long-term rates are necessarily market-determined. We see that this need not be the case. It is possible under these assumptions for the monetary authorities, here defined generally as the central bank plus the Treasury department, to fix both the short and the long rates, r_b and r_{bL}. In other words, it is possible for the monetary authorities to set the yield curve. Indeed, for a long time, monetary authorities were keen in fixing both the bill rate and the bond rate. This was particularly the case right after the Second World War, when government debts were enormous, as a result of the huge war effort that had produced large annual government deficits. It was then important for rates of interest to be pegged at low rates, to avoid an excessive

---

[7] Expectations in a discrete time model, by contrast to a continuous time model, can be tricky. What we assume here is that there is a time sequence in household decisions. Households make their consumption decisions early on during the current period, at a time when they don't know yet what their exact regular income for the period will be, and when they don't yet have information about the bond prices of the current period. This is why they rely on the regular income of the previous period and on the wealth that they had accumulated at the end of the previous period. By contrast, when households decide to allocate their wealth, we assume this is done towards the end of the current period, at which point they have proper information about the interest rates that they are being offered and the current bond prices.

amount of debt servicing. Because investors knew that the long-term interest rate was pegged, it could be set at very low levels, because investors did not fear capital losses.

In the United States, the Treasury-Fed Accord of 1951 freed the Federal Reserve from its obligation to peg both short and long rates (Hetzel and Leach 2001). Gradually, elsewhere in the world, monetary authorities renounced intervention so as to fix the long-term rate of interest, letting it fluctuate according to the so-called market forces. Central banks kept a direct control on short rates only – the Treasury bill rate initially, and then the inter-bank overnight rate (called the federal funds rate in the United States).

But the present model implies that it is quite possible for monetary authorities to set both the short and the long rates, as the chairman of the Fed, Alan Greenspan, reminded us in 2003. All that is needed, as shown by equations (5.13) and (5.14), is for the central bank to purchase the Treasury bills left over by the households, at the set bill rate, while the Treasury supplies whatever long-term bonds are demanded by households, matching demand whatever it is at the bond price (and hence bond rate) set by the Treasury or the monetary authorities. Things are made easier when the public accepts the new bond price (equation 5.20 then applies), but we shall see later what happens when the public holds on to its expectations about future bond prices (when equation 5.20A applies).

5.7   The short-run and long-run impact of higher interest rates on real demand

Suppose there is an unexpected increase in the interest rates set by the monetary authorities, taking all participants in financial markets by surprise. There is no difficulty in incorporating such an increase in the bill rate, but things are a bit more tricky with respect to bonds. We emphasized that the demand for bonds depends on the expected rate of return. If financial participants expect a fall in the price of bonds, that is, they expect high rates of interest on bonds, this implies a low, possibly, a negative rate of return on existing bonds. Households, expecting such a low rate of return, would reduce the size of their bond holdings. However, if the Treasury *unexpectedly* decides to lower the price of long-term bonds, thus increasing the long rate, then there ought to be an increase in the demand for bonds, since, as long as no further negative changes in bond prices are anticipated, the expected rate of return is now higher, equal to the new rate of interest on long-term bonds. Indeed this is precisely what will occur if equation (5.20) holds, that is, when $p_{bL}^e = p_{bL}$ at all times.

Assume that this is what occurs, with the Treasury bill rate rising from 3% to 4%, while the new price of bonds is such that the long rate is hiked from 5% to 6.66% (the price of bonds drops from 20 to 15 dollars), with the expected rate of return on bonds rising by the same amount, due to the assumed expectation that no further change in bond prices will be forthcoming. The most important point of this experiment is that the fall in bond prices induces an immediate reduction in wealth. Interest rates have a big effect on asset prices and this is one of the main conduits for monetary policy – working in the conventional way. A rise in interest rates reduces demand for a time – in Model *LP* this is achieved by a reduction in consumption expenditures, with a lag, through the reduction in the wealth term that appears in the consumption function. And this puts the earlier unconventional result of Chapter 4 into a proper perspective. Model *LP* shows that interest rate increases do have a negative effect on real demand, but this negative effect is only a temporary one (which may still last for quite a long time). In a longer period, the effect of higher interest rates is positive as we said before.

Once again, it is easy to ascertain the steady-state (implicit) solutions of the model, by noting that in the stationary state the government budget must be in balance. Starting from equations (5.14) and (5.3), a balanced budget implies that:

$$(G + r_b \cdot B_h^* + BL_s^*) = T = \theta \cdot (Y + r_b \cdot B_h^* + BL_h^*)$$

Therefore GDP in the stationary state is equal to:

$$Y^* = \frac{\{G + (r_b \cdot B_h^* + BL_s^*) \cdot (1 - \theta)\}}{\theta} = \frac{G_{NT}}{\theta}$$

where, as in Chapter 4, G_{NT} stands for total government expenditures, including all interest payments to households, *net* of taxes, and where G_{NT}/θ is the *fiscal stance*.

The following figures, which should be considered together, illustrate what happens. Figure 5.2 shows the effect on the wealth to disposable income ratio. There is an extremely large initial reduction because the fall in the prices of long-term bonds has caused a huge capital loss for households. The fall in this ratio is quickly made good because, one period later, as Figure 5.3 shows, there is a large fall in disposable income (and GDP) – the result of lower consumption via the wealth effect. However, as with Model *PC* of Chapter 4, the long-run effect of increasing interest rates is to raise aggregate income, despite the initial negative wealth effect. The steady-state income level (GDP or household disposable income) is still a positive function of the rates of interest, for reasons similar to those detailed in Chapter 4. Finally,

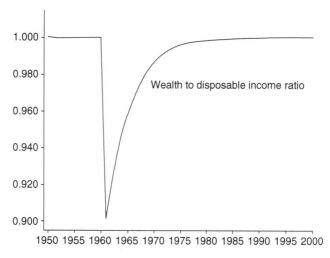

Figure 5.2   Evolution of the wealth to disposable income ratio, following an increase in both the short-term and long-term interest rates, with Model *LP1*

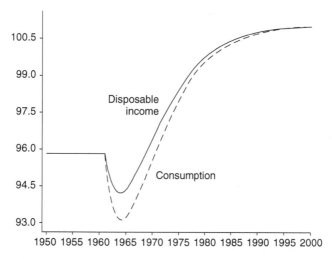

Figure 5.3   Evolution of household consumption and disposable income, following an increase in both the short-term and long-term interest rates, with Model *LP1*

Figure 5.4 shows how wealth is allocated between the two kinds of securities. The share taken by long-term securities rises, since we assumed a more substantial increase in the yield on bonds, notwithstanding the capital loss on the opening stock, so the government must be held to issue long-term securities on a potentially massive scale to match increased demand.

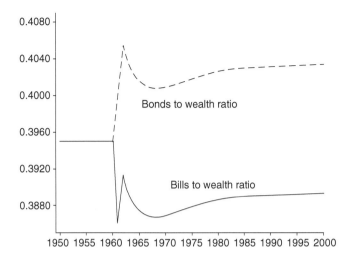

Figure 5.4 Evolution of the bonds to wealth ratio and the bills to wealth ratio, following an increase from 3% to 4% in the short-term interest rate, while the long-term interest rate moves from 5% to 6.67%, with Model *LP1*

5.8 The effect of household liquidity preference on long rates

5.8.1 Targeted proportions of the liabilities of Government

The Treasury must issue or retire long bonds on a massive scale whenever there is a substantial change in the price of bonds targeted by the Treasury, or alternatively, when the public modifies its expectations about the future level of bond prices. This may help to explain why, in the real world, long-term rates of interest tend to be under the control of market forces. The purpose of this section is to explain how the preferences or the expectations of households could have an impact on the differential between the Treasury bill rate and the bond rate.

In the previous sections, with equation (5.20), it was assumed that households never considered a change in the future price of bonds relative to the current price. It is now time to give more leeway to household liquidity preference. Assume that the evolution of expectations regarding future bond prices follows the following rule:

$$\Delta p^e_{bL} = -\beta_e (p^e_{bL-1} - p_{bL}) + add \qquad (5.20B)$$

This difference equation insures that in the long run realized and expected values are equal. The random element *add* gives a boost one way or another, when we wish to introduce some independent change in liquidity preference on the part of households (meaning here a change in what households consider future normal bond yields will be). The future bond price that is expected by households may thus differ from the current bond price, either because the current price was modified by a decision of the government, or because households have modified their views with regard to the future.

We now introduce a mechanism that would explain how the liquidity preference of the public could have an impact on the price of long-term bonds, even when the central bank is trying to set both the bill rate and the price of bonds. The mechanism, one among many possible ones, is described with the help of four equations, one that replaces a previous equation of Model *LP*, and three new equations. We now assume that the price of bonds set by the Treasury is not a constant anymore, so that we drop the last equation of Model *LP*, equation (5.24), and replace it by the following equations:

$$p_{bL} = (1 + z_1 \cdot \beta - z_2 \cdot \beta) \cdot p_{bL-1} \tag{5.24A}$$

$$z_1 = 1 \quad \text{iff } TP > top \tag{5.25}$$

$$z_2 = 1 \quad \text{iff } TP < bot \tag{5.26}$$

$$TP = \frac{BL_{h-1} \cdot p_{bL-1}}{BL_{h-1} \cdot p_{bL-1} + B_{h-1}} \tag{5.27}$$

The price of bonds depends on whether a certain target proportion, here called *TP*, is kept within its target range. The proportion in question is the ratio of the value of long-term bonds outstanding to the total value of bonds and bills in the hands of households, as defined by equation (5.27). When the targeted proportion exceeds the top of the range, called *top*, the Treasury lets bond prices float upwards. When the targeted proportion falls below the bottom of the range, called *bot*, the Treasury lets bond prices float downwards.

The logic behind this behaviour is the following. Although the monetary authorities passively provide households with the assets of their choice, at the interest rates set by the monetary authorities or the Treasury, it is presumed that the Treasury prefers to preserve the composition of its debt towards the general public within a certain range, preferring not to have all of its eggs in the same basket. The value of its long-term debt should not exceed a certain target value as a ratio of its total debt held by households; and similarly, the value of its short-term debt, as a percentage of its total debt *vis-à-vis* the households, should not exceed a certain percentage.

The reader may note a certain degree of similarity with the assumption which is sometimes entertained in some macroeconomic models, where it is assumed that the government or the monetary authorities wish to restrain the proportion of the government deficit that is financed by issuing money, as was recalled in Chapter 4. Here it is assumed that government wishes to restrain the proportion of its stock of debt which is financed by bills issued to the private sector. In both cases, interest rates (here long-term rates only) become endogenous, because the preferences of households may not be consistent with the proportions set as a target by the government sector.

So what happens is the following. Suppose, for some reason, that the share of the value of outstanding long-term bonds is exceeding the upper part of the range targeted by the monetary authorities, called *top*. Since this share is essentially demand determined, this implies that there is a high demand, by households, for such a kind of asset. The monetary authorities will respond by letting the prices of bonds drift upwards, thus moving along the lines drawn by market forces. The Treasury is thus leaning with the wind. When demand is low and the share of long-term bonds is falling below the lower part of the range, below *bot*, the Treasury will respond by letting bond prices drift downwards.

We may conduct two different experiments. In the first experiment, assume that the government decides to increase the bill rate, but this time without modifying bond yields. This should lead to a fall in the demand for bonds and hence a fall in the *TP* ratio, the bonds to bills ratio. If the ratio falls below the bottom range, this will induce the central bank to let the price of bonds fall. This will drive up the bond yield r_{bL} and generate temporary expected capital gains; these two effects in turn will induce households to hold more bonds, thus driving the economy back towards the target *TP* range. As a result, in this model, a permanent one-shot increase in the bill rate generates in the end a higher bond rate, as one would expect. There is a link between the two interest rates. All this is shown in Figures 5.5 and 5.6 which illustrate the consequences of the initial increase in the bill rate.

As a second experiment, assume that household portfolio holders now expect a fall in the price of bonds, believing that a new, higher, long rate of interest ought to rule the economy. The random element of equation (5.20A) now kicks in. This change in the value of the expected price of bonds implies that long-term bond holders expect a capital loss. The expected rate of return on bonds is thus lower than the yield on bonds. We have the inequality: $ERr_{bL} < r_{bL}$. This implies, from equations (5.9A), (5.10) and (5.11), that households now desire to hold fewer bonds, and more bills and cash money. As long as we assume that the government and the central bank are impervious to any change in the composition of the debt, this would have no effect whatsoever on the long-term rate of interest. However, in the modified model – Model *LP2* – the change in the expectations of households, if large enough, will have repercussions on the price of bonds and hence on the long interest rate. With expectations of a fall in the price of bonds, less long-term

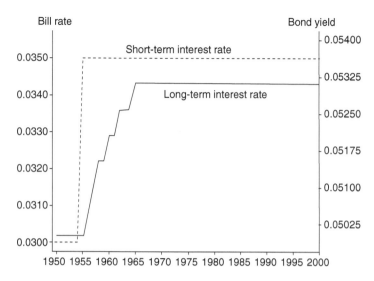

Figure 5.5 Evolution of the long-term interest rate (the bond yield), following an increase in the short-term interest rate (the bill rate), as a result of the response of the central bank and the Treasury, with Model *LP2*

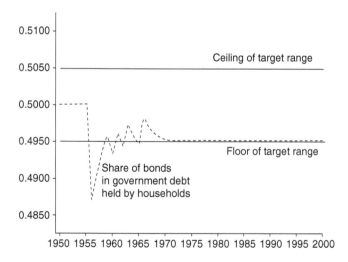

Figure 5.6 Evolution of the target proportion (TP), that is the share of bonds in the government debt held by households, following an increase in the short-term interest rate (the bill rate) and the response of the central bank and of the Treasury, with Model *LP2*

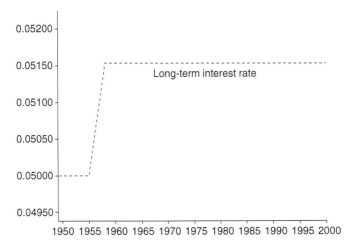

Figure 5.7 Evolution of the long-term interest rate, following an anticipated fall in the price of bonds, as a consequence of the response of the central bank and of the Treasury, with Model *LP2*

bonds will be demanded by households, and if this change is large enough, the proportion *TP* of bonds to total securities held by households will fall below the bottom of the targeted range, inducing the Treasury to reduce the price of bonds that it sets.

The reduction in the price of bonds will have two stabilizing effects that will take place in the next period. First, the fall in bond prices will lead to an increase in the rate of interest on long-term bonds r_{bL} as is well-known, and as illustrated with Figure 5.7. Second, since households adjust their expectations with regard to future bond prices only gradually, the expected capital loss will have been reduced by virtue of the decrease in the actual bond price. This is shown in Figure 5.8. As a result, in the next period, the expected rate of return on long-term bonds will have risen, and the demand for bonds by households will pick up, eventually leading the proportion *TP* back inside its target range, as shown in Figure 5.9.

Figures 5.7 and 5.9 shows that market expectations may have an impact on realized financial outcomes, if the monetary authorities are swayed by the pressures exercised by market participants. It should be emphasized however that this is a discretionary decision of the monetary authorities, based on a convention – the target range of long-term bonds as a proportion of the government debt towards the public. Long-term interest rates react to modifications in the liquidity preference of households because the monetary authorities and the Treasury wish to enforce the convention that they have imposed upon themselves.

158

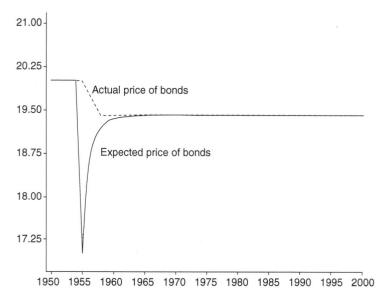

Figure 5.8 Evolution of the expected and actual bond prices, following an anticipated fall in the price of bonds, as a consequence of the response of the central bank and of the Treasury, with Model *LP2*

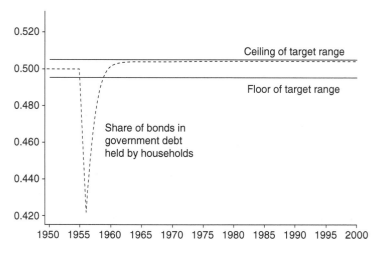

Figure 5.9 Evolution of the target proportion (*TP*), that is the share of bonds in the government debt held by households, following an anticipated fall in the price of bonds, as a consequence of the response of the central bank and of the Treasury, with Model *LP2*

5.8.2 Various explanations of the yield curve

The above exercise clearly shows that the liquidity preference of households can have an impact on real flows and the distribution of asset stocks. With the expanded model, Model *LP2*, we understand more easily why long-term bond rates may be left to the vagaries of the conventions used by private agents: governments may have decided in advance the proportions of short- and long-term debt that they wish to be responsible for, and hence they will accept to lean with the wind when these proportions threaten to get out of range.

The above model also shows that, as long as assets are not perfect substitutes, which is an assumption embedded in the Tobin portfolio model that we use here, there are *relative asset supply effects*. If the Treasury provides more long-term securities, the long-term yield diminishes compared to the bill rate. In our model, it is possible for the monetary authorities and the Treasury to modify the yield curve by changing relative asset supplies.[8]

Model *LP* thus potentially illustrates all possible explanations of the interest rate term structure, also called the time yield curve. On the one hand, there is the *expectations* theory, which says that long-term rates should reflect expected future short-term rates. On the other hand, there is the *market segmentation* theory or the *preferred habitat* theory, which claim that agents have strong preferences for some types of assets, for instance short-term assets, in which case these theories can also be associated with a *liquidity premium* theory, which asserts that the yield curve is normally upward-sloping. In the case of the segmentation theory, because assets are far from being perfect substitutes, 'the shape of the yield curve will be affected by "local" supply and demand conditions' (Howells and O'Hara 1999: 555), as is the case here.

In our portfolio equations, as shown in their matrix form, the segmentation or liquidity theories are reflected by the presence of the λ_{i0} vector of coefficients, which indicates the proportions in which agents would like to hold the various assets, regardless of their rates of return. By contrast, the λ_{ij} matrix that applies to the various rates of return reflects the impact of expectations regarding future interest rates on asset demand functions. With the expectations theory of the yield curve, if agents expect a string of higher short-term interest rates on bills, they will be indifferent to purchasing bonds only if long-term interest rates rise as well. On the basis of such a rise in long-term rates, they will expect falling bond prices, and hence agents will entertain a lower expected rate of return on bonds. This, as we have seen in the previous simulation with our expanded Model (*LP2*), should indeed lead to a steeper yield curve. Hence the steeper yield curve could be explained by future interest rate expectations, or by a change in liquidity preference.

---

[8] The extreme version of this model, whereby governments fix the supply of bonds, rather than the price of bonds, can be found in Appendix 5.3.

5.9   Making government expenditures endogenous

A key feature of all the models presented up to now is that pure government expenditures G are assumed to be exogenous. In fact, this assumption is required for a determinate solution of the model to exist. Without exogenous pure government expenditures, there would be no multiplicand.

Still, there is no reason to believe that pure government expenditures are impervious to what is going on in the rest of the economy. For instance, in an otherwise growing economy, one would believe that pure government expenditures would also be growing. What we want to underline in the present context is the sensitivity of pure government expenditures to the budget position of government. Previous experiments have shown, as one would expect, that increased interest rates on long-term bonds initially lead to a fall in the value of long-term bonds and in the value of household wealth. The increase in interest payments on bills also leads, initially, to an increase in the budget deficit of government. This effect on public deficits is further reinforced, in the initial stages, by the negative effects that high interest rates have on wealth. Because consumption depends on wealth, the large capital losses induced by the higher interest rates induce a reduction in consumption and national income, and this in turn leads to falling tax revenues for the government sector, and hence to even larger deficits.

These negative effects on the government budget are eventually reversed, because households gradually reconstruct their wealth through saving, so that government revenues rise again, so much that in the new steady state, national income is now higher, due to the larger payments on the debt. But this result is achieved because it has been assumed all along that pure government expenditures were impervious to the apparition of large budget deficits.

But this may not necessarily be so. Atul Sood (1999) has shown that high real interest rates lead to higher government deficits in the short-run, as must obviously be the case, but he has also shown that these higher interest rates often lead to reduced primary deficits, that is to higher primary surpluses, which are defined as the difference between government tax income and pure government expenditures $(T - G)$. In other words, at some point, when the deficit gets too large, governments aim at controlling public deficits, and to do so they reduce their pure government expenditures – the services that they offer on education, wealth, transport and so on.

Sood (1999) shows these results using the so-called *Granger-causality* analysis. This econometric method attempts to assess causality from a temporal point of view. For instance, interest rates are said to 'cause' deficits if it can be shown that past values of interest rates add some explanatory power to the past values of deficits in explaining current deficit values. In that specific meaning of causality, Sood shows that higher real interest rates 'cause' larger overall deficits, more precisely higher deficit to GDP ratios, but then also 'cause' larger primary surpluses and larger primary surplus to GDP ratios, when governments decide to cut down on pure government expenditures in an effort to fight off the public deficits.

Of course, such behaviour does not necessarily occur in all countries, but Sood shows that it describes fairly well the evolution of the fiscal stance of major countries such as the United States, Canada, France and Germany, as well as that of a few less developed countries such as India, over the last thirty years of the twentieth century.

Such government behaviour can be easily modelled within the framework of Model *LP* – in *LP3*. This behaviour is described by equations (5.28) to (5.31).

$$PSBR = (G + r_{b-1} \cdot B_{s-1} + BL_{s-1}) - (T + r_{b-1} \cdot B_{cb-1}) \tag{5.28}$$

$$z_3 = 1 \quad \text{iff} \quad \left(\frac{PSBR_{-1}}{Y_{-1}} \right) > 3\% \tag{5.29}$$

$$z_4 = 1 \quad \text{iff} \quad \left(\frac{PSBR_{-1}}{Y_{-1}} \right) < -3\% \tag{5.30}$$

$$G = G_{-1} - (z_3 + z_4) \cdot \beta_g \cdot PSBR_{-1} + add_2 \tag{5.31}$$

It has been assumed that politicians are concerned with the deficit to GDP ratio, here called $PSBR/Y$.[9] When this ratio exceeds a certain threshold, this triggers fiscal austerity, as governments reduce their pure government expenditures relative to the level achieved in the previous period. The reduction is assumed to be a certain fraction β_g of the deficit incurred in the previous period. In the current case, this occurs automatically when the ratio exceeds 3%, as suggested in various documents pertaining the European union, in particular in the Treaty of Maastricht. We also assume that there is a symmetric response when there is a large budget surplus.

All this could have been made more complicated. We could have assumed for instance that government expenditures are also reduced whenever the government has a large debt ratio, for instance 60%, once again as suggested in the Maastricht Treaty, even when it is running modest deficits relative to

[9] Since the deficits of governments involve the issue of assets, government deficits are often known under the name of *public sector borrowing requirement*. From hence arises the acronym *PSBR* that is often used in discussions of public policy and that we have also picked up to designate the size of government budget deficits.

the size of GDP.[10] We could also have further assumed that governments trigger ever harsher austerity policies when both the debt and the deficit ratios are being exceeded. Possibilities can quickly be multiplied with these sorts of conditional reaction functions.

What is important to note is that the model so developed, Model *LP3*, is an instance of *hysteresis*. The model offers determinate steady-state solutions only as long as the austerity measures are not triggered. As soon as these are triggered, pure government expenditures *G*, which in all the previous formalizations were the key multiplicand exogenous variable, also become an endogenous variable. As a result there is no *determinate* steady-state solution to the model. The system does tend towards a long-run equilibrium, but this steady-state solution is not independent of the path taken by the system. The steady state depends on the past history of the economic system under study. It depends on the values taken by the various endogenous variables, in particular the deficit to income ratio (and the debt to disposable income ratio if this ratio were to be taken into account). The model is now *path-dependent*. To find out the steady-state values to be taken by the various endogenous variables, one needs to know the exact path taken by the economy. Such a system, where the exogenous variables become in fact endogenous and dependent on the previous values taken by the main endogenous variables, is an instance of *deep endogeneity*. In such a case, the 'evolution of a system may be best described, not by equilibria, but by "contemporaneous" values of variables, expressed in terms of their own past history' (Setterfield 1993).

In previous formalizations of Model *LP*, the amplitude of the recession induced by a negative shock had no impact whatsoever on the final steady-state equilibrium. This stationary state only depended on the new rate of interest, the level of government expenditures, the tax rate, and various saving and portfolio parameters. Eventually, the economy would get to this pre-defined new stationary state. For instance, as shown by Figure 5.10, decrease in the propensity to save has a negative short-run impact on gross domestic product, but eventually, as was discussed in great detail in Chapter 4, the larger amounts of government debt payments lead to higher household disposable income and national income in the new stationary state.

With the present formalization, as described by equations (5.28) to (5.31), the amplitude and possibly the length of the recession might have an impact

---

[10] Dealing with the debt of government is however more complicated than dealing with its deficit since the recorded debt, based on historical accounts, will be different from the value of debt, as measured here, since the latter depends on its market value, which will be different from its historically measured value whenever there have been changes in the prices of long-term bonds. Presumably, it is this historically measured debt – the sum of past deficits – which is of concern to accountants, rating agencies and government bureaucrats.

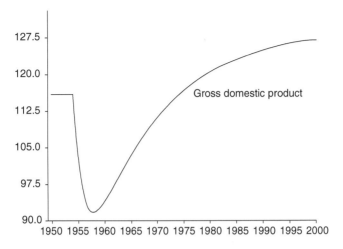

Figure 5.10 Evolution of national income (GDP), following a sharp decrease in the propensity to consume out of current income, with Model *LP1*

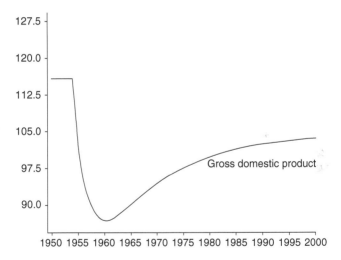

Figure 5.11 Evolution of national income (GDP), following a sharp decrease in the propensity to consume out of current income, with Model *LP3*

on the final stationary state. If the recession induced by higher rates of interest trigger large government deficits, relative to income, these deficits will induce the politicians and bureaucrats to cut into government expenditures. As a result, the new stationary state might turn out to be one with lower national

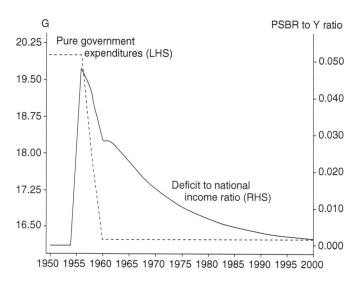

Figure 5.12 Evolution of pure government expenditures and of the government deficit to national income ratio (the PSBR to GDP ratio), following a sharp decrease in the propensity to consume out of current income, with Model *LP3*

income, rather than one with higher national income, as was the case with previous formalizations of Models *PC* and *LP*.

This is illustrated with the help of Figures 5.11 and 5.12. Figure 5.11 shows the evolution of national income. Gross domestic product falls into a recession, but the recovery is insufficient to reach the initial steady state, or even to go beyond it, in contrast to the situation described by Figure 5.10. With Model *LP3*, what happens is that the recovery is hindered by the austerity triggered by the high deficit to income ratio *(PSBR/Y)*. Figure 5.12 shows the evolution of the deficit to income ratio, and that of government expenditures (measured on a different scale). Government expenditures start to drop in the period that follows the exceedingly high deficit to income ratio, that is whenever that ratio exceeds the 3% rate. The final equilibrium – the new steady state – will thus depend on the reaction parameter of the government, and it will depend on what governments consider to be an unacceptable deficit to GDP ratio. There is thus time-dependence. The new stationary state depends on what happens in the transitional states.

Standard Keynesian policy requires that governments increase their expenditures (or reduce tax rates) when the economy enters a recession, or even better, whenever the economy threatens to slow down. This is Abba Lerner's *functional finance*. While it is far from certain that governments followed these principles even in the heyday of Keynesianism, in the 1980s several governments (but not the American governments of Ronald Reagan and

George H.W. Bush!) have reverted to the so-called *Treasury view*, that Keynes objected so much to in the 1930s. When following the *Treasury view*, governments reduce their pure expenditures when their tax revenues decrease, thus acting like most households would when their incomes drop. The advocates of the *Treasury view* argued that governments ought to reduce their expenditures and the fiscal deficit in a slowdown because by doing so, the government would provide room for the private sector, allowing the private sector to collect the funds and the saving necessary for its investment expenditures – so that it does not *crowd-out* the private sector. In the models presented up to now, there is no private sector investment, so this kind of argument cannot really be debated. However, we have seen that it is possible for the central bank to set the interest rate of its choice, whatever the budgetary position of government. The rate of interest on bills or bonds can be made independent of the deficit or the debt ratios. In other words, in our models, the rate of interest is not determined by debt or deficit ratios; rather, changes in interest rates will have an impact on the evolution of government deficits and government debt.

Appendix 5.1: Equations of Model *LP*

$$Y \equiv C + G \tag{5.1}$$

$$YD_r \equiv Y - T + r_{b-1} \cdot B_{h-1} + BL_{h-1} \tag{5.2}$$

$$T = \theta \cdot (Y + r_{b-1} \cdot B_{h-1} + BL_{h-1}) \quad \theta < 1 \tag{5.3}$$

$$V \equiv V_{-1} + (YD_r - C) + CG \tag{5.4}$$

$$CG = \Delta p_{bL} \cdot BL_{h-1} \tag{5.5}$$

$$C = \alpha_1 \cdot YD_r^e + \alpha_2 \cdot V_{-1} \quad 0 < \alpha_2 < \alpha_1 < 1 \tag{5.6}$$

$$V^e \equiv V_{-1} + (YD_r^e - C) + CG^e \tag{5.7}$$

$$H_h = V - B_h - p_{bL} \cdot BL_h \tag{5.8}$$

$$H_d = V^e - B_d - p_{bL} \cdot BL_d \tag{5.9}$$

$$\frac{H_d}{V^e} = \lambda_{10} + \lambda_{12} \cdot r_b + \lambda_{13} \cdot ERr_{bL} + \lambda_{14} \cdot \left(\frac{YD_r^e}{V^e}\right) \tag{5.9A}$$

$$\frac{B_d}{V^e} = \lambda_{20} + \lambda_{22} \cdot r_b + \lambda_{23} \cdot ERr_{bL} + \lambda_{24} \cdot \left(\frac{YD_r^e}{V^e}\right) \tag{5.10}$$

$$\frac{BL_d \cdot p_{bL}}{V^e} = \lambda_{30} + \lambda_{32} \cdot r_b + \lambda_{33} \cdot ERr_{bL} + \lambda_{34} \cdot \left(\frac{YD_r^e}{V^e}\right) \tag{5.11}$$

$$B_h = B_d \tag{5.12}$$

$$BL_h = BL_d \tag{5.13}$$

$$\Delta B_s \equiv B_s - B_{s-1} \equiv (G + r_{b-1} \cdot B_{s-1} + BL_{s-1}) - (T + r_{b-1} \cdot B_{cb-1})$$

$$- \Delta BL_s \cdot p_{bL} \tag{5.14}$$

$$\Delta H_s \equiv H_s - H_{s-1} \equiv \Delta B_{cb} \tag{5.15}$$

$$B_{cb} = B_s - B_h \tag{5.16}$$

$$BL_s = BL_h \tag{5.17}$$

$$ERr_{bL} = r_{bL} + \chi \cdot \frac{(p_{bL}^e - p_{bL})}{p_{bL}} \tag{5.18}$$

$$r_{bL} = \frac{1}{p_{bL}} \tag{5.19}$$

$$p_{bL}^e = p_{bL} \tag{5.20}$$

$$CG^e = \chi \cdot (p_{bL}^e - p_{bL}) \cdot BL_h \tag{5.21}$$

$$YD_r^e = YD_{r-1} \tag{5.22}$$

$$r_b = \bar{r}_b \tag{5.23}$$

$$p_{bL} = \bar{p}_{bL} \tag{5.24}$$

Hidden equation: $H_s = H_h$

Expanded Model LP2:

$$\Delta p_{bL}^e = -\beta_e \cdot (p_{bL-1}^e - p_{bL}) + add \tag{5.20b}$$

$$p_{bL} = (1 + z_1 \cdot \beta - z_2 \cdot \beta) \cdot p_{bL-1} + add1 \tag{5.24A}$$

$$z_1 = 1 \quad \text{iff } TP > top \tag{5.25}$$

$$z_2 = 1 \quad \text{iff } TP < bot \tag{5.26}$$

$$TP = \frac{BL_{h-1} \cdot p_{bL-1}}{(BL_{h-1} \cdot p_{bL-1} + B_{h-1})} \tag{5.27}$$

Expanded Model LP3:

$$PSBR = (G + r_b \cdot B_{s-1} + BL_{s-1}) - (T + r_b \cdot B_{cb-1}) \tag{5.28}$$

$$z_3 = 1 \quad \text{iff} \quad \left(\frac{PSBR_{-1}}{Y_{-1}} \right) > 3\% \tag{5.29}$$

$$z_4 = 1 \quad \text{iff} \quad \left(\frac{PSBR_{-1}}{Y_{-1}} \right) < -3\% \tag{5.30}$$

$$G = G_{-1} - (z_3 + z_4) \cdot \beta_g \cdot PSBR_{-1} + add2 \tag{5.31}$$

Appendix 5.2: The liquidity trap

We first assume that it is possible for the monetary authorities to set any interest rate on long-term bonds although we have already identified possible qualification to this hypothesis: what if the Treasury is targeting a certain range with regard to the proportion of its debt that ought to be held in the form bills by the general public? We have seen that if households entertain expectations about the price of bonds which are different from the actual price, this will imply possibly massive switches of holdings between bonds and bills, thus inducing the monetary authorities to change bond prices in the direction expected by households.

It should also be pointed out that, when long-term interest rates are low, massive transfers from bonds to bills are more likely. The reason for this is that a very small differential between the expected rate and the current rate, when the current rate is low, is bound to engineer large capital losses for those holding bonds, and hence lead to a large negative expected rate of return on long-term bonds. This can be seen quite easily. Recall that the holder of a perpetuity is to receive one dollar of interest revenue at the end of the following year. What change in bond prices would be sufficient for the expected capital loss to wipe out the actual interest revenue? Obviously, the required change in bond prices is just one dollar. If the actual bond price is $25, a fall in the expected bond price to $24 will do the trick; and similarly, an expected bond price of $9 when the actual price is 10$ will also bring the expected rate of return down to zero. The implications for the expected change in the long-term rate of interest are quite different in both cases, however. With a $25 bond price, the long-term rate is 4%, and the required change is 16.6 percentage points, or an expected interest rate of 4.166%; when the bond price is $10, the long-term rate is 10%, and the required change in the long-term rate is 111 percentage points, or an expected long-term rate of 11.11%. This is the so-called *squares law* that Keynes (1936: 202, 207) associated with the possibility of a liquidity trap in the case of long-term assets.

At low long-term rates of interest, a small variation in the expected future rate will cause a substantial drop in the expected rate of return on long-term securities, and hence massive transfers from bonds to bill holdings by households. If the monetary authorities wish to peg low long-term rates, they must be willing to absorb these massive transfers. At higher rates of interest, the effects of a similar variation in expected future rates will have much a minor impact on the expected rate of return and on portfolio allocation. Thus it will be much more difficult for the monetary authorities to peg low long-term interest rates compared to high long-term rates. The cause of this is not the low yield, but rather the fear of a substantial capital loss that a small variation in the actual long-term rate could impose (Kregel 1985: 136).

Keynes's squares law can easily be shown. Start with the definition of the relationship of the yield of a bond (call it simply r) and its price:

$$r = \frac{1}{p_{bL}} \tag{5.19}$$

and recall the definition of the expected rate of return on long-term bonds:

$$ERr_{bL} = r + \frac{(p_{bL}^e - p_{bL})}{p_{bL}} \tag{5.18}$$

From these two equations we obtain:

$$ERr_{bL} = r + \left(\frac{1}{r^e} - \frac{1}{r}\right) \cdot r = \frac{[r \cdot r^e + (r - r^e)]}{r^e}$$

where r^e is the long rate expected to be realized in the next period.

What we now want to know is the size of the expected change in long-term interest rates which is sufficient to bring the expected rate of return down to zero. Setting to zero the above equation, we obtain:

$$(r - r^e) = -r \cdot r^e$$

or

$$r^e = \frac{r}{(1 - r)}$$

And since,

$$r^e = r + \Delta r^e$$

we obtain:

$$\Delta r^e = \frac{r^2}{(1 - r)}$$

The expected change in the long-term interest rate which is required to create a capital loss that wipes out interest income from a perpetuity is roughly equal to the square of the current long-term interest rate. This justifies the two examples given above.

Appendix 5.3: An alternative, more orthodox, depiction of the bond market

As was pointed out in the main text, while it is possible for governments and monetary authorities to control both the short rates and the long rates of interest, control over long rates has been relinquished by most central banks in the 1950s. It is quite possible to set forth a model of the economy where central banks set the bill rate, while they let market forces determine the price of long-term bonds. What we need to assume is that the supply of bonds is a given, rather than assume, as was done in Model *LP*, that

Table A5.1 Changes required to achieve an alternative orthodox Liquidity Preference model (*LPNEO*)

Model *LP*	Model *LPNEO*	Changes required in *LPNEO*
$BL_s = BL_h$	$BL_s = \overline{BL}_s$	(5.17A) The supply of bonds is a given
$p_{bL} = \bar{p}_{bL}$	$BL_d = BL_s$	(5.24A) This is the market equilibrium condition
$BL_d \cdot p_{bL}/V^e = \lambda_{30} + \lambda_{32} \cdot r_b$ $+ \lambda_{33} \cdot ERr_{bL}$ $+ \lambda_{34} \cdot (YD_r^e/V^e)$	$BL_d \cdot p_{bL}/V^e = \lambda_{30} + \lambda_{32} \cdot r_b$ $+ \lambda_{33} \cdot ERr_{bL}$ $+ \lambda_{34} \cdot (YD_r^e/V^e)$	(5.11A) The unknown is now p_{bL} instead of BL_d

the quantity of bonds was supplied on demand. The following equations then need to be rewritten.[11]

This orthodox variant of Model *LP* (Table A5.1) can itself be modified to incorporate the fact that the central authorities may decide to reduce the supply of bonds when they find that long rates are too high compared to short rates. The rationale behind such a move is that governments would wish to reduce the cost of servicing the debt. When long rates are high, it makes sense to finance a larger proportion of the debt through short-term bills. In such a case, equation (5.17A) could be replaced by:

$$BL_s = (1 - z_1 \cdot \beta + z_2 \cdot \beta) \cdot BL_{s-1} \qquad (5.17B)$$

$$z_1 = 1 \quad \text{iff } Spread > tops \qquad (5.17C)$$

$$z_2 = 1 \quad \text{iff } Spread < bots \qquad (5.17D)$$

$$Spread = r_{bL-1} - r_{b-1} \qquad (5.17E)$$

These reaction functions of the authorities are built in symmetry with the expanded Model *LP2* of Appendix 5.1. When the discrepancy between short rates and long rates is back to its normal range, the number of outstanding bonds remains constant. Thus, in this model, although the central authorities have some control over the spread between short and long rates, the long rate relative to the short rate is free to move within the range delimited by the parameters *tops* and *bots*.

---

[11] Note that the hidden equation remains, as before, $H_s = H_h$.

6
Introducing the Open Economy

6.1 A coherent framework

This chapter extends the closed economy framework developed in previous chapters to describe two economies which trade merchandise with one another. Our methodology differs from the usual textbook approach, according to which models of individual closed economies are eventually 'opened', but which give no consideration to what other countries must be held to be doing and how a full set of interactions between all countries might be characterized. The excuse is that the open economy under study is presumed to be small compared to the rest of the world, so that the feedback effects can be assumed to negligible. But then not much can be said about the US economy, the size of which surely guarantees large feedback effects on the rest of the world, nor about the European community or the block of Asian countries including Japan. This partial equilibrium approach is the more surprising because international trade theory is usually treated within a relatively sophisticated two-country and two-good framework. We shall discuss open economy macro-economics using models of an economic system which, taken as a whole, is closed, with all flows and all stocks fully accounted for wherever they arise.[1]

One devastating feature of one-country-open-macro is that in the array of asset demand functions, which will be developed later in this book, the demand for overseas assets must be treated net; yet net overseas assets may move from positive to negative, making it impossible to construct a sensible array of asset demand functions. What is required, here again, is a

---

[1] This method is put forward in particular in Godley (1999b). It was first adumbrated in Tobin and De Macedo (1980), and later developed in Allen and Kenen (1980), Kenen (1985), and Branson and Henderson (1985), although all of this work, in our view, falls short of solving a dynamic model which evolves through time with multiple feedbacks.

Table 6.1 Balance sheet of two-region economy (Model *REG*)

	North households	South households	Government	Central bank	Σ
Cash money	$+H_h^N$	$+H_h^S$		$-H$	0
Bills	$+B_h^N$	$+B_h^S$	$-B$	$+B_{cb}$	0
Wealth (balancing item)	$-V_h^N$	$-V_h^S$	$-V_g$	0	0
Σ	0	0	0	0	0

systemic approach, methodologically identical with the closed economy models already presented.[2] Our open-economy models will evolve organically in stages from model *PC* in Chapter 4. We start off with the very same (closed) economy described by model *PC*, and then imagine how the economies of two component regions, which together make up the total, interact with one another and with the government. This will be Model *REG*. In subsequent sections we deal with a two-country system, each with its own currency. This will be Model *OPEN*.

6.2 The matrices of a two-region economy

We introduce open-economy macroeconomics by splitting a closed economy into two parts, the 'North' and the 'South' but retaining a single government, a single fiscal and monetary system and (of course) a single currency. The economy described here is the very same economy as in Model *PC*; we just disaggregate it into two regions, which will be differentiated by adding the S superscript sign to symbols describing one (the 'South') and N to describe the other (the 'North').

Table 6.1 shows the balance sheet of this two-region economy. Table 6.1 is no different from Table 4.1, except that households have been subdivided into two groups, the households living in the North and those in the South. V_g represents the net wealth of the federal government and it takes on a negative value, since the government has no asset and only a liability, represented by B. As a consequence V_g describes total net wealth acquired by the households of both regions.

---

[2] See also Gray and Gray (1988–89: 241) for the advantages of adopting a flow-of-funds matrix for the world, thus identifying the 'constraints and interdependencies which must characterize the international financial system' and transforming 'balance-of-payments analysis from a partial to a general framework'.

Table 6.2 Transactions-flow matrix of two-region economy (Model *REG*)

	North households	North production	South households	South production	Government	Central bank	Σ
Consumption	$-C^N$	$+C^N$	$-C^S$	$+C^S$			0
Govt. exp.		$+G^N$		$+G^S$	$-G$		0
North Exports to South		$+X^N$		$-IM^S$			0
South Exports to North		$-IM^N$		$+X^S$			0
GDP	$+Y^N$	$-Y^N$	$+Y^S$	$-Y^S$			0
Interest payments	$+r_{-1} \cdot B^N_{h-1}$		$+r_{-1} \cdot B^S_{h-1}$		$-r_{-1} B_{-1}$	$+r_{-1} \cdot B_{cb-1}$	0
Profits of central bank					$+r_{-1} \cdot B_{cb-1}$	$-r_{-1} \cdot B_{cb-1}$	0
Taxes	$-T^N$		$-T^S$		$+T$		0
Change in cash	$-\Delta H^N_h$		$-\Delta H^S_h$			$+\Delta H$	0
Change in bills	$-\Delta B^N_h$		$-\Delta B^S_h$		$+\Delta B$	$-\Delta B_{cb}$	0
Σ	0	0	0	0	0	0	0

Table 6.2 shows the transactions-flow matrix of our two-region economy. There are two main changes compared to the single-region economy of Table 4.2. First, as was the case with the balance sheet, households and production firms are subdivided into two groups. Second, there are two new rows in the matrix which represent the exports that each region expedites to the other. As with all other rows, each of these two rows must sum to zero, and here they do by definition. The addition of the export and import entries does not modify the all-important principle that all columns of the transactions-flow matrix must sum to zero.[3]

Exports from the North are denoted as X^N. From the point of view of the importing region, these exports are denoted as IM^S, since they are the imports into the South. Thus, by definition, $X^N = IM^S$, and this explains why the row 'North exports to the South' must sum to zero. Similarly, the exports of the South are the imports of the North, and hence we have $X^S = IM^N$, which explains why the next row also sums to zero.

There is another delicate accounting point that should be mentioned. In Table 6.2, imports (into the North, say), only appear in the column of producing firms, and not in the column of the household sector. It seems, then, that only firms import goods from the other region, while households in the North only consume goods produced by firms located in the North. In other words, it would seem that imports are only made up of intermediate goods, while households do not directly consume imported goods. Now this would be a rather bizarre assumption for we know that consumers do purchase imported goods. Another interpretation of Table 6.2 is possible. Remembering that most goods are purchased in shops, one can say that all imported goods transit through firms of the North, which act as intermediaries, purchasing these goods from the firms of the South, and then selling them to the Northern household consumers.

6.3 The equations of a two-region economy

It turns out to be surprisingly easy to adapt Model *PC* from Chapter 4 to describe the behaviour of the two-region system which constitutes Model *REG*. The equations can all be found in Appendix 6.1.

The first two equations define national income in an open economy, as the transactions matrix shows. Equation (6.1) defines national income in the North. It equals consumption and government expenditures, plus net exports, that is, the exports of the North to the South minus the imports of the North from the South, where X and IM stand for exports and imports. Exports are part of production and income, whereas imports are

---

[3] To save space, the current and the capital accounts of the central bank have been amalgamated.

goods or services that come from abroad and hence that must be subtracted from national income. The national income of the South is described in a symmetric way.

$$Y^N = C^N + G^N + X^N - IM^N \tag{6.1}$$

$$Y^S = C^S + G^S + X^S - IM^S \tag{6.2}$$

$$IM^N = \mu^N \cdot Y^N \tag{6.3}$$

$$IM^S = \mu^S \cdot Y^S \tag{6.4}$$

$$X^N = IM^S \tag{6.5}$$

$$X^S = IM^N \tag{6.6}$$

The next four equations are new, and determine imports and exports. Imports are assumed to be simple proportions of the output of each region. For instance, in equation (6.3), the imports into the North from the South, IM^N, are assumed to be a fraction μ^N of the production of the North Y^N. The parameter μ^N is the propensity of the North region to import goods and services. In general, we expect the propensities to import of the North and of the South regions to be different. Thus, in general, we have $\mu^N \neq \mu^S$, where μ^S is the import propensity of the South.

The value of the exports of each region follow by identity, as we pointed out when describing the flow matrix of our two-region economy. For instance, equation (6.5) is simply saying that exports from the North to the South, X^N, are identically equal to imports into the South from the North. Equation (6.6) similarly describes exports from the South to the North.

Equations (6.7) to (6.18) are similar to the equations that arose from Model PC, but each equation is now split into two equations and each equation describes one of the two regions. Thus to each region corresponds regional disposable income, taxes, wealth, consumption, a regional money demand function and a regional bill demand function. However, as can be seen from equations (6.9) and (6.10), despite having two regions, we still have a single tax rate θ and a single rate of interest on bills r. In other words, there is a single monetary and fiscal policy applying to the whole country. Although the first assumption corresponds to the monetary institutions of all countries, the second assumption is not a necessary one. Many countries, especially federations, apply different tax rates to different parts of the country.

$$YD^N = Y^N - T^N + r_{-1} \cdot B^N_{h-1} \tag{6.7}$$

$$YD^S = Y^S - T^S + r_{-1} \cdot B^S_{h-1} \tag{6.8}$$

$$T^N = \theta \cdot (Y^N + r_{-1} \cdot B^N_{h-1}) \quad 0 < \theta < 1 \tag{6.9}$$

$$T^S = \theta \cdot (Y^S + r_{-1} \cdot B^S_{h-1}) \quad 0 < \theta < 1 \tag{6.10}$$

$$V^N = V^N_{-1} + (YD^N - C^N) \tag{6.11}$$

$$V^S = V^S_{-1} + (YD^S - C^S) \tag{6.12}$$

$$C^N = \alpha^N_1 \cdot YD^N + \alpha^N_2 \cdot V^N_{-1} \quad 0 < \alpha_2 < \alpha_1 < 1 \tag{6.13}$$

$$C^S = \alpha^S_1 \cdot YD^S + \alpha^S_2 \cdot V^S_{-1} \quad 0 < \alpha_2 < \alpha_1 < 1 \tag{6.14}$$

$$H^N_h = V^N - B^N_h \tag{6.15}$$

$$H^S_h = V^S - B^S_h \tag{6.16}$$

$$\frac{B^N_h}{V^N} = \lambda^N_0 + \lambda^N_1 \cdot r - \lambda^N_2 \cdot \left(\frac{YD^N}{V^N}\right) \tag{6.17}$$

$$\frac{B^S_h}{V^S} = \lambda^S_0 + \lambda^S_1 \cdot r - \lambda^S_2 \cdot \left(\frac{YD^S}{V^S}\right) \tag{6.18}$$

We have differentiated the behaviour of households of the North from that of households in the South so the various parameters describing consumer behaviour (α_1 and α_2) and portfolio behaviour (λ_0, λ_1 and λ_2), as they appear in equations (6.9) and (6.10), as well as (6.17) and (6.18), carry an exponent identifying each region. When building the data bank of the model we assumed symmetric behaviour in each region. We shall however conduct one experiment changing this assumed symmetry, since we do not, in general, expect households from different regions to behave identically.

The next four equations, equations (6.19) to (6.22) are definitions, the aggregates T, G, B_h and H_h being made up of two regional components. In particular, pure government expenditures, G, must now be split into two components. Government expenditure takes place partly in the North and partly in the South, and how much is spent in each region is a policy decision. In the model the two pure governmental flows are separate exogenous variables. On the other hand, as could be seen in equations (6.7) and (6.8), the expenditures arising from servicing the debt are split according to the amount of bills held by the households of each region.

$$T = T^N + T^S \tag{6.19}$$

$$G = G^N + G^S \tag{6.20}$$

$$B_h = B_h^N + B_h^S \tag{6.21}$$

$$H_h = H_h^N + H_h^S \tag{6.22}$$

Finally, the last group of four equations closes the model. All of these equations are the same as the equivalent equations in Model *PC*. Equation (6.23) is the overall budget constraint of the government sector. Equation (6.24) reflects the balance-sheet constraint of the central bank. Equation (6.25) tells us that the central bank is the residual purchaser of bills. Any outstanding bill not purchased by the households of both regions will be purchased by the central bank. This behavioural equation allows us to close the model with equation (6.26), that is, it allows us to assume that the central bank sets the rate of interest on bills of its choice. The rate of interest on bills is an exogenous variable in this model, as it was in the previous models.

$$\Delta B_s = B_s - B_{s-1} = (G + r_{-1} \cdot B_{s-1}) - (T + r_{-1} \cdot B_{cb-1}) \tag{6.23}$$

$$\Delta H_s = H_s - H_{s-1} = \Delta B_{cb} \tag{6.24}$$

$$B_{cb} = B_s - B_h \tag{6.25}$$

$$r = \bar{r} \tag{6.26}$$

As in all our previous models, there is a 'missing' or 'redundant' equation, that is, an equation that arises from the complete accounting framework put forth here. This last equation, which can be deduced from all the others, is, once again:

$$H_s = H_h \tag{6.27}$$

The supply of money, and the end-of-period demand for money, are necessarily equal, without any price-equilibrating mechanism. Once more, we emphasize that the redundant equation cannot be incorporated into the computer model, for otherwise the model would be over-determined.

To sum up, there are 26 variables in Model *REG*, all to be found on the left-hand side of the 26 equations of Appendix 6.1. The fiscal position of central government is given by three parameters: the tax rate θ, and the regional (pure) expenditures, G^N and G^S.

6.4   The steady-state solutions of Model *REG*

How will such a two-region economy behave? Due to the large number of variables, the discussion is perhaps best organized by considering the steady state to which the model will converge. Assuming away continuous growth, this model, like previous models, implies that a stationary state is reached when household wealth remains constant. In other words, a stationary state is reached when the change in household wealth is equal to nil, that is when $\Delta V = 0$. Naturally in such a stationary state, the government budget of this two-region economy is also in balance and issues no further liability. However, as we shall see, while the government taken overall has a balanced budget, unless a very special and unlikely stationary state has been reached, its operations in one region will carry a deficit while its operations in the other region will carry a surplus of equal size.

Take the case of the North. Making use of equations (6.11) and (6.7), and as can be read from the first row of Table 6.2, the change in the wealth of Northern households is equal to:

$$\Delta V^N = Y^N + r_{-1} \cdot B^N_{-1} - T^N - C^N$$

Substituting Y^N by its value in equation (6.1), we obtain another expression for the change in household wealth:

$$\Delta V^N = (G^N + r_{-1} \cdot B^N_{-1}) + X^N - T^N - IM^N \tag{6.28}$$

Making the following definition:

$$G^N_T = G^N + r_{-1} \cdot B^N_{h-1} \tag{6.29}$$

hence defining G^N_T as the total government expenditures injected in the North region, including both pure government expenditures and the cost of servicing the debt held by Northern households, we obtain the following equation:

$$\Delta V^N = (G^N_T + X^N) - (T^N + IM^N) = (G^N_T - T^N) + (X^N - IM^N) \tag{6.30}$$

This equation is a very important one in flow-of-funds analysis. It says that at all times the change in household wealth is equal to the sum of two terms: the government deficit and the trade surplus. This equation generates constraints as to what can be said or what cannot be said when analysing macroeconomic sectoral balances, and we shall pay particular attention to these when conducting simulations.

In the meantime note that there is no more change in the wealth of households living in the North, $\Delta V^N = 0$, when the following condition is fulfilled:

$$G^N_T + X^N = T^N + IM^N \tag{6.31}$$

Condition (6.31) can also be rewritten as:

$$G^N_T - T^N = IM^N - X^N \tag{6.32}$$

Equation (6.32) is a well-known expression, which has given rise to considerable debate, under the name of the *twin-deficit situation*. From equation (6.32), we can see that, *in the stationary state*, a government budget deficit is necessarily accompanied by an equivalent trade deficit. If the left-hand side of equation (6.32) is negative, so must be the right-hand side. This equation, which necessarily arises in the stationary state, has sometimes been interpreted to imply that government deficits *generate* trade deficits. No such causality is implied here. On the contrary, we mostly emphasize causation running in the opposite direction. With our experiments, trade deficits cause government deficits.

Equation (6.31) gives rise to another important relationship. First, as an intermediate step, we define *net total* government expenditures in the North as:

$$G_{NT}^N = G^N + r_{-1} \cdot B_{h-1}^N - \theta \cdot r_{-1} \cdot B_{h-1}^N = G^N + (1 - \theta) \cdot r_{-1} \cdot B_{h-1}^N$$

(6.33)

implying that net total government expenditures include interest payments to Northern households net of taxes on these interest payments.

From equation (6.9) we know that the value of T^N is a direct function of Y_T^N. If imports IM^N were also a direct function of this total income, Y_T^N, we could easily derive an equation defining the steady-state level of total income. Things are slightly more complicated because imports are a function of GDP, that is Y^N. Making use of equations (6.9) and (6.3), equation (6.31) can be rewritten as a function of GDP, so that we obtain the following relationship, taking into account our new definition of net government expenditures:[4]

$$Y^{N*} = \frac{(G_{NT}^N + X^N)}{(\theta + \mu^N)}$$

(6.34)

This says that, in a stationary state, GDP in the North depends on 'total' government expenditures (net of income taxes on interest payments) in the North plus the exports of the North, divided by the sum of the general tax

---

[4] The proof is simple. Start off with equation (6.31), linking the right-hand side to equations (6.9) and (6.3):

$$G_T^N + X^N = \theta \cdot (Y^N + r_{-1} \cdot B_{h-1}^N) + \mu Y^N$$

$$(G_T^N - \theta \cdot r_{-1} \cdot B_{h-1}^N) + X^N = \theta Y^N + \mu Y^N$$

and now recall the definition of net total government expenditures:

$$G_{NT}^N + X^N = (\theta + \mu) Y^N$$

rate and the import propensity of the North. This important relationship is the foreign trade multiplier, or Harrod multiplier, since it was first suggested by Roy Harrod (1933).[5]

Equation (6.34), as is the case of the previous equations, is not a fully developed solution, since total income and total government expenditures depend on the amount of bills held by Northern households. In addition, the exports of the North themselves depend on the income of the South region. However, equation (6.34) is informative, since it gives us the main elements that determine regional income: the higher government expenditures, on goods and in servicing the debt, and the higher the exports, the higher regional income; the higher the tax rate and the propensity to import, the lower regional income.

While economic forces will drive the economy to the point where the government budget deficit (or surplus) for the North region is exactly equal to the trade deficit (or surplus) of the North region, *nothing will lead the system towards balanced trade.* For a steady state in which regional trade is balanced, it must be the case that $X^N = IM^N$ and therefore, by (6.32), that $G_T^N = T^N$. In that peculiar steady state, we have a kind of *super* stationary state since trade and government regional budget are both balanced, so we have the following equality:[6]

$$Y^{N**} = \frac{G_{NT}^N}{\theta} = \frac{X^N}{\mu^N} \tag{6.35}$$

This is to say that each region's 'trade performance ratio', defined for the North as X^N/μ^N – exports relative to import penetration – must be exactly equal to the fiscal stance (G_{NT}^N/θ for the North) if trade is to be balanced in the stationary state. But there is nothing in the model to make this happen.

So what, in general, does the stationary state look like? Needless to say, all the additional equations presented for the North – equation (6.28) to (6.35) – could be rewritten for the South, with the appropriate superscripts. In the general case, there will be a convergence to the state described by equation (6.31) and (6.32) – that is, the sum of government expenditures and exports must equal the sum of tax receipts plus imports. The government's regional budget deficit (surplus) in the stationary state will *exactly* equal that region's trade deficit (surplus) with the other region. Each region

---

[5] The relationship was resurrected in the 1970s by the work of the Cambridge Economic Policy Group (which included Wynne Godley), that of Kaldor, and by the growth equations unveiled by Tony Thirlwall (1979) and McCombie and Thirlwall (1994).

[6] Obviously $X^N = IM^N$ implies that $Y^{N**} = X^N/\mu^N$. In addition, $G_T^N = T^N$ implies that $G_T^N = \theta \cdot (Y^N + r_{-1} \cdot B_{h-1}^N)$, and hence that $G_T^N - \theta \cdot r_{-1} \cdot B_{h-1}^N = \theta \cdot Y^N$, which is: $G_{NT}^N = \theta \cdot Y^N$.

achieves its own wealth target, with no need for any adjustment to monetary policy – at given interest rates – by virtue of the fact that the government is exactly replenishing (or for the surplus region depleting) the stock of wealth which is being lost (gained) through inter-regional transactions with exactly compensating fiscal transfers (Kaldor 1970b).

While the 'balance of payments' of a relatively unsuccessful region deteriorates as its imports rise, no balance of payments financing *problem* can possibly arise. This is because in any new stationary state, as well as in any period of transition, the regionally differentiated government deficit (surplus) makes good, or finances, any part of the payments deficit that the private sector does not wish to finance and ditto *mutatis mutandis* for the surplus region. Not only is there no balance of payments financing problem, the inhabitants of each region have no knowledge of any surplus or deficit beyond, perhaps, some generally perceived change of prosperity because their income and wealth have changed.

6.5   Experiments with Model *REG*

6.5.1   An increase in the propensity to import of the South

Various simulations can be conducted, to illustrate how Model *REG* works. All we need to do is to change some parameters. The most obvious experiment to conduct is to increase the propensity to import of one of the regions. Let us assume, then, that the propensity to import of the South region, μ^S, is increased. The simulations illustrate the interdependence between the two regions.

The reader may recall that, by identity and hence *in all circumstances*, as shown in equation (6.30), the private sector surplus (ΔV) in each region is necessarily equal to the government's regional deficit ($G_T - T$) plus the balance-of-payments surplus of the region ($X - IM$). Figure 6.1 shows the government's regional budget balance: when the budget balance is negative, as shown in Figure 6.1, the government is running a deficit in that region. The figure shows that, *in the new stationary state*, the government's regional deficit is exactly equal to the region's balance of payments deficit. Thus, in the new stationary state of the South, the propensity to import which underwent an increase in its value, generates a *twin-deficit situation*. During the intervening, transitional, period, the balance of payments of the deficit region (the South) recovers somewhat after its initial fall, because output in the surplus region (the North) rises, thanks to the North's higher exports induced by the South's higher propensity to import. But the higher level of output in the North, in due course, brings about some recovery in the deficit region's exports. During the transitional period the government regional deficit automatically makes up any difference between the other two balances of the region.

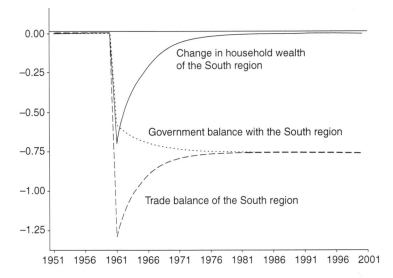

Figure 6.1   Evolution of the balances of the South region – net acquisition of financial assets by the household sector, government budget balance, trade balance – following an increase in the propensity to import of the South region

The evolution of output in each region, as described in the preceding paragraph, is illustrated in Figure 6.2. It shows that the step increase in the propensity to import of the South generates a sudden increase in output in the North, and a corresponding decrease in the South's output. The changes, however, quickly taper off, because the model incorporates the counter-active feedback effects that each region is imposing upon the other. These feedback effects are such that a new steady state is soon reached, each region producing a constant output.

While demand in the South region falls when its import propensity rises, demand in the North region rises, and this may be inflationary if it starts off fully employed. This may induce a central government to take deflationary fiscal measures even though output and employment in the South have fallen. It should be possible to draw conclusions along Kaldorian lines about the beneficial effect of regionally differentiated fiscal policy (Kaldor 1970b). Note too that in reality taxes are progressive and that government outlays are automatically differentiated because the central government is responsible for all unemployment benefit. This implies, *de facto*, some kind of regionally differentiated fiscal policy, provided the tax system is sufficiently progressive and the unemployment benefits are sufficiently generous.

These are, we believe, important 'real' results which, with only a little imagination, can be applied to the current discussion of the European Monetary Union (EMU) and its common currency – the Euro. It sheds light on the vexed

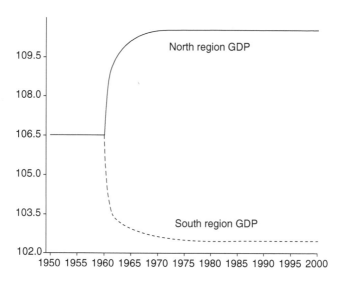

Figure 6.2   Evolution of GDP in the North and the South regions, following an increase in the propensity to import of the South region

question of what is the difference between a balance-of-payments deficit which exists between two parts of a single country which has a unitary fiscal and monetary system – not, however, the current euro zone arrangements – and one which exists between two different economies. These differences will be clearer when we present a similar model of two economies, each with its own currency.

In the meantime, the dramatic consequences of the *twin-deficit* accounting proposition in all stationary states should be noted, especially within the context of the EMU. In the example illustrated with Figures 6.1 and 6.2, it is clear that any region, or country within the EMU, which experiences an increase in the propensity to import, will end up with a regional government deficit, even though it started out with a balanced budget. *In the steady state*, or rather, in a *stationary* steady state without growth, and excluding any third party, it is impossible for both regions of a country, or for both countries of a monetary union, to simultaneously enjoy government budget surpluses or balanced budgets.

This proposition is rarely understood, in contrast to another, more obvious proposition, that says that all countries in the world cannot simultaneously enjoy a trade surplus or a balance-of-payments surplus. In Model *REG*, it is obvious that the South and the North regions cannot simultaneously, in or out of the stationary state, enjoy a positive trade balance. One of them must have a deficit, since the conditions required for balanced trade, as seen with equation (6.35), are so stringent.

But while everyone knows that, in a two-country monetary union, one of the partners will be running a trade deficit, it is not always understood that in that same two-country monetary union, the laws of accounting are such that the country running a trade deficit must be running a government budget deficit as well once the steady-state position is reached. Despite this mathematical necessity, all countries of the EMU are strongly encouraged, with financial penalties being imposed otherwise, to run balanced budgets or budgets with surpluses. Such a rule must presuppose that countries that are part of the eurozone are running balance-of-payments surpluses relative to the rest of the world. But why should this be the case? Taking all the countries of the eurozone as a whole, equation (6.32) shows that a rule forbidding all countries to run a budget deficit in the long run, and hence in the stationary state, makes no economic sense.

6.5.2 An increase in the government expenditures of the South

In the previous experiment, the causality inherent to equation (6.32) and its twin-deficit proposition ran from the trade deficit to the budget deficit. But what about causality going the other way around? Could budget deficits cause trade deficits? This can be easily assessed by running another experiment, based on an increase in government expenditures. Let us assume then, that, starting from a stationary state with balanced budgets and balanced trade, that the central government decides to increase government expenditures in the South, for instance in an attempt to increase the level of output and employment in this region. What will be the consequences on regional output and regional balances?

As one would expect, both regions will benefit from an increase in economic activity, but because the impact is more direct in the South, GDP output will react more in the South than in the North (Figure 6.3). As a result of the increase in income and disposable income, the target level of household wealth will be higher and households will save during the transition to the new steady state, as can be seen from Figure 6.4. Once the steady state is reached, the trade account of the South and the central government balance with the South will both be permanently negative, but no one is likely to notice since in the South GDP will now be higher, in line with the objective of the initial change in central government expenditures (symmetrically, the trade account of the North region and the central government balance with the North region will be positive, and of equal size, so that the overall central government budget position will be balanced).

6.5.3 An increase in the propensity to save of the Southern households

When studying Model *PC*, we discovered a puzzling result, at least from a Keynesian perspective, that an increase in saving propensities eventually led

184

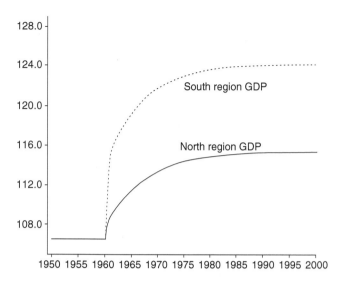

Figure 6.3 Evolution of GDP in the South and the North regions, following an increase in the government expenditures in the South region

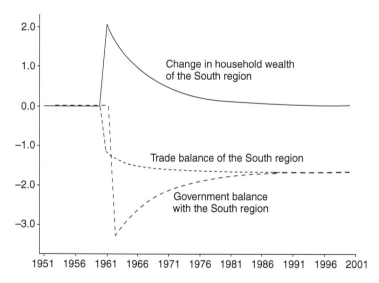

Figure 6.4 Evolution of the balances of the South region – net acquisition of financial assets by the household sector, government budget balance, trade balance – following an increase in the government expenditures in the South region

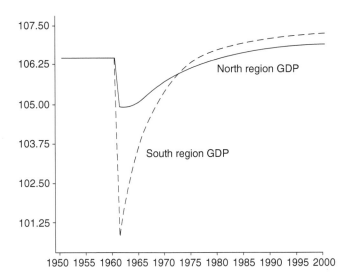

Figure 6.5 Evolution of GDP in the North and South regions, following an increase in the propensity to save of South region households

to a higher steady-state level of output. What happens now in our two-region economy if the households in one region decide to increase their propensity to save? This is the subject of our third experiment. Let us assume, again starting from a steady state with balanced trade and balanced budgets, that the households of the South decide to reduce their propensity to consume out of current income – the α_1 parameter. What happens to output levels, trade balances, and fiscal positions?

Figure 6.5 shows that there is a slowdown in economic activity in the South. Because of the interdependence of the two regions, a similar but less abrupt slowdown also occurs in the North, since their exports to the South will decrease. However, as in Model *PC*, both regions eventually recover, and the long-run steady-state effect of this increase in the propensity to save turns out to be slightly positive.

Figure 6.6 shows that the higher degree of thriftiness on the part of the South region households leads to an accumulation of additional wealth, which is compensated both by the central government deficit in the South and the trade surplus of the South, both of which appear as a result of the economic recession occurring in the South region. Eventually, all balances approach equilibrium. Figure 6.6 however shows that twin deficits, or twin surpluses, only *need* to occur in (quasi) stationary states. During the transition, before a stationary state is reached, a government surplus in the region may well accompany a trade deficit, or vice-versa.

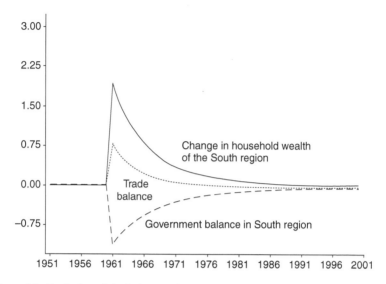

Figure 6.6 Evolution of the balances of the South region – net acquisition of financial assets by the household sector, government budget balance, trade balance – following an increase in the propensity to save of South region households

6.5.4 A change in the liquidity preference of the Northern households

A final experiment with Model *REG* assumes that the Southern households reduce their liquidity preference. Within the context of our model, this means that households from the South now wish to hold a larger proportion of their portfolio in the form of bills, which implies that the λ_0^S coefficient in the bill demand equation (6.17) is now higher. This difference in the values taken by the two parameters λ_0^N and λ_0^S is in fact what one would expect when comparing a rich and a poor region, assuming now the richer area is the South region. The rest of the parameters can remain as they are. What will now happen to output, trade balances and fiscal positions?

In this model even a fairly large reallocation of wealth towards bills will only generate a small increase in the output of the South (and an even smaller one – hardly distinguishable – in the North). What happens, as can be seen in Figure 6.7, is that central government will now be compelled to make more interest payments to the households residing in the South. This increases both the government deficit and disposable income in the South. This in turn leads to higher consumption and higher GDP in the South, the latter inducing both wealth accumulation and a trade deficit for the South. Both the government deficit in the South and the trade deficit of the South will be sustained in the (quasi) steady state. The conclusion is that the reduction

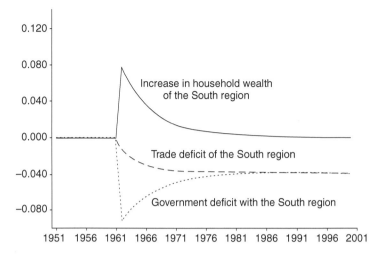

Figure 6.7 Evolution of the balances of the South region – net acquisition of financial assets by the household sector, government budget balance, trade balance – following a decrease in the liquidity preference of South region households

in liquidity preference by Southern households has some positive economic repercussions on the South, as it now benefits from higher total government expenditures. But all these effects are of a second-order magnitude.

6.6 The matrices of a two-country economy

The next stage is to turn Model *REG* into a two-country model with no over-arching or federal, government. This will be Model *OPEN*. However, moving in steps, it will for the time being be assumed that the private residents of each country are not allowed to hold any kind of foreign asset. The matrices for the regional model must be changed so that each country has its own government and its own central bank. The main change, however, is that we now assume that the currencies in the two countries are different from one another; hence all transactions between them require conversion so that the transaction can be made in common units. It will also be assumed that exchange rates are fixed, so any discrepancy between sales and purchases on the exchange market are made good by transactions of the central banks.

As always we introduce this new model by presenting the balance sheet matrix and the transactions-flow matrix. These are shown in Tables 6.3 and 6.4.

Table 6.3   Balance sheet matrix of two-country economy (Model *OPEN*)

	North house-holds	North Govt.	North central bank	South house-holds	South Govt.	South central bank	Σ
Cash money	$+H_h^N$		$-H_h^N$	$+H_h^S$		$-H_h^S$	0
Bills	$+B_h^N$	$-B^N$	$+B_{cb}^N$	$+B_h^S$	$-B^S$	$+B_{cb}^S$	0
Gold reserves			$+or^N \cdot p_g^N \cdot xr$			$+or^S \cdot p_g^S$	$or^N \cdot p_g^N \cdot xr$ $+or^S \cdot p_g^S$
Wealth (balancing item)	$-V_h^N$	$-V_g^N$	0	$-V_h^S$	$-V_g^S$	0	$-(or^N \cdot p_g^N \cdot xr$ $+or^S \cdot p_g^S)$
Σ	0	0	0	0	0	0	0

Each country now has its own government which issues bills, and each country has a central bank which issues its own currency. But in addition, each central bank owns a stock of gold reserves which, not being financial assets, have no liability as their counterpart. This is why the value of the gold reserves appearing in the Σ column is not zero. Despite that, central banks have zero net worth, as they did in the previous model without gold reserves.

As with Model *REG*, all the variables relevant to the North have an N superscript, while all the variables relevant to the South have an S superscript. The value of gold reserves is given by a physical quantity ('*or*') times the price of gold (p_g) expressed in the appropriate currency.[7] The exchange rate *xr* is defined as the number which converts North values and prices into their equivalents in the currency ruling in the South. For example, if North values are in dollars, while South values are in yen, with one dollar being exchanged for 100 yen, then the exchange rate *xr* is equal to 100.

When adding items in a given column, we need not worry about the exchange rate, because all items are in the same currency. This is not the case when dealing with rows. However, because, as a simplification device, we have assumed that the inhabitants of each country can only purchase domestic assets, each half of each row sums to zero (the half dealing with domestic assets), so that we need not worry about the exchange rate when

---

[7] In French, *or* means gold.

summing the elements of each row, except for the row dealing with gold reserves. In the case of gold reserves, we must add gold reserves which are valued in different currencies. To avoid adding apples and oranges, the gold reserves of the North must be converted in the currency of the South country, so that the gold reserves of the North and of the South can be added together. This is done by multiplying the value of the gold reserves of the North by the exchange rate xr, as shown in the middle column, so as to obtain a measure of these gold reserves valued with the South currency.

In the absence of inter-country fiscal transfers (such as took place without anyone knowing or noticing when there was a federal government) there must be a means by which international debts can be settled. As the residents of neither country hold the currency of the other, when they receive payments denominated in foreign currency for their exports, they are considered to exchange the proceeds into their own currency; and when they make payments in foreign currency for imports, they must obtain the means of payment from the central bank. Any excess of (private sector) payments for imports over receipts from exports must therefore have an identical counterpart in transactions involving the two central banks, using some internationally acceptable means of payment – assumed here to be sales or purchases of gold bars valued at some fixed rate in terms of its own currency. With a fixed exchange rate and no restrictions on trade, each central bank must be willing to buy or sell gold on any scale at that fixed rate.

Within the present international monetary system, gold bars are not traded anymore. Although some central banks still hold gold reserves, the reserves of central banks are mainly made up of foreign currencies, mainly US dollars, and it is these foreign currencies that are used whenever central banks decide to intervene in foreign exchange markets to maintain the exchange rate of their home currency *vis-à-vis* some other currency (often the US dollar) or basket of currencies. There was a time, however, where gold reserves provided the main international acceptable means of payment. This time is known as the *gold standard period*, which occurred between 1880 and 1913 – the heyday of the gold standard – and then again from 1922 to 1938. The model to be presented here, Model *OPEN*, can thus either be understood as a representation of the gold standard period, or be understood as a rough and over-simplified version of the current international monetary system.

Whatever the chosen interpretation, we may now examine the transactions-flow matrix of this two-country economy, which appears in Table 6.4. As with all transactions-flow matrices, each row and column of Table 6.4 must sum to zero. As in Table 6.3, we need not worry about the currency in use when summing the items in each column, since all such items are in domestic currency. Summing the rows is a bit more complicated. As was the case with the balance sheet, there is no problem for many of the rows, since each half of these rows, linked to domestic transactions only, sums to zero anyway. However, this is not the case of all rows, and in particular this

Table 6.4 Transactions-flow matrix of two-country economy (Model OPEN)

	North country				South country				Σ
	Households	Producers	Govt.	Central bank	Households	Producers	Govt.	Central bank	
Consumption	$-C^N$	$+C^N$			$-C^S$	$+C^S$			0
Govt. exp.		$+G^N$	$-G^N$			$+G^S$	$-G^S$		0
North Exports to South		$+X^N$		$\cdot xr$		$-IM^S$			0
South Exports to North		$-IM^N$		$\cdot xr$		$+X^S$			0
GDP	$+Y^N$	$-Y^N$			$+Y^S$	$-Y^S$			0
Interest payments	$+r_{-1}\cdot B^N_{h-1}$		$-r_{-1}\cdot B^N_{-1}$	$+r_{-1}\cdot B^N_{cb}$	$+r_{-1}\cdot B^S_{h-1}$		$-r_{-1}\cdot B^S_{-1}$	$+r_{-1}\cdot B^S_{cb-1}$	0
Profits of central bank			$+r_{-1}\cdot B^N_{cb-1}$	$-r_{-1}\cdot B^N_{cb-1}$			$+r_{-1}\cdot B^S_{cb-1}$	$-r_{-1}\cdot B^S_{cb-1}$	0
Taxes	$-T^N$		$+T^N$		$-T^S$		$+T^S$		0
Change in cash	$-\Delta H^N_h$			$+\Delta H^N$	$-\Delta H^S_h$			$+\Delta H^S$	0
Change in bills	$-\Delta B^N_h$		$+\Delta B^N$	$-\Delta B^N_{cb}$	$-\Delta B^S_h$		$+\Delta B^S$	$-\Delta B^S_{cb}$	0
Change in reserves				$-\Delta or^N\cdot p^N_g$	$\cdot xr$			$-\Delta or^S\cdot p^S_g$	0
Σ	0	0	0	0	0	0	0	0	0

is not the case with the export rows and the row dealing with changes in gold reserves. For these rows, an additional column must be introduced, that multiplies the domestic values of the North country by the exchange rate *xr*, to obtain values measured in the South currency. All the items in the row may then be summed, since they are being expressed in the same *numéraire*. As all other rows, the rows dealing with exports and changes in gold holdings must then all sum to zero, thanks to this currency adjustment.[8]

It is a feature of Table 6.4 which may surprise for an instant that neither country has or needs a column describing its current balance of payments. However the coherence enforced by double entry accounting ensures that total flows in each country always exactly equal total outflows. Thus trade flows, which are to be found in the two rows describing exports, make up the balance of payments on current account, which is, in turn, exactly equal to the sum of each country's transfers of gold described in the row called 'change in reserves'. The logic of the double entry system implies that the entries in the final line sum to zero; hence as both entries in the 'change in reserves' row have a negative sign, one country's gold stock can only rise if the other's falls to an exactly equal extent.

6.7 The equations of a two-country economy

It is easy to adapt the equation system from Model *REG*, to transform it into a two-country model. This is done in Appendix 6.2, where equations have been renumbered starting with equation (6.O.1) to underline the fact that we are now dealing with Model *OPEN*.

A lot of the equations of Model *OPEN* are identical to those of Model *REG*. Thus, equations (6.O.1) to (6.O.4), (6.O.7), (6.O.8), and (6.O.11) to (6.O.18) are identical to equations (6.1) to (6.4), (6.7), (6.8), and (6.11) to (6.18).[9] Only a few changes are required to complete the model. First, the export and import identities must reflect the fact that there now exist two currencies instead of one. The imports and exports of the North are thus adjusted by being multiplied by the exchange rate, as shown in equations (6.O.5) and (6.O.6).

$$X^N = \frac{IM^S}{xr} \tag{6.O.5}$$

$$X^S = IM^N \cdot xr \tag{6.O.6}$$

---

[8] Changes in gold holdings must also sum to zero. If gold was being produced by the production sector, and purchased by one of the central banks, this would have to enter the matrix, but we would still be left with zero-sum columns and rows.
[9] It cannot be assumed however that the consumption and the portfolio parameters are identical in the two regions, which are now two separate countries.

Next, one must delete from Model *REG* all references to a general government and a unique central bank. We now have two separate governments and two different central banks. Each government can set its own tax rate, as shown in equations (6.O.9) and (6.O.10).

$$T^N = \theta^N \cdot (Y^N + r^N_{-1} \cdot B^N_{h-1}) \quad 0 < \theta^N < 1 \tag{6.O.9}$$

$$T^S = \theta^S \cdot (Y^S + r^S_{-1} \cdot B^S_{h-1}) \quad 0 < \theta^S < 1 \tag{6.O.10}$$

Third, the four equations of Model *REG* that were defining the aggregates of the two-region economy – equations (6.19) to (6.23) – are now meaningless in the two-country economy of Model *OPEN*, and must be deleted. Because there are now two governments and two central banks, the financial variables related to these institutions double in size: there are now eight such variables, namely the supply of bills by each of the two governments, the demand for bills and the supply of cash money by each central bank, and finally the rate of interest set by each central bank. There are also four additional variables, that did not exist in Model *REG*: the change in gold holdings by each central bank, and the price of gold in each country. The exchange rate may be considered as the last additional variable, but we have assumed fixed exchange rates, so that the exchange rate is a constant. We thus have 13 additional variables, and so we must define 13 extra equations to determine Model *OPEN*. This is the task that we now tackle.

$$\Delta B^N_s = B^N_s - B^N_{s-1} = (G^N + r^N_{-1} \cdot B^N_{s-1}) - (T^N + r^N_{-1} \cdot B^N_{cb-1}) \tag{6.O.19}$$

$$\Delta B^S_s = B^S_s - B^S_{s-1} = (G^S + r^S_{-1} \cdot B^S_{s-1}) - (T^S + r^S_{-1} \cdot B^S_{cb-1}) \tag{6.O.20}$$

$$B^N_{cb} = B^N_s - B^N_h \tag{6.O.21}$$

$$B^S_{cb} = B^S_s - B^S_h \tag{6.O.22}$$

$$\Delta or^{N.} \cdot p^N_g = \Delta H^N_s - \Delta B^N_{cb} \tag{6.O.23}$$

$$\Delta or^{S.} \cdot p^S_g = \Delta H^S_s - \Delta B^S_{cb} \tag{6.O.24}$$

$$H^N_s = H^N_h \tag{6.O.25}$$

$$H^S_s = H^S_h \tag{6.O.26}$$

Equations (6.O.19) and (6.O.20) describe the budget constraint of each government; there is nothing new here. Equations (6.O.21) and (6.O.22) are not new either: they say that each central bank is ready to purchase any bill outstanding which is not bought by households of its constituency. Equations (6.O.23) and (6.O.24) reflect the balance-sheet constraint of the central bank. While the balance sheet constraint of the central bank was already used in Model *PC* and Model *REG*, these two equations are new insofar as they incorporate changes in gold holdings by each central bank. But now, because gold holdings appear on the left-hand side of the equations, while the supply of cash money by the central bank appears on the right-hand side of these two equations, we need two new equations in determining the supply of cash money in each country. These two equations are equations (6.O.25) and (6.O.26). They indicate that each central bank is supplying the amount of cash money which is demanded by households and explicitly reflect the proposition that money is endogenous, in the sense that it is demand-led, determined by the portfolio choice of households.

Five more equations need to be found. Two of these are straightforward. The price of gold in each country must be determined. With equation (6.O.27) we assume that the price of gold in the North is a given, expressed in the currency ruling in the North and set by the North central bank. By the law of one price, the price of gold in the South is determined by the exchange rate, given the price of gold in the North, as shown in equation (6.O.28). Since we have room for three more equations, this means that, in addition to a fixed exchange rate, as shown by equation (6.O.29), it is possible for both central banks to set the rate of interest of their choice, as reflected by equations (6.O.30) and (6.O.31). In other words, despite each country being an open economy with a fixed exchange rate, the rates of interest in each country can be set exogenously. The rates of interest do not need to play any price-equilibrating mechanism.

$$p_g^N = \bar{p}_g^N \qquad (6.O.27)$$

$$p_g^S = p_g^N \cdot xr \qquad (6.O.28)$$

$$xr = \overline{xr} \qquad (6.O.29)$$

$$r^N = \bar{r}^N \qquad (6.O.30)$$

$$r^S = \bar{r}^S \qquad (6.O.31)$$

The redundant equation is now the one which describes the equivalence between reserve gains by one country and reserve losses by the other, as can be assessed from the row 'Change in reserves' in the transactions-flow matrix of Table 6.4. That is to say, the structure of the model implies that:

$$\Delta or^S = -\Delta or^N \qquad (6.O.32)$$

and in the simulations this is invariably found to be true, although it does not appear as an equation in the model.

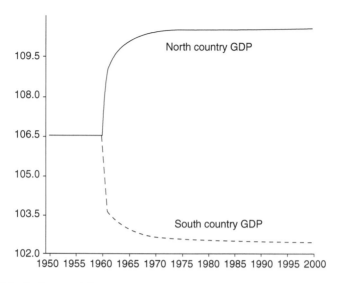

Figure 6.8 Evolution of GDP in the North and in the South countries, following an increase in the South propensity to import

6.8 Rejecting the Mundell–Fleming approach and adopting the *compensation* approach

6.8.1 Ever-falling gold reserves

When the two-country model is simulated, we find that a rise in the propensity to import of the South country has effects which, initially, are identical with those in the regional model. The two countries reach a kind of stationary state, which we shall call a *quasi stationary state*, where there is no change in the financial assets held by the households of each country, and where there is no change in the income level of both countries. The income of the North country is now higher, and that of the South country is now lower, as shown in Figure 6.8, which is identical to Figure 6.2.

Once again the South is subjected to the twin-deficit situation. The effects on the balance of trade, the private sector's financial balance and the budget deficit are identically the same as those illustrated in Figure 6.1 – reproduced here as Figure 6.9 with obvious small amendments to the headings.

However, whereas in the regional model the balance-of-payments deficit is automatically financed by fiscal transfers between regions by the central government and which can continue for ever, in the two-country model the deficit is financed by a loss of reserves which exactly matches its trade deficit, step by step, in the quasi stationary state. This must be the case, by the laws of logic, since changes in reserves

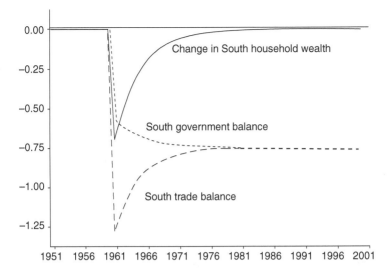

Figure 6.9   Evolution of the balances of the South country – net acquisition of financial assets by the household sector, government budget balance, trade balance – following an increase in the South propensity to import

are the only international transactions on capital account. The reader will recall that when building our transactions and balance sheet matrices, we assumed capital flows away – implying fully fledged capital controls.

In the country with the trade surplus, the gold reserves are continuously rising, while in the trade deficit country they are diminishing. In addition, the government of the deficit country sees the size of its public debt continuously rising, thus facing a rising public debt to income ratio. This is why we may call the resulting situation a *quasi* stationary state, since some of the main variables or ratios are still changing, and also because it is impossible for the situation to persist indefinitely. 'As a long-term proposition the hypothesis of ever-increasing government debt relative to income accompanied by continuous external deficits is implausible' (Godley and Cripps 1983: 297).

The interesting thing to emerge from the simulations is that, beyond reducing income in the weaker country via the mechanism of the foreign trade multiplier, as shown in Figure 6.8, the private sector receives no signal that anything is wrong at all. Yet the central bank is suffering an unsustainable loss of reserves which can only go on for as long as there are reserves to lose. As there are no private international capital transactions and as we have, so far, a strictly fixed exchange rate system, the government will be forced eventually to do one of three things: to deflate demand to the point where the external deficit is eliminated; to borrow reserves from abroad; or administratively to restrict imports to what can be paid for with exports.[10] It would be possible to work out how much deflation there would have to be – if this is the route adopted – by setting the change in reserves to zero and endogenizing government expenditures (or the tax rate). This would ensure that the economy must be deflated to the point where the balance of payments is also zero.

Until a government runs out of reserves and has to take drastic restrictive action, the signals the private sector receives *are almost identical to the ones it gets in the regional model*; the deficit country suffers a loss of income and a generalised loss of wealth and employment, as in the regional model. The only other additional information is that the government running the country with the trade deficit is facing a permanent budget deficit, despite a constant national income. The rising public debt to income ratio might induce households to reduce their holdings of government bills. But this, in itself, cannot stop the central bank from keeping the interest rates at a constant level. Indeed, in the (quasi) stationary state, the new public debt is all being financed by the sales of bills to the central bank. The value of bills purchased by the central bank is exactly equal to the value of gold losses that it incurs, as indicated by equations (6.O.23) and (6.O.24). Otherwise, there is no automatic correction mechanism of any kind to stem the trade deficit.

This finding is profoundly at odds with the influential body of literature which has its genesis in the Mundell–Fleming models of fixed exchange rate economies and the body of doctrine known as 'the monetary approach to the balance-of-payments', which turn out to be modern extensions of the 'price-specie flow' mechanism outlined by David Hume, back in the eighteenth century. A central contention of these theories is that there is some automatic feedback mechanism that gradually brings back an equilibrium balance-of-payments whenever a surplus or a deficit position occurs, even if nominal exchange rates are fixed. The feedback mechanism is usually presented with the following arguments. A balance-of-payments deficit in a fixed exchange rate regime means a loss of reserves. In Hume's time, the balance-of-payments deficit meant a loss of gold, and this was said to lead to a fall in prices, which made the products of the deficit country more competitive and hence allowed it to recover balanced trade.

In the modern world, claim the proponents of the Mundell–Fleming approach, this loss of reserves, which appears on the asset side of the balance sheet of the central bank, is said to induce an equivalent depletion of

---

[10] Another option would be devaluation, or a decision to move to a flexible exchange rate regime.

the monetary base, which constitutes the liability side of the central bank. The falling monetary base – the falling supply of high-powered money – leads to a falling money supply, and hence to higher interest rates. These rates will keep on rising until balance-of-payments equilibrium is restored, because as long as the external balance is not restored the monetary base keeps being depleted. These feedback mechanisms mimic the 'price-specie flow' mechanism that was said to rule in Hume's time and in the heyday of the gold standard regime of international settlements, when gold was the main if not the only instrument of foreign reserves. Despite the neat graphical representations of the mainstream models via the well-known IS/LM/BP framework, these standard models are difficult to penetrate, precisely because they are never set forth in a comprehensive system of accounts, with every equation and every equilibrium condition made explicit.

6.8.2   A gold standard with non-existent rules of the game

The interesting thing to emerge from Model *OPEN* is that although a deficit country loses gold reserves, this loss has no independent effect on anything else at all. This is the more surprising because Model *OPEN* retains the main features of the gold exchange standard, which provides the institutional background which is said to be the most favourable to the functioning of the *rules of the game*, that is, the mechanism which ensures that a balance-of-payments deficit will lead to a fall in base money and the money supply, as well as a rise in interest rates, and hence to the recovery of a balanced external position. Model *OPEN* runs under the gold standard, since any trade deficit must be made good by a transfer of gold between central banks. Still, *the rules of the game* just do not and cannot apply. There is no endogenous mechanism eliminating the balance-of-payments deficit. Hume's 'price-specie flow' mechanism just does not seem to have any bite. [11]

The point that mainstream authors seem to be missing is that when there is a loss of reserves, as illustrated in Figure 6.9, there will be, after the first kerfuffle as the private sector adapts, a budget deficit which is exactly equal to this loss of reserves. The asset stocks adjust to a new, lower level, in line with the lower income flow but thereafter they exhibit no change at all. The compensatory mechanism from the budget deficit thus removes all leverage which

[11] It must be pointed out that Mundell (1961), whose other works are often invoked to justify the relevance of the rules of the game in textbooks and the IS/LM/BP model, was himself aware that the automaticity of the *rules of the game* relied on a particular behaviour of the central bank. Indeed he lamented the fact that modern central banks were following the *banking principle* instead of the *bullionist principle*, and hence adjusting 'the domestic supply of notes to accord with the needs of trade' (1961: 153), which is another way to say that the money supply was endogenous and that central banks were concerned with maintaining the targeted interest rates. This was in 1961!

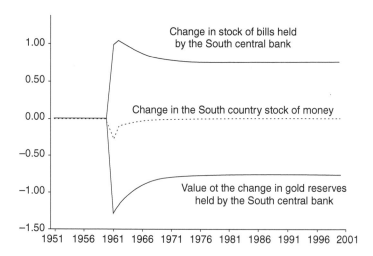

Figure 6.10 Evolution of the three components of the balance sheet of the South central bank – gold reserves, domestic Treasury bills and money – following an increase in the South propensity to import

the loss of reserves is supposed to be exercising on the monetary system. Although there is no deliberate 'sterilization' of falling reserves by the central bank, the fall in foreign reserves is nonetheless continuously offset by the increase in the amount of bills held by the central bank, as is shown in Figure 6.10. This increase is entirely endogenous to the behaviour of the central bank and of the entire economic system. One could say that it arises as a consequence of the decision by the central bank to keep the rate of interest on bills constant. But beyond that, the relative constancy of the money supply in the new steady state is not the result of a discretionary decision made in an attempt to keep the money supply constant, as 'sterilization' is portrayed by mainstream authors.

A very similar process is arising in the North, which, with its trade surplus, sees its foreign reserves rise continuously. The rise in these reserves is counterbalanced by the fall in the amount of bills that the North central bank is required to hold. This is known as the *compensation* thesis (Lavoie 2001b: 206). The compensation principle asserts that changes in foreign reserves will generally be compensated by endogenous mechanisms that are tied to the normal behaviour of the central bank and to that of the other economic agents in the economy. The compensation principle would also operate in an open economy with private bank money.

6.8.3 Two kinds of money supply endogeneity

Mainstream economists usually hold that, whereas otherwise it may be considered to be an exogenous variable, the money supply is endogenous in the case of an open economy with fixed exchange rates. This instance of endogeneity of the money supply process has nothing to do however with the endogenous money supply process that has been presented in this book and by post-Keynesian authors in general. In the Mundell–Fleming approach and in the so-called 'monetary approach to the balance-of-payments', the money supply is said to be endogenous in the case of fixed exchange rates, but this endogeneity process is *supply-led*. There, the stock of money falls or rises because the amount of foreign reserves falls or rises. In the open economy case described by mainstream authors, the money supply increases endogenously, but independently, of the demand for money expressed by the economic agents. Changes in interest rates then adapt the endogenous, but autonomous, increase in the money supply to the unchanging money demand schedule.

This sort of endogeneity of the money supply is totally at odds with the type of endogeneity underlined here. In the post-Keynesian approach and in Model *OPEN* in particular, the money supply is endogenous because it is *demand-led*. In Model *OPEN*, the money supply grows (or diminishes) because more (or less) of it is being demanded by the households of the domestic economy. When agents desire more cash money, the central bank provides the banknotes to the users of the monetary system. Assets are supplied, at given interest rates, on demand and in exactly the right proportions. The number of equations and unknowns in the model is such that there is no way to describe (net) asset supplies other than as passive responses to demand (Lavoie 2001b).

In the case described by Figures 6.8 to 6.10 – the case of the deficit country – it would seem at first that the Mundell–Fleming story is vindicated. Starting from an external balance and a balanced budget, the increase in the propensity to import leads to a trade and balance-of-payments deficit, and also, in the initial stages of the transition, to a fall in the stock of money balances, as the Mundell–Fleming model would predict. As is clear from Table 6.5, which shows the first-period effect of the jump in imports on the balance sheet of the South central bank, the induced fall in the stock of money (-0.29) is much smaller than the decrease in gold reserves (-1.28); indeed it is about five times smaller. The difference is *compensated* by an increase in the stock of Treasury bills held by the central bank $(+0.99)$. This is because the fall in the stock of money is not 'caused' by the drop in the supply of foreign reserves; rather it is entirely demand-determined. It comes about as a result of the fall in the flow of income induced by the higher propensity to import. The fall in the level of income brings about a fall in the target level of wealth, and hence in the amount of desired money balances. To achieve this lower wealth target, households dissave. These effects, as can be seen from Figures 6.9 and 6.10, however, are only temporary ones. When income and wealth reach their new stationary levels after a few periods, the amount of money held by households remains constant while the trade deficit continues unabated, with the central

Table 6.5   First-period effect of the jump in imports on the balance sheet of the South central bank

Assets	Liabilities
Change in gold reserves −1.28	Change in high-powered money −0.29
Change in Treasury bills +0.99	

bank experiencing a continuous drain on its gold reserves. The Mundell–Fleming story, or the 'income-specie flow' mechanism as Mundell (1961: 159) calls it, and the 'price-specie flow' mechanism both turn out to be erroneous after all.

This finding is in line with the claim made by Arestis and Eichner (1988: 1015) that 'so long as it is recognized that money supply is credit-driven and demand-determined, the exchange rate regime is of absolutely no consequence in the determination of money and credit'. Interest rates can be set by the central bank and money is demand-determined in this fixed exchange rate regime.[12]

6.8.4   A further example of the compensation thesis: increasing the propensity to save

Let us assume that South households decide to increase their propensity to save, thus increasing their target wealth to income ratio. The impact of such a decision on GDP is identical to what was described with Figure 6.5 in the case of the two regions, with both the South and the North countries GDP dropping briskly, only to rise to a slightly higher level in the new stationary state. Similarly, the impact on the household financial balance, trade balance and government budget of the South are identical to that described in Figure 6.6. In other words, the short-term recession in the South initially generates a government deficit and a trade surplus. This trade balance however gets reversed in the long run, since the higher steady-state GDP in the South generates constant trade deficits and government deficits of equal size.

The new results of this two-country economy, relative to the two-region economy, can be found in Figure 6.11, which illustrates what happens to the three components of the balance sheet of the South central bank. The evolution of gold holdings reflect the evolution of the trade balance. Gold

---

[12] This was recognized by earlier Keynesian authors, such as Meade. As Allen and Kenen (1980: 8), point out, 'Meade instructs the central bank to maintain a constant interest rate; the bank's open market operations offset changes in the supply of money caused by movements of reserves and offset changes in the demand for money caused by the movements in domestic income'.

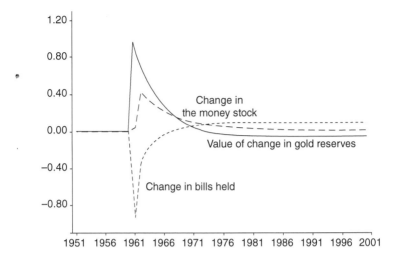

Figure 6.11 Evolution of the components of the balance sheet of the South central bank, following an increase in the South propensity to consume out of current income

holdings initially rise, but this is gradually replaced by an outflow of gold, since a quasi stationary state is reached, with a constant trade deficit. The stock of high-powered money initially increases, reflecting the increase in desired wealth by Southern households, and it then remains constant reflecting the quasi stationary state with no change in the wealth of households. As to the amount of bills held by the central bank, it is this component of the central bank that adjusts to the fluctuations in the other components of its balance sheet. To maintain a given rate of interest, the South central bank compensates the quasi steady-state outflow of gold reserves by increasing domestic credit, that is by increasing its holdings of domestic Treasury bills. By contrast, during the recession, the inflow of gold, which was accompanied by a modest increase in the money supply arising from the decision of Southern households to increase their two wealth components, was compensated by a reduction in the stock of bills held by the South central bank, thus illustrating once more the compensation principle.

6.9 Adjustment mechanisms

6.9.1 The super stationary state

Over recent years, a group of heterodox economists (see McCombie and Thirlwall 1994) has been arguing, both for theoretical and empirical reasons, that the long-run rate of growth of any open economy is essentially constrained by a ratio, which is the rate of growth of its exports divided by the income elasticity of imports of that country. This implies that, over the long run, the trade account of these countries is roughly balanced. In fact, in the original study of Thirlwall (1979), Japan was the only country the actual rate of growth of which did not turn out to be closely related to the prediction of his simple equation because Japan had a large trade account surplus over a large number of years.

We have claimed above that no automatic economic forces would push the economy towards a balanced trade account. But this of course is true only as long as there are spare foreign reserves. When a country with a balance-of-payments deficit runs out of reserves, something must be done. As pointed out earlier, the government of the deficit country can decide to pursue fiscal austerity in order to establish a balanced trade position, by reducing national income and hence imports. This kind of decision is particularly likely, because of the twin-deficit problem: the country with a trade deficit will also be facing, at least when the steady state is reached, a government budget deficit. Recalling equation (6.35), modified to take into account the fact that the tax rate now applies to a single country, it is quite simple to understand what will occur.

$$Y^{\mathrm{N}} = \frac{G^{\mathrm{N}}_{\mathrm{NT}}}{\theta^{\mathrm{N}}} = \frac{X^{\mathrm{N}}}{\mu^{\mathrm{N}}} \qquad (6.35\mathrm{A})$$

Assuming that exports are exogenous, and that the propensity to import cannot be modified, the only way to reach the super stationary state, for a country with a trade deficit, is to reduce pure government expenditures or to increase the tax rate. This will be done until the $G^{\mathrm{N}}_{\mathrm{NT}}/\theta^{\mathrm{N}}$ ratio, which is too high relative to the $X^{\mathrm{N}}/\mu^{\mathrm{N}}$ ratio, is reduced to the level of the latter. If such policies are indeed pursued, it is clear that the world economy suffers from a recession bias, since the reduction in autonomous expenditures in one country eventually leads to the reduction in the exports of the other countries. As to the countries with a trade and budget surplus, they will have little incentive to speed up pure government expenditures, although lately, strong pressures have been exerted, to use any government surplus to reduce tax rates. These pressures ought to be successful in keeping the recession bias at bay, but at the same time, the forces in play are asymmetrical. In the case of vanishing foreign reserves, something *must* be done to slow down imports and deflate the economy. In the case of the economy with a trade surplus, there is no such urgency. Politicians and bureaucrats are quite content with trade and government budget surpluses. They probably feel that nothing needs to be done to correct the trade surplus, and they can easily withstand pressures to increase government services or to cut tax rates. This is because, among other factors, some of the constituencies which are so enthusiastic about tax cuts – the rentiers – are also worried about the consequences of such tax cuts, fearing that the cuts would generate an overheated economy and accelerating price inflation.

6.9.2 Adjustment through pure government expenditures

Still, let us consider the possibility of an adjustment through changes in pure government expenditures. Let us first model some partially symmetric adjustment mechanism, that leads to a decrease in pure government expenditures whenever gold reserves are falling, and that leads to a relatively smaller increase in pure government expenditures whenever gold reserves are rising. This adjustment mechanism may be written in a quite simple way. We could have:

$$G^N = G^N_{-1} + \varphi^N \cdot (\Delta or^N_{-1} \cdot p^N_{g-1}) \tag{6.0.33}$$

$$G^S = G^S_{-1} + \varphi^S \cdot (\Delta or^S_{-1} \cdot p^S_{g-1}) \tag{6.0.34}$$

where the φs are positive.

Such an adjustment mechanism is stabilizing, as can be seen from Figure 6.12. As in the previous figures, we assume that, having started from a super stationary state, there is an increase in the South propensity to import. As its net exports decrease, the South economy slows down and must face both losses of gold reserves and government deficits. However, this time round, the losses and the budget deficits do not last forever, for the decreasing pure government expenditures slow down the economy and bring it back both to a balanced trade position and to a balanced budget – with some overshooting as can be seen from Figure 6.12.

The only problem with this stabilizing mechanism is that the economy must slow down, so that, in the new steady state, the income level in the deficit country – the South – is lower than what it was before or than what it would have been had pure government expenditures been left at a constant level. This can be verified by comparing the new steady-state value taken by the GDP of the South country in Figure 6.13 with that of Figure 6.8, where an identical experiment was conducted, but without the adjustment mechanism. Of course, in the North economy, the reverse occurs: the income level rises, both because of its improved trade position, and because of its increased government expenditures. If there had been no symmetrical process, (i.e. had the North not reacted to its trade surplus by increasing its government expenditures) income in the South would have fallen even more, but balanced trade would have been achieved nonetheless.

As the use of fiscal policy to curb trade imbalances yields strong stabilizing properties, it is no surprise to discover that the World Bank and the IMF are quite keen on using such an adjustment tool and in imposing it when they

204

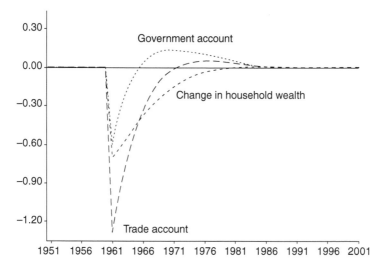

Figure 6.12 Evolution of the balances of the South country – net acquisition of financial assets by the household sector, government budget balance, trade balance – following an increase in the South propensity to import, with fiscal policy reacting to changes in gold reserves

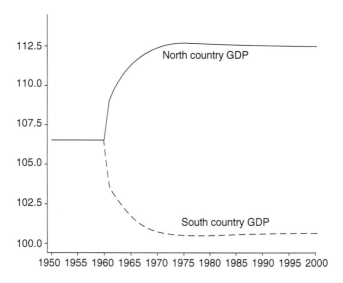

Figure 6.13 Evolution of GDP in the South and the North countries, following an increase in the South propensity to consume, with fiscal policy reacting to changes in gold reserves

propose adjustment packages to third-world countries that have balance-of-payments disequilibria. The danger is that all balance-of-payments deficit countries use such an adjustment mechanism while all surplus countries decline to inflate their economies, in which case the world economy will be biased towards depression.

6.9.3   Adjustments through interest rates

World Bank adjustment packages usually contain another element – interest rate hikes. Are these interest rate increases stabilizing? In standard World Bank adjustment packages, the higher (real) interest rates are there to slow down the economy, so as to help solving a negative trade balance, and they are intended to attract foreign capital as well as to induce domestic asset holders to keep their assets in the domestic financial markets. Within the present model, it is clear that interest rate hikes would serve no purpose. There are two reasons for this. In Model *OPEN*, private economic activity does not depend on interest rates; in addition, capital flows between countries are ruled out, so there are no foreign capital flows to attract or no domestic capital flows to keep within.

Still, what would happen if interest rates were to react to changes in gold reserves? We can put forward an adjustment equation which is similar to the one proposed above. We would have:

$$r^N = r^N_{-1} - \varphi^N \cdot (\Delta o r^N_{-1} \cdot p^N_{g-1}) \tag{6.O.30A}$$

$$r^S = r^S_{-1} - \varphi^S \cdot (\Delta o r^S_{-1} \cdot p^S_{g-1}) \tag{6.O.31A}$$

The rate of interest is not set exogenously anymore; however, within the framework that we have set up, it is still possible for the monetary authorities to set the rate of interest at their discretion. In other words, equations (6.O.30A) and (6.O.31A), which replace equations (6.O.30) and (6.O.31), are the reaction functions of the central banks.

One would normally suppose that the change in the rate of interest ought to be a negative function of the change in gold reserves. This is why there is a minus sign in front of the φ parameters. For instance, a decrease in gold reserves ought to lead to an increase in the rate of interest.

It would seem that we are back to the 'price-specie' mechanism, and to the Mundell–Fleming automatic adjustment mechanism. As pointed out in previous sections, these mechanisms lead to spontaneous increases in rates of interest whenever gold reserves are falling. But precisely, the above equations have nothing automatic or natural about them. They are reaction functions, which require a discretionary decision and a purposeful action from the central bank. Rates of interest move up, not as a result of some spontaneous market mechanism, but rather as a consequence of the deliberate

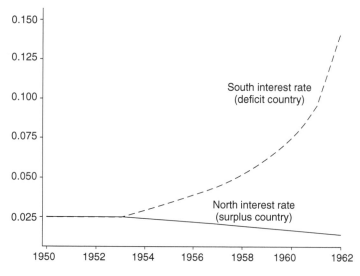

Figure 6.14   Evolution of interest rates, following an increase in the South propensity to import, with monetary rules based on changes in gold reserves

policy choice of the monetary authorities. Equations (6.O.30) are monetary rules that the central banks have decided to put in place.

The other key question is whether such an increase in interest rates, whenever a trade deficit arises, will have stabilizing effects. It turns out that such an adjustment mechanism is fundamentally non self-righting. It is formally unstable, as simulation experiments quickly reveal. Figure 6.14 shows that this is so because the interest rate in the South rises ever faster (while interest rates in the North keep falling, more slowly, on the basis of an asymmetric rule). Figure 6.15 shows that the trade imbalances between the South and the North only worsen, with the government deficit in the South getting ever worse. Indeed, when submitted to such monetary adjustment rules, the program crashes.

Such a result is not surprising. High rates of interest cannot attract foreign capital, since capital flows have been excluded by assumption. High interest rates do not slow down the economy either, and hence cannot reduce the trade deficit, since interest rates are assumed not to have any negative impact on the private economy. Indeed, an increase in interest rates worsens the budget deficit of government, and it fuels the consumption expenditures and the imports of the private economy, by reason of equations (6.O.3) and (6.O.7), thus leading to a further deterioration of the balance of trade.

The instability of this interest rate adjustment still occurs if we let interest rates have a negative impact on aggregate consumption. Assume for instance that, as was done with Model *PC* of Chapter 4, a higher interest rate leads to

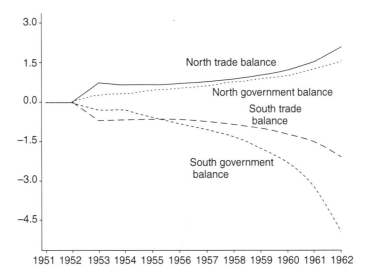

Figure 6.15 Evolution of the trade accounts and government balances of both countries, following an increase in the South propensity to import, with monetary rules based on changes in gold reserves

a lower propensity to consume out of disposable income. In the case of the South economy, we would have:

$$\alpha_1^S = \alpha_{10}^S - \iota^S \cdot r^S \qquad (6.O.35)$$

We have experimented with several different values for the ρ and φ parameters. The model becomes rather chaotic, and the results vary considerably from one set of parameters to another. Sometimes the model explodes, sometimes it converges to a quasi steady state, as shown here in Figures 6.16 and 6.17, sometimes it seems to go nowhere. Thus we can only conclude that adjustments through interest rates do not seem to be reliable, even when higher interest rates slow down the economy in the short run.

6.10 Concluding thoughts

We could, at this stage, make further experiments and examine what happens to the South if its government were to decide to increase expenditures, or if households from the North were to reduce their liquidity preference. We are not going to pursue the matter further at this point because our model is still very scanty. In particular, the production sector does not invest, and there are no private banks. But the assumptions made are not *so* scanty that they cannot be used to describe a certain range of real historical situations. One can easily think of episodes, like 1931 when Britain was forced off the

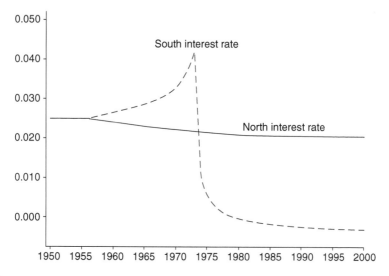

Figure 6.16 Evolution of interest rates, following an increase in the South propensity to import, with interest rates acting on propensities to consume and reacting to changes in gold reserves

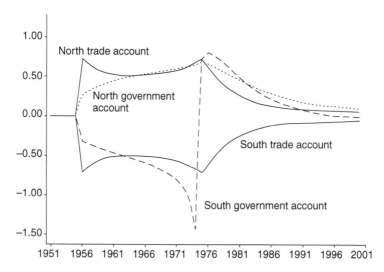

Figure 6.17 Evolution of trade accounts and government balances, following an increase in the South propensity to import, with interest rates acting on propensities to consume and reacting to changes in gold reserves

gold standard because she ran clean out of reserves at a particular hour and minute, which gives us courage to believe that we are on the right track. In addition, there is a large amount of empirical and descriptive evidence supporting the compensation principle which can be found for periods during which the gold exchange standard was ruling – the regime considered to be most favourable to enforce the so-called rules of the game. Studies have provided data that run contrary to what would occur if the rules of the game had been followed during the gold exchange standard era.[13] This shows that the price-specie flow mechanism and the rules of the game are bad theories and bad descriptions of what occurs in the real world. The point made here is that these theories are failures because they lack a proper and coherent accounting framework.

The current framework can be easily extended to include capital flows or other institutional set-ups. For instance, in Lavoie (2003), the present framework is modified by including private capital flows between countries in a world with two governments and one central bank (something akin to Europe). Also, in Lavoie (2006c), there is a discussion within a two-country framework of the currency board institution, so popular before the Argentinian debacle.[14] Izurieta (2003) also develops the case of dollarization along similar lines.

One could argue that the *OPEN* model or these offsprings are oversimplified and omit too many realistic features. We shall show in Chapter 12 however, that the main mechanisms and results of the *OPEN* model are still vindicated in more sophisticated models, for instance when there is free capital mobility between countries, and when central banks hold foreign assets instead of gold as foreign reserves. In that chapter, we shall also go beyond fixed exchange rates, by analysing what occurs when the model is transformed into a flexible exchange rate model, with changing exchange rates having an impact on various price indices. A simplified version of that model has been presented in Godley and Lavoie (2005–6), where a slightly different pedagogical approach has been followed to help readers understand the logic of the compensation principle or that of endogenous sterilization.

Appendix 6.1: Equations of Model *REG*

$$Y^N = C^N + G^N + X^N - IM^N \tag{6.1}$$

$$Y^S = C^S + G^S + X^S - IM^S \tag{6.2}$$

$$IM^N = \mu^N \cdot Y^N \tag{6.3}$$

---

[13] See Appendix 6.3 for further details.
[14] More is said about this in Appendix 6.4.

$$IM^S = \mu^S \cdot Y^S \tag{6.4}$$

$$X^N = IM^S \tag{6.5}$$

$$X^S = IM^N \tag{6.6}$$

$$YD^N = Y^N - T^N + r_{-1} \cdot B_{h-1}^N \tag{6.7}$$

$$YD^S = Y^S - T^S + r_{-1} \cdot B_{h-1}^S \tag{6.8}$$

$$T^N = \theta \cdot (Y^N + r_{-1} \cdot B_{h-1}^N) \quad 0 < \theta < 1 \tag{6.9}$$

$$T^S = \theta \cdot (Y^S + r_{-1} \cdot B_{h-1}^S) \quad 0 < \theta < 1 \tag{6.10}$$

$$V^N = V_{-1}^N + (YD^N - C^N) \tag{6.11}$$

$$V^S = V_{-1}^S + (YD^S - C^S) \tag{6.12}$$

$$C^N = \alpha_1^N \cdot YD^N + \alpha_2^N \cdot V_{-1}^N \quad 0 < \alpha_2^N < \alpha_1^N < 1 \tag{6.13}$$

$$C^S = \alpha_1^S \cdot YD^S + \alpha_2^S \cdot V_{-1}^S \quad 0 < \alpha_2^S < \alpha_1^S < 1 \tag{6.14}$$

$$H_h^N = V^N - B_h^N \tag{6.15}$$

$$H_h^S = V^S - B_h^S \tag{6.16}$$

$$\frac{B_h^N}{V^N} = \lambda_0^N + \lambda_1^N \cdot r - \lambda_2^N \cdot \left(\frac{YD^N}{V^N} \right) \tag{6.17}$$

$$\frac{B_h^S}{V^S} = \lambda_0^S + \lambda_1^S \cdot r - \lambda_2^S \cdot \left(\frac{YD^S}{V^S} \right) \tag{6.18}$$

$$\frac{H_h^N}{V^N} = (1 - \lambda_0^N) - \lambda_1^N \cdot r + \lambda_2^N \cdot \left(\frac{YD^N}{V^N} \right) \tag{6.15A}$$

$$\frac{H_h^S}{V^S} = (1 - \lambda_0^S) - \lambda_1^S \cdot r + \lambda_2^S \cdot \left(\frac{YD^S}{V^S} \right) \tag{6.16A}$$

$$T = T^N + T^S \tag{6.19}$$

$$G = G^N + G^S \tag{6.20}$$

$$B_h = B_h^N + B_h^S \tag{6.21}$$

$$H_h = H_h^N + H_h^S \tag{6.22}$$

$$\Delta B_s = B_s - B_{s-1} = (G + r_{-1} \cdot B_{s-1}) - (T + r_{-1} \cdot B_{cb-1}) \tag{6.23}$$

$$\Delta H_s = H_s - H_{s-1} = \Delta B_{cb} \tag{6.24}$$

$$B_{cb} = B_s - B_h \tag{6.25}$$

$$r = \bar{r} \tag{6.26}$$

Hidden equation:

$$H_s = H_h \qquad\qquad (6.27)$$

Appendix 6.2: Equations of Model *OPEN*

$$Y^N = C^N + G^N + X^N - IM^N \qquad\qquad (6.O.1)$$

$$Y^S = C^S + G^S + X^S - IM^S \qquad\qquad (6.O.2)$$

$$IM^N = \mu^N \cdot Y^N \qquad\qquad (6.O.3)$$

$$IM^S = \mu^S \cdot Y^S \qquad\qquad (6.O.4)$$

$$X^N = \frac{IM^S}{xr} \qquad\qquad (6.O.5)$$

$$X^S = IM^N \cdot xr \qquad\qquad (6.O.6)$$

$$YD^N = Y^N - T^N + r^N_{-1} \cdot B^N_{h-1} \qquad\qquad (6.O.7)$$

$$YD^S = Y^S - T^S + r^S_{-1} \cdot B^S_{h-1} \qquad\qquad (6.O.8)$$

$$T^N = \theta^N \cdot (Y^N + r^N_{-1} \cdot B^N_{h-1}) \quad 0 < \theta^N < 1 \qquad\qquad (6.O.9)$$

$$T^S = \theta^S \cdot (Y^S + r^S_{-1} \cdot B^S_{h-1}) \quad 0 < \theta^S < 1 \qquad\qquad (6.O.10)$$

$$V^N = V^N_{-1} + (YD^N - C^N) \qquad\qquad (6.O.11)$$

$$V^S = V^S_{-1} + (YD^S - C^S) \qquad\qquad (6.O.12)$$

$$C^N = \alpha^N_1 \cdot YD^N + \alpha^N_2 \cdot V^N_{-1} \quad 0 < \alpha_2 < \alpha_1 < 1 \qquad\qquad (6.O.13)$$

$$C^S = \alpha^S_1 \cdot YD^S + \alpha^S_2 \cdot V^S_{-1} \quad 0 < \alpha_2 < \alpha_1 < 1 \qquad\qquad (6.O.14)$$

$$H^N_h = V^N - B^N_h \qquad\qquad (6.O.15)$$

$$H^S_h = V^S - B^S_h \qquad\qquad (6.O.16)$$

$$\frac{B^N_h}{V^N} = \lambda^N_0 + \lambda^N_1 \cdot r^N - \lambda^N_2 \cdot \left(\frac{YD^N}{V^N}\right) \qquad\qquad (6.O.17)$$

$$\frac{B^S_h}{V^S} = \lambda^S_0 + \lambda^S_1 \cdot r^S - \lambda^S_2 \cdot \left(\frac{YD^S}{V^S}\right) \qquad\qquad (6.O.18)$$

$$\frac{H^N_h}{V^N} = (1 - \lambda^N_0) - \lambda^N_1 \cdot r^N + \lambda^N_2 \cdot \left(\frac{YD^N}{V^N}\right) \qquad\qquad (6.O.15A)$$

$$\frac{H^S_h}{V^S} = (1 - \lambda^S_0) - \lambda^S_1 \cdot r^S + \lambda^S_2 \cdot \left(\frac{YD^S}{V^S}\right) \qquad\qquad (6.O.16A)$$

$$\Delta B_s^N = B_s^N - B_{s-1}^N = (G^N + r_{-1}^N \cdot B_{s-1}^N) - (T^N + r_{-1}^N \cdot B_{cb-1}^N) \tag{6.O.19}$$

$$\Delta B_s^S = B_s^S - B_{s-1}^S = (G^S + r_{-1}^S \cdot B_{s-1}^S) - (T^S + r_{-1}^S \cdot B_{cb-1}^S) \tag{6.O.20}$$

$$B_{cb}^N = B_s^N - B_h^N \tag{6.O.21}$$

$$B_{cb}^S = B_s^S - B_h^S \tag{6.O.22}$$

$$\Delta or^{N \cdot} \cdot p_g^N = \Delta H_s^N - \Delta B_{cb}^N \tag{6.O.23}$$

$$\Delta or^{S \cdot} \cdot p_g^S = \Delta H_s^S - \Delta B_{cb}^S \tag{6.O.24}$$

$$H_s^N = H_h^N \tag{6.O.25}$$

$$H_s^S = H_h^S \tag{6.O.26}$$

$$p_g^N = \bar{p}_g^N \tag{6.O.27}$$

$$p_g^S = p_g^N \cdot xr \tag{6.O.28}$$

$$xr = \overline{xr} \tag{6.O.29}$$

$$r^N = \bar{r}^N \tag{6.O.30}$$

$$r^S = \bar{r}^S \tag{6.O.31}$$

Redundant or hidden equation:

$$\Delta or^S = -\Delta or^N \tag{6.O.32}$$

Possible additional equations to Model *OPEN*

OPENG

$$G^N = G_{-1}^N + \varphi^N (\Delta or_{-1}^N \cdot p_{g-1}^N) \tag{6.O.33}$$

$$G^S = G_{-1}^S + \varphi^S (\Delta or_{-1}^S \cdot p_{g-1}^S) \tag{6.O.34}$$

OPENM

$$r^N = r_{-1}^N - \varphi^N \cdot (\Delta or_{-1}^N \cdot p_{g-1}^N) \tag{6.O.30A}$$

$$r^S = r_{-1}^S - \varphi^S \cdot (\Delta or_{-1}^S \cdot p_{g-1}^S) \tag{6.O.31A}$$

OPENM3

$$r^N = r_{-1}^N - \varphi^N \cdot (\Delta or_{-1}^N \cdot p_{g-1}^N) \tag{6.O.30A}$$

$$r^S = r_{-1}^S - \varphi^S \cdot (\Delta or_{-1}^S \cdot p_{g-1}^S) \tag{6.O.31A}$$

$$\alpha_1^N = \alpha_{10}^N - \iota^N \cdot r \qquad\qquad (6.O.35)$$

$$\alpha_1^S = \alpha_{10}^S - \iota^S \cdot r \qquad\qquad (6.O.37)$$

Appendix 6.3: Historical and empirical evidence concerning the compensation principle

Some authors advocate a return to the gold standard, believing that it would restore the rules of the game, and hence that it would help to restore stability and balance-of-payments equilibria throughout the world. This is not the opinion however of the main modern proponents of the compensation principle, who point out that the compensation phenomenon which can be observed in modern economies could already be observed in the nineteenth century. This opinion is confirmed by studies on the gold standard period, between 1880–1913 and 1922–38. Bloomfield (1959: 49) shows that when looking at year-to-year changes in the period before the First World War – the heyday of the gold standard – the foreign assets and the domestic assets of central banks moved in opposite directions 60% of the time. Foreign assets and domestic assets moved in the same directions only 34% of the time for the eleven central banks under consideration. The prevalence of a negative correlation thus shows that the so-called rules of the game were violated more often than not, even during the heyday of the gold standard. Indeed, 'in the case of *every* central bank the year-to-year changes in international and domestic assets were more often in the *opposite* than in the same direction' (Bloomfield 1959: 49–50).

Almost identical results were obtained in the case of the 1922–38 period. Ragnar Nurkse (1944: 69) shows that the foreign assets and the domestic assets of twenty-six central banks moved in opposite direction in 60% of the years under consideration, and that they moved in the same directions only 32% of the time. Studying the various episodes of inflows or outflows of gold and exchange reserves, Nurkse (1944: 88) concludes that 'neutralization was the rule rather than the exception'. Without saying so, Nurkse adopts the compensation principle as the phenomenon ruling central banks in an open economy. The rules of the game as they were to be endorsed in the modern IS/LM/BP models of Mundell are an erroneous depiction of reality.

> There is nothing automatic about the mechanism envisaged in the 'rules of the game'. We have seen that automatic forces, on the contrary, may make for neutralization. Accordingly, if central banks were to intensify the effect of changes in their international assets instead of offsetting them or allowing them to be offset by inverse changes in their domestic assets, this would require not only deliberate management but possibly even management in opposition to automatic tendencies.
> (Nurkse 1944: 88)

Nurkse's account of the negative correlation between foreign and domestic assets of central banks in various dramatic instances is particularly interesting because he rejects the standard interpretation in terms of a 'sterilization' operation initiated by the central bank. Nurkse considers that it would be 'quite wrong to interpret [the inverse correlation] as a deliberate act of neutralization' on the part of the central bank.

Instead, Nurkse considers that the neutralization (or sterilization) of shifts in foreign reserves is caused by 'normal' or 'automatic' factors. Well-known authors have implicitly or explicitly endorsed the principle of compensation. Nicholas Kaldor (1980: 309) has provided some econometric evidence in support of the principle. When speaking of the various determinants of the monetary base within the balance sheet of the central bank, Charles Goodhart (1984: 192) points out that there is 'some tendency towards negative covariation in these flows, that is, they seem to interact in a way that produces some partial compensation, which alleviates some of the difficulties facing the authorities. A large foreign exchange inflow usually encourages sales of gilts and also reduces company demand for bank credit'.

Appendix 6.4: Other institutional frameworks: the currency board

Currency boards are central banks deprived of the power to grant credit to domestic borrowers. Their sole responsibility is to make sure that the amount of domestic currency issued is fully covered by their foreign reserves. Such currency boards were first set up in colonial times, in the first half of the nineteenth century, when Britain wished to reduce the costs and inconvenience generated by the use of its currency by the far-away colonies of its huge empire. Currency boards were highly popular until the end of the Second World War, at which stage they went out of fashion, being a symbol of outmoded colonialism, and were replaced by standard central banks. Except for Hong-Kong and Singapore, currency boards virtually disappeared until 1991, when Argentina adopted a currency board kind of monetary arrangement, which has since been imitated in a few other countries, such as Bulgaria or Lithuania (Ponsot 2002).

Currency boards have been proposed as a quick-fix solution to the recurrent problems that have been met by various countries to maintain price and exchange rate stability, in particular in South America and in Eastern Europe, especially in Russia. Currency boards are said to provide credibility to a currency, since, at least in theory, the issue of currency is limited by the availability of foreign reserves. In other words, domestic currency is backed by foreign reserves. 'Pure' currency boards hold a single type of asset – foreign reserves, gold or foreign currencies such as the American dollar or the euro. They make no domestic credit and, in contrast to central banks, they make no advances to the domestic private sector nor do they hold domestic government assets. Any increase in the stock of high-powered money must be accompanied by an influx of foreign reserves, that is, a favourable balance of payments.

Currency boards are thus the means to restore the automatic adjustment mechanisms that neo-classical economists have been longing for. According to its proponents, the currency board is said to restore the *Rules of the game* that ought to regulate any properly designed open financial system, notably one based on the gold exchange standard. Within such a system, any deficit in the balance of payments would generate gold losses, which are then said to induce reductions in the money supply and higher interest rates, and hence a slowdown in economic activity and in imports, and ultimately an equilibrated balance of payments. Lavoie (2006c) shows that a currency board does not quite behave in this simple way. Its functioning is barely any different from that of an ordinary central bank; the currency board may also function along the lines of a stable endogenous-money economy, but it may do so within a more restricted zone. Outside this zone, either fiscal policy must be given up or interest rate behaviour will generate instability.

More surprisingly, within the stock-flow consistent approach which is advocated here, Lavoie (2006c) shows that it is possible for the currency board to set interest rates, even though it is defending a fixed exchange rate on one hand, and refusing on the other hand to grant loans to its domestic economy. This is recognized by the officials of some currency boards.

In the case of Bulgaria again, the Bulgarian National Bank 'announces the base interest rate', whereas the standard belief is that under a currency board or more generally a fixed exchange rate, 'the market alone should determine interest rates' (Dobrev 1999: 14). This result is rather remarkable, for it goes against accepted opinions. Take the following statement for instance, drawn from a well-known survey of exchange rate economics:

> Under a currency board arrangement, the board normally agrees to supply or redeem domestic base money against a foreign currency without limit at a fixed exchange rate. Thus a pure currency board arrangement is essentially equivalent to a fixed exchange rate arrangement in which sterilization is prohibited and the monetary authorities have no autonomy over interest rates. (Isard 1995: 213)

The currency board described by Lavoie (2006c) is indeed a pure currency board; it sustains a fixed exchange rate and it does not engage in standard sterilization operations, that is, it does not engage into open market operations since it neither sells nor purchases bills and bonds. Still, the currency board has full control over interest rates. This is made possible by the fluctuations in the money deposits of government, held on the books of the currency board, which allow for the flexibility of the currency board arrangement. Whenever foreign exchange reserves (gold reserves) are increasing faster than the domestic household demand for cash money, the slack between the two is taken by an increase in government deposits held at the currency board. Symmetrically, when the demand for money by households is rising faster than the foreign exchange reserves of the currency board, or when foreign exchange reserves are falling faster than the household demand for domestic cash money, the discrepancy is taken care of by a reduction in government deposits held at the currency board. The compensation principle is just as valid in the case of a currency board as it was in the case of the *OPEN* economy model with a central bank compelled to hold constant the exchange rate.

Appendix 6.5: How to easily build an open model

- Start with two identical economies, both at the super stationary state. Indeed, you may start with the same numbers that were used for a closed economy (the *PC* model).
- Use the super steady-state equations to determine income, net total government expenditures, exports (and imports), from the chosen tax rate and the propensity to import. Use nice rounded numbers.
- Assume some arbitrary level of bills held by households and an exogenous rate of interest. This will help set pure government expenditures.
- Compute disposable income.
- From the propensities to consume, compute the steady-state wealth to disposable income ratio, and hence household wealth.
- By difference, compute the amount of cash held by households.
- This determines the amount of cash issued by the central bank. In the *PC* model, this would then determine the amount of bills held by the central bank, and by

adding bills held by households, this would fix the total amount of government debt.

- But in an open economy, you must proceed differently. You can now set an arbitrary level of debt for the government, the residual amount of bills held by the central bank, and the appropriate value of gold held by the central bank, provided all these values respect the central bank balance-sheet constraints.

- Set the parameters of the portfolio equations in a manner that is consistent with the values already determined.

- To add some asymmetry to the model, you may modify the propensities to consume of one of the two countries, making sure that the α_3 coefficient so computed corresponds indeed to the wealth to disposable income ratio that you started with.

7
A Simple Model with Private Bank Money

7.1 Private money and bank loans

As pointed out earlier, money is created in two fundamentally different ways. In Chapters 3–6, we only dealt with *government* money – indifferently called high-powered money, central bank money, cash money or outside money. This kind of money had a peculiar characteristic: it carried no interest yield. It is now time to introduce *private* money, that is, the money created by private banks. Although private, or commercial, banks could also print cash money or banknotes, as they indeed were allowed to do in the past before central banks were awarded the monopoly, we shall assume that all private money takes the form of money deposits. We shall further assume that these bank deposits carry an interest yield.

In previous chapters we saw that the creation of government money was associated with government deficits. In the case of private money, the creation of money is tied to banks granting new loans. Although loans could be granted to firms, households or the government sector, we shall suppose, at least initially, that all loans are granted to production firms. These loans carry an interest yield, which must be paid by the firms which have borrowed from the banks. The reader may wonder why private money has not been brought into the picture any sooner. These interest payments, which must be made by firms, are the major cause. They add some complications to the accounting framework, complications that did not exist when only the government sector had to make interest payments on its debt.

Why do production firms need to borrow from banks? Why are firms in debt vis-à-vis the banking system, whereas there was no such debt in the previous chapters? The previous chapters described a service economy, where no capital goods were required for the firms to produce. This service economy was a kind of pure labour economy, where labour was the only input. Production did not require fixed capital, and it was assumed that all services could be produced on demand, without any need to hold inventories of goods or services. In a sense, production was instantaneous; it did not require time. These simplifying and artificial assumptions allowed us to move quickly forward in Chapters 3–6. They allowed us to circumvent relatively difficult accounting problems, such as cost accounting, inventory accounting, inflation accounting, as well as delicate economic questions, such as investment behaviour and the distribution of property income. It is now time to face some of these real-world problems. In the real world, firms require fixed capital and working capital. As a result, they need to borrow from private banks.

In this chapter, we present the *BMW* model, the simplest *bank-money world* model. There is only one kind of financial asset, the money deposits held by households, and only fixed capital expenditures will be taken into account. This will allow us to circumvent, until the next chapter, the complications associated with inventories valuation and inflation accounting.

7.2   The matrices of the simplest model with private money

7.2.1   The balance sheet matrix

As usual, we start with the balance sheet matrix of Model *BMW* – the simplest model with private money. The entire public sector has been assumed away, so as to concentrate on the workings of the private economy. Thus both the pure government sector and the central bank have been taken out of the matrix. We have also reverted to a closed economy. We assume that households do not borrow, and that they accumulate all their savings in the form of money deposits. Reciprocally, we assume that firms do not hold money balances, and that they borrow from banks to finance their new capital expenditures. Finally, we assume, for simplicity, that neither the firms nor the banks have any net worth. This means, by implication, that no asset revaluation has taken place in the past. In other words, prices have been assumed to remain constant. Indeed, in the equations of the model, the price level will be a constant, set equal to one.

All these assumptions are reflected in the balance sheet matrix of Table 7.1. As usual, all rows related to financial assets or liabilities sum to zero. This is the case of the M row, which deals with money deposits at banks; and it is also the case of the loans taken by firms, the L row. By contrast, the row relevant to tangible capital, the K row of fixed capital, does not sum to zero. This is a phenomenon that we observed in Chapter 2, when balance sheet matrices were first presented. Tangible capital appears in the assets of production firms, but they are not counterbalanced by the liabilities of another sector. Tangible capital is only an asset; it is not simultaneously an asset and a liability, as is the case of financial capital.

Table 7.1   Balance sheet of Model *BMW*

	Households	Production firms	Banks	Σ
Money deposits	$+M$		$-M$	0
Loans		$-L$	$+L$	0
Fixed capital		$+K$		$+K$
Balance (net worth)	$-V_h$	0	0	$-V_h$
Σ	0	0	0	0

As usual, also, we add a balancing item, net worth, which ensures that all columns sum to zero. In the very simple model presented here, neither the production sector nor the banking sector are assumed to make any net profits. As a result, the net worth of both the production and the banking sectors is nil. Only the household sector has a positive net worth, its wealth V_h, and by the laws of accounting, that net wealth must be exactly equal to the existing amount of tangible capital K. Thus in the present simplified model, money deposits are equal to bank loans, and each of these two items is equal to the value of tangible capital.

7.2.2   The transactions-flow matrix

Let us now deal with the transactions-flow matrix, as shown in Table 7.2. As with the other transactions matrix, this matrix has components of the National Income and Product Accounts arranged as transactions between sectors above the first horizontal line. Below this line are the changes in financial assets and liabilities which correspond to the Flow-of-Funds Account. Columns and rows all sum to zero.

There are two novelties compared to the transactions-flow matrices of the previous models. First, there is a private banking sector, with both a current and a capital account. The current account registers the payments that the banking sector must make or receive. The capital account registers the additions or the subtractions, to assets and liabilities. The other novelty is the capital account of the sector of production firms. Firms now accumulate fixed capital goods, so long as a stationary state has not been reached. This accumulation of capital goods, and how it is financed, is registered in this capital account. The current account only registers output sales and production costs.

What happens is that, unlike consumption or government expenditures, investment in fixed capital (or in inventories, when these will be introduced) does not originate from other sectors, so that, in a double entry system of accounts, they have to come from a capital account from within the firm

Table 7.2 The accounting transactions-flow matrix of Model *BMW*

	Households	Production firms Current	Capital	Banks Current	Capital	Σ
Consumption	$-C$	$+C$				0
Investment		$+I$	$-I$			0
[Production]		$[Y]$				
Wages	$+WB$	$-WB$				0
Depreciation allowances		$-AF$	$+AF$			0
Interest on loans		$-r_{l-1} \cdot L_{-1}$		$+r_{l-1} \cdot L_{-1}$		0
Interest on deposits	$+r_{m-1} \cdot M_{-1}$			$-r_{m-1} \cdot M_{-1}$		0
Change in loans			$+\Delta L$		$-\Delta L$	0
Change in deposits	$-\Delta M$				$+\Delta M$	0
Σ	0	0	0	0	0	0

sector. The funds to pay for these capital expenditures, in turn, will have to come from somewhere, as we shall see.

Reading the matrix horizontally, we note that any source of income must have a counterpart somewhere. For instance, the interest income on money deposits paid by banks must have as a counterpart the interest income received by the households. Similarly, the wage bill of firms are the wages received by households. The main new entry is the *gross* investment entry *I*. Firms sell the fixed capital goods they produce, and this appears with a plus sign in the current account column, since this is a source of income. But they also acquire these fixed capital goods – their investment – and these appear with a minus sign in the capital account column, since these investment goods purchases are a use of fund. The funds to finance the acquisition of capital goods come from two sources, and this is what the other entries in the capital account column of firms show : these two sources are the amortization funds and funds borrowed from the banking sector.

The amortization funds are the funds that the firms set aside in each period to fund replacement investment, that is, to replace tangible capital that is being worn out. In other words, the amortization funds *AF* play a role which is no different from retained earnings, except that it is assumed that these amortization funds are intended to cover only the replacement cost of

Table 7.3 The behavioural transactions matrix of Model *BMW*

	Households	Production firms Current	Production firms Capital	Banks Current	Banks Capital	Σ
Consumption	$-C_d$	$+C_s$				?
Investment		$+I_s$	$-I_d$			?
[Production]		[Y]				
Wages	$+WB_s$	$-WB_d$				?
Depreciation allowances		$-AF$	$+AF$			0
Interest on loans		$-r_{l-1} \cdot L_{-1}$		$+r_{l-1} \cdot L_{-1}$		0
Interest on deposits	$+r_{m-1} \cdot M_{-1}$			$-r_{m-1} \cdot M_{-1}$		0
Change in loans			$+\Delta L_d$		$-\Delta L_s$	?
Change in deposits	$-\Delta M_h$				$+\Delta M_s$	?
Σ	0	0	0	0	0	0

worn-out capital, whereas retained earnings could be used to finance new additions to tangible capital. Here, by contrast, any acquisition of fixed capital goods, beyond the amounts required to replenish the existing stock, leads to an increase in loans of an equivalent amount.[1]

7.2.3 The behavioural transactions matrix

Because we are now introducing private bank money, no short cut will be taken in the present chapter. Once again, as we did with Model *SIM* in Chapter 3, a fully fledged model is going to be presented, where the supply and the demand sides of the main variables are distinct from each other. In order to do this, we shall once more start off from a behavioural transactions matrix, here shown in Table 7.3.

As was the case with Model *SIM*, the behavioural transactions matrix of Table 7.3 incorporates suffixes to the main variables. Take the case of the first

---

[1] The introduction of capital depreciation complicates the model somewhat, but adds a great deal of realism. As we shall see, a reduction in the stationary level of income requires a smaller stock of capital, but a reduction in the capital stock cannot be achieved without capital depreciation, unless one assumes the far-fetched possibility of negative investment output.

row. Because the demand for consumption goods C_d may be different from the sales of consumption goods C_s, the entry in the summation cell carries a question mark. Until we provide a mechanism explaining how these two variables turn out to be equal, we cannot be sure that the row sums to zero. Similar question marks arise for the two rows dealing with financial assets. We must explain, for instance, why the changes in the supply of loans respond to the changes in the demand for loans. On the other hand, the rows associated with interest payments on loans or on deposits have their summation cell equal to zero. It is rather obvious, for instance, that the interest payments on deposits made by the banks are by necessity equal to the amounts that depositors receive, and no adjusting mechanism is required here.

The behavioural matrix will be particularly useful when we outline the equations that define the model.

7.3 The equations of Model *BMW*

As mentioned in the previous section, output prices are assumed to remain constant throughout, to avoid dealing with revaluation complications right away. While all variables are expressed in nominal values, these values may also be interpreted as real magnitudes, by setting the price level equal to unity.

The model is made up of 19 equations, with 19 variables, excluding the price variable. These equations can all be seen at a glance in Appendix 7.1. To help handling the system of equations, every variable appears on the left-hand side of an equation. The first four equations describe the mechanisms that adjust the various supply variables to their demand equivalent. The next seven equations are drawn from the transactions matrix, while the last eight equations reflect definitions or behaviour.

Once again we start with the four equations that equalize supply to demand.

$$C_s = C_d \tag{7.1}$$

$$I_s = I_d \tag{7.2}$$

$$N_s = N_d \tag{7.3}$$

$$\Delta L_s = \Delta L_d \tag{7.4}$$

Equations (7.1) and (7.2) reflect once more the assumed existence of an instantaneous quantity adjustment process. Producers supply the consumption goods which are being demanded and the investment goods which have been ordered. As was explicit in Model 1, equation (7.3) reflects the assumption that there is an infinite reserve army of unemployed workers, who are ready to work at constant productivity if they are being offered employment, whatever the wage rate. Finally, equation (7.4) reflects the hypothesis that the banks will supply the loans which are being demanded by the firms. In other words, there is no credit rationing in this model. The supply of loans is whatever the demand for loans is. In this simple world, there is no credit restrictions, or if there was, it would be reflected in the value taken by the parameter γ in equation (7.18). If production firms knew that some credit restrictions were existing, they would take this into consideration and would adjust more slowly to their targeted stock of capital, thus requesting smaller amounts of loans.

We now move to definitional equations which are implied by the transactions matrix, starting with the column of the current account of production firms. These definitional equations are given below:

$$Y = C_s + I_s \tag{7.5}$$

$$Y = WB_d + r_{-1} \cdot L_{d-1} + \delta \cdot K_{-1} \tag{7.6A}$$

$$WB_d = Y - r_{-1} \cdot L_{d-1} - \delta \cdot K_{-1} \tag{7.6}$$

Total gross production is defined in the standard way used in all national accounts, as the sum of all expenditures on goods and services, here consumption and investment goods, as shown in equation (7.5), or as the sum of all payments of factor income, as shown in equation (7.6A). Factor income is made up of three components: the wage bill, the amortization funds, and the interest payments of firms on their debt.[2] While the wage bill and the interest payments of firms are fairly straightforward, we need to say a bit more about AF – the amortization funds. We shall assume that these amortization funds are a constant proportion δ of the value of the stock of tangible capital at the beginning of the current period. Thus we write:

$$AF = \delta \cdot K_{-1} \tag{7.7}$$

For the purpose of the model, equation (7.6) rather than equation (7.6A) is the relevant one. It says that, in the present model, the wage bill is a residual. With a given unit price, and a certain level of production, the wage bill must be what is left once amortization funds and the interest payments to the banks have been taken care of. These are set at the beginning of the period, for a given rate of interest on loans, since the stock of debt L_{-1} and the stock of capital K_{-1} are given by history.

We still remain with the identities of the firm sector in the transactions matrix. Equation (7.8) is the budget constraint of the capital account of the

---

[2] We could say, in broad terms, that the interest payments and the amortization funds constitute the profits of the economic system, but the net 'profits' – net of interest and amortization – are zero.

production sector. Since firms make no net profits – amortization funds only finance the replacement of used-up capital – net investment must be entirely financed by loans obtained from the banking sector.

$$\Delta L_d = I_d - AF \tag{7.8}$$

The transactions matrix also yields the definition of income relevant to households. Equation (7.9) defines the disposable income of households. Since there is no government and no taxes, the disposable income of households is simply the sum of their wages and the interest payments that they receive on their deposits. It may be noted that household disposable income YD is different from national income, because of the presence of depreciation allowances in the definition of gross domestic product Y.

$$YD = WB_s + r_{m-1} \cdot M_{d-1} \tag{7.9}$$

The budget constraint of the household sector is shown in equation (7.10). In this simplified world, whatever income is not spent on consumption goods is added to the existing stock of bank deposits. Equation (7.10) describes the wealth accumulation function of households.

$$\Delta M_h = M_h - M_{h-1} = YD - C_d \tag{7.10}$$

Finally, equations (7.11) and (7.12) reflect respectively the capital account constraint and the current account constraint of the banking sector. Banks have a single asset – bank loans – and a single liability – bank deposits. There are no bonds, no central bank reserves, and private banks do not accumulate capital reserves since they have been assumed to make zero profits. As a result, the supply of bank money must be precisely equal to the supply of bank loans, and the rate of interest on deposits must be set equal to the rate of interest on loans.

$$\Delta M_s = \Delta L_s \tag{7.11}$$

$$r_m = r_l \tag{7.12}$$

We next move to three definitions related to the wage bill. Equation (7.13) makes the obvious definition of the wage bill, as the product of the wage rate times the level of employment. Equation (7.14) tells us what the level of employment will be, given the production level Y. Recall that Y represents both a nominal magnitude and real production, since the price level has been set equal to one. We assume, again for simplicity, a linear relationship between production and employment. The parameter *pr* represents labour productivity, being equal to output per unit of labour.[3] Finally, equation (7.15) tells us what the wage rate is, both in nominal and real terms, since, as already pointed out, the price level is a constant set equal to unity. Given the wage bill, as it appears in equation (7.6), and given the level of employment, as implied by equation (7.14), the real wage is determined by equation (7.15). More will be said about this in a later section.

$$WB_s = W \cdot N_s \tag{7.13}$$

$$N_d = \frac{Y}{pr} \tag{7.14}$$

$$W = \frac{WB_d}{N_d} \tag{7.15}$$

We now move to the equations that have some link with the behaviour of the various agents. We start with the behaviour of households, namely their consumption behaviour. The proposed consumption function, equation (7.16), is slightly different from the one that we have used in all previous models. An autonomous term has been added to our standard consumption function. Hence, as before, there are two induced terms, those that depend on current disposable income and past accumulated wealth. But consumption depends also in part on an exogenous element. It is this autonomous component of consumption that will allow our model to remain determinate. Otherwise, if consumption were fully induced, there would be no anchor to the model since investment expenditures are also induced, and as we shall see, converge to zero near the stationary state. It turns out that the exogenous term α_0 in the consumption function of our private money model plays the role of the exogenous government expenditures G, in the closed models with government money.

$$C_d = \alpha_0 + \alpha_1 \cdot YD + \alpha_2 \cdot M_{h-1} \tag{7.16}$$

The investment behaviour of firms is dealt with in the next equations. Equation (7.17) is another definition. It recalls that the change in the stock of fixed capital is equal to gross investment in fixed capital I_d minus the stock of machines used up during the current period through wear, tear and obsolescence – depreciation allowances – which we note as DA. Normally, a machine would wear out after a certain number of years of use, and so the depreciation allowance used to compute net investment should depend on the exact time-path of past investments. For instance, if all machines were designed to last for 20 years, with normal use and maintenance, the precise

[3] In mainstream terms, both the marginal and the average products of labour are constant.

amount of *disinvestment*, that is, the precise number of machines vanishing from the existing tangible capital stock would equal the exact number of machines that were put into service 20 years before. We shall assume otherwise however. For simplicity we shall assume that a constant proportion of the existing stock of machines either wears out or becomes obsolescent. Thus we have a constant rate of depreciation δ. This rate is applied to the stock of machines existing at the beginning of the current period, which is the stock of machines that ended up remaining at the end of the previous period, K_{-1}, and hence depreciation allowances shall be defined as in equation (7.18). Comparing equations (7.18) and (7.7), it should be obvious that we are assuming, for simplicity once again, that amortization funds and depreciation allowances are exactly equal. The funds that firms set aside to replace their used-up capital is just equal to the amount that is necessary to replace used-up capital. Combining equations (7.17) and (7.18), we obtain equation (7.18A), which says that the stock of machines at the end of the current period is equal to the stock of capital at the beginning of the current period, plus net investment.

$$K = K_{-1} + (I_d - DA) \tag{7.17}$$

$$DA = \delta \cdot K_{-1} \tag{7.18}$$

$$K = (1 - \delta) \cdot K_{-1} + I_d = K_{-1} + (I_d - \delta \cdot K_{-1}) \tag{7.18A}$$

Continuing with investment behaviour, equation (7.19) below is saying that production firms target a certain capital stock K^T. This targeted capital stock depends on the sales achieved in the previous period. The implicit assumption made here is that entrepreneurs, when they decide on their orders of investment goods, see overall sales of the previous period as the indicator of the overall sales in the coming period, and attempt to maintain a normal rate of utilization of their capacity.[4]

$$K^T = \kappa \cdot Y_{-1} \tag{7.19}$$

Finally, there is the investment function itself. The proposed investment function is quite standard: it is the partial adjustment accelerator model. Equation (7.20) says that *net* investment adjusts *partially* ($\gamma < 1$) to the discrepancy between the targeted capital stock K^T and the stock of machines that was inherited from the end of the previous period. *Gross* investment I_d is the sum of that net investment plus the investment required to replace the used-up machines. When the past stock of machines is larger than the targeted stock, gross investment will be smaller than replacement investment,

---

[4] If $Y_{-1} = Y_N$, the normal output, then the capital to full capacity ratio will be $\kappa \cdot u_N$ where u_N is the normal rate of capacity utilization.

in which case net investment will be negative. Of course, the model must be so constrained that *gross* investment cannot be negative. Its minimum value is zero.[5]

$$I_d = \gamma \cdot (K^T - K_{-1}) + DA \qquad (7.20)$$

The last equation of the model is the equation defining the rate of interest on loans. Because we have a degree of freedom left, the rate of interest on loans can be set by the banking system, at the level that it sees fit. The rate of interest on loans is not the result of a market-clearing price mechanism.

$$r_l = \bar{r}_l \qquad (7.21)$$

As should be the case in all coherent models, there is a redundant equation, which can be deduced from the other equations of the model, but which need not to be included within the model, for otherwise it would be over-determined. This equation can be deduced from the all the conditions that have been imposed on our behavioural transactions matrix. Because we have found the mechanisms that insure that all the columns and rows, but one, of the behavioural transactions matrix must sum to zero, we know that the last row must sum to zero as well, despite the absence of such an explicit mechanism for this last row. Here the last row is that of the changes in bank deposits. The redundant equation is:

$$\Delta M_h = \Delta M_s \qquad (7.22)$$

There are two distinct processes that explain the issue of new bank deposits by the banking system on the one hand (equation 7.11), and the additional amount of bank deposits that households decide to hold on the other hand (equation 7.10). By virtue of the tight accounting of the model, these two processes must yield the same answer, without any equilibrium condition being imposed.

7.4 The steady state

7.4.1 Income in the steady state

We now explore the steady-state solutions of our model. Because the model is so simple, it is possible to obtain analytically the steady-state solutions of the main variables. The steady state here is a stationary state, with no growth. This implies that, in the steady state, net investment is zero while gross investment is equal to depreciation allowances, and household saving is also zero. This insures, as in our previous models of a closed economy,

---

[5] More will be said about this in a later section.

that there is no asset accumulation in the steady state, so that stocks do not change while flows are kept constant.

The fact that household saving is zero in the steady state implies that once this state has been reached, household consumption must be equal to disposable income, as can be ascertained from the transactions matrix. Thus in the steady state, the consumption function (7.16) can be rewritten as:

$$YD^* = \alpha_0 + \alpha_1 \cdot YD^* + \alpha_2 \cdot M_h^* \tag{7.23}$$

where the stars denote steady-state values. There is no need to incorporate a time suffix to the money variable M_h, since in the steady state the value taken in the current period is the same as that of the previous period.

Another substitution can be made. In the steady state, net investment is zero, which implies, from equation (7.20), that the target level of capital is equal to the achieved stock of capital. This implies that $K^{T*} = K^*$. But we also know from the balance sheet matrix of Table 7.1 that, in our simple model, the wealth of households must never be different from the stock of tangible capital. The stock of wealth of households is entirely composed of money deposits. This implies that the following equality must hold at all times:

$$V_h = M_h = K \tag{7.24}$$

From equation (7.19), we also know that in the steady state the following equality will hold:

$$K^{T*} = \kappa \cdot Y^* \tag{7.25}$$

so that equation (7.23) can be rewritten as:

$$YD^* = \alpha_0 + \alpha_1 \cdot YD^* + \alpha_2 \cdot \kappa \cdot Y^* \tag{7.26}$$

Before we can find the steady-state value of disposable income YD^*, we need to establish the relationship between gross domestic product Y and household disposable income YD. In the case of our model, with the various conditions imposed, the difference is simply that the second variable is equivalent to net domestic product rather than gross domestic product. The difference then is the amount of capital depreciation. We may thus write:

$$Y = YD + \delta \cdot K_{-1} \tag{7.27}$$

In the steady-state, the previous, current and target stocks of wealth are all equal. Thus, with the help of equation (7.25), we can rewrite equation (7.27) in its steady-state version:

$$Y^* = YD^* + \delta \cdot \kappa \cdot Y^*$$

so that we have:

$$Y^* = \frac{YD^*}{(1 - \delta \cdot \kappa)} \qquad (7.28)$$

Substituting equation (7.28) into equation (7.26), we obtain the steady state value of disposable income:

$$YD^* = \frac{\alpha_0 (1 - \delta \cdot \kappa)}{(1 - \alpha_1) \cdot (1 - \delta \cdot \kappa) - \alpha_2 \cdot \kappa} \qquad (7.29)$$

and from there the value of the gross domestic product:

$$Y^* = \frac{\alpha_0}{(1 - \alpha_1) \cdot (1 - \delta \cdot \kappa) - \alpha_2 \cdot \kappa} \qquad (7.30)$$

Obviously, for these values to be positive, there must be some restrictions on the values taken by the various parameters. For gross domestic product Y^* to be positive, its denominator needs to be positive, which implies that the propensities to consume out of disposable income and out of wealth need to be small enough. Similarly, the target capital to income ratio κ and the rate of depreciation of capital δ cannot be too large.[6] Thus, the model makes sense only if the following restriction on the values taken by the various parameters is fulfilled:

$$\frac{(1 - \alpha_1)}{\alpha_2} > \frac{\kappa}{(1 - \delta \cdot \kappa)} \qquad (7.31)$$

In words, the ratio of the households' marginal propensity to save out of disposable income to the marginal propensity to consume out of wealth needs to be large enough compared to the values taken by the other (production) parameters of condition (7.31).[7]

7.4.2 The paradox of thrift recovered

A quick look at equation (7.30) is enough to verify the factors that have no impact and those that have an impact on the steady state level of income (and employment). It is remarkable that the rate of interest on deposits or loans has no impact whatsoever on the steady state level of income. Neither does the real wage level. This result is quite obvious, since the target level of capital is the result of a straightforward accelerator mechanism, which does

---

[6] Obviously, in the simplified case without depreciation, $\delta = 0$, and equation (7.30) simplifies to: $Y^* = \alpha_0/(1 - \alpha_1 - \alpha_2 \cdot \kappa)$, while condition (7.31) below becomes: $\kappa < (1 - \alpha_1)/\alpha_2 = \alpha_3$. The target capital to sales ratio set by firms must be smaller than the target wealth to disposable income set by households.
[7] This implies, if $\kappa = 2$ for instance, that the propensity to save out of disposable income must be more than twice the propensity to consume out of wealth.

not depend on the rate of interest being charged on loans, as could be seen from equation (7.19). In addition, there is a single propensity to consume out of disposable income, whether this income comes from wages or from interest revenue. Similarly, it may noticed that the γ parameter of the investment function (7.20), which represents the reaction speed of entrepreneurs when facing any discrepancy between the target and the actual capital stock, does not determine the steady state level of income.

Equation (7.30) shows quite clearly the role played by the α_0 parameter, which represents autonomous consumption expenditures. These autonomous consumption expenditures play the role previously played by government expenditures. They are the multiplicand of the model. The multiplier depends on the values taken by the propensities to consume α_1 and α_2, the target capital to income ratio κ, and the depreciation rate δ. It is obvious that the higher any of these parameters, the higher the steady state level of income, for a given amount of autonomous consumption expenditures.

Post-Keynesian authors have long underlined the role played by autonomous demand. The exogenous component of demand was of course emphasized by Keynes himself, but his followers have been struck by the key role that it plays in modern economies (Godley and Cripps 1983; Davidson 1994). Kaldor (1983: 9) has argued that, precisely because of autonomous demand, a capitalist economy is not necessarily self-adjusting. An increase in potential output will not 'automatically induce a corresponding growth of actual output. This will only be the case if exogenous demand expands at the same time to the required degree; and this cannot be taken for granted ...'. In our model, α_0 represents the autonomous component of demand. Figure 7.1 illustrates the obvious fact that any increase in autonomous consumption α_0 leads to an increase in disposable income and in overall consumption.

Figure 7.1 also illustrates the cyclical dynamics generated by investment behaviour. Income or disposable income overshoot their new steady state values because the increase in output during the transition induces positive net investment in fixed capital, these investments being made to insure that future capacity stays in line with expected demand. When the economy approaches its new steady state, net investment falls back towards zero, and as a result national income and disposable income drop below the values attained during part of the transition. Figure 7.2 illustrates the cyclical behaviour of investment, as generated by the accelerator equation. In the initial steps of the transition, net investment quickly moves up, first as a reaction to the increased sales induced by the hike in autonomous consumption expenditures, and then by the increased investment expenditures needed to replace the worn-out machines of the growing stock of capital; eventually however, net investment falls to zero, and all investment is replacement investment.

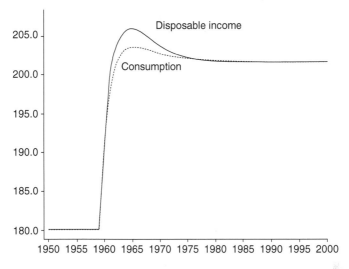

Figure 7.1 Evolution of household disposable income and consumption, following an increase in autonomous consumption expenditures, in Model *BMW*

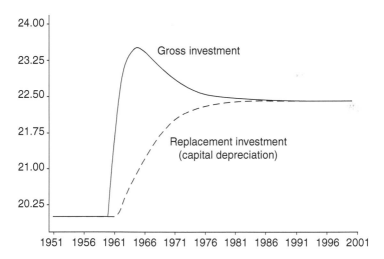

Figure 7.2 Evolution of gross investment and disposable investment, following an increase in autonomous consumption expenditures, in Model *BMW*

The positive impact of a higher propensity to consume on the steady state level of income is also worthy of being noted. In Model *SIM* of Chapter 3, an increase in the propensity to consume only had a temporary positive impact on national income, and no impact whatsoever on the steady state level of income. In Model *PC* of Chapter 4, an increase in the propensity to consume had a *negative* impact on the steady state level of income. These results contradicted the famous *paradox of thrift*, that had been highlighted by Bernard Mandeville in his famous *Fable of the Bees* and by Keynes in his *General Theory*. In the model with private money and no government that is developed in the current chapter, the paradox of thrift is recovered. An increase in thrift, that is, an increase in the propensity to save out of current income or out of wealth will reduce the current level of income as well as the steady state level of income.

What occurs is that the reduction in consumption reduces income, which leads in the next period to a reduction in the target stock of fixed capital, and in investment. In the end, provided the model is stable, the lower stock of tangible capital will be associated with lower financial wealth on the part of households, and this will generate a lower stationary level of income. All this is shown in Figure 7.3. Starting from a stationary state, it is assumed that a campaign of thrift is successful, so that households decide to decrease permanently their propensity to consume out of disposable income. The figure shows the negative impact on gross domestic income and disposable income, both at the beginning of the thrift campaign and in the new stationary state.

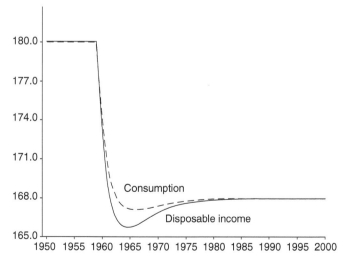

Figure 7.3 Evolution of household disposable income and consumption, following an increase in the propensity to save out of disposable income, in Model *BMW*

7.4.3 Capital and the money stock in the steady state

We have not yet discussed the values taken by tangible capital and money deposits. From the balance sheet of Table 7.1, we know that all times $K = M_h = L$. Therefore, it must be the case that $K^* = M_h^*$ in the stationary state. However, this equality is not an obvious one, since capital accumulation and the accumulation of financial assets appear to be determined by two entirely different processes. In the case of capital accumulation, we have already seen with equation (7.25) that:

$$K^{T*} = K^* = \kappa \cdot Y^* \tag{7.25}$$

so that in the steady state the amount of tangible capital, following equation (7.30), must be equal to:

$$K^* = \kappa \cdot \frac{\alpha_0}{(1 - \alpha_1) \cdot (1 - \delta \cdot \kappa) - \alpha_2 \cdot \kappa} \tag{7.32}$$

Seen from the household point of view, the accumulation of financial assets seems to follow a completely independent path. We know that in the stationary state $C^* = YD^*$ and $M_h = M_{h-1}$, so that, from the consumption function, equation (7.16), we obtain:

$$M_h^* = \left\{ \frac{(1 - \alpha_1)}{\alpha_2} \right\} \cdot YD^* - \frac{\alpha_0}{\alpha_2} \tag{7.33}$$

Equations (7.32) and (7.33) appear to be entirely different determinants of wealth. Still, the endogenous values of Y^* and YD^* will be such that $K^* = M_h^*$.

7.5 Out-of-equilibrium values and stability analysis

7.5.1 Out-of-equilibrium values

As we pointed out in Chapter 3, a key question is whether the solution of the model, when it exists, will ever be attained if the economy starts away from it. This is the issue of stability. To study it, we must first obtain the out-of-equilibrium values for the two main variables – the level of income and the stock of wealth. We can proceed in a way which at first is similar to that followed when we searched for the stability conditions of Model *SIM* in Chapter 3. That is, we identify a difference equation for the stock of tangible capital, and another one for the income level.

The difference equation for the stock of capital is fairly simple to obtain. We simply combine the relations relevant to investment behaviour, equations (7.17) to (7.20), to obtain:

$$K = (1 - \gamma) \cdot K_{-1} + \gamma \cdot \kappa \cdot Y_{-1} \qquad (7.34)$$

The present capital stock (or money balances, since, by equation (7.27), these need to be the same), is a function of the stock of tangible capital and income level from the previous period.

Let us now find the difference equation relevant to the gross national product. By combining equations (7.5), (7.16) and (7.20), that is by making use of the fact that gross national product is the sum of consumption and investment expenditures, we obtain present income as a function of present disposable income, past wealth, the past stock of tangible capital, and the capital stock target.

$$Y = \alpha_0 + \alpha_1 \cdot YD + \alpha_2 \cdot M_{h-1} + \gamma \cdot (K^T - K_{-1}) + \delta \cdot K_{-1}$$

Recalling equations (7.19), (7.24) and (7.27), that is, recalling that the target stock of capital depends on the realized income level of the previous period, that the gross domestic product is disposable income plus the depreciation allowances, and that the held money balances are exactly equal to the value of tangible capital, the above equation becomes equation (7.35), which describes national income in the current period as a function of national income and of the stock of capital of the previous period.

$$Y = \frac{\alpha_0 + \{(1 - \alpha_1) \cdot \delta + (\alpha_2 - \gamma)\} \cdot K_{-1} + \gamma \cdot \kappa \cdot Y_{-1}}{(1 - \alpha_1)} \qquad (7.35)$$

This is the second of our two difference equations. Thus given the capital stock of the previous period, and the level of income that was achieved in the previous period, it would be possible to figure out the income level and the money balances held in the next period, if all parameters, given variables and reaction coefficients were to remain the same. Starting from some random position, it is thus possible, with the help of equations (7.34) and (7.35), to follow the path taken by the economy in all these out-of-equilibrium positions.

7.5.2 Stability conditions

Now things are more complicated than they were when the stability of Model *SIM* was studied in Chapter 3, because there current income was only a function of previous wealth, so that everything could be brought back to a single equation in one variable. Here, current income is also a function of its past value. So what we have is a system of two difference equations, with two variables, both based on the past value taken by each variable. Thus we have a recursion with two variables, which in general could be written as:

$$z_t = \mathbf{A} \cdot z_{t-1} + \mathbf{c} \tag{7.36}$$

where z is a vector of two variables (here capital and income), while $\mathbf{A}$ is a matrix of coefficients and $\mathbf{c}$ is a vector that represents the constant terms.

In the matrix form given by (7.36), the two recursion equations (7.34) and (7.35) may thus be written as:

$$\begin{bmatrix} K \\ Y \end{bmatrix} = \begin{bmatrix} 1 - \gamma & \gamma \kappa \\ \dfrac{(1 - \alpha_1)\delta + (\alpha_2 - \gamma)}{1 - \alpha_1} & \dfrac{\gamma \kappa}{1 - \alpha_1} \end{bmatrix} \begin{bmatrix} K_{-1} \\ Y_{-1} \end{bmatrix} + \begin{bmatrix} 0 \\ \dfrac{\alpha_0}{1 - \alpha_1} \end{bmatrix}$$

The stability conditions are more difficult to handle in the case of difference equations than they are in the case of differential equations.[8] Let us first use the following notation to represent the two-variable system,

$$\mathbf{A} = \begin{bmatrix} a_{11} & a_{12} \\ a_{21} & a_{22} \end{bmatrix}$$

The determinant of the system is:

$$detA = a_{11} \cdot a_{22} - a_{21} \cdot a_{12};$$

the trace is:

$$trA = a_{11} + a_{22};$$

the discriminant is:

$$\Delta = (trA)^2 + 4 \cdot detA.$$

The system is unstable if the absolute value of the determinant is equal to or greater than one ($|detA| \geq 1$). A *necessary* condition for stability is thus that the absolute value of the determinant be less than unity. In the case of our model, stability requires the following condition:

$$(1 - \alpha_1) > \frac{(1 - \alpha_2)\gamma \kappa}{(1 + \delta \gamma \kappa)} \tag{7.37}$$

---

[8] See Gandolfo (1977: 136–9, 273–9) for more precise conditions in the case of difference and differential equation systems respectively.

If this is verified, then the system will be stable whenever the discriminant is non-negative ($\Delta \geq 0$). But this is difficult to verify with algebraic values, because of the squared term of the discriminant. In addition, the system can be stable with a negative discriminant, provided the trace is smaller than 2 ($trA < 2$), if and only if $-detA < 1 - |trA|$. It is not obvious that the latter condition would be fulfilled at all times in our model. But assuming that the parameters are such that this condition is realized, the only remaining issue would be whether the trace is sufficiently small, that is smaller than 2 as said above, and thus stability may also involve the following condition:

$$(1 - \alpha_1) > \frac{\gamma \cdot \kappa}{(1 + \gamma)} \tag{7.38}$$

Condition (7.38) essentially says that the model converges to its stable solution provided the propensity to save is larger than the product of the capital/output ratio κ and the γ reaction parameter, with the product being deflated by $(1 + \gamma)$. This is a classic result with this kind of a model based on an accelerator theory of investment.[9] Had we dealt with differential equations instead, condition (7.38) would have been a necessary and sufficient condition for stability, since the other condition for stability in a differential system is identical to the existence condition, as defined in (7.31).[10]

The lesson to be drawn from this stability analysis, by looking at both conditions (7.37) and (7.38), is that some weighted product of the target capital to output ratio κ and the reaction parameter γ need be small enough, compared to the saving ratio on disposable income. When working capital is considered, that is, inventories of finished goods, the capital to output ratio is relatively small, much smaller than unity, so that firms are often assumed to respond quite quickly to any discrepancy between the existing stock of inventories and the desired stock (the γ parameter may be near unity). By contrast, when fixed capital is taken into account, this involves capital to output ratios that are much larger than unity, around 3 perhaps; if models based on some

---

[9] The accelerator model, and its more general variant – the capital stock adjustment model – are studied in great detail in many works, in particular Gandolfo (1977). We do not attempt to find out how the model is approaching its long run solution. In other words, we do not attempt to find the parameter values that will guarantee that the model converges without exhibiting oscillations. Our simulations will demonstrate whether the chosen parameter values lead or not to oscillations. For instance, when γ is moved up from 0.15 to 0.25, the model converges but oscillates.

[10] In other words, in a system of differential equations, condition (7.31) corresponds to the stability condition that the determinant of the system be positive, while condition (7.38) corresponds to the stability condition that the trace be negative.

Table 7.4 Stability conditions

	α_1	α_2	γ	κ	δ	Eq. (7.31) Existence	Eq. (7.37) Determinant	Eq. (7.38) Trace
BMW model	0.75	0.10	0.15	1	0.10	0.25 > 0.111	0.25 > 0.133	0.25 > 0.130
Gandolfo	0.75	0.10	0.10	3	0.10	0.25 < 0.428		
Alternative	0.75	0.10	0.10	2	0.10	0.25 = 0.25	0.25 > 0.176	0.25 > 0.182
Alternative	0.75	0.10	0.15	1.916	0.10	0.25 > 0.237	0.25 < 0.251	0.25 = 0.25

form of the accelerator are to yield stable solutions, one needs to assume that entrepreneurs are responding slowly to any discrepancy between actual and desired capacity (the γ parameter has to be a small percentage). Indeed, Gandolfo (1977: 157) claims that empirically, 'the value of the reaction coefficient has been found to be normally about 0.10'. This is only partly reassuring regarding whether conditions (7.37) and (7.38) are normally fulfilled, because even when $\gamma = 0.10$, the required conditions are rather stringent, as can be seen in Table 7.4 above.[11]

Our *BMW* model is set up in such a way that all conditions are fulfilled. Introducing a target capital output ratio of 3 in that model would negate the existence condition. Jacking up the reaction parameter of producers in such a way that the trace condition is respected could still leave the existence condition unfulfilled. And finally, in the last line of Table 7.3, we have a case where the determinant condition only would go unfulfilled if the target capital to output ratio were raised sufficiently.

7.5.3 An approximate and intuitive stability condition

Condition (7.38) is the result of the simultaneous interaction of two difference equations. If one only wishes to get some estimate of the condition required for stability, then one may use a short-cut. An approximate stability condition – a partial equilibrium stability condition so to speak – can be easily obtained by following a method put forth by Keynesian economists. The trick is that a model should be stable if saving reacts more strongly to changes than does investment. Here for instance, investment reacts to a change in income through the target capital stock. Similarly, any change in disposable income will also induce a change in saving. Thus in general, a model is stable provided $dSAV/dY > dI/dY$, where *SAV* represent saving (if positive solutions exist). We must thus compare how the investment function and the saving function react to a change in income.

---

[11] Readers may wish to derive more intuitive results by assuming that $\delta = 0$.

Take the investment function, given by equation (7.20). With the appropriate substitutions provided by equations (7.18) and (7.19), we obtain:

$$I_d = \gamma \cdot (\kappa_{\cdot -1} - K_{-1}) + \delta \cdot K_{-1}$$

Taking the partial derivative of this equation with respect to Y_{-1}, we obtain:

$$\frac{dI}{dY_{-1}} = \gamma \cdot \kappa$$

We now consider the saving function, which is the complement of the consumption function (7.16). Given equations (7.24), it can be rewritten as:

$$SAV = -\alpha_0 + (1 - \alpha_1) \cdot (Y - \delta \cdot K_{-1}) - \alpha_2 \cdot M_{h-1}$$

Taking the partial derivative of this expression with respect to Y, we obtain:

$$\frac{dSAV}{dY} = (1 - \alpha_1)$$

Thus, as an approximation, for the model to be stable we want saving to react more promptly than investment to a change in income. The two income variables in the derivative are from a different time period, but still, as an approximation, we may say that we wish $dSAV/dY$ to be larger than dI/dY_{-1}. This implies then that:

$$(1 - \alpha_1) > \gamma \cdot \kappa \tag{7.38A}$$

Obviously, equation (7.38A) so obtained resembles one of the true stability condition of the overall model, defined by equation (7.38), but it is only an approximation of it (indeed it is more stringent than (7.38)). Still the shortcut so taken, despite its partial equilibrium features, is a useful estimate, for it easily provides an approximate stability condition and an intuitive interpretation of stability, in terms of the amplitude in the reaction of the investment and saving functions to changes in income.

Stability conditions closely resembling equation (7.38A) are to be found in a large number of heterodox models, in particular the growth and income distribution models that have been developed by the earlier post-Keynesians (Kaldor, Robinson) and more recently by Kaleckian authors (Lavoie and Godley 2001–2).

7.5.4 An additional condition to achieve smoothly the steady state

Achieving steady states requires an additional condition however. When parameters are such that the new stationary capital stock is higher than before, no additional condition is needed. But when the new stationary level of capital is lower than before, the new stationary state will be achieved by having negative net investment. Under such circumstances, part of the used-up capital will not be replaced. In other words, replacement investment will be below disinvestment – what we called depreciation allowances.

Still, while net investment can be negative when firms decide not to replace all the tangible capital stock that has vanished because of obsolescence and wear and tear, gross investment can never be negative. Gross investment must thus be zero or a positive amount. Putting together equations (7.17A) and (7.19), we obtain the following condition:

$$(\gamma - \delta) \cdot \left(\frac{K_{-1}}{Y_{-1}} \right) \leq \gamma \cdot \kappa \qquad (7.39)$$

Obviously, such a condition is always fulfilled when the γ parameter is smaller than the δ parameter. In words, this means that gross investment would never become negative provided the percentage of the gap between the target and the existing stock of capital that the entrepreneurs wish to close in every period is smaller than or equal to the percentage of tangible capital that gets used up in every period. Otherwise the following condition has to be fulfilled:

$$\frac{Y_{-1}}{K_{-1}} > \frac{(\gamma - \delta)}{(\gamma \cdot \kappa)}. \qquad (7.40)$$

What this means is that, when the economy takes a negative shock, the shock needs to be not too large and the rate of capacity utilization must not fall below a certain level, for otherwise entrepreneurs would wish for a negative amount of gross investment. This would induce a forced adjustment in the γ parameter. The new steady state would still eventually be reached, but the parameter structure of the model would need to be changed, to take into account the non-negative constraint on gross investment. In other words, the desired negative adjustment to the capital stock could not be achieved. This could be handled in a simulation package, and it would introduce non-linearities.

In the meantime, Figure 7.4 illustrates the evolution of the output to capital ratio (Y/K_{-1}), which is some proxy of the rate of utilization of capacity, following a decrease in the propensity to consume, which, as we already know, entails a negative shock on the economy. As can be seen from Figure 7.4, the recession generated by the increase in the propensity to save is accompanied by a drop in the rate of capacity utilization, but as

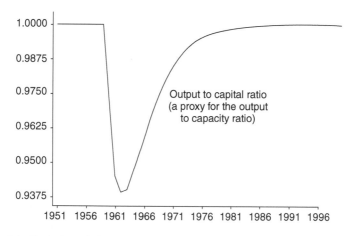

Figure 7.4 Evolution of the output to capital ratio (Y/K_{-1}), following an increase in the propensity to save out of disposable income, in Model *BMW*

the economy goes towards its new steady state, the output to capital ratio goes back to its desired level, and hence the rate of utilization goes back to its initial level.

7.6 The role of the rate of interest

7.6.1 The rate of interest and the real wage

Having shown that the model converges to its solution, at least for some restricted set of parameter values, we may now pursue further the question of comparative statics. In section 7.4.2, it was already pointed out that the paradox of thrift had been recovered, both in the short run and while comparing steady states. However, it was also pointed out that the rate of interest had no impact whatsoever, neither on the short-run solution nor on the steady state one. This was attributed mainly to the fact that the rate of interest had no impact on the target stock of capital (i.e. on the target capital/output ratio) and was not a component of the consumption function. It is now time to reconsider the latter assumption.

However, before we do so, it is interesting to study the relationship in the model between prices, interest rates, and real wages. This will give rise to a version of the famous wage/profit frontier which has been developed by classical economists, and which underlines the possible conflict over income distribution between wage recipients and profit-recipients, in the present case interest-recipients. It will also allow us to note the lack of realism of the simple model without residual profits which has been suggested here, which will lead us in future chapters to propose a pricing behaviour which is more reasonable and more realistic.

Let us recall the equations which define the real wage:

$$WB_d = Y - r_1 \cdot L_{d-1} - \delta \cdot K_{-1} \tag{7.6}$$

$$WB_s = W \cdot N_s \tag{7.13}$$

$$N_d = \frac{Y}{pr} \tag{7.14}$$

$$W = \frac{WB_d}{N_d} \tag{7.15}$$

$$N_s = N_d \tag{7.3}$$

The last of these five equations shows that we can ignore the distinction between N_s and N_d, and WB_s and WB_d. Combining equations (7.13) and (7.14), we equalize the two expressions of the wage bill, seen from the supply and the demand side:

$$Y - r_1 \cdot L_{d-1} - \delta \cdot K_{-1} = \frac{W \cdot Y}{pr}$$

so that, recalling that at all times $L = K$, we have:

$$W = pr \left\{ 1 - (r_1 + \delta) \cdot \left(\frac{K_{-1}}{Y} \right) \right\} \tag{7.41}$$

It is now obvious that the real wage is directly proportional to the productivity of labour, measured by pr, and that it is inversely related to the rate of interest on loans, the rate of depreciation of capital, and to the capital/output ratio of the period. Thus, for a given productivity of labour, the higher the rate of interest, the rate of depreciation, and the capital/output ratio, the lower the real wage must be. The evolution of the real wage rate, as represented by equation (7.41) is illustrated in the case of an increase in the propensity to save, with the help of Figure 7.5. As we saw with Figure 7.4, the slowdown in the economy induces a temporary reduction in the rate of capacity utilization, more precisely in the Y/K_{-1} ratio. This means a temporary increase in the K_{-1}/Y ratio and hence a reduction in the real wage rate W. By contrast, in the steady state, the real wage takes a specific constant value, for in the steady state the actual capital/output ratio is the target capital/output ratio. Formalized, this implies that the steady-state real wage is equal to, as shown in Figure 7.6:

$$W^* = pr\{1 - (r_1 + \delta) \cdot \kappa\} \tag{7.42}$$

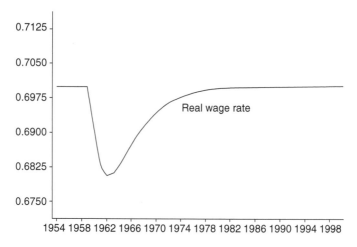

Figure 7.5 Evolution of the real wage rate (W), following an increase in the propensity to save out of disposable income, in Model *BMW*

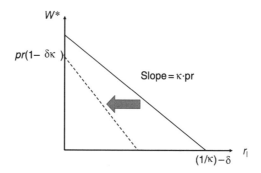

Figure 7.6 The relationship between the real wage and the interest rate on loans

It may be noted that equations (7.41) and (7.42) represent the classical wage/profit frontiers, the latter one being the steady state wage/profit frontier. The wage/profit frontier illustrates the negative relationship which is necessarily said to exist between the real wage and the rate of profit. Here, since there is no net profit, the relationship exhibited by equations (7.41) and (7.42) is the negative relation between the real wage and the rate of interest. An increase in one must lead to the reduction of the other, *all other things equal*. In other words, the increase in interest payments must necessarily lead to a fall in the wage bill and in the real wage. This is in perfect symmetry to the arguments that were made by neo-classical authors and that were

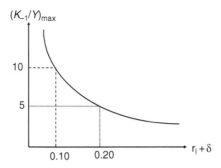

Figure 7.7 The maximum capital to output ratio that can be attained during the transition, for a given interest rate on loans

criticized by Keynes in *The General Theory*, according to which 'profits will necessarily go up because wages have gone down' (Keynes 1936: 258). As we have seen with equations (7.30) and (7.35), the interest rate has no impact on either short-run income or its steady state value, although it reduces the real wage.

The relationship between the real wage and the rate of interest on loans introduces another constraint on the values that can take the various parameters and variables, both in the steady state and during any transition path towards the steady state. Since the real wage is a residual, the real wage is an endogenous variable that depends on the values taken by the other parameters and variables. The real wage however, just like gross investment, cannot be negative. In the steady state, as illustrated in Figure 7.7, the rate of interest on loans cannot be larger than a certain value, such that the maximum steady-state rate of interest on loans is:

$$r_{l-max} = \frac{(1 - \kappa \cdot \delta)}{\kappa} \qquad (7.43)$$

Thus, the larger the target capital to output ratio, and the greater the rate of capital depreciation, the smaller the maximum level of the rate of interest (here the real rate, since price inflation has been assumed away).

Similar limits can be imposed when the economy has not yet reached the steady state. The conditions imposed by the fact that the wage rate cannot fall to zero can be drawn from equation (7.42). Considering now the rate of interest on loans and the rate of depreciation as given variables, let us see what maximum value can be taken by the capital to output ratio in any time during the transition path. The real wage rate will not fall to zero provided the following condition is fulfilled:

$$\left(\frac{K_{-1}}{Y}\right)_{max} = \frac{1}{(r_l + \delta)} \qquad (7.44)$$

Thus the larger the rate of interest and the rate of depreciation, the smaller the maximum value that can be taken during the transition by the capital to output ratio. This relationship is illustrated with the help of Figure 7.7. The curve drawn there is a rectangular hyperbola. If the sum of the rate of interest and the rate of depreciation doubles, the maximum capital to output ratio is halved. This implies, once more, that for the model to make sense, negative shocks on the economy cannot be too large, for otherwise they would propel the utilization of capital to very low rates. As a result of these very low rates, firms would be unable to pay their workers, for interest payments on their debt would be so large, relative to production, that they would take over the entire national product. In the real world, such circumstances are unlikely, but equation (7.41) clearly shows that real wages are under threat whenever real interest rates rise, whenever capital becomes rapidly outmoded, and whenever there is a fall in production relative to the existing stock of capital.

7.6.2   The interest rate and the mark-up

Now, what is the relationship between these wage–profit frontiers and the mark-up pricing formula? Students who are familiar with the post-Keynesian or Kaleckian literature know that prices there are often expressed as a mark-up over unit costs. In the simplest models, prices are said to arise from a mark-up over unit labour costs, more precisely their variable unit labour costs. Firms have their accountants compute these unit costs, and multiply the found unit cost by some conventional constant to arrive at prices. Formally we have:

$$p = (1 + \varphi) \cdot \left(\frac{W}{pr} \right) \tag{7.45}$$

where p is the price and φ is the percentage costing mark-up on unit labour costs W/pr.

Our model has a peculiar feature, however, which is that it is assumed that prices are equal to unity, that is, $p = 1$ at all times. This assumption was made, it may be recalled, to avoid all the complications associated with price re-evaluations. However, because of the fixed prices assumption, it follows that the real wage, starting from the mark-up equation (7.45), can be rewritten as:

$$W = \frac{pr}{(1 + \varphi)} \tag{7.46}$$

We thus have two equations that determine the real wage: equation (7.41) which follows from the structure of the model, and equation (7.46), which arises from a mark-up procedure. Combining these two equations, we obtain the value of the mark-up:

$$\varphi = \frac{(r_l + \delta) \cdot \left(\dfrac{K_{-1}}{Y} \right)}{1 - (r_l + \delta) \cdot \left(\dfrac{K_{-1}}{Y} \right)} \tag{7.47}$$

In the present model, the mark-up is not a constant, it is an endogenous variable, which depends on the exact value taken by the capital/output ratio. This result lacks realism, of course, because we need to assume one of two unlikely hypotheses, either that firms know their sales Y in advance or that the real wage of workers is set as they reach out for consumer goods. However, there is no other way out, until the model becomes more sophisticated and allows for the presence of residual profits, something that will be done in the next chapters. In the meantime, we may note that the mark-up becomes a constant only in the steady state, in which case it is equal to:

$$\varphi^* = \frac{(r_{l-1} + \delta) \cdot \kappa}{1 - (r_{l-1} + \delta) \cdot \kappa} \tag{7.48}$$

Obviously, in symmetry to the real wage, the higher the rate of interest, the rate of depreciation, and the target capital/output ratio, the higher is the mark-up.

7.6.3 The rate of interest with a modified consumption function

We now come back to the singular feature of our model, which says that changes in the rate of interest charged on firms or paid to depositors will have no impact on the level of income, neither in the short-run nor in the steady state. This feature was attributed to the fact that changes in the interest rate had no impact on either the demand for capital or the demand for consumption goods.

It is easy however to remedy to this. Let us assume that households make a distinction between their labour income and their interest income, and that the propensity to consume out of wages is larger than their propensity to consume out of interest payments. Let us call α_{1w} the former and α_{1r} the latter. The consumption function now becomes:

$$C_d = \alpha_0 + \alpha_{1w}.WB_s + \alpha_{1r} \cdot r_{m-1} \cdot M_{h-1} + \alpha_2 \cdot M_{h-1} \tag{7.16A}$$

which may also be rewritten as:

$$C_d = \alpha_0 + \alpha_{1w} \cdot WB_s + (\alpha_{1r} \cdot r_{m-1} + \alpha_2) \cdot M_{h-1} \tag{7.16B}$$

or:

$$C_d = \alpha_0 + \alpha_{1w} \cdot WB_s + \{\alpha_2(r_{m-1})\} \cdot M_{h-1} \qquad (7.16C)$$

Consumption function (7.16C) is often to be found in mainstream textbooks. It says, as interpreted from equation (7.16B), that households consume a proportion α_2 of their wealth. However, here in contrast to what is usually assumed in mainstream theory, the consumed proportion α_2 is a positive function, instead of a negative one, of the rate of return on wealth, given by r_m.

But let us go back to equation (7.16A). It is in effect a modified Kaldorian consumption function, or a Cambridge consumption function, for it distinguishes between labour income and property income, attributing a differentiated propensity to consume to each kind of income. This distinction between labour income and property income has led to a whole series of models, mainly models of growth and distribution, as can be found in Kaldor (1956), Robinson (1956), Kalecki (1971) and many other Cambridge authors. These models, because they embody both the multiplier effects and class or income distinctions, are in the Keynesian and Marxist traditions. A key assumption in these models is that the propensity to consume out of labour income is larger than the propensity to consume out of property income. Thus, with equation (7.16A), we must add:

$$\alpha_{1w} > \alpha_{1r} \qquad (7.49)$$

Condition (7.49) is in line with the so-called *classical* consumption function, where the propensity to save out of wages is zero, while the propensity to save out of interest or profit income is equal to one, or at least positive.

What will now be the impact of an increase in interest rates in such a Kaldorian model (called *BMWK*)? The impact is almost obvious, following the analysis of the preceding sub-section. The increase in the interest rate on loans forces firms to reduce the real wage rate, in line with equations (7.42) and (7.43), and Figure 7.6. This redistribution of income, away from workers and towards rentiers (since the interest rate on deposits rises with that of the rate on loans), reduces consumption demand. Thus the impact of an increase in interest rates is a negative one. Income and employment fall, and this reduction also remains when steady states are compared. By taking income distribution into account in the consumption function, we have thus recovered what is considered to be an intuitive result. Increases in interest rates reduce aggregate demand and output, but not through the investment function. The negative impact of the increase in interest rates, when income distribution enters the consumption function, is illustrated with the help of Figure 7.8.

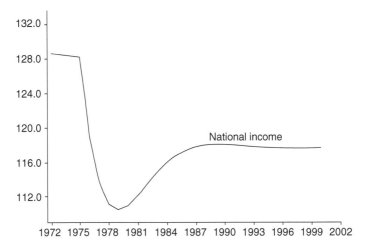

Figure 7.8 Evolution of Gross Domestic Income (Y), following an increase in the interest rate, in Model *BMWK*

7.7   A look forward

The present chapter has introduced privately issued money created by banks. We have examined in detail some of the stability issues and existence issues that are linked with stock-flow models. These questions could be analytically dealt with precisely because of the relative simplicity of Model *BMW*. We have seen that the dynamics of models that ignore the government sector are quite different from those that take into account government debt in a stock-flow consistent manner. The main drawback of our model, however, was the unavoidable implicit hypothesis that the wage rate was an endogenous variable of the model, the value of which could only be known once the equilibrium level of income of the period had been reached. This was forced upon us because we needed to assume that the price level was set at a constant level, to avoid dealing with price changes. This hypothesis is obviously in contradiction with the real world. The next chapters will remedy to this, by introducing additional realistic features, in particular the residual profits and the inventories of firms.

Appendix 7.1: The equations of Model *BMW*

Basic behavioural equations

$$C_s = C_d \tag{7.1}$$

$$I_s = I_d \tag{7.2}$$

$$N_s = N_d \tag{7.3}$$

$$\Delta L_s = \Delta L_d \tag{7.4}$$

Transactions of the firms

$$Y = C_s + I_s \tag{7.5}$$

$$WB_d = Y - r_{l-1} \cdot L_{d-1} - AF \tag{7.6}$$

$$AF = \delta \cdot K_{-1} \tag{7.7}$$

$$\Delta L_d = I_d - AF \tag{7.8}$$

Transactions of households

$$YD = WB_s + r_{m-1} \cdot M_{d-1} \tag{7.9}$$

$$\Delta M_h = M_h - M_{h-1} = YD - C_d \tag{7.10}$$

Transactions of the banks

$$\Delta M_s = \Delta L_s \tag{7.11}$$

$$r_m = r_l \tag{7.12}$$

The wage bill

$$WB_s = W \cdot N_s \tag{7.13}$$

$$N_d = \frac{Y}{pr} \tag{7.14}$$

$$W = \frac{WB_d}{N_d} \tag{7.15}$$

Household behaviour

$$C_d = \alpha_0 + \alpha_1 \cdot YD + \alpha_2 \cdot M_{h-1} \tag{7.16}$$

The investment behaviour

$$\Delta K = I_d - DA \tag{7.17}$$

$$DA = \delta \cdot K_{-1} \tag{7.18}$$

$$K^T = \kappa \cdot Y_{-1} \tag{7.19}$$

$$I_d = \gamma \cdot (K^T - K_{-1}) + DA \tag{7.20}$$

The behaviour of banks

$$r_l = \bar{r}_l \tag{7.21}$$

Model *BMWK*

Replace equation (7.16) by

$$C_d = \alpha_0 + \alpha_{1w} \cdot WB_s + \alpha_{1r} \cdot r_{m-1} \cdot M_{h-1} + \alpha_2 \cdot M_h \tag{7.16A}$$

8
Time, Inventories, Profits and Pricing

8.1 The role of time

We shall not present a model in this chapter. Instead the chapter will be entirely devoted to the measurement of profits, costs and inventories, together with an analysis of the way in which firms' pricing decisions distribute the national income. The subject matter is intricate and potentially controversial because there are so many ways in which accounts are kept. Our guiding light will be that the concepts and definitions will always meet the consistency requirements of the double entry matrices which underlie all our work. In particular, the definition of profits and the way in which appropriations are recorded must fit into a transactions matrix describing a whole economy so that all rows and all columns sum to zero. This will guarantee that our concepts are *sufficiently* good even if they are occasionally controversial since we shall ensure that the sum of all inflows will always be equal to the sum of all outflows.

The behavioural and accounting problems we shall encounter stem largely from the fact that, in contrast with all the models so far presented, we shall not assume any more that whatever is being produced will be sold within the accounting period. We now deal with the more general case where, except in the stationary state, the amount of goods produced in a given period will be different from the amount sold in the same period. This will allow us to take the concept of *time* much more seriously.[1] Introducing time in economic models forces the economist to take into account aspects of the economy which are often brushed aside, such as uncertainty, credit finance and inventories. The following is a good statement of that claim.

---

[1] Some economists argue that this concern with time is a defining tenet of post-Keynesian economics (Davidson 1982: 14; Henry 1993).

Firms require revolving finance from banks, not only because production and distribution take time while wages have to be paid in advance of sales being made, but also because they cannot know exactly what their sales are going to be .... It is unrealistic to suppose ... that what is produced in one period will automatically be sold in the next. (Godley 1999a: 396)

It will be a very important part of our story that firms initiate production, that the production process takes time and therefore that firms need finance in advance of their receiving anything from sales. Firms engage in production in the expectation that they will be able to set a price and achieve enough sales at that price to generate some target level of profits.

In each period, there is thus a possibility that what has been produced will not be sold. This can arise for three major reasons. First, production takes time, and hence what has been produced during the accounting period may yet be unfinished and not ready for sale. The unfinished product will thus be added to the stock of goods that are carried by the firm – it will be added to the inventories of the firm. Second, the product may be finished within the accounting period, but it may require some time to be distributed and sold (the market period is not simultaneous with the production period).[2] Our model will underline a third cause of the discrepancy between production and sales within a period, which is uncertainty.

Because production takes time, firms must anticipate their sales for the current or the next period. They can only rely on their best estimates of these sales, and they cannot forecast them with perfect certainty. Because production takes time, the goods that they expect to sell must be produced in advance. Because demand by customers may exceed production, firms must set aside stocks of produced goods that will generally make it possible to satisfy demand whenever it exceeds production. These precautionary stocks of goods are the inventories of the firm. Based on their past experience and best-practice management techniques, firms will set a target inventories to sales ratio, which should allow them to respond fully to any peak in demand, while minimizing the costs which are associated with the carry of finished but unsold goods. Consumers see examples of these every day: in grocery shops, in furniture stores, in the lots of auto dealers.

In any period, except in a stationary steady state, even without forecasting mistakes, there will be a discrepancy between the production and the sales of the period. This is because firms are continuously building up or reducing

---

[2] Some economists (e.g. Shaikh (1989); Smithin (1986)) assume that goods produced at time t − 1 are all sold at time t. We are uncomfortable with this assumption because part of what is sold in period t may also have been produced in period t. Also the assumption denies to inventories their 'buffering' role to which we attach so much importance.

the size of their inventories, in an attempt to achieve their inventory targets. In addition, when forecasting mistakes occur, there is a discrepancy between what is sold and what was expected to be sold when the production decision had to be taken. This implies a change in actual inventories, even if the target inventories to sales ratio had been previously reached.

In general, forecasting errors will occur. The main exception is when firms produce to order. In some industries firms only engage in production when orders have been received from customers, where the latter enter into a contract which ensures that they can purchase the ordered goods as soon as they are ready. This occurs mainly in the case of fixed investment goods and specific intermediate or finished goods. In the industries that produce to order, the key issue is that of capacity output: these firms must make sure that they have enough capacity and a wide enough labour pool to respond to any additional order, for otherwise they are likely to lose that order to a competitor. In general, a firm might produce some goods on order, and the rest in advance, based on a forecast. In the case of diaries for instance, some companies order thousands of diaries for their employees and faithful customers. The diary producer produces these on order, months in advance. On the other hand, the diaries sold to individuals in retail outlets are not produced to order; they must also be produced in advance, way before the beginning of the New Year, but the production run will be based on demand forecasts and past sales. Here stocks of finished products are being held for precautionary reasons, to ensure that unanticipated fluctuations in sales can be absorbed without any disruption.

The analysis which follows involves some concepts (including profits,[3] inventories and inventory valuation) which are not usually given much attention. The presence of inventories complicates the analysis and the accounting, but they add a dose of realism to our understanding of both macroeconomics and the business firm.

8.2 The measure of profits

8.2.1 The conceptual framework

We usually open our analysis with balance sheet and transaction matrices which define the institutional structure of a model. In the present case, because we wish to focus on features of firms operating in the production sector, we start with a partial transaction matrix, indeed that part of the matrix that is relevant to the operations of the production firms. This is shown in Table 8.1.

---

[3] It is standard practise to assume that profits are timelessly equal to the marginal product of capital times the stock of capital. Inventories play no role in market-clearing models – nor in 'disequilibrium' non-market clearing models!

Table 8.1 The operations of production firms in a simplified setting

Components	Production firms	
	Current account	Capital account
Sales	$+S$	
Change in the value of inventories	$+\Delta IN$	$-\Delta IN$
Wages	$-WB$	
Interest on loans	$-r_{l-1} \cdot L_{-1}$	
Entrepreneurial profits	$-F$	
Change in loans		$+\Delta L$
Σ	0	0

The above matrix offers the simplest accounts involving a firm that holds inventories. As was pointed out in previous chapters, we deal with a vertically integrated sector, and hence ignore all intermediate goods. This has the advantage of simplification, but of course it sets aside all the production and pricing interdependencies between goods that are to be found in a Leontief input-output model or in the Sraffian model.[4] Be that as it may, we assume in what follows that the only production costs of firms are their labour costs.

In the period under consideration, the firm makes sales to customers, the value of which is S. This item carries a plus sign, of course, since it is a source of funds. These are sales of goods that have been produced in the current or in the previous period. Some produced goods are not sold. From the standpoint of accountants, these yet-to-be-sold goods are considered as if they had been sold by the production department of the firm (linked to the current account) to another department, the acquisition department of the firm (linked to the capital account). This is why they appear with a plus sign as well. On the other hand, the opening stock of inventories is assumed to be disposed of, in other words it has been repurchased by the production department to be sold to customers. So the net transaction here involves the change in the value of inventories, which is given by ΔIN. In the capital account, the change in the value of inventories ΔIN appears with a negative sign, because the acquisition department of the firm acquires the unsold goods, and so from that angle it is a use of funds. And how are the unsold goods acquired? They must be purchased with the help of bank loans, because at this stage this is the only source of finance; firms do not have retained earnings. This means

---

[4] This is underlined by Lee (1998: ch. 12). Eichner (1987) offers a complete presentation of these input-output links in the context of macroeconomics.

Table 8.2 Starting from scratch: all produced goods enter inventories

Components	Production firms	
	Current account	Capital account
Sales	0	
Change in the value of inventories	$+\Delta IN$	$-\Delta IN$
Wages	$-WB$	
Interest on loans		
Entrepreneurial profits	0	
Change in loans		$+\Delta L$
Σ	0	0

that in the balance sheet of our simple firm, the value of inventories *IN* has to be exactly equal to the value of bank loans L.[5]

Why do inventories need to be financed through bank loans? It is simply the result of the fact that the costs of obtaining inventories are not offset by some other income flow, unless a money flow is provided by bank loans. This is best shown with the help of Table 8.2, which reproduces Table 8.1, but starting from scratch, at the very beginning of the life of a producing firm, in its very first period of operation. Assume that all the goods that have been produced in this first period, at cost *WB*, have not yet been sold. There are no sales ($S = 0$), but wages have been paid, and all produced goods appear as increases in the value of inventories. These inventories are temporarily acquired by the firm itself. Since the firm is just starting from scratch, all of the inventories must obviously be financed by advances – bank loans. Table 8.2 also makes clear a principle that was established in Chapter 2, that inventories must be valued at cost, since that is what production actually did cost, thereby measuring the amount of finance which was needed. This principle will soon be put to use.

8.2.2 Entrepreneurial profits versus total business profits

Going back to the current account of Table 8.1, we turn to the negative elements of the column. During the period, the firms have engaged in paying out wages *WB* (as already pointed out). But because of operations that occurred in previous periods, they also had to pay interest on their outstanding stock of loans, which, as claimed above, means they had to make interest payments by reason of their holdings of inventories. The difference

[5] When accountants realize that the goods in stock cannot ever be sold (as when diaries are outdated), or must be dumped at a price which is lower than their cost, the value of inventories fall, and hence firms must announce a one-time loss.

between the sources of funds of the producing firms and their uses of funds constitutes the entrepreneurial profits F, which as said before, is assumed to be entirely distributed as dividends to households, so that no profits are retained within the firm. Hence, directly from the matrix describing the operations of producing firms, we get the first definition of profits – *entrepreneurial* profits:

$$F = S - (WB - \Delta IN + r_{l-1} \cdot IN_{-1})$$ (8.1)

In the present case, what is being assumed is that the interest costs on held inventories are considered as unavoidable costs.[6] Even if an individual firm (like Microsoft) were able to self-finance its interest costs on inventories, it would be facing an opportunity cost, given by the interest payments it could receive if it were lending these funds.

Entrepreneurial profits, F, as given by equation (8.1), is our preferred definition of profit. First, it is our contention that profit is the sum of money which can be periodically extracted from a set of business operations and distributed while leaving the balance sheet of the concern unchanged.[7] Second, entrepreneurial profits are directly derived from the transactions-flow matrix, as shown by a subset of it – Table 8.1. Third, we shall argue later that when firms make pricing decisions they are primarily concerned with entrepreneurial profits.

There are however other possible definition of profits besides equation (8.1). If we consider gross business profits, before interest payments, then we get a second definition of profits, that of *total* business profits, which we find less relevant:[8]

$$F_T = S - (WB - \Delta IN)$$ (8.2)

---

[6] It is assumed that the value of inventories is the same as the value of loans. In real life this may not be the case, as inventories may be financed by reductions in cash balances or short-term financial assets, in which case the cost of financing assets must be interpreted as an opportunity cost – the interest payments foregone to finance inventories. In addition, within a more general framework, firms have to make interest payments on bank loans obtained for the initial finance of investment or on issued securities (corporate paper, corporate bonds). These interest payments will not be distinguished from interest payments on inventories in the accounts of firms. We shall suggest a way of handling this problem in Chapter 11.

[7] Entrepreneurial profits for firms are here defined by analogy with the Haig–Simons definition of disposable income. Households' income is the amount that can be consumed without diminishing their wealth; entrepreneurial profit is the amount that can be distributed without diminishing the assets of the firm.

[8] This would correspond to EBITDA, or earnings before interest, (corporate) taxes, and depreciation allowances. As we know since the scandals of Enron or Nortel, among other accounting tricks, managers of these firms used this defective concept to hide the huge losses that they were suffering because of their high interest payments.

These two definitions, as given by equations (8.1) and (8.2), are far from intuitive. In a world without changes in the value of inventories, when $\Delta IN = 0$, we get the standard result that profits are the discrepancy between sales and costs. In the case of gross profits, it is the discrepancy between sales and the wage bill, and in the case of entrepreneurial profits, the interest cost is added to the wage cost. Why are changes in the value of inventories subtracted from the wage bill cost of the current period? A full answer will soon be forthcoming.

The above formula defining profits is occasionally, though mistakenly, taken to imply that a physical addition to inventory accumulation adds to profits. But this it cannot possibly do. If the addition to inventories takes place with no addition to sales, no difference at all is made to profits; the increased inventory must be exactly matched by an addition to outlays. If the physical rise in inventory takes place because of a fall in sales, this must *reduce* profits. There will be an increase in inventories but this will have a lower value than the sales foregone. In particular, when there are no sales, profits are nil, as we saw in Table 8.2.

8.2.3 The definition of historic costs

In an attempt to understand the meaning of profits, let us define as the *historic wage cost* the terms which are in parentheses in equation (8.2) above. In other words, the historic wage cost *HWC* is defined as:

$$HWC = (WB - \Delta IN) \tag{8.3}$$

In addition, let us define as the *total historic costs* the terms which are found in the parentheses of equation (8.1). Total historic costs *HC* are thus historic wage costs plus the interest costs on inventories:

$$HC = (WB - \Delta IN) + r_{l-1} \cdot IN_{-1} \tag{8.4}$$

What these equations are thus implying is that gross business profits (total business profits) are the difference between sales and historic wage costs, while entrepreneurial profits are the difference between sales and total historic costs. While defining profits in a general way as the difference between sales and costs, the definition of historic costs or of historic wage costs is not so obvious. Why should the historic wage cost *HWC* be equal to the sum of the current wage bill *WB* and the *change* in the value of inventories ΔIN?

To help us answer this question let us consider two further identities. First, let us consider an identity in the realm of physical objects. Let us assume that all firms produce 'widgets', which can be counted as identical physical objects. These physical objects, which can be expressed in real units, will always be identified with the help of lower case letters. By contrast their value equivalents, in dollars, will be identified, as they were before, with upper case letters. Then there is an identity that says that any change in the physical stock of inventories (*in*) at the end of a period is equal to production (*y*) less sales (*s*), when everything is measured in common 'widget' units, that is in real terms.

$$\Delta in = in - in_{-1} = y - s \tag{8.5}$$

We now need some relations to move smoothly from physical units to dollar values. The nominal value of inventories, which we have called *IN*, now in upper case letters, is thus equal to the volume of physical units of inventories, *in*, valued at cost. That this must be so is once more related to the fact that this is actually how much it cost to produce and get the inventories. We must thus consider the unit cost *UC* of producing widgets in the current period. We thus have:

$$IN = in \cdot UC \tag{8.6}$$

with

$$UC = \frac{WB}{y} \tag{8.7}$$

telling us how much it costs per widget to produce *y* widgets in the current period.

The relationship between the various measures of inventory levels and changes may be summarized, once again using the invaluable Ostergaard diagram, first presented in Chapter 5:

$$\Delta IN = in \cdot UC - in_{-1} \cdot UC_{-1} = \Delta in \cdot UC + \Delta UC \cdot in_{-1} \tag{8.8}$$

This identity shows that only the 'first-in first-out' method of accounting for stocks of inventories (FIFO) is consistent with economic logic, for it is clear that the widgets leftover at the end of each period were all produced in that period and hence that they should be valued at the current unit cost of production.

The change in the value of inventories ΔIN, which is the value of inventories at the end of this period less the value of inventories at the end of the previous period, is identically equal to the physical change in inventories measured at cost plus the change in unit cost times the opening number of widgets in stock. This last term (the second term on the outmost right-hand side of the above equation) is known among national accountants as 'stock appreciation' or *inventory valuation adjustment (IVA)*, and more will be said about it when we discuss the national accountants' definition of profits in the next section. In the meantime, the relationship given by (8.8) will make it easier to understand the meaning of historic wage costs and historic costs.

Given that overlapping production cycles of varying duration are taking place, it follows that a proportion σ_S of objects sold in any period was produced in the previous period, and therefore that the proportion $(1 - \sigma_S)$ of objects sold this period was made this period. By definition, we have:

$$s = \sigma_s \cdot s + (1 - \sigma_s) \cdot s \tag{8.9}$$

The objects made, but not sold, last period (the first term on the right-hand side of 8.9) constitute the number of objects in stock with which firms started the period. In other words, they were the physical inventories left at the end of the previous period. The proportion σ_s is thus a stock-flow ratio in real terms; it is the inventories to sales ratio (bearing in mind that σ_s is an *ex post* ratio, not a target parameter, since sales s are only known after the fact, at the end of the period). Formally we have:

$$\sigma_s = \frac{in_{-1}}{s} \tag{8.10}$$

We now can give an intuitive definition of historic wage costs *HWC*. The historic wage cost is the wage cost encountered when producing the goods that have been sold this period. Since a proportion σ_s were produced in the previous period, their wage cost is given by the unit cost of the previous period, UC_{-1}. The rest, the proportion $(1 - \sigma_s)$, were produced in the current period, at the unit cost *UC*. The historic wage cost is thus:

$$HWC = \sigma_s \cdot s \cdot UC_{-1} + (1 - \sigma_s) \cdot s \cdot UC \tag{8.11}$$

It still needs to be shown that this intuitive definition, equation (8.11), is identical to the definition that arose from total business profits and the study of Table 8.1, that is equation (8.3). In other words, is the following equality true?

$$\sigma_s \cdot s \cdot UC_{-1} + (1 - \sigma_s) \cdot s \cdot UC = (WB - \Delta IN)$$

From equations (8.7) and (8.8), we can rewrite the RHS of the above equation as:

$$(WB - \Delta IN) = y \cdot UC - (\Delta in \cdot UC + \Delta UC \cdot in_{-1})$$

Because of equation (8.5), we have:

$$(WB - \Delta IN) = s \cdot UC + \Delta in \cdot UC - (\Delta in \cdot UC + \Delta UC \cdot in_{-1})$$

Expanding Δin and ΔUC, this can be further rewritten as:

$$(WB - \Delta IN) = s \cdot UC + in \cdot UC - in_{-1} \cdot UC - in \cdot UC + in_{-1} \cdot UC$$
$$- UC \cdot in_{-1} + UC_{-1} \cdot in_{-1}$$
$$= (s - in_{-1}) \cdot UC + UC_{-1} \cdot in_{-1}$$
$$= (1 - \sigma_s) \cdot s \cdot UC + \sigma_s \cdot s \cdot UC_{-1}$$

because of equation (8.9).

We thus have demonstrated that equation (8.3) is identical to (8.11). This shows that the wage costs encountered by firms *historically*, over their volume of sales of the current period, is indeed equal to the expression $(WB - \Delta IN)$. It follows that the difference between the value of realized sales S and this expression is indeed equal to the gross business profits of the firm.

If we add interest costs on inventories to this expression, $(WB - \Delta IN)$, we get total historic costs HC over sales of the current period, as was claimed in equation (8.4), so that we may write:

$$HC = (1 - \sigma_S) \cdot s \cdot UC + (1 + r_{l-1}) \cdot \sigma_S \cdot s \cdot UC_{-1} \qquad (8.12)$$

We may also wish to define the historic unit cost, HUC, which is the total historic cost per sold unit. Dividing equation (8.12) by s, we get:

$$HUC = \frac{HC}{s} = (1 - \sigma_S) \cdot UC + (1 + r_{l-1}) \cdot \sigma_S \cdot UC_{-1} \qquad (8.13)$$

8.2.4 Entrepreneurial profits as a share of sales

We now show that entrepreneurial profits can be defined as a share of sales. What we wish to show is that 'if prices are in a fixed ratio to the historic cost of producing what is sold, then profits in any period will be a constant proportion of the value of sales in that period' (Godley and Cripps 1983: 74–5). From equations (8.1) and (8.4) we know that:

$$S = F + HC \qquad (8.14)$$

Ex post it is always possible to claim that entrepreneurial profits are a fraction φ' of the total historic costs encountered in the production of the goods that were sold in the current period. We have:

$$F = \varphi' \cdot HC \qquad (8.15)$$

so that combining the last two equations we get:

$$S = (1 + \varphi') \cdot HC \qquad (8.16)$$

which implies that:

$$\frac{F}{S} = \frac{\varphi'}{(1 + \varphi')} \qquad (8.17)$$

Finally, combining (8.12) and (8.16), we have:

$$S = (1 + \varphi')\{(1 - \sigma_S) \cdot s \cdot UC + (1 + r_{l-1}) \cdot \sigma_S \cdot s \cdot UC_{-1}\} \qquad (8.18)$$

Dividing through by s, and remembering that:

$$S = s \cdot p \qquad (8.19)$$

we have at last an expression which *defines* the price level as a mark-up on current and lagged unit costs, with weights determined by their respective shares in total sales:

$$p = (1 + \varphi') \cdot HUC = (1 + \varphi') \cdot \{(1 - \sigma_s) \cdot UC + (1 + r_{l-1}) \cdot \sigma_s \cdot UC_{-1}\}$$

$$(8.20)$$

It cannot be too strongly emphasized that (8.20) is nothing more than a definition, though one that is very suggestive. It is saying, for instance, that if firms wished to collar a proportion of the value of sales equal to $\varphi'/(1 + \varphi')$, this would exactly be achieved if they were to set prices as a mark-up equal to φ' on *actual* historic unit costs. We shall see later why target markups may not be achieved in practice, although (in our opinion) they do come pretty close.

Equation (8.20) is useful for the measurement of markups because entrepreneurial profits and business sales can be looked up in accounts directly whereas the historic wage costs can only be estimated by indirect calculations. 'The theorem holds irrespective of how prices are actually fixed. For example, if competitive market processes cause prices to settle at levels which yield a constant share of profits in the value of sales, then prices must move in exactly the same manner *as if* they had been set by adding constant percentage markups to historic costs' (Godley and Cripps 1983: 75).

8.2.5 The distinction between entrepreneurial profit and cash flow

We have shown that entrepreneurial profit is the difference between sales and the total historic cost of producing what was sold. We have, repeated for convenience:

$$F = S - THC = S - (WB - \Delta IN + r_{l-1} \cdot IN_{-1})$$

$$(8.2)$$

In all likelihood the accountants of the entrepreneurs tell them that their firm has made a profit equal to the above amount. The entrepreneurs then decide to distribute the entire profit amount to their families. Will they be able to do so?

The answer is that in general they will not, unless there is no increase in the value of inventories, or unless the increase is entirely financed by borrowing. To distribute the entire amount of entrepreneurial profits in the form of dividends, firm owners need to borrow from banks the equivalent of the change in the value of inventories. This brings forth the important distinction between entrepreneurial profits and cash flow. The cash flow of the firm is equal to:

$$CF = S - WB - r_{l-1} \cdot IN_{-1}$$

$$(8.21)$$

The cash flow of firms within a period is equal to its sales minus the costs that were encountered within the period – the wage bill and the interest payments on the stock of inventories. The cash flow is the net inflow of money into the firm, disregarding any bank loan or other financial transactions. The difference between the entrepreneurial profit and the cash flow is the increase in the value of inventories ($F - CF = \Delta IN$). In most standard models this distinction plays no role since the existence of inventories is assumed away. The distinction between entrepreneurial profits and cash flow becomes relevant only when there are changes in the value of inventories.

The discrepancy between the cash flow and entrepreneurial profits becomes an important issue when the value of inventories changes quickly. From equation (8.8), $\Delta IN = \Delta in \cdot UC + \Delta UC \cdot in_{-1}$, we know that this will happen under two sets of conditions. First, it can arise because the cost of inventories is rising at a high pace – the case of inflation ($\Delta UC \cdot in_{-1}$). Second, it can also happens when fast-growing firms require fast-growing volumes of inventories ($\Delta in \cdot UC$). Under these circumstances, while firms may be making large profits, they are continuously required to borrow large amounts from outside sources if they wish to distribute all of their entrepreneurial profits. Indeed, examples can be easily built where profitable firms, with looming profits, face negative cash flows because of their fast-rising inventories (Godley and Cripps 1983: 70).

The distinction between cash flow and entrepreneurial profits helps to explain the role of credit money. Without credit money – unless inventories valued at cost are matched one for one for loans from the banks – it would be impossible for firms to distribute dividends or at least to distribute as dividends the entire amount of their entrepreneurial profits. Bank loans are a systemic requirement of the monetary production economy.

8.2.6   The definition of National account profits

Up to now we have focussed our attention on profits as perceived by business accountants. National accountants, as exemplified in the National Income and Product Accounts, or NIPA for short, have however a different definition of profits. Their definition derives from the fact that the whole national accounting system is being built around the concept of production. The point of view of the national accountants is that national income should remain the same if production and sales – measured in real terms, here measured in units of widgets – do not change. Recalling that the whole of output is made up of real sales and the value of the increase in physical inventories:

$$y = s + \Delta in \tag{8.5}$$

nominal GDP must be made up of these two components, valued at their appropriate price. In the case of inventories, this means that they must be valued at their unit cost. GDP in a closed economy without government thus starts from the value of consumption and investment (here investment in new inventories):

$$Y = C + I = p \cdot s + UC \cdot (\Delta in) = S + \Delta IN - \Delta UC \cdot in_{-1} \tag{8.22}$$

The first two components on the outmost right-hand side of equation (8.22) are identical to the first two components of the current account column of Table 8.1. However, there is also a third component, the $\Delta UC \cdot in_{-1}$ term, which is known among national accountants as 'stock appreciation' (*SA*) or *inventory valuation adjustment* (*IVA*), and which represents the increase in the value of the opening stock of inventories.

$$SA = \Delta UC \cdot in_{-1} \tag{8.23}$$

Net investment, in our world without fixed investment, is thus equal to the value of the change in physical inventories, $UC \cdot (\Delta in)$, and not to the change in the value of inventories, ΔIN. It follows that total profits, as measured by the national accountants, must also be reduced by the amount of this 'stock appreciation'. When computing national account profits, national accountants behave as if all sold output had been produced at the current cost – the replacement cost. For national accountants, total profits are thus equal to:

$$F_{\text{nipa}} = S - WB + \Delta IN - SA \tag{8.24}$$

so that the sum of factor incomes (wages plus profits) is indeed equal to the value of production:

$$Y = WB + F_{\text{nipa}} \tag{8.25}$$

The current treatment of profits in NIPA is thus consistent with the general principle that holding gains or losses, real or nominal, whatever their origin, should not influence the measure of income, saving or value added, which are flows, and hence should be relegated to revaluation accounts. In the view of the national accountants, stock appreciation *SA* is akin to a capital gain, and cannot be included within national income, which measures flows. Thus the overriding justification for deducting stock appreciation both from profits and changes in the value of inventories is that national accountants need a concept both of aggregate income and aggregate expenditure which is conceptually identical to production – as there is no counterpart to stock appreciation in production.

This is the national accounts definition of profits that has been adopted by the SNA since 1953. It must be said however that when the first national accounts came out, their progenitor, Richard Stone (1947: 45,62), did include stock appreciation in the profits of productive firms, using F_T as in equation (8.2), presumably as a direct transposition of business accounting. This is because from the point of view of the firm stock appreciation is not really a capital gain. Although a revaluation has taken place, there is no capital gain in the ordinary sense because all inventories are valued at cost and all have been be paid for by the firm as they were accumulated, giving rise to additional borrowing – just as much as the accumulation of physical stocks gave rise to borrowing. What is actually happening is that the objects in stock, even if stationary in aggregate, are all the time revolving; so inventories purchased at one time are continuously being used up and replaced by objects newly purchased at a different price. If this is not perfectly clear, we have written out in an Appendix an elaborate arithmetical example which, hopefully, illustrates the whole issue with precision.

While the deduction of stock appreciation from NIPA profits achieves consistency of one kind, it is defective from another viewpoint because it does not conform with a definition of profits as a distributable surplus and because, since stock appreciation is not a transaction, it cannot be fitted into a transactions matrix. This criticism of the NIPA definitions does not apply to the US flow-of-funds accounts where, in the table describing firms' appropriation accounts, *IVA* is added back to 'book' profits to obtain total funds available to firms and then included again in investment expenditure as a component of firms' outlays.[9] In a sense this is not surprising since financial accounts are based on the same logic as our transactions-flow matrix, from which our definition of entrepreneurial profits has arisen.

8.3   Pricing

8.3.1   Generic cost-plus pricing

Up till now, we have described the values that various variables ought to take – in particular the profit variables – at given production costs and prices. Thus we dealt with realized or actual values. We now wish to tackle an entirely different issue, that of price setting. What are firms trying to do when they set prices? Our general answer to this question is that they aim, taking one year with the next, to make enough profits to pay for fixed investment and to distribute enough to satisfy shareholders. But for present purposes, in this initial step, we assume that their objective is to secure profits equal to some proportion of sales. Thus we tackle the following question: At given production costs, if firms wish to achieve a certain level of profits, what price will they have to set?

The pricing decision is based on expectations and conventions. Price setting is based on some measure of unit cost, to which is added a costing margin. This is the generic principle of *cost-plus pricing*, which is generally endorsed by heterodox economists, who reject marginal cost pricing. Here, as in other heterodox works, prices are assumed to be based on the principle of *cost-plus pricing*. Prices are seen as an income distribution mechanism, in

---

[9] See Flow-of-Funds Table F.102, lines 7 and 13.

the hands of the firms. By marking up costs, firms attempt to achieve a certain amount of profits, or a certain profit share, which will allow them to meet their goals. Prices are not the anonymous result of a market-clearing mechanism where prices rise rapidly when demand rises and fall when demand falls. We know that in reality noting at all like this happens, except in auction markets.[10] Prices do not exist to clear markets, as they are conceived in the Walrasian story of the commissaire-priseur who calls prices, to find the one that will perfectly equate demand and supply. As Hicks (1965: 79) points out: 'The existence of stocks has a great deal to do, in practice, with the possibility of keeping prices fixed. If, when demand exceeds output, there are stocks that can be thrown in to fill the gap, it is obvious that the price does not have to rise; a market in which stock changes substitute for price changes (at least up to a point) is readily intelligible'.

Firms have two kinds of decisions to make, costing and pricing. 'Costing refers to the procedures that a business enterprise employs to determine the costs that will be used in setting the selling price of a good before actual production takes place and hence the actual costs of production are known.... Pricing refers to the procedures the business enterprise uses to set the price of a good before it is produced and placed on the market. That is, starting with the costs determined by its costing procedures, the business then adds a costing margin to costs or marks up the costs to set the price' (Lee 1998: 10).

Another important decision of the firm is whether it sets a *gross* or a *net* costing margin. This depends on whether firms are concerned with total business profits F_T or entrepreneurial profit F, as defined in the previous section. Assuming that firms target a certain costing margin on their sales, is that margin gross or net of the unavoidable interest costs that must be met to carry inventories? In other words, for a given amount of expected sales, do firms target a certain amount of total business profits or do they target an amount of entrepreneurial income, net of the interest cost?

---

[10] Godley and Gillion (1965) went through the individual quotations making up the United Kingdom's wholesale price index. We took a serial sample (every tenth observation) and found that individual quotations only changed at rare intervals and that the monthly changes, when they did occur, clustered around 5%. It could be said, by and large, that changes in the overall index were determined by the number of individual quotations which had increased by 5% that month. This finding conforms with the common observation that firms issue price lists at discrete intervals of time. Indeed any other behaviour would be disorderly and expensive. These findings have been confirmed by more recent survey studies initiated by Alan Blinder (1991) and reproduced in several countries (see Amirault *et al.* 2004–2005). While the survey results seem to be anomalies from a neo-classical point of view, they are fully consistent with post-Keynesian pricing theory (Downward and Lee 2001).

It is clear that different answers to this question will generate different price and income share dynamics. If entrepreneurs target their entrepreneurial income, any increase in interest costs will be carried into higher prices.[11] In other words, increases in interest rates will not lead to a fall in the share of income going to entrepreneurial profit, but it will lead to a fall in the real wage rate and in the share of wages, as we assumed it did in section 6 of Chapter 7. By contrast, if entrepreneurs target total business profits, an increase in interest cost will lead neither to an increase in prices nor to a fall in the real wage rate; it will only lead, *ceteris paribus*, to a decrease in the share of entrepreneurial income. In this world, interest income is limited by the extent of total business profit. This is the hypothesis that has been endorsed by a majority of post-Keynesian authors, who omit the impact of interest costs on the costing margin, implicitly assuming that firms are concerned with total business profits rather than entrepreneurial profits. In the models of the next chapters, by contrast, we shall assume that entrepreneurs set their costing margins and prices while targeting entrepreneurial income.

8.3.2   Mark-up pricing

Let us first deal with the simplest of all pricing methods, that of mark-up pricing. As pointed out above, this method is particularly appropriate if firms are only concerned with their total business profits, gross of interest payments, or if firms are generally unable to pass on interest costs. It is also appropriate under the assumption that unit costs are constant, whatever the level of output or the level of sales. This is the assumption which is usually found in post-Keynesian mark-up models. In most post-Keynesian models, costing is done on the basis of *variable* costs, which, are approximately the same thing as the so-called *direct* or *prime* costs. In that case, unit costs are usually constant or nearly so, at a moment of time, for different levels of output. In the simple vertically integrated models with which we deal, the constant unit cost is the unit labour cost.[12] We already presented this simple mark-up pricing model in Chapter 7 as:

$$p = (1 + \varphi) \cdot \left(\frac{W}{pr} \right) = (1 + \varphi) \cdot UC \tag{8.26}$$

---

[11] What is meant here is any increase in unavoidable interest costs on inventories. In the more general case where firms borrow for other purposes, such as purchases of fixed capital goods, then a target return pricing formula could apply, with some target rate of return on capital. An increase in interest rates may or may not induce an increase in the target rate of return.

[12] As already pointed out, this does not mean that we believe that firms set prices on the basis of labour unit costs only; we do recognize that firms base their prices on unit direct costs, which include the cost of intermediate goods (see Coutts, Godley and Nordhaus 1978). But the model here is a vertically integrated model.

where φ is a percentage costing margin, and where W/pr is the unit labour cost of producing one widget, or what we called UC in the previous subsections – the unit cost.

Even when unit labour costs are changing from one period to the next, it could be that firms are still using formula (8.26) to set prices. This would be the case of *replacement cost pricing*, whereby firms adjust the selling price instantaneously to changes in unit costs (Coutts, Godley and Nordhaus 1978: 36). This form of pricing would go hand in hand with last-in first-out (LIFO) accounting principles.

In the present chapter, and in most chapters to follow, we emphasize the fact that unit labour costs may change from one period to the next. We also showed in the previous subsections how total business profits depend on historic wage costs, and how entrepreneurial profits depend on overall historic costs. Because of the existence of inventories, the goods sold in a period have been produced in part only during the current period; the rest of the goods have been produced in an earlier period. The unit cost of the sold goods thus varies depending on whether they originate from past inventories or current production. As a consequence, the average unit cost of the sold goods varies as well, depending on the proportion of the sold goods that comes out of inventories. For every different level of sales, the average unit cost of producing the sold goods is different. This is true even if we consider labour costs only.

But even if unit labour costs turned out to be constant from one period to the next, because there were no wage inflation and no change in labour productivity, the actual average unit cost would vary depending on the scale of the sales. This is because total historic costs HC, in contrast to historic wage costs HWC, contain an element of fixed costs – the interest costs linked to inventory holding. When the level of widget sales is larger, the fixed costs are spread over a larger number of units, and as a result the average unit cost is lower.

So, on what basis can these average or unit costs be computed, knowing that every different level of sales generates a different unit cost? There are two possible answers to this question: *normal-cost pricing* and *full-cost pricing*.[13] We start with full-cost pricing.

8.3.3 Historic full-cost pricing

Godley (1999a) accounts for variations in average unit cost by using what we may call *historic full-cost pricing*. This is a variant of *full-cost pricing*, which was first proposed by Hall and Hitch (1939). In full-cost pricing, prices are based on average unit costs, including overheads (or fixed costs) such as interest

---

[13] See Lavoie (2001a) and Lee (1998, part 2) for more details on these two pricing views.

costs on inventories, computed at the expected volume of *output*. Here we propose a variant of full-cost pricing, by assuming that prices are based on average unit cost computed at the expected *sales* volume. More precisely, the average unit cost involved is the *historic* unit cost computed at the expected or forecast *sales* volume, or the *expected historic unit cost*. Calling HUC^e this expected historic unit cost, the pricing formula that we propose in this chapter is given by:

$$p = (1 + \varphi) \cdot HUC^e \tag{8.27}$$

where

$$HUC^e = \frac{HC^e}{s^e} \tag{8.28}$$

The variables s^e and HC^e are the expected sales volume and the total historic costs that would be encountered at this expected sales volume. Note that φ is the *target* (ex ante) mark-up, in contrast to the *realized* (ex post) mark-up φ' that was defined in section 8.2.

What is the expected historic unit cost equal to? There are three components to it. The first two components arise from the historic wage costs, or more precisely from the expected historic wage costs. The first component is the unit cost of previously produced goods that will be sold in the current period. Inventories make up this component. The second component is the unit cost of the goods to be produced in the current period. The average wage unit cost is thus a weighted average of these two components. What will the weights be? Note that we can write the following definition:

$$\sigma_{se} = \frac{in_{-1}}{s^e} \tag{8.29}$$

At the beginning of the period firms hold inventories of an amount in_{-1}. If they expect a volume of sales s^e, this implies that they expect a proportion σ_{se} of their sales to stem from inventories, at the lagged unit cost UC_{-1}. These lagged unit costs will thus be factored by the weight σ_{se}. By the same token, this also implies that firms expect a proportion $(1 - \sigma_{se})$ of their sales volume to be provided by goods produced in the current period, at the current unit cost UC. The current unit costs thus carry a weight $(1 - \sigma_{se})$. This is in perfect analogue with our computations of realized historic wage costs HWC, as was found in equation (8.11).

The third component is the interest cost on the value of inventories accumulated at the end of the previous period. Thus in analogue with the actual historic unit cost, HUC, given by equation (8.13), the expected historic unit cost is:

$$HUC^e = (1 - \sigma_{se}) \cdot UC + \sigma_{se} \cdot (1 + r_{l-1}) \cdot UC_{-1} \tag{8.30}$$

Ultimately, putting together equations (8.28) and (8.30), the price equation, assuming full-cost historic pricing, is given by:

$$p = (1 + \varphi) \cdot \{(1 - \sigma_{se}) \cdot UC + \sigma_{se} \cdot (1 + r_{l-1}) \cdot UC_{-1}\} \qquad (8.31)$$

This pricing formula says that prices will be set according to expected sales, on the basis of expected historic unit costs and the percentage mark-up φ.[14]

8.3.4 The possibility of perverse pricing

There are two features of formula (8.31) worth noticing. First, any change in the expected sales to inventories ratio σ_{se} induces a change in prices. Prices will thus be changing all the time. Another, more annoying feature of pricing formula (8.31) is that if firms expect sales to be higher, assuming no difference between UC_{-1} and UC, this leads to a lower expected historic unit cost, and hence, for a given mark-up φ, this yields a lower price p. The culprit, so to speak, is the σ_{se} ratio once again. This is called 'perverse pricing'. Perverse pricing, as Gardiner Means (1991: 326) defined it, implies that higher sales are associated with lower prices, while lower sales are associated with higher prices. This may occur with historic full-cost pricing. It is for this reason – the inverse link between expected demand and the price level – that some heterodox authors are reluctant to use full-cost pricing or any of its variants.[15]

There are two possible cases of perverse pricing, associated with the denominator and the numerator of the σ_{se} ratio, as defined in equation (8.29). Obviously, when there is an exogenous increase in expected sales s^e, the σ_{se} ratio is lower, and this leads to falling prices according to formula (8.31), unless unit costs UC increase during the period. Thus, if realized sales are equal to expected sales, higher sales will indeed be associated with lower prices – a case of perverse pricing. The second case of perverse pricing is caused by an unanticipated increase in demand in the previous period. This will generate a reduction in the realized level of inventories in_{-1}, and hence once more a reduction in the σ_{se} ratio – the more so if expected sales s^e react positively to the realized increase of the previous period. Thus in the experiments that we have conducted using the historic full-cost formula, an

---

[14] Because costs are related to prices and profits in this very specific way, the lag between costs and prices cannot be just anything – as the econometricians assume. That is, they assume that the lag can be anything at all and that they are uniquely qualified to discover what it is. This is one of the reasons the work of Godley and Nordhaus (1972), who imposed lags based on stock/output ratios in preference to estimating them econometrically, was never really influential – it was an implicit challenge to econometric methodology.

[15] It should be pointed out, however, that when current unit costs are higher than lagged unit costs, the sign of the relation between expected sales and the price level becomes uncertain.

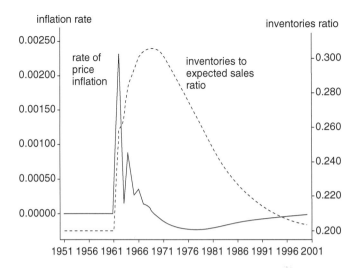

Figure 8.1 Evolution of price inflation and the inventories to expected sales ratio, following a decrease in autonomous demand

increase in demand is usually accompanied by a small dip in the price level, or in the level of inflation when an inflation equation is added.[16] Figure 8.1 shows inversely that when autonomous demand briskly falls, the inflation rate is momentarily boosted up, as a result of the increase in the inventories to expected sales ratio ($\sigma_{se} = in_{-1}/s^e$).

8.3.5 Normal-cost pricing

The drawback of perverse pricing can be avoided by the use of *normal-cost pricing*, where normal costs are defined in reference to a *normal* level of output or a *normal* level of capacity utilization, as was initially proposed by Andrews (1949) and Andrews and Brunner (1975). Normal-cost pricing is an alternative to historic full-cost pricing, that retains the main positive features of the latter while avoiding the drawback just mentioned. With normal-cost pricing, firms measure costs by reference to a *normal* or *standard* level of capacity utilization. Normal costs are then defined as the level at which total costs would be, if output were at its *normal* or trend level (Coutts, Godley and Nordhaus 1978: 22–3). Prices are thus set as a costing margin over normal unit costs, which we can denote as *NUC*. Formally, this can be written as:

$$p = (1 + \varphi) \cdot NUC \qquad (8.32)$$

---

[16] The dip is very small, but exists nonetheless. For instance when autonomous demand goes up by 25%, prices decrease at once by about 0.25% with our numbers.

With normal-cost pricing, there is no presumption that the normal output level will be the realized output level of the period, nor that sales will be equivalent to this normal output level. In addition, the expected output level and the expected level of sales could both be different from the normal output level. As a consequence, both the expected and the realized level of entrepreneurial profits could be quite different from the profit measure implicit to the pricing formula based on the normal output level, as given by equation (8.32). This is the main disadvantage of the normal-pricing formula. Its advantage is that firms that use normal-cost pricing can base their pricing decision on a convention or a rule of thumb – the normal or standard level of output – and need not make forecasts about future sales volumes when setting prices.[17] Moreover it will always be possible for firms to adjust the costing margin if actual and normal costs diverge for a long time, as we shall show in the model deployed in Chapter 11.

Within our simplified framework, what will be the normal unit cost? With historic full-cost pricing, the expected historical unit cost depends on past and current unit labour costs, the rate of interest, and the current inventories to expected sales ratio σ_{se}. As was shown above, it is this ratio that causes perverse pricing. A company that would set prices neither on actual costs nor on expected costs would have to forsake σ_{se} and use instead what it considers to be the *normal* inventories to sales ratio. What is this normal ratio? It is the *target* inventories to sales ratio, which, as we shall see in the next chapter, drives the behaviour of firms in inventory accumulation, and which is equal to:

$$\sigma^T = \frac{in^T}{s^e} \tag{8.33}$$

The σ^T ratio is the ideal *end-of-period* inventories to *expected sales* ratio that firms would like to achieve in the long run. It is a target parameter that firms set as a convention. This target parameter is realized only when firms reach the stationary state – in the long period. We suggest that firms set normal unit costs on the basis of this convention. Normal unit costs are the same as historical unit costs when the target inventories to expected sales parameter σ^T is realized. Thus by using normal-cost pricing, firms act as if the target inventories to sales ratio was the realized one at all times, or rather they act as if the target inventories to sales ratio was realized on average. Normal-cost prices are thus, in that sense, long-period prices (Lee 1985). They do not reflect

---

[17] One of us has directed a great deal of research effort in an attempt to ascertain whether prices move up or down relative to 'normal' historical unit costs, defined as unit costs as they would be if output were reckoned at a normal, or trend level. See Godley (1959), Neild (1963), Godley and Nordhaus (1972), Coutts, Godley and Nordhaus (1978).

non-systematic forces tied to fortuitous variations in sales or inventories. They are prices that reflect historical unit costs as they would be in the long period. With normal-cost pricing, firms know that the income distribution implicit in the pricing formula will not be realized in general, even when their sales forecasts are correct. The only exception is the stationary state.

When fixing prices, firms need not make forecasts about future sales volume. They need only know the past and current unit labour costs, the rate of interest, and the conventional inventories to sales σ^T ratio. By analogy with the full-cost pricing formula, given by (8.31), we obtain the normal-cost pricing equation:

$$p = (1 + \varphi) \cdot NHUC \tag{8.34}$$

with the normal historic unit cost *NHUC* being equal to:

$$NHUC = (1 - \sigma^T) \cdot UC + \sigma^T \cdot (1 + r_{l-1}) \cdot UC_{-1} \tag{8.35}$$

The only thing still left unexplained is the costing margin φ. This will be remedied in Chapter 11.[18]

8.3.6 Some noteworthy features of historic full-cost pricing and normal-cost pricing

Equations (8.31) and (8.34) have several noteworthy features, at least four. To start with, full-cost pricing and normal-cost pricing are based on information that firms possess or search for at the time that they must make their pricing decisions. First, firms give themselves a percentage mark-up φ, more about which will be said in a moment. Second, in the case of normal-cost pricing, the σ^T parameter is also a convention set by firms themselves. In the case of historic full-cost pricing, firms easily estimate the weight σ_{se}, since they know the level of inventories accumulated at the end of the previous period, and by making a forecast of sales, based in particular on the sales of the previous period. Third, the firms collect information on labour unit costs; accountants have carefully calculated lagged unit costs, and entrepreneurs know the wage rate to be paid to workers in the current period, and they would have some estimate of their productivity. Fourth, and finally, firms would know what interest rate r_{l-1} they are being charged to finance their inventories, since this rate is set at the end of the previous period.

---

[18] Here we assumed that the normal historic unit cost *NHUC* is based on unit costs proper, *UC* and UC_{-1}. However, if we were to add more realistic features such as cyclically changing productivity growth, so that current unit costs could not be known at the beginning of the period, when prices are set, *NHUC* would need to be based on a conventional *normal* unit cost, *NUC* and NUC_{-1}, which would depend on some estimate of trend productivity.

A second noteworthy feature of our two pricing formulas is that interest costs come explicitly into these pricing formulas. It is clear that any increase in the rate of interest charged to manufacturing firms that carry and finance inventories with bank loans will be passed on to consumers, through higher prices, provided firms do not simultaneously decrease the mark-up φ. The impact of the rate of interest is even more obvious, when pricing formulas (8.31) or (8.34) are rewritten while assuming that unit costs do not change from one period to the next. Assuming that $UC = UC_{-1}$, pricing formula (8.31) for instance becomes:

$$p = (1 + \varphi) \cdot (1 + r_l \cdot \sigma_{se}) \cdot UC \qquad (8.36)$$

Equation (8.36) illustrates very clearly the principles of cost-plus pricing. The price is based on a measure of direct costs, the labour unit costs given by UC; then there is a percentage mark-up, given by $r_l \cdot \sigma_{se}$, which is designed to cover the overhead costs arising from the unavoidable interest costs; finally there is the entrepreneurial profit percentage mark-up, given by φ.

With such a pricing formula, the monetary and the real sides of the economy are intertwined. *All else equal*, when interest rates rise, prices rise. There is a long tradition of heterodox economists, who, at some time or another, have taken this view: Thomas Tooke and the Banking School, Harrod, Kaldor, Sylos Labini, Graziani, Garegnani, Pivetti and even, for a time, Joan Robinson. In the United States, it is known as Senator Patman's view (see Taylor 2004a: 88–90). Kaldor (1982: 63), for instance, wrote that 'interest costs are passed on in higher prices in much the same way as wage costs'.

What is the meaning of the percentage mark-up φ and what economic interpretation can we attribute to it? The answer is quite obvious once we compare the pricing equations to the identity derived from the transactions-flow matrix. We have:

$$p = (1 + \varphi) \cdot HUC^e = (1 + \varphi)\{(1 - \sigma_{se}) \cdot UC + \sigma_{se} \cdot (1 + r_{l-1}) \cdot UC_{-1}\} \qquad (8.27)$$

$$p = (1 + \varphi) \cdot NHUC = (1 + \varphi)\{(1 - \sigma^T) \cdot UC + \sigma^T \cdot (1 + r_{l-1}) \cdot UC_{-1}\} \qquad (8.34)$$

on one hand, and on the other hand:

$$p = (1 + \varphi')HUC = (1 + \varphi')\{(1 - \sigma_s)UC + \sigma_s(1 + r_{l-1})UC_{-1}\} \qquad (8.20)$$

where

$$\frac{F}{S} = \frac{\varphi'}{(1 + \varphi')} \qquad (8.17)$$

Thus, by saying that firms set a percentage mark-up equal to φ over expected historic unit costs (or normal historic unit costs), we imply that firms aim at securing as entrepreneurial profit a proportion $\varphi/(1 + \varphi)$ of the value of sales. That is, firms set a price such that their expected entrepreneurial profit is a proportion $\varphi/(1 + \varphi)$ of the expected value of sales. For instance, if $\varphi = 0.5$, it implies that firms target entrepreneurial profits that represent $(.5)/(1.5) = 33.3\%$ of the expected value of sales.

Another interesting property of the historic cost pricing formula given by equation (8.31) is that the actual share of entrepreneurial profits in the value of sales, $\varphi'/(1 + \varphi')$, will always turn out to be a close approximation of the desired share $\varphi/(1 + \varphi)$, whatever the realized value of sales. Changes in the actual share compared to the targeted share are due either to mistaken estimates of the current period productivity of workers or to mistaken forecasts of expected sales.[19] The latter make the interest cost per sold unit different from its expected cost, and it also modifies the realized weight between lagged and current unit labour costs, making it different from the one incorporated into the pricing equation. This last effect is only relevant when unit costs UC differ from one period to the next.

Of course these properties of historic cost pricing extend to normal-cost pricing. The normal-cost pricing formula implies that entrepreneurs expect profits to be a proportion φ of sales when the stationary state is reached with the realized inventories to sales ratio no different from the target inventories to sales ratio.

8.3.7 Historic unit costs and inflation

Our historic full-cost and normal-cost pricing formulas have a final noteworthy feature. These formulas are impervious to inflation. To demonstrate this we shall focus on the case of the historic full-cost pricing formula. Even when unit costs UC differ from one period to the next, due to cost inflation for instance, the pricing formula may still be rewritten as equation (8.36), that is on the basis of the current unit cost UC only. All that is required is a reinterpretation of the interest rate r_l paid on loans to finance inventories. The rate must now be reinterpreted not as the nominal rate, but rather as the real rate of interest, defined with respect to the rate of cost inflation. To demonstrate this remarkable feature of pricing formulas (8.31) and (8.34) based on expected or normal historic unit costs, we start by making the following two definitions.

First, we define the rate of cost inflation π_c as being equal to:

$$\pi_c = \frac{(UC - UC_{-1})}{UC_{-1}} = \left(\frac{UC}{UC_{-1}} \right) - 1 \tag{8.37}$$

The rate of cost inflation measures the rate of growth of unit costs. This rate of growth is (nearly exactly) the difference between the rate of growth of

---

[19] In the model to be built for this chapter, we will assume that when entrepreneurs set prices they make correct forecasts of labour productivity pr and that they have finalized the wage bargain with their workers, hence knowing what the nominal wage W is.

nominal wages minus the rate of growth of labour productivity. The above equation implies that lagged unit costs can be rewritten as:

$$UC_{-1} = \frac{(UC)}{(1 + \pi_c)} \tag{8.38}$$

The real rate of interest, here called rr_c to reflect the fact that it is the rate of interest net of cost inflation, is usually given by the equation $rr_c = r_l - \pi_c$. This however is only an approximation. To find out the exact real rate of interest, let us assume that the agent owns a monetary asset, say M. At the end of the period, thanks to the interest payment, the agent is now left with an amount $(1 + r_{l-1})M$. In real terms, however, this amount must be deflated by $(1 + \pi_c)$ under the assumption that prices have risen at the rate π_c. The interest income, net of inflation, is thus:

$$\left\{ \frac{(1 + r_{l-1})}{(1 + \pi_c)} \right\} \cdot M - M$$

Dividing the above expression by the initial value of the asset M, we obtain the real rate of interest, which is defined by the following relation:

$$rr_{c-1} = \frac{(1 + r_{l-1})}{(1 + \pi_c)} - 1 \tag{8.39}$$

so that we can write:

$$(1 + r_{l-1}) = (1 + rr_{c-1}) \cdot (1 + \pi_c) \tag{8.40}$$

We can now substitute the values of equations (8.38) and (8.40) into the historic full-cost pricing formula (8.31). We nearly directly obtain:

$$p = (1 + \varphi) \cdot (1 + rr_{c-1} \cdot \sigma_{se}) \cdot UC \tag{8.41}$$

By analogy, the normal-cost pricing equation may also be rewritten in terms of current unit labour costs only, as was done with the historic full-cost pricing equation. With the real rate of interest rr_c we obtain the simple equation:

$$p = (1 + \varphi) \cdot (1 + rr_{c-1} \cdot \sigma^T) \cdot UC \tag{8.42}$$

Where price inflation and cost inflation are equal, the historic full-cost pricing and normal-cost pricing equations may be rewritten strictly in terms of current unit costs; lagged unit costs need not be taken explicitly into consideration. But the nominal rate of interest must be replaced by the real interest rate in the pricing formulas, with no change whatsoever to the costing mark-up. The new formula is nearly identical to equation (8.36) that we had obtained when assuming that unit costs did not change. The only difference is that the *real* rate of interest, as defined in equation (8.39) must now enter the pricing formula.

One may wonder whether price inflation and cost inflation are ever equal. They will be equal whenever there is no change in the parameters φ, rr_c and σ_{se} of the pricing formula (8.41).

Equations (8.41) and (8.42) clearly show that the margin over *current* labour unit costs UC depends on the *real* rate of interest, and not on the nominal rate of interest.[20] Indeed these equations show that one purpose of pricing is to determine the shares of real incomes. This can be seen even more clearly in the following way. Take equation (8.41), divide it by p, and multiply it by y – the real output. We obtain:

$$y = (1 + \varphi) \cdot (1 + rr_{c-1} \cdot \sigma_{se}) \cdot UC \cdot \frac{y}{p}$$

Remembering that unit costs are the wage bill per unit produced, or $UC = WB/y$, and calling wb the real wage bill, $wb = WB/p$, the above equation becomes:

$$y = (1 + \varphi) \cdot (1 + rr_{c-1} \cdot \sigma_{se}) \cdot wb \qquad (8.43)$$

This equation is a behavioural equation. It sets forth a relation of fundamental significance. It shows that when firms set prices, they intend to determine exhaustively the distribution of real national income between wage income, entrepreneurial income and rentier income. The intended shares of each of these is given by the following ratios:

the share of real wage income: $\quad \dfrac{wb}{y}$;

the share of rentier income: $\quad rr_{c-1} \cdot \sigma_{se} \cdot \dfrac{wb}{y}$

the share of entrepreneurial income: $\quad \varphi \cdot (1 + rr_{c-1} \cdot \sigma_{se}) \cdot \dfrac{wb}{y}$

$$= \frac{\varphi}{(1 + \varphi)}$$

As soon as any of these two quantities are determined, the third is automatically determined as well. The formula has the very important implication that *if* firms have the power to set a mark-up of their choice, and *if* banks can set nominal rates of interest at a level which ensures that the real interest rate does not change, then there is no way in which the real wage bill (for a

---

[20] There seems to be some confusion in this regard among some authors who claim that higher nominal interest rates could lead to higher prices, in particular in Dutt (1992) and Graziani (2003). See Lavoie (1995: 157) for a clear assertion that real rates of interest are the correct variable to consider. The proof offered here had already been provided by Godley and Cripps (1983: 193).

given output) or the wage share can be changed as a result of the nominal wage bargain. These results were established with the historic full-cost pricing formula. By analogy, identical results would be obtained in the case of normal-cost pricing as we defined it.[21]

8.4 Numerical examples of fluctuating inventories

8.4.1 The impact of changing sales on profits: a numerical example without inflation

The purpose of this section is to provide readers with two simple examples of fluctuating sales. They will underline the impact that fluctuating sales, for a given amount of production, inflict on various measures of profit and its share in the value of sales or in the value of national income. In this example, a most simple one, we assume that the unit cost *UC* is constant from one period to the next. This implies that there is no inventory valuation adjustment ($IVA = 0$) and that the price level is constant. We further assume that firms have reached a stationary level of output, equal to 100 units, and hence that the target level of inventories has been achieved. Assuming that firms still expect sales to remain at 100, this means that they will produce 100 units, having no intention to increase or diminish their inventories voluntarily. On the matter of distribution, we assume that the price level is equal to unity ($p = 1$), that unit costs are $UC = .70$, and that the overall interest cost is equal to $2. This could be the case, for instance, if the value of inventories (IN_{-1}) at the beginning of the period were equal to 40 while the rate of interest on loans was 5%. This implies that the target share of entrepreneurial profits *F* in sales is 28%, as indicated at the top of Table 8.3.

One can draw several lessons from this table. First, we note that all but one measure of profit shares rise when sales exceed expectations, that is, when there is a business upswing (case 2). Second, it is quite obvious that measures of shares relative to sales are much more stable than measures of shares relative to national income. The share of total business profits stay at their target 30%, while the share of *realized* entrepreneurial profits $\varphi'/(1+\varphi')$ stay very close to their target $\varphi/(1 + \varphi) = 28\%$, despite large fluctuations in sales and inventories.[22] By contrast the share of entrepreneurial profit relative to GDP oscillates between 25.77% and 30.10%, most of the slack being taken by the share of wages in GDP. The share of interest costs in national income, which is 2% when sales expectations are realized, falls to 1.96% when sales rise to 110 units.

---

[21] We only need to substitute σ^T for σ_{se} in the equations above.

[22] Note once again that while the percentage net costing margin is φ (ex ante), φ' is the percentage profit margin (the realized, ex post, margin).

Table 8.3 A numerical example of varying sales, without inflation

Hypotheses:
$s^e = 100$; $UC = UC_{-1} = .70$; $p = 1$; $\varphi/(1 + \varphi) = 28\%$

		Case 1	Case 2	Case 3
Production	y	100	100	100
Sales volume	s	100	110	90
Value of the change in inventories	$\Delta in \cdot UC$	0	−7	+7
National income	$Y = s \cdot p + \Delta in \cdot UC$	100	103	97
Wage bill	WB	70	70	70
Historic wage cost	HWC	70	77	63
Interest costs	$r_{l-1} \cdot IN_{-1}$	2	2	2
Gross profits	F_T	30	33	27
Entrepreneurial profits	F	28	31	25
Profit shares wrt sales	F_T/S	30%	30%	30%
	$F/S = \varphi'/(1 + \varphi')$	28%	28.18%	27.77%
Profit shares wrt national income	F_T/Y	30%	32.04%	27.97%
	F/Y	28%	30.10%	25.77%

Now in reality, sales at the macroeconomic level will never go through swings as large as those described here. Nevertheless there is a further lesson to be drawn from the table. When carrying out studies of cyclical profit shares through the business cycle, economists would be well advised to look at profit shares relative to sales rather than profit shares relative to national income. These studies often attempt to assess whether workers manage to raise their bargaining power in a boom. The fact that the profit share relative to GDP rises in the first part of the upswing, and diminishes in the second part of the boom, is no necessary indication of the evolution of the bargaining power of workers; it may simply reflect unexpected movements in sales relative to output. The evolution of profits relative to sales would seem to be a better possible indicator of the changes in the relative strength of workers and their employers.

8.4.2 The impact of changing sales on profits: a numerical example with cost inflation

We again explore the impact of changing sales, with a given production level, on the various measure of profits, but this time with a time-varying unit cost, which involves the computation of an inventory valuation adjustment

Table 8.4 A numerical example of varying sales, with cost inflation

Hypotheses:

$UC = .70$; $UC_{-1} = .66$; $\pi_c = 6.06\%$

$p = 1$; $\varphi/(1 + \varphi) = 28\%$; $\varphi = .388$

$\sigma_{se} = 0.5$; $s^e = 100$; $in_{-1} = 50$; $(1 + r_{c-1} \cdot \sigma_{se}) = 1.0286$

$rr_{c-1} = 5.71\%$

$r_{l-1} = 12.12\%$

Production	y	100	100	100
Sales volume	s	100	110	90
Value of the change in inventories	$\Delta in \cdot UC$	0	−7	+7
National income	$Y = s \cdot p + \Delta in \cdot UC$	100	103	97
Stock appreciation	$SA = \Delta UC \cdot in_{-1}$	2	2	2
Wage bill	WB	70	70	70
Historic wage cost	HWC	68	75	61
Interest costs	$r_{l-1} \cdot IN_{-1}$	4	4	4
Gross profits	F_T	32	35	29
Entrepreneurial profits	F	28	31	25
NIPA profits	F_{nipa}	30	33	27
Profit shares wrt sales	F_T/S	32%	31.81%	32.22%
	$F/S = \varphi'/(1 + \varphi')$	28%	28.18%	27.77%
NIPA profit shares	F_{nipa}/Y	30%	32.04%	27.83%
	F_{nipa}/S	30%	30%	30%

(*IVA*), also called stock appreciation (*SA*). The hypotheses used are inserted in Table 8.4.

Once more we see that profit shares relative to sales do not move or barely move, whereas the profit share relative to national income experiences larger fluctuations.

Appendix 8.1: A numerical example of inventory accounting

The store: no production, just purchases and sales

First imagine a store which buys goods from a manufacturer and subsequently sells them to the public. Counting merchandise as numbers of identical physical objects, which we shall call 'widgets', we may first imagine the store's operations being recorded in the way shown in the first four columns of Table A8.1. These four columns only deal with physical objects. Note that we always use upper case letters to designate variables in nominal values while lower case letters are used for real variables (physical objects, or deflated nominal values, as the case may be).

The store starts operations in the first quarter of year 1. It buys 12 widgets in that quarter and in each of the subsequent quarters of year 1, shown as y in column 1. It sells nothing during the first year, so inventories, accounted as the number of physical

Table A8.1 A numerical example with inventories

	Objects				Dollars							
Row	1	2	3	4	5	6	7	8	9	10	11	12
Quarter, year	Purchases or production	Sales	Inventories (change and level)		Unit costs	Wage bill (1×5)	Price	Sales value (2×7)	Inventories at cost (level and change)		Historic wage costs	Profit 8–11
	y	s	Δin	in	UC	WB	p	S	IN	ΔIN	HWC	F_T
1	12	0	12	12	1	12	–	0	12	12	0	0
2	12	0	12	24	1	12	–	0	24	12	0	0
3	12	0	12	36	1	12	–	0	36	12	0	0
4	12	0	12	48	1	12	–	0	48	12	0	0
Year 1	48	0	48	48	1	48	–	0	48	48	0	0
1	12	12	0	48	1	12	1.5	18	48	0	12	6
2	12	12	0	48	1	12	1.5	18	48	0	12	6
3	12	12	0	48	1	12	1.5	18	48	0	12	6
4	12	12	0	48	1	12	1.5	18	48	0	12	6
Year 2	48	48	0	48	1	48	1.5	72	48	0	48	24
1	12	24	–12	36	1	12	1.5	36	36	–12	24	12
2	12	24	–12	24	1	12	1.5	36	24	–12	24	12
3	24	24	0	24	1	24	2.0	48	24	0	24	24
4	24	24	0	24	1	24	2.0	48	24	0	24	24
Year 3	72	96	–24	24	1	72	1.75	168	24	–24	96	72
1	24	24	0	24	1.2	28.8	2.0	48	28.8	4.8	24	24
2	24	24	0	24	1.2	28.8	2.0	48	28.8	0	28.8	19.2
3	24	24	0	24	1.2	28.8	2.0	48	28.8	0	28.8	19.2
4	24	24	0	24	1.2	28.8	2.0	48	28.8	0	28.8	19.2
Year 4	96	96	0	24	1.2	115.2	2.0	192	28.8	4.8	110.4	81.6

objects in store, rise by 12 widgets every quarter, reaching 48 at the end of the year as shown in columns 3 and 4. These inventories, in real terms, are noted *in*, while the change in real inventories is noted Δin. Sales (noted *s* in column 2) begin in the first quarter of year 2 and continue through the year at the rate of 12 widgets per quarter so, as purchases remain at 12, there is a zero change in inventories and their level is again 48 at the end of the year. In year 3, sales jump to 24 per quarter and stay at that level for the rest of the example. Purchases remain at 12 for two quarters, so inventories initially fall by 12 per quarter. Then purchases jump to 24 and stay at that level so there are no further changes in the level of inventories. The level of inventories falls to 24 in the second quarter of year 3 and remains at that level thereafter.

Beyond introducing an identity linking purchases, sales and increases in physical inventories, the numbers illustrates an important theorem – that in a stationary steady state, the inventory to sales ratio measures the average time an object remains in stock. Through years 1 and 2 it obviously takes exactly four quarters for any object to be sold using a 'first-in first-out' method of accounting for stocks of inventories (FIFO). For instance, the 12 widgets that had been purchased in the first quarter of year 1 are sold in the first quarter of year 2, and hence they remain in stock for exactly four quarters. Similarly the 12 widgets purchased in the second quarter of year 1 are sold in the second quarter of year 2. One may think of the objects being put onto a conveyor belt when they are bought and later taken off and sold in the order in which they were bought.

If the objects are not sold in the order they were purchased, for instance if they are sold following the 'last-in first-out' principle (LIFO), the *mean* period they remain in stock is still given by the stock/sales ratio; at the end of year 2 the mean period is 48:12 (or 4) on a quarterly basis and 48:48 (or 1) on an annual basis. In years 3 and 4 the mean lag has shortened to a single quarter. At the end of both these years, the mean period is 24:24 (or 1) on a quarterly basis and 24:96 (or 1/4) on a yearly basis.

The manufacturing firm and inventory accounting

To interpret the columns which follow, imagine the business to be not a store but a manufacturing firm which produces the widgets it sells; the meaning of the symbol *y* therefore changes from purchases to production of widgets. If we assume that produced goods can only be sold under the 'first-in first-out' principle, and assuming away the presence of precautionary inventories, then the fourth year of the numerical example of Table A8.1 describes a case where the goods produced in one quarter, say quarter 1 of year 4, can only be sold in the next quarter (in quarter 2 of year 4). A time lag of one period between production and distribution would indeed be introduced, but this time lag is of only one quarter. If the accounting period of our model is one year, then the inventories to sales ratio is only 0.25, giving the impression that there is no time lag whatsoever between production and sales, and that some of the goods that have been consumed in one period had been produced within the same period. But this is an illusion based on the fact that the production and the accounting periods are of different length.

The dollar amounts in columns 5 and 6 assume, for simplicity, that productivity is fixed at one widget per worker per period, so the number of employees is always equal to the number of widgets produced – *y* in column 1. The wage rate starts at $1 per quarter and rises in a jump to $1.2 per quarter at the beginning of year 4. As productivity is assumed to be constant, the unit cost (*UC* in column 5) is equal to the wage rate.

Column 7 gives the selling prices p measured in dollars which firms charge per widget; and column 8 gives the total dollar value of sales. As shown in the table, this is column 2 times column 7.

Column 9 gives the dollar value of the inventory of widgets *measured at cost*, noted *IN* – what it cost the firm to build those inventories. These measures are pretty straightforward during the first three years, since there is no change in the unit cost of produced widgets. Any change in the dollar value of inventories must be attributed to a change in the number of physical widgets in stock. Things are more complicated in the first quarter of year 4. There, although there is no change in the volume of inventories *in*, that is, there is no change in the number of widgets in stock, there is a change in their value measured at cost. There is an increase from $24 to $28.8, hence an increase of $4.8 as shown in column 10, because 24 widgets valued at $1 each have been taken out of stock and sold; these have been replaced with an inventory of 24 newly produced widgets which have cost, and are therefore valued at, $1.2 each. Column 10 gives the change in the value of the widget stock, once more measured at cost, noted ΔIN.

The relationship between the various measures of inventory levels and changes may be summarized by equation (8.8):

$$\Delta IN = \Delta in \cdot UC + \Delta UC \cdot in_{-1} \tag{8.8}$$

ΔIN (column 10) is identically equal to the physical change in inventories measured at cost (column 3 times column 5) plus the change in unit cost times the opening number of widgets in stock – the 'stock appreciation' or *inventory valuation adjustment (IVA)*.

As there is no change at all in the volume of inventories in the first quarter of Year 4, the whole of the increase in the value of inventories takes the form of stock appreciation. Note that, notwithstanding the suggestive name 'stock appreciation' and notwithstanding that the value of inventories has gone up without there being any change in the volume of inventories, nothing in the nature of capital appreciation has occurred which is in any way comparable with appreciation of shares in the stock market. The reason for this is that we are watching a revolving process in which old inventories purchased at one price are replaced by new inventories purchased at another (higher) price. There is no capital appreciation in the ordinary sense because everything comprised within the concept of *IN* is valued at the price which was actually paid for it. Still, as we shall see later, the increase in the value of inventories has, in some other sense, some similarity with the capital gains on stock market shares.

The measure of profits

We now address a major question. How much profit has the firm made through the first four years of its operations? As pointed out in the main text, the conventional *business* answer to this question is that total profits of firms, named F_T, in each period are equal to the dollar value of sales less the value of outlays in the same period plus the change in the value of inventories between the beginning and end of the period, knowing that inventories are always valued at cost.

$$F_T = S - WB + \Delta IN \tag{8.2}$$

These profits F_T appear in column 12 of Table A8.1. They are the sum of columns 8 (sales) and 10 (the change in the value of inventories at cost), from which column 6 (the wage bill) has been subtracted. They are also column 8 minus column 11.

We have so far omitted to mention a feature of the transactions described in Table A8.1. In the sequence of events described, firms have to pay out wages for the whole of year 1 before they get anything back at all. So the whole process cannot get started, nor can it proceed, unless there is an external source of funds to finance these initial outlays. It is natural to suppose that this external finance comes from commercial banks. At the end of year 1 the firm has made a zero profit, but it has had to lay out $48 with no offsetting receipts at all. It will only have been possible to carry out these operations if a loan of $48 has been obtained; but if such a loan has indeed been obtained, the firm is fully solvent from a balance sheet point of view, with an asset at the end of the period (the inventory stock valued at $48) which is exactly equal to the liability (the loan it has received). And for the rest of the example, what are recorded as profits can always be extracted leaving assets equal to liabilities if, and only if, there is a loan equal to the stock of inventory.

National accounts

It is possible to present another numerical example, which arises from that of Table A8.1, but which takes into account the national income definitions. This is done in Table A8.2. Column 1 represents sales, which in this case are akin to consumption expenditures (it is directly taken from column 8 of Table A8.1). Column 2 measures the change in the value of inventories, as measured by businesses, ΔIN (it is taken from column 10 of Table A8.1). Column 3 is the inventory valuation adjustment. This adjustment only occurs in the first quarter of year 4, since it is only in that year that unit costs change. Column 4 is investment, as measured by national accountants,

Table A8.2 A numerical example of the national accounts

Row	1	2	3	4	5	6	7
Quarter	$C = S$	ΔIN	$SA = -IVA$	$I = \Delta in \cdot UC$	$Y = \text{GDP } (1+4)$	WB	F_{nipa}
Q1	0	12	0	12	12	12	0
Q2	0	12	0	12	12	12	0
Q3	0	12	0	12	12	12	0
Q4	0	12	0	12	12	12	0
Year 1	0	48	0	48	48	48	0
Q1	18	0	0	0	18	12	6
Q2	18	0	0	0	18	12	6
Q3	18	0	0	0	18	12	6
Q4	18	0	0	0	18	12	6
Year 2	72	0	0	0	72	48	24
Q1	36	−12	0	−12	24	12	12
Q2	36	−12	0	−12	24	12	12
Q3	48	0	0	0	48	24	24
Q4	48	0	0	0	48	24	24
Year 3	168	−24	0	−24	144	72	72
Q1	48	4.8	4.8	0	48	28.8	19.2
Q2	48	0	0	0	48	28.8	19.2
Q3	48	0	0	0	48	28.8	19.2
Q4	48	0	0	0	48	28.8	19.2
Year 4	192	4.8	4.8	0	192	115.2	76.8

since we have excluded fixed investment in the present chapter. Column 5 is the gross domestic product, GDP, which we have denoted previously by the letter Y. Domestic income, seen from the side of expenditures, is the sum of consumption and investment; but seen from the side of income, it is the sum of wages and profits. This is what the next two columns indicate, since the sum of column 6 (the wage bill, taken from column 6 of Table A8.1) and column 7 (NIPA total profits) must equal GDP. Note that NIPA profits (column 7) are different from total profits (column 12 of Table A8.1) on only one occasion, when the unit cost of widgets changes, in the first quarter of year 4. Seen from the national accountant's point of view, we must have the following equalities:

$$Y = C + I = S + (\Delta IN - SA) = s \cdot p + \Delta in \cdot UC = WB + F_{\text{nipa}} \qquad (8.22)$$

It is important to note that the same produced good takes on a different value depending on whether it has been sold or not, as can be seen from the $s \cdot p + \Delta\ in \cdot UC$ term. When the good is sold, it is valued at its selling price p; when it is unsold, being added to the stock of inventories, the produced good is valued at its unit cost UC.

The numerical example of Table A8.1 is built in such a way that the unit cost to price ratio is constant between the first quarter of year 2 and the second quarter of year 3, as can be seen by matching columns 5 and 7; similarly the profits to sales ratio is constant at 33% during the same time period, as can be checked with columns 12 and 8. By contrast, there are wide swings in the ratio between profits and wages in national income, as can be seen by comparing columns 5 and 6 of Table 8.2. In the last quarter of year 2, profits represent 33% of national income, whereas in the first quarter of year 3, they represent 50% of national income. These swings arise as a result of the large fluctuations in sales relative to production; when sales exceed production, as in the first quarter of year 3, the profit share rises.

9
A Model with Private Bank Money, Inventories and Inflation

9.1 Introduction

The present chapter applies the accounting lessons and the pricing behaviour that we discussed in Chapter 8. A preliminary model describing a closed economy with no government is deployed, based on 'inside' money created by banks. After having explored its main features, we will be able to move on to two more realistic models of a whole modern industrial monetary economy, those of Chapters 10 and 11, that deal simultaneously with privately issued money and government-issued money.

Three propositions are central to the argument of this chapter. First, as we are now describing an industrial economy which produces goods as well as services, we must recognize that production takes time. As workers have to be paid as soon as production starts up, while firms cannot simultaneously recover their costs through sales, there arises a systemic need for finance from outside the production sector. Second, when banks make loans to pay for the inventories which must be built up before sales can take place, they must simultaneously be creating the credit money used to pay workers which they, and the firms from which they buy goods and services, find acceptable as a means of payment. Third, we are about to break decisively with the standard assumption that aggregate demand is always equal to aggregate supply. Aggregate demand will now be equal to aggregate supply plus or minus any change in inventories. Hicks (1989) noted the high theoretical importance of this proposition because it destroys the market clearing condition which is central to general equilibrium theory, though he did so with a marked lack of rhetoric. For this reason our new model will be called Model *DIS* because it deals with disequilibrium (of a kind) in the goods market.

As always, we start with balance sheet and transactions matrices which describe the accounting structure of the model and define the nominal variables which it comprises. As Table 9.1 shows, the only form of wealth owned by households is (credit) money. Firms are assumed to operate without any fixed capital but they own a stock of finished goods and work-in-progress

Table 9.1 Balance sheet of Model *DIS*

	Households	Production firms	Banks	Σ
Money deposits	$+M$		$-M$	0
Loans		$-L$	$+L$	0
Inventories		$+IN$		$+IN$
Balance (net worth)	$-V_h$	0	0	$-V_h$
Σ	0	0	0	0

Table 9.2 The transactions-flow matrix of Model *DIS*

	Households	Production firms		Banks		Σ
		Current	Capital	Current	Capital	
Consumption	$-C$	$+C$				0
Change in the value of inventories		$+\Delta IN$	$-\Delta IN$			0
Wages	$+WB$	$-WB$				0
Interest on loans		$-r_{l-1} \cdot L_{-1}$		$+r_{l-1} \cdot L_{-1}$		0
Entrepreneurial profits	$+F$	$-F$				0
Bank profits	$+F_b$			$-F_b$		0
Interest on deposits	$+r_{m-1} \cdot M_{-1}$			$-r_{m-1} \cdot M_{-1}$		0
Change in loans			$+\Delta L$		$-\Delta L$	0
Change in deposits	$-\Delta M$				$+\Delta M$	0
Σ	0	0	0	0	0	0

(inventories) which is exactly matched by a liability in the form of bank loans.[1] The banks 'owe' money and their assets consist entirely of loans. Table 9.2 – the transactions-flow matrix of Model *DIS* – is nearly identical to Table 7.2. The only difference is that entrepreneurial profits and bank profits are now distributed to households.

9.2 The equations of Model *DIS*

The present model, like all our models, is a representation of a complete, interdependent dynamic system. We shall break into the causal circle at a

---

[1] The core of Model *DIS* is similar to that of Model *BMW*. As a result, there is just one essential difference between the balance sheet of Table 7.1 and that of Table 9.1. The tangible capital item previously called *fixed capital* is replaced by the item that represents *inventories*.

critical point and discuss the behaviour of each part of the model individually. We then solve the model and learn how it works as a whole, bolstering such analytic results as we can grind out with numerical simulations.

9.2.1 The production decision

Two fundamental postulates of this model are, first, that firms decide each period, in advance of knowing what their sales will be, how much (in terms of physical quantities) they will produce; second, that they set the unit price which they are going to charge. These production and price decisions are interdependent; the firm must believe that the price it charges is consistent with its expectation about how many units it will sell, while the whole operation generates profits which are some target share of sales.

Since there is a lag between firms' outlays and their receipts from sales, the whole production/sales process necessarily involves the accumulation of inventories. However, inventories do not come into existence solely because production takes time, they also rise and fall because firms make mistakes about the amount they are going to sell.

Accordingly we write the production decision as:

$$y = s^e + in^e - in_{-1} = s^e + \Delta in^e \tag{9.1}$$

where y, s, and in are respectively output, sales and inventories, measured as physical objects. The superscript e means that the number in question is what firms expect to happen, or, in the case of inventories, what they plan. The equation says that firms decide to produce what they expect to sell plus any planned increase in inventories.

We assume that there is some long-run desired ratio of inventories to expected sales, just as in Chapter 7 we had a fixed capital to output target ratio, which we shall call σ^T. Thus, on the basis of their expected sales for the period, firms set a long run target for inventories, in^T, such that:

$$in^T = \sigma^T \cdot s^e \tag{9.2}$$

However firms know that their expectations may be mistaken, so they aim to recover only a proportion γ of the distance between the targeted and actual inventory levels in any one period. The level of inventories in^e that firms desire to hold at the end of the period is given by:

$$in^e = in_{-1} + \gamma(in^T - in_{-1}) \tag{9.3}$$

No problem of stability can in practise arise, as it did in Chapter 7, because the inventory to sales ratio is so small.[2]

---

[2] In the United States, the inventory/sales ratio is below 0.2. We will say no more about stability, considering that the issue has been dealt in sufficient detail for a very similar model, in Chapter 7.

Any change in the physical stock of inventories is equal to production less what is actually sold:

$$in = in_{-1} + (y - s) \tag{9.4}$$

Putting (9.1) and (9.4) together, it follows that realized inventories differ from expected inventories by the difference between expected and actual sales. Inventories will turn out to be lower than expected to the extent that sales turn out to be higher than expected, and vice versa, so we have the following additional equation, which we can use instead of equation (9.4):

$$in - in^e = s^e - s \tag{9.4A}$$

Expected sales could be randomly distributed around past sales. Alternatively sales expectations could be adaptive, which is the form that we adopt here, where entrepreneurs revise their past sales expectations in light of the sales that occurred in the previous period:

$$s^e = \beta s_{-1} + (1 - \beta) \cdot s^e_{-1} \tag{9.5}$$

What about realized sales? As in previous models, we assume that firms sell the exact amount of consumer goods demanded by households but this assumption has now become realistic because firms carry stocks into which they can dig whenever demand exceeds production. We need only assume that households never demand more in a period than the sum of inventories accumulated at the beginning of the period plus current production. Provided this condition is fulfilled, rationing will never occur so it is legitimate to assume that:

$$s = c \tag{9.6}$$

where c is the real demand for consumer goods by households.[3]

We next define four variables related to production which have already been discussed extensively. The number of people employed N is determined by the number of physical units firms decide to produce divided by labour productivity pr, which is assumed to be constant.

$$N = \frac{y}{pr} \tag{9.7}$$

The wage bill WB is given by the number of people employed times the nominal wage rate W (measured by dollars per employee per period), the latter assumed initially to be exogenous.

$$WB = N \cdot W \tag{9.8}$$

---

[3] In other words, we assume that at all times: $(y + in_{-1}) > c$.

The unit cost of production, *UC*, is the wage bill divided by the quantity produced.

$$UC = \frac{WB}{y} \tag{9.9}$$

This definition of unit costs enables us to infer the total value (measured at cost) of the goods in stock, which have so far been measured in physical units, so long as the accounting period is longer than the production period.

$$IN = in \cdot UC \tag{9.10}$$

All the variables which make up unit cost will be known to the firm.

9.2.2 The pricing decision

The previous chapter was mainly devoted to an analysis of the pricing decision, so we only briefly present the relevant equations here. The key relation is that firms aim to secure as entrepreneurial profit, net of interest costs, a certain proportion, $\varphi/(1 + \varphi)$, of the value of sales S defined as the number of objects sold s times their price p measured as dollars per object.

$$S = p \cdot s \tag{9.11}$$

To achieve their objective, firms use normal-cost pricing, with a percentage mark-up φ over normal historical unit costs such that:

$$p = (1 + \varphi) \cdot NHUC \tag{9.12}$$

where normal historical unit costs, *NHUC*, are defined as:

$$NHUC = (1 - \sigma^T) \cdot UC + \sigma^T \cdot (1 + r_{-1}) \cdot UC_{-1} \tag{9.13}$$

with σ^T being the conventional inventories to sales target ratio which firms would like to achieve over the long run.

Realized profits F, as shown in the previous chapter, are equal to:

$$F = S - WB + \Delta IN - r_{-1} \cdot IN_{-1} \tag{9.14}$$

all of which are immediately distributed to households.

9.2.3 Banks, loans and money

If production takes time and if firms are to distribute profits in full, they must have recourse to borrowing, and we assume that loans from banks are indeed obtained on a scale which exactly corresponds to the level of inventories.

But what exactly does this mean? From the workers' point of view the receipt of income consists of an accumulating credit balance at the bank which is exactly equal to the loans taken on by firms; it is implied that workers find the acquisition of credit balances at banks a credible means of payment for their services, and that they have confidence that businesses will, in turn, accept payment in the form of cheques which draw down those credit balances when they buy goods.

The banks' operations in this simplified world are easily characterized. As can be seen from the balance sheet matrix of Table 9.1, the demand for loans by firms is:

$$L_d = IN \tag{9.15}$$

We assume that banks open lines of credit to firms such that the stock of loans is automatically increased when inventories grow and automatically repaid when they fall.

$$L_s = L_d \tag{9.16}$$

The quantity of credit money outstanding or (in neo-classical terminology) '*supplied*' is always exactly equal to the stock of loans, as implied by the banks' balance sheet:

$$M_s = L_s \tag{9.17}$$

Banks charge interest on loans and pay interest on money. We shall assume that both rates of interest are determined by banks and that the lending rate is above the deposit rate, so that banks make profits.

$$r_1 = \bar{r}_1 \tag{9.18}$$

$$r_m = r_1 - add \tag{9.19}$$

Banks' profits, F_b, arise from the difference between the interest that they receive on loans and the interest they pay on deposits. As with non-financial firms, we assume that banks distribute all their profits to households immediately.

$$F_b = r_{1-1} \cdot L_{-1} - r_{m-1} \cdot M_{h-1} \tag{9.20}$$

9.2.4 Household behaviour

Total personal income, YD, the disposable income of households, there being no taxes, consists of wages, profits paid over by firms and banks, and receipts of interest on money held at the beginning of the period

$$YD = WB + F + F_b + r_{m-1} \cdot M_{h-1} \tag{9.21}$$

The stock of money which households find themselves holding at the end of each period is determined by the opening stock plus total income less the value of consumption, C. As in Chapters 3 and 4, we use the h subscript to denote the actual stock of money held, measured ex post. Thus we have:

$$\Delta M_h = YD - C \tag{9.22}$$

Our hypothesis regarding consumers expenditure is identical with that proposed in Chapter 3, namely that households consume a certain proportion of their expected income each period subject to their eventually achieving some desired level of wealth (in this case entirely consisting of bank deposits) relative to their income. There is, however, an important difference between the Chapter 3 formulation and the present one in that the present model incorporates the idea that prices change, either because the mark-up changes or (potentially) because wage rates or interest rates change. Our modified hypothesis regarding household behaviour is that *the wealth target is formulated in real terms*; if the price level goes up this reduces the real value of the existing stock of wealth/money *pro tanto*, making it necessary to save a little more in nominal terms in order to achieve a given amount of wealth in real terms. In other words, households are assumed *not* to suffer from money illusion. This will be explained in more detail in the next subsection.

To incorporate these ideas, we may start by reformulating the Haig–Simons definition of income, which was first presented in Chapter 5 when discussing capital gains. Here there are no capital gains, but households are experiencing a real capital loss on their past accumulated wealth when prices rise. As a result, the Haig–Simons definition of income will come very handy when prices change. According to Haig (1921) and Simons (1938), income is defined as the sum of consumption and the increase in wealth. Up to the present chapter, however, we assumed output prices would be constant, and hence we did not need to distinguish between real and nominal income. How is the Haig–Simons definition of income to be reinterpreted in a world where output prices change? In other words, what is the Haig–Simons definition of *real* income? In symmetry to our previous definition, we shall define *real* disposable income as the sum of *real* consumption plus the increase in the stock of *real* wealth. In other words, *real* disposable income is the flow of income measured in real terms, which, if entirely consumed, will leave the *real* stock of wealth intact. Hence we have the Haig–Simons definition of real disposable income:

$$yd_{hs} = c + (m_h - m_{h-1}) \tag{9.23}$$

where:

$$C = c \cdot p \tag{9.24}$$

and

$$m_h = \frac{M_h}{p} \tag{9.25}$$

The variables c and m_h are the straightforward values of the flow of consumption C and the stock of money M_h, both deflated by the price level of the current period.[4] Since we assume that the only assets held by households are their money balances at banks, these money deposits make up the entire stock of household wealth.

To complete the model, we only need two additional equations. As before, we shall assume that consumption depends on disposable income and the real stock of accumulated wealth. In the present context, with the possibility of price changes, we assume, as already said, that consumption or saving decisions are taken in real terms. If households had perfect foresight, their real consumption demand would depend on their realized real (Haig–Simons) income and on the past accumulated real stock of money. We would have:

$$c = \alpha_0 + \alpha_1 \cdot yd_{hs} + \alpha_2 \cdot m_{h-1} \qquad (9.26A)$$

However we assume that households make their consumption decisions on the basis of their *expected* real disposable income, yd_{hs}^e, so the consumption function is:

$$c = \alpha_0 + \alpha_1 \cdot yd_{hs}^e + \alpha_2 \cdot m_{h-1} \qquad (9.26)$$

We now have to say how expectations about real disposable income are formed. As usual, a multitude of possibilities are open. In a well-wrought stock-flow model, expectations by firms and households about sales and income have a secondary practical importance. We could assume entirely exogenous and constant expectations.[5] We could assume that these expectations are randomly formed around the past level of real disposable income. We shall assume here that expectations about the current period real disposable income is a weighted average of the past realized level of real disposable income and the past level of expected real disposable income, so that we have:

$$yd_{hs}^e = \varepsilon \cdot yd_{hs-1} + (1 - \varepsilon) \cdot yd_{hs-1}^e \qquad (9.27)$$

The model of inventories with private bank money is now complete. We have 27 equations and 27 variables. If we wish to deal with national income, as defined by the national accountants, we could add an auxiliary equation of definition, which would play no causal role in the model:

$$Y = s \cdot p + \Delta in \cdot UC$$

The reader should note once again that national income is not such that $Y = p \cdot y$, since the nominal value of output y is different depending on whether output has been sold (s) or has been added to inventories (Δ in).

---

[4] It should be noted, as will be pointed out later, that: $\Delta m_h \neq \Delta M_h / p$.

[5] In this case, however, real output in the stationary state would depend on how optimistic entrepreneurs are. See Appendix 9.2.

9.2.5   The redundant equation

Although the model is now complete, there is no equation which makes the 'demand' for money, M_h in (9.22), equal to its 'supply', M_s in (9.17). The demand for credit money is determined by the spending and saving decisions of households while the supply of money is determined by a quite different process, namely the need of firms to build and finance adequate inventories and their decision to distribute all their profits. Yet once again the equivalence of money 'supplied' by banks with the money which households 'demand' is guaranteed by the coherence of the system as a whole. There is neither need nor place for an equilibrium condition which makes the demand for money equal to supply. So in this model the hidden equation is:

$$M_s = M_h \qquad\qquad (9.28)$$

The so-called money supply M_s, which is created as a result of the banks granting loans to finance the inventories of firms, always turns out to be exactly equal to money held by households. And once again, this equation cannot be included in the computer program for otherwise the model would be over determined.

In general, the stock of money that households end up holding at the end of the period will be different from the end-of-period amount of money that they expected to hold when they took their consumer decisions at the beginning of the period. Any error in expectations about income will have, as its precise counterpart, an error in the expected end-of-period stock of nominal money. Just as errors in sales expectations by firms have, as their counterpart, deviations in inventories (and hence loans) from their expected values, so do errors in expectations about incomes by households have as their counterpart deviations in money stocks from their expected values. It is inventories on the one hand, and money stocks on the other, which provide the essential flexible elements – the 'buffers' – which enable the whole system to function in a world of uncertainty. What occurs essentially is that when households over-estimate their disposable income, they spend more than they should have, and hence end up with bank balances smaller than expected. And because households have spent more than expected, firms wind up with smaller than expected inventories, and hence with smaller requirements for loans to finance inventories. This 'buffering' does not merely enable the system to function, it also generates a kind of auto pilot whereby unexpected (and unwanted) stocks of money and inventories result in a corrective mechanism which comes into play during subsequent periods.

Two final points are in order, before we tackle a few simulations. The model in its present form implies that firms can collar any proportion whatever of the national income by raising the mark-up. But this is a consequence of our assumption up to this point that nominal wages are exogenous. Second, our assumption that firms seek to make profits equal to some proportion of sales is only appropriate to a world in which there is no fixed capital investment. In future models firms will have different objectives and we shall have to modify the mark-up formula to accommodate these.

9.3 Additional properties of the model

9.3.1 An inflation-accounted definition of household's real disposable income

Now that we have introduced the possibility of price changes, and the Haig–Simons definition of real disposable income, we must make an important point about the properties of this definition of real income. What we wish to demonstrate is that the real income of households, using the Haig–Simons definition, which we called yd_{hs}, is not simply the deflated value of their nominal income YD. Formally, what we wish to show is that $yd_{hs} \neq YD/p$. To demonstrate this, we must take a somewhat roundabout route.

First, let us again resort to the Ostergaard diagram to decompose ΔM_h on the basis of equation (9.24), which says that: $M_h = m_h \cdot p$. We get:

$$\Delta M_h = \Delta m_h \cdot p + \Delta p \cdot m_{h-1} \tag{9.29}$$

However, from the definition of nominal disposable income, given by equation (9.22), we also know that the change in money balances and hence the above expression are equal to:

$$\Delta m_h \cdot p + \Delta p \cdot m_{h-1} = YD - C$$

Dividing through by p we obtain:

$$\Delta m_h + (\Delta p) \cdot \frac{m_{h-1}}{p} = \frac{YD}{p} - \frac{C}{p}$$

Recalling the definitions of equations (9.22) and (9.23), we obtain:

$$\Delta m_h + c = yd_{hs} = \frac{YD}{p} - (\Delta p) \cdot \frac{m_{h-1}}{p}$$

If we multiply and divide the last term on the right-hand side by p_{-1}, we further obtain:

$$yd_{hs} = \frac{YD}{p} - \left(\frac{\Delta p}{p_{-1}}\right) \cdot \left(\frac{p_{-1} \cdot m_{h-1}}{p}\right)$$

$$= \frac{YD}{p} - \left(\frac{\Delta p}{p_{-1}}\right) \cdot \left(\frac{M_{h-1}}{p}\right) = \frac{YD}{p} - \frac{\pi \cdot M_{h-1}}{p} \tag{9.23A}$$

with π the rate of price inflation. Or alternatively, we can write:

$$yd_{hs} = \frac{YD}{p} - \text{л} \cdot m_{h-1} \tag{9.23B}$$

with $\text{л} = \Delta p/p$ defining an expression which is close to the proper definition of the inflation rate π, while not being quite identical.

The above two equations show quite clearly that the Haig–Simons definition of real income is indeed such that $yd_{hs} \neq YD/p$ when there is price inflation. These equations also yield an explicit 'inflation accounted' definition of real disposable income yd_{hs}. The first term – the positive one – is the flow of regular income (wages plus profits plus interest receipts), deflated by p – the current price level. The second term – the negative one – as shown in equation (9.23A), is the nominal stock of money of the previous period, deflated by the current price level and multiplied by the rate of inflation in output prices, given by $\Delta p/p_{-1}$. This second term is sometimes referred as the 'inflation tax' or the 'inflation loss'. Thus in general the real disposable income is equal to the deflated flow of regular income less the loss, properly deflated, in the purchasing power of the stock of wealth/money inherited from the previous period.[6] In simple terms, Haig–Simons real disposable income is the deflated flow of regular income minus the deflated inflation loss.[7]

9.3.2 A real wealth target

Under the assumption that households have a wealth target expressed in real terms, what is this targeted level of wealth? As was the case with nominal magnitudes in Chapter 3, it is a simple matter to compute the targeted level of real wealth. First, note that by similarity with the realized real disposable income of equation (9.23), we may write the expected real disposable income as:

$$c = yd_{hs}^{e} - \Delta m_d = yd_{hs}^{e} - (m_d - m_{h-1}) \tag{9.30}$$

where m_d is the desired real amount of money balances, or what is often called the demand for real money balances.

Combining equation (9.30) with the consumption function in real terms, given by equation (9.26), and collecting terms, we obtain a wealth adjustment function, as we had in Chapter 3, but this time with all variables expressed in real terms:

$$\Delta m_d = \alpha_2 \cdot \left\{ \left[\frac{(1 - \alpha_1)}{\alpha_2} \right] \cdot yd_{hs}^{e} - m_{h-1} \right\} - \alpha_0 \tag{9.31}$$

---

[6] A slightly different generalization will be needed with capital gains, as we shall see in Chapter 10.

[7] The inflation loss in *nominal* terms is $\pi \cdot M_{h-1}$ while the *deflated* loss is $\pi \cdot M_{h-1}/p$.

In the stationary, where $\Delta m_d = 0$, and where $yd_{hs} = yd_{hs}^e$, we have the following relation between the real money stock desired by households, and real disposable income:

$$m_d^* = \left\{ \frac{(1 - \alpha_1)}{\alpha_2} \right\} \cdot yd_{hs}^* - \left(\frac{\alpha_0}{\alpha_2} \right) = \alpha_3 \cdot yd_{hs}^* - \left(\frac{\alpha_0}{\alpha_2} \right) \tag{9.32}$$

where $\alpha_3 = (1 - \alpha_1)/\alpha_2$.

The relationship between the steady-state real money stock and the real disposable income of households is the same as that established in nominal terms with the help of equation (7.33) of Chapter 7.

9.4 Steady-state values of Model *DIS*

9.4.1 The impact of an increase in the mark-up φ

Let us now proceed with a simple experiment with Model *DIS*. Let us impose an increase in the costing mark-up φ. The obvious impact of such a change is an increase in the price p relative to unit labour costs UC (which are unchanged), as is obvious from equations (9.12) and (9.13).

The less obvious impact of the increased costing margin is illustrated in Figure 9.1, where the change is imposed upon a stationary state. The immediate impact is a reduction in Haig–Simons real income and in real consumption. Indeed, because the fall in real disposable income was unexpected, real consumption falls one period later and it does not fall as much as real income. What happens is that the one-time price increase has deflationary short-run consequences, because the price hike leaves households with a lower real stock of money balances, and hence a lower real Haig–Simons income, as can be seen from equation (9.23A).

Figure 9.1 also shows that the price increase generated by the higher costing margin φ induces a new – lower – stationary level of real income and consumption. In other words, the long-run consequences of the relative price increase is a lower real income, and also, as could be shown, lower real money balances and lower employment. Why is this so, when we have argued that introducing the Haig–Simons definition of real income in the consumption function ought to make the model impervious to nominal changes?

9.4.2 The steady-state value of real output

To find out, it is best to derive the steady-state value of the real income variable, as we did for the steady-state value of disposable income in Chapter 7. To do so, we shall use the consumption function (recalling that in the stationary state the expected and realized values will be the same) and both

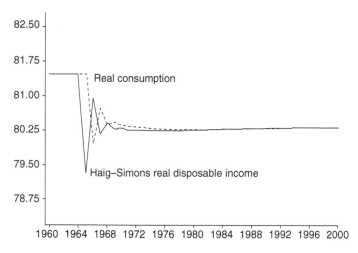

Figure 9.1   Evolution of (Haig–Simons) real disposable income and of real consumption, following a one-shot increase in the costing margin

definitions of real Haig–Simons income.

$$c = \alpha_0 + \alpha_1 \cdot yd_{hs} + \alpha_2 \cdot m_{h-1} \qquad (9.26A)$$

$$yd_{hs} = \frac{YD}{p} - \pi \cdot m_{h-1} \qquad (9.23B)$$

$$yd_{hs} = c + (m_h - m_{h-1}) \qquad (9.23)$$

Putting the first two equations together we obtain:

$$c = \alpha_0 + \alpha_1 \cdot \{yd - \pi \cdot m_{h-1}\} + \alpha_2 \cdot m_{h-1} \qquad (9.35)$$

where we define yd to be the deflated flow of regular income:

$$yd = \frac{YD}{p} \qquad (9.36)$$

Recalling that in the steady state there is no change in real wealth, from the two equations (9.23) we must have in the stationary state only:

$$c^* = yd^* - \pi \cdot m_h^* = yd_{hs}^* \qquad (9.37)$$

Equation (9.37) implies that in the stationary state there is no real saving by households, although households save nominal amounts of money in each period when prices increase (recall that $\pi = \Delta p / p$). In the stationary state, households receive a flow of nominal income YD (which grows with inflation), and they set aside an amount $\Delta M_h = \Delta p \cdot M_{h-1}$. But this amount only serves to replenish real cash balances and preserve the existing level of real wealth. There is no real saving. Real consumption is equal to real income correctly measured, that is measured with the Haig–Simons lens, and hence in that sense there is no saving by households.

Putting together equations (9.35) and (9.37), and remembering that we look for the stationary state, we obtain:

$$yd^*_{hs} = \alpha_0 + \alpha_1 \cdot yd^*_{hs} + \alpha_2 \cdot m^*_h \qquad (9.38)$$

We now only need to express m_h in terms of yd_{hs}. It must be remembered that, at all times, the nominal wealth of households in this model is exactly equal to the nominal value of inventories, as can be deduced from equations (9.15) to (9.17). Thus we have:

$$IN = M_h$$

with:

$$IN = in \cdot UC \qquad (9.10)$$

$$M_h = p \cdot m_h \qquad (9.25)$$

These three equations imply that:

$$m_h = in \cdot \frac{UC}{p}$$

Assuming a stationary state where expected sales are equal to realized sales,[8] equation (9.2) becomes:

$$in = in^T = \sigma^T \cdot s^* = \sigma^T \cdot c^* = \sigma^T \cdot yd^*_{hs}$$

and hence we obtain:

$$m_h = \sigma^T \cdot yd_{hs} \cdot \left(\frac{UC}{p}\right)$$

Substituting this value of m_h back into the consumption function, we obtain the stationary value of real disposable income.

$$yd^*_{hs} = \frac{\alpha_0}{1 - \alpha_1 - \alpha_2 \cdot \sigma^T \cdot (UC/p)} \qquad (9.39)$$

In the present experiment, the increase in prices is a one-time increase; this implies that in this stationary state there is no permanent inflation, that

---

[8] This assumption is not as obvious as it looks. With exogenous sales expectations, a steady state will be reached even though realized sales are not equal to expected sales. See Appendix 9.2.

is $\Delta p = \pi = 0$. So the Haig–Simons definition of real income is no different from the deflated flow of income in this steady state.

The stationary solution of real Haig–Simons income given by equation (9.39) is very close to that obtained in Chapter 7 with equation (7.29). The multiplicand is given by the autonomous real consumption expenditures α_0, and the multiplier is given by the inverse of the denominator. The main difference with the solution given by nominal magnitudes is that real disposable income depends as well on the level of prices p relative to unit costs UC. In other words, in deriving the solution, one must be careful to distinguish between the nominal value of inventories, which is real inventories evaluated at unit costs, and the nominal value of sold finished goods, which are evaluated at price, as it appears in equations (9.10) and (9.25) above.

Equation (9.39) shows that an increase in the mark-up, which leads to a fall in the UC/p ratio, ultimately leads to a fall in the stationary level of real income, and hence to a fall in the stationary level of consumption, production and employment. The cause of this decrease is the change in the long-run multiplier effect of inventory accumulation, which is reduced by an increase in the costing margin φ.

9.4.3 Long-run impact of other parameter changes

The long-run effects of changing other parameters are obvious, once we make use of equation (9.39). Obviously, an increase in autonomous consumption expenditures will lead to an increase in real disposable income and in the other real quantity variables. Also, an increase in the propensities to consume will lead to an increase in real quantities. Similarly, as shown in Figure 9.2, a higher target inventories to sales ratio (σ^T) will generate a brisk increase in real income and then in consumption. These two variables will keep increasing for a while, with a bit of overshooting, until a new stationary state, with higher economic activity is reached. Figure 9.3 helps to explain why income keeps increasing for a while: firms do not try to achieve the new inventories target right away, since inventories follow a partial adjustment process, as described by equation (9.3). While there is a brisk increase in desired inventories and realized inventories, firms continue to desire an increase in physical inventories for a number of periods. Figure 9.3 also shows that the change in realized inventories is systematically inferior to the desired change, because of the adaptative expectations of households. Naturally, in this model, changes in the money stock and in the stock of loans fully espouse – to the tune of a multiplicative constant – the changes in realized inventories. Physical inventories, loans and money balances all play the role of a buffer.

Why is steady-state real output higher when the target inventories to sales ratio is higher? The answer is not immediately obvious. Initially, during the transition, the higher level of output is due to the investment in inventories required by the gradual attempt to achieve the higher inventories to sales ratio. But in the stationary state, this investment in inventories is brought

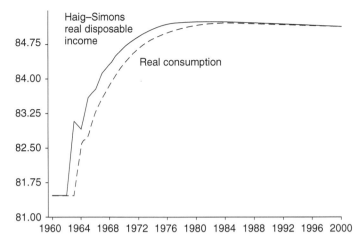

Figure 9.2 Evolution of (Haig–Simons) real disposable income and of real consumption, following an increase in the target inventories to sales ratio

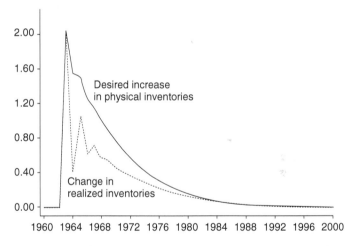

Figure 9.3 Evolution of the desired increase in physical inventories and of the change in realized inventories, following an increase in the target inventories to sales ratio

back down to zero, since investment and saving are back to zero in the new stationary state. So higher investment cannot be the cause of the higher steady-state real output. Why does the economy end up with a higher steady-state real income? The reason is quite simple. While transitory income is higher, firms accumulate new circulating capital and households save part of their income, thus accumulating wealth. It is this higher accumulated wealth, which is one of the arguments of the consumption function, which in the end drives up the stationary level of real consumption and real income.

On the other hand, a one-time increase in the wage rate W will not generate any steady-state change, since such a change will have no impact on the parameters contained in equation (9.39). For the same reasons, an increase in productivity will have no long-run impact on all real variables save one: employment will be reduced since an equal amount of goods can be produced with less labour.

Not so obvious is the fact that an increase in the rate of interest will also lead to a reduction in real variables and in real disposable income in particular. Again, this can be attributed to the role played by the UC/p term in equation (9.39). A one-time increase in the rate of interest leads to an increase in historic unit costs, and hence to prices, relative to unit labour costs. As a result, the ratio UC/p falls whenever interest rates rise, and this reduces the stationary value of real disposable income, as can be read from equation (9.39). But this effect is negligible in model *DIS*, given reasonable parameters, even for substantial changes in the rate of interest.

9.5   Dealing with inflation in (a slightly modified) Model *DIS*

9.5.1   Nominal and real interest rates

The final paragraph of the previous section introduces the importance of interest rate setting in a world of inflation. While the rate of interest has no direct impact on consumption or investment in Model *DIS* – it enters neither the consumption function nor the target inventories function – it has however an indirect impact on income, through the UC/p ratio, by changing the value of the multiplier. As long as there is no inflation, we need only be concerned with nominal rates and one-time changes in these rates. However, with inflation, as we saw in the previous chapter, it is the real rate of interest that determines the unit labour cost to price ratio. Therefore, thanks to equation (9.39), we know that any change in the real rate of interest that would have been generated by an inflation process has an impact on steady-state real output and employment. A lower real interest rate would be associated with a larger stationary level of output.

We could tackle inflation with Model *DIS* as it exists. But given the fact that a constant nominal rate of interest modifies the UC/p ratio whenever there is a change in the rate of inflation, it might be better at this stage to introduce the hypothesis of a constant real rate of interest on loans (and hence on money deposits). To make this assumption however, we need to modify somehow the logic of the model. In particular, we need to assume that the banking system automatically modifies the nominal interest rates that apply to the stock of loans (and deposits) outstanding at the end of the previous period, in line with the rate of inflation on unit labour costs of the current period. We have already defined the rate of cost inflation π_C as:

$$\pi_C = \frac{(UC - UC_{-1})}{UC_{-1}} = \left(\frac{UC}{UC_{-1}}\right) - 1 \tag{9.I.1}$$

The real rate of interest on loans, rather than the nominal rate, is now a constant:

$$rr_C = \overline{rr}_C \tag{9.I.2}$$

And the nominal rate of interest on loans is given by the Fisher formula:

$$r_l = (1 + rr_C) \cdot (1 + \pi_C) - 1 \tag{9.I.3}$$

while as before the nominal rate of interest on deposits is equal to the nominal rate of interest on loans.

This means that the nominal rate of interest on loans, set by the banks in period t, are now effective in period t (rather than in period $t + 1$, as in Model *DIS*), meaning that interest payments that have to be made in period t depend on the rate of cost inflation which has occurred in period t. In other words, both the *ex ante* and the *ex post* real rates of interest are exogenous. The nominal lending rate is now assumed to be floating, being adjusted to the rate of inflation of costs immediately.[9]

As was shown in the previous chapter, with continuously changing costs, the pricing equations (9.12) and (9.13) can be replaced by equation (9.I.4), where the price level only depends on *current* unit labour costs and the *real* rate of interest on loans, and, as before, on the costing margin and the inventories to sales target ratio.

$$p = (1 + \varphi) \cdot \left(1 + rr_C \cdot \sigma^T\right) \cdot UC \tag{9.I.4}$$

All these changes insure that, in our forthcoming discussion of the impact of inflation on the real variables of the economy, the ratio UC/p does not change when the rate of inflation is modified, and hence does not bias the achieved results.

9.5.2 Endogenous inflation and the supply side

Until the present chapter, inflation was carefully kept aside. This may have annoyed a number of readers, first because inflation and inflation control

[9] This seems to correspond to current monetary policy since central banks, in their fight against inflation, focus their attention on real rates of interest rather than on nominal ones.

is an important feature of modern economies and current monetary policy, and second because the inflationary process is viewed as a kind of supply constraint on output, so that these constraints have been assumed away altogether in all of our previous models. We could not do otherwise however. This is due to the fact that changes in unit costs and in prices, along with changes in inventories, create substantial and complex accounting difficulties, which we wished to avoid in order to focus on the main elements of a formalized monetary macro economy. But now that price changes are being considered, there is no obstacle to considering continuous price changes, that is price inflation.

How are wage rates determined? We assume, realistically, that wage rates only change at discrete intervals of time and, for convenience, that they only change at the beginning of each period. In what follows we propose a simplified version of a wage inflation theory which has been broadly espoused by a large number of economists (Cripps and Godley 1976; Rowthorn 1977; Sawyer 1982; Layard *et al.* 1991).[10] We assume that workers and their unions target a real wage, which is a function of the productivity level and the level of effective demand – here proxied by the rate of employment compared to the level of full employment, N_{fe}.[11] In addition, we suppose that the rate of growth of nominal wages is a function of the difference between this target real wage rate and the real wage actually achieved in the previous period. These two ideas are formalized by the two following equations, which provide the simplified component of an endogenous determination of inflation in our model.

$$\omega^T = \left(\frac{W}{p}\right)^T = \Omega_0 + \Omega_1 \cdot pr + \Omega_2 \cdot \left(\frac{N}{N_{\text{fe}}}\right) \tag{9.I.5}$$

$$W = W_{-1} \cdot \left(1 + \Omega_3 \cdot \left(\omega^T_{-1} - \frac{W_{-1}}{p_{-1}}\right)\right) \tag{9.I.6}$$

where ω^T is the target real wage of workers.

Taking these wage equations in combination with the price equations, we can now establish a coherent series of sequences in time. Workers obtain

---

[10] Although our little model of conflict inflation does resemble the one of Layard, Nickell and Jackman (1991), we think it contrasts with their approach which concentrates on a putative wish of firms to engineer a desired real wage, or real wage share, without any regard at all to what will be the effects on profits – or what profits need or desire to achieve.

[11] Of course, it should be admitted that our definition of *full employment* is one where statistical agencies would still find unemployed labour. Full employment is here defined as the rate of unemployment which neither encourages nor discourages the population to enter the labour force.

awards at discrete intervals. They have a real wage target, in principle measurable as a money wage rate divided by the price level. Workers succeed in getting a money award which goes some way towards meeting their immediate real wage aspiration. Then firms fix prices as a mark-up on normal historic costs which will erode some part of the real wage at the time the last bargain was struck. This sequence of events ensures that firms get the profits they need and that real wages always rise by something close to the normal rise in productivity in the economy as a whole. In our simulation models we assume that firms always successfully apply that mark-up which secures the share of real output they need to carry on business, normally making real wages the residual. But it is recognized that lots of things can change the story. If the economy is an open one, firms may be unable to retain the mark-up without a reduction in sales while import prices may affect the total cost of production. Wages may come to be partially or wholly indexed in which case the whole process may accelerate out of control.[12]

The fact that the real value of the money wage bargain is partially eroded between settlements does not necessarily mean that workers' expectations about their real wages over the forthcoming period have been disappointed. It is more likely that they come to expect the thing that normally does actually happen, given that settlements occur at discrete intervals while inflation is continuous, namely that there turns out to be a rise in real wages which roughly matches the rise in productivity in the economy as a whole. The outcome of the wage bargaining processes in terms of inflation will obviously be dependent on the quasi-parameters Ω_i which may be very different at different times.

This inflation story is based on the notion that workers look for a *fair* pay (Wood 1978). As shown by equation (9.I.5), productivity increases lead workers to target a higher real wage, since they might feel that these increases are partially the result of their hard work. These are the *normative* pressures. However, what Wood calls the *anomic* pressures, essentially the pressures of supply and demand, also have an impact on the fair real wage. High rates of unemployment will lead to a reduction of the target real wage, and hence in the level of wage inflation negotiated between the workers and the firms. Equation (9.I.6) says that workers try to catch up. Wage inflation depends on how large is the discrepancy between what workers perceive to be fair pay (based on economic information collected at the end of the previous period) and the actual real wage rate of the previous period.[13]

---

[12] On this see Godley and Cripps (1983: ch. 10) and Taylor (2004b: 68–78).

[13] In contrast to mainstream authors who assume that wage inflation depends on the expected rate of price inflation, we assume instead that wage inflation depends on the previous evolution of prices. In other words, post-Keynesians believe that workers'

Inflation under these assumptions does not necessarily accelerate if employment stays in excess of its 'full employment' level. Everything depends on the parameters and whether they change. Inflation will accelerate if the value of Ω_2 rises through time or if the interval between settlements shortens. If Ω_2 turns out to be constant then a higher pressure of demand will raise the inflation rate without making it accelerate. An implication of the story proposed here is that there is no vertical long-run Phillips curve. There is no NAIRU. When employment is above its full-employment level, unless the parameter Ω_2 moves up there is no acceleration of inflation, only a higher rate of inflation.

The following quote reflects fairly well the beliefs and the understanding of both authors regarding empirical literature on this topic: 'Indeed *if* it is true that there is a unique NAIRU, that really is the end of discussion of macroeconomic policy. At present I happen *not* to believe it and that there is no evidence of it. And I am prepared to express the value judgment that moderately higher inflation rates are an acceptable price to pay for lower unemployment. *But I do not accept that it is a foregone conclusion that inflation will be higher if unemployment is lower*' (Godley 1983: 170).

Adding the above two equations to the equations that set real and nominal rates of interest yields a modified *DIS* model, which we shall call the *DISINF* model, to be described extensively in Appendix 9.3.

9.5.3 The possibility of non-neutral inflation

The stationary solution that we have derived in section 9.4 allows us to deal explicitly with the consequences of price inflation. Equation (9.39) yields the stationary solution for real disposable income, real consumption and real output in an inflationary environment. For convenience, it is repeated here:

$$yd^*_{hs} = \frac{\alpha_0}{1 - \alpha_1 - \alpha_2 \cdot \sigma^T (UC/p)} \tag{9.39}$$

Since these real variables only depend on given parameters, plus the endogenous UC/p ratio equation, we can assert that equation (9.39) shows, as long as real interest rates are kept constant so that the UC/p ratio remains unchanged, that price inflation has no impact whatsoever on real variables in our modified *DIS* model – the *DISINF* model.

It is important to point out that such a result was achieved because we made the hypothesis that households are not being fooled by inflation. Households take consumption decisions based on expected real Haig–Simons disposable income. It is this notion of income which enters the consumption function. When making consumption or saving decisions, households take full account

organizations try to recover past increases in cost-of-living indices; they do not attempt to forecast future increases.

of the inflation loss, or inflation tax, which takes its toll on the existing stock of wealth held by households. With these hypotheses, in particular the key consumption equation (9.26), price inflation has neither a positive nor a negative impact on real variables, such as real consumption, production, or employment.[14] Generating an exogenous continuous increase in unit costs and prices, without any change in the costing margin φ, will have no impact whatsoever on the relevant real variables.

Could it be otherwise? Indeed it could be. Let us examine the case where households are blind to the capital losses that are being inflicted by continuously rising prices. This would imply that households are being fooled by inflation. To incorporate such a behaviour, one only needs to modify the consumption function, and assume that households consume a proportion of their deflated regular income, $yd = YD/p$, rather than a proportion of their (expected) Haig–Simons real income. In this case, the consumption function becomes:

$$c = \alpha_0 + \alpha_1 \cdot yd + \alpha_2 \cdot m_{h-1} \qquad (9.26B)$$

We may now find again a steady-state solutions. As before, a steady state is achieved when real wealth does not change anymore, that is when real consumption equates the Haig–Simons real disposable income. With the inflation-blind consumption function given by equation (9.26B), the steady-state real consumption and real Haig–Simons disposable income are equal to:

$$yd^*_{hs} = \frac{\alpha_0 + \alpha_1 \cdot \unicode{0x05D0} \cdot m^*_h}{1 - \alpha_1 - \alpha_2 \cdot \sigma^{\mathrm{T}} \cdot (UC/p)} \qquad (9.40)$$

Obviously the inflation term ($\unicode{0x05D0} = \Delta p/p$) appears in the numerator with a positive coefficient. Thus, with inflation-blind households, inflation leads to an *increase* in the steady-state values taken by the real variables. Inflation in this case leads to an increase in real consumption and real (Haig–Simons) disposable income, as shown in Figure 9.4. Naturally this implies that output and employment rise as well. This simulation is done with Model *DISINF*, using the revised consumption function (9.26B). Figure 9.5 shows how this increase was accomplished. Since households are blind to the capital losses inflicted by inflation, they do not quite realize that they spend more than what is required to keep their real wealth constant – in other words their propensity to save out of properly measured real disposable income is lower,

---

[14] It was also assumed that the target inventories to sales ratio, in volumes, given by equation (9.2), remained unaffected by inflation (see Godley and Cripps 1983: 238).

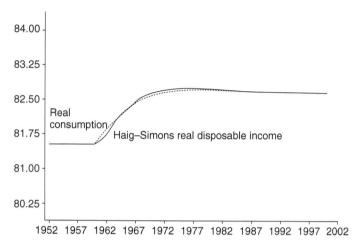

Figure 9.4 Evolution of (Haig–Simons) real disposable income and of real consumption, following an increase in the rate of inflation, in a variant where households are blind to the capital losses inflicted by price inflation

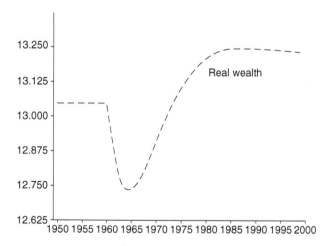

Figure 9.5 Evolution of real wealth, following an increase in the rate of inflation, in a variant where households are blind to the capital losses inflicted by price inflation

and as a result their real wealth initially decreases. However, this lower propensity to save, as predicted by Keynesian economics, leads to higher real income and output, and hence the new value of steady-state wealth becomes higher than its initial value.

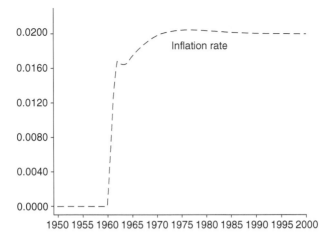

Figure 9.6 Evolution of the rate of price inflation, following a one-shot increase in the target real wage of workers

In the simulation, the move from zero inflation to a positive inflation rate, here approximately 2% as charted in Figure 9.6, arises from imposing a one-time increase in the autonomous term Ω_0 in the target real wage equation (9.I.5). As a result, workers ask for higher nominal wages, and this translates into permanent cost and price inflation. What happens is that the target real wage becomes higher than the one which is made possible by the costing margin set by firms and the real rate of interest. Inflation picks up slightly during the transition period, since equation 9.I.5 assumes that the target real wage rate reacts positively to increases in the employment rate, with the latter variable increasing until the new steady state is reached.

9.5.4 Implications of endogenous money

The fact that exogenously imposed inflation has no effect or a positive impact on real income and employment contradicts the well-known Pigou effect. As some readers may recall, Pigou (1943) had argued that full employment in a stationary state – which is precisely the steady state described here – could be recovered if wage costs and hence prices could fall enough. His idea was that unemployment, if there was no impediment to competition between workers, would lead to a continuous fall in money wages, and consequently in prices. Pigou's argument was that real money balances were part of the consumption function, as they have in all our own consumption functions, in particular equations (9.26) and (9.26B). With falling prices, Pigou argued, real money balances would become larger and would generate higher consumption expenditures; this real balance effect on consumption would push up production and employment until the latter reached its full employment level.

It was quickly pointed out by Kalecki (1944: 131) that one of Pigou's key assumptions is that the nominal stock of money is a constant in his framework. This assumption lacks consistency in a fully determined macroeconomic model, as we have tried to show with even the simplest model of Chapter 3. As also pointed out by Kalecki (1944), money deposits are backed by loans made to firms. These loans, within our simple framework, are determined by the value of inventories required by firms. If the cost of inventories diminishes, so will the required nominal amounts of loans, and hence so will the nominal amounts of money balances held by households. In other words, money is endogenous, and cannot be assumed to remain constant when unit labour costs and prices are diminishing. Thus the error of Pigou and of all those who rely on a real cash balances effect through the consumption function is to assume that nominal money balances are exogenous variables which remain at a constant level whatever happens to unit costs and prices. As pointed out by Moore (1988: 327), 'in a credit money economy there is no Pigou effect'.

The analysis of the previous section, and the analysis presented here, clearly shows that falling unit labour costs and prices have no positive effect on output and employment in a closed economy with only private agents. But Model *DISINF* is a highly simplified model, which omits any reference to a government sector. We shall see in the next chapter that when government expenditures are taken into consideration, the possible effects of inflation or deflation are contingent on several factors, besides the behaviour of households. But whatever the long-run impact of inflation on the real economy that will be ascertained in Chapter 10, it cannot be attributed to some version of the Pigou effect since money is endogenous in our models.

Appendix 9.1: Equation list of Model *DIS*

The production decision

$$y = s^e + in^e - in_{-1} = s^e + \Delta in^e \tag{9.1}$$

$$in^T = \sigma^T \cdot s^e \tag{9.2}$$

$$in^e = in_{-1} + \gamma \cdot (in^T - in_{-1}) \tag{9.3}$$

$$in = in_{-1} + (y - s) \tag{9.4}$$

$$s^e = \beta s_{-1} + (1 - \beta) \cdot s^e_{-1} \tag{9.5}$$

$$s = c \tag{9.6}$$

$$N = \frac{y}{pr} \tag{9.7}$$

$$WB = N \cdot W \tag{9.8}$$

$$UC = \frac{WB}{y} \tag{9.9}$$

$$IN = in \cdot UC \tag{9.10}$$

The pricing decision

$$S = p \cdot s \tag{9.11}$$

$$p = (1 + \varphi) \cdot NHUC \tag{9.12}$$

$$NHUC = \left(1 - \sigma^{T}\right) \cdot UC + \sigma^{T} \cdot (1 + r_{l-1}) \cdot UC_{-1} \tag{9.13}$$

$$F = S - WB + \Delta IN - r_{l-1} \cdot IN_{-1} \tag{9.14}$$

The banking system

$$L_{d} = IN \tag{9.15}$$

$$L_{s} = L_{d} \tag{9.16}$$

$$M_{s} = L_{s} \tag{9.17}$$

$$r_{l} = \bar{r}_{l} \tag{9.18}$$

$$r_{m} = r_{l} - add \tag{9.19}$$

$$F_{b} = r_{l-1} \cdot L_{-1} - r_{m-1} \cdot M_{h-1} \tag{9.20}$$

The consumption decision

$$YD = WB + F + F_{b} + r_{m-1} \cdot M_{h-1} \tag{9.21}$$

$$\Delta M_{h} = YD - C \tag{9.22}$$

$$yd_{hs} = c + (m_{h} - m_{h-1}) \tag{9.23}$$

$$C = c \cdot p \tag{9.24}$$

$$m_{h} = \frac{M_{h}}{p} \tag{9.25}$$

$$c = \alpha_{0} + \alpha_{1} \cdot yd_{hs}^{e} + \alpha_{2} \cdot m_{h-1} \tag{9.26}$$

$$yd_{hs}^{e} = \varepsilon \cdot yd_{hs-1} + (1 - \varepsilon) \cdot yd_{hs-1}^{e} \tag{9.27}$$

The redundant equation is

$$M_{s} = M_{h}$$

Appendix 9.2: The peculiar role of given expectations

In Chapter 3, we found that expectations in a stock-flow model did not play any role in defining steady-state values. The stationary state depended on more fundamental variables. However, in the current model, when pursuing steady-state values, as obvious as it may look, we cannot just assume that planned inventories will be realized in the stationary state, unless expectations are endogenized. With *exogenous* expected sales ($s^e = \bar{s}^e$), we could reach a steady state where expected and realized sales are different, and hence where desired, targeted and realized inventories are different. For instance, exogenous over-optimistic sales expectations lead to a rise in steady-state output and sales. The new steady-state sales would be below sales expectations, and realized steady-state inventories would exceed expected and targeted inventories. Indeed, in the stationary state, we would have the following relation: $(s^e - s) = (in^e - in^T) \cdot (\gamma/(1-\gamma))$. Here, entrepreneurs wind up with inventories that are higher than expected (desired in the period), and expected inventories are higher than the level targeted over the long run. In every period they try to reduce their inventories (by the amount $\gamma \cdot (in_{-1} - in^T)$), but the amount by which they try to reduce their inventories, in the stationary state, is just equal to the amount by which they overestimate sales ($s^e - s$), so that output and inventories remain constant.

The proof is the following. In the stationary state, sales equal output and inventories remain constant:

Let us start by noting that at all times:

$$in - in^e = s^e - s \tag{9.4A}$$

and

$$in^e = in_{-1} + \gamma \cdot (in^T - in_{-1}) \tag{9.3}$$

This last equation can be rewritten as:

$$in_{-1} - in^e = -\gamma \cdot (in^T - in_{-1}) \tag{A9.1}$$

Solving for in_{-1}, we get:

$$in_{-1} = \frac{in^e - \gamma \cdot in^T}{1 - \gamma} \tag{A9.2}$$

Note also that in the stationary state, inventories must remain constant, so that:

$$in = in_{-1} \tag{A9.3}$$

From (A9.3), equations (A9.1) and (9.4A) have the same terms on the left-hand side, so that their right-hand sides are equal. We get:

$$s^e - s = \gamma \cdot (in_{-1} - in^T) \tag{A9.4}$$

As pointed out above, the difference between expected and actual sales is just equal to the amount by which entrepreneurs try to reduce their inventories. In other words, equation (A9.4) can be rewritten as:

$$s^e + \Delta in^e = s \tag{A9.5}$$

But this, through equation (9.1) that defines the output decision, implies that sales and output are equal. Despite the fact that sales expectations always turn out to be mistaken, we do have:

$$y = s \qquad\qquad (A9.6)$$

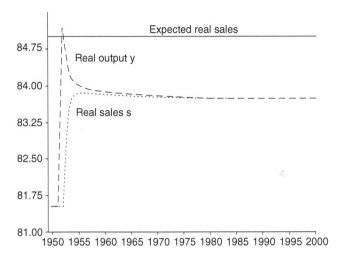

Figure A9.1 Evolution of real output and real sales following a permanent upward shift in the level of expected real sales

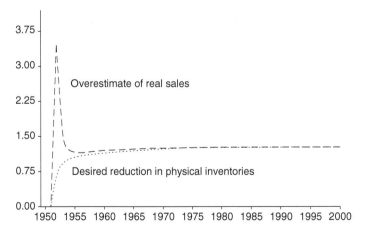

Figure A9.2 Convergence of the overestimate of real sales with the desired reduction in physical inventories following a permanent upward shift in the level of expected sales

Putting the value of in_{-1} given by equation (A9.4) into equation (A9.5), we get what we are looking for, that is:

$$(s^e - s) = (in^e - in^T) \cdot \left\{ \frac{\gamma}{(1-\gamma)} \right\}$$
(A9.6)

All this is illustrated with Figures A9.1 and A9.2, which start from a stationary state perturbed by a higher level of expected sales, which in the experiment moves up, permanently, to $s^e = 85$. Figure A9.1 shows that in the new stationary state output and sales converge to each other, even though sales diverge from expected sales. Figure A9.2 illustrates the convergence towards the equality described by equation (A9.4): the overestimate of real sales and the desired reduction in physical inventories converge towards each other.

Appendix 9.3: Equation list of Model *DISINF*

The production decision

$$y = s^e + in^e - in_{-1} = s^e + \Delta in^e$$
(9.1)

$$in^T = \sigma^T \cdot s^e$$
(9.2)

$$in^e = in_{-1} + \gamma(in^T - in_{-1})$$
(9.3)

$$in = in_{-1} + (y - s)$$
(9.4)

$$s^e = \beta s_{-1} + (1 - \beta)s^e_{-1}$$
(9.5)

$$s = c$$
(9.6)

$$N = \frac{y}{pr}$$
(9.7)

$$WB = N \cdot W$$
(9.8)

$$UC = \frac{WB}{y}$$
(9.9)

$$IN = in \cdot UC$$
(9.10)

The pricing decision

$$S = p \cdot s$$
(9.11)

$$F = S - WB + \Delta IN - r_l \cdot IN_{-1}$$
(9.14)

$$p = (1 + \varphi) \cdot (1 + rr_c \cdot \sigma^T) \cdot UC$$
(9.I.4)

The banking system

$$L_d = IN$$
(9.15)

$$L_s = L_d$$
(9.16)

$$M_s = L_s$$
(9.17)

$$r_m = r_l - add$$
(9.18)

$$F_b = r_{l-1} \cdot L_{-1} - r_{m-1} \cdot M_{h-1} \tag{9.20}$$

$$\pi_c = \frac{(UC - UC_{-1})}{UC_{-1}} = \left(\frac{UC}{UC_{-1}}\right) - 1 \tag{9.I.1}$$

$$rr_c = \bar{r}r_c \tag{9.I.2}$$

$$r_l = (1 + rr_c) \cdot (1 + \pi_c) - 1 \tag{9.I.3}$$

The consumption decision

$$YD = WB + F + F_b + r_m \cdot M_{h-1} \tag{9.21}$$

$$\Delta M_h = YD - C \tag{9.22}$$

$$yd_{hs} = c + (m_h - m_{h-1}) \tag{9.23}$$

$$yd = \frac{YD}{p} \tag{9.36}$$

$$C = c \cdot p \tag{9.24}$$

$$m_h = \frac{M_h}{p} \tag{9.25}$$

$$c = \alpha_0 + \alpha_1 \cdot yd_{hs}^e + \alpha_2 \cdot m_{h-1} \tag{9.26}$$

$$c = \alpha_0 + \alpha_1 \cdot yd + \alpha_2 \cdot m_{h-1} \tag{9.26B}$$

$$yd_{hs}^e = \varepsilon \cdot yd_{hs-1} + (1 - \varepsilon) \cdot yd_{hs-1}^e \tag{9.27}$$

The inflation process

$$\omega^T = \left(\frac{W}{p}\right)^T = \Omega_0 + \Omega_1 \cdot pr + \Omega_2 \cdot \left(\frac{N}{N_{fe}}\right) \tag{9.I.5}$$

$$W = W_{-1}\left(1 + \Omega_3 \cdot \left(\omega_{-1}^T - \frac{W_{-1}}{p_{-1}}\right)\right) \tag{9.I.6}$$

10
A Model with both Inside and Outside Money

10.1 A model with active commercial banks

The following chapter combines Model *PC*, which described an economy in which there was portfolio choice but only with government (or 'outside') money, with Model *DIS* in which there were inventories but only credit (or 'inside') money. We shall call the model to be developed the *INSOUT* Model, since it combines inside and outside money. In the process we shall describe the main ways in which the central bank exercises control over commercial banks. In addition, the description of commercial banks will go beyond the simple equality between loans and deposits, with which we were content in the previous chapters. In the present chapter, commercial banks will actually need to take decisions of their own.

The contents of this chapter have a special interest because now, for the first time in this book, we describe a whole monetary economy which, though still very much simplified and mechanical, begins to approach the one which exists in the real world. It stands in stark opposition to that deployed in the mainstream literature and in mainstream textbooks – which have it that 'outside' money is directly under the control of the authorities and that a determinate amount of credit money is created via the 'money multiplier' as banks 'loan up'. In these mainstream models, the 'demand for money' has to be brought into equivalence with the exogenous 'money supply' via an equilibrium condition which determines the rate of interest.[1]

This chapter will repeat much material from earlier chapters. But what we now have is a core model of such importance that it has seemed desirable to

---

[1] As pointed out in earlier chapters, some mainstream authors, for example Romer (2000), now argue that this model of exogenous money supply with endogenous interest rates should be forsaken and replaced by another model where money is endogenous and where the central bank sets real interest rates as a function of the discrepancy between the actual and the targeted rates of inflation. This is actually what John B. Taylor (2004) does in his chapter on monetary policy. However, in the chapter

include, at this stage, a complete statement which has a unified focus. Most of the originality of the present chapter, beyond bringing together inside and outside money, resides in developing a more sophisticated and realistic portfolio choice for households and in extending the role of commercial banks.

10.2 Balance sheet and transaction matrices

The two matrices below (See Tables 10.1 and 10.2) describe the accounting structure of our new model. So far as households are concerned, the difference, compared with our earlier models, is that the array of assets which they can choose to hold – or find themselves holding – has been extended to include three kinds of money (cash H, checking accounts $M1$, and deposit accounts $M2$) in addition to bills and bonds, with counterpart flows of investment income. Firms are not different from those in Model *DIS*, except that they collect indirect taxes (now the only form of taxation) and pay them over to the government. Stocks and flows generated by the government now include a number of transactions with commercial banks. First of all, on occasion, commercial banks have to obtain advances A from the central bank. Commercial banks, in addition to loans made to firms, have two more assets:

Table 10.1 The balance sheet of Model *INSOUT*

	Households	Firms	Govt.	Central bank	Banks	Σ
Inventories		+IN				+IN
HPM	+H_h			−H	+H_b	0
				+A	−A	
Checking deposits	+$M1_h$				−M1	0
Time deposits	+$M2_h$				−M2	0
Bills	+B_h		−B	+B_{cb}	+B_b	0
Bonds	+$BL_h \cdot p_{bL}$		−BL · p_{BL}			0
Loans		−L			+L	0
Balance	−V	0	+GD	0	0	−IN
Σ	0	0	0	0	0	0

on money creation, Taylor reverts to the traditional story based on money multipliers and reserve-constrained creation – seemingly not realizing that this is inconsistent with his previous institutional description of the central bank.

Table 10.2 Transactions matrix of Model INSOUT

	Households	Firms Current	Firms Capital	Govt.	Central bank Current	Central bank Capital	Banks Current	Banks Capital	Σ
Consumption	$-C$	$+C$							0
Government expenditures		$+G$		$-G$					0
Δ in the value of inventories		$+\Delta IN$	$-IN$						0
Sales tax		$-T$		$+T$					0
Wages	$+WB$	$-WB$							0
Entrepreneurial profits	$+F_f$	$-F_f$							0
Bank profits	$+F_b$						$-F_b$		0
Central bank profits				$+F_{cb}$	$-F_{cb}$				0
Interest on advances					$+r_{a-1}\cdot A_{-1}$		$-r_{a-1}\cdot A_{-1}$		0
Interest on loans		$-r_{l-1}\cdot L_{-1}$					$+r_{l-1}\cdot L_{-1}$		0
Interest on deposits	$+r_{m-1}\cdot M2_{-1}$						$-r_{m-1}\cdot M2_{-1}$		0
Interest on bills	$+r_{b-1}\cdot B_{h-1}$			$-r_{b-1}\cdot B_{-1}$	$+r_{b-1}\cdot B_{cb-1}$		$+r_{b-1}\cdot B_{b-1}$		0
Interest on bonds	$+BL_{h-1}$			$-BL_{-1}$					0
Change in the stocks of advances						$-\Delta A$		$+\Delta A$	0
loans			$+\Delta L$					$-\Delta L$	0
cash	$-\Delta H_h$					$+\Delta H$		$-\Delta H_b$	0
checking deposits	$-\Delta M1_h$							$+\Delta M1$	0
time deposits	$-\Delta M2_h$							$+\Delta M2$	0
bills	$-\Delta B_h$			$+\Delta B$		$-\Delta B_{cb}$		$-\Delta B_b$	0
bonds	$-\Delta BL_h\cdot p_{bL}$			$+\Delta BL\cdot p_{bL}$					0
Σ	0	0	0	0	0	0	0	0	0

Treasury bills B_b and cash balances H_b which they hold at the central bank – the latter constituting the banks' reserves. And banks 'owe' two kinds of money – checking and time deposit accounts, of which only the latter are assumed to bear interest. As before, banks earn profits, called F_b, which are the excess of their interest receipts over their interest payments, and which, like the profits F_f of producing firms, are assumed to be distributed instantaneously to households. As was the case with some of the previous models, the central bank is making a profit, called F_{cb}, because its assets generate interest revenues while its liabilities pay no interest, and the profit of the central bank is pocketed by the government sector. Otherwise the two matrices here replicate the features that have been observed in the previous chapters.

Already, at the level of concepts, the system deployed here differs sharply from the mainstream model – which makes no reference either to bank profits or to the rather obvious fact that, in order to explain bank profits, there must be several different rates of interest; in addition to the bill rate of interest there must be a money rate which banks pay on deposits and a loan rate which banks charge on what they lend. We shall find that without the profits of banks and banks' adjustment of those rates of interest over which they have direct control (i.e. those on loans and deposit money) it would be impossible to solve the model.

It is not too early to emphasize two key features of the logical structure displayed in the transactions matrix. Every column sums to zero – from which it follows that once every variable in a column bar one has been determined that last variable is logically implicit. It might be supposed that this logical constraint on the sum of a sector's activities has no causal implications at all. However it will be found, with all decisions having to be made in an uncertain world, that there has to be, for every sector, some component of their transactions which flexibly takes on the character of a residual and which cannot be directly controlled. Thus (to let the cat straight out of the bag) for households the residual process will be mainly the way in which their holdings of non-interest bearing credit money (checking accounts) change; for firms the residual will be the amount of loans from the banking system; for banks it will be holdings of bills and on occasion the advances that they take from the central bank; for the government, it will be new issues of bills; for the central bank, it will be the issue of base, or high-powered, money to banks, as well as the amount of its advances to commercial banks.

Second, this model like all our models is a complete system with all rows as well as columns summing to zero so that once every variable bar one is determined (in the model as a whole not just the sectoral columns), the value of that last variable is logically implied by all the others. In other words, there must always be an implicit equation, which has to be 'dropped' when the model comes to be solved.

10.3 Producing firms

The model is now so complex and has such a high degree of dynamic inter-dependence that its exposition in words presents considerable difficulties. While each individual outcome will always be heavily dependent on what happens in other sectors, we proceed by initially discussing each sector separately. By the standard of textbook models ours is large, having eighty odd equations. Yet the economic assumptions are still crude and restrictive. The reader is asked to exercise imagination.

The following four sections discuss in turn firms, households, the government and its central bank, and commercial banks. Each subsection opens with a list of the model equations which are most relevant to the sector in question. Then each sector's motivation, the system properties which constrain it and the determinants of what actually happens are discussed verbally. Having run through the sectors individually, we discuss how the system as a whole behaves. Simulation experiments will provide a solid armature around which a narrative can be rigorously set forth.

The reader may take note of the following conventions. The superscript 'e' denotes an expected value, the superscript 'T' denotes a target, while for households we still distinguish between on the one hand demanded, expected or planned values, which are denoted by a 'd' subscript, and on the other hand realized values, which carry an 'h' subscript. Stars still denote steady-state values. Capital letters for income and expenditure components denote current prices, the lower case denotes volumes (the number of physical objects in the case of production and expenditures) or deflated values (such as would be the case for wealth). Variables without subscripts are all realized values. Greek letters are parameters (or what are considered as such in the model).

10.3.1 Equations describing the decisions of firms

Box 10.1 Firms' equations

$y = s^e + (in^e - in_{-1})$	y is output, s sales, in inventories (measured as physical objects);	(10.1)
$N = \dfrac{y}{pr}$	N is employment, pr productivity;	(10.2)
$WB = N \cdot W$	WB is the wage bill, W the nominal wage rate;	(10.3)
$UC = \dfrac{WB}{y}$	UC is the unit cost of producing one object;	(10.4)
$s^e = \beta \cdot s_{-1} + (1 - \beta) \cdot s^e_{-1}$	Adaptative expectations, or the following alternative:	(10.5)

$s^e = [s_{-1} \cdot (1 + RA1)]$	RA1 is a random variable with mean $= 0$, normally distributed;	(10.5A)
$in^T = \sigma^T \cdot s^e$	in^T is long-run targeted inventories of widgets;	(10.6)
$\sigma^T = \sigma_0 - \sigma_1 \cdot r_1$	The target inventories to sales ratio depends on r_1, the *nominal* rate of interest on loans;	(10.7)
$r_1 = \dfrac{(1 + r_1)}{(1 + \pi)} - 1$	the Fisher discrete time formula for the real rate of interest where π is the inflation rate;	(10.8)
$in^e = in_{-1} + \gamma \cdot (in^T - in_{-1})$	in^e is the short-run planned level of widget inventories;	(10.9)
$p = (1 + \tau) \cdot (1 + \varphi) \cdot NHUC$	NHUC is the normal historic unit cost, defined as:	(10.10)
$NHUC = (1 - \sigma^T) \cdot UC + \sigma^T \cdot (1 + r_1 \cdot) \cdot UC_{-1}$	where σ^T is defined as in (10.7);	(10.11)
$F_f^e = \left\{ \dfrac{\varphi}{(1 + \varphi)} \right\} \cdot \left\{ \dfrac{1}{(1 + \tau)} \right\} \cdot p \cdot s^e$	Expected profits of firms.	(10.11A)

The equations in Box 10.1 that describe the behaviour of firms are no different from those that we used in Chapter 9. Firms produce what they expect to sell plus any change in the stock of inventories which they plan to bring about (10.1). The production decisions of firms imply a demand for labour which is determined by production in combination with exogenous productivity (10.2). The wage bill is determined by employment and exogenous wage rates (10.3). The unit cost of producing objects is defined as in the two previous chapters (10.4). The volume of inventories is assumed to adjust towards some desired ratio to sales, which, as a slight complication, is inversely related to the nominal rate of interest on loans (10.6, 10.7, 10.9). The assumption is that higher interest rates induce firms to economize on their inventories (Malinvaud 1982: 208; Trivedi 1970).[2]

Sales expectations depend on some adaptative behaviour (10.5); or we may wish to introduce random variations in the volume of expected sales (10.5A).

[2] There is a lot of contradictory empirical evidence on this, with many studies showing that the nominal rate of interest seems to be the relevant rate, rather than the real rate as theory would tell us.

We do not have much to say about how expectations are formed. With randomly generated variations in expectations, which have been tested in model simulations, one can observe how a system can operate if actual and expected values differ from one another all the time in an unpredictable way – there is no suggestion that expectations are indeed formed like this (that is the reason why equation 10.5A has been put into square brackets). If sales are above or below expectation, there will be a corresponding fall or rise in inventories which will give a quantity signal to firms to raise or reduce output in later periods (if there has been no further change in sales expectations).

We now come to a slight variation compared to Model *DIS* of Chapter 9. Firms are still assumed to set their prices as a mark-up on normal historic unit costs (10.11, 10.12), which are defined with the help of the target inventories to sales ratio parameter σ^T, as defined in equation (10.7). But we now assume away personal income taxes, and introduce instead a sales tax. This indirect tax is levied on the ex-tax value of sales at a proportional rate of τ. For instance, if $\tau = 0.1$ a widget the value of which is \$10 before tax, has a final sale price of \$11. The share of taxes in the value of sales is thus $\tau/(1+\tau)$. In the present instance, the share of taxation would be 9.09%. As a result, firms set prices at a level which, if their sales expectations and inventories to sales target ratio are fulfilled, ensure that they will realize, in the form of entrepreneurial profits, some proportion $\varphi/(1+\varphi)$ of the total ex-tax value of sales, that is, a proportion $\varphi/(1+\varphi)$ of the value of sales left over once sales taxes have been deducted, as shown in equation (10.11A).[3]

10.3.2 Equations describing realized outcomes

Box 10.2 Firms' equations

$s = c + g$	Realized sales volume equals consumption plus government expenditures;	(10.12)
$S = s \cdot p$	Realized sales value, in \$;	(10.13)

---

[3] The assumption that prices are a mark-up on expected or normal historic unit costs is very much weaker than it might appear. It was explained in Chapter 9 why the ratio of the value of sales to the historic cost of producing what was sold (which determines the profit margin) is equal to the ratio of the price level to the historic unit cost of production (*HUC*). In other words, whenever it is the case that profits are a constant proportion of (ex-tax) sales it is also the case that prices are a constant mark-up on historic unit cost. Econometric studies of 'the price equation' very commonly treat lags as entirely contingent phenomena, to be discovered by econometric criteria alone, with no regard for the implied distribution of income between profits and other factor incomes.

$in - in_{-1} = y - s$	Realized change in inventories;	(10.14)
$\sigma_s = \dfrac{in_{-1}}{s}$	Realized inventories to sales ratio;	(10.15)
$IN = in \cdot UC$	Realized inventories valued at current unit cost;	(10.16)
$L_d = IN$	Amount of loans required by firms;	(10.17)
$F_f = S - T - WB$ $+ \Delta IN - r_l \cdot IN_{-1}$	Realized entrepreneurial profits of firms;	(10.18)
$\pi = \dfrac{(p - p_{-1})}{p_{-1}}$	π is the rate of price inflation.	(10.19)

Up to equation (10.11) we have discussed the way in which firms' key decisions – that is, decisions about output, employment and prices – are made. The remaining equations in this section describe how realized outcomes come about, although these cannot be justified comprehensively until we have completed our account of how other sectors behave. For instance households' consumption seems at this stage to be exogenously determined but that will change when we get to the household sector.

Realized sales by firms are equal to the sum of personal and government consumption demand (10.12, 10.13) (Box 10.2). As usual we assume that what is demanded is provided by firms, the more so since firms now let inventories respond to unexpected fluctuations in demand. Realized inventories are equal to the opening stock of inventories plus (realized) sales less production (10.14). This of course can be tied to the inventories to realized sales ratio, σ_s, which we defined in Chapter 8 (here equation 10.15).

That there is a difference between expected and actual sales, which leads to unexpected changes in inventories, has enormous theoretical importance because it removes any need (for either the businessman or the economist) to seek an equilibrium condition which would clear the market for goods by finding the right price. The price of goods, in our model, is not a market-clearing mechanism. The purpose of pricing is to assign shares of income to the various constituents. There should be no argument about how inventories ought to be valued in the present context since inventories valued at historic cost correctly measure the scale of the costs incurred and therefore of the finance which has been required (equation 10.16). As inventories fluctuate violently in the short term, their equivalence with loans implies that the latter are available, instantaneously, to match these fluctuations (equation 10.17). For reasons of convenience (to economize on equations and functions) it is assumed, finally, that firms never hold any money or securities; it is not strictly necessary for them to do so given our assumptions that loans match inventories one-for-one instantaneously and that all profits are immediately distributed.

Realized profits (10.18) are a residual quantity over which firms have no direct control. Profits are equal to the value of sales less wages, indirect taxes and interest charges paid in respect of inventories during the period plus the change during the period in inventories valued at historic cost. We have already explained (in great detail in Chapter 8) that this definition is logically equivalent to saying that profits are the difference between the ex-tax value of sales and the historic cost of producing what was sold. *As it is only possible for firms to distribute all their profits if inventories valued at cost are matched one for one by loans from outside the sector*, inventory fluctuations generate a systemic need for finance, all of which is assumed to be provided by the banking system. This implies, as already mentioned above, that firms use lines of credit to finance inventories automatically.[4]

Finally, equation (10.19) defines the rate of price inflation π that could arise as a result, for instance, of an exogenous and continuous rise in the nominal wage rate.

10.4 Households

10.4.1 Equations describing realized or *ex post* outcomes

Box 10.3   Households' equations

$YD_r = F + WB + r_{m-1} \cdot M2_{h-1}$ $+r_{b-1} \cdot B_{hh-1} + BL_{h-1}$	YD_r is the realized nominal regular income of households – the sum of factor income plus interest receipts; (10.20)
$CG = \Delta p_{bL} \cdot BL_{h-1}$	CG is the capital gain on long-term bonds; (10.21)
$YD_{hs} = YD_r + CG$	YD_{hs} is the Haig–Simons nominal disposable income; (10.22)
$F = F_f + F_b$	F_f and F_b are the net profits of firms and of banks; (10.23)
$\Delta V = YD_{hs} - C$	This is the change in realized nominal wealth; (10.24)
$V_{nc} = V - H_{hh}$	V_{nc} is realized wealth, net of cash; (10.25)

---

[4] The issue of credit rationing will be discussed in Chapter 11. Suffice it to say at this stage that, as discussed in Chapter 2, if firms are to start up production and accumulate inventories, these will need to be financed. Thus, in our view, which is that of the French circuitists, if credit rationing occurs, it will occur at the very beginning of the production process, stopping entrepreneurs from producing.

$$yd_r = \frac{YD_r}{p} - \pi \cdot \frac{V_{-1}}{p}$$

yd_r is realized real regular disposable income; (10.26)

$$yd_{hs} = c + \Delta v = c + (v - v_{-1})$$

yd_{hs} is realized real Haig–Simons income; (10.27A)

$$yd_{hs} = \frac{YD_r}{p} - \pi \cdot \frac{V_{-1}}{p}$$
$$+ \Delta p_{bL} \cdot \frac{BL_{h-1}}{p}$$

The extended version; (10.27)

$$v = \frac{V}{p}$$

v is realized real wealth; (10.28)

This time we start with the realized outcomes. Nominal disposable income is once again given two possible definitions. First, there is regular disposable income YD_r, given by equation (10.20) (Box 10.3), which only includes regular flows – wage income, three kinds of interest income, and distributed profits F, including both the realized profits of firms F_f and those of banks F_b as shown in equation (10.23). All these sources of income can be found in the first column of the transactions matrix of Table 10.2. Capital gains CG on bonds, as defined in equation (10.21), are excluded from this regular income. The sum of regular income and capital gains constitutes the Haig–Simons definition of nominal income Yd_{hs}, as shown in equation (10.22).

Changes in the stock of household wealth, in equation (10.24), are equal to the gap between actual disposable income, in its Haig–Simons measure, and the value of consumption. As shown in equation (10.25), from this stock of wealth, we deduct transactions-determined cash (banknotes) H_{hh} to obtain wealth net of cash, V_{nc}, which is available for asset allocation. Thus we assume that there is a strict transactions demand for cash money – for petty transactions – which when realized is given by H_{hh}. This arises as a result of the use of banknotes when making some daily consumption expenditures. It is assumed (given modern transactions technology) that the amount of cash held by households is not part of the wealth allocation process and is determined entirely by the need to finance transactions. In other words, while banknotes are part of household wealth, they are not part of the wealth that households allocate to various assets on the basis of rates of return.

The next three equations define real values. Equation (10.26) defines the realized real regular disposable income of households. As was explained in detail in section 3 of Chapter 9, real regular disposable income is not simply a deflated nominal regular income, in other words, $yd_r \neq YD_r/p$. Consistency makes it necessary to deduct the loss in real wealth caused by price inflation, which is what equation (10.26) says. The Haig–Simons definition of income is at the origin of this consistency requirement. Equation (10.27A) provides the standard Haig–Simons definition of realized real disposable income yd_{hs}, which is the sum of real consumption and the realized change in real wealth.

Equation (10.27) defines the same Haig–Simons real disposable income, but this time in an extensive manner, with the help of equations (10.21) and (10.22). Equation (10.28) defines real household wealth, which is simply the deflated amount of nominal wealth.

10.4.2 Equations describing the decisions of households

Box 10.4 Households' equations

$$c = \alpha_0 + \alpha_1 \cdot yd_r^e + \alpha_2 \cdot v_{-1}$$ *c* is real consumption, that depends on expected real disposable regular income, and past real wealth;   (10.29)

$$yd_r^e = \varepsilon \cdot yd_{r-1} + (1 - \varepsilon)yd_{r-1}^e$$ Expected real disposable regular income;   (10.30)

$$yd_r^e = [yd_{r-1}(1 + RA2)]$$ An alternative to 10.30 using a random variation;   (10.30A)

$$C = p \cdot c$$ *C* is the $ value of consumptions;   (10.31)

$$YD_r^e = p \cdot yd_r^e + \pi \cdot \frac{V_{-1}}{p}$$ Expected nominal regular disposable income;   (10.32)

$$V^e = V_{-1} + (YD_r^e - C)$$ Expected nominal wealth;   (10.33)

$$H_{hd} = \lambda_c \cdot C$$ Households' demand for cash;   (10.34)

$$V_{nc}^e = V^e - H_{hd}$$ Expected nominal wealth net of cash.   (10.35)

We now move to the equations describing the decisions of households (Box 10.4). Their decisions to consume are assumed to depend on the stock of real wealth inherited from the previous period in combination with the real regular disposable income they expect to receive during the period (equation 10.29). Alternatively stated, it is assumed that households have a target for their regular income-wealth ratio towards which they move, subject to temporary deviations owing to mistaken expectations, at a rate consistent with their need for consumption during the current period.[5] Equations (10.30) and (10.30A) explain how households arrive at their expected real regular disposable income. Two variants are offered. The first is based on some adaptative process, while the second assumes some random process.

The next equations define nominal variables that will be useful when we reach the portfolio decisions. Consumption expenditures, in nominal terms, are given by equation (10.31). Equation (10.32) yields expected nominal

---

[5] As $\Delta v = yd_r - c$, equation (10.29) implies $\Delta v = \alpha_2 \cdot [\alpha_3 \cdot yd_r^e - v_{-1}]$ where $\alpha_3 = (1 - \alpha_1)/\alpha_2$ which in turn implies $v^* = \alpha_3 \cdot yd_r^*$. Targeted real wealth depends on real regular disposable income.

regular disposable income, which depends on both expected real regular income and the inflation loss on wealth, in symmetry with equation (10.26). The actual current price level and inflation rate are assumed to be known when such expected incomes are formulated. The assumption is that output prices are set by firms at the beginning of the period, on the basis of normal historic unit costs, as explained in the previous subsection, and hence that price stickers are out when households make their consumption and portfolio decisions during the period.

Once households have planned their consumption expenditures in nominal terms, and having made forecasts with regard to their nominal regular disposable income, they are able to make an estimate of the wealth they will have accumulated by the end of the period. This expected wealth V^e depends on past wealth V_{-1}. It should also depend on expected capital gains of the current period, as was the case in Chapter 5, but we shall simplify this part of the model by assuming away expectations about capital gains and changing bond prices.

Finally, as mentioned when discussing realized outcomes, households' desire to hold a certain quantity of banknotes H_{hd}. This cash is proportional to the consumption expenditures that occur, and constitutes the strict transactions demand for money (equation 10.34). Deducting this cash money from expected wealth yields expected wealth net of cash, V^e_{nc} (equation 10.35). This net amount of wealth will be the key variable in the description of the households' allocation of their wealth.

Box 10.5 Households' portfolio equations, based on nominal rates

$$\frac{M1_d}{V^e_{nc}} = \lambda_{10} + \lambda_{12} \cdot r_m + \lambda_{13} \cdot r_b + \lambda_{14}$$
$$\cdot ERr_{bL} + \lambda_{15} \cdot \left(\frac{YD^e_r}{V^e_{nc}}\right) \tag{10.36}$$

$$\frac{M2_d}{V^e_{nc}} = \lambda_{20} + \lambda_{22} \cdot r_m + \lambda_{23} \cdot r_b + \lambda_{24}$$
$$\cdot ERr_{bL} + \lambda_{25} \cdot \left(\frac{YD^e_r}{V^e_{nc}}\right) \tag{10.37}$$

$$\frac{B_{hd}}{V^e_{nc}} = \lambda_{30} + \lambda_{32} \cdot r_m + \lambda_{33} \cdot r_b + \lambda_{34}$$
$$\cdot ERr_{bL} + \lambda_{35} \cdot \left(\frac{YD^e_r}{V^e_{nc}}\right) \tag{10.38}$$

$$\frac{(p_{bL} \cdot BL_d)}{V^e_{nc}} = \lambda_{40} + \lambda_{42} \cdot r_m + \lambda_{43} \cdot r_b + \lambda_{44}$$
$$\cdot ERr_{bL} + \lambda_{45} \cdot \left(\frac{YD^e_r}{V^e_{nc}}\right) \tag{10.39}$$

While our account of household behaviour up to this point has already been covered in Model *DIS*, new ground is broken with respect to the array of assets between which households can allocate their wealth, although we adopt the same methodology for asset allocation as that described in Chapter 5 with Model *LP* – that is, we use the 'adding-up' constraint and various other constraints originally proposed by James Tobin. In addition to cash, households can now hold checking account money, time deposit money, government bills and government bonds (here assumed once more to be perpetuities). It is a profoundly important feature both of households' wealth allocation plans, and of the subsequent outcome, that all wealth goes into one or other of these five categories. Households cannot, given their income and their consumption, reduce their holdings of one type of asset without increasing the sum of all their other holdings; nor can they consistently plan to reduce one without increasing the other.

There is a positive transactions demand for checking account money, based on expected income relative to expected wealth net of cash, (YD_r^e/V_{nc}^e), with corresponding negative effects on other asset demands. The planned allocation of expected wealth (net of cash holdings) between each kind of money and each type of government security is determined principally by the rate of return on each asset: r_m the current rate of interest on time deposits $M2$ (which is implicitly assumed to prevail in the next period), r_b the short-term of interest or the rate of return on bills, and r_{bL} the long-term interest rate which will also be the rate of return on bonds as long as bond prices do not change. We assume that checking account deposits $M1$ carry no interest. The nominal rate of return on checking deposits is thus zero. This is why the rate of return on checking balances is nowhere to be found in the portfolio equations (10.36) to (10.39). But as we shall soon see, it is of the greatest importance to assign a consistent value to the four λ_{i1} parameters that are implicitly attached to this zero nominal rate of return on checking deposits in the four portfolio equations (Box 10.5).

As expressed, the four portfolio equations take the *nominal* rates of return on all four assets. The question naturally arises as to whether the *real* rates of return or the nominal ones ought to be taken into consideration into the portfolio equations. In Godley (1999a), for instance, real rates of return appear in the portfolio equations. In the *PC* and *LP* models of Chapters 4 and 5, we did not deal with this issue, because we were assuming a world with constant prices. But in the present model, where price and wage inflation could arise, the question has to be squarely faced.

Our answer is that, as long as the portfolio set-up is consistent and the various adding-up constraints are respected, we may indifferently use real or nominal rates of return. Either sort of rates of return will yield the same results with the same set of parameters. From a purely realistic point of view, households will be comparing nominal rates; and hence from that point of view it may seem better to use nominal rates, as in equations (10.42) to (10.45). From a formal point of view, some economists may prefer to use real rates of return, as shown in Box 10.6, or in the following matrix, because this presentation carries explicitly the rate of return on checking deposits and its associated λ coefficients.

As is well-known, ideally, it is the rate of inflation *expected* now for the next time period that should enter into the portfolio equations, since portfolio decisions are always forward looking. We shall simplify however, and assume that the expected rate of inflation of the next period is precisely equal to the realized rate of price inflation of the current period.

In a world with price inflation, non-interest bearing money has a negative rate of return – approximately equal to the inflation rate π. The real rate of return on checking deposits is exactly equal to $-\pi/(1 + \pi)$, according to Fisher's discrete time formula that we developed in Chapter 8. The real rates of return used in this alternative representation of the portfolio decision (Box 10.6) which appears in equations (10.36A) to (10.39A) are defined in equations (10.36B) to (10.39B). The advantage of this presentation using real rates of return, as already pointed out, is that it highlights the importance of assigning consistent values to the λ_{i1} parameters that only appear implicitly in the equations defining portfolio choice in nominal terms.

Box 10.6   Households' portfolio equations, based on real rates

$$\frac{M1_d}{V_{nc}^e} = \lambda_{10} + \lambda_{11} \cdot \left(-\frac{\pi}{(1 + \pi)} \right) + \lambda_{12} \cdot rr_m + \lambda_{13} \cdot rr_b$$

$$+ \lambda_{14} \cdot rr_{bL} + \lambda_{15} \cdot \left(\frac{YD_r^e}{V_{nc}^e} \right) \tag{10.36A}$$

$$\frac{M2_d}{V_{nc}^e} = \lambda_{20} + \lambda_{21} \cdot \left(-\frac{\pi}{(1 + \pi)} \right) + \lambda_{22} \cdot rr_m + \lambda_{23} \cdot rr_b$$

$$+ \lambda_{24} \cdot rr_{bL} + \lambda_{25} \cdot \left(\frac{YD_r^e}{V_{nc}^e} \right) \tag{10.37A}$$

$$\frac{B_{hd}}{V_{nc}^e} = \lambda_{30} + \lambda_{31} \cdot \left(-\frac{\pi}{(1 + \pi)} \right) + \lambda_{32} \cdot rr_m + \lambda_{33} \cdot rr_b$$

$$+ \lambda_{34} \cdot rr_{bL} + \lambda_{35} \cdot \left(\frac{YD_r^e}{V_{nc}^e} \right) \tag{10.38A}$$

Continued

Box 10.6   Continued

$$\frac{(p_{bL} \cdot BL_d)}{V_{nc}^e} = \lambda_{40} + \lambda_{41} \cdot \left(-\frac{\pi}{(1+\pi)}\right) + \lambda_{42} \cdot rr_m + \lambda_{43} \cdot rr_b$$

$$+ \lambda_{44} \cdot rr_{bL} + \lambda_{45} \cdot \left(\frac{YD_r^e}{V_{nc}^e}\right) \tag{10.39A}$$

$$-\frac{\pi}{(1+\pi)} = \frac{(1+0)}{(1+\pi)} - 1 \quad \begin{array}{l}\text{the negative rate of return on} \\ \text{M1 deposits;}\end{array} \tag{10.36B}$$

$$rr_m = \frac{(1+r_m)}{(1+\pi)} - 1 \quad \text{real rate on term deposits;} \tag{10.37B}$$

$$rr_b = \frac{(1+r_b)}{(1+\pi)} - 1 \quad \text{real rate on bills;} \tag{10.38B}$$

$$rr_{bL} = \frac{(1+r_{bL})}{(1+\pi)} - 1 \quad \text{real rate on long-term bonds.} \tag{10.39B}$$

10.4.3   The adding-up constraints

As we found in Chapter 5, it may be prudent to indicate explicitly what the adding-up constraints must be. First we have the following two vertical summation constraints, that are relevant to the constant shares of assets in net wealth and to the impact of the regular income to net wealth ratio:

$$\lambda_{10} + \lambda_{20} + \lambda_{30} + \lambda_{40} = 1 \tag{ADUP.1}$$

$$\lambda_{15} + \lambda_{25} + \lambda_{35} + \lambda_{45} = 0 \tag{ADUP.2}$$

The next four vertical adding-up constraints deal with the parameters of the rates of return matrix:

$$\lambda_{11} + \lambda_{21} + \lambda_{31} + \lambda_{41} = 0 \tag{ADUP.3}$$

$$\lambda_{12} + \lambda_{22} + \lambda_{32} + \lambda_{42} = 0 \tag{ADUP.4}$$

$$\lambda_{13} + \lambda_{23} + \lambda_{33} + \lambda_{43} = 0 \tag{ADUP.5}$$

$$\lambda_{14} + \lambda_{24} + \lambda_{34} + \lambda_{44} = 0 \tag{ADUP.6}$$

We could also include the *horizontal* adding-up constraints underlined by Godley (1996). But as we saw in Chapter 5, the horizontal adding-up constraints can be replaced by the more restrictive *symmetry* constraints suggested by Friedman (1978), since the symmetry constraints, given the vertical constraints above, also fulfil the horizontal adding-up constraints. We thus also impose the following six symmetry constraints:

$$\lambda_{12} = \lambda_{21} \tag{ADUP.7}$$
$$\lambda_{13} = \lambda_{31} \tag{ADUP.8}$$
$$\lambda_{23} = \lambda_{32} \tag{ADUP.9}$$
$$\lambda_{14} = \lambda_{41} \tag{ADUP.10}$$
$$\lambda_{24} = \lambda_{42} \tag{ADUP.11}$$
$$\lambda_{34} = \lambda_{43} \tag{ADUP.12}$$

Readers can build any example that fits all these adding-up constraints.[6] They will find that the representations in terms of the real and nominal rates of return yield the same results.

10.4.4 Realized portfolio asset holdings

Box 10.7 Households' equations

$H_{hh} = H_{hd}$	intentions regarding cash are fulfilled;	(10.40)
$B_{hh} = B_{hd}$	intentions regarding bills are fulfilled;	(10.41)
$BL_h = BL_d$	intentions regarding bonds are fulfilled;	(10.42)
$M1_{hN} = V_{nc} - M2_d$ $-B_{hd} - p_{bL} \cdot BL_d$	The *notional* amount of bank checking accounts people would find themselves holding;	(10.43)

Continued

---

[6] The horizontal constraints would be:

$$\lambda_{11} = -(+\lambda_{12} + \lambda_{13} + \lambda_{14}) \tag{ADUP.13}$$
$$\lambda_{22} = -(+\lambda_{21} + \lambda_{23} + \lambda_{24}) \tag{ADUP.14}$$
$$\lambda_{33} = -(+\lambda_{31} + \lambda_{32} + \lambda_{34}) \tag{ADUP.15}$$
$$\lambda_{44} = -(+\lambda_{41} + \lambda_{42} + \lambda_{43}) \tag{ADUP.16}$$

Box 10.7 Continued

$M1_h = M1_{hN} \cdot z_1$	These two equations say that	(10.44)
$z_1 = 1$ iff $M1_{hN} \geq 0$	the bank checking deposits held are	
	zero if they would turn out to be	
	negative according to equation	(10.45)
	(10.43);	
$M2_h = M2_d \cdot z_1 + (V_{nc} - B_{hh} - p_{bL} \cdot BL_d) \cdot z_2$		(10.46)
$z_2 = 1$ iff $M1_{hN} < 0$	if checking deposits were to be	
	negative, households would	
	adjust them back to zero by	
	decreasing time deposits.	(10.47)

It is assumed that all plans with regard to the disposition of expected net wealth between cash, time deposit money, bills and bonds are *generally* realized (equations 10.41, 10.42, and 10.43) as shown in Box 10.7. Hence all mistaken expectations about income and wealth determine the deviations, from what was originally planned, in checking account money deposits (equation 10.43). We have here, in fluctuations in checking account deposits, an exact analogue to the fluctuations in inventory accumulation consequent upon firms never knowing exactly what their sales are going to be. As is the case of firms' expectations about sales, the way expectations by households about their real disposable income are actually formed is no big deal; if actual income is lower than expected, this will show up instantaneously as lower-than-expected wealth in the form of checking account money and result (by the consumption equation 10.29) in corrective action in subsequent periods. The stocks of money and wealth which are created put households on a kind of autopilot. Mistakes about income get communicated and hopefully rectified by the arrival of a bank statement!

Equations 10.43 to 10.47 however take into account the possibility of the checking account balance getting into the red. With some large mistakes in expectations, it could be the case that the *notional* amount of checking deposits $M1_{hN}$ falls to a negative number. We assume that households are forbidden to borrow, that they benefit from no credit line, and that banks will not allow the checking accounts of their individual customers to become negative. If this were to happen, the banks would take funds away from the time deposits of households and transfer them to the checking account of the same customers. Equations 10.43 to 10.47 provide a (slightly complicated) mechanism that insures that checking account deposits $M1_h$ actually held by households are either positive or equal to zero. When this mechanism must be put into action, actual checking deposits are brought back to zero and time deposits become the residual element that adjusts realized outcomes to expected ones.

10.5 The government sector and the central bank

10.5.1 The government sector

Box 10.8 Government's equations

$T = \tau \cdot (S - T) = S \cdot \dfrac{\tau}{(1 + \tau)}$ Realized tax revenue from sales tax;   (10.48)

$G = p \cdot g$ Nominal and real pure government expenditures;   (10.49)

$PSBR = G + r_{b-1} \cdot B_{s-1} + BL_{s-1} - (T + F_{cb})$ Government deficit;   (10.50)

$B_s = B_{s-1} + PSBR - \Delta(BL_s) \cdot p_{bL}$ New issues of bills;   (10.51)

$BL_s = BL_d$ Bonds are supplied on demand;   (10.52)

$p_{bL} = \dfrac{1}{r_{bL}}$ The price of long-term bonds is the inverse of their yield;   (10.53)

$r_{bL} = \bar{r}_{bL}$ The yield on long-term bonds is set exogenously.   (10.54)

The government collects revenues through a sales tax (Box 10.8), the rate of which is $\tau/(1 + \tau)$, as discussed earlier (equation 10.48). The government also buys part of the output of firms, g in terms of widgets, at the price set by firms (equation 10.49). The government's fiscal deficit, which we called *PSBR* for *public sector borrowing requirement*, as per equation (10.50), is equal to the balance between all outlays (pure expenditures plus interest payments on both kinds of debt) and all revenues, which include tax receipts and the profits F_{cb} of the central bank which are returned to the government.

There are different ways in which the government's management of its debts can be described. We assume that the government and the monetary authorities hold both the long and the short interest rate constant – something that was shown could conceivably be done with Model *LP* in Chapter 5 – which is another way of saying that they buy and sell bills and bonds without limit at those rates of interest. So, at fixed interest rates, we shall see that the central bank acts as the residual supplier or purchaser of Treasury bills. Likewise the government supplies bonds on demand to households, as shown by equation (10.52), which implies that the long-term interest rate (or the price of bonds) is set exogenously (equations 10.53 and 10.54). The supply of bills by government is determined by its budget constraint. The change in the supply of bills is the difference between the public sector borrowing requirement and the yield value of the current period issue of long-term bonds, as shown in equation (10.51).

10.5.2   The central bank

Box 10.9   The central bank's equations

$H_s = B_{cb} + A_s$	the balance sheet of the central bank;	(10.55)
$H_{bs} = H_s - H_{hs}$	the supply of cash (HPM) has two components: the supply to banks and the supply to households;	(10.56)
$B_{cb} = B_s - B_{hh} - B_{bd}$	the central bank is the residual purchaser of bills;	(10.57)
$r_b = \bar{r}_b$	The rate of interest on bills is set exogenously;	(10.58)
$A_s = A_d$	Advances to commercial banks are provided on demand;	(10.59)
$r_a = r_b$	For simplification, the rate on advances is the same as the rate on Treasury bills;	(10.60)
$F_{cb} = r_{b-1} \cdot B_{cb-1} + r_{a-1} \cdot A_{s-1}$	The profits of the central bank.	(10.61)

We now turn to the equations which are directly tied to the central bank. Equation (10.55) reflects the very simple balance-sheet constraint of the central bank (Box 10.9). The value of its assets – the bills that it holds and the advances that it has made to commercial banks – must be equal to the total amount of high-powered money H_s that it supplies. High-powered money is made up of two components: the cash that is supplied to households, indirectly, through the banking system, for their transactions when purchasing consumer goods, and the reserves which private banks must hold in the form of deposits at the central bank, as shown in equation (10.56).

On the bills market, the central bank is a residual purchaser, at the rate of interest on bills that the monetary authorities have decided to enforce. The central bank buys any bill which is not demanded by banks or the households. These two hypotheses are formalized with the help of equations (10.57) and (10.58).

In addition, the central bank provides, on demand, advances to commercial banks, as reflected by equation (10.59). Within our framework, as discussed in the next section, those loans to commercial banks are required when systemic conditions in the financial system are such that commercial banks would otherwise wind up with fewer liquid assets (Treasury bills) than they minimally desire (or possibly with negative holdings). Central banks then provide advances to banks, which allow banks to keep their minimal amount of bills instead of selling them on the open market to fulfill their clearing obligations. In so doing the size of the balance sheet of central banks does not change, but that of commercial banks does. For simplification purposes, and also because in the real world they are virtually equal, the rate of interest on advances is assumed to take the same value as the interest rate on Treasury bills (equation 10.60). Knowing the balance sheet of the central bank allows us to deduce the profit equation of the central bank, given by equation (10.61).

Why can't the monetary authority determine the issue of base money and make some other component of its balance sheet the residual, flexible, variable? In theory this is indeed a possibility, at least in the context of a mechanical model such as ours. However, it will be found that in practise the issue of base money could only be exogenously determined as a policy instrument if there were unbelievably large fluctuations in interest rates – so large that the simple linear functions which we have used to describe asset demands would break down, as would the system itself.

Thus, to sum up the situation of the government sector with that of its central bank, the fiscal and monetary authorities determine their pure expenditures, the rate of taxation, and interest rates – both short and long.

The government has a further instrument of policy in that it can (at least in theory) change the reserve requirement of banks. This is discussed in the following section.

10.6 The commercial banking system

10.6.1 The duties of the commercial banks

We now arrive at the most innovative part of Model *INSOUT*, at least compared with all our previous models, the origins of which can be found in Godley (1997, 1999a).[7] This subsection is original because it goes much beyond the simple one-asset and one-liability commercial bank that had been first introduced in Chapters 7 and 9, with models *BMW* and *DIS*. Here we introduce a more sophisticated commercial banking system, closer to reality, with two kinds of deposits, two assets and compulsory reserve requirements (although such reserve requirements no longer exist in several countries, such

---

[7] A further discussion about the difference between the present representation of bank behaviour and that of neo-classical economists can be found in Lavoie and Godley (2006).

as Canada). The behaviour of banks is given particular attention and is also an original feature of Model *INSOUT*

In other models that attempt to integrate bank behaviour to a full-fledged macroeconomic model, specifically that of Brainard and Tobin (1968) and Tobin (1969), banks are essentially agents operating in financial markets who do nothing but make an asset choice exactly like the asset choice of households and conducted according to the same principles. The role of banks is thus nothing more than to extend the range of asset and liability choice open to households. Tobinesque banks are treated like financial intermediaries. Their main function is not to create loans which make possible the expansion of production and the financing of inventories. Their main role rather is to allocate assets and to decide whether they are prepared to take on any additional liabilities. This view of banks is a rather artificial one, and it leads Tobin (1969: 337) to make some strange constructions, such as a deposit supply function which describes 'the quantity of deposits banks wish to accept at any given deposit rate', or to argue that the rate of interest on loans adjusts to clear the credit market (Backus *et al.* 1980: 265). As pointed out by Goodhart (1984: 268), the concept of a supply function for bank deposits is a dubious one and does not seem to properly describe the activity of banks: 'In what manner do banks supply demand deposits?'.

We are proposing something entirely different here. We are saying that banks respond passively to the needs of business for loans (within the limits imposed by creditworthiness, which will not be modelled here however) and to the asset allocation activities of households, as well as providing the means of payment. Banks make profits not by deciding what kind of asset to invest in, but rather by setting prices that insure a profit margin; they do this by setting the loan and deposit rates of interest relative to the bill rate and relative to each other in such a way that profits will be forthcoming. In addition, banks modify the interest rates over which they have some control in response to quantity signals relative to the 'liquidity ratio' or profitability rules of thumb that they assign themselves, presumably on the basis of past experience. In short, banks are price takers with regard to the interest rates they receive on bills and price makers with regard to the interest rates they charge on loans and pay on money deposits (Godley 1999a: 397). It is our view, and also that of Goodhart (1984: 195–6) and Docherty (2005), that such a depiction of commercial banks is much more realistic than as an asset allocator, and it yields much more profound insights. How exactly banks decide on the amount of profit that they can reasonably expect will not be discussed here, and will await the next chapter. In the meantime, despite this lack of precision, we believe that the present model of bank behaviour offers enough innovations to be worth presenting.

Box 10.10   Commercial banks' equations

$H_{hs} = H_{hd}$	cash supplied on demand;	(10.62)
$M1_s = M1_d$	checking deposits supplied on demand;	(10.63)
$M2_s = M2_d$	time deposits supplied on demand;	(10.64)
$L_s = L_d$	loans supplied on demand;	(10.65)
$H_{bd} = \rho_1 \cdot M1_s + \rho_2 \cdot M2_s$	the reserve requirements of banks.	(10.66)

The first three equations (10.62–10.64) in Box 10.10 describe 'supplies' of all three kinds of money to households, which are assumed to passively match 'demands', which are all determined in the way explained in the household section above. Equations (10.63) and (10.64) say banks passively accept the money that is being deposited with them. With equation (10.62), we assume that the central bank provides all the cash that is demanded by consumers. The central bank never refuses to provide commercial banks with the banknotes that their clients need for transacting. As in the real world, banknotes can always be obtained through automatic teller machines. Hence in reality, banknotes issued by the central bank are supplied to households who demand them through the services of private banks, in exchange for bank deposits.

We retain the word 'supply' because this accords with conventional usage, although it does not properly convey the nature of the processes we are trying to depict. What these equations are saying is something very simple, with which everyone is familiar – that banks will exchange any of three kinds of money for one another on demand; that they will always accept deposits, and that they will always transfer money paid by households as a whole to another sector in exchange for goods (purchased from firms) or for bills and bonds (purchased from the government or from banks themselves). There may in reality be some restriction on the speed with which money in time deposit accounts can be spent for any purpose, but we assume for present purposes that there is no delay.

Equation (10.65) makes the strong assumptions that loans are instantaneously available for the finance of inventories as these fluctuate; also that loans are made for no other purpose. Obviously loans in the real world are made for many other reasons. But here, as we begin to build up towards a realistic picture, we concentrate on what we believe to be the most basic rationale for the existence of commercial banks; without finance, production in an industrial economy could not function. Hence we assume that all firms are provided with a line of credit – overdrafts – that is sufficiently large to respond to any fluctuation in inventories. Consumer credit will figure in the next chapter.

It is assumed in equation (10.66) that banks are obliged, by order, to hold reserves in the form of 'vault cash' or balances with the central authorities which are equivalent to cash; and that these reserves must always be some proportion of their liabilities – that is, there is a compulsory reserve ratio ρ_1 on checking deposits $M1$, and another such ratio ρ_2 on time deposit $M2$. In most countries where such reserve requirements are imposed, the required ratio on time deposits is much smaller, and hence generally we have $\rho_2 < \rho_1$, but there is no harm is supposing that $\rho_1 = \rho_2 = \rho$. The banks' reserves, together with banknotes in the hands of private agents, make up what is called base money or high-powered money. It is always open to the government, at least in theory, to change the compulsory reserve requirement from one proportion to another. As the mainstream account of how credit money is created hinges entirely upon the way in which an increase in banks' reserves leads to a rise in the money supply via the so-called 'money multiplier', we shall be particularly interested in simulations of what happens following a change in the statutory reserve requirements.

10.6.2   The balance-sheet constraint of commercial banks

We reach now a key point in our exposition of the way banks function. Equation (10.67) describes the collective balance-sheet restraint of commercial banks. We can ascertain from the transactions matrix at the head of this chapter that changes in the sum of banks' assets must always equal changes in the sum of banks' liabilities. The foregoing paragraphs of this section have argued that levels and therefore changes in all the components of banks' consolidated balance sheet except for one are determinate; the determined variables are money (all kinds) held by households, loans to firms and banks' own reserves with the central bank. It follows by the laws of logic that the remaining variable – banks' holdings of (or, if you must, 'demand' for) bills is determined as well. Each of the other components of the banks' balance sheet is likely to be bobbing around, individually subject to quite distinct influences. It now turns out that it is banks' holdings of bills which has to be the fluctuating counterpart of the sum of all these diverse transactions. Checking deposits played the role of a buffer for households; in the case of the banking system, Treasury bills play the role of a buffer.[8] As Goodhart (1984: 196) says, 'the demand by banks for bonds [bills] emerges as a residual'.

Commercial banks must hold a sufficiently large stock of bills to absorb any fluctuation in money deposits or in loans. There will be circumstances

---

[8] In Appendix 10.1, we show that such a financial system is often called an 'asset-based' financial system, and is typical of the Anglo–Saxon world. Typically, in most other countries, private banks carry no bills and are freely allowed to borrow from the central bank, provided they can show some collateral, usually in the form of discounted commercial paper.

however where the fluctuations in the assets and liabilities of banks are such that the stock of bills will fall below the minimum level targeted by banks. Under some circumstances, the stock of bills held by commercial banks would even have to turn negative, if it weren't for the advances of the central bank. Thus equation (10.67) represents the *notional* (rather than the *actual*) stock of bills that would be left in the hands of commercial banks, because the stock of bills held by banks cannot become negative (Box 10.11).

Box 10.11 Commercial banks' equations

$$B_{bdN} = M1_s + M2_s - L_s - H_{bd} \qquad \text{Notional balance-sheet constraint of banks;} \qquad (10.67)$$

$$BLR_N = \frac{B_{bdN}}{(M1_s + M2_s)} \qquad \text{Net bank liquidity ratio;} \qquad (10.68)$$

$$A_d = \{bot \cdot (M1_s + M2_s) - B_{bdN}\} \cdot z_4 \qquad \text{Advances needed by banks;} \qquad (10.69)$$

$$z_4 = 1 \quad \text{iff } BLR_N < bot \qquad (10.70)$$

$$B_{bd} = A_d + M1_s + M2_s - L_s - H_{bd} \qquad \text{Actual balance-sheet constraint of banks;} \qquad (10.71)$$

$$BLR = \frac{B_{bd}}{(M1_s + M2_s)} \qquad \text{Actual (or gross) bank liquidity ratio.} \qquad (10.72)$$

The financial system taken as a whole thus needs an additional buffer, and that will be the advances provided by the central bank to the banking institutions. Indeed, here we will further assume that banks do wish to hold a minimum amount of bills under all circumstances, and hence advances from the central bank will be used both to ensure that the stock of bills held by commercial banks does not turn negative, but also to ensure that the amount of bills that they hold is at least equal to the targeted minimum. When, for instance, agents wish to transform their money deposits into an excessive amount of bills or high powered money, the banks manage to hold on to their bills by getting advances from the central bank. In other words the banks are acquiring high-powered money by borrowing it from the central bank. What we called the notional stock of bills is in fact the stock of bills held by banks *net* of the amount of advances taken from the central bank.

All this is represented with the help of equations (10.67–10.72). We assume through equation (10.68) that banks are concerned with a *net bank liquidity ratio*, BLR_N. The denominator of this ratio is the overall amount of bank deposits while the numerator is the net amount of bills held by banks, that is the actual amount of bills they hold minus the advances taken by the private banks at the central bank. As indicated by equations (10.69) and (10.70), when this notional bank liquidity ratio falls below a minimum value, a bottom value called *bot*, banks get advances A_d from the central bank, thus allowing them to restore the minimum *bot* ratio. The *actual* balance-sheet constraint of the banks, as can be seen from Table 10.2, is thus given by equation (10.71), which includes advances from the central bank. These advances, as we saw with equation (10.59), are provided on demand. As a result, the actual (or gross) bank liquidity ratio, *BLR*, is given by equation (10.72).

Inventories played the role of a buffer for firms; these firms had the ability to restore their target level of inventories in the long run, by adequate changes in production relative to the expected sales. Similarly, while there is not much that the banks can do in the short run besides borrowing from the central bank, in the long run banks do have the ability to restore their buffer of bills to the level that they judge appropriate without resorting to central bank advances. This is what we come to see next.

10.6.3   The determination of interest rates set by banks

Box 10.12   Commercial banks' equations

$r_m = r_{m-1} + \Delta r_m + \zeta_b \cdot \Delta r_b$	Deposit rates move with bill rates and also depend on	(10.73)
$\Delta r_m = \zeta_m(z_4 - z_5)$	whether the BLR_N is within its target	(10.74)
	range;	
$z_4 = 1$ iff $BLR_{N-1} < bot$		(10.75)
$z_5 = 1$ iff $BLR_{N-1} > top$		(10.76)
$F_b = r_{l-1} \cdot L_{s-1} + r_{b-1} \cdot B_{bd-1}$ $\quad - r_{m-1} \cdot M2_{s-1} - r_{a-1} \cdot A_{d-1}$	profits of banks;	(10.77)
$r_l = r_{l-1} + \Delta r_l + \Delta r_b$	loan rates move with bill rates and also depend on	(10.78)
$\Delta r_l = \zeta_l(z_6 - z_7)$	whether bank profitability is within its target	(10.79)
	range;	
$z_6 = 1$ iff $BPM < botpm$		(10.80)
$z_7 = 1$ iff $BPM > toppm$		(10.81)
$BPM = \dfrac{(F_b + F_{b-1})}{\{M1_{s-1} + M1_{s-2} \\ + M2_{s-1} + M2_{s-2}\}}$	Mean profit margin of banks.	(10.82)

There are only two main variables that need to be explained, and those are the interest rate on term deposits, r_m, and the interest rate on loans, r_l. While both interest rates are assumed to move up following an increase in the base rate set by the central bank[9] – here the Treasury bill rate r_b – we shall further assume that two different mechanisms are at work to explain the possibly diverging evolution of these two administered interest rates (Box 10.12). We shall assume that variations of the rate of interest on term deposits, relative to the bill rate, depend on the evolution of the notional bank liquidity ratio BLR_N. By contrast variations in the rate of interest on loans, relative to the bill rate, depend on the evolution of some measure of bank profits.

Embedded in the model is a hierarchy of interest rates. This hierarchy was put forth by Godley and Cripps (1983: 160). They argued that banks would be looking for 'an appropriate or sensible' composition of their portfolios of assets. The bill rate would determine what the rates set by banks ought to be. 'Thus bank lending rates must be higher than [bill rates] (otherwise banks would not want to lend to the private sector) and rates on interest-bearing bank deposits must be lower than [bill rates] (otherwise neither the public nor banks would want to hold [bills])'.

*How is the rate on deposit money determined? The mechanism to be described closely follows the rules suggested in Godley (1997, 1999a). Our key assumption, as pointed out in the previous subsection, is that banks keep the bank liquidity ratio a positive number above some minimum target, asking for central bank advances if needed. In the longer run however, we shall assume that banks do not wish to be indebted to the central bank, and hence that banks aim to keep the notional or net bank liquidity ratio BLR_N within some quite narrow range, the floor and the ceiling of this range being *bot* and *top*. If the sum of the other balance sheet items has driven the bill holdings of banks below the bottom of this range, they must raise the deposit rate. This mechanism, described by equations (10.73) to (10.76), will have the effect of inducing people to sell a proportion of their holdings of government securities and invest the proceeds in term deposit accounts. This leads to an expansion in the liabilities of the commercial banks, who can then purchase government securities and obtain an equivalent increase in their assets (or reduce the amount of advances that they took from the central bank, in which case there is no expansion in the balance sheet of commercial banks), as can be checked from the balance sheet identity of banks (equations 10.67 and 10.71). The bank liquidity ratio will now be higher.[10]

---

[9] Lending rates increase or decrease one-for-one with changes in the bill rate, while changes in deposit rates only represent a proportion ζ_b of the change in the bill rate, as shown in equation (10.73).

[10] This behaviour seems to be compatible with the evidence uncovered by Forman, Groves and Eichner (1985), who show that the higher the degree of liquidity pressure, relative to its trend value, the higher the interest rates. Since the degree of liquidity pressure is defined by Forman *et al.* as the ratio of loans to deposits, it is nearly the complement of the bank liquidity ratio defined here.

Conversely if the bank liquidity ratio rises above the safety range so that banks are holding more bills than they need, banks will reduce the interest rate on term deposits so that people hold a smaller share of wealth in money deposits and a higher share in securities. Banks will wish to hold as few bills as they safely can, because the rate of interest on these is lower than that on loans to the private sector. In our simulation model we have made up crude rules governing the banks' responses which will always keep the net bank liquidity ratio moving towards the designated safety band, while the actual bank liquidity ratio is always at or above the minimum ratio.

And so we come to banks' profits, defined in equation (10.77) as the sum of all interest receipts less the sum of all interest payments. Our argument is that banks can ensure that all their operations are profitable, notwithstanding the passivity in their responses which we have assumed, by appropriate adjustments in at least one of the rates of interest over which they have control. We shall assume that banks raise the rate they charge on loans, relative to the bill rate, whenever their profitability falls below a certain threshold, here called *botpm*. Similarly, when profitability exceeds some upper threshold – called *toppm* – they reduce their lending rates, for fear of government legislation or consumer outrage.

The behaviour of lending rates, as expressed in equations (10.78)–(10.81), is symmetric to that of deposit rates. The fluctuations of lending rates, relative to those of the bill rate, do not however depend on the bank liquidity ratio; rather they depend on the value taken by the bank profit margin – called *BPM*. This bank profit margin is defined as the ratio of banks' profits relative to the stock of deposits of the previous period. We shall assume, as appears in equation (10.82), that banks check the mean value of this profitability index over two periods, instead of acting on the basis of the value of a single year, so as to avoid unnecessary gyrations in the lending rate.

Our model is now complete in the sense that, with government expenditure, the tax rate, the short and the long rates of interest, as well as productivity taken as exogenous variables, there is an equation to explain the behaviour of every other variable (the nominal wage will be explained next). As in all of our models, there is one additional equation, the *redundant* equation, that need not be incorporated in the model. To find it, note that there are equations both in banks' demand for reserves (equation 10.66) and in the supply of reserves to banks (equation 10.56). And here we have, at last, our redundant equation for the system as a whole:

$H_{bs} = H_{bd}$ the redundant equation: supplies of reserves are found
to be equal to demand   (10.83A)

Banks' demand for cash and the central bank's supply of cash to banks will invariably be found to be of identical magnitude although there is no equation to make this happen. Banks demand reserves on the basis of legal requirements tied to the size of their deposit liabilities; central banks provide reserves apparently on the sole basis of their balance-sheet constraint. Still the amount supplied will necessarily be equal to the amount demanded. It is our belief that this is a finding which confirms the imaginative insights of some post-Keynesian monetary economists, such as Le Bourva, Kaldor and Moore, who did not use formal methods of exposition. The quantity of reserves supplied by the government to banks cannot be directly controlled. All that the government can control is the rate of interest it charges when it finds itself making funds available.[11]

The redundant equation of the model – equation (10.83A) – helps us to understand why some countries, such as Canada or Switzerland, are able to run monetary policy and keep control over interest rates despite the compulsory reserve ratio being equal to zero. In Canada, for instance, there are no reserve requirements whatsoever. Canadian chartered banks are provided with the banknotes that they need to operate the automatic teller machines and their counter operations. Canadian banks do not hold any deposits at the Bank of Canada. Still, despite the lack of compulsory (and free) reserves, the Bank of Canada is able to set the overnight rate at which individual chartered banks lend or borrow from each other. In our model, if the ρ ratios representing the required reserve ratios were equal to zero, nothing in how the model functions would be changed. It is true that the stock of high-powered money H_b held by banks would be zero, and hence that the liability side of private banks would be further simplified. But this would have no effect on the ability of the central bank to set the bill rate, and it would have no direct effect on how banks set interest rates on loans and deposits.

10.6.4 Introducing inflationary forces

The INSOUT model may be finalized by introducing the same determinants of inflation that we added to the DIS model of Chapter 9. We can assume that workers or their unions have some real wage target in mind, which depends positively on labour productivity of the previous period as well on the observed lagged employment rate. The rate of wage inflation will depend on how wide is the discrepancy between the target real wage and real wage of the previous period, as workers try to catch up by raising nominal wages. The following two equations describe this mechanism.

$$\omega^T = \left(\frac{W}{p}\right)^T = \Omega_0 + \Omega_1 \cdot pr + \Omega_2 \cdot \left(\frac{N}{N_{fe}}\right) \tag{10.84}$$

$$W = W_{-1}\left(1 + \Omega_3 \cdot \left(\omega^T_{-1} - \frac{W_{-1}}{p_{-1}}\right)\right) \tag{10.85}$$

Since the focus of the present chapter is the ability of the private banks to absorb short-run fluctuations in the components of their balance sheet, while still maintaining, in the long run, both their profitability and their liquidity ratio within their desired range, not too much will be said about inflation rates. Furthermore, since we have assumed that central banks set nominal rates, without introducing a central bank reaction function that would include inflation rates and employment rates – as in the Taylor rule – the true consequences of inflation cannot be taken fully into account.

Finally, for accounting purposes, we should recall the definition of gross domestic product, Y, which, as we saw in Chapter 8, is the sum of the dollar value of sales and of the value of the change in inventories:

$$Y = p \cdot s + UC \cdot \Delta in \tag{10.86}$$

10.7   Making it all sing with simulations

10.7.1   The steady state

In this section we try to convey, by simulation experiments, how the system as a whole behaves. It may be as well first to recall that the model has a well defined stationary steady state to which it will tend if all the exogenous variables are held constant. This full steady state must be one in which all stocks and all flows are constant. But if stocks of government debt are constant it would seem to be the case that all outflows from the government are equal to all inflows (that is, tax receipts). Using the above notation it would seem to be the case that:

$$G + r_b \cdot B^* + BL^* = T \tag{10.87}$$

where $r_b = r_{b-1}$.

We shall see in a latter subsection that equation (10.87), as a condition for stationarity, only holds when prices are constant. When there is inflation, real variables must be taken into account rather than nominal magnitudes, and hence the equilibrium level of output derived in equation (10.89) below only holds in a world without inflation.

As taxes are levied on the ex-tax, current price, value of sales, and as, in the stationary state, there is zero investment in inventories so that output is equal to sales ($y = s$) it follows that:

$$T = s \cdot p \cdot \frac{\tau}{(1 + \tau)} \tag{10.88}$$

We can therefore infer that, assuming away continuous inflation, the stationary value for real output is:

$$y^* = (G + r_b \cdot B^* + BL^*) \cdot \frac{(1 + \tau)}{(p \cdot \tau)} \tag{10.89}$$

The stationary real level of output depends on the tax rate, pure government expenditures and debt servicing, but the number of bills and bonds issued are themselves endogenous variables.[12] To find out exactly what is going on in the model, we need to use simulations.

10.7.2 Simulation 1: An increase in the targeted inventories to sale ratio

In our first simulation experiment we explore what would happen if, starting from a stationary steady state, the inventory to sales target ratio σ^T were to move up in a step, following an increase in the parameter σ_0 of equation (10.7). This change will give us the opportunity to handle nearly all the interesting features of our more sophisticated financial system. Note first that, in contrast to the large steady-state increase that was observed with the help of Figure 9.2 in the case of a pure private economy, the real output of this mixed economy will move back after the disturbance to a new steady-state which should be close to the original one, by reason of equation (10.89) above, which defines stationary real output. As we shall see, real output will not in general move back to exactly its original level because stocks of government debt will have changed. After a detour through a pure private economy without government, we see that the main result obtained in our most simplified models of Chapters 3 or 4 with only government money, returns to haunt us in the present complex mixed economy.

Figure 10.1A shows the evolution of the dollar value of inventories, and hence the evolution of the stock of bank loans granted to firms (since inventories are financed by bank loans). An approximate 10% increase in the target inventory to sales ratio does lead to a substantial increase in inventories and bank loans, with some overshooting, as inventory investment (the change in the stock of inventories) first jumps up, then declines, even reaching negative values. The response of consumption and total output follows the characteristic pattern generated by the multiplier process; both of them rise and both gradually fall back, consumption initially trailing output, tracking the impetus given by inventory investment, as can be seen in Figure 10.1B, where real output and real consumption are charted as a ratio of their original values before the change.[13]

---

[12] Equation (10.89) is not entirely correct since we have omitted the revenues that the government collects out of the profits of the central bank. But this is a second-order error.

[13] A credible reason as to why the increase in the target inventories to sales ratio generates a slight reduction in the long-run value of real output will have to await the derivation of equation (10.98).

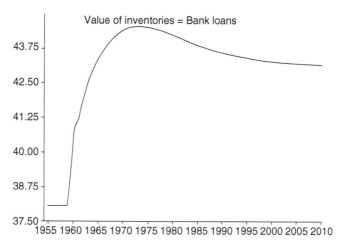

Figure 10.1A   Evolution of inventories (and hence bank loans), following an increase in the target inventories to sales ratio

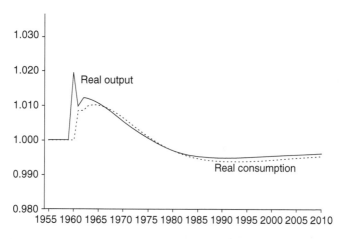

Figure 10.1B   Evolution of real output and real consumption, relative to their initial steady state values, following an increase in the target inventories to sales ratio

Next consider what happens to the balance sheet of households and banks. Figure 10.1C tracks the additions, relative to the original steady state, to the various components of household wealth immediately after the step increase in the target inventories to sales ratio that was imposed (in the 1960 period, as shown in the chart). This increase, as we saw in the previous figure, led to a brisk increase in output. As the addition to income was unexpected, no active portfolio choice is immediately made (in 1960) and consequently

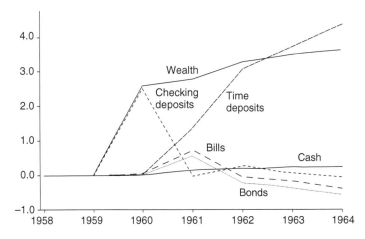

Figure 10.1C Evolution of household wealth and of its various components, relative to their initial steady state values, during the first periods that follow an increase in the target inventories to sales ratio

the entire accretion to wealth fetches up in the first period as an addition to holdings of checking bank deposits (non-interest bearing money). In the present instance, the notion of the initial rise in money being a response to an increase in the 'demand' for it is particularly wide of the mark; holdings of non-interest bearing money have gone up by default, because income recipients have been taken by surprise.

In the next period (in 1961), the process of active asset reallocation begins. There is a tiny addition to holdings of cash by households which is needed for transactions purposes. Besides this, there is, at least in 1961, an increase in the holdings of bills and bonds of households that echoes the increase in wealth. The most noticeable change is that of the interest-bearing money balances – the term deposits. It can be observed that there is a sharp rise in the term deposits held by households, to the point that by 1963, their increase even exceeds the increase in wealth, implying a decrease in the absolute amounts of checking deposits, bills and bonds held by households.[14] This new change in the structure of the household portfolio is due to the increase in the interest rate on term deposits, an increase illustrated in Figure 10.1D. But why does this rate increase?

[14] All these changes, besides those of the first period, are indicative of what could happen; their magnitude depends on the exact values taken by the portfolio parameters. For instance it could be that checking deposits remain above their starting value.

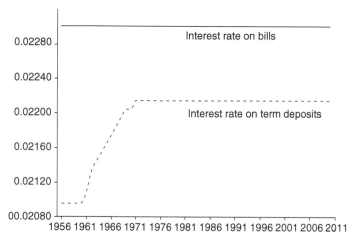

Figure 10.1D   Evolution of the interest rate on term deposits, following an increase in the target inventories to sales ratio

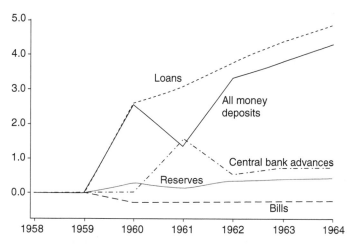

Figure 10.1E   Evolution of the various components of the balance sheet of commercial banks, relative to their initial steady state values, during the first periods that follow an increase in the target inventories to sales ratio

Figure 10.1E gives us clues as to why this could happen. The figure charts the changes, relative to the original steady state, of the various components of the balance sheet of banks. Loans, tracking inventories, briskly increase. The stock of money deposits, in the first period (1960), increases by the exact same amount, as the French circuitists and Basil Moore (1988) would argue. But in the second period (1961), households reallocate their newly acquired wealth and rectify their consumption behaviour in accordance with their higher incomes, thus getting rid of part of the newly acquired deposits, which do not keep up with the rising level of loans made to firms. The banks' compulsory reserves move upwards, in proportion to the overall amount of money deposits. Since banks only have a limited amount of bills to absorb these fluctuations in their balance sheet, they are forced to take advances from the central bank. This then induces banks to raise interest rates on term deposits, as was shown in Figure 10.1D, in an effort to attract depositors, so that money deposits catch up somewhat with bank loans.

Figure 10.1F shows that these actions initiated by banks will eventually be successful in reestablishing an acceptable bank liquidity ratio. As pointed out in the previous section, the notional bank liquidity ratio is the net amount of bills held by banks divided by the amount of banks' deposits. The net amount of bills is the actual amount held minus the value of the advances taken at the central bank. The large increase in loans granted by the banks is only partially absorbed by an increase in bank deposits, and as a result the net bank liquidity ratio drops below its minimum acceptable level – the bottom of the target range – as can be seen in Figure 10.1F. Advances from the central bank keep the actual or gross bank liquidity ratio at this minimum level. But with time, thanks to the higher deposit rates, plus the fact that inventories and hence loans drop back somewhat, banks manage to recover a net bank liquidity ratio which stands within the target range. This is when the interest rate on deposits becomes constant once again.

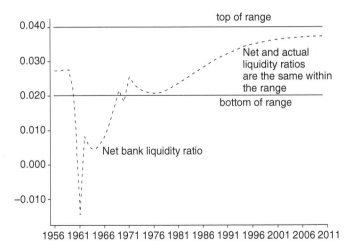

Figure 10.1F Evolution of the net bank liquidity ratio, relative to its target range, following an increase in the target inventories to sales ratio

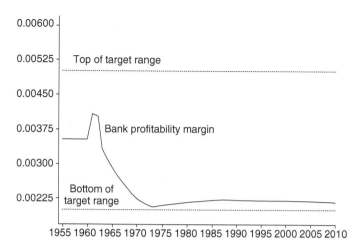

Figure 10.1G   Evolution of the bank profitability margin, relative to its target range, following an increase in the target inventories to sales ratio

We did not show the evolution of interest rates on loans, because the simulation did not induce any change in them. The cause of this is that, although the transformation of the balance sheet of banks has led to variations in the profits of banks, and in the new steady state to lower profits, mostly as a consequence of the higher interest rates on deposits, at no point did the bank profit margin fall below the minimally acceptable level. This is shown in Figure 10.1G. Of course, all of this is indicative. Had the premia on lending rates been any different, or had the profitability thresholds been any tighter, lending rates would have followed the upward movement of deposit rates.

In the new steady state, inventories, loans and deposit accounts are all higher than before. The stock of government securities is lower than before however. Total government debt has been reduced because, through most of the transition period, the government has been running a budget surplus, as shown in Figure 10.1H. With lower government debt, the steady-state flow of aggregate income, expenditure and output are all (very slightly) lower than before the shock, as illustrated in Figure 10.1B.

The central bank also has to adapt its balance sheet to the changing needs of the financial system, as well as the desires of portfolio holders and the public sector borrowing requirement. Figure 10.1I illustrates the evolution. By responding to the demands of the financial system, that is by allowing fluctuations in its holdings of Treasury bills, and also by granting advances to banks on demand, the monetary authorities are able to keep control over the bill rate (and, to a lesser degree, over all the other rates that move in sync with it), keeping it exactly at its target level.

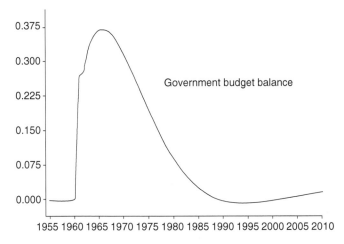

Figure 10.1H Evolution of the government budget balance, relative to its initial steady state value, following an increase in the target inventories to sales ratio

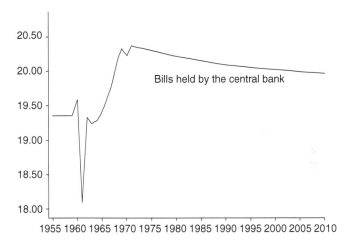

Figure 10.1I Evolution of the stock of Treasury bills held by the central bank, following an increase in the target inventories to sales ratio

In our model, notwithstanding that there is a fractional reserve rule in place, the entire chain of causality is reversed compared with the standard textbook neo-classical story. And although the supply of credit leads to an endogenous creation of money while the demand for money appears to be determined by a completely independent process, at no stage of the analysis can we say that there is an excessive supply of money. The reason for this is that we have formalized the existence of buffer mechanisms, which preclude the necessity of continuous equilibrium relationships.

10.7.3   Simulation 2: An increase in pure government expenditures

In our second simulation, we repeat an experiment that was made in our very first model, Model *SIM*. We suppose that the fiscal authorities decide to increase (permanently) pure real government expenditures g in a single step. The steady-state impact of such a change is quite obvious, if we look at the steady-state determinant of real output, as given by equation (10.89). Figure 10.2A shows the evolution of real (Haig–Simons) disposable income and that of real consumption. In the initial stages following the change, consumption lags behind disposable income, but then catches up and even goes beyond disposable income. As a result, real wealth increases in the early stages, but decreases in the later stages, where it converges towards real disposable income since we assumed a real wealth to real disposable income target ratio equal to unity. This cyclical behaviour, following an increase in government expenditures, is not a necessary feature of the model; running a similar model with different parameters yields a smooth convergence between real wealth and disposable income (Godley 1997). But Figure 10.2A shows that more complex models, compared to the simpler model of Chapter 3 for instance, where oscillations could not arise, can yield more complicated trajectories.

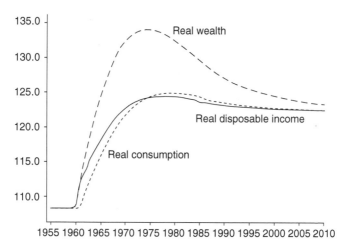

Figure 10.2A   Evolution of household real wealth, real disposable income and real consumption, following a one-step permanent increase in real government expenditures

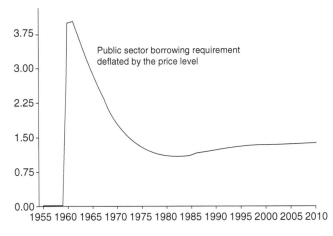

Figure 10.2B Evolution of the public sector borrowing requirement, deflated by the price level, following a one-step permanent increase in real government expenditures

In the stationary state, as discussed time and again, real consumption is equal to real (Haig–Simons) disposable income, and hence real household wealth is constant. In the stationary state, we would also expect the government budget balance to be zero. Figure 10.2B illustrates the evolution of the deflated value of the public sector borrowing requirement $(PSBR/p)$. As one would expect, the more expansionary fiscal stance initially generates a large budget deficit, with the government being forced to borrow.[15] The chart however indicates that the borrowing requirement in real dollars converges to a positive number in the stationary state. Isn't there a contradiction with everything we have claimed in the previous chapters and in equation (10.87)? In the stationary state, when the wealth of the private sector is constant, shouldn't the public debt be constant as well?

What happens is that the *INSOUT* model entertains an inflation mechanism, found in equations (10.84) and (10.85). In the base stationary state, the inflation rate has been set at zero. However, the larger real government expenditures generate higher outputs and higher levels of employment. These in turn generate higher rates of inflation, which mimic the higher output, as shown in Figure 10.2C. Inflation however modifies public sector accounting since inflation erodes public debt. Inflation reduces real debt, where real debt is nominal debt deflated by current prices. One must thus make a distinction

---

[15] The *fiscal stance*, as it was already defined in Chapter 3, is the ratio of overall government expenditures to the share of tax revenues in national income (the average tax rate).

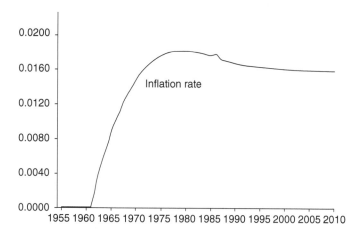

Figure 10.2C Evolution the price inflation rate, following a one-step permanent increase in real government expenditures

between nominal and real debt, and between a nominal and a real budget balance. A stationary state with permanent inflation implies a constant stock of real debt, and hence a zero real budget balance, but a nominal budget deficit. This is the exact counterpart of the situation of households, who, because they hold assets that are being eroded by inflation, must have zero real saving in the stationary state, but a positive nominal amount of saving to keep their real wealth intact. While the government is running a nominal budget deficit, either measured in current dollars (*PSBR*) or measured in deflated dollars (*PSBR/p*), its real budget stance must take inflation gains on debt into consideration. Thus the real government budget balance is given by:

$$\frac{-PSBR + (\Delta p) \cdot (B_{s-1} + BL_{s-1} \cdot p_{bL-1})}{p}$$

When the government balance is measured in this manner, as shown in Figure 10.2D, it does indeed converge towards zero as the economy approaches the steady state. This implies that the real debt of government, is constant. Indeed, when we check the evolution of the public debt to GDP ratio in this closed economy, looking at Figure 10.2E, we observe that the discretionary increase in government expenditures has led to a temporary increase in the public debt to GDP ratio, but that this ratio is driven back to its original level when all the dynamic effects of this change have run their course, when the economy reaches the new stationary state. Still, output, income, consumption and employment all stand at a higher level in this new stationary state. And of course, so do the stocks of loans, money and securities.

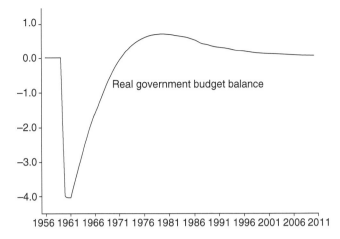

Figure 10.2D Evolution of the real government budget balance, taking into account the capital gains due to the erosion of the public debt by price inflation, following a one-step permanent increase in real government expenditures

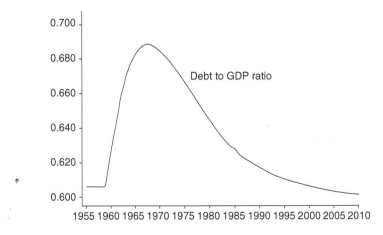

Figure 10.2E Evolution of the debt to GDP ratio, following a one-step permanent increase in real government expenditures

As in the previous experiment, we can look at the consequences of the higher activity and the larger financial stocks on interest rates and on the profitability of banks. Figure 10.2F shows the evolution of the main interest rates. Initially, there is a drop in inventories and hence in bank loans, as firms get surprised by the amplitude of aggregate demand, caused by the brisk increase in government expenditures. One period later, as firms react

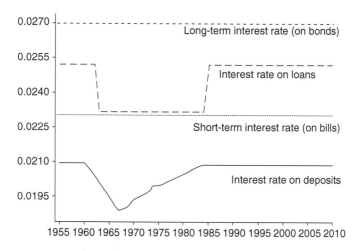

Figure 10.2F Evolution of interest rates on bank loans and term deposits, relative to short and long-term rates on government securities, following a one-step permanent increase in real government expenditures

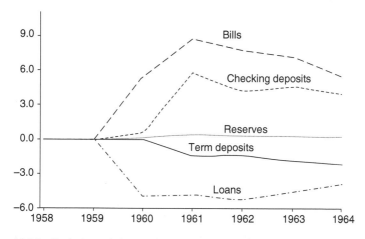

Figure 10.2G Evolution of the various components of the balance sheet of private banks, relative to their initial steady state values, during the first periods that follow an increase in the real government expenditures

to this drop in inventories by jacking up production, households are also taken by surprise, as their actual income turns out to be much greater than their expected income, leading to a substantial increase in checking deposits. Both of these effects, shown in Figure 10.2G, drive up the bank liquidity ratio beyond the top of its target range as illustrated in Figure 10.2H, thus

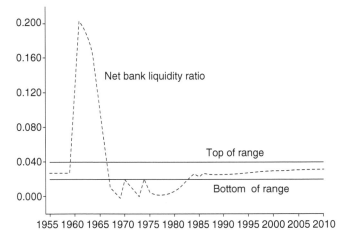

Figure 10.2H Evolution of the net bank liquidity ratio, relative to its target range, following a one-step permanent increase in real government expenditures

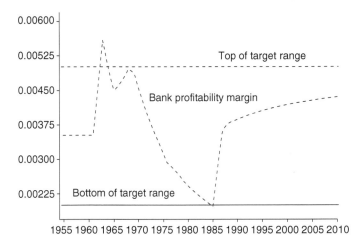

Figure 10.2I Evolution of the bank profitability margin, relative to its target range, following a one-step permanent increase in real government expenditures

inducing reductions in the interest rate on term deposits. In the meantime, as a consequence of the changes in the composition of bank balance sheets, and also as a result of the lower deposit rates, bank profitability also shoots up, beyond the top of its target range (Figure 10.2I). This drives down interest rates on loans. Eventually, as expectations adapt to actual conditions, and as the government deficit vanishes, both deposit rates and lending rates are driven back to their original steady-state levels, and banks are even driven to the discount window, being forced to take advances from the central bank on occasion (on Figure 10.2H the net bank liquidity ratio drops below the bottom of the target range, implying that banks borrow from the central bank to keep the actual bank liquidity ratio at its minimal level).

It is interesting to note that, in the new steady state, with higher activity and higher loans and money stocks, both in nominal and in real terms, interest rates are no higher than they were in the starting steady state. This occurs even though we have assumed that banks are concerned by the levels of their bills to money ratio – the net bank liquidity ratio. This goes against the claim, made by proponents of structural endogeneity such as Chick and Dow (2002) or Wray (1990), that an economy in a boom or with higher activity ought to be associated with higher interest rates since the bank liquidity ratio of banks would need to be lower. Things are much more complex in a fully consistent model which has several interdependencies that cannot always be fully appreciated within the context of a partial analysis. A fortiori, in a world where banks would be little concerned by such a ratio, as some horizontalist authors like John Smithin or Le Bourva (1992) would put it, there is little evidence that interest rates ought to rise. In fact, as we can see from Figure 10.2F, despite the huge increase in government debt, the central bank and the government have no difficulty in keeping the bill rate and the bond rate at the constant level of their choice. But this requires, as can be seen in Figure 10.2J, that the central bank accept wide variations in the composition of its

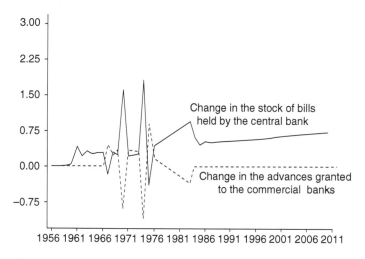

Figure 10.2J Period-by-period changes in the stock of Treasury bills held by the central bank and in the advances granted to commercial banks, following a one-step permanent increase in real government expenditures

balance sheet, so as to accommodate changes in the demand for reserves and in the demand for bills, and granting advances to commercial banks on demand.

10.7.4 Simulation 3: An increase in the compulsory reserve ratios

In our third experiment, the banks' statutory reserve requirement is assumed to rise from 10% to 20%, for both checking and term deposits. It would appear that, according to the ubiquitous 'money multiplier' model, such a change should cut the 'money supply' in half. Our view is that nothing remotely like that could possibly happen.

Figure 10.3A shows changes, compared with what would otherwise have happened, in the banks' balance sheet in the periods immediately following the postulated change. According to our model, the immediate consequence of raising the reserve requirement is that reserves themselves do all the adjusting. In advance of any change in interest rates, households have no motive to change any of their asset holdings and firms have no motive to cut their borrowing. So the instantaneous counterpart of the change in the reserve requirement is a 100% increase in reserves. This should be accompanied by an equivalent fall, measured in dollars, in the net stock of bills held by banks. However, as can be seen in Figure 10.3A, advances from the central bank play the main buffer role in the first period (1960) and in the following two periods. In the system as configured here, banks are initially forced to borrow

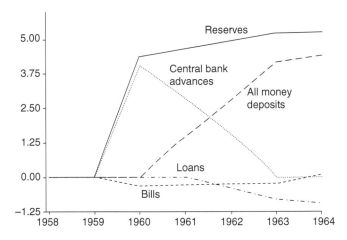

Figure 10.3A Evolution of the various components of the balance sheet of commercial banks, relative to their initial steady state values, during the first periods that follow an increase in the compulsory reserve ratios

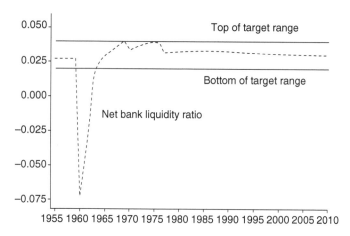

Figure 10.3B Evolution of the net bank liquidity ratio, following an increase in the compulsory reserve ratios

most of the newly required reserves. Instead of depleting their stock of Treasury bills, commercial banks prefer to take advances from the central bank.

In the second period (1961), banks having seen their bank liquidity ratio fall below the bottom of its target range, as shown in Figure 10.3B, they will raise their interest rate on deposits, in an effort to attract more household term deposits and restore their bank liquidity ratio. The consequence of this, as can be seen in Figure 10.3A, is that the stock of money deposits – including both checking and term deposits – increases instead of briskly decreasing, in contrast to the traditional money multiplier story. This will lead to a further increase in the amount of reserves, since compulsory reserves are a fraction of money deposits.

Furthermore, Figure 10.3A also shows that there is a small drop in the amount of loans. This can be attributed to the increase of the interest rate on loans, in the third period, as shown in Figure 10.3C. This increase in lending rates leads to a reduced target inventories to sales ratio, which induces a reduction in inventories and hence in bank loans needed by firms. This increase in the lending rate is due to the fall in the bank profitability margin, as shown in Figure 10.3D, that has been induced by the large unfavourable changes in the structure of the balance sheet of the banks, imposed by the more severe compulsory reserve requirements. In addition, bank profits get hurt by the higher deposit rates needed to reestablish an adequate net bank liquidity ratio. As bank profits get mauled, banks need to raise lending rates to get the bank profitability margin back to its target range.

In the new stationary state, as there has been a switch from government securities to money deposits, there will actually be more money in existence

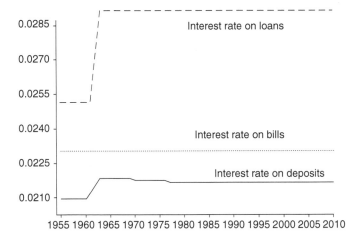

Figure 10.3C Evolution of the interest rate on deposits and the interest rate on loans, for a given interest rate on bills, following an increase in the compulsory reserve ratios

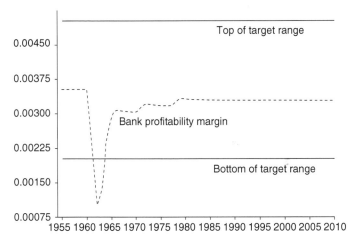

Figure 10.3D Evolution of the bank profitability margin, following an increase in the compulsory reserve ratios

as a result of the whole operation than there would have been without it! This can be seen in Figure 10.3E. Although the stock of money deposits gets somewhat reduced, as firms reduce the size of their inventories, the new steady-state stock of money deposits remains higher than in the original steady state. The higher compulsory reserve ratio has had no negative impact on the stock of money, and no impact to speak of on real output. Its only

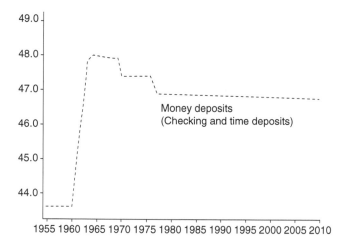

Figure 10.3E   Evolution of the stock of money deposits, following an increase in the compulsory reserve ratios

noticeable impact, as observed in Figure 10.3B, is a larger spread between deposit rates and lending rates. The compulsory reserve requirements on bank deposits act as a tax, which banks pass on to borrowers, as banks retain their profitability by raising lending rates when the compulsory reserve ratio is hiked up by the monetary authorities.

10.7.5   Simulation 4: An increase in the acceptable bank liquidity ratio

Our fourth experiment describes what happens when banks turn out to show a higher preference for liquidity. What will be the consequences of banks targeting a higher bank liquidity ratio? What if banks wish to hold a safer portfolio? Recall that the bank liquidity ratio is the ratio of bills to deposits, or, as an approximation, the ratio of bills to total liabilities. Since total liabilities must be equal to total assets, this implies that banks wish to hold a larger proportion of their assets in the form of bills. In other words, it means that banks wish to hold more bills relative to loans than they held before.[16] In terms of equations (10.75) and (10.76), this means that banks set the *bot* and

---

[16] This hopefully answers some of the queries made by some authors such as Sheila Dow (1997: 66) and Jörg Bibow (2000). They insist that banks show some liquidity preference. This can either mean that banks wish to modify the 'disposition of the asset side of the bank's balance sheet' (Dow 1997: 66), substituting government securities in place of loans to the private sector, or it could imply that banks wish to change the size of their balance sheet altogether. Here we illustrate the case where an increased bank liquidity preference can be tied to bigger balance sheets.

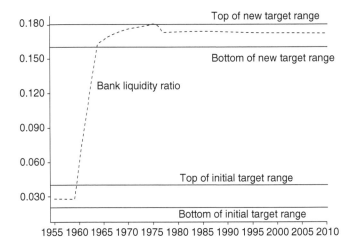

Figure 10.4A Evolution of the bank liquidity ratio, following an increase in the liquidity preference of banks, proxied by an upward shift of the liquidity ratio target range

the *top* parameters to higher levels – in other words the bottom and top of the target range of the bank liquidity ratio are set at a higher level.

Now that we understand the structure of the model, we can guess at least some of the consequences of such a change in the liquidity preference of banks. Since banks wish to hold a larger proportion of bills among their assets, as shown in Figure 10.4A, they will have to increase interest rates on money deposits relative to those on bills to induce households to relinguish the bills that banks desire to acquire. The consequences on interest rates are pretty straight-forward. Despite a constant bill rate, still set by the central bank, the deposit rate rises. If this increase is large enough, and if the required changes in the balance sheet of banks is important enough, the higher bank liquidity ratio targets will draw the bank profitability margin below its target range, and as a consequence the lending rates will also be raised, as is the case in Figure 10.4B, so that the bank profitability margin comes back towards its target range, as shown in Figure 10.4C. Thus, higher bank liquidity preference will mean both a higher bank liquidity ratio and higher deposit and lending rates relative to the bill rate.

In our model, it is assumed that when banks do decide to raise the minimum acceptable bill to deposit ratio, this minimum ratio will be achieved regardless of what needs to be done to achieve it. In the present case, as shown in Figure 10.4D, banks will even take advances from the central bank to modify the composition of their assets. Generally speaking, the attempt by banks to increase their target liquidity ratio will induce an increase in the size of their balance sheet, as either larger central bank advances or money

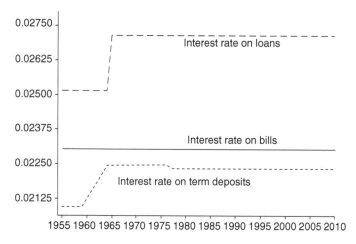

Figure 10.4B Evolution of the interest rates on deposits and loans, following an increase in the liquidity preference of banks, proxied by an upward shift of the liquidity ratio target range

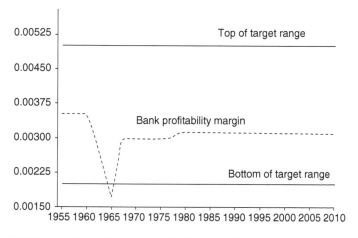

Figure 10.4C Evolution of the bank profitability margin, following an increase in the liquidity preference of banks, proxied by an upward shift of the liquidity ratio target range

deposits will accompany the larger amounts of Treasury bills held by private banks. Loans, which are a systemic requirement, cannot be called back or cut down at the initiative of the banks; indeed, when they do diminish at a later stage, as shown in Figure 10.4D, it is as a result of the negative impact of lending rates on the inventories to sales ratio.

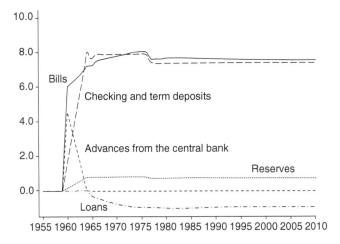

Figure 10.4D Evolution of the various components of the balance sheet of commercial banks, relative to their initial steady state values, following an increase in the liquidity preference of banks, proxied by an upward shift of the liquidity ratio target range

10.7.6 Simulation 5: A decrease in the propensity to consume out of real disposable regular income

We now repeat an experiment which we did on a number of occasions in previous chapters. We assume that some campaign in favour of thriftiness has been successful, and that the propensity to consume out of expected real disposable regular income suddenly drops down permanently in a step (this is the parameter α_1 in equation 10.29). It turns out that the results that we obtained in smaller and simpler models, notably in Chapter 4 and 5, still hold up with the more complete model – the *INSOUT* model. We had already observed with the help of Figure 5.10 that a decrease in the propensity to consume out of income initially leads to a fall in output and disposable income, as Keynesians would expect, but in the long run, when comparing steady states, this change leads to higher output and disposable income, provided no other parameter changes. Figure 10.5A, which illustrates the discrepancy between real disposable income and consumption, and thus the positive change in households' wealth, is very similar to Figure 5.10, despite the fact that the *INSOUT* model takes into account a much more complex private sector. As a counterpart to the rising household wealth, the short-run slowdown in economic activity provoked by reduced consumption generates a deficit in the government budget balance (see Figure 10.5B). This enlarges the size of the public debt and that of the interest payments on public debt, thus leading ultimately, in the long run, to an increase in economic activity,

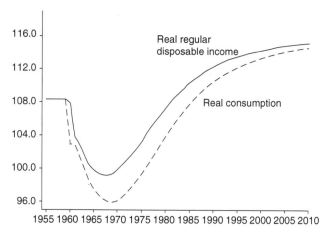

Figure 10.5A   Evolution of real regular disposable income and of real consumption, following a decrease in the propensity to consume out of (expected) real regular disposable income

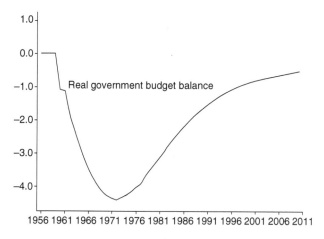

Figure 10.5B   Evolution of the real government budget balance, following a decrease in the propensity to consume out of (expected) real regular disposable income

as per equation (10.89).[17] Whether there are no private banks and no private investment, as in Chapters 4 and 5, or whether these exist as in the current model, does not alter this fundamental principle arising from the requirements of stock-flow consistency.

---

[17] Equation (10.98) will demonstrate this more formally.

10.7.7 Simulation 6: An exogenous increase in the rate of inflation

In this last simulation, we reproduce an experiment that we carried out in Chapter 9. Once again we impose a one-time increase in the autonomous term Ω_0 in the target real wage equation (10.84). As a consequence, although nothing else has changed, workers ask for higher nominal wages, and this translates after some adjustment into permanent cost and price inflation. The results that we obtain in the current chapter, with a more complete *INSOUT* model that incorporates a government sector, are however quite different from those that were obtained with the Chapter 9 *DISINF* model where the government sector was simply assumed away. In Chapter 9, persistent inflation had either a *positive* effect on the stationary level of real income if households were blind to the capital losses inflicted by inflation, or *no effect at all* if households were aware of these losses. In the *INSOUT* model with the government sector, where it is assumed that households are fully aware of inflation losses, persistent inflation is likely to have *no effect* or a *negative* impact on the stationary level of real income. The explanations of why this new result emerges will give us another opportunity to check the evolution of the real government budget balance, which we briefly discussed in subsection 10.7.3.

Figure 10.6A shows the boost in the rate of price inflation generated by the higher target real wage rate. Figure 10.6B shows that the higher inflation rate generates a lower stationary real national income. This is accompanied, as illustrated in Figure 10.6C, by a government budget deficit that exists even

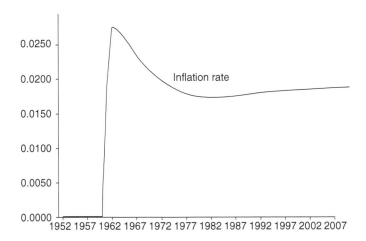

Figure 10.6A Evolution of the rate of price inflation, following a one-step increase in the target real wage rate

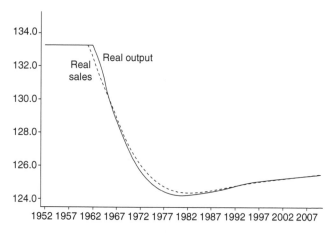

Figure 10.6B   Evolution of real sales and real output following a one-step increase in the target real wage that generates an increase in the rate of inflation

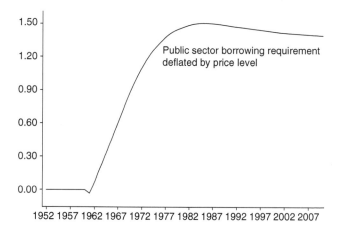

Figure 10.6C   Evolution of the public sector borrowing requirement, deflated by the price level, following a one-step increase in the target real wage that generates an increase in the rate of inflation

in the stationary state. But Figure 10.6D demonstrates that this is a *nominal* budget deficit, and that when the budget balance is measured in the appropriate way, by taking into account the inflation gains on the existing stock of debt, the real budget stance does converge towards zero. In other words, in the stationary state, where the real wealth of households remains constant, the real debt of the government also remains constant, meaning that the *real* deficit, net of the inflation capital gains on the existing debt, is zero.

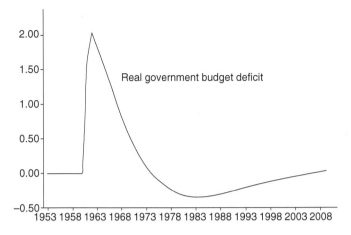

Figure 10.6D Evolution of the real government budget deficit, taking into account the capital gains due to the erosion of the public debt by price inflation, following a one-step increase in the target real wage that generates an increase in the rate of inflation

As we have seen in the earlier chapters which were based on state money, the stationary state in a closed economy is achieved when the financial position of the public sector is such that the public sector does not create new liabilities any more. Thus the stationary state is achieved when the public sector is in balance. In a world without inflation, this meant that the government sector ran no budget deficit (nor a surplus), and hence that government expenditures, including interest payments, were equal to its revenues (mainly taxes).

In a world with inflation, things are slightly more complicated, since inflation erodes the burden of a given stock of public debt. In other words, inflation reduces real debt, where real debt is nominal debt deflated by current prices. One must thus make a distinction between nominal and real debt, and between a nominal and a real budget balance. A stationary state with permanent inflation implies a constant stock of real debt, and hence a zero real budget balance, but a nominal budget deficit. This is the exact counterpart of the situation of households, who, because they hold assets that are being eroded by inflation, must have zero real saving in the stationary state, but a positive nominal amount of saving to keep their real wealth intact.

10.7.8 The steady state with price inflation

Let us derive once more the stationary value of real output (as was done in equation 10.89), but this time by taking into account the possibility of price inflation. Let us start from an identity arising from the balance sheet of Table 10.1. Reading off from the 'Balance' line, we see that:

$$V = GD + IN \tag{10.90}$$

which says that nominal household wealth has two counterparts, nominal government debt *GD* and nominal private debt, *IN*, which is the value of inventories that firms must carry as debt in the form of bank loans. This of course also implies that the value of public debt is exactly equal to the amount of household wealth, from which we must subtract the value of the inventories of firms:

$$GD = V - IN \tag{10.90A}$$

The same equation can be rewritten in differences:

$$\Delta GD = \Delta V - \Delta IN \tag{10.91}$$

Assuming away capital gains or losses arising from changes in interest rates, as in any event we shall concern ourselves with the steady-state solution where such changes will be excluded, the change in nominal government debt can be written as:

$$\Delta GD = G + \check{r} \cdot GD - T = G + \check{r} \cdot (V - IN) - T \tag{10.92}$$

where $\check{r}$, as in Chapter 4, is the average interest rate on government debt.

Making use again of the Ostergaard formula, the changes in wealth and in inventories, once again assuming away capital gains or losses arising from changing interest rates, can be written as:

$$\Delta V = p \cdot \Delta v + \Delta p \cdot v_{-1} \tag{10.93}$$

$$\Delta IN = UC \cdot \Delta in + \Delta UC \cdot in_{-1} \tag{10.94}$$

Focussing on the stationary state, we know that in such a state real wealth and real inventories remain constant, so that $\Delta v = \Delta in = 0$.

Applying this condition to equations (10.93) and (10.94), making use of equation (10.92), and using real variables times their price, equation (10.91) can be rewritten as:

$$g \cdot p + \check{r} \cdot p \left[v - in \cdot \left(\frac{UC}{p} \right) \right] - T = \Delta p \cdot v - \Delta UC \cdot in \tag{10.95}$$

or better still, by moving taxes on the right-hand side, dividing by *p*, and taking note that in the steady-state $\Delta p/p = \Delta UC/UC$, we obtain:

$$g + \check{r} \left[v - in \cdot \left(\frac{UC}{p} \right) \right] - \left(\frac{\Delta p}{p} \right) \left[v - in \cdot \left(\frac{UC}{p} \right) \right] = \frac{T}{p} \tag{10.96}$$

This equation demonstrates that, once the stationary state has been reached, the overall level of tax revenues (in real terms) will be equal to real government expenditures, including debt servicing, minus the inflation gain on government debt.[18] With inflation, *ceteris paribus*, the *real* fiscal stance gets reduced, since 'the government receives an inflation gain on its debt which makes the inflation-adjusted government deficit smaller than its cash deficit' (Godley and Cripps 1983: 244). In other words, the government share of *real* national income exceeds the tax revenues, because of the inflation gain (or alternatively real outlays are diminished by the inflation gain). This explains why the public sector borrowing requirement (*PSBR*) is positive (there is a nominal government deficit, as expenditures exceed tax revenues) once a stationary state with positive price inflation is reached, as was the case in Figures 10.2B and 10.6B. As pointed out by Godley and Cripps (1983: 245), 'what emerges is that the faster the rate of inflation the larger the government's cash deficit must be in order to keep real debt constant'. In the new stationary state, the higher the rate of inflation, the larger is the discrepancy between deflated government expenditures and deflated government revenues, that is the larger the apparent deflated deficit.

But now we are in a position to find the stationary level of real output because we know that in the stationary state, $s^* = y^*$ and $c^* = yd_r^* = yd_{hs}^*$. Furthermore, we know that:

$$T = s \cdot p \cdot \frac{\tau}{(1 + \tau)} \tag{10.88}$$

$$in^* = \sigma^T \cdot s^* \tag{10.6A}$$

$$v^* = \alpha_3 \cdot yd_r^* \tag{10.97}$$

$$s = c + g \tag{10.13}$$

Using the four above equations, from equation (10.96) we derive the stationary level of real output of Model *INSOUT* when taking into account price inflation. This long-run equilibrium level of income is:

$$y^* = \frac{g - \alpha_3 \cdot (\breve{r} - \text{n})}{\left[\dfrac{\tau}{1 + \tau}\right] - \left[\alpha_3 - \sigma^T \cdot \left(\dfrac{UC}{p}\right)\right](\breve{r} - \text{n})} \tag{10.98}$$

where $\text{n} = \Delta p/p$, as defined in Chapter 9.[19]

---

[18] 'The government's real fiscal stance may be defined, by analogy with the money fiscal stance, as the ratio of real government spending ... to the government's share of *real* national income. This differs from the money fiscal stance not only because spending is measured in real rather than in money terms but also because the government's share of real income includes the inflation gain mentioned above which is ignored in the money accounts' (Godley and Cripps 1983: 244).

[19] It is also possible to calculate the stationary government debt to real GDP ratio, which we may wish to call gd^*/y^*, where gd is the real government debt, by recalling

The possible long-run implications of price inflation are now clear.[20] Taking the partial derivatives, we find:

$$\frac{dy^*}{d\mathfrak{n}} < 0$$

and

$$\frac{dy_*}{d\check{r}} > 0$$

Suppose we move from a stationary equilibrium with no inflation ($\pi = \mathfrak{n} = 0$) to a new stationary equilibrium with inflation. If there is no change in the nominal rate of interest (and no change in the distribution of public debt), then $\check{r}$ remains at its initial value, and inflation then generates a decrease in the stationary level of real output, and hence a fall in real income and employment.[21]

The cause of this fall is that real government expenditures, when netting out the capital gains that have occurred on the public debt because of inflation, have decreased, thus leading to a fall in the multiplicand of the multiplier process. To avoid such a decrease in the multiplicand, the alternative is for the government to increase its expenditures on debt servicing. Indeed, we can see from equation (10.98) that provided that $\Delta(\check{r} - \mathfrak{n})$ is zero, that is provided the increase in the average interest rate $\check{r}$ is equal to the inflation proxy value $\mathfrak{n}$, *and also provided there is no change in real pure government expenditures g*, inflation will generate no change in the long-run value of real output.[22] In this case, an inflation-neutral fiscal stance could

---

that $gd = v - in \cdot (UC/p)$, and making use of the stationary values and equations (10.12) and (10.97). We obtain that:

$$gd^* = \alpha_3(y^* - g) - in^* \cdot (UC/p)$$

while the gd^*/y^* expression can be obtained by substituting the value of y^* from equation (10.98).

[20] And so of course are the implications of changes in the other parameters of equation (10.98). An increase in the target inventories to sales ratio σ^T leads to a lower long-run real output, as long as $(\check{r} - \mathfrak{n}) > 0$, which is what we assumed in our first experiment. Also an increase in the target wealth to regular disposable income ratio α_3 leads to a higher long-run real output, as was observed in Figure 10.1B and 10.5A, also as long as $(\check{r} - \mathfrak{n}) > 0$.

[21] There will be a small second-order change in the UC/p ratio. See Chapter 8.

[22] Here we thus recover the result that was achieved in Model *DISINF* of Chapter 9, which did not include a government sector. It should be recalled that consumption equation (10.29), based on the definition of real regular disposable income (equation 10.26), assumes that households are fully aware of inflation losses. If, as

be achieved.[23] 'Provided the real interest rate is maintained ... this happens automatically through the variation in nominal interest payments' (Godley and Cripps 1983: 245).

While an inflation-neutral fiscal stance seems something that could easily be achieved by governments, especially now with modern central banks being keen on increasing nominal interest rates in line with inflation rates, so that real interest rates and the expression $(\check{r} - \Pi)$ would remain approximately unchanged, reality is often otherwise, at least judging by the experience of the 1970s. One important cause for this is the fact that the increase in nominal interest rates will generate a slowdown of the economy during the transition to the new steady state. The higher interest rates imply a fall in the prices of long-term bonds, and hence inflict large capital losses to the bond holders. As a result household real consumption will drop and the economy will slow down. In the *INSOUT* model, in addition, the target inventories to sales ratio is sensitive to the value taken by the nominal interest rate, so that higher interest rates will also induce a reduction in planned investment in inventories, and hence a further reduction in short-run output.

All these effects are illustrated in Figures 10.7, which reproduce the impact on Model *INSOUT* of an autonomous increase in the rate of inflation, as was shown in Figures 10.6, but this time under the assumption that both the short-term and the long-term interest rates are increased approximately in line with the increase in inflation. Figure 10.7A tracks the short-run drop in real sales and their long-run recovery towards the initial steady-state level. Figure 10.7B shows the evolution of the real wealth of households and the government stock of real debt, both of which diminish considerably in the short run following the increase in long-term interest rates. Finally, Figure 10.7C shows the deflated government budget balance, adjusted and unadjusted for inflation gains. In the short run, the former moves into a surplus position while the latter goes into an apparent deficit.

As a result of the slowdown, the nominal government deficit will be even higher than it would be in its steady state with inflation, and this may induce the government to take restrictive fiscal measures, raising tax rates or reducing pure real government expenditures. As pointed out by Godley and Cripps (1983: 245, 247), 'the increased cash deficit required in the presence of inflation are regarded with suspicion by adherents of the "balanced budget" ... . The *real* fiscal stance may tighten in response to inflation, while the cash

---

in Chapter 9, we assume that households are blind to inflation losses, it is as if the α_3 parameter were revised upwards. The revised α_3 parameter takes the value: $\alpha_3/(1 - (\alpha_1/\alpha_2) \cdot \Pi)$. In this case inflation would have a positive impact on the long-run level of real output.

[23] However there will be a small second-order effect on σ^T, since the value of this parameter will be pushed down by the higher nominal interest rate. See equation (10.7).

372

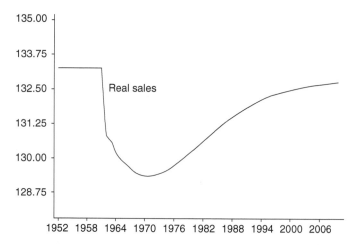

Figure 10.7A Evolution of real sales and real output following a one-step increase in the target real wage that generates an increase in the rate of inflation, accompanied by an increase in nominal interest rates that approximately compensates for the increase in inflation

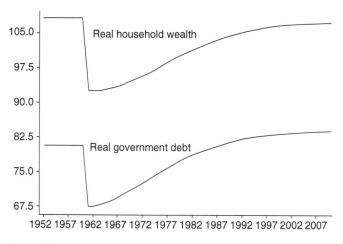

Figure 10.7B Evolution of real household debt and real government debt following a one-step increase in the target real wage that generates an increase in the rate of inflation, accompanied by an increase in nominal interest rates that approximately compensates for the increase in inflation

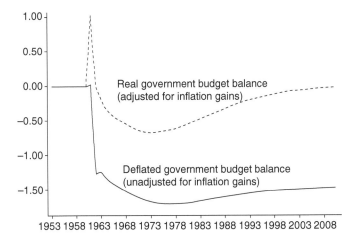

Figure 10.7C Evolution of the deflated government budget balance, adjusted and unadjusted for inflation gains, following a one-step increase in the target real wage that generates an increase in the rate of inflation, accompanied by an increase in nominal interest rates that approximately compensates for the increase in inflation

deficit expands'. This we believe is what happened in a large number of countries in the 1970s and early 1980s, and it may have contributed to the appearance of stagflation.

With the growth of nominal deficits and nominal debt, governments decided to reduce their operating expenditures, reducing health and education services, in an effort to control what seemed like an uncontrollable expansion of debt ratios. Thus, while in the mid 1970s real interest rates fell, thus reducing the contribution of the government sector to effective demand, thereafter it was the reductions in *g* that directly weakened the contribution of the public sector to real demand.

Governments were thus caught in a Catch-22 situation. With rising inflation rates and no increase in nominal interest rates, the real fiscal stance becomes more restrictive on its own, and this drives down the long-run real output level. If governments do raise nominal interest rates in line with inflation rates, a neutral real fiscal stance can be achieved, so there is no decrease in the long-run output level, but the higher interest rates will generate large capital losses on long-term bonds which, in the short run, will cause an economic recession and large government deficits. The only way out is for the government to increase its operating expenditures in real terms, but this is unlikely in a situation where nominal government deficits are already rising.

10.8 Conclusion

We have gone a long way with the introduction of realistic banks which make decisions. But the model still lacks some key features of the real world. For instance, in the *INSOUT* model producing firms and banks distribute all of profits and have no retained earnings. In addition, the stock market with its equities and speculators has been left out. These important features of the real world are introduced in the growth model of the next chapter, since retained earnings, for instance, are a major characteristic of a growing corporate economy.

Appendix 10.1: Overdraft banking systems

Anglo–saxon textbooks typically describe what we can be called *asset-based* financial systems, which are characterized by a large government debt, some of which is held by all sectors of the economy. Adjustments in the liquidity of both firms and banks is done, or is presumed to be done, through changes in the assets, namely changes in the holdings of government bills. This is said, probably rightly so, to characterize financial systems of the Anglo–Saxon world.

As was pointed out in Chapter 2 however, most countries fail to have asset-based adjustment mechanisms. Both firms and banks adjust their liquidity position by changes on their liability side. Indeed, even Anglo-Saxon financial systems have experienced such a kind of adjustment over the last twenty or thirty years, and indeed such a phenomenon has been called *liability management*. Now it should be noted that liability management has always been pursued by large New York banks, which are indebted towards the rest of the American banking systems. Most of the adjustment in their liquidity position is done by varying the size of their advances that they borrow from the rest of the financial system. These banks only keep a minimum amount of Treasury bills – the minimum required to conduct their clearing operations safely. Other countries also experience this division in bank tasks: some banks seem to specialize in collecting deposits, and carry large amounts of bills, thus adjusting their liquidity position on the asset side; other banks specialize in making loans, are largely in debt *vis-à-vis* other banks, and adjust their liquidity position on the liability side, by discharging debt or adding debt. Because the banking sector is represented by a single homogeneous sector, we cannot model this institutional distinction within our framework.

There are also countries where the entire banking system is structurally in debt *vis-à-vis* the central bank. These banking systems are the so-called *overdraft* systems. In these overdraft systems, banks carry no bills, or no bills in excess of the amounts required to operate safely and conveniently within the bank payments clearing system.[24] Since bills cannot be used as a buffer, the entire adjustment mechanism relies on liability management, whereas private banks obtain *advances* from the central

---

[24] Indeed, large value payment clearing systems, which operate in real time, instead of clearing on the books of the central bank at the end of the day, require the possession of these Treasury bills as a guarantee for the finality of the payment. Indeed such use of Treasury bills has generated the generalization of the use of *repos*,

bank. For instance, if households decide to reduce their bank deposits in exchange for cash money, without any change in loans, private banks obtain the additional cash money that households long for by borrowing it from the central bank. In that case, the advances of the central bank to the commercial banking system increase. Most countries of the world, including a large number of European countries, have their banking system in an overdraft position.

In our *INSOUT* model we have taken the decision to describe a banking system that has some functions of both financial systems – the asset-based and the overdraft financial system.[25] We have assumed that banks in the short-run are free to get advances from the central bank, paying no specific penalty relative to short-term assets of similar duration, hence describing features of overdraft economies. But we have also assumed that banks desire to hold a certain proportion of their assets in the form of Treasury bills, and that in the long run they will act in such a manner that this proportion will be achieved without being structurally indebted to the central bank, thus describing features that are more pertinent to the asset-based system. It is our belief that, with globalization and the new operating procedures followed by a large number of central banks, financial systems are gradually moving towards this hybrid structure, and hence that the reaction rules that we attribute to central banks and private banks go a long way towards describing actual processes.

The modelling of the pure asset-based system is to be found in Godley (1999a). Zezza and Dos Santos (2004) take on the case of the pure overdraft system, where banks hold no bills whatsoever. Within this framework, it is possible to see how deposit rates would evolve endogenously. We could assume that private banks in a pure overdraft system keep a check on a *bank liquidity pressure ratio – BLPR*. This variable would be the ratio of the funds that banks have borrowed from the central bank to the sum of the deposits being held in banks. The higher the liquidity pressure ratio, the more banks must rely on the funds borrowed from the central bank. In general we would expect the central bank rate on advances r_a to be higher than the rate of interest r_m paid on time deposits of households. Hence, if banks are to hold on to their profits, there is an inducement for them to raise the rate of interest on time deposits whenever the bank liquidity pressure ratio exceeds what is considered to be its normal range.

This procedure should help to bring the ratio back to its normal range. The mechanism that leads to such a result is the following. By raising the interest rate on time deposits, banks induce households to switch from checking deposits to time deposits, thus reducing the overall amount of compulsory reserve requirements, and hence reducing the demand of banks for high-powered money as long as the reserve requirements on time deposits are less stringent than those on checking deposits. In addition, the increase in the rate on time deposits induces households to sell their bills and to acquire time deposits instead. This, by virtue of the balance-sheet constraint of banks, allows them to reduce their advances from the central bank, thus bringing the bank liquidity pressure ratio back towards its normal range.

whereby Treasury bills are sold with a promise to repurchase them back within 24 or 48 hours. Thus, in fact, Treasury bills are lent for a day or two.

[25] See Levy-Garboua and Maarek (1978) for a more traditional formalization of an overdraft financial system.

Appendix 10.2: Arithmetical example of a change in portfolio preference

It may help readers if we provide an arithmetical example of the interdependencies that occur when there is a change in the portfolio preferences of households. This will also help us to understand the *quadruple entry system* advocated by Copeland (1949), as discussed in Chapter 2. Start by assuming that for some reason, everything else being held constant, households decide to hold $100 more in the form of money, splitting this into a $90 increase in bank deposits (denoted [1] in Table A10.1, which is a simplified balance sheet matrix of model *INSOUT*) and a $10 increase in cash (denoted [2]). This implies that households have reduced their holding of government securities, and we will assume here that households sold $80 worth of bills [3] and $20 worth of long-term bonds [4].

If this happens, there have to be no less than seven simultaneous changes in the balance sheets of commercial banks, the central bank and the government. First the money deposits 'owed' by banks to their depositors must obviously rise by $90, which, being a liability, appear as a negative item [5] in the balance sheet of the banks. Assuming the existence of a compulsory fractional reserve ratio, set at 10%, commercial banks must acquire additional central bank deposits equal to $9 to fulfill their reserve requirements [6]. By their (vertical) balance sheet identity, this means that banks can now acquire $81 worth of Treasury bills [7]. Banks will acquire bills, which act as the residual buffer for banks, instead of granting loans, because post-Keynesians assume that banks grant loans on demand, to all credit-worthy borrowers, which implies that the appearance of new bank deposits does not, in contrast to the mainstream money multiplier story, induce or allow commercial banks to grant more loans since there is no reason to believe that the additional deposits will transform unworthy potential borrowers into credit-worthy ones.

Turning now to the central bank, the horizontal row at the top tells us that the central bank must issue additional amounts of high-powered money (HPM), the sum of the demanded cash and central bank deposits, that is $19 [8]. Once again, as these are liabilities to the central bank, this amount appears with a negative sign. Since the size of the central bank liabilities has increased by $19, the asset side must increase by an identical amount, leading the central bank to purchase $19 worth of bills [9]. To keep the interest rate on bills constant, the demand for and the supply of bills must remain equal to one another, and hence, since the net demand for bills has grown

Table A10.1 Arithmetical example of a change in portfolio preference

	Households	Firms	Govt.	Central bank	Banks	Σ
HPM	+10 [2]			−19 [8]	+9 [6]	0
Bank deposits	+90 [1]				−90 [5]	0
Bills	−80 [3]		−20 [10]	+19 [9]	+81 [7]	0
Bonds	−20 [4]		+20 [11]			0
Loans						0
Σ	0	0	0	0	0	0

by $20, the government must issue $20 worth of new bills [10], which appear with a negative sign since this is a liability for the government. Finally, the last change in the matrix, [11], can be inferred in two ways.

Reading vertically, since the size of the government debt is among the *ceteris paribus* variables, the government must retire $20 worth of government bonds to compensate for the $20 increase in the outstanding amount of bills (this will appear with a plus sign, since this is a reduction in liabilities).

Alternatively, reading horizontally, to keep bond prices constant, the government must reduce the value of its debt denominated in bonds since the household demand for bonds has been reduced by $20, purchasing back the bonds that households do not wish to hold anymore.

11
A Growth Model Prototype

11.1 Prolegomena

This is by far the most ambitious chapter of the book. It sets out a rigorous basis for the integration of Keynesian–Kaleckian macroeconomics (with constant or increasing returns to labour, growth, mark-up pricing, etc.) with a model of the financial system comprising banks, loans, credit money and equities, together with a model of inflation. Central contentions of the chapter are that, with trivial exceptions, there are no equilibria outside financial markets and that the role of prices is to distribute the national income, with inflation sometimes playing a key role determining the outcome.

The model deployed here describes a growing economy which does not spontaneously find a steady state even in the long run, but which requires active management of fiscal and monetary policy if full employment without inflation is to be achieved. Its main new features are as follows.

As the model describes a growing economy, firms now undertake fixed investment and their pricing mark-up is endogenous, depending on the rate at which dividends are paid and the proportion of investment that firms wish to finance through retained earnings. Second, firms now issue stock market shares – equities.[1] Third, there is now a distinction between unit costs and normal unit costs, the former being actual labour costs per unit produced. When production is above normal, actual unit costs will be lower than normal unit costs, which depend on trend productivity. It will now be assumed that households as well as firms borrow from banks, and that the gross flow of new personal loans (before repayments) is exogenously determined as a

---

[1] We first introduced retained earnings and stock equities in a growth model in Lavoie and Godley (2001–2). See also Taylor (2004a: ch. 8) for an analytical version of that model.

proportion of disposable income.[2] As a result, consumption will depend on net lending as well as real disposable income and wealth. Finally banks will have to face the fact that some corporate borrowers default on their loans. As a result, banks retain part of their profits, accumulating own funds that allow them to absorb capital losses while fulfilling regulation obligations related to capital adequacy ratios. The loan rate will once more be determined endogenously as a mark-up on the deposit rate.

As in any growth model, some of the most crucial equations are those determining how growth arises. First, we assume an exogenous – unexplained – trend rate of growth in labour productivity, while the potential labour force is assumed to be constant. Second, we initially assume that real pure government expenditure (excluding interest payments) – grows at a constant rate, initially the same rate at which labour productivity is growing. Third, we assume that the rate of accumulation of fixed capital is a function of the rate of capacity utilisation and of the real rate of interest. The rate of growth of fixed capital is thus an endogenous variable, which adjusts to the growth rate of pure government expenditures.

11.2 Balance sheet, revaluation and transactions-flow matrices

As always, we start the description of the model with its balance sheet and transactions-flow matrices to which we add a revaluation matrix. Table 11.1

Table 11.1 The balance sheet of Model GROWTH

	Households	Firms	Govt.	Central bank	Banks	Σ
Inventories		$+IN$				$+IN$
Fixed capital		$+K$				$+K$
HPM	$+H_h$			$-H$	$+H_b$	0
Money	$+M$				$-M$	0
Bills	$+B_h$		$-B$	$+B_{cb}$	$+B_b$	0
Bonds	$+BL \cdot p_{bL}$		$-BL \cdot p_{BL}$			0
Loans	$-L_h$	$-L_f$			$+L$	0
Equities	$+e \cdot p_e$	$-e \cdot p_e$				0
Bank capital	$+OF_b$				$-OF_b$	0
Balance	$-V_h$	$-V_f$	$-V_g$	0	0	$-(IN+K)$
Σ	0	0	0	0	0	0

[2] Households nowadays borrow substantial amounts from banks, as much if not more than firms, so any realistic account of what is going on in modern economies should incorporate personal bank loans. See Howells (1999).

provides the balance-sheet of the model, which we shall call Model *GROWTH*. The economy is again divided into five sections – households, firms, banks, a central bank and a government, each of which has distinct functions and objectives. The household column has three new features. First, households are now indebted to banks. Second, they now hold stock market equities (or shares) issued by firms, e shares each valued at price p_e. The third new feature of this column is the term OF which describes the own funds of banks – the value of their equity. It is assumed that whereas production firms are corporations valued by the stock market, banks are privately held companies, which do not issue stocks. As a result, the net worth of these banks belongs to the private owners of the banks, and must appear as part of the net wealth of households.

It may be useful to recall some accounting issues which were discussed at the beginning of Chapter 2. The description of the Firms column here corresponds with that in Table 2.2 where the net worth of firms is defined as the difference between all their assets and all their liabilities including the market value of equities. As a consequence the net worth of firms V_f can be either positive or negative. By contrast, the Banks column corresponds to the one in Table 2.3 where the net worth of banks is calculated as the difference between all assets and liabilities, excluding equities (since we assumed away their existence!). This is the own funds of banks, or their equity capital. For the bank to be solvent, this net worth must be positive. However these own funds of the bank, OF_b, belong to the owners of the banks, and for this reason, while they enter with a negative sign in the balance sheet of the banks they also enter with a plus sign in the balance sheet of households.

The other components of the balance sheet have already been introduced in previous models. Firms own both kinds of tangible asset needed for production – inventories and fixed capital.

We now move to a new matrix, the revaluation matrix, given by Table 11.2 which was also discussed in Chapter 2. In previous models, the revaluation

Table 11.2 Revaluation matrix of Model *GROWTH*: Changes in assets arising from revaluation gains

	Households	Firms	Government	Central bank	Banks	Σ
Bonds	$+\Delta p_{bL} \cdot BL_{-1}$		$-\Delta p_{bL} \cdot BL_{-1}$			0
Equities of firms	$+\Delta p_e \cdot e_{-1}$	$-\Delta p_e \cdot e_{-1}$				0
Bank equity	$+\Delta OF_b$				$-\Delta OF_b$	0
Fixed capital		$+\Delta p \cdot k_{-1}$				$+\Delta p \cdot k_{-1}$

matrix comprised only one entry, the capital gains or capital losses on holdings of long-term bonds. In the *GROWTH* model, four components may be revalued. Besides bonds, stock market equities are also liable to capital gains and losses. Third, banks accumulate own funds, but these funds belong to the owners of the banks, so that they are treated as a liability of the banks. From the standpoint of the bank owners, since this is a closed rather than a publicly owned corporation, the own funds accumulated by the bank during a period are treated as a capital gain. From a Haig–Simons point of view, the bank's own funds are part of the wealth of household owners, because if the bank were to be liquidated, their owners would be left with the bank capital – the own funds of the bank. Finally, the fourth line of the matrix shows an automatic revaluation of the value of firms' fixed capital, arising from price inflation.

Table 11.3 describes net transactions between all five sectors in some given period of time, measured at current prices. Start with the first seven items in the top half of the second column, written in bold characters. This list is the national income identity comprising the major expenditure categories (government expenditure, personal consumption and investment) and flows of factor income (wages and profits). Every item in this column is a transaction with another sector or with a different part of the same sector (e.g. when firms buy investment goods from other firms or profits are retained in the business), so a new column, the capital account column has been created to record these capital transactions.

The columns describing the government and central bank are no different from those of Table 10.2. Indeed, every entry in the top half of the matrix has already been encountered in previous chapters and is self-explanatory, except for two unusual features relating to national income accounting conventions. First, in the row called 'financing cost of inventories', in column 2, the loan rate of interest multiplied by the opening stock of inventories has been substituted for conventional stock appreciation (or IVA). Second, interest payments by firms, other than with respect to loans for the finance of inventories, are included in line seven as a component of distributed profits. The reasons for making these entries have already been explained in detail in Chapter 8, where we dealt with various possible definitions of profits, and the distinction between the requirements of business and national accounts. Banks and producing firms distribute dividends to their owners (FD_b and FD_f), and keep part of their profits undistributed, in the form of retained earnings (FU_b and FU_f).

The bottom of the first half of the Table describes the various interest payments on deposits, bills, bonds and personal loans. The latter is a new entry. It is assumed that households obtain personal loans from banks (L_h) on which they make interest payments. These payments carry a negative sign, since they are a use of funds, being subtracted from the personal income of households.

Table 11.3 Transactions matrix of Model GROWTH

	Households	Firms		Central bank		Govt.	Banks		Σ
		Current	Capital	Current	Capital		Current	Capital	
Consumption	$-C$	$+C$						0	0
Government expenditures		$+G$				$-G$		0	0
Fixed investment		$+I$	$-I$					0	0
Inventory accumulation		$+\Delta IN$	$-\Delta IN$					0	0
Income tax	$-T$					$+T$		0	0
Wages	$+WB$	$-WB$						0	0
Inventory financing cost		$-r_{l-1} \cdot IN_{-1}$					$+r_{l-1} \cdot IN_{-1}$	0	0
Entrepreneurial Profits	$+FD_f$	$-F_f$	$+FU_f$				$+r_{l-1} \cdot (L_{f-1} - IN_{-1}) - r_{l-1} \cdot NPL$	0	0
Bank profits	$+FD_b$						$-F_b$	$+FU_b$	0
Central bank profits				$-F_{cb}$		$+F_{cb}$		0	0
Interest on — personal loans	$-r_{l-1} \cdot L_{h-1}$						$+r_{l-1} \cdot L_{h-1}$	0	0
deposits	$+r_{m-1} \cdot M_{-1}$						$-r_{m-1} \cdot M_{-1}$	0	0
bills	$+r_{b-1} \cdot B_{h-1}$					$-r_{b-1} \cdot B_{-1} + r_{b-1} \cdot B_{cb-1}$	$+r_{b-1} \cdot B_{b-1}$	0	0
bonds	$+BL_{-1}$					$-BL_{-1}$		0	0
Change in the stocks of — loans	$+\Delta L$		$+\Delta L$					$-\Delta L$	0
cash	$-\Delta H_h$				$+\Delta H$			$-\Delta H_b$	0
money deposits	$-\Delta M$							$+\Delta M$	0
bills	$-\Delta B_h$				$-\Delta B_{cb}$	$+\Delta B$		$-\Delta B_b$	0
bonds	$-\Delta BL \cdot p_{bL}$					$+\Delta BL \cdot p_{bL}$		0	0
equities	$-\Delta e \cdot p_e$		$+\Delta e \cdot p_e$					0	0
Loan defaults			$+NPL$					$-NPL$	0
Σ	0	0	0	0	0	0	0	0	0

The lower part of the transactions-flow matrix describes the flow-of-funds. Checking the first column, that of households, there are two new items. Besides acquiring cash balances, money deposits, bills and bonds, households purchase stock market shares newly issued (Δe). In addition, when households increase their borrowing, they have a new source of funds in the form of personal bank loans. The other new entry is 'Loan defaults' (*NPL*) which describe non-performing loans. It is assumed that a certain proportion of loans made to firms turn bad. The new loans (ΔL_f) that firms obtain as residual finance for changes in inventories and fixed investment will be reduced by the amount of defaulted loans. These non-performing loans will also appear in the capital account of banks.

11.3   Decisions taken by firms

11.3.1   An overview of firms decisions

The following sections outline the behaviour and motivation of each of the five sectors. These will be followed by an assessment of how the postulated economy as a whole functions.

Firms continuously have to take a complex and interdependent set of decisions regarding output, investment, costing, prices, employment and finance. As was argued earlier, firms must continuously *decide* how much they are going to produce and what prices they will charge. These decisions will be based on the quantity they expect to sell at those prices and the change in inventories they intend to achieve. Firms must also decide how much fixed investment they will undertake depending (for instance) on their 'animal spirits' and the existing pressure on capacity together with expectations about financial conditions and profitability. The stylized facts are that, subject to an upward trend in productivity, there are roughly constant returns to labour in the long run and increasing returns in the short run. The demand for labour has an obvious implication for the wage bill which firms have to pay. Further stylized facts are that the prices which firms charge are insensitive to short-run fluctuations in aggregate demand, as argued in Coutts, Godley and Nordhaus (1978). As a result, pro-cyclical fluctuations in demand and output tend to be associated with pro-cyclical fluctuations in profits. The prices set by firms must be consistent, not only with their expectation about the quantity they will sell (at those prices), it must also be such, relative to wage costs, as to generate enough profit to pay for some target proportion of their fixed investment while distributing enough to satisfy shareholders and creditors.[3]

---

[3] The line of argument here accords with an enormous body of theoretical work, notably by Kalecki, Kaldor and Tobin. One of the authors derived his arguments from personal conversations with the last two of these characters. The link between retained earnings and investment can also be found in the works of Wood (1975), Eichner (1976)

Finally, the prices which firms charge, and the profits they hope to make and distribute, are not independent of the recourse which they must have to banks and financial markets as a residual source of funds for investment in fixed and working capital.

This whole syndrome of firms' decisions is presented in the following formal model. We shall discuss, in turn, firms' decisions regarding output and employment, investment, pricing and financing requirements. While the modelling of behaviour is crude, the accounting is solid and we shall reach conclusions which, when integrated into sub-models of other parts of a closed economy, will reveal some key features of the *modus operandi* of a modern industrial economy together with an account of the financial system and credit money. The main purpose of having a formal model, based on transactions accounts which have no black holes, is that one is forced to consider how each part of an economy is interconnected with every other part.[4] For instance, pro-cyclical productivity combined with normal-cost pricing must have counterparts in the monetary system since the sudden increase in profits when demand rises is likely to reduce the demand for loans without there being a comparable fall in the demand for money, thereby threatening banks' profits.

In the sections that immediately follow we divide the decisions of firms into four components: those related to output, inventories and investment; costing decisions; pricing decisions; and financing implications. We close the section with accounting identities describing realized outcomes.

11.3.2 Output and investment decisions

Box 11.1 shows the equations relevant to output, inventories and fixed investment. The first five equations are familiar, since they were described in Chapter 9. The only new equation is (11.2), where it is assumed that expected sales are a weighted average of current sales and past sales, the latter being augmented by trend productivity growth which is deemed to represent secular tendencies in sales.

Equation (11.6) says that fixed capital accumulates at the rate gr_k. This growth rate, as can be seen in the next equation, depends on some constant reflecting animal spirits, on the real rate of interest on loans rr_l, as well as a proxy for the rate of utilization of capacity u (here really an output to capital ratio, as shown in equation 11.7). This choice of investment function is arbitrary. The purpose here is not to argue for one specification against another

---

and Harcourt and Kenyon (1976). See also Godley (1993) and Lavoie (1992: 109–18) for descriptions of such a link.

[4] Keynes (1936: 297) knew all about this since he emphasizes that when analysing a particular problem we should keep all related problems 'at the back of our heads'. We are hoping that the computer makes it possible to do this in a formal way and even to bring those problems round to the front of the heads of lesser mortals.

Box 11.1 Firms' equations

$y = s^e + (in^e - in_{-1})$	Real output decision;	(11.1)
$s^e = \beta \cdot s + (1 - \beta) \cdot s_{-1} \cdot$	Expected real sales;	(11.2)
$(1 + gr_{pr})$		
$in^T = \sigma^T \cdot s^e$	Long-run inventory target;	(11.3)
$in^e = in_{-1} + \gamma \cdot (in^T - in_{-1})$	Short-run inventory target;	(11.4)
$in = in_{-1} + (y - s)$	Actual (real) inventory;	(11.5)
$k = k_{-1} \cdot (1 + gr_k)$	Real capital stock;	(11.6)
$gr_k = gr_0 + \gamma_u \cdot u - \gamma_r \cdot rr_l$	Growth of real capital stock;	(11.7)
$u = \dfrac{y}{k_{-1}}$	Capacity utilization proxy;	(11.8)
$rr_l = \left\{ \dfrac{(1 + r_l)}{(1 + \pi)} \right\} - 1$	Real interest rate on loans;	(11.9)
$\pi = \dfrac{(p - p_{-1})}{p_{-1}}$	Rate of price inflation;	(11.10)
$i = (gr_k + \delta) \cdot k_{-1}$	Real gross investment.	(11.11)

---

but to show how, given the investment decision, firms have to validate it by successfully generating the needed finance.[5] Finally, equation (11.11) defines real gross investment, which depends on the rate of accumulation and the rate of depreciation of capital δ.

We end this section with a few identities, found in Box 11.2. Sales are made up of consumption, government and gross investment (equation 11.12). The other identities transform quantities into values taking note, once more, that goods in stock are valued at their cost of production *UC*, not at the price that they could fetch if they were sold in the current period. This has the implications for the measure of nominal GDP first discussed in Chapter 9.

---

[5] Here we simply follow Dos Santos and Zezza (2005). Lavoie and Godley (2001–2) propose a more sophisticated investment function. Empirical work seems to show that an essential component of all investment functions is the rate of capacity utilization, either for reasons related to the standard accelerator, or because rates of capacity utilization are a fair proxy for the realized rate of profit, thus alleviating liquidity constraints on producing firms.

Box 11.2 Firms' equations

$s = c + g + i$	Actual real sales;	(11.12)
$S = s \cdot p$	Nominal value of realized sales;	(11.13)
$IN = in \cdot UC$	Inventories valued at current cost;	(11.14)
$I = i \cdot p$	Nominal gross investment;	(11.15)
$K = k \cdot p$	Nominal value of fixed capital;	(11.16)
$Y = s \cdot p + \Delta in \cdot UC$	Nominal GDP.	(11.17)

11.3.3 Costing decisions

Box 11.3 Firms' equations

$$\omega^T = \left(\frac{W}{p}\right)^T = \Omega_0 + \Omega_1 \cdot pr$$
$$+ \Omega_2 \cdot \{ER + z_3(1 - ER) - z_4 \cdot bandT + z_5 \cdot bandB\}$$

Real wage aspiration assessed at bargaining table; (11.18)

$$ER = \frac{N_{-1}}{N_{fe-1}}$$

Employment rate ; (11.19)

$$z_3 = 1 \quad \text{if } 1 - bandB \le ER \le 1 + bandT$$
$$z_4 = 1 \quad \text{if } ER > 1 + bandT$$
$$z_5 = 1 \quad \text{if } ER < 1 - bandB$$

(11.20)

$$W = W_{-1} + \Omega_3 \cdot (\omega^T \cdot p_{-1} - W_{-1})$$

Nominal wage; (11.21)

$$pr = pr_{-1} \cdot (1 + gr_{pr})$$

Labour productivity (gr_{pr} is productivity growth); (11.22)

$$N^T = \frac{y}{pr}$$

Desired employment; (11.23)

$$N = N_{-1} + \eta \cdot (N^T - N_{-1})$$

Actual employment; (11.24)

$$WB = N \cdot W$$

Nominal wage bill; (11.25)

$$UC = \frac{WB}{y}$$

Actual unit cost; (11.26)

$$NUC = \frac{W}{pr} \qquad \text{Normal (trend) unit cost;} \qquad (11.27)$$
$$NHUC = (1 - \sigma^N) \cdot NUC + \sigma^N \cdot$$
$$(1 + r_{lN} \cdot) \cdot NUC_{-1} \qquad \text{Normal historic unit cost.} \qquad (11.28)$$

The costing decisions that firms need to take are to be found in Box 11.3. As discussed in Chapter 9, inflation is essentially a conflicting-claims phenomenon, with workers coming to the bargaining table with an aspiration to obtain a real wage rate ω^T, the size of which depends on trend labour productivity and on the pressure of demand for labour.[6] The nominal wage then reacts to the discrepancy between the target wage and the actual nominal wage (equation 11.21). However, we believe the real-world process to be highly contingent, going beyond mechanical equations. Indeed the evidence relating to the UK with regard to the years prior to 1975 as well as the evidence in several countries over the last few years supports the view that there is quite a range of employment or unemployment values within which the inflation rate will be unmoved (or even move perversely).

We thus complicate equation (11.18) by adding a logical function (11.20), which says that when the rate of employment ER (as defined in equation 11.19), is within a certain band, there will be no additional pressures on the target real wage and hence on the rate of inflation. What these equations are saying is represented in Figure 11.1, which shows a kind of Phillips curve with a horizontal segment, which corresponds to the situation where $z_3 = 1$. Such a horizontal segment has been suggested recently, among others, by Tobin (1995), Hein (2002) and Palascio-Vera (2005). There is also an ever-growing

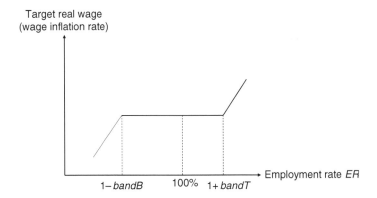

Figure 11.1   Phillips curve with horizontal mid-range segment

[6] In the actual model, equation (11.18) is expressed in logarithmic form.

number of empirical studies that support middle-range flat segments (Eisner 1996; Filardo 1998; Barnes and Olivei 2003).

The growth rate of trend labour productivity is still assumed to be an exogenous variable (equation 11.22).[7] This trend productivity level and the output decision have a direct implication for desired employment, N^T (equation 11.23). By contrast, actual employment, N, follows a partial adjustment process towards its normal relationship to output, as described by equation (11.24). In this way there will be a short-term increase in productivity when output rises above trend in accordance with a well established stylized fact. As total output fluctuates about its trend, there is a tendency for labour productivity to move pro-cyclically. This may be simply because there is a lag between unusual movements in output (which may turn out to be temporary) and the response of firms in terms of hiring. It may alternatively come about because the total labour force comprises a category of 'overhead' employees which does not respond – only sluggishly – to short- and medium-term fluctuations in output (Lavoie 1992: ch. 5).

The distinction between trend and actual productivity allows us to make a distinction between actual unit costs UC, as defined by equation (11.25) and (11.26), and trend or normal unit costs NUC, as given by equation (11.27). We assume that normal unit costs enter into the determination of normal historic unit costs $NHUC$, (11.28), which is based on past and current normal unit costs, and on what firms consider to be the normal inventories to sales target σ^N and the normal interest rate r_{lN}.[8] It is this normal historic unit cost which will be the multiplicand upon which the costing margin will be applied when firms set prices.

11.3.4 Pricing decisions

Box 11.4 Firms' equations

$p = (1 + \varphi) \cdot NHUC$	Normal-cost pricing;	(11.29)
$\varphi = \varphi_{-1} + \varepsilon \cdot (\varphi^T_{-1} - \varphi_{-1})$	Actual mark-up;	(11.30)

---

[7] Thus, although we believe that the rate of technical progress is influenced by effective demand, we disregard for simplicity the point made by both Kaldor (1960: 237) and Robinson (1956: 96), that 'the natural rate of growth is ultimately endogenous to the demand-determined actual rate of growth ... . The natural rate is not an attractor in demand-led growth models' (Setterfield 2002: 5). See also Lavoie (2006d: 180–1) and Godley and Cripps (1983: 253–4).

[8] In a static model, this normal ratio σ^N would be the long-run inventories to sales target σ^T already defined in equation (11.3), as it was in Chapter 10. However, with growth this long-run target is never achieved, so that the realized inventories to sales ratio in steady-state growth is always different from this target σ^T. Thus in the base run, we have set $\sigma^N = \{\sigma^T/(1+gr_{pr})\}/(in/in^T)$.

$$\varphi^{\text{T}} = \frac{F_{\text{f}}^{\text{T}}}{HC^{\text{e}}} \qquad \text{Ideal mark-up;} \qquad (11.31)$$

$$\begin{aligned} HC^{\text{e}} &= (1 - \sigma_{\text{se}}) \cdot s^{\text{e}} \cdot UC \\ &\quad + \sigma_{\text{se}} \cdot (1 + r_{l-1}) \cdot s^{\text{e}} \cdot UC_{-1} \end{aligned} \qquad \text{Expected historical costs;} \qquad (11.32)$$

$$\sigma_{\text{se}} = \frac{in_{-1}}{s^{\text{e}}} \qquad \begin{aligned} &\text{Opening inventories to} \\ &\text{expected sales ratio;} \end{aligned} \qquad (11.33)$$

$$\begin{aligned} F_{\text{f}} &= S - HC = S \\ &\quad -\{(1 - \sigma_{\text{s}}) \cdot s \cdot UC + \sigma_{\text{s}} \cdot \\ &\quad \ s \cdot (1 + r_{l-1}) \cdot UC_{-1}\} \end{aligned} \qquad \begin{aligned} &\text{Realized entrepreneurial} \\ &\text{profits;} \end{aligned} \qquad (11.37\text{A})$$

$$\begin{aligned} F_{\text{f}}^{\text{T}} &= FU_{\text{f}}^{\text{T}} + FD_{\text{f}} + r_{l-1} \cdot \\ &\quad (L_{\text{fd}-1} - IN_{-1}) \end{aligned} \qquad \begin{aligned} &\text{Planned entrepreneurial} \\ &\text{profits of firms;} \end{aligned} \qquad (11.34)$$

$$FU_{\text{f}}^{\text{T}} = \psi_{\text{U}} \cdot I_{-1} \qquad \begin{aligned} &\text{Planned retained} \\ &\text{earnings of firms;} \end{aligned} \qquad (11.35)$$

$$FD_{\text{f}} = \psi_{\text{D}} \cdot F_{\text{f}-1} \qquad \text{Dividends of firms.} \qquad (11.36)$$

We assume that prices are based on normal historical unit costs to which a mark-up φ is applied (equation 11.29) as shown in Box 11.4. The mark-up is still arbitrary to some extent, depending on business know-how and experience, but it evolves through a partial adjustment mechanism towards a target mark-up φ^{T} (equation 11.30). This target mark-up itself evolves through time (equation 11.31). The target mark-up is some kind of ideal mark-up, that would generate the target amount of entrepreneurial profits F_{f}^{T} desired by firms when realized sales s are exactly equal to expected sales s^{e}, for in this case expected historical costs HC_{e} would be exactly equal to actual historical costs, as can be seen from a comparison of equations (11.32) and (11.37A).[9] As pointed out in Chapter 8, the costing margin φ^{T} in the price equation would, under these conditions turn out to be exactly equal to the realized costing margin φ'. The rule of thumb mark-up φ, will not, in general, generate the required level of profits. So to the extent that profits are too high or too low, the partial adjustment process of equation (11.30) will drive the system, along with the adjustment process that ties production to actual sales, towards a steady state where $\varphi = \varphi^{\text{T}}$, ensuring that profits are generally sufficient to pay for investment as well as dividends and interest.

In contrast to the previous chapters, we suggest here an explanation of the (ideal) costing margin φ^{T} (in other words, the ideal entrepreneurial profit

[9] Equation (11.37A), as all equations with an 'A' suffix, does not enter the model. In the model, it is being replaced by the more standard equation (11.37). But we have shown in Chapter 8 that these two equations are identical. Note that $\sigma_{\text{s}} = in_{-1}/s$.

share, $\varphi^T/(1+\varphi^T)$). Given historic costs, the target mark-up depends on target entrepreneurial profits. Target entrepreneurial profits, as shown by equation (11.34), must cover target retained earnings FU_f^T, distributed dividends FD_f and interest payments on loans other than those generated by inventories (which have already been taken into account as part of historic costs). We suppose, in line with stylized facts and as several previous post-Keynesian authors have claimed, that firms attempt to finance most of their gross fixed investment expenditures through their gross retained earnings. Indeed, equation (11.35) sets target undistributed profits as a proportion ψ_U of gross nominal investment in fixed capital of the previous period. Distributed dividends are a fraction ψ_D of entrepreneurial profits earned in the previous period (equation 11.36), and this, actual distributed dividends, rather than a target amount, enters into the target profits equation. It is assumed that firms will distribute dividends only once they have obtained verified accounts of their activities.[10]

11.3.5   Financial implications for the firms

Box 11.5   Firms' equations

$$F_f = S - WB + \Delta IN - r_1 \cdot IN_{-1}$$
Realized entrepreneurial profits of firms;   (11.37)

$$FU_f = F_f - FD_f - r_{l-1} \cdot (L_{fd-1} - IN_{-1}) + r_{l-1} \cdot NPL$$
Retained earnings of firms;   (11.38)

$$L_{fd} = L_{fd-1} + I + \Delta IN - FU_f - \Delta e_s \cdot p_e - NPL$$
Demand for loans by firms;   (11.39)

$$NPL = npl \cdot L_{fd-1}$$
Defaulted (non-performing) loans;   (11.40)

$$e_s = e_{s-1} + (1 - \psi_U) \cdot \frac{I_{-1}}{p_e}$$
Supply of equities issued by firms;   (11.41)

---

[10] Final sales will be known at best on the 31st of December, and the income and profit statement of the firm needs to be verified by accountants before any dividend decision can be taken. Indeed, in many countries, dividends are announced only on the 30th of June, after attorneys and accountants have checked the numbers, because it would be illegal to distribute dividends that are greater than profits (Vallageas 2001). Thus the dividends distributed in period t arise from the activity of period $t - 1$.

$$r_K = \frac{FD_f}{(e_{s-1} \cdot p_{e-1})} \qquad \text{Dividend yield of firms;} \qquad (11.42)$$

$$PE = \frac{p_e}{(F_f / e_{s-1})} \qquad \text{Price earnings ratio;} \qquad (11.43)$$

$$q = \frac{(e_s \cdot p_e + L_d)}{(K + IN)} \qquad \begin{array}{l}\text{Tobin's } q \text{ ratio or} \\ \text{Kaldor's valuation ratio.}\end{array} \qquad (11.44)$$

The rules of thumb which firms adopt will never exactly generate required profits because sales, inventories and interest rates will all undergo unexpected short-term variations. Realized entrepreneurial profits F_f, as defined in equation (11.37), which reproduces the analysis conducted in Chapter 8, will thus, in general, be different from targeted profits (Box 11.5). Because distributed dividends and interest payments on bank debt are set amounts, dependent on values taken in the previous period, any windfalls in entrepreneurial profits will go into actual retained earnings FU_f. Equation (11.38), which describes undistributed profits, includes an additional term, $r_{l-1} \cdot NPL$. Those are the interest payments that firms defaulting on their loans did not pay to banks. As a result entrepreneurial profits are enlarged by this amount, *ceteris paribus*.[11] It is assumed that a proportion *npl* of previous bank loans default every year (equation 11.40).

Finally coming to the firm sector's *financial requirements*, equation (11.39) describes required bank loans, L_{fd}. The change in loans that firms require can be computed from their capital account column in Table 11.3. Loans, once again, act as a buffer, absorbing unexpected changes in financial requirements. Any (positive) windfall in entrepreneurial profits will be reflected in a decrease in the demand for loans. Required loans will also be diminished when some firms default on their loans (*NPL*), and when firms make new stock issues ($\Delta e_s \cdot p_e$). We have assumed that if firms plan that a proportion ψ_U of nominal investment expenditures will be financed through retained earnings, then a proportion $(1 - \psi_U)$ – this expression being a small percentage – will be financed through new issues of shares (equation 11.41).

---

[11] The *ceteris paribus* clause normally would not apply because the inventories usually provide the collateral backing the bank loans provided to firms. If firms default on their loans, either the banks should get hold of the inventories or these inventories have become worthless (because they are outdated merchandise), and hence, if non-performing loans amount to *NPL* dollars, this implies that firms should lose *NPL/UC* units of real inventories. In other words, equation (11.5) ought to be written as:

$$in = in_{-1} + (y - s) - \frac{NPL}{UC}$$

As a result, on average, only *additional* investment expenditures, relative to those of the previous period, will be financed through bank loans, so that apart from these, bank loans are essentially financing inventories.

The last three equations of Box 11.5 yield some well-known financial ratios. The dividend yield, r_k, is the ratio of the dividends distributed this period over the stock market value of the shares outstanding at the end of the previous period. This ratio will enter the portfolio decisions of households. Equation (11.43) gives the price earnings ratio, which is the current equity price divided by profits per share. It is also interesting to define the (average) q ratio, as Tobin called it, or the valuation ratio under Kaldor's terminology (equation 11.44). In our model, as we believe also in the real world, there is no mechanism to make the q ratio converge towards unity. The evolution of the q ratio, as well as that of the price earnings ratio, will depend to a large extent on the desire of households to hold equities compared to their desire to hold other financial assets, an issue which is discussed in the next section.

11.4 Decisions taken by households

The decisions of households will be split into three subsections. The first subsection is by now familiar and deals with personal income, disposable income, changes in wealth and consumption. The second is new, describing how households get into debt. The third deals with usual portfolio decisions.

11.4.1 Income and consumption decisions

Box 11.6 Households' equations

$$YP = WB + FD_f + FD_b$$
$$+ r_{m-1} \cdot M_{h-1} + r_{b-1} \cdot$$
$$B_{hd-1} + BL_{d-1} \qquad \text{Nominal personal income;} \qquad (11.45)$$

$$T = \theta \cdot YP \qquad \text{Income taxes;} \qquad (11.46)$$

$$YD_r = YP - T$$
$$- r_{l-1} \cdot L_{hd-1} \qquad \begin{array}{l}\text{Nominal regular} \\ \text{disposable income;}\end{array} \qquad (11.47)$$

$$YD_{hs} = YD_r + CG \qquad \begin{array}{l}\text{Haig–Simons nominal} \\ \text{disposable income;}\end{array} \qquad (11.48)$$

$$CG = \Delta p_{bL} \cdot BL_{d-1}$$
$$+ \Delta p_e \cdot e_{d-1} + \Delta OF \qquad \text{Capital gains;} \qquad (11.49)$$

$$V = V_{-1} + YD_{hs} - C \qquad \text{Nominal wealth;} \qquad (11.50)$$

$$v = \frac{V}{p} \qquad \text{Real stock of wealth;} \qquad (11.51)$$

$$C = p \cdot c \qquad \text{Nominal consumption;} \qquad (11.52)$$

$$
\begin{aligned}
c &= \alpha_1 \cdot (yd_r^e + nl) \\
&\quad + \alpha_2 \cdot v_{-1}
\end{aligned}
\qquad \text{Real consumption;} \qquad (11.53)
$$

$$
\begin{aligned}
yd_r^e &= \varepsilon \cdot yd_r + (1 - \varepsilon) \cdot \\
&\quad yd_{r-1} \cdot (1 + gr_{pr})
\end{aligned}
\qquad \begin{aligned}&\text{Expected real regular}\\&\text{disposable income;}\end{aligned} \qquad (11.54)
$$

$$yd_r = \frac{YD_r}{p} - \frac{\pi \cdot V_{-1}}{p} \qquad \begin{aligned}&\text{Real regular}\\&\text{disposable income.}\end{aligned} \qquad (11.55)$$

This subsection is familiar territory, but it contains a few innovations as a consequence of the introduction of personal loans to households (Box 11.6). Nominal personal income YP is the sum of wages, dividends and interest payments received on deposits, bills and bonds (equation 11.45). Income taxes, the only kind of taxes in Model $GROWTH$, are paid on this personal income (equation 11.46). Nominal regular disposable income YD_r is what households are left with once they have paid their income taxes and once they have made their interest payments on the personal loans they have taken from banks (equation 11.47). Haig-Simons nominal disposable income YD_{hs} is the sum of regular disposable income and capital gains (equation 11.48). The latter, as mentioned in our discussion of the revaluation matrix, comprises capital gains on bonds and equities, as well as the increase in the own funds of banks, which belong to households (equation 11.49). As a result, the change in nominal wealth is defined in the usual way, as the sum of Haig-Simons disposable income and capital gains (equation 11.50).

As in our other models with changing prices, we suppose that consumption decisions are taken in real terms. Real consumption, as shown by equation (11.53) depends on expected real regular disposable income and on a new element, nl, which is the deflated net lending to households by banks. In other words, it is assumed that a portion of the funds obtained from banks by households are consumer loans, while the rest is used to purchase financial assets. The nl variable will be explained in the next subsection. As to expected real regular disposable income yd_r^e, in symmetry with expected real sales, we suppose that it is a weighted average of the real regular disposable income of the current period and that of the previous period, augmented by the secular trend in the growth rate of productivity (equation 11.54). Real regular disposable income yd_r, in line with previous chapters, is itself defined as deflated regular disposable income minus the capital losses inflicted by price inflation (equation 11.55).

11.4.2   Personal loans decisions

Box 11.7   Households' equations

$$GL = \eta \cdot YP$$ Gross amount of new personal loans;   (11.56)

$$\eta = \eta_0 - \eta_r \cdot rr_l$$ New loans to personal income ratio;   (11.57)

$$NL = GL - REP$$ Net amount of new personal loans;   (11.58)

$$REP = \delta_{rep} \cdot L_{hd-1}$$ Personal loan repayments;   (11.59)

$$L_{hd} = L_{hd-1} + NL$$ Demand for personal loans;   (11.60)

$$nl = \frac{NL}{p}$$ Real amount of new personal loans;   (11.61)

$$BUR = \frac{(REP + r_{l-1} \cdot L_{hd-1})}{YP}$$ Burden of personal debt.   (11.62)

Box 11.7 shows the operations linked to personal loans. Equation (11.56) says that the gross flow of new personal loans is a fraction η of nominal personal income. This fraction may be interpreted as some limit which households assign to themselves or as a limit which banks impose on households, following some rule of thumb. The fraction η is itself inversely related to the real rate of interest on loans, as shown in equation (11.57), in line with the now vast literature on credit rationing.

As equation (11.58) shows, net lending to households within a period is equal to gross new loans minus repayments, (*REP*). Principal repayments are a fraction δ_{rep} of the outstanding stock of personal loans (equation 11.59). The end-of-period stock of loans of the current period is thus equal to the stock of loans at the beginning of the period, L_{hd-1}, plus the net flow of new loans *NL* (equation 11.60).

The last two equations of Box 11.7 define ratios. The *nl* variable that we encountered in the equation describing real consumption is here defined as the nominal flow of net lending *NL*, deflated by the price index. Equation (11.62) yields a potentially useful measure of the burden of debt on households. This burden, *BUR*, is the sum of interest payments and principal repayments as a fraction of personal income. It is the debt-service burden.

11.4.3 Portfolio decisions

Box 11.8 Households' equations

$$\frac{M_d}{V_{fma-1}} = \lambda_{10} + \lambda_{11} \cdot r_m - \lambda_{12} \cdot r_b$$
$$- \lambda_{13} \cdot r_{bL} - \lambda_{14} \cdot r_K + \lambda_{15} \cdot \left(\frac{YP}{V_{fma-1}}\right); \quad (11.63)$$

$$\frac{B_{hd}}{V_{fma-1}} = \lambda_{20} - \lambda_{21} \cdot r_m + \lambda_{22} \cdot r_b$$
$$- \lambda_{23} \cdot r_{bL} - \lambda_{24} \cdot r_K - \lambda_{25} \cdot \left(\frac{YP}{V_{fma-1}}\right); \quad (11.64)$$

$$\frac{(p_{bL} \cdot BL_d)}{V_{fma-1}} = \lambda_{30} - \lambda_{31} \cdot r_m - \lambda_{32} \cdot r_b$$
$$+ \lambda_{33} \cdot r_{bL} - \lambda_{34} \cdot r_K - \lambda_{35} \cdot \left(\frac{YP}{V_{fma-1}}\right); \quad (11.65)$$

$$\frac{(p_e \cdot e_d)}{V_{fma-1}} = \lambda_{40} - \lambda_{41} \cdot r_m - \lambda_{42} \cdot r_b$$
$$- \lambda_{43} \cdot r_{bL} + \lambda_{44} \cdot r_K - \lambda_{45} \cdot \left(\frac{YP}{V_{fma-1}}\right); \quad (11.66)$$

$$M_h = V_{fma} - B_{hd} - p_{bL} \cdot$$
$$BL_d - p_e \cdot e_d \quad \text{Money deposits - a residual;} \quad (11.67)$$

$$V_{fma} = M_d + B_{hd}$$
$$+ p_{bL} \cdot BL_d + p_e \cdot e_d \quad \text{[11.66 rewritten];} \quad (11.68A)$$

$$V_{fma} = V + L_{hd} \quad \text{Financial market asset}$$
$$- H_{hd} - OF \quad \text{(investible) wealth;} \quad (11.68)$$

$$H_{hd} = \lambda_c \cdot C \quad \text{Households' demand for cash;} \quad (11.69)$$

$$e_d = e_s \quad \text{Stock market equilibrium.} \quad (11.70)$$

Households' allocate expected disposable income between consumption and wealth accumulation while simultaneously allocating wealth between the various assets listed in the accounting matrices. As households' expected income is always different from realized income there must be a flexible component in the wealth allocation process which takes on a buffering role. Cash is not a good candidate for this role in the days of credit cards and electronic payments from and into bank deposit accounts. A better candidate is bank deposits which act as the passive variable giving signals in much the same way as inventories give signals to firms and reconciles actual with expected sales.

Financial assets, or rather what we now call market financial assets, V_{fma}, are allocated in line with Tobinesque principles, with the appropriate adding-up constraints, as described by equations (11.63) to (11.66) (Box 11.8). Financial market assets comprise four kinds of assets: money deposits, bills, bonds and equities, as shown by equation (11.68A). The financial market asset component of household wealth V_{fma} can be read off from the first column of Table 11.1. Because the gross wealth of households is equal to their net wealth V plus their liabilities, in this case bank loans L_{hd}, the wealth that can be invested in market financial assets is equal to the net wealth of households V, plus the funds borrowed from the banks L_{hd}, minus household wealth which is stuck in the own funds, OF, of the banks and the wealth which is kept in the form of cash, H_{hd}. This identity arising from Table 11.1 is found in equation (11.68).

In this model we do away with complex calculations of expected wealth and simply assume that expected investible wealth is the market financial asset wealth of the previous period (V_{fma-1}). We further assume that the demands for financial assets are always realized, except for the demand for money M_d, since money deposits held by households are a residual which reconciles expected with actual outcomes . The stock of money deposits that households end up with is thus M_h (not M_d), and its value is defined by equation (11.67) instead of equation (11.63).[12] By contrast, the demand for cash H_{hd} is always realized, being related to transactions arising from nominal consumption (equation 11.69).

Finally, equation (11.70) reflects the fact that the demand for equities, given in (11.66), has to be confronted with the supply of equities arising from firms' needs, as determined in equation (11.41), which gives rise to the model's only equilibrium condition. Since the number of shares on the stock market is determined by decisions made by firms, it is the number of shares demanded, e_d, that has to adjust to the supply of shares e_s, and not the reverse. A change in stock market prices p_e is the mechanism that will

[12] More specifically, due to the adding up properties, we have: $M_d = V_{fma-1} - B_{hd} - p_{bL} \cdot BL_d - p_e \cdot e_d$, and in general V_{fma-1} and V_{fma} will be different.

bring demand into equivalence with supply, and hence in that case, and in that case only, we have a true price-clearing mechanism. In other words, in the portfolio equation (11.66), the right-hand side variable – the endogenous variable – is the price of equities, p_e, which will make e_d equal to e_s by (11.70).

11.5 The public sector

11.5.1 The government sector

Box 11.9 Government's equations

$T = \theta \cdot YP$	Income taxes [already given];	(11.46)
$G = p \cdot g$	Nominal pure government expenditures;	(11.71)
$g = g_{-1}(1 + gr_g)$	Real pure government expenditures;	(11.72)
$PSBR = G + r_{b-1} \cdot$ $\dfrac{(B_{hs-1} + B_{bs-1})}{+ BL_{s-1} - T}$	Nominal government deficit;	(11.73)
$B_s = B_{s-1} + PSBR$ $- \Delta BL_s \cdot p_{bL}$	New issues of bills;	(11.74)
$GD = B_{hs} + BL_s + H_s$	Nominal government debt.	(11.75)

We now move to the public sector, composed of the government and the central bank (Box 11.9). All the equations relevant to the government sector will be familiar to readers, except equation (11.72) which defines the evolution of real pure government expenditures. It is initially assumed these expenditures grow at the rate gr_g, a rate that the government can change in a discretionary attempt to raise its share of national expenditures or to raise the growth rate of the economy.[13] In addition, the government may wish to change the tax rate θ.

---

[13] It will be found that, in our model, with no population growth, pure government expenditures, over a long period, must grow at the trend rate of productivity growth ($gr_g = gr_{pr}$).

11.5.2 The central bank

Box 11.10 The central bank's equations

$F_{cb} = r_{b-1} \cdot B_{cbd-1}$	Central bank profits;	(11.76)
$BL_s = BL_d$	Bonds are supplied on demand;	(11.77)
$B_{hs} = B_{hd}$	Household bills supplied on demand;	(11.78)
$H_{hd} = H_{hs}$	Cash supplied on demand;	(11.79)
$H_{bs} = H_{bd}$	Reserves supplied on demand;	(11.80)
$H_s = H_{bs} + H_{hs}$	Supply of high powered money;	(11.81)
$B_{cbd} = H_s$	Central bank bills (balance sheet);	(11.82)
$B_{cbs} = B_{cbd}$	Central bank buys bills that it demands;	(11.83)
$r_b = r_b$	The rate of interest on bills is set exogenously;	(11.84)
$r_{bL} = r_b + add_{BL}$	The long-term interest rate;	(11.85)
$p_{bL} = \dfrac{1}{r_{bL}}$	Price of long-term bonds.	(11.86)

In Model *GROWTH*, central banks have been simplified compared to the *INSOUT* model. The central bank only holds Treasury bills as assets while its liabilities are only made up of bank reserves and banknotes. As a result the profits of central banks, as given by equation (11.76), are equal to the interest payments they receive on their bill holdings. The next seven equations of Box 11.10, equations (11.77) to (11.83) are 'supply equals demand' conditions, in other words all supplies of assets passively match all demands. The various equations that describe how government securities or central bank liabilities are supplied on demand, allow the interest rates on Treasury bills and government bonds to be treated as exogenous variables, which is what equations (11.84) and (11.85) are saying, with the long-term rate assumed equal to the short-term rate plus a fixed mark-up.[14]

---

[14] This is obviously a simplifying assumption. A more complex representation of the evolution of the bond rate was presented in Chapter 5.

11.6   The banking sector

11.6.1   Deposit rates, monetary and credit aggregates

Box 11.11   Commercial banks' equations

$M_s = M_h$ | Bank deposits supplied on demand; | (11.87)

$L_{fs} = L_{fd}$ | Loans to firms supplied on demand; | (11.88)

$L_{hs} = L_{hd}$ | Personal loans supplied on demand; | (11.89)

$H_{bd} = \rho \cdot M_s$ | Reserve requirements of banks; | (11.90)

$B_{bs} = B_s - B_{hs} - B_{cbs}$ | Bills supplied to banks; | (11.91)

$B_{bd} = M_s - L_{fs} - L_{hs} - H_{bd} + OF_b$ | Balance-sheet constraint of banks; | (11.92)

$B_{bs} = B_{bd}$ | The redundant equation; | (11.110A)

$BLR = \dfrac{B_{bd}}{M_s}$ | Bank liquidity ratio; | (11.93)

$r_m = r_{m-1} + \Delta r_m$ | Deposit interest rate; | (11.94)

$\Delta r_m = \zeta_m \cdot (z_1 - z_2)$ | Change in deposit rate; | (11.95)

$z_1 = 1$ iff $BLR < bot$ | Logical functions dependent on whether the bank; | (11.96)

$z_2 = 1$ iff $BLR > top$ | liquidity ratio is within its *bot* and *top* range. | (11.97)

We now tackle the banking sector. The innovative part is mainly to be found in the equations of Box 11.12. All of the equations of Box 11.11 are familiar to readers of Chapter 10. Equation (11.87) indicates that money deposits are endogenous, being created on demand, which is to say that banks will always credit (debit) the account of a householder who receives (pays) a cheque from (to) another party, including the government, or exchange credit money for cash and vice versa. But when we say that banks accommodate households in this way, their function is not well described by saying that they are 'supplying' money to households, and the whole notion of a supply of credit money which is distinct from demand is chimerical, as Kaldor used to maintain so vehemently.

Equations (11.88) and (11.89) tell us that loans, both personal and corporate ones, are also supplied on demand to all creditworthy borrowers (firms that cannot get loans would not even be able to start production). Banks must also accumulate reserves proportional to their deposits, either in the form of deposits at the central bank or as banknotes in vaults and automatic teller machines (equation 11.90).

The stock of bills held by banks can be seen from two points of view, both arising from the identities of the balance sheet matrix. On one hand the supply of bills to banks can be seen as the supply left over after taking into account the bills supplied to households and the central bank (equation 11.91). On the other hand, there is a demand for bills by banks that arises from the balance sheet constraint of banks, given by equation (11.92). This equation is helpful for it establishes a link between the aggregates in the banks' balance sheet and the interest rate which is paid on bank deposits. Since deposits and loans are supplied on demand, while banks' reserves are predetermined and while banks' own funds OF_b are not under the full control of the banks, as we shall see with Box 11.12, it follows that the banks' holdings of bills, B_{bd}, must be the buffer that absorbs unequal fluctuations in the assets and liabilities of the banks.

But while banks have no direct control over the number of bills they hold, they have an indirect control, through changes in the spread between the deposit interest rate (which they administer) and the bill rate (which is administered by the central bank). As we saw with experiments of Chapter 10, the banks are able to bring back the bank liquidity ratio – the bill to deposit ratio – within an acceptable range, and this is the justification for equations (11.93) to (11.97). If the liquidity ratio drops below the acceptable range, the banks' response must be to raise the rate of interest they pay on money deposits relative to the given bill rate.

11.6.2 The determination of lending rates

Box 11.12 Commercial banks' equations

$r_l = r_m + add_l$	Loan interest rate;	(11.98)
$OF_b^T = NCAR \cdot (L_{fs-1} + L_{hs-1})$	Long-run own funds target;	(11.99)
$OF_b^e = OF_{b-1} + \beta_b \cdot (OF_b^T - OF_{b-1})$	Short-run own funds target;	(11.100)

$$FU_b^T = OF_b^e - OF_{b-1} + npl^e \cdot L_{fs-1}$$

Target retained earnings of banks; (11.101)

$$npl^e = \varepsilon_b \cdot npl^e_{-1} + (1 - \varepsilon_b)npl_{-1}$$

Expected proportion of non-performing loans; (11.102)

$$FD_b = \lambda_b \cdot Y_{-1}$$

Dividends of banks; (11.103)

$$F_b^T = (FD_b + FU_b^T)$$

Target profits of banks; (11.104)

$$F_b = r_{l-1} \cdot (L_{fs-1} + L_{hs-1} - NPL) + r_{b-1} \cdot B_{bd-1} - r_{m-1} \cdot M_{s-1}$$

Actual profits of banks; (10.105)

$$add_l = \frac{\{F_b^T - r_{b-1} \cdot B_{bd-1} + r_{m-1} \cdot (M_{s-1} - (1 - npl^e) \cdot L_{fs-1} - L_{hs-1})\}}{\{(1 - npl^e) \cdot L_{fs-1} + L_{hs-1}\}}$$

Lending mark-up over deposit rate; (11.106)

$$FU_b = F_b - FD_b$$

Actual retained earnings; (11.107)

$$OF_b = OF_{b-1} + FU_b - NPL$$

Own funds of banks; (11.108)

$$CAR = \frac{OF_b}{(L_{fs} + L_{hs})}$$

Actual capital adequacy ratio; (11.109)

$$B_{bd} = B_{bs}$$

Redundant equation. (11.110A)

We now arrive at an innovative part of Model *GROWTH*, at least when compared to the model of the previous chapter. As pointed out earlier in the chapter, banks target a certain level of profits, they retain part of these profits, and they accumulate equity capital so that they can manage fluctuations in the proportion of defaulting loans and also to fulfil the *capital adequacy ratios* which have been imposed on internationally-active banks by the Bank for International Settlements (BIS). Similar rules have also been imposed on banks operating domestically by most central banks or national regulatory agencies. As a result of these, banks are forced to hold a minimum amount of their own funds as a proportion of their liabilities. With this protection, the BIS hopes that any payment default will not spread to international banks, thus avoiding domino effects that could have devastating effects on the world financial system. Thus banks need to make enough profits to cover dividend payments that their private owners deem desirable, and to augment their own funds in line with the BIS rules on capital adequacy ratios. These two requirements, given the interest rates administered by the central bank, determine the spread between the rate of interest on loans and the rate of interest on deposits. Equation (11.98) of Box 11.12 says precisely this: the lending rate is equal to the deposit rate plus a spread, add_l, which remains to be determined.

The next equation (11.99) specifies required own funds, according to the rules set forth by the BIS in 1988. These rules say that banks must secure a minimum amount of capital (own funds) relative to their assets. The value of assets, for the purpose of this regulation, is weighted according to the presumed risk of these assets. In the case of our banks, there are only three kinds of asset: cash reserves held at the central bank, bills issued by central government, and loans made to the private sector. Cash reserves and Treasury bills carry a 0% risk weight, since they are liabilities of a sovereign government. Loans made to private firms and individuals carry a 100% risk weight.[15] Thus in our case, the minimum amount of required own funds must be a certain percentage of corporate and personal loans. This ratio, called the *capital adequacy ratio* or the *target standard ratio*, was initially set at 8%.[16] We assume that banks attempt to fulfil this ratio by targeting a ratio that is slightly higher than 8%, this ratio being the *normal capital adequacy ratio, NCAR*. The *NCAR* applies to the loans outstanding at the beginning of the current period (the loans owed at the end of the previous period), as shown in equation (11.99), because, when banks set their targets and take their interest rate decisions, they do not yet know the stocks of loans and deposits that will be realized at the end of the period. In this way, there is a strong likelihood that they will achieve the target standard ratio set by the BIS. We also assume that firms do not attempt to achieve the normal capital adequacy ratio all at once, and that they respond to a partial adjustment mechanism described by equation (11.100). Thus, in symmetry with the inventory adjustment process, OF_b^T is the own funds long-run target, while OF_b^e is the short-run target for the current period.

To increase their own funds, firms need to set aside undistributed profits.[17] As shown by equation (11.101), banks decide on a target for retained earnings

---

[15] Things have become more complicated in the *New Capital Adequacy Framework*, issued for comments by the BIS in March 2000, with its latest update in November 2005 (Basel Committee 2005). The new framework, called *Basel II*, is scheduled to be operational at the end of 2007. In Basel II, a lower risk weight is attributed to claims on corporations with AAA, AA and A ratings by rating agencies, while sovereign governments without a AAA or AA rating carry a positive risk weight (instead of a zero weight as was the case for OECD governments in Basel I). Other measures were already in place to take into account off-balance items, such as guaranteed credit lines arrangements or securitization of loans.

[16] 'The Committee confirms that the target standard ratio of capital to weighted risk assets should be set at 8% .... ' (Basel Committee, 1988: 14).

[17] We assume that bank owners do not put up funds of their own any more. Indeed, the BIS defines bank capital as *equity capital* and the past accumulation of retained earnings.

FU_b^T by computing the additional amount of own funds needed to fulfil the own funds short-run target and by making an estimate of the amount of own funds that will be lost through bad loans. Retained earnings must cover these two elements. The estimate of the percentage of non-performing loans, npe^e, is assumed to be based on past estimates and the past proportion of non-performing loans (equation 11.102).

On this basis, banks set themselves a target level of profits, F_b^T, which includes the target retained earnings that they need, plus additional profits to pay out distributed dividends FD_b, as seen in equation (11.103), this latter amount here being crudely assumed to be some fraction of the previous period's GDP (equation 11.104).[18]

So far we have only dealt with target profits. What then are realized profits? They are given by equation (11.105). Banks get revenues from the bills they hold and the loans they have made (more exactly those loans that did not default), while they must pay out interest on money deposits. All these rates are predetermined, since they were set in the previous period. Similarly, all stocks of assets and liabilities are predetermined, except for the size of non-performing loans that will not be known in the current period. As a consequence, bank profits in the current period are (nearly completely) predetermined from the actions and pricing decisions that were taken in the previous period. It follows that when banks are assessing their target of profits, they are really making an attempt to achieve profits and retained earnings for the next period. There is nothing they can do about the profits that will be announced at the end of the current period.

On the other hand banks can compute the spread between the deposit rate and the lending rate that would have generated the targeted level of profits had there been no mistake in their estimates. The formula for this spread is given by equation (11.106). This spread, on average, will allow the banks to meet their profit and capital adequacy objectives. To compute the required interest spread add_l, we equate the profit targets with the expected bank profits, thus obtaining:

$$F_b^T = r_{l-1} \cdot (L_{fs-1} + L_{hs-1} - npl^e \cdot L_{fs-1})$$
$$+ r_{b-1} \cdot B_{bd-1} - r_{m-1} \cdot M_{s-1}$$

---

[18] Indeed, it has been shown by Hubbard, Kuttner and Palia (2002) that banks with low realized capital adequacy ratios are prone to set higher lending rates, thus providing direct empirical justification for the equation determining the interest rate on loans that we suggest further down.

We then rewrite the loan rate r_l as a function of the deposit rate and the spread, as in equation (11.98). We get:

$$F_b^T = (r_{m-1} + add_l) \cdot (L_{fs-1} + L_{hs-1} - npl^e \cdot L_{fs-1})$$
$$+ r_{b-1} \cdot B_{bd-1} - r_{m-1} \cdot M_{s-1}$$

Rearranging and solving for the spread add_l, we obtain equation (11.106).

Actual retained earnings of the current period will turn out to be the difference between actual bank profits and distributed dividends (11.107). Knowing this, it is possible to compute the actual own funds of the banks at the end of the current period. The banks' capital will be equal to their own funds of the previous period, plus the retained earnings of the current period, minus the actual amount of defaulting loans in the current period, as shown by equation (11.108). Finally, at the end of the period, it will be possible to compute the actual capital adequacy ratio, *CAR*, the end-of-period own funds to loans ratio given by equation (11.109), and compare it with the target capital ratio set by the BIS or with the normal capital adequacy ratio targeted by banks.

We cannot close the presentation of Model *GROWTH* without mentioning the redundant equation of the model. A quick look at Box 11.11 will reveal that we have two equations dealing with the stock of bills held by banks, B_{bs} given by equation (11.91), while B_{bd} is given by equation (11.92). These two quantities, the supply of and the demand for bills, are reached by quite distinct routes. It might for a moment, be supposed that an equilibrium condition, equation (11.110A) of Box 11.11, is required to bring supply into equivalence with demand and thereby, conceivably, making the bill rate of interest endogenous. But no such equilibrium condition is required. We have reached the point at which every other demand has been matched by supply, and therefore under quasi-Walrasian principles, this last must hold as well by the logic of the comprehensive accounting system, without any equation to making this happen. So the solution to the problem, as usual, is simply to drop (11.110A) from the computer model. The equality between demand and supply for bills from and to banks (verified in every simulation experiment) provides the inconspicuous headstone which validates the entire logical structure of the model.

11.7 Fiscal and monetary policies

11.7.1 Preliminaries

Up to now our style of exposition has not been enormously different from the narrative style used by most post-Keynesian authors as well as by Keynes himself. Equations have been attached to all substantial propositions, but there has been little suggestion that these are more than decorations. However the building of a fully articulated simulation model has been the fundamental tool which has made this work possible. Starting from models similar to Godley (1999a), Lavoie and Godley (2001–2), Dos Santos and Zezza (2005) and Godley and Lavoie (2006), the computer model underlying this paper has grown by accretion; and without it, it would have been impossible to be even remotely sure that the system functioned as an organic whole when the individual propositions were strung together.

Not only does the model exist, it solves freely, it satisfies all the accounting constraints (including the identity between demand and supply of the bank's holdings of bills, although there is no equation to make this happen) and it has, when simulated, all the properties claimed for it. For instance, when shocked from its steady state, prices do not immediately respond either way, yet profits are generated which in due course are sufficient to pay for fixed investment and to make adequate distributions to creditors and shareholders.

We end by describing some of the main findings, noting that alternative solutions to the model all start from a *'base line'* solution extending over seventy odd 'years' in which a steady state has been reached with all stocks and all flows rising at the same rate – namely 3% per period (per annum). The nominal wage rate rises by about 3.25% per annum, normal productivity by exactly 3% and prices by about 0.25%. All shocks to the system will be imposed in the 'year' 1965.

11.7.2   An autonomous increase in wage inflation

We conduct our first experiment by considering the case of an autonomous increase in the rate of wage inflation, because it will be of some relevance for all the experiments that follow. Such an experiment was also conducted in Chapter 10, where we concluded that an autonomous increase in the target real wage rate, generating a persistent higher rate of inflation, would induce a fall in the level of real output, as long as nominal interest rates remain constant and households are aware of the capital losses inflicted by inflation. Does a similar result occur in our growth model, where households do take inflation losses into account?

To find out, we impose an exogenous increase in the real wage aspiration of workers, hiking up the Ω_0 parameter of equation (11.18). This induces a somewhat symmetric increase in wage inflation and price inflation, which persists in the long run, as shown in Figure 11.2A. The impact on real output and its main components, relative to their base line solutions, can be observed in Figure 11.2B. While real investment is barely affected, because of the fall in the real interest rate which is part of the argument of the investment function, real consumption is greatly diminished (relative to the base line case), and hence real output remains below its base line solution in the steady state. Thus, in our growth model, inflation generates a persistently lower real GDP level.

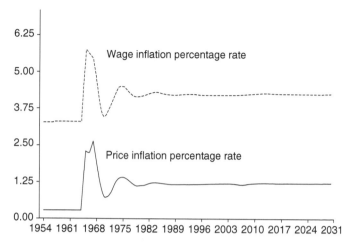

Figure 11.2A Evolution of wage inflation and price inflation, following an autonomous increase in the target real wage

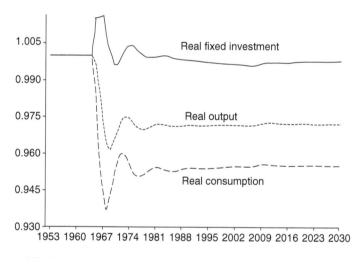

Figure 11.2B Evolution of real gross fixed investment, real output and real consumption, all relative to the base line solution, following an autonomous increase in the target real wage

The lower real output, relative to the base line solution, can be attributed to the fact, already identified in Chapter 10, that the real balance of the government sector gets reduced by inflation, thus reducing its contribution to effective demand.

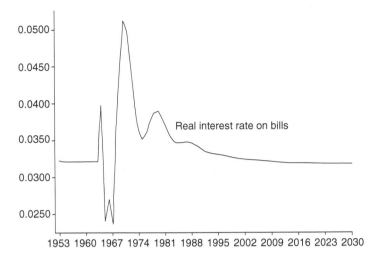

Figure 11.2C Evolution of the real interest rate on bills, following an autonomous increase in inflation, when the nominal bill rate is set so as to ensure a long-run real rate which is no different from the real rate of the base line solution

In a second experiment, with the same autonomous increase in wage inflation, we simultaneously modify the nominal rate of interest on bills, to insure that the real bill rate and the real bond rate, in the new steady state, are approximately equal to what they were in the original steady state. This is shown in Figure 11.2C, where after some sharp fluctuations, the real bill rate converges to its starting value. However, the negative consequences of inflation remain, as can be seen in Figure 11.2D. Indeed, real output relative to its base line solution barely changes compared with the situation described in Figure 11.2B, where the nominal bill rate was constant. This can be ascribed to the brisk fall in the real wealth of households (which enters the consumption function). This fall can be attributed to two effects. First, the increase in the nominal bond rate that accompanies inflation reduces bond prices and hence the wealth of households. Second, the higher rates of return on deposits, bills and bonds reduce the demand for equities, as can be read from portfolio equation (11.66), thus inducing capital losses on the stock market.

Thus, in the case of a growth model, the negative effects of inflation on real output remain, whether nominal interest rates stay constant or move up with inflation.[19] And this must be kept in the back of our mind as we analyse

---

[19] Assuming that households do not take inflation losses into account does not change this conclusion.

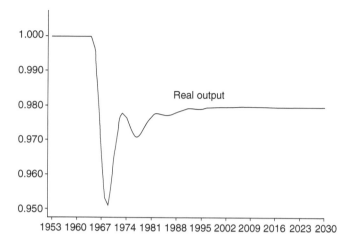

Figure 11.2D   Evolution of real output, relative to the base line solution, following an autonomous increase in inflation, when the nominal bill rate rate is set so as to ensure a long-run real rate which is no different from the real rate of the base line solution

the impact of parameter changes that may involve substantial changes in the inflation rate.

11.7.3   A one-period increase in the growth rate of pure government expenditures

We start our various fiscal experiments by imposing a one-period boost to the growth rate in real pure government expenditures g. In other words, the growth rate in real pure government expenditures moves from 3% to 3.5% in 1965, only to come back right away to 3% in all the following years. This simply means that the share of real government expenditures in real output moves up in 1965. The implications of such a change are illustrated with a series of Figures 11.3.

In Figure 11.3A, real pure government expenditure and real output y are expressed relative to the levels which these two variables take in the base line solution. From 1965 on, government expenditures are nearly one percent higher than the value that they took in the base line case. The immediate effect on real output is less than the addition to government expenditure because the shock was unexpected so inventory accumulation turns negative, but the multiplier effects gradually take effect. Real output also becomes nearly one percent higher than its base line solution. The graph indicates that fiscal policy can be quite successful in increasing the level of output.

The following Figure 11.3B, illustrates the same outcome, but seen from the labour market. The one-year increase in government expenditures that was imposed achieves a permanent increase in the employment rate, which

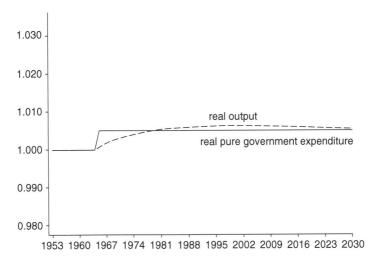

Figure 11.3A Evolution of real output and real consumption, relative to the base line solution, following an increase in the rate of growth of real pure government expenditures for only one year

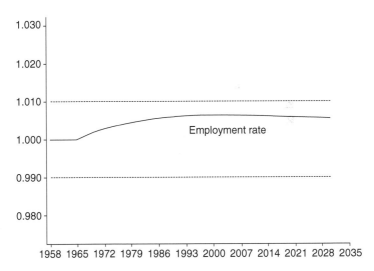

Figure 11.3B Evolution of the employment rate, assumed to be at unity in the base line solution, following an increase in the rate of growth of real pure government expenditures for only one year

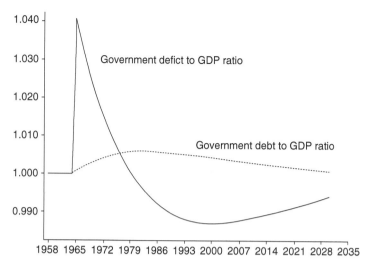

Figure 11.3C   Evolution of the government deficit to GDP ratio and of the government debt to GDP ratio, relative to the base line solution, following an increase in the rate of growth of real pure government expenditures for only one year

rises gradually nearly one percent above the value of its base line solution (which was assumed to be 100%, i.e. 'full' employment). In the present case, the employment rate remains within the range where higher employment does not generate any additional change in the target real wage rate, and as a consequence there is no change to speak of in the rate of price inflation. This insures that the problems linked with higher inflation rates, evoked in the previous subsection, are being avoided. Fiscal policy is thus able to generate a moderate increase in the rate of employment, or a reduction in the unemployment rate.

Figure 11.3C shows the implications of this one-time expansionary fiscal policy on the fiscal indicators which are being watched by financial analysts. Once again these two indicators are shown relative to the base line solution, where both the deficit to GDP ratio and the debt to GDP ratio reach steady percentages. Somewhat surprisingly, both of these ratios go back to their base line values. In other words, as long as the rate of inflation remains unaffected, the one-shot increase in the growth rate of government expenditures will have no long-run impact on the debt to GDP ratio and the deficit to GDP ratio, although it will generate a brisk increase in the short-run deficit to GDP ratio. What this demonstrates is that, to a large extent, these two ratios are determined by factors that are out of the direct control of the government.

Finally Figure 11.3D gives some further, less obvious, implications of the one-time increase in government expenditures. The expansion of output and

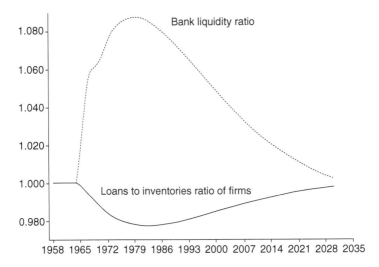

Figure 11.3D Evolution of the bank liquidity ratio and of the loans to inventories ratio of firms, relative to the base line solution, following an increase in the rate of growth of real pure government expenditures for only one year

employment during the transition to a new steady state improves the debt position of firms temporarily. Their loans to inventories ratio becomes lower than in the base line case, in particular because the loans needed by firms decrease relative to the base line solution. The implication for banks is that their liquidity ratio – their bill to deposit ratio – rises relative to the base line solution in the early steps of the transition, because of the relative fall in loans to firms and because of the relative increase in the quantity of bills which they hold. However, in the later steps of the transition, the banks' liquidity ratio gradually converges back to its initial level, endogenously, without any need to change the interest rate on deposits.

We conclude this subsection with a reminder that tax policy could achieve similar results. Figure 11.3E illustrates the relative impact on consumption and output of a one-shot permanent decrease in the income tax rate θ. The impact on relative output is similar to that described in Figure 11.2A. In addition, there is virtually no long-run impact on the government deficit to GDP ratio and on the government debt to GDP ratio. Thus, fiscal policy, meaning here taxation, is able to bring back the economy to full employment or keep it there.

11.7.4 A permanent increase in the growth rate of pure government expenditures

We now pursue a similar but different experiment, assuming that the growth rate of real pure government expenditures g moves up permanently from

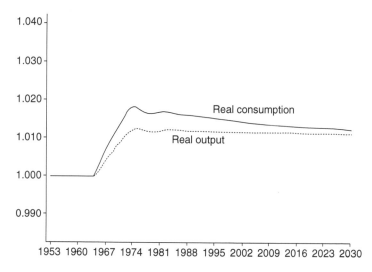

Figure 11.3E   Evolution of real consumption and real output, relative to the base line solution, following a permanent one-shot decrease in the income tax rate

3.0% to 3.5% in 1965. Since the labour force is constant, while the rate of growth of normal labour productivity remains at 3%, the rate of employment rises forever, as is illustrated in Figure 11.4A. This is accompanied by a rise in the rate of inflation, also shown in the right-hand side vertical axis of Figure 11.4A, as the rise in the employment rate encourages workers to target real wage increases that go beyond productivity increases.

Figure 11.4B only shows growth rates of real variables. Initially, all three real variables (pure government expenditures, capital and output) grow at the same rate. The growth rate of real pure government expenditures is then forever hiked up. Surprisingly, while the rate of output growth initially seems to follow the tracks of pure government expenditures, it then drops and oscillates towards a steady growth rate at about 3.1%, much below the 3.5% growth rate of real pure government expenditures, and this despite the fact that the real rate of capital accumulation does seem to be moving towards the 3.5% figure.

There is nothing surprising about the rise in the rate of capital accumulation, since the rising inflation rate generates falling real interest rates, which are part of the argument of the investment function, given by equation (11.7), remembering that by construction the *nominal* bill rate (the king-pin of the monetary system) is exogenous and, in this simulation, fixed.[20] What is

---

[20] Since the growth rate of output in the later years is lower than the growth rate of capital, this implies that the rate of capacity utilization is gradually falling.

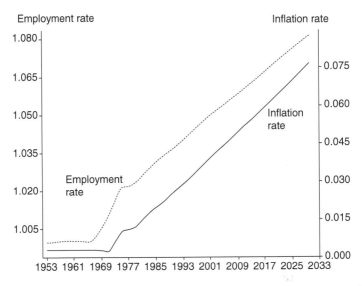

Figure 11.4A Evolution of the employment rate and of the inflation rate, with the growth rate of real pure government expenditures being forever higher than in the base line solution

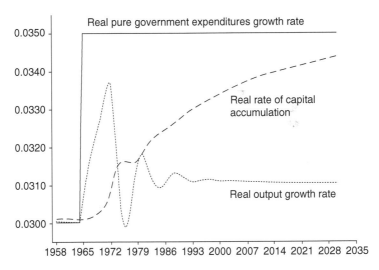

Figure 11.4B Evolution of the real rate of capital accumulation and of the growth rate of real output, with the growth rate of real pure government expenditures being forever higher than in the base line solution

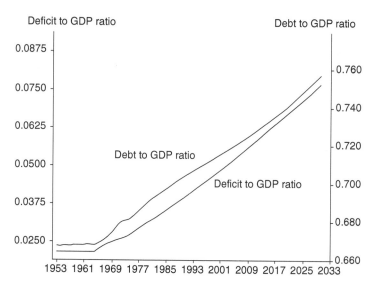

Figure 11.4C   Evolution of the government deficit to GDP ratio and of the government debt to GDP ratio, with the growth rate of real pure government expenditures being forever higher than in the base line solution

surprising is the fact that the growth rate of output would not converge to the growth rate of real pure government expenditures. This is due to the fact, already noted in Chapter 10, that government expenditures are made up of two components: pure expenditures and debt servicing expenditures. With a constant nominal interest rate, the debt servicing expenditures cannot rise at the pace set by pure expenditures.

The consequences for the financial ratios of the government sector are quite devastating. These are shown in Figure 11.4C. The government deficit to GDP ratio, as shown on the left-hand side of the vertical axis, rises continuously through time, showing no tapering sign. Similarly, the debt to GDP ratio keeps moving up, thus indicating that the overall government expenditures grow faster than national income.

One may wonder what would occur if the real bill rate, rather than the nominal bill rate, were the exogenous variable. Before we examine this case, let us first see what happens when there is an increase in the nominal bill rate. This will help us to understand the case of an endogenous interest rate.

11.7.5   A permanent increase in the bill rate of interest

In this third experiment, we assume that the central bank decides to crank up the interest rate on bills by 25 basis points every two periods, with four consecutive hikes, starting in 1965. The bill rate thus moves from 3.5% in 1964 up to 4.5% in 1971, where it remains thereafter. The evolution of the bill

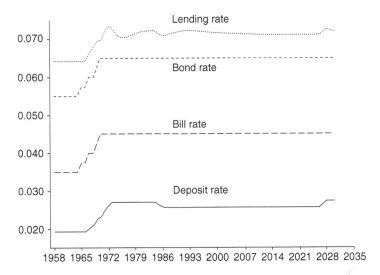

Figure 11.5A Evolution of the lending rate, the deposit rate, and the bond rate, when the (nominal) bill rate is being hiked up in steps and then kept at this higher level

rate is shown in Figure 11.5A, which also illustrates the bond rate, the deposit rate and the lending rate, which all follow, to a greater or lesser degree, the increase in the bill rate.

Since investment and new personal loans are a function of the real lending rate (which also rises, since inflation is either steady or initially decreases), and since consumption depends on wealth, the value of which is negatively influenced by the increase in the bond rate, the restrictive monetary policy initially does its work, as can be seen from Figure 11.5B. Real output and real consumption (as well as the employment rate) relative to the base line case decrease rapidly, as most economists would expect, but the negative effects only last for a few periods. In the medium run real consumption and real output (as well as the employment rate) overtake the base line solutions until a new steady state is reached, with higher relative levels. Thus, just as we had observed on many occasions in our previous models with stationary long-run equilibria, the short-run impact of higher interest rates is negative, but the long-run impact is positive. There is no change in the long-run growth rate of the economy, but once the transition period is over, real GDP values are higher than the base line solutions. This surprising result can once again be attributed to the fact that overall government expenditures, which are the multiplicand of the multiplier process, are now larger because of the larger interest payments that are necessary to service the government debt.

Let us now look at some of the financial implications of the central bank decision to hike up interest rates. Figure 11.5C shows that in the medium

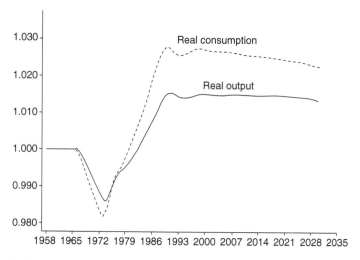

Figure 11.5B   Evolution of real consumption and real output, relative to the base line solution, when the (nominal) bill rate is set at a higher level

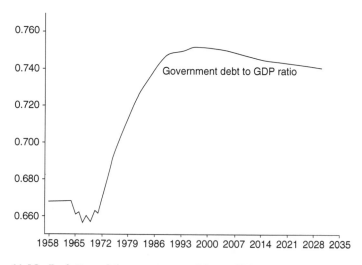

Figure 11.5C   Evolution of the government debt to GDP ratio, when the (nominal) bill rate is set at a higher level

and long run, higher interest rates lead to rising government debt to GDP ratios, starting at 66.7%, dropping temporarily at 65.6% because of the fall in the value of bonds, then peaking at 75.2% until it converges to a steady state around 74%. One can guess that if the increase in interest rates had

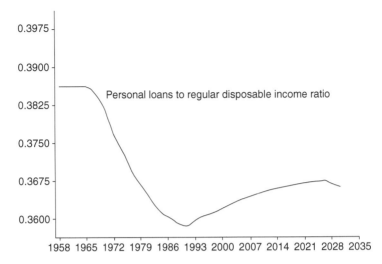

Figure 11.5D Evolution of the personal loans to regular disposable income ratio, when the (nominal) bill rate is set at a higher level

been more than 100 basis points, the impact on public debt ratios would have been quite devastating.[21]

The impact on the finances of households can also be examined. First, Figure 11.5D shows that higher interest rates discourage households from borrowing, as assumed in equation (11.57). The personal loans to regular disposable income ratio drops through time. As to the debt-service burden of personal debt, *BUR*, which is defined in equation (11.62) as the weight of interest payments and debt repayment, it is initially driven up as shown in Figure 11.5E, because of higher interest payments, but then driven down as households decline to take on new loans.

11.7.6 Expansionary fiscal policy and neutralized monetary policy

Let us now come back to our second experiment, where the growth rate of real pure government expenditures was pushed up permanently from 3% to 3.5%. We now assume that the central bank abandons its nominal peg of the bill rate. We shall be assuming two different kinds of behaviour on the part of the central bank.

---

[21] With our parameters, when the bill rate moves from 3.5% to 8.5%, the kind of increase that OECD countries have experienced in the 1980s or early 1990s, the steady-state public debt to GDP ratio moves from 66% to 99% – a change which has also been experienced by several countries in those years.

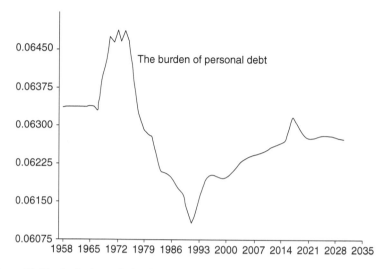

Figure 11.5E Evolution of the burden of personal debt (the weight of interest payments and principal repayment, as a fraction of personal income), when the (nominal) bill rate is set at a higher level

First, we assume that the central bank attempts to keep real rates, more precisely the bill rate, at a constant level. Will this be helpful and help the economy to stabilize towards the growth rate engineered by the fiscal authorities? We insert into Model *GROWTH* an adjustment mechanism by which the central bank retains an approximately constant real bill rate, quickly adjusting the nominal bill rate to any realized change in the inflation rate. We have the following equations:

$$r_b = (1 + rr_b) \cdot (1 + \pi) - 1 \tag{11.111}$$

$$rr_b^T = \frac{(1 + r_b)}{(1 + \pi)} - 1 \tag{11.112}$$

$$rr_b = rr_{b-1} + \varepsilon_b \cdot (rr_b^T - rr_{b-1}) \tag{11.113}$$

with r_b the nominal bill rate, rr_b^T the target real bill rate, and rr_b the actual real bill rate.[22]

Such a mix of fiscal and monetary policies will be rather unsuccessful, as it generates a wild oscillating pattern in real output and in nominal interest

_____

[22] We are aware that these equations do not adequately the forward-looking behaviour of central banks nowadays, but we are doubtful that central banks are able to correctly predict future inflation rates anyway.

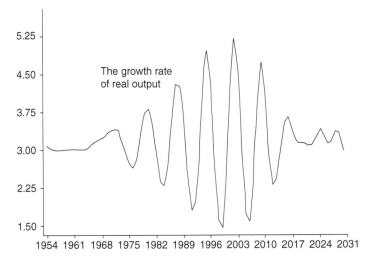

5.25

4.50   The growth rate
of real output

3.75

3.00

2.25

1.50

1954 1961 1968 1975 1982 1989 1996 2003 2010 2017 2024 2031

Figure 11.6A Evolution of the growth rate of real output, with the growth rate of real pure government expenditures being forever higher than in the base line solution, when the central bank attempts to keep the real interest rate on bills at a constant level, but with a partial adjustment function

rates (Figures 11.6A and 11.6B). This cyclical behaviour can be explained in the following way. The increase in nominal rates of interest at first generates negative effects, but these are wiped out by the positive effects arising from the larger multiplicand associated with larger government debt servicing. But as further increases in interest rates are required, new negative effects arise, followed by still more new positive effects, thus generating the cycle.[23]

Let us now assume a different behaviour on the part of the central bank. The central bankers may figure that the fiscal authorities are mistaken in their decision to have real pure government expenditures growing at 3.5%, and attempt to rectify the situation by raising interest rates in such a way that monetary restrictions exactly counter-balance the expansionary effects of fiscal policy. In other words, by trial and error we construct a series of bill rate changes that keeps the employment rate at its initial full employment level, with the additional goal of keeping the inflation rate constant, despite

---

[23] A similar cyclical pattern emerges if we repeat our very first experiment, with a temporary boost in the rate of growth of real pure government expenditures which, this time, is sufficient to get the employment rate outside the flat range of the Phillips curve. The oscillations in the employment rate (and consequently in the inflation rate) generated by the attempt of the central bank to keep the real interest rate constant will become ever larger, despite the fact that real pure government expenditures are growing at the appropriate 3% rate.

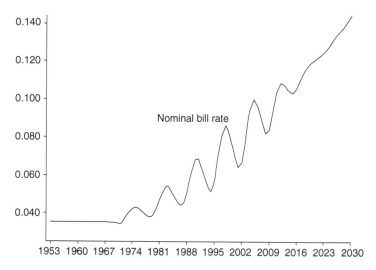

Figure 11.6B Evolution of the nominal bill rate, with the growth rate of real pure government expenditures being forever higher than in the base line solution, when the central bank attempts to keep the real interest rate on bills at a constant level, but with a partial adjustment function

the overly expansionary fiscal policy. Thus we grant the central bank the power to forecast correctly future real output and real employment, and to act accordingly in a forward-looking way, managing to keep the employment rate constant (as shown in Figure 11.6C). What then will happen?

Figure 11.6D traces the evolution of nominal interest rates. It is assumed that expansionary fiscal policy starts in 1960, but that the central bank avoids overheating by making a pre-emptive strike and raising the bill rate in 1959. As the fiscal authorities maintain an expansionary stance, interest rates must be raised again in the following years. It is visually clear that this combination of fiscal and monetary policies forces the central bank to raise the bill rate exponentially, with accelerating real rate increases.[24] The model is in an exploding mode.

We are far from being able at this stage to draw conclusions about the conduct of fiscal and monetary policy in the real world, in particular because the model under discussion describes a closed economy which is not being buffeted by external, or other, shocks. Nevertheless, the results illustrated in

---

[24] Indeed, despite the employment rate being constant, the rate of inflation decreases after a while, since the higher real lending rates reduce the incentive to accumulate capital, thus leading to a reduction in the ideal mark-up (since relatively less retained earnings are needed), and hence to a reduction in price inflation.

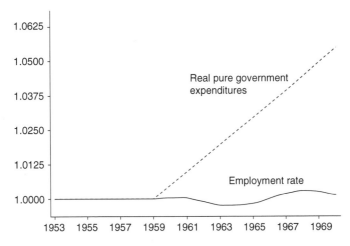

Figure 11.6C Evolution of real pure government expenditures and of the employment rate, relative to the base line solution, with the growth rate of real pure government expenditures being forever higher than in the base line solution, when the central bank attempts to keep the employment rate at a constant level in a forward-looking manner

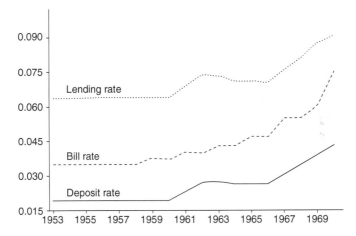

Figure 11.6D Evolution of the lending rate, the bill rate and the deposit rate, with the growth rate of real pure government expenditures being forever higher than in the base line solution, when the central bank attempts to keep the employment rate at a constant level in a forward-looking manner

Figure 11.6D are interestingly suggestive. They carry the implication, using this particular model, that, *given average tax rates*, government expenditure must normally be made to grow at the same rate as the (growing) steady state of the economy and that there is a (nearly) unique *level* of government expenditure which is the counterpart of full employment. If fiscal policy (the relationship between government expenditure and tax rates) is set in some other way, monetary policy is unable to keep the economy on an even keel for more than a short time.

Despite the misgivings that have been expressed over the last thirty years or so, fiscal policy, in our opinion, is the key instrument to drive and maintain the economy to a full employment position with low inflation.[25]

11.8 Households in the model as a whole

We now move on to experiments involving changes in household decisions. We shall do three of these. The experiments will revolve around the propensity to consume, the willingness to acquire new loans, and portfolio preferences.

11.8.1 An increase in the propensity to consume out of regular income

In this subsection, we repeat an experiment that was conducted with several earlier models. We impose an increase in the propensity to consume out of the regular disposable income that households expect to obtain in the current period. This propensity is parameter α_1 in equation (11.53). Indeed, the parameter applies not only to regular disposable income but also to the value of net new loans that households obtained in the current period.

The reader may recall that in models devoid of a government sector, Keynes's paradox of thrift held up: an increase in the propensity to consume led to an increase in national income; by contrast, in models with a government sector, a higher propensity to consume led, in the long run, to reduced national income. What will be the result of a higher propensity to consume in a growth model such as ours?

The answer is provided by Figure 11.7A. The higher propensity to consume initially propels consumption and real GDP upwards relative to the base line solution. In the long run, however, real consumption and real output go

---

[25] We believe that central banks have been able to keep inflation under control as a result of a combination of factors, including the high rates of unemployment that most OECD countries have faced in the 1980s and early 1990s and the modified competitive environment arising from world globalization, both of which have restricted the ability and willingness of labour unions and employees to demand higher wages, even in times of high employment and high economic activity.

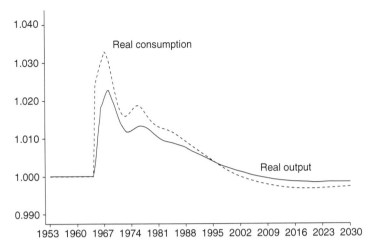

Figure 11.7A Evolution of real consumption and real output, relative to the base line solution, following a one-step permanent increase in the propensity to consume out of regular income

back to the levels that they would have achieved in the base line case. This implies that the growth rates of real output and consumption are temporarily above 3%, then temporarily below 3%, and back to 3% in the long run. What has happened is that, for a time, consumers' intake is more than they would have had, had the propensity to consume remained at its initial level. And similarly, the employment rate, which roughly follows the path of real output, is higher than in the base line case for a number of periods, going back to its 'full employment' level in the long run. We may thus conclude that a higher propensity to consume has a positive impact on the economy (meaning real GDP) in the short run, and no impact (or no discernible impact) in the long run. In other words, in this model, there is no trade off between present consumption and future consumption.

Figure 11.7B, shows how this consumer binge can be achieved. The real wealth of households relative to the base line case diminishes during the transition, until real wealth starts growing once more at the rate given by the base line case. The long-run impact of the increase in the propensity to consume is thus a smaller amount of household wealth.

Figure 11.7C illustrates the impact of a higher propensity to consume on the inflation rate. When consumption and production are speeded up, with the employment rate going beyond the upper limit of the flat portion of the Phillips curve, the inflation rate moves up; but it gradually falls back to a level which is comparable to that of the base line case. It is interesting to note that the initial increase in economic activity leads to a small *decrease* in the rate of

424

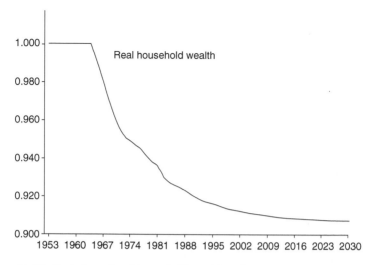

Figure 11.7B Evolution of real household wealth, relative to the base line solution, following a one-step permanent increase in the propensity to consume out of regular income

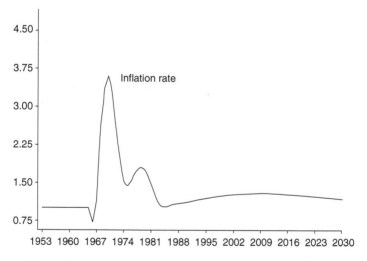

Figure 11.7C Evolution of the inflation rate, relative to the base line solution, following a one-step permanent increase in the propensity to consume out of regular income

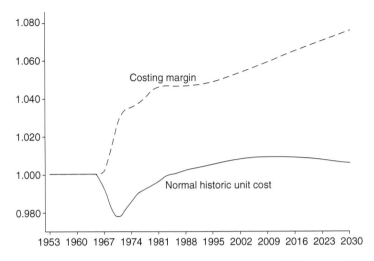

Figure 11.7D Evolution of the costing margin of firms and of their normal historic unit costs, relative to the base line solution, following a one-step permanent increase in the propensity to consume out of regular income

inflation (in the 'year' 1966, one period after the demand shock). The cause of this decrease is to be found in Figure 11.7D. While the costing margin of firms stays put in the first one or two periods, for a number of years there is a decrease in the normal historic unit cost *NHUC* relative to the base line solution. The cause of this is mainly that, as output rises above trend, there is a short-term increase in labour productivity which reduces the normal unit cost *NUC* relative to the base line case – a well-known stylized fact that our model is able to reproduce.

The short-run speed-up in economic activity is also reflected in the financial ratios of producing firms. As shown in Figure 11.7E, the retained earnings to fixed investment ratio, both terms being expressed in gross terms, moves up in the short run, as firms achieve higher than trend profits due to the relative increase in economic activity. Figure 11.7E also shows that this can be attributed in part to the fact that stocks of inventories (relative to the base line case) decline in the upward part of the business cycle. Both of these series get back to normal when the economy goes back to its new steady state.

What are the other implications for the economy as a whole? Figure 11.7F charts the relative evolution of the government deficit to GDP ratio and the government debt to GDP ratio. Both decrease in the short run, and both reach a new steady state, at levels that are lower than the base line solution. While this is something that is to be expected, it is noteworthy, as it shows that the evolution of these government financial ratios depend to a large extent on the saving desires of the community. If households increase their

426

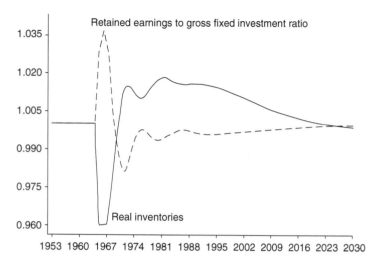

Figure 11.7E Evolution of the retained earnings to gross fixed investment ratio and of real inventories, relative to the base line solution, following a one-step permanent increase in the propensity to consume out of regular income

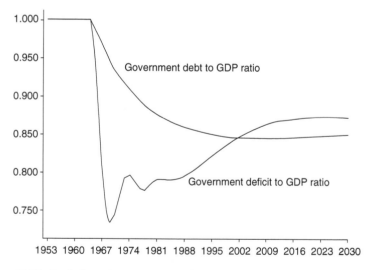

Figure 11.7F Evolution of government deficit to GDP ratio and of the government debt to GDP ratio, relative to the base line solution, following a one-step permanent increase in the propensity to consume out of regular income

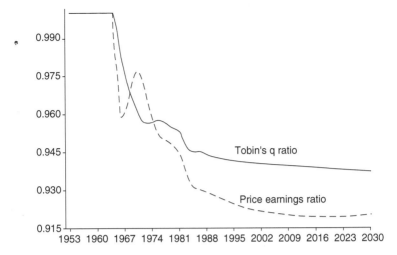

Figure 11.7G Evolution of Tobin's *q* ratio and of the price-earnings ratio, relative to the base line solution, following a one-step permanent increase in the propensity to consume out of regular income

propensity to consume out of regular income, or in other words reduce their implicit wealth to disposable income target ratio, this will have consequences for the government steady-state debt to GDP ratio. The relationship between household wealth and government debt is not a one-to-one relation, since the private sector, most notably the producing sector, also holds debt, and since part of this debt is liable to capital gains, but there is a close relation nonetheless.[26]

Finally in Figure 11.7G we draw the implications of the fall in the propensity to consume out of regular income for two private financial ratios – Tobin's *q* ratio (or Kaldor's valuation ratio) and the price-earnings ratio, which is a standard measure in financial economics. These two ratios are defined in equations (11.44) and (11.43). Both ratios drop to a lower value in the new steady state. The cause of this drop is that the higher propensity to consume reduces the flow of placements into financial assets, thus reducing the price of equities on the stock market relative to the base line case,[27] and helping to explain the fall in real wealth that was observed in Figure 11.7B.

[26] More precisely, it can be assessed from Table 11.1 that:

$$V = DG + L_{fd} + e_d \cdot p_e,$$

and more will be said about this in the conclusion of the chapter.

[27] This result is identical to the one found in the Kaleckian growth model of Godley and Lavoie (2001–2: 298).

11.8.2   An increase in the gross new loans
to personal income ratio

We now proceed to a new experiment, making use of the equations of Box 11.7 devoted to the determination of personal loans. The major parameter of household behaviour with respect to debt is η. This parameter represents the gross value of new loans as a portion of personal income that households are willing to take on, or are allowed to take on, in every period, as defined by equations (11.56) and (11.57). The parameter η is itself dependent on the real rate of interest on loans, so that the true exogenous parameter is η_0, and this is the parameter that is augmented in the next experiment.

Figure 11.8A shows, as one would expect, that the increase in the willingness to take on new loans leads to an increase in both the personal loans to personal income ratio and the debt-service burden of personal debt, *BUR*. Households thus decide to take on more debt as a proportion of their personal income, and this debt carries a heavier weight – interest and principal repayment – relative to their personal income. What are the consequences of this greater household willingness to go into debt (or the greater willingness of banks to grant credit to the household sector)?

Figure 11.8B shows the consequences for real consumption and real output. In the short run, this greater willingness to borrow leads to higher consumption and higher real GDP relative to the base line case. This positive effect, however, is only temporary. It is followed by a reversal, so that in the new

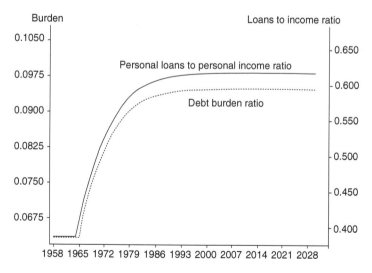

Figure 11.8A   Evolution of the personal loans to personal income ratio and of the burden of personal debt, following an increase in the gross new loans to personal income ratio

steady state, real consumption and real output (and hence the employment rate) are lower than they would have been in the base line scenario. These results thus give support to the arguments advanced by Palley (1996: 213), who wrote that, in the case of household debt, 'the crux of the argument is that borrowing initially serves to increase aggregate demand and output, but that debt service payments subsequently serve to reduce them'.

The picture shown in Figure 11.8B has interesting repercussions for the evolution of many OECD countries, most notably the United States and Canada, where aggregate demand over the last ten years or so has been sustained by a continuous expansion in the personal debt of households relative to their personal income (Godley 1999c; Godley and Zezza 2006; Papadimitriou *et al.* 2005; Papadimitriou *et al.* 2006; Seccareccia 2005). Several authors have wondered whether such a regime, where the growth of the economy is essentially driven by the willingness of households to accept ever higher debt to income ratio, could go on much longer. Figure 11.8B illustrates the fact that, even if households do nothing to reduce their debt to personal income ratio or their debt-servicing ratio, letting them rise towards their steady-state levels, there is some likelihood that aggregate demand in the future will be negatively affected by past decisions to increase the flow of new loans relative to personal income.

We next explore the implications of higher personal debt ratios for other sectors of the economy. Figure 11.8C shows what happens to the main ratios of the banking sector. Despite the increase in loans to the private sector,

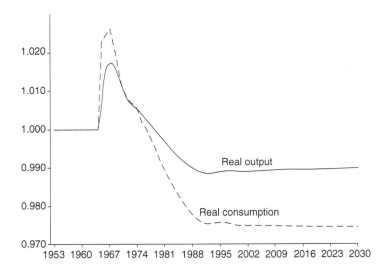

Figure 11.8B Evolution of real output and real consumption, relative to the base line solution, following an increase in the gross new loans to personal income ratio

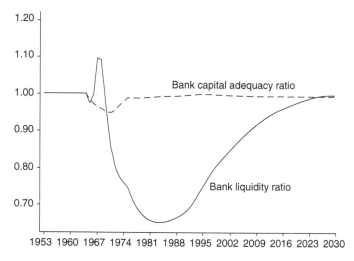

Figure 11.8C   Evolution of the bank capital adequacy ratio and of the bank liquidity ratio, relative to the base line solution, following an increase in the gross new loans to personal income ratio

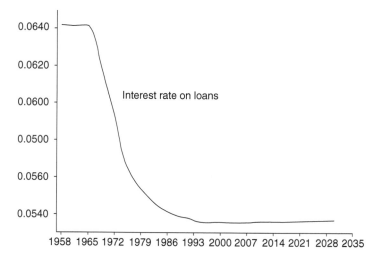

Figure 11.8D   Evolution of the lending rate set by banks, following an increase in the gross new loans to personal income ratio

banks have no trouble keeping their capital adequacy ratios at the proper level (indeed the lending rate does not even need to be raised; it falls as shown in Figure 11.8D). On the other hand, there are some large fluctuations in the bank liquidity ratio, but this ratio returns to its initial position endogenously,

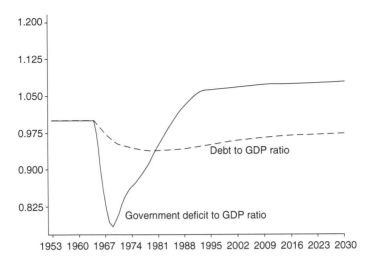

Figure 11.8E Evolution of the government deficit to GDP ratio and of the government debt to GDP ratio, relative to the base line solution, following an increase in the gross new loans to personal income ratio

without any change in the deposit interest rate. Thus the banking sector is able to absorb quite large fluctuations in loans to the personal sector.

The consequences for the finances of the public sector are shown in Figure 11.8E. In the short run, when the economy speeds up thanks to the borrowing binge of the household sector, the government deficit to GDP ratio drops, and so does the government debt to GDP ratio. However, as the negative effects of increased household borrowing take their toll on the economy, the government deficit ratio moves back up to an even higher level than in the base line case. Thus once more, we can see that the evolution of the financial ratios of the government sector do depend heavily on the saving or borrowing decisions of households.

11.8.3 An increase in the desire to hold equities

We now discuss changes in household liquidity preference. The innovative feature of this chapter with respect to portfolio choices is the introduction of equity prices. We thus shock our growth model by introducing a decrease in the preference for liquidity. This implies a higher λ_{40} parameter in portfolio equation (11.66). Since the sum of the λ_{i0} parameters must be equal to one, this implies that at least one of the other λ_{i0} parameters must be reduced. We assume for simplicity that only the λ_{10} parameter is correspondingly reduced, implying that households reduce their money deposits to acquire more stock market equities.

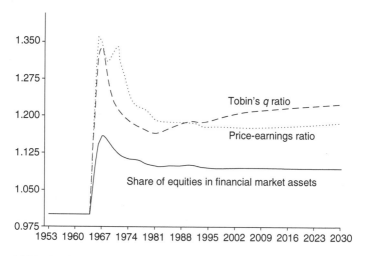

Figure 11.9A   Evolution of Tobin's *q* ratio, the price-earnings ratio and the share of equities in household wealth held in the form of financial market assets, all relative to the base line solution, following an increase in the household desire to hold stock market equities

The implications of such a change, relative to the base line solution, are illustrated in Figure 11.9A. First, the share of equities in the wealth of households which is held in the form of financial market assets (money deposits, bills, bonds and equities) does rise, nearly by definition. The increase in the demand for equities gets reflected in higher equity prices. Hence, as a result, the price-earnings ratio jumps, and so does Tobin's *q* ratio. There is some over-shooting in the reaction of all these ratios, but long-run steady-state values are all greater than in the base line case, as one would expect.

The reduction in liquidity preference leads to other substantial consequences. As shown in Figure 11.9B, real consumption and real output relative to the base line case increase, since real wealth, which has increased considerably because of large capital gains on stock market equities, is an argument of the consumption function. Surprisingly, in the long-run, the level of real output, relative to the base line case, is not any higher – indeed it is somewhat lower. This would seem to be best explained by the fact that gross real investment, relative to the base line case, is dropping.

Why is the rate of accumulation dropping below the trend rate of growth? The answer must be found within the banking system. A quick look at the banking system reveals that the bank liquidity ratio has taken a hard hit, due to the fact that households have reduced the size of their bank deposit holdings in their attempt to purchase additional stock market shares. Banks can absorb this deposit drain, but the buffer is made up of their bill holdings,

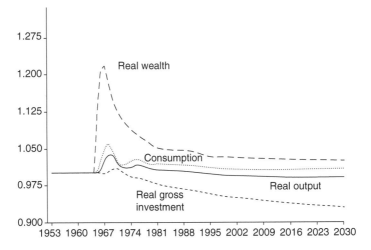

Figure 11.9B Evolution of real wealth, real consumption, real output and real gross investment, all relative to the base line solution, following an increase in the household desire to hold stock market equities

which must decline drastically.[28] To recover a proper bank liquidity ratio, banks must raise the deposit rate, and this is what they do, as can be seen in Figure 11.9C. But since banks must also preserve their profitability and their own funds, banks must also raise the lending rate, thus driving up the real rate of interest that enters into the accumulation function. This is why investment drops relative to the base case.

But things would have been completely different had households switched to stock market equities by reducing their holdings of government bonds and bills instead of reducing the size of their bank deposits. Figure 11.9D shows what would have had happened in this case. The bank liquidity ratio is driven up, as households sell their bonds and bills, with some of the latter being acquired by banks. As a result, with the liquidity ratio beyond the upper threshold, banks reduce the deposit rate in an attempt to get the liquidity ratio back to its normal range, and the lending rate follows the decrease in deposit rates.

Comparison of Figures 11.9C and 11.9D explains why it is important to be explicit about all portfolio equations. The implications for interest rates of an increase in the propensity to hold stock market equities turn out to be

---

[28] In the present experiment, the number of bills held by banks even becomes negative, which implies that banks must borrow them from the central bank, but the mechanism has not been made explicit, in contrast to the system described in Chapter 10.

434

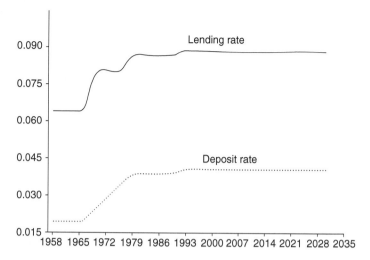

Figure 11.9C Evolution of the lending rate and the deposit rate, following an increase in the household desire to hold stock market equities, when this desire is offset by a drop in the desire to hold bank deposits

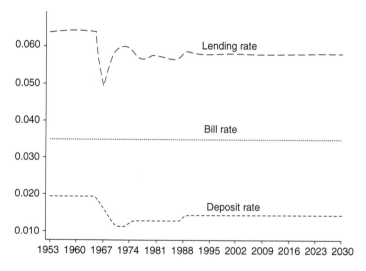

Figure 11.9D Evolution of the lending rate and the deposit rate, following an increase in the household desire to hold stock market equities, when this desire is offset by a drop in the desire to hold bills and bonds

quite different depending on whether the counterpart to this increase is to be found in a decrease in the propensity to hold money deposits, which was the residual equation in the portfolio system, or in a decrease in the propensity to hold bills and bonds. If the last portfolio equation is not explicit, then any increase in the desire to hold equities will be automatically reflected in a desire to hold a smaller proportion of money deposits. As Brainard and Tobin (1968: 103) point out, 'if this is an assumption one would not make deliberately, neither should he make it inadvertently'.

11.9 Financial decisions in the model as a whole

We close this chapter by making experiments related to financial issues. We discuss the target proportion of investment to be financed by internal funds; the proportion of loans that default; and the normal capital adequacy ratio of banks.

11.9.1 An increase in the target proportion of gross investment financed by retained earnings

Recall that it was assumed, in Box 11.4, that the ideal or target mark-up is a positive function of planned retained earnings of firms which are set as a proportion ψ_U of gross investment expenditures undertaken in the previous period. The complement of this proportion, $(1 - \psi_U)$, is to be raised on the capital markets, by issuing new shares. A possible experiment is thus to assume an increase in the target proportion of investment to be financed by internal funds. Such an increase simultaneously implies a reduction in the new issue of equities issues, thus reducing the relative quantity of equities on the stock market. Under such circumstances, we would expect the price of equities to rise, as when the preference for equities was on the rise. Is this what is observed?

Let us first deal with the ideal mark-up. Since the mark-up is now designed to generate more profits, a higher target proportion of gross investment financed by retained earnings generates a higher ideal costing margin. Indeed, in the experiment we move the ψ_U proportion up to 100%, implying that no new shares are issued from 1965 on.

The increase in the ideal costing margin can indeed be observed with the help of Figure 11.10A, with the brisk increase in the actual costing margin φ. The increase in prices and price inflation, and hence the reduction in the real wage caused by this higher costing margin immediately generates wage inflation, as shown in Figure 11.10B, thus yielding another example of conflict inflation, where inflation is driven by conflicting claims over the distribution of income. In the present case, the real wage target of workers is being frustrated by the increase in the costing margin. Wage demands are however tempered by the slowdown in economic activity, but still, in the

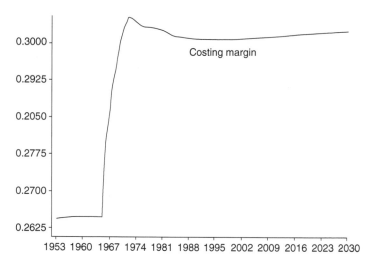

Figure 11.10A   Evolution of the costing margin of firms, following an increase in the target proportion of gross investment being financed by gross retained earnings

Figure 11.10B   Evolution of the wage inflation rate, following an increase in the target proportion of gross investment being financed by gross retained earnings

long run, wages rise at about 4.25% whereas they were rising at 3.25% in the initial steady state.

Figure 11.10C shows that real consumption and the employment rate (and hence real output) drop like a rock in the short run, only to partially recover

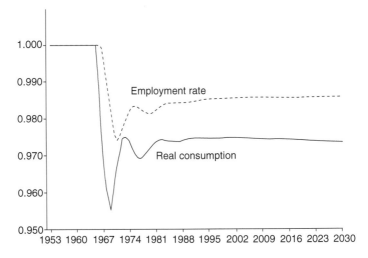

Figure 11.10C   Evolution of the employment rate and of real consumption, relative to the base line solution, following an increase in the target proportion of gross investment being financed by gross retained earnings

in the following periods, reaching new steady-state levels which are still lower than those of the base line solutions, most likely because of the increase in the inflation rate as we demonstrated with our very first experiment. Even though we have not assumed propensities to consume that are differentiated on the basis of income sources or social classes, the reduction in the real wage arising from the higher costing margin does have negative consequences for output and the employment rate. The lesson to be drawn from this is that for higher costing margins to have no negative impact on the economy, they must be accompanied by higher investment expenditures that sustain effective demand or that speed up productivity growth.

Finally, as mentioned at the beginning of this subsection, the smaller issues of stock market shares do lead to an increase in the price earnings ratio, and to a more obvious increase in Tobin's q ratio, as shown in Figure 11.10D. Figure 11.10E shows the evolution of the growth rate in equity prices, deflated by the overall price index, as well as that of some weighted average of the growth rate in entrepreneurial profits of firms, deflated in the same manner. As one would expect, deflated profits start by growing at 3%, as all real variables do in the base line steady state, and they end back growing at 3% in the new steady state. By contrast, it may noted that equity prices were initially growing at only 1.50%, and that they hiked up to above 5% when firms took the decision not to issue shares anymore. The (deflated) growth rate of equity prices then gravitates towards a 3% rate. Why then didn't equity prices grow at 3% in the base line steady state? It is because, in a steady state, the value

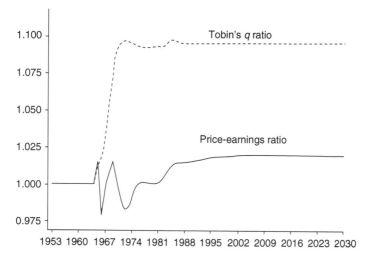

Figure 11.10D Evolution of Tobin's *q* ratio and of the price-earnings ratio, relative to the base line solution, following an increase in the target proportion of gross investment being financed by gross retained earnings, which also corresponds to a decrease in the proportion of investment being financed by new equity issues

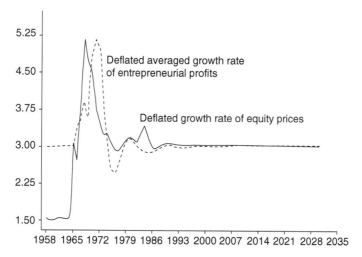

Figure 11.10E Evolution of the deflated averaged growth rate of the entrepreneurial profits of firms and of the deflated growth rate of equity prices, following an increase in the target proportion of gross investment being financed by gross retained earnings and no new equity issues

of all portfolio assets must grow at the same rate. But the value of equities is made up of a price times the number of equities. The growth rate of the value of equities is thus made up of three components, the growth rate of equity prices, the growth rate of equity numbers, and the product of these two growth rates. In the base line solution, firms did issue new equities, and as a consequence the deflated growth rate of equity prices had to be smaller than 3%.

11.9.2 Banks capital adequacy ratios

Another innovative feature of Model *GROWTH* is that it contains a parameter that tracks the percentage of bank loans to firms that default every period. This is the parameter *npl* first introduced in equation (11.40). What happens when this percentage rises?

The answer is provided in Figure 11.11A. The increase in the percentage of non-performing loans brings about a sharp decline in the banks capital adequacy ratio. Banks however manage to bring back the actual capital adequacy ratio towards its normal level within a short-time period. How is this accomplished? Figure 11.11B shows us how. The spread between the lending rate and the deposit rate is pushed up. Surprisingly however, while the capital adequacy ratio falls, the bank liquidity ratio rises, and this is why the deposit rate moves down, thus allowing the banks to keep the lending rate at a level which is not much higher than the base line solution lending rate.

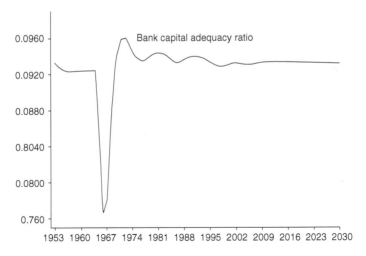

Figure 11.11A Evolution of the actual bank capital adequacy ratio, following an increase the percentage of non-performing loans (defaulting loans)

440

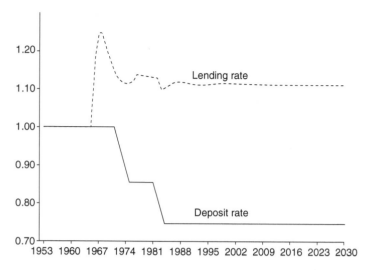

Figure 11.11B Evolution of the lending rate and deposit rate, relative to the base line solution, following an increase the percentage of non-performing loans (defaulting loans)

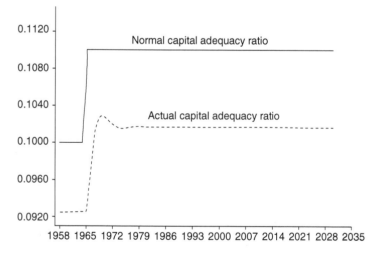

Figure 11.11C Evolution of the actual bank capital adequacy ratio, following a one-time permanent increase in the normal capital adequacy ratio

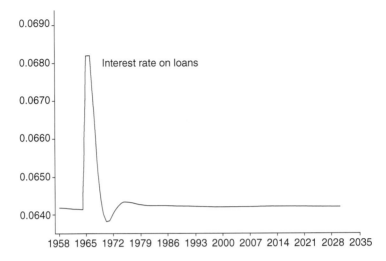

Figure 11.11D Evolution of the interest rate on loans set by banks, following a one-time permanent increase in the normal capital adequacy ratio

Similarly, if higher compulsory capital adequacy ratios were to be imposed on banks, or if they were to self-impose higher normal capital adequacy ratios, actual capital adequacy ratios could very quickly adapt to these new norms, described as *NCAR* in the model, as shown in Figure 11.11C. The higher actual ratio would be achieved by raising the interest rate, as shown in Figure 11.11D. In this case, however, in contrast to the case describing an increase in the percentage of defaulting loans, the increase in the lending rate would only be of a temporary nature.

11.10 A concluding recap

Our model is rooted in a solid, comprehensive and realistic accounting frame-work and, as we believe, accords with many stylized facts backed up by a lot of theory well grounded in the post-Keynesian tradition. In short, our conjecture is that subject to admitted major simplifications, the model does indeed provide important insights regarding the evolution of a modern industrial economy through historical time and the way in which the financial system fulfils an essential role, given that production takes time and all decisions have to be taken under conditions of uncertainty. Still, we are concerned because our most realistic model, which has been described in detail and illustrated with simulations, remains rather indigestible. Is it possible to grind out some analytic propositions which convey simply how the system as a whole works? Here is a suggestion.

The balance sheet matrix given in Table 11.1 tells us that household wealth turns out to be equal to the liabilities of the other two non-financial sectors, that is government debt and the liabilities of the producing firms. As pointed out in an earlier footnote, we have:

$$V = GD + L_{fd} + e_d \cdot p_e \tag{11.114}$$

The liabilities of firms can be rewritten in terms of their assets (fixed capital and inventories), through Tobin's q ratio equation. The previous equation, with the help of equation (11.44), can thus be rewritten as:

$$V = GD + q \cdot (K + IN) \tag{11.115}$$

so that the nominal government debt, by definition, has to be equal to:

$$GD = V - q \cdot (K + IN) \tag{11.116}$$

Dividing through by the price level, and recalling that $IN = in \cdot UC$, this identity becomes:

$$gd = v - q \cdot \left[k + in \left(\frac{UC}{p} \right) \right] \tag{11.117}$$

where gd is the real government debt. Dividing through by real output y, we obtain the government debt to GDP ratio:

$$\frac{gd}{y} = \frac{v}{y} - q \cdot \left[\left(\frac{k}{y} \right) + \left(\frac{in}{y} \right) \cdot \left(\frac{UC}{p} \right) \right] \tag{11.118}$$

But every one of the ratios on the right hand-side of the equation is perfectly determined, or nearly perfectly determined in the case of v/y, by a stock-flow norm in the steady state. In the case of in/y, making use of equations (11.3) and (11.5), we have:

$$\frac{in^*}{y^*} = \frac{(1+gr) \cdot \sigma^T}{\{1 + gr \cdot (1 + \sigma^T)\}} \tag{11.119}$$

where gr is the steady-rate of growth of the economy. The ratio k^*/y^* arises from equations (11.6)–(11.8):

$$\frac{k^*}{y^*} = \frac{(1+gr) \cdot \gamma_u}{(gr - gr_0 + \gamma_r)} \tag{11.120}$$

As to the v/y ratio, it is a rather complicated expression, but we can more easily get a similar ratio in terms of yp where $yp = YP/p$. With the help of equations (11.47)–(11.55), and omitting interest payments on personal loans, we obtain:[29]

$$\frac{v^*}{yp^*} = \frac{(1-\theta)\cdot(1-\alpha_1)\cdot(1+gr)}{\alpha_2 + gr + \pi - \dfrac{[(1+gr)\cdot(cg-\alpha_1\cdot nl)]}{v}} \tag{11.121}$$

where cg are the deflated capital gains (besides inflation losses).

As a reasonable approximation, we can say that the main difference between personal income and national income is made up of the internal funds retained by firms. As an approximation, with the help of equation (11.35) we an say that:

$$yp = \left[1 + gr - \psi_U \cdot gr\left(\frac{k}{y}\right)\right]\cdot y \tag{11.122}$$

so that:

$$\frac{v^*}{y^*} = \frac{(1-\theta)\cdot(1-\alpha_1)\cdot(1+gr)\cdot\left[1+gr-\psi_U\cdot gr\cdot\left(\dfrac{k^*}{y^*}\right)\right]}{\alpha_2 + gr + \pi - \dfrac{[(1+gr)\cdot(cg-\alpha_1\cdot nl)]}{v}} \tag{11.123}$$

Thus in the steady state with growth the ratio of government debt to GDP is given by the following expression,

$$\frac{gd^*}{y^*} = \frac{v^*}{y^*} - q^*\cdot\left[\left(\frac{k^*}{y^*}\right) + \left(\frac{in^*}{y^*}\right)\cdot\left(\frac{UC^*}{p^*}\right)\right] = \alpha_4 \tag{11.124}$$

where the ratio gd^*/y^* is in no degree an aspiration or policy decision of the government but a logical implication of the sum of private sector aspirations (mainly stock-flow norms), over which the government has no direct control.

This ratio, α_4, can be evaluated, using the numbers in our simulation model, as 0.667, from which it follows that the real budget deficit (the growth of real government debt), since the postulated economy is growing at 3%, is just under 2% of real GDP and the nominal deficit a bit more than 2% of nominal GDP.

We can use the formula given in the appendix of Chapter 3 to calculate the mean lag between the changes in the real fiscal stance and real output. We define the real fiscal stance, fs, as

$$fs = \frac{g'}{\theta'} \tag{11.125}$$

---

[29] When capital gains, personal loans and inflation losses are omitted, this equation comes down to equation A3.3.3 of Chapter 3.

where g' is total government outlays in real terms (inflation accounted) and θ' describes the ratio of tax receipts to GDP.

The mean lag, *ML*, is given by the expression:

$$ML = \frac{\alpha_4}{\theta'} \qquad (11.126)$$

which can be evaluated as a bit over 3 years.

Readers who reproduce the steady state of our simulation model will be able to verify that real output does indeed track the fiscal stance one for one with a lag of three years. While the mean lag formula is quite general, as pointed out by Godley and Cripps (1983: 125), it normally has no descriptive power during any transition to the steady state, if one occurs, when the fiscal stance is given a shock, as some of the lag weights typically become negative.

We conclude that the level and growth rate of the fiscal stance is predetermined if economic growth at full employment is to be achieved. But the government's budget deficit is equal, by identity, to personal saving plus firms' net saving (undistributed profits less investment in fixed and working capital) which we call 'private net saving'. There is no way in which the government can change private net saving measured at full employment, which will normally be positive. It necessarily follows that the steady state budget deficit is determined by private net saving, rather than the other way round, and that the budget balance must normally be in deficit. This is in accordance (or at least consistent) with one of Minsky's major contentions, but it is quite inconsistent with the ignorant assumption often made by politicians that the budget balance should be zero; it is also inconsistent with the Maastricht fiscal rules. It is a major anomaly that governments' fiscal policies, throughout the world, are judged by their budget deficits, measured *ex post*, over which they have little more control than over the money supply, while the fiscal stance itself is a number which is not often calculated, let alone admitted to the public discussion.

12
A More Advanced Open Economy Model

12.1 Introduction

The open economy model deployed in Chapter 6 was very much simplified, with fixed exchange rates and no private transactions in foreign assets, while central banks held all their foreign exchange reserves in the form of gold. In this chapter we add a number of realistic features.[1] Private agents trade foreign assets. Official account imbalances are settled normally by transactions in dollar-denominated assets, with gold only playing a small role. International trade depends both on national output and relative prices, implying a distinction between nominal and real values.[2] A minimum of five prices are considered: export prices, import prices, the price of sales, a domestic sales price and a GDP deflator. Fixed and flexible exchange rate regimes will both

---

[1] Our methodology, which is based on stock and flow matrices which embody all transactions within and between two or three countries, was developed by Godley during the nineties. The first paper published was Godley (1999b) which formed the basis for Taylor (2004a). There are now some models with three countries. Lequain (2003) has built a model with two countries sharing a single central bank (Europe), operating with a fixed exchange rate regime with a third country (the USA), the money of which is the international currency. Godley and Lavoie (2006b) have built a similar model, but operating with a flexible exchange rate regime. Zhao (2006) built a model with the first two countries (China and the USA) tied up by a fixed exchange rate, while a third country (Europe) is on a flexible exchange rate regime with these other two countries. None of these models (apart from Godley (1999b)) deal explicitly with prices. We have benefited from Lequain's formalization of a dollar exchange regime (an international monetary system based on the dollar rather than on gold), as can be seen in Godley and Lavoie (2003).

[2] This explains why a flexible exchange rate regime was not considered in Chapter 6. A flexible exchange rate regime implies changing price indices, and these could best be handled only after Chapter 8, where prices were first introduced. See Godley and Lavoie (2005–6) for a more heuristic but less formal attempt at handling a flexible exchange rate regime, without making use of prices.

be explored. But many simplifying assumptions remain. There are only two countries, there is no domestic or foreign investment in fixed or working capital,[3] firms do not hold financial assets, there is no endogenous wage inflation, there are no commercial banks or credit money, and the treatment of expectations is rudimentary. Yet we already need nearly one hundred equations to close the model and for inclusion of further realistic features we would require several more.

The present model, like all our previous models, evolves through time, solving dynamically from one period to the next. There are two parties to each transaction, while every financial balance has a counterpart change in balance sheets, making the model complete in the vitally important sense that the nth equation is logically implied by the other $n - 1$. This completeness provides some ostensive justification for the model by comparison with others which do not use a comprehensive accounting framework. Indeed the logical structure of the model and the need to find an equation for each of its one hundred odd variables brings some degree of inevitability to its overall properties, which might survive alternative specifications of key behavioural relationships, for instance the equations describing international trade or the consumption function.[4]

As in other chapters, we start by setting out the model's balance sheet and the transactions-flow matrices. We then present sets of equations describing how individual components of the model work on various different assumptions about how it is closed (fixed versus floating exchange rates). Various simulation experiments are then conducted which illustrate how the systems as a whole work.

12.2   The two matrices

Table 12.1 sets out the balance sheets of two economies, which will be called 'the United States' and 'the United Kingdom', as a single complete system. As no physical capital exists apart from foreign exchange reserves held in the form of gold, every asset is a financial asset which has a counterpart liability. Household wealth in each country has three components: cash (in the domestic currency only), bills issued at home and bills issued abroad. We use notations that are similar to those of Chapter 6, but instead of a North and South terminology, we have recourse to a dollar ($) and pound sterling denomination (£).

Bills issued by the government of one country can be held either by households or by the central bank of the other country. When describing bills,

[3] So we can revert to using stationary models without a major loss of insight.
[4] The model presented here is a heavily revised version of Godley (1999b) and Godley and Lavoie (2003).

Table 12.1 Balance sheets of the two economies

	Households	Firms	Govt.	Central bank	Exch. rate	Households	Firms	Govt.	Central bank	Sum
	UK (£ country)					US ($ country)				
Money	$+H^£$			$-H^£$		$+H^\$$			$-H^\$$	0
£ Bills	$+B_£^£$		$-B^£$	$+B_{cb£}^£$	$\cdot xr^£$	$+B_\$^£ \cdot xr^£$				0
$ Bills	$+B_£^\$ \cdot xr^\$$			$+B_{cb£}^\$ \cdot xr^\$$	$\cdot xr^£$	$+B_\$^\$$		$-B^\$$	$+B_{cb\$}^\$$	0
Gold				$+or^£ \cdot p_g^£$	$\cdot xr^£$				$+or^\$ \cdot p_g^\$$	$\Sigma or \cdot p_g^\$$
Balance	$-V^£$		$-NW_g^£$	$-NW_{cb}^£$	$\cdot xr^£$	$-V^\$$		$-NW_g^\$$	0	$-\Sigma or \cdot p_g^\$$
Sum	0	0	0	0	$\cdot xr^£$	0	0	0	0	0

a symbol indicating the issuing country will appear as a superscript, while the country where the asset is held will be indicated by a subscript. Thus, for instance, $B_\pounds^\$$ describes a bill owned by a UK household but issued in the United States and $B_{\text{cb}\pounds}^\$$ denotes a bill held by the UK central bank (the Bank of England) and issued in the United States. Second, supplies of bills are always denominated in the currency where the bills were issued while demand is always denominated in the currency of the country where the asset is held. Thus the supply of bills described by $B_\pounds^\$$ is denominated in dollars but the demand for them is denominated in pounds.

In the balance sheets shown in Table 12.1, every entry in the US section on the right is denominated in dollars (\$), and every entry in the UK section on the left is denominated in pounds (£). To obtain stocks of US bills held in United Kingdom and valued in pounds, their supply must be multiplied by the value of the US dollar in pounds (the exchange rate $xr^\$$). So the summation of rows (apart from cash which is not exchanged internationally) requires a multiplicative factor, the exchange rate $xr^\pounds$, which represents the value of one unit of the £ currency (the pound) in terms of dollars (the number of dollars per pound), and stands between the two halves of the matrix. Thus all the sterling data in the left half of the matrix are transformed into dollars, which can then be added to the dollar values on the right half. To get the hang of the accounting it may be useful to follow the trek taken by $B_\pounds^\$$, that is UK holdings of dollar bills $B^\$$ in Table 12.1. This variable starts off life as part of the total supply of dollar bills $B^\$$, denominated in dollars, in column 8. When it shows up as an asset owned by UK households in column 1 it has had to be multiplied by $xr^\$$ to convert it to pounds. But then to bring all items in row 3 into equivalence with one another it must be multiplied by $xr^\pounds$ in the middle of the table to convert it back to dollars.

Table 12.1 shows that firms hold no assets or liabilities and that governments issue only bills to finance their deficits. The liabilities of central banks consist of cash money while their assets consist of bills and gold (described by '*or*', as in Chapter 6). On the assumption that the price of gold in US dollars remains constant, the net worth of the US central bank has to be zero. By contrast, the net worth of the UK central bank may become positive (negative) when exchange rates vary, because of capital gains (losses) when the dollar currency appreciates (depreciates). This is because the price of gold is assumed to be set in dollars, and because the UK central bank holds bills denominated in dollars.

The flow matrix in Table 12.2 uses a double entry format to describe all transactions within and between the two economies and defines all the nominal variables which we shall use. All rows and all columns must sum to zero by accounting identity. As with the stock matrix, the left half of Table 12.2 describes all UK transactions measured in pounds (the £ currency); the right half describes US transactions measured in dollars (the \$

Table 12.2 Transactions-flow matrix of the two economies

	Households	Firms	Govt.	Central bank	Exch. rate	Households	Firms	Govt.	Central bank	Sum
	UK (£ country)					US ($ country)				
Consumption	$-C^£$	$+C^£$				$-C^\$$	$+C^\$$			0
Govt. Exp.		$+G^£$	$-G^£$				$+G^\$$	$-G^\$$		0
Trade		$-IM^£$ $+X^£$			$\cdot xr^£$ $\cdot xr^£$		$+X^\$$ $-IM^\$$			0
GDP	$+Y^£$	$-Y^£$				$+Y^\$$	$-Y^\$$			0
Taxes	$-T^£$		$+T^£$			$-T^\$$		$+T^\$$		0
Interest payments	$+r^£ \cdot B_£^£$ $+r^\$ \cdot B_£^\$ \cdot xr^\$$		$-r^£ \cdot B^£$	$+r^£ \cdot B_{cb£}^£$ $+r^\$ \cdot B_{cb£}^\$ \cdot xr^\$$	$\cdot xr^£$ $\cdot xr^£$	$+r^£ \cdot B_\$^£ \cdot xr^£$ $+r^\$ \cdot B_\$^\$$		$+r^\$ \cdot B^\$$	$+r^\$ \cdot B_{cb\$}^\$$	0
CB profits			$+F_{cb}^£$	$-F_{cb}^£$				$+F_{cb}^\$$	$-F_{cb}^\$$	0
Changes in:										
Money	$-\Delta H^£$			$+\Delta H^£$		$-\Delta H^\$$			$+\Delta H^\$$	0
£ Bills	$-\Delta B_£^£$		$+\Delta B^£$	$-\Delta B_{cb£}^£$	$\cdot xr^£$	$-\Delta B_\$^£ \cdot xr^£$				0
$ Bills	$-\Delta B_£^\$ \cdot xr^\$$			$-\Delta B_{cb£}^\$ \cdot xr^\$$	$\cdot xr^£$	$-\Delta B_\$^\$$		$+\Delta B^\$$	$-\Delta B_{cb\$}^\$$	0
Gold				$-\Delta or^£ \cdot p_g^£$	$\cdot xr^£$				$-\Delta or^\$ \cdot p_g^\$$	0
Sum	0	0	0	0		0	0	0	0	0

currency). There are seven entries common to both countries, those in rows 3, 4, 7, 8, 11, 12 and 13, and in each case (accounting) equivalence is brought about by the exchange rate, shown in the central column. The top section of the table gives, for each country, simplified components of the national income accounts. The middle section of Table 12.2 describes flows of interest payments. The lower third of the table describes transactions in assets – the flow-of-funds accounts.

The assumption that there are no private holdings of foreign cash implies that any payments or receipts of foreign currency from trade in goods or assets are simultaneously exchanged by the central bank into domestic currency. How the central bank and the government then respond to the implied *ex ante* change in foreign reserves will have profound consequences for the overall outcome.

12.3 Equations of the generic model

In this section we set out the equations which are common to all the closures of the model – the fixed and the flexible exchange rate regimes. In the section after this one, we will add the equations required to close the flexible exchange regime model, and we will show that it is a relatively simple task to move on to a fixed exchange regime.

12.3.1 Identities describing arterial flows

We begin with income and wealth definitions, in the spirit of Chapter 10. Regular disposable income (net of taxes), YD_r, is defined in Column 1 of the transactions-flow matrix; Haig–Simons disposable income, YD_{hs}, adds to regular income the capital gains obtained from holdings of foreign bills and caused by fluctuations in the exchange rate; the accumulation of private wealth, V in nominal terms, is equal to (Haig–Simons) disposable income less consumption. All these definitions apply first to the UK economy:

$$YD_r^£ = Y^£ + r_{-1}^£ \cdot B_{£s-1}^£ + r_{-1}^\$ \cdot B_{£s-1}^\$ \cdot xr^\$ - T^£ \tag{12.1}$$

$$YD_{hs}^£ = YD_r^£ + (\Delta xr^\$) \cdot B_{£s-1}^\$ \tag{12.2}$$

$$\Delta V^£ = YD_{hs}^£ - C^£ = (YD_r^£ - C^£) + (\Delta xr^\$) \cdot B_{£s-1}^\$$$
$$= NAFA^£ + CG^£ \tag{12.3}$$

where Y is total factor income, T is taxes, r is the bill rate of interest, C is consumption, B is Treasury bills, $NAFA$ is the net accumulation of financial assets by the household sector, and CG represents capital gains of the household sector.

Equation (12.1) gives the definition of regular disposable income denominated in pounds, hence interest payments on US bills (the third term on the right-hand side) is converted from dollars into pounds using the exchange rate, as can be read off from Column 1 in Table 12.2. Capital gains, which are included in equation (12.2), describe the change in the pound value of previously issued US bills measured in dollars; note once again that capital gains are not transactions and therefore have no place in the columns of the transactions-flow matrix given by Table 12.2.

Equations (12.4) to (12.6) give exactly comparable definitions for the US economy.

$$YD_r^\$ = Y^\$ + r_{-1}^\$ \cdot B_{\$\,s-1}^\$ + r_{-1}^\pounds \cdot B_{\$\,s-1}^\pounds \cdot xr^\pounds - T^\$ \tag{12.4}$$

$$YD_{hs}^\$ = YD_r^\$ + (\Delta xr^\pounds) \cdot B_{\$\,s-1}^\pounds \tag{12.5}$$

$$\Delta V^\$ = YD_{hs}^\$ - C^\$ = (YD_r^\$ - C^\$) + (\Delta xr^\pounds) \cdot B_{\$\,s-1}^\pounds$$

$$= NAFA^\$ + CG^\$ \tag{12.6}$$

We assume that governments only tax regular income, ignoring capital gains, so

$$T^\pounds = \theta^\pounds \cdot (Y^\pounds + r_{-1}^\pounds \cdot B_{\pounds\,s-1}^\pounds + r_{-1}^\$ \cdot B_{\pounds\,s-1}^\$ \cdot xr^\$) \tag{12.7}$$

$$T^\$ = \theta^\$ \cdot (Y^\$ + r_{-1}^\$ \cdot B_{\$\,s-1}^\$ + r_{-1}^\pounds \cdot B_{\$\,s-1}^\pounds \cdot xr^\pounds) \tag{12.8}$$

The identities describing the national income at current prices (Columns 2 and 6) are:

$$Y^\pounds = C^\pounds + G^\pounds + X^\pounds - IM^\pounds \tag{12.9}$$

$$Y^\$ = C^\$ + G^\$ + X^\$ - IM^\$ \tag{12.10}$$

where G is (pure) government expenditure, X is exports and IM is imports.

As central banks have no interest-paying liabilities, their profits (F_{cb}) are equal to total interest receipts from any domestically issued bills, plus, as is the case for the UK central bank, any foreign Treasury bills, $B_{cb\pounds}^\$$, which they hold, as shown in Columns 4 and 9 of the matrix.

$$F_{cb}^\pounds = r_{-1}^\pounds \cdot B_{cb\pounds\,s-1}^\pounds + r_{-1}^\pounds \cdot B_{cb\pounds\,s-1}^\$ \cdot xr^\$ \tag{12.11}$$

$$F_{cb}^\$ = r_{-1}^\$ \cdot B_{cb\$\,s-1}^\$ \tag{12.12}$$

Given that central bank profits are all paid back to the government, we can write the (government) budget constraints (Columns 3 and 8) as:

$$\Delta B_s^\pounds = G^\pounds - T^\pounds + r_{-1}^\pounds \cdot B_{s-1}^\pounds - F_{cb}^\pounds \tag{12.13}$$

$$\Delta B_s^\$ = G^\$ - T^\$ + r_{-1}^\$ \cdot B_{s-1}^\$ - F_{cb}^\$ \tag{12.14}$$

where, recall, B_S is the total outstanding stock of bills – the sole liability of the government, as distinct from the whole public sector including the central bank.

Payments by the US government on US Treasury bills held by the UK central bank are comprised within total interest payments by the US government, $r_{-1}^{\$} \cdot B_{s-1}^{\$}$, the third term on the right-hand side of (12.10), as is clear from line 8 of the transactions matrix. Hence interest payments on US Treasury bills appear as a credit to the UK central bank but not as a debit to the US central bank.

It is a feature of Table 12.2 which may seem surprising that neither country has a column describing its balance of payments. However the coherence enforced by double entry accounting ensures that total flows into each country always exactly equal total outflows, *whether measured as current (trade etc.) flows or as capital account transactions.* Thus trade flows (lines 3 and 4 of the transactions matrix) plus interest payments (lines 7 and 8) make up the balance of payments on current account which is, in turn, exactly equal to the sum of each country's transactions in capital assets shown in lines 11–13. To link the transactions described in Table 12.2 to the balance sheets in Table 12.1, it is necessary to take into account capital gains (or losses) arising from changes in the exchange rate. The balance of payments identities, which are not shown in the matrix, are:

$$CAB^{£} = X^{£} - IM^{£} + r_{-1}^{\$} \cdot B_{£s-1}^{\$} \cdot xr^{\$}$$
$$- r_{-1}^{£} \cdot B_{\$s-1}^{£} + r_{-1}^{\$} \cdot B_{cb£s-1}^{\$} \cdot xr^{\$} \tag{12.15}$$

$$KABOSA^{£} = +\Delta B_{\$s}^{£} - \Delta B_{£s}^{\$} \cdot xr^{\$} - \{\Delta B_{cb£s}^{\$} \cdot xr^{\$} + \Delta or^{£} \cdot p_{g}^{£}\} \tag{12.16}$$

$$CAB^{\$} = X^{\$} - IM^{\$} + r_{-1}^{£} \cdot B_{\$s-1}^{£} \cdot xr^{£}$$
$$- r_{-1}^{\$} \cdot B_{£s-1}^{\$} - r_{-1}^{\$} \cdot B_{cb£s-1}^{\$} \tag{12.17}$$

$$KABOSA^{\$} = +\Delta B_{£s}^{\$} + \Delta B_{cb£s}^{\$} - \Delta B_{\$s}^{£} \cdot xr^{£} - \{\Delta or^{\$} \cdot p_{g}^{\$}\} \tag{12.18}$$

CAB is the current account balance, which by the normal NIPA conventions, only records transactions and takes no account of capital gains. The current account balance is equal to the trade balance $(X - IM)$ plus the balance of 'invisibles' – the balance in investment income from and to the foreign economy.

KABOSA is the capital account balance, defined such that $CAB + KABOSA = 0$. In other words, *KABOSA* includes the official settlements account (*OSA*), which itself includes the negative of changes in official reserves, this change being the term between French brackets. Once again, as long as the US dollar, rather than gold, is the international currency, increases in the official reserves of United Kingdom (the £ country) will not be matched by a decrease in the foreign reserves of the Fed (the central bank of the \$ country), as can be observed by checking the terms inside the brackets in equations (12.16) and (12.18). There is thus an asymmetry here, which impacts on the definition of a non-tautologic balance of payments (one which is not always equal to zero by definition). If we exclude capital account transfers involving any of the two central banks, that is taking away the payments related to what is usually called the official settlements account, then we get another definition of the capital account balance:

$$KAB^{\pounds} = +\Delta B^{\pounds}_{\$\,s} - \Delta B^{\$}_{\pounds\,s} \cdot xr^{\$} \tag{12.19}$$

$$KAB^{\$} = +\Delta B^{\$}_{\pounds\,s} - \Delta B^{\pounds}_{\$\,s} \cdot xr^{\pounds} \tag{12.20}$$

12.3.2 Trade

We now enter a subsection which will look familiar to students of international trade, but which will be given an original twist. Trade prices, here more specifically the trade prices of the United Kingdom, are assumed to be determined in the following way:

$$\boldsymbol{p^{\pounds}_{m}} = v_0 - v_1 \cdot \boldsymbol{xr^{\pounds}} + (1 - v_1) \cdot \boldsymbol{p^{\pounds}_y} + v_1 \cdot \boldsymbol{p^{\$}_y} \qquad 0 < v_1 < 1 \tag{12.21}$$

$$\boldsymbol{p^{\pounds}_{x}} = v_0 - v_1 \cdot \boldsymbol{xr^{\pounds}} + (1 - v_1) \cdot \boldsymbol{p^{\pounds}_y} + v_1 \cdot \boldsymbol{p^{\$}_y} \qquad 0 < v_1 < 1 \tag{12.22}$$

where p_m is import prices, p_x is export prices, p_y is the GDP deflator, while bold characters denote natural logs of these variables.

The justification for the constraints on the parameters derives from the following thought experiments:

1. If there were a simultaneous additions of some given amount to domestic inflation in both countries with no change in the exchange rate, then there would surely be an equivalent addition to export and (therefore) import prices in each country – hence the constraint that the coefficients on domestic and foreign inflation sum to unity. This explains the $(1 - v_1) \cdot p^{\pounds}_y + v_1 \cdot p^{\$}_y$ part of the price of imports equation, and its equivalent terms in the export price equation.
2. If currency depreciation (a negative change in $xr^{\pounds}$) were accompanied by a simultaneous and equal addition to domestic inflation, it is reasonable to expect that import prices would rise by the full amount of the depreciation – hence the sum of the (absolute values) of the coefficients on the exchange rate and domestic inflation should also sum to unity. This explains the constraint on the $-v_1 \cdot xr^{\pounds} + (1 - v_1) \cdot p^{\pounds}_y$ part of the import price equation.
3. It is well established empirically that, following depreciation, and given no immediate effect on domestic inflation, export and import prices denominated in home currency rise, but there will normally be some deterioration in the terms of trade (i.e. $v_1 > v_1 > 0$ implying that import prices will rise faster than export prices) and vice versa for appreciation. Presumably exporters in both countries adjust prices in order to maintain or achieve

some desired market share when exchange rates change (as shown by Bloch and Olive 1996).

Import and export prices for the United States now follow by symmetry, since, for instance, the export prices of the United Kingdom are the import prices of the United States, once exchange rates are taken into consideration:

$$p_x^\$ = p_m^£ \cdot xr^£ \tag{12.23}$$

$$p_m^\$ = p_x^£ \cdot xr^£ \tag{12.24}$$

Trade flows, measured at constant prices, are determined, very conventionally, by relative price and income elasticities, with bold variables again representing logs.

$$\boldsymbol{x^£} = \varepsilon_0 - \varepsilon_1 \cdot (\boldsymbol{p_{m-1}^\$} - \boldsymbol{p_{y-1}^\$}) + \varepsilon_2 \cdot \boldsymbol{y^\$} \tag{12.25}$$

$$\boldsymbol{im^£} = \mu_0 - \mu_1 \cdot (\boldsymbol{p_{m-1}^£} - \boldsymbol{p_{y-1}^£}) + \mu_2 \cdot \boldsymbol{y^£} \tag{12.26}$$

Equation (12.25) says that the volume of UK exports ($x^£$) responds with an elasticity of ε_1 with respect to US import prices ($p_m^\$$) relative to US domestic prices ($p_y^\$$) – both expressed in dollars – and ε_2 with respect to US domestic output ($y^\$$). Equation (12.26) says that UK imports ($im^£$) respond with elasticities μ_1 with respect to import prices ($p_m^£$) relative to domestic prices ($p_y^£$) – both expressed in pounds – and μ_2 with respect to domestic output ($y£$).

As with prices, these equations imply, logically, what dollar export and import volumes must be since the exports of one country are the imports of the other:

$$x^\$ = im^£ \tag{12.27}$$

$$im^\$ = x^£ \tag{12.28}$$

Finally the four identities generating the values of trade flows in own currency are:

$$X^£ = x^£ \cdot p_x^£ \tag{12.29}$$

$$X^\$ = x^\$ \cdot p_x^\$ \tag{12.30}$$

$$IM^£ = im^£ \cdot p_m^£ \tag{12.31}$$

$$IM^\$ = im^\$ \cdot p_m^\$ \tag{12.32}$$

It is often assumed that the sum of the elasticities with respect to relative prices must sum to at least one if the trade balance is to improve following devaluation (the Marshall-Lerner condition). But in verity the sum of these elasticities need be no greater than the elasticity of terms of trade with respect to devaluation. If there were no change at all in the terms of trade following a 10% devaluation – for instance if both import and export prices in US dollars went up by 6%, not an impossible outcome – the sum of the elasticities need be no greater than *positive* for the balance of trade to improve.[5] If the deterioration in the terms of trade were 40% of the devaluation, then the sum of the price elasticities need be no more than 0.4. This would occur if the 10% devaluation in the value of the dollar caused import prices in the US, $p_m^\$$, to rise by 7% while export prices in US dollars, $p_x^\$$, rose by 3%.

12.3.3 Income and expenditures

The consumption function, with the wealth acquisition function that this implies, is central to the way in which the system is driven towards a stationary state, as with our other models. We still assume that households set their real consumption decisions as a function of their real disposable income and past accumulated real wealth. But how are these to be measured? In particular what is the relevant price index? We suggest that the relevant price is that of domestic sales, p_{ds}, since this is the price that consumers face when they purchase goods. It is, in our model, the nearest equivalent to consumer prices.

Real wealth will thus be defined as nominal wealth V, as already defined in equations (12.3) and (12.6), deflated by domestic prices.

$$v^£ = \frac{V^£}{p_{ds}^£} \tag{12.33}$$

$$v^\$ = \frac{V^\$}{p_{ds}^\$} \tag{12.34}$$

Real (inflation accounted) disposable income (yd_{hs}), once again in line with the Haig–Simons definition of disposable income, must take possible inflation losses into account, and is therefore given by:

$$yd_{hs}^£ = \frac{YD_{hs}^£}{p_{ds}^£} - v_{-1}^£ \cdot \frac{\Delta p_{ds}^£}{p_{ds}^£} \tag{12.35}$$

$$yd_{hs}^\$ = \frac{YD_{hs}^\$}{p_{ds}^\$} - v_{-1}^\$ \cdot \frac{\Delta p_{ds}^\$}{p_{ds}^\$} \tag{12.36}$$

[5] The standard interpretation of the Marshall-Lerner condition seems to be based on the assumption that export prices, expressed in the domestic currency, won't change following a depreciation of the home currency, while import prices will increase in line with the depreciation. In other words, prices are assumed to be always fixed in the currencies of the exporters. This implies that the terms of trade go down by the full amount of the depreciation.

since we know that, properly measured, Haig–Simons disposable income must be such that: $yd_{hs} = c + (v - v_{-1})$.

Real consumption is determined by expected real disposable income and the opening stock of (real) wealth. As before, we assume a two-stage decision, where households decide on an overall flow of saving, and then choose how they will allocate their expected wealth.

$$c^£ = \alpha_1^£ \cdot yd_{hse}^£ + \alpha_2^£ \cdot v_{-1}^£ \tag{12.37}$$

$$c^\$ = \alpha_1^\$ \cdot yd_{hse}^\$ + \alpha_2^\$ \cdot v_{-1}^\$ \tag{12.38}$$

where the subscript 'e' denotes an expected value.

The formation of expectations about income (and therefore wealth) is no big deal in a well wrought stock-flow model. Any way of forming expectations that is not downright perverse (such as would be the case if expectations were to move in a way that ignores or compounds previous errors) will eventually lead to the same result. This is because errors lead to unwanted changes in stocks of wealth which lead, in turn, to self-correcting adjustments in subsequent periods. We shall assume for simplicity that expected real disposable income is some average of this and last period's income.

$$yd_{hse}^£ = \frac{(yd_{hs}^£ + yd_{hs-1}^£)}{2} \tag{12.39}$$

$$yd_{hse}^\$ = \frac{(yd_{hs}^\$ + yd_{hs-1}^\$)}{2} \tag{12.40}$$

The limited role of expectations is made clearer when one notices, once more, that the consumption function may alternatively be written as a wealth adjustment function, $\Delta v_e = \alpha_2(\alpha_3 \cdot yd_{hse} - v_{-1})$, where $\alpha_3 = (1 - \alpha_1)/\alpha_2$. The system will come to rest (of a kind) when the changes in the real stock of wealth are zero, implying that wealth targets, v^*, have been met, that is, when $v = \alpha_3 \cdot yd$.

For the rest of this section we have a raft of equations, most of them identities, which set out how real wealth accumulation and real consumption are inter-related with all the current price variables.

The total volume of sales, s, is equal to the sum of its components:

$$s^£ = c^£ + g^£ + x^£ \tag{12.41}$$

$$s^\$ = c^\$ + g^\$ + x^\$ \tag{12.42}$$

The value of sales is:

$$S^£ = s^£ \cdot p_s^£ \tag{12.43}$$

$$S^\$ = s^\$ \cdot p_s^\$ \tag{12.44}$$

where p_S is the average price of all sales.

The price level of sales, p_S, is determined as a mark-up, φ, on unit costs:

$$p_S^£ = \frac{(1 + \varphi^£) \cdot (W^£ \cdot N^£ + IM^£)}{s^£} \tag{12.45}$$

$$p_S^\$ = \frac{(1 + \varphi^\$) \cdot (W^\$ \cdot N^\$ + IM^\$)}{s^\$} \tag{12.46}$$

where W is the nominal wage rate and N is employment. All profits earned as a result of the mark-up are assumed to be distributed immediately to the household sector.

The price of domestic sales is:

$$p_{ds}^£ = \frac{(S^£ - X^£)}{(s^£ - x^£)} \tag{12.47}$$

$$p_{ds}^\$ = \frac{(S^\$ - X^\$)}{(s^\$ - x^\$)} \tag{12.48}$$

The remaining relationships in this section are those necessary to complete the income/expenditure flow system. They are tedious but necessary steps. They describe, in turn, domestic sales value, DS; domestic sales volume, ds; nominal GDP, Y; real GDP, y; the GDP deflator, p_y; the value of consumption, C; the value of government expenditure, G; the tax yield, T, and employment, N.

$$DS^£ = S^£ - X^£ \tag{12.49}$$

$$DS^\$ = S^\$ - X^\$ \tag{12.50}$$

$$ds^£ = c^£ + g^£ \tag{12.51}$$

$$ds^\$ = c^\$ + g^\$ \tag{12.52}$$

$$Y£ = S^£ - IM^£ \tag{12.53}$$

$$Y^\$ = S^\$ - IM^\$ \tag{12.54}$$

$$y^£ = s_£ - im^£ \tag{12.55}$$

$$y^\$ = s^\$ - im^\$ \tag{12.56}$$

$$p_y^£ = \frac{Y^£}{y^£} \tag{12.57}$$

$$p_y^\$ = \frac{Y^\$}{y^\$} \tag{12.58}$$

$$C^£ = c^£ \cdot p_{ds}^£ \tag{12.59}$$

$$C^\$ = c^\$ \cdot p_{ds}^\$ \tag{12.60}$$

$$G^\pounds = g^\pounds \cdot p_{ds}^\pounds \tag{12.61}$$

$$G^\$ = g^\$ \cdot p_{ds}^\$ \tag{12.62}$$

$$T^\pounds = \theta^\pounds \cdot (Y^\pounds + r_{-1}^\pounds \cdot B_{\pounds s-1}^\pounds + r_{-1}^\$ \cdot B_{\pounds s-1}^\$ \cdot xr^\$) \tag{12.63A}$$

$$T^\$ = \theta^\$ \cdot (Y^\$ + r_{-1}^\$ \cdot B_{\$ s-1}^\$ + r_{-1}^\pounds \cdot B_{\$ s-1}^\pounds \cdot xr^\pounds) \tag{12.64A}$$

$$N^\pounds = \frac{y^\pounds}{pr^\pounds} \tag{12.65}$$

$$N^\$ = \frac{y^\$}{pr^\$} \tag{12.66}$$

where *pr* is labour productivity.

12.3.4 Asset demands

Up to this point, thanks mainly to the simplifying assumption that there is no inventory investment, we have been able to assume that the supply of output, as well as the supply of labour, is instantaneously equal to demand. How about asset demands and supplies?

Outside a stationary steady state, all stocks and flows will be changing. Demands for assets will originate from the private sectors' wealth accumulation and asset allocation. Supplies of assets originate from the balance of both governments' transactions. The way in which demands are brought into equivalence with supplies will determine how the system as a whole behaves. The manner of this reconciliation, which can take many forms, comprises the core of what this chapter has to say.

The equations summarizing how nominal wealth is created for the private sector were given right at the beginning of this section. The private sector's *ex ante* allocation of wealth between the three categories of available financial assets is determined according to Tobin's principles, as should now be standard for the reader:

$$B_{\pounds d}^\pounds = V^\pounds \cdot (\lambda_{10} + \lambda_{11} \cdot r^\pounds - \lambda_{12} \cdot (r^\$ + dxr_e^\$)) \tag{12.67}$$

$$B_{\pounds d}^\$ = V^\pounds \cdot (\lambda_{20} - \lambda_{21} \cdot r^\pounds + \lambda_{22} \cdot (r^\$ + dxr_e^\$)) \tag{12.68}$$

$$H_d^\pounds = V^\pounds \cdot (\lambda_{30} - \lambda_{31} \cdot r^\pounds - \lambda_{32} \cdot (r^\$ + dxr_e^\$)) \tag{12.69A}$$

$$B_{\$ d}^\$ = V^\$ \cdot (\lambda_{40} + \lambda_{41} \cdot r^\$ - \lambda_{42} \cdot (r^\pounds + dxr_e^\pounds)) \tag{12.70}$$

$$B_{\$ d}^\pounds = V^\$ \cdot (\lambda_{50} - \lambda_{51} \cdot r^\$ + \lambda_{52} \cdot (r^\pounds + dxr_e^\pounds)) \tag{12.71}$$

$$H_d^\$ = V^\$ \cdot (\lambda_{60} - \lambda_{61} \cdot r^\$ - \lambda_{62} \cdot (r^\pounds + dxr_e^\pounds)) \tag{12.72A}$$

where, for each country, the sum of the constants is equal to one and the sum of the coefficients in each remaining column is equal to zero, bearing in mind that for bills the assumption is that the coefficient on its own interest rate will be positive and that on other interest rates will be negative.[6] As we know, when consumption is based on expectations which will typically be falsified, these conditions can best be taken into account by removing one of the portfolio equations for each country (those identified with an A suffix), and rewriting them as

$$H_d^£ = V^£ - B_{£\,d}^£ - B_{£\,d}^\$ \tag{12.69}$$

$$H_d^\$ = V^\$ - B_{\$\,d}^\$ - B_{\$\,d}^£ \tag{12.72}$$

The subscript 'd' denotes demand and, where the asset is issued abroad, this subscript signifies that the asset is denominated in the currency where the asset is held and this is why exchange rates do not enter the portfolio equations. The subscript 'e' denotes an expected value, while the prefix '*d*' denotes a proportional rate of change – thus the expected rate of return on bills issued abroad equals the foreign rate of interest plus the change in the exchange rate which is expected to occur *by the next period* – and hence we have by definition:

$$dxr_e^£ = \frac{\Delta xr_e^£}{xr^£} \tag{12.75}$$

$$dxr_e^\$ = \frac{\Delta xr_e^\$}{xr^\$} \tag{12.76}$$

We could make the conventional assumption that the expected rate of exchange is equal to the difference between domestic and foreign rates of interest, thereby establishing equivalence between expected total rates of return on the two assets. This would imply:

$$xr_e^£ = xr_{-1}^£ + (r^\$ - r^£) \cdot xr_{-1}^£$$
$$xr_e^\$ = xr_{-1}^\$ + (r^£ - r^\$) \cdot xr_{-1}^\$$$

These equations imply that uncovered interest parity (UIP) holds. But according to the views of foreign exchange traders, they give no indication of the expected future spot rate; rather they define the forward rate, as set by bankers and traders for their clients (Isard 1995: 78). The forward rate,

[6] To cut down the number of equations and focus on the essential elements, portfolio equations are assumed to depend on realized wealth rather than expected wealth. The transactions demand for money, dependent on disposable income, has been omitted.

relative to the spot rate, gives no indication of how the spot rate will move in the future, as has been repeatedly shown in empirical tests (Moosa 2004).[7] As traders say – this is the so-called *cambist* view – the forward rate cannot be the expected future spot rate, and hence the conventional closure based on UIP is not helpful (Lavoie 2000; 2002–3).[8]

We are thus left with two (simple) possibilities. We can assume that the expected exchange rate is a given (xr_e = a constant), which might correspond to some fundamental exchange rate that investors believe will be realized sooner or later; or we can assume, as we implicitly did in the portfolio equations, that investors have an opinion about possible *changes* in the exchange rate, in which case the term dxr_e may be positive or negative, and will be nil in the neutral case.

12.3.5   Asset supplies

What of asset supplies? The government, having taken decisions about tax rates and public expenditure authorizations and commitments, has no control over its surplus/deficit nor over the issue of bills to which this gives rise, as shown in equations (12.13) and (12.14); nor has it any control over where the bills go to. Central banks will always exchange cash for bills and vice versa. This is equivalent to saying that the supply of all assets to the private sector of each country passively matches demand. This is the closure which corresponds to the assertion that the money supply is endogenous and demand-led, with central banks setting or steering interest rates rather than attempting to target money supplies or the supply of securities, an assumption which we believe to be realistic and best able to describe the actual behaviour of central banks.

There are many different ways to arrange the equilibrium conditions for assets, since we are free to choose the appropriate redundant equation – the equation that arises from the fulfilment of every other equation of the model.

---

[7] Isard (1995: 81–2) says that it is 'widely acknowledged that interest differentials explain only a small proportion of subsequent changes in exchange rates' and 'often mispredict the direction of change'. Tobin (1982b: 124) himself provides some anecdotal evidence against the view that the forward rate is a predictor of future spot rates.

[8] While the method that we use is similar to the one used by Taylor (2004a; 2004b, ch. 10) in his open-economy models, there is a crucial difference: Taylor still assumes endogenously determined interest rates, while ours are set exogenously by central banks. Thus these target rates of interest act as an anchor. This difference may help explain why Taylor (2004b, p. 333) believes that, in contrast to what we claim, 'the exchange rate is not set by temporary macro equilibrium conditions. It must evolve over time subject to rules based on expectations about its future values in the future'. This forces Taylor to introduce UIP to close his model, on the basis that UIP relies on 'arbitrage arguments that "should be true"' (*ibid*, p. 333), while acknowledging earlier that UIP 'does not fit the data' (*ibid*, p. 315)!

And accounting identities can also be arranged in different ways. Here we choose the set of equations that we used for the fixed exchange rate variant of our model in Godley and Lavoie (2005–6).

We start with those assets issued by US institutions, government and central bank, which are acquired by the domestic central bank and by the domestic private sector, thus writing the following issuing requirements:

$$H_s^\$ = H_h^\$ \tag{12.77}$$

$$B_{\$\,s}^\$ = B_{\$\,d}^\$ \tag{12.78}$$

$$B_{cb\,\$\,s}^\$ = B_{cb\,\$\,d}^\$ \tag{12.79}$$

where the subscript 's' denotes supply.

In the case of assets issued by UK institutions, and acquired by the domestic central bank and the domestic private sector, we may write, symmetrically:

$$H_s^\pounds = H_h^\pounds \tag{12.80}$$

$$B_{\pounds\,s}^\pounds = B_{\pounds\,d}^\pounds \tag{12.81}$$

$$B_{cb\,\pounds\,s}^\pounds = B_{cb\,\pounds\,d}^\pounds \tag{12.82}$$

Le us now deal with the components of the balance sheet identity of the central banks. In the case of the US central bank, column 9 of the balance sheet matrix (Table 12.1) yields the following identity:

$$B_{cb\,\$\,d}^\$ = H_s^\$ - or^\$ \cdot p_g^\$ \tag{12.83}$$

while in the case of the UK central bank, column 4 of the transactions-flow matrix (Table 12.2) gives:

$$\Delta B_{cb\,\pounds\,d}^\pounds = \Delta H_s^\pounds - \Delta B_{cb\,\pounds\,s}^\$ \cdot xr^\$ - \Delta or^\pounds \cdot p_g^\pounds \tag{12.84}$$

The US central bank's equation can be represented using levels, because there is no possibility of capital gains (or losses) within the Fed's balance sheet. The Fed has no foreign asset or liability, and we shall assume for simplicity that the price of gold in dollars, $p_g^\$$, is pegged at some constant value. By contrast, the balance sheet of the Bank of England must be set in differences, because it includes bills issued abroad, which are susceptible to capital gains when the dollar appreciates. In addition, if this occurs, the price of gold in pounds ($p_g^\pounds$) rises, creating a second possible source of appreciation for the Bank of England.

The model is nearly complete. In all variants we shall assume that no gold is traded between central banks ($\Delta or = 0$), gold being kept simply as a remnant of the long-gone Bretton Woods regime.[9] The law of one price is applied to the price of gold, under the assumption, already mentioned above, that the price of gold in dollars, $p_g^\$$, is given. Thus the price of gold in pounds depends on the exchange rate, as shown in equation (12.85). Also, obviously, the dollar exchange rate, that is the number of pounds per dollar, is the reciprocal of $xr^\pounds$.

$$p_g^\pounds = p_g^\$ \cdot xr^\$ \tag{12.85}$$

$$xr^\$ = \frac{1}{xr^\pounds} \tag{12.86}$$

We now deal with conditions of supply and demand that involve the exchange rate, and that we had voluntarily omitted when we dealt with conditions of supply and demand that only involved domestic agents. Three conditions need to be realized, the third one, equation (12.89) being in fact part of the equations that will identify a closure.

$$B_{\$s}^\pounds = B_{\$d}^\pounds \cdot xr^\$ \tag{12.87}$$

$$B_{cb\pounds d}^\$ = B_{cb\pounds s}^\$ \cdot xr^\$ \tag{12.88}$$

$$B_{\pounds s}^\$ = B_{\pounds d}^\$ \cdot xr^\pounds \tag{12.89}$$

The generic model as such is complete. We now move to the different possible closures.

12.4   Alternative closures

12.4.1   A flexible exchange rate closure

We first deal with the flexible exchange rate closure. The £ central bank, faced with a step-up in imports, refuses to intervene in foreign exchange markets, so that it does not lose any of its foreign exchange reserves. The exchange rate $xr^\pounds$ is endogenous (equation 12.89FL), while the amount of foreign reserves, measured in dollars, becomes a constant (equation 12.91FL). US Bills supplied to foreign bond holders are a residual (equation 12.90FL). The closure is made up of the following three equations, plus the redundant

[9] Otherwise, we need another equation, $\Delta or^\$ = -\Delta or^\pounds$.

equation, equation (12.82A).[10]

$$xr^£ = \frac{B^\$_{£\,s}}{B^\$_{£\,d}} \tag{12.89FL}$$

$$B^\$_{£\,s} = B^\$_s - B^\$_{cb\,£\,s} - B^\$_{\$\,s} - B^\$_{cb\,\$\,s} \tag{12.90FL}$$

$$B^\$_{cb\,£\,s} = constant \tag{12.91FL}$$

$$B^£_{cb\,£\,s} = B^£_s - B^£_{£\,s} - B^£_{\$\,s} \tag{12.82A}$$

while equation (12.84) simplifies down to:

$$\Delta B^£_{cb\,£\,d} = \Delta H^£_s \tag{12.84FL}$$

These four FL equations, with the other 87 remaining equations, constitute the *OPENFLEX* model. This model has over ninety equations, despite commercial banks having been assumed away!

Equations (12.82A) and (12.90FL) are accounting identities which can be read from rows 2 and 3 of the balance sheet matrix given by Table 12.1.

Equation (12.89FL) might seem to imply that the exchange rate is determined in a unique market, the market for $B^\$_£$ bills. But this is not the case. The exchange rate, like every other endogenous variable, is only allowed to appear a single time on the left hand side of an equation. But the system is a fully interdependent one such that the solution of the model as a whole requires and ensures that every equation in which the exchange rate appears is satisfied at the same time. Thus equations (12.89FL) and (12.87) must simultaneously be satisfied. And the exchange rate determined in (12.89FL) will be found to satisfy all the trade equations in which it appears and also to influence personal consumption through its effect on capital gains.

12.4.2 A fixed exchange rate closure, with endogenous foreign reserves

We shall define three different closures of the fixed exchange rate regime. Here we show that it is a simple task to move from the flexible exchange rate closure to a fixed exchange rate closure with freely changing endogenous reserves, that is, what most people would consider to be the standard fixed exchange rate regime. This closure constitutes what we can call Model *OPENFIX*. There are many different ways to bump successive equations to arrive at the new fixed exchange rate closure, but here we suggest a

---

[10] This is now the redundant equation because equation (12.82) already has an equation with $B^£_{cb\,£\,s}$, the supply of domestic bills to the Bank of England (the UK central bank), on the left-hand side.

particularly simple one, that involves inverting only three equations. The three equations to be inverted are the ones we identified in the previous subsection,

$$xr^£ = \frac{B^\$_{£s}}{B^\$_{£d}} \tag{12.89FL}$$

$$B^\$_{£s} = B^\$_s - B^\$_{cb£s} - B^\$_{\$s} - B^\$_{cb\$s} \tag{12.90FL}$$

$$B^\$_{cb£s} = constant \tag{12.91FL}$$

which become:

$$xr^£ = constant \tag{12.91F}$$

$$B^\$_{£s} = B^\$_{£d} \cdot xr^£ \tag{12.89F}$$

$$B^\$_{cb£s} = B^\$_s - B^\$_{£s} - B^\$_{\$s} - B^\$_{cb\$s} \tag{12.90F}$$

Equation (12.91F) specifies explicitly that the exchange rate is an exogenous variable, and hence that we are within a fixed exchange regime closure. Equation (12.89F) inverts equation (12.89FL). As to equation (12.90F), it describes the evolution of UK foreign reserves. Alternatively expressed, equation (12.90F) describes the purchases of US Treasury bills which the UK central bank must make in order to prevent its exchange rate from floating up or down.

12.4.3   An alternative fixed exchange rate closure: the deficit country lets its interest rate become endogenous

An alternative way of fending off devaluation, in theory, is to raise the interest rate. Once again, it is easy to adapt the equations of the model to show how this would have to happen. We start from the main fixed exchange rate closure, but impose upon it that the central bank declines to use its foreign reserves, as if the country were on a flexible exchange rate. Hence another variable, which was previously assumed to be constant, now needs to be made endogenous and that will be the rate of interest on UK bills $r^£$. As in the previous subsection, we show the four equations of the fixed exchange rate closure that need to be modified, and the four new equations of this new closure, plus equation (12.91F) which defines a fixed exchange rate regime and remains as is. These equations are:

$$B^\$_{£s} = B^\$_{£d} \cdot xr^£ \tag{12.89F}$$

$$B^\$_{cb£s} = B^\$_s - B^\$_{£s} - B^\$_{\$s} - B^\$_{cb\$s} \tag{12.90F}$$

$$xr^{£} = constant \tag{12.91F}$$

$$r^{£} = constant \tag{12.92}$$

$$B^{\$}_{£d} = V^{£} \cdot (\lambda_{20} - \lambda_{21} \cdot r^{£} + \lambda_{22} \cdot (r^{\$} + dxr^{\$}_{e})) \tag{12.68}$$

which become:

$$B^{\$}_{£d} = B^{\$}_{£s} \cdot xr^{\$} \tag{12.89R}$$

$$B^{\$}_{£s} = B^{\$}_{s} - B^{\$}_{cb£s} - B^{\$}_{\$s} - B^{\$}_{cb\$s} \tag{12.90R}$$

$$xr^{£} = constant \tag{12.91}$$

$$B^{\$}_{cb£s} = constant \tag{12.92R}$$

$$r^{£} = \frac{\lambda_{20} + \lambda_{22} \cdot (r^{\$} + dxr^{\$}_{e}) - B^{\$}_{£d}/V^{£}}{\lambda_{21}} \tag{12.68R}$$

so that once more all variables can only be found once on the left-hand side. This would be Model *OPENFIXR*.

12.4.4 Another alternative fixed exchange rate closure: one country sets its government expenditures endogenously

Governments can also avoid devaluation by reducing public expenditures. The second possible additional fixed exchange rate closure is also very simple to arrive at. It is relatively easy to rearrange the equations, following the procedure outlined in the previous subsection, so as to show how fiscal policy could be adjusted to preserve a fixed rate of exchange despite a deteriorated trade balance. The new fiscal stance has to be such that after allowing for all lags and feedbacks, the level of domestic output is reduced to such an extent that the value of imports exactly equals that of exports.

Once more we start from the main closure with a fixed exchange rate, but impose upon it that the central bank declines to use its foreign reserves, as if the country were on a flexible exchange rate. Hence another variable, which was previously assumed to be constant, now needs to be made endogenous and that will be the (pure) government expenditures in the UK, $g^{£}$. As in the previous section, we can show the equations of the generic model that need to be changed, as well as the equations that define the main fixed exchange regime closure. The following equations

$$g^{£} = constant \tag{12.93}$$

$$G^{£} = g^{£} \cdot p^{£}_{ds} \tag{12.61}$$

$$\Delta B_s^\pounds = G^\pounds - T^\pounds + r_{-1}^\pounds \cdot B_{s-1}^\pounds - F_{cb}^\pounds \tag{12.13}$$

$$B_{\pounds s}^\$ = B_{\pounds d}^\$ \cdot xr^\pounds \tag{12.89F}$$

$$B_{cb\pounds s}^\$ = B_s^\$ - B_{\pounds s}^\$ - B_{\$ s}^\$ - B_{cb\$ s}^\$ \tag{12.90F}$$

$$xr^\pounds = constant \tag{12.91F}$$

$$B_{cb\pounds s}^\pounds = B_s^\pounds - B_{\pounds s}^\pounds - B_{\$ s}^\pounds \tag{12.82A}$$

become:

$$B_{cb\pounds s}^\$ = constant \tag{12.93G}$$

$$g^\pounds = \frac{G^\pounds}{p_{ds}^\pounds} \tag{12.61G}$$

$$G^\pounds = \Delta B_s^\pounds + T^\pounds + F_{cb}^\pounds - r_{-1}^\pounds \cdot B_{s-1}^\pounds \tag{12.13G}$$

$$B_{\pounds s}^\$ = B_{\pounds d}^\$ \cdot xr^\pounds \tag{12.89F}$$

$$xr^\pounds = constant \tag{12.91F}$$

$$B_s^\pounds = B_{\$ s}^\pounds + B_{\pounds s}^\pounds + B_{cb\pounds s}^\pounds \tag{12.82AG}$$

$$B_{cb\pounds s}^\$ = B_s^\$ - B_{\pounds s}^\$ - B_{\$ s}^\$ - B_{cb\$ s}^\$ \tag{12.90GA}$$

Here, *nominal* government expenditures are constrained by equation (12.13G). Real government expenditures are thus adjusted to accord with the nominal amount, through equation (12.61G). We use the redundant equation (12.82A) of the fixed exchange rate model to determine the supply of bills of the UK government (as in 12.82AG), and hence as a result, we must find a new redundant equation for our new closure, which will be equation (12.90GA). Equations (12.89F) and (12.91F) that defined a fixed exchange rate closure are still part of this new closure, which we can call Model *OPENFIXG*.

12.5   Experiments with the main fixed exchange rate closure

12.5.1   An increase in the US propensity to import

We now run some experiments, starting with the main fixed exchange rate closure, which assumes that foreign reserves are endogenous, so that readers can compare the results with those achieved in the simpler model of Chapter 6. Our simulation procedure is to start from a full stationary state, with all government budget balances and current account balances at zero, introduce a disturbance, and then inspect a sequence of solutions which will lead either to a new full stationary state or to a hopefully intelligible form of instability. In the first exhibit we assume that 'the United Kingdom' achieves an uncovenanted addition to exports in a step which is maintained indefinitely (ε_0 in equation (12.25) moves up). Assuming that fiscal policy (the parameters θ and g for each country), monetary policy (the rates of interest in both countries), the exchange rate and gold reserves are all fixed, the consequences for the UK trade account balance and current account balance (*CAB*), as well as for the government budget balance and the net accumulation of financial assets (*NAFA*) by the private sector are shown in Figure 12.1A.

We already know from Chapter 6 that the GDP of the successful exporter – here United Kingdom – will rise to a new stationary level, while the GDP of the other country will decrease to a new lower constant level. The increase in domestic income will generate an increase in UK wealth, which is reflected in the positive net accumulation of financial assets by UK households, shown by the *NAFA* continuous line in Figure 12.1A. As GDP reaches its new constant level, this accumulation of financial assets tapers back to zero, and when it actually does reach zero, the quasi stationary state has been reached. The UK trade balance rises to a surplus position. Because monetary and fiscal policy and also the exchange rate are all fixed, there is no corrective mechanism in operation, so the trade balance remains indefinitely at its new higher level. But the current account balance, which includes interest flows on foreign assets or liabilities, while initially improving by the same amount as the trade balance, proceeds thereafter to increase by ever larger – and accelerating – amounts as the Bank of England holdings of US Treasury bills increase, generating ever larger flows of interest payments. The UK government's budget

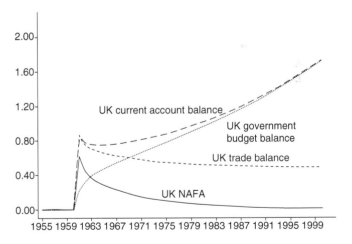

Figure 12.1A Effect of an increase in the US propensity to import on UK variables, within a fixed exchange rate regime with endogenous foreign reserves: net accumulation of financial assets, current account balance, trade balance and government budget balance

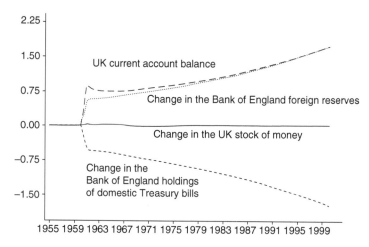

Figure 12.1B   Effect of an increase in the US propensity to import, within a fixed exchange rate regime with endogenous foreign reserves, on the UK current account balance and elements of the balance sheet of the Bank of England (the UK central bank): change in foreign reserves, stock of money, holdings of domestic Treasury bills

balance, after a period of transition, moves into surplus which is exactly equal to the UK current account surplus, thus getting into a *twin-surplus* situation. These two variables increase exponentially.[11] Exactly the same thing is happening in reverse in the United States. The US government deficit and the US current account deficit are both increasing without limit, even though the trade deficit remains constant.

Figure 12.1B shows the current account balance and the change in the value of US Treasury bills held by the Bank of England (its foreign reserves). Initially the two series differ because there is a change in the private income flows in both countries which leads to a counterpart adjustment in stocks of US assets held privately in the United Kingdom and vice versa. In particular, since UK households earn higher revenues, they purchase additional bills, among which are bills issued in the United States. As a result, the negative capital account balance (net of the acquisition of official foreign reserves), partly compensates for the current account surplus for a while. Eventually, however, the income flow settles down at a new constant level and the changes in private wealth revert to zero. But the UK current account balance remains in surplus, while the overall government sector (including the central bank)

---

[11] This result is also achieved by Lequain (2003). This is the main difference from previous models where gold stocks, carrying no interest, were the only means to hold foreign reserves, as in Godley (1999b) or Chapter 6. In those models, the current account surplus remained constant, so that foreign reserves rose linearly.

keeps accumulating foreign assets on an equivalent scale, so the amount of reserves (US bills) being acquired by the Bank of England comes to exactly match the UK current account surplus.

There is no intrinsic limit to these processes. The Bank of England does not lose control of its own monetary policy as it buys US Treasury bills, and there is no flooding of their economy with liquidity. This again can be seen in Figure 12.1B, by checking the continuous line illustrating changes in cash money issued by the Bank of England, which quickly reverts to zero. This roughly constant stock of money occurs despite the enormous and exponential increase in foreign reserve assets. This is because the increase in holdings of US Treasury bills is being *compensated* by the decrease in the UK central bank holdings of domestic bills, as can also be seen in Figure 12.1B. The increases in private disposable income, consumption, output and the pressure of demand in the United Kingdom are no more than can be accounted for by the increase in exports and the multiplier effects of this. The increase in private wealth, and its allocation between cash and bills of each kind, is in no way different from what would have taken place had the increase in income originated in a quite different way, for instance as a result of a relaxation of fiscal policy.

All the same things are happening in reverse to the US economy. Initially, there is a slight reduction in the stock of cash and the stock of US bills held by the Fed, as a result of a decrease in GDP, but afterwards all these remain constant, despite the current account deficit. Because the US dollar is the international currency, there is no need for the Fed to 'sterilize' anything. There is no fall in the foreign reserves of the US central bank; the financial assets that have to be provided, as a counterpart to the current account deficit, are being provided by the US Treasury, the debt of which is increasing. The accumulation of US Treasury bills by the Bank of England, and the payment of interest on these bills to it by the US government, is an entirely self-contained process which at no point affects private stocks and flows in either country. That this is the case can actually be observed in the introductory system describing arterial flows, in equations (12.11)–(12.14) together with the text which immediately follows, where it is shown that receipts by the UK government derived from bills issued by the US government $(r^\$_{-1} \cdot B^\$_{cb\pounds-1} \cdot xr^\$)$ are components of both governments' budget balance and also of both countries' current account balance (equations 12.15 and 12.17) – but they do not enter the flows of private disposable income which are comprehensively given by equations (12.1) and (12.4).

To judge from its recent behaviour (in the early years of 2000), it is not implausible to suppose that under such circumstances the US government would, in practise, relax fiscal policy enough to keep the level of GDP where it would otherwise have been, thereby generating an even larger trade deficit and an even larger public sector deficit. Under these circumstances the 'real' thing that would be happening is that US residents would be producing the same amount as before but absorbing more goods and services than they are producing. UK residents would be producing more but absorbing less than they produce.[12] There may be solid political or strategic reasons why both countries are happy to let the whole thing go on indefinitely.[13]

The situation being described here with the help of Figures 12.1 seems to approximate the current situation of the Chinese economy. Hence let us now attribute to China what is being described in the charts under the name of UK. Is it right to call such accumulation of reserves by the Chinese central bank 'intervention'; and is it right to describe the process as one in which the US is *'having to attract \$x billion per day'* to finance its deficit? Not really. What is happening, surely, is that Chinese exporters receive, for their increased sales abroad, an additional flow of dollars which they exchange with their central bank for their own currency. The Chinese central bank (the People's Bank of China) finds itself with an equivalently rising stock of dollar balances which it exchanges for US Treasury bills. Beyond these two exchanges the People's Bank of China neither needs nor wants to do anything at all.

12.5.2 Theoretical implications

These findings are profoundly at odds with much conventional wisdom and with the received view that arises from the standard Mundell–Fleming model. Peter Kenen (1985: 669) writes, as many others: '... Reserve flows alter the money stock, undermining the influence of monetary policy .... The monetary approach to the balance of payments is built on this basic proposition'.[14] But the monetary approach does not have a fully articulated monetary system in which the private sector allocates its wealth between money and other assets. In both countries, the private sector's accumulation of wealth and its allocation between available assets is not in any way affected by these central bank operations beyond what is implied by the step change in disposable income.

Some would say that the People's Bank of China will be 'sterilizing' foreign reserves, by selling Chinese Treasury bills on the open market. In a way, this is true. While the Chinese central bank's foreign reserves are sky-rocketing, its holdings of domestic bills are dwindling, as already pointed out. But this

[12] We are grateful to Randy Wray for pointing this out.

[13] It could be argued, as we did in Chapter 6, that at some point domestic and foreign investors will be scared by the rising debt to GDP ratio of the US government, or by the large foreign debt to GDP ratio of the US economy, and hence will reduce their demand for US bills. But as long as the Bank of England is willing to hold its foreign reserves in the form of US bills, this portfolio reshuffle can be handled within the described system, that is, with fixed exchange rates and unchanged interest rates.

[14] Similarly, in a recent IMF paper, Prasad and Wei (2005: 13) write that 'the capital inflows that are reflected in reserve accumulation could increase liquidity in the banking system, creating potential problems'.

is not the result of any intentional policy, where central bankers are actively intervening in financial markets. The Chinese central bank, just like the US one, is simply attempting to keep interest rates constant. Bills are provided to those who demand them at the set rate of interest. The central bank provides cash on demand to its citizens. The reduction in domestic bills holdings by the People's Bank of China is essentially the consequence of the reduction in the amount of outstanding debt of the Chinese government. This can go on indefinitely without any negative implication for the Chinese economy.

Others argue that sterilization in countries with external surpluses cannot go on forever because rates of interest on the liabilities of the central bank are bound to be higher than rates of interest on US T-bills; this, it is argued, would lead to operating losses (or opportunity costs) to the sterilizing central bank. As Prasad and Wei (2005: 13) put it: 'Sterilization of capital inflows to avoid this outcome [increased liquidity] could generate fiscal costs as the rate of return on domestic sterilization instruments is typically higher than that earned on reserve holdings'. This argument certainly does not apply to countries such as China, as Prasad and Wei (2005) recognize, since Chinese interest rates are administered and can be set at levels lower than in the United States. Also, why would interest rates in surplus countries be any higher than interest rates in countries facing current account deficits? One would have thought that countries faced with external deficits would be the ones who might be tempted by high or rising interest rates!

Indeed, as can be seen in Figure 12.1C, the surplus country (the UK, as shown, or China, as is currently the case) sees its debt to GDP ratio fall

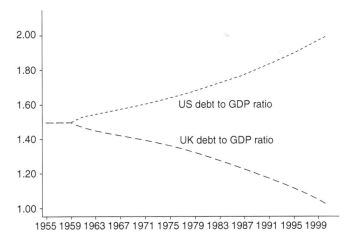

Figure 12.1C Effect of an increase in the US propensity to import on the US debt to GDP ratio and on the UK debt to income ratio, within a fixed exchange rate regime with endogenous foreign reserves

continuously, while the deficit country (the US) has a rising debt to GDP ratio. If anything, we would expect, based on standard risk analysis, that (long-term) interest rates in the US would be pressured up, while interest rates in the surplus countries would be pressured down by market forces. From the standpoint of the surplus country, there is thus nothing to stop the situation from continuing.

12.6   Experiments with alternative fixed exchange rate closures

12.6.1   An endogenous interest rate

If surplus countries can accumulate foreign reserves without any restriction, the reverse case is not possible. Deficit countries losing foreign reserves will eventually run out of them. Faced with dwindling foreign reserves, many central banks raise interest rates. We have described such a possible mechanism in the first of our alternative fixed exchange rate closure, in section 4, whereby the central bank – let us call it the UK central bank (or the Bank of England) from now on – lets interest rates become endogenous, in its attempt to preserve the existing fixed exchange rate without losing any additional foreign reserves, in the hope of attracting foreign capital. A rise in domestic interest rates will thus generate positive capital account flows that will compensate for the negative trade and current accounts.

But a single adjustment to interest rates of this kind will only keep the asset market and the balance of payments in equilibrium for a single period. If the 'UK' goes on having an external deficit – in other words, as long as there is no slowdown of the economy or as long as exports don't become more competitive – there will have to be a further rise in the UK interest rate, to induce yet higher foreign inflows of capital. As there is no mechanism in play to correct the trade deficit, we end up with an unstable situation – the interest rate has to go on rising for ever to maintain an adequate inflow of capital. Meanwhile, the trade balance remains negative, while the current account keeps getting ever more negative, at an exponential rate, due to the rising burden of interest payments that need to be made abroad. This is all shown in Figures 12.2A and 12.2B, where in addition it is shown that the deficit country will be faced with a rising debt to GDP ratio that mirrors the exponential rise in domestic interest rates.

The attempt to stabilize the system through interest rate changes generates instability, as is always the case in our kind of open economy models (Izurieta 2003; Godley and Lavoie 2006b), and as we already observed towards the end of Chapter 6.

12.6.2   Endogenous real government expenditures

To avoid devaluation without losing reserves, governments may decide to use fiscal rather than monetary policy. This alternative closure, where foreign

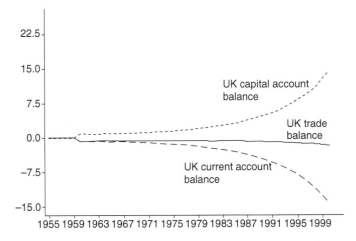

Figure 12.2A Effect of an increase in the UK propensity to import, within a fixed exchange rate regime with endogenous UK interest rates, on UK variables: capital account balance, trade balance, and current account balance

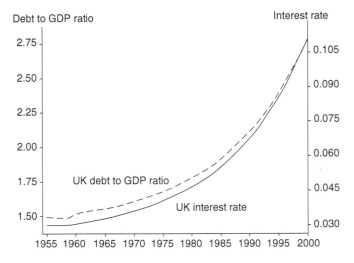

Figure 12.2B Effect of an increase in the UK propensity to import, within a fixed exchange rate regime with endogenous UK interest rates, on the UK interest rate and on the UK debt to GDP ratio

reserves are assumed to remain constant, implies that nominal government expenditures are now an endogenous variable, as described in section 5. The fiscal stance of the UK government depends on how many extra bills can be unloaded on financial markets (as determined by equation 12.82AG). The UK government is financially constrained. It is as if there existed some kind of loanable funds constraint. The intuition is that fiscal policy always adjusts so that the total supply of UK bills is such that the market absorbs them willingly at given interest rates. Fiscal policy is adjusted in such a way that the UK government is running a deficit only if the financial markets are ready to take in more UK bills at the given interest rate. Alternatively, this new closure can be understood as a situation where the rising debt of the deficit country is judged to be unsustainable by 'the markets', and that, as a result of this, fiscal policy of the deficit country and the amount of new government debt issued is 'constrained' by the financial markets.

This kind of fiscal policy response by the deficit country will have a negative impact on the surplus country, as shown in Figure 12.3A. While real GDP obviously falls in the trade-deficit ridden UK, real GDP also ends up being lower in the US, despite its initial export-led boost. Thus, as pointed out by a large number of observers, the current IMF-led international monetary system where deficit countries are encouraged to cut down on government expenditures imposes a deflationary bias to the world economy as a whole.

Second, as a counterpart, this type of fiscal policy does achieve what is intended. As UK imports progressively fall because of lower UK incomes, the current account imbalance goes towards zero, and so does the trade balance which even becomes positive at some point, because during the transitional period the country has increased its net foreign debt, which now has to be serviced. Figure 12.3B shows all this, as it also illustrates how the balance of payments problems of the UK get alleviated.

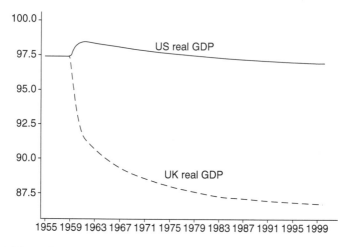

Figure 12.3A Effect of an increase in the UK propensity to import, within a fixed exchange rate regime with endogenous UK government expenditures, on the US and UK real GDP

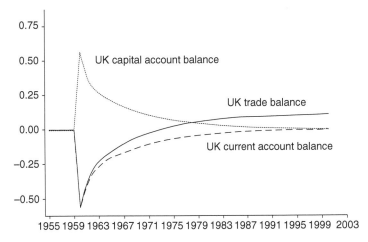

Figure 12.3B Effect of an increase in the UK propensity to import, within a fixed exchange rate regime with endogenous UK government expenditures, on various UK variables: the capital account balance, the current account balance and the trade balance

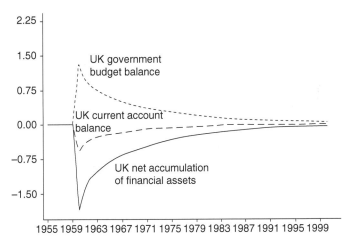

Figure 12.3C Effect of an increase in the UK propensity to import, within a fixed exchange rate regime with endogenous UK government expenditures, on various UK variables: the current account balance, the government budget balance, and the net accumulation of financial assets

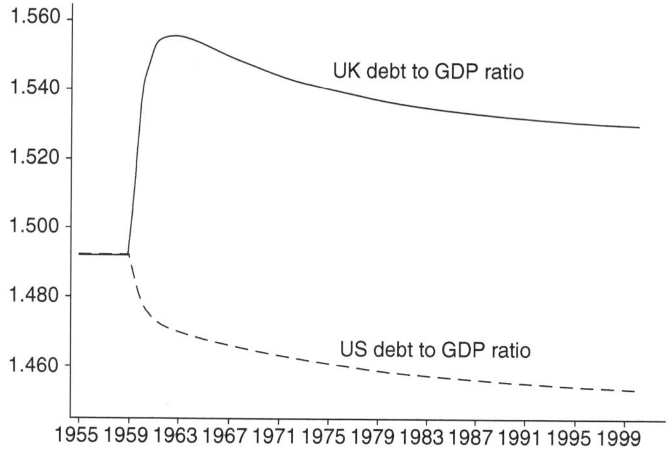

Figure 12.3D   Effect of an increase in the UK propensity to import, within a fixed exchange rate regime with endogenous UK government expenditures, on the UK and US debt to GDP ratios

Figure 12.3C helps us to understand how such an improvement can arise. It is due to the fact that UK households, through their lower disposable incomes generated by the fiscal austerity policies (which propel the government budget balance into a surplus position), are being forced to dissave, thus selling some of their holdings of both domestic and foreign securities. Mainly as a result of this, the capital account balance becomes positive. Finally, as shown with Figure 12.3D, while the debt to GDP ratio of the UK rises at first (despite government surpluses), because of the large fall in domestic output, the austere fiscal policy eventually stabilizes the debt to GDP ratios of both countries, in contrast to what was occurring in Figures 12.1C and 12.2B.

12.6.3   A one-step devaluation

In this subsection we simulate what happens when a country gets into a trade deficit situation, with falling foreign reserves and resolves its predicament by devaluing currency in a step. As in previous experiments, we assume that the UK suddenly starts importing more foreign goods, and hence is faced with a trade and balance of payments deficit. The government believes that the pressures on the existing parity are too strong, and decides to devalue. What will then happen?

Figure 12.4A describes the evolution of the UK trade balance and current account balance. As the trade deficit is on its way to settling towards a stationary level, the UK government decides to devalue. In the first two periods following the devaluation, there is no improvement in the trade and the

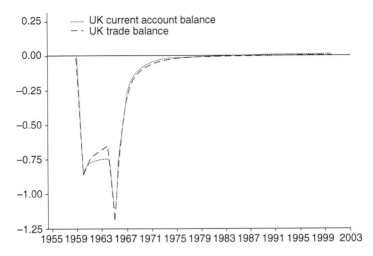

Figure 12.4A Effect on the UK current account balance and trade balance of a successful one-step devaluation of the sterling pound, following an increase in the UK propensity to import, within a fixed exchange rate regime with endogenous foreign reserves

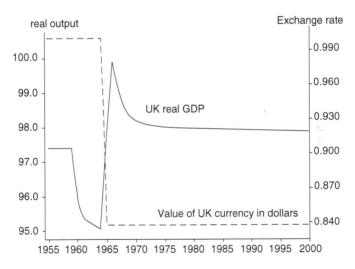

Figure 12.4B Effect of a successful one-step devaluation of the sterling pound on UK real GDP, following an increase in the UK propensity to import, within a fixed exchange rate regime with endogenous foreign reserves

current account balances; actually both of them worsen.[15] However, starting with the third period, external deficits decrease. Here, with the simulation shown in Figure 12.4A, the government has properly identified the size of the devaluation that is required to get the economy back to a balanced current account position. Figure 12.4B shows that, in the circumstances described by the parameters of the model, the UK economy escapes the stagnation that would otherwise have been in prospect due to its poor trading performance. With its currency devaluation, GDP in the UK rises and even achieves a long-term level which is higher than that of the original stationary state.

12.7 Experiments with the flexible exchange rate closure

12.7.1 A step fall in the UK exports

We now turn to the other main closure, the one with a flexible exchange rate regime. Let us assume once more that the UK experiences a downturn in its exports. This will initially create a trade and current account deficit and the economic slowdown will create as well a government budget deficit. The increase in the supply of assets abroad causes sterling (the £ currency) to fall in order to clear the market in all assets simultaneously. This is shown in Figure 12.5A and 12.5B

But the dynamic response of the system as a whole is only just beginning. A train of sequences ensues – and continues until the balance of payments and all changes in stock variables revert to zero. For as long as the balance of payments is non-zero this must be generating a change in the net supply of foreign denominated assets in each country causing a further change in the exchange rate. When exchange rates change, the absolute and relative prices of exports and imports all change, so trade volumes and values, income flows and accumulations of wealth all change. Some of these processes are shown in Figure 12.5C, where we see how export and import prices both rise measured in sterling, accompanied by a deterioration in the terms of trade, as sterling depreciates at a decelerating rate until a new equilibrium is restored (Figure 12.5B).

Figure 12.5A shows how the current account balance deteriorates initially but then reverts to zero, while the trade balance, thanks to the depreciating currency, becomes positive. As a result, as shown in Figure 12.5D, the fall in UK domestic output, as a result of the direct and indirect (multiplier) effect of the fall in net export demand, is only temporary. The deterioration in the terms of trade and the rise in import prices act so as to make real exports

---

[15] This is in part due to the lagged effect on imports, some of the price effects arising before the quantity effects. The evolution of the trade balance in Figure 12.4A is a representation of the famous J-curve effect, whereby the trade deficit widens at first, and gets narrowed only after a delay.

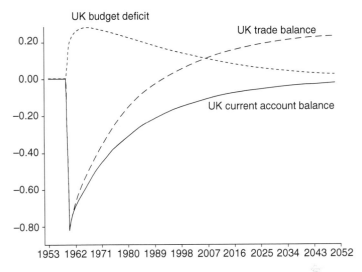

Figure 12.5A Effect of a decrease in the UK propensity to export, within a flexible exchange rate regime, on various UK variables: current account balance, trade balance and government budget deficit

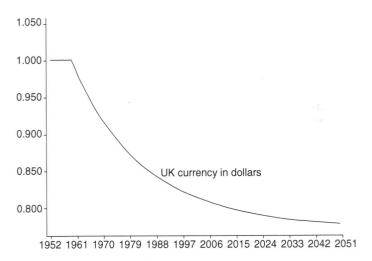

Figure 12.5B Effect on the sterling exchange rate of a decrease in the UK propensity to export, within a flexible exchange rate regime

Figure 12.5C Effect of a decrease in the UK propensity to export, within a flexible exchange rate regime, on various UK price indices: export prices, import prices and domestic sales prices

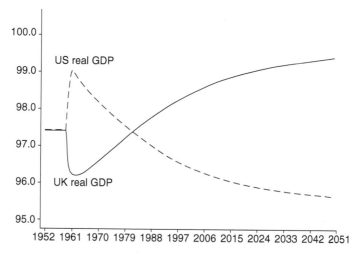

Figure 12.5D Effect of a decrease in the UK propensity to export, within a flexible exchange rate regime, on the UK and US real GDP

exceed real imports in the new steady state. As the trade balance goes into a surplus position, the total demand for domestic product rises above what it was in the first place (with our parameters).

12.7.2 A step increase in US government expenditures

Let us now turn to the US economy, and assume that the US government decides to increase it real public expenditures $g^\$$. Real output in the US rises, as can be seen in Figure 12.6A. As a result, US imports rise and the US current account balance becomes briskly negative, as shown in Figure 12.6B.[16] In addition, taxes collected in the US rise (because of the rise in GDP) but less that government expenditures, so the US government budget goes into deficit. This means that there has to be an increase in the stock of bills issued by the US Treasury. Because $B^\$_{\$\,d}/V^\$$ and $H^\$_d/V^\$$ are fixed (there being no change in interest rates by assumption, and since we simplified by assuming away the transactions demand for money), the net accumulation of financial assets by US households is insufficient to absorb all the bills being newly issued by the US Treasury. As a result, there has to be an increase in $B^\$_{\pounds\,s}$, the amount of US Treasury bills which are supplied abroad. But a similar situation is occurring in the United Kingdom. Because interest rates are fixed, $B^\$_{\pounds\,d}/V^\pounds$ and $B^\pounds_{\pounds\,d}/V^\pounds$ are also both fixed, as shown in Figure 12.6C. In addition, because the one-period change in UK output is small, the demand by UK households for Treasury bills issued by the US government, $B^\$_{\pounds\,d}$, hardly changes. The increase in the supply of these US Treasury bills to foreign households, as can be seen also in Figure 12.6C, must thus be absorbed through a change in the exchange rate. The exchange rate, $xr^\$$, as can be deduced from equation (12.89FL), must fluctuate in a way which makes the supply of US Treasury bills abroad equal to the overseas demand for them, when expressed in the same currency. In other words, $xr^\$$ – the dollar exchange rate (the value of the dollar in £ currency) depreciates, as shown in Figure 12.6D.

Next, the change in the exchange rate feeds into both import functions, reducing the import propensity in the United States and raising it in the United Kingdom, thus eventually generating a balanced current account (Figure 12.6B). In addition, the falling dollar generates capital losses for UK residents and capital gains for US residents. These revaluations of wealth stocks will feed into the asset demands in both countries in the same period, and affect consumption expenditures in the succeeding period, through a wealth effect. While the responses in the two countries are symmetrical they

---

[16] There is initially a relatively small increase the output of the UK because its exports have increased, as can be seen in Figure 12.6A. Its budget position improves, but only by a very small amount.

482

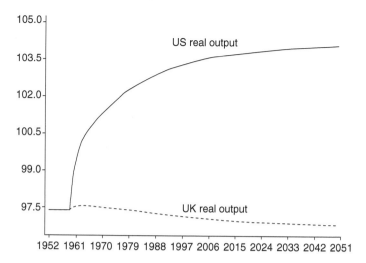

Figure 12.6A Effect of a step increase in real US government expenditures, within a flexible exchange rate regime, on the US and UK real GDP

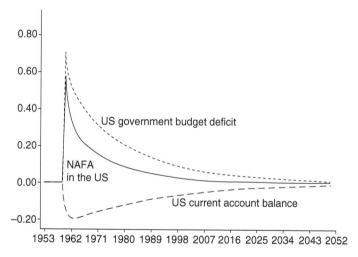

Figure 12.6B Effect of a step increase in real US government expenditures, within a flexible exchange rate regime, on the main US balances: net accumulation of financial assets, government budget deficit, current account balance

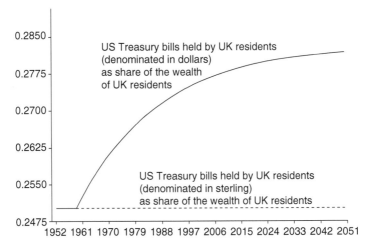

Figure 12.6C Effect of a step increase in real US government expenditures, within a flexible exchange rate regime, on the share of the wealth of UK residents held in the form of US Treasury bills, when denominated in dollars and then in sterling

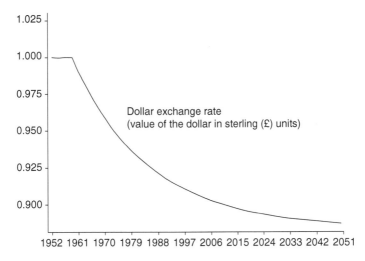

Figure 12.6D Effect on the dollar exchange rate of a step increase in real US government expenditures, within a flexible exchange rate regime

will not in general be identical. The coefficients in the asset demand functions will in general be entirely different as between the two countries, yet there has to be only a single exchange rate to satisfy all the relevant responses.

The one-period solution which this model generates when shocked does not, in general, simultaneously generate a new overall stationary state in which the balance of payments imbalance is eliminated. Rather a new current account deficit/surplus will occur which will in turn generate a new, and similar, set of responses. So long as the exogenous variables do not change, the exchange rate will go on falling at a reducing rate until a new full stationary state is achieved. Fiscal policy and also monetary policy in the form of interest rates both remain under the full control of each government.

The result that we achieved with fiscal policy could be derived from the standard IS-LM-BP graph of a modified Mundell–Fleming model. Assume that the LM curve is flat, while the other two curves have their usual shapes. An increase in government expenditures shifts the IS curve to the right, thus leading to a new internal equilibrium which is situated below the BP curve, inducing a depreciation of the domestic currency and hence inducing further rightward shifts of the IS and BP curves. This reverses the standard results achieved with the Mundell–Fleming model, where fiscal policy is relatively ineffective with flexible exchange rates. In addition, higher government expenditures here lead to a depreciation of the domestic currency, because of the induced trade deficit. By contrast (provided the BP curve is flat, when securities are perfect substitutes, or at least flatter than the LM curve), the Mundell–Fleming model concludes that higher government expenditures lead to an appreciation of the domestic currency, arising from a capital account surplus. This surplus is generated by higher interest rates, caused by crowding-out, a result that arises from the unrealistic assumption that central banks hold the money supply constant despite an increased demand for money.

12.7.3   Liquidity preference and exchange rate expectations

Changes in interest rates, liquidity preference or exchange rate expectations can all be represented within a similar framework. An increase in the liquidity preference of asset holders in favour of US Treasury bills (through the constants λ_{i0}) and an expected increase in the dollar exchange rate, just as an increase in the interest rate on US Treasury bills, lead to an attempt by households to increase their share of US securities in their portfolios.

The rise in the desire of investors to hold US assets immediately leads to a brisk hike in the dollar exchange rate, the value of the dollar in sterling units. In other words, there is a sudden appreciation of the dollar, as can be seen in Figure 12.7A. As Figure 12.7B shows, and as is implied by the portfolio equations, the share of dollar bills in UK resident portfolios immediately rises and that of UK bills in UK resident portfolios falls by an equivalent amount so long as both shares are measured in sterling. However this conceals the fact

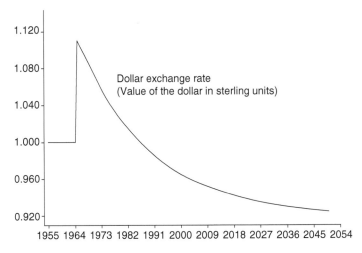

Figure 12.7A   Effect on the dollar exchange rate of an increase in the desire to hold US Treasury bills, within a flexible exchange rate regime

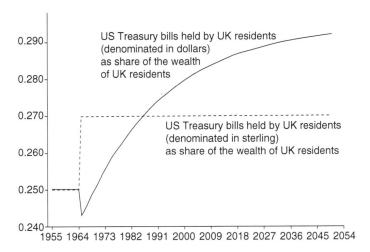

Figure 12.7B   Effect of an increase in the desire to hold US Treasury bills, within a flexible exchange rate regime, on the share of the wealth of UK residents held in the form of US Treasury bills, when denominated in dollars and then in sterling

that because the exchange rate has changed, the share of US bills measured in dollars initially falls, rising only at a later stage. The initial fall is due to the fact that, since there is an approximately constant supply of US Treasury bills in the entire world, not all households will succeed in increasing their share of wealth held in the form of US Treasury bills, when measured in dollars, since US residents are also increasing their share of US Treasury bills. UK residents will thus initially hold fewer US Treasury bills, when measured in dollars, but they will succeed in holding more of them, when measured in their domestic currency. This will be achieved through an appreciated dollar.

Such changes induce a momentary slowdown of the US economy (and a momentary boost of the UK economy) through the exchange rate channel (Figure 12.7C). The stronger dollar will disturb the whole system by generating fiscal and trade imbalances (Figure 12.7D). US residents will experience capital losses on their holdings of foreign Treasury bills due to the depreciation of the sterling currency. US residents will thus save more on their regular income, generating a net accumulation of financial assets that will also slow down the US economy. One period later, because the stronger dollar induces higher US imports, the US economy will start running a current account deficit. The latter, along with the slowdown in US consumption, reduce US GDP and propel the US government budget into deficit. Because of this, US Treasury bills will have to be newly issued. The system, by inducing a US government deficit (see Figure 12.7D), creates the US government assets that the investors desire. The outstanding stock of $B_S^\$$ will rise gradually, and thus respond to the higher demand for this security.

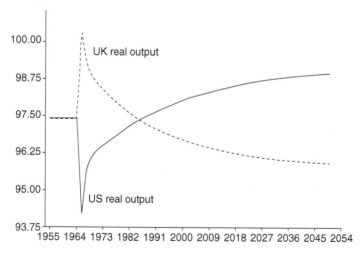

Figure 12.7C   Effect on UK and US real GDP of an increase in the desire to hold US Treasury bills, within a flexible exchange rate regime

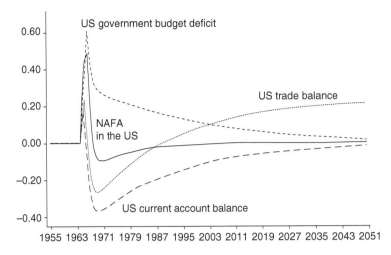

Figure 12.7D   Effect of an increase in the desire to hold US Treasury bills, within a flexible exchange rate regime, on various US variables: net accumulation of financial assets, government budget deficit, current account balance and trade balance

As a result, the value of the dollar will revert towards its original value (Figure 12.7A), and so will US real output (Figure 12.7C). Indeed, because of the additional costs of servicing the now larger external debt, the US current account balance will be brought back to zero only if the trade balance remains positive, as can be seen from Figure 12.7D. As a consequence, the new steady state value of the dollar exchange rate is lower than its original steady state value, and the new US GDP steady state value is higher than what it was before the change in portfolio preferences.

12.8   Lessons to be drawn

We have presented a model of a two-country economy that makes up a whole world. The model is set up with one country, the 'US', which provides Treasury bills which are accepted as a reserve asset by the central bank of the other country. Goods are freely traded, and financial assets, although they are not perfect substitutes, are freely exchanged between countries. The main model and its alternative closures are all based on a rigorous and watertight system of stock and flow accounts. Income, consumption, government deficits, exports and imports of both countries are all endogenous variables in these models, as are the various price indices. In addition, wealth, the stock of money and the stock of bills held by households, or the stock of bills held by the central banks are all endogenous variables. Depending on the chosen closure, foreign reserves, the exchange rate or one rate of interest can be made endogenous. The model evolves through time, solving dynamically from one period to the next.

In the main model with fixed exchange rates, we have shown that it is perfectly feasible for a country like the United States to run a trade deficit, as well as a current account deficit, while setting the rate of interest of its choice and without losing any control over the supply of high-powered money. Reciprocally, when other countries are running current account surpluses or balance of payments surpluses, their central banks can also peg interest rates at the level of their choice while still keeping the supply of money in line with the demand for it arising from private agents. Despite the fact that growing interest payments will enlarge the US current account deficit at an exponential rate, GDP and the stock of high-powered money will converge to constant levels in both countries. On the other hand, when countries other than the US run balance of payments deficits, pressures to modify fiscal or monetary policy, or to move unto a floating exchange regime will be mounting, as official reserves gradually vanish and approach some minimal level.

Our view of the impact of balance of payments surpluses or deficits on the money stock can be contrasted with the standard view, which is conveyed by the authors of most textbooks and in the usual Mundell–Fleming IS/LM/BP model. Of course it could be objected to us that the Mundell–Fleming model is not anymore the model in use in top-tiered journals, but Isard (1995: 116) in his recent survey points out that 'the Mundell–Fleming model remains the "workhorse" in academic discussions of stabilization policy for the open economy'.

The standard view is generally justified on the basis of a partial analysis of the balance sheet of the central bank, where its assets, among them foreign reserves, are said to supply-determine the stock of money. One of these authors for instance says: 'Let us conclude this section by reiterating its central and fundamental message: in order to maintain a fixed exchange rate, a central bank must engage in foreign exchange transactions that prevent it from managing the monetary base so as to achieve other macroeconomic objectives' (McCallum 1996: 139). Our complete stock-flow model shows that such a statement is far from the truth. When the US is running a deficit and the rest of the world a surplus, central banks can clearly set interest rates at the level they feel is most appropriate. In our view, there is no 'price-specie flow' mechanism of any kind at work.

It is of course recognized by textbook authors that 'central bank interventions in the foreign exchange market may not affect the home-country money stock if they are sterilized' (McCallum 1996: 138). But such sterilization is then said to be 'weak and short-lived', or it is claimed that such 'sterilization' will lead to modified holdings by the private sector of claims on the US government or on foreign governments (Isard 1995: 140–3). We have argued in contrast that the so-called sterilization process is entirely self-contained and affects neither the flows nor the stocks of the private economy. In addition, we object to such a process being called sterilization, and believe that the expression 'compensation' process is much more appropriate. At most, one can speak of 'endogenous sterilization'.

As long as the central bank wishes to peg the exchange rate and its main interest rate, a compensation mechanism will operate quite automatically, as part of the defensive operations conducted daily to maintain clearing balances at their required level. The central bank will neutralize the net impact of any public flow between its balance sheet and that of the financial system (through repos or any other means at its disposal) in order to keep the overnight rate (the federal funds rate) at or near its target rate (Eichner 1986; Howard 1998). In one of its background papers, the Bank of Canada (2004) explains that when it conducts exchange rate operations, moderating a decline in the Canadian dollar for instance, it must sterilize its purchases of Canadian dollars by 'redepositing the same amount of Canadian-dollar balances in the financial system', in order 'to make sure that the Bank's purchases do not take money out of circulation and create a shortage of Canadian dollars, which could put upward pressures on Canadian interest rates'. Thus sterilization is not a matter of choice, it is a necessity as long as the central bank wants to keep the interest rate at its target level.

In the rest of the paper, we have shown that the main model could be quickly modified to yield alternative closures, using the same method, with no black holes. Flexible fiscal policy yielded a stable model, while endogenous interest rates generated instability, as they did in Chapter 6. Flexible exchange rates also seemed to be conducive to stabilizing external disequilibria, as long as speculative capital markets were not taken into consideration. With the flexible exchange rate closure, we had to be very careful in distinguishing short-run effects from long-run ones.

It must be emphasized that the use of the different closures, as presented here, does not correspond in any straightforward way to different policy regimes. The closures are not in any general sense alternatives to one another. It would, for instance, be perfectly possible for a country which had a depreciating currency to switch course and use fiscal policy or put up interest rates. Government expenditures would be gradually reduced, or interest rates would be pushed up, as long as the depreciation goes on. One could also assume a fixed exchange regime, where government expenditures and interest rates are gradually modified by the fiscal and the monetary authorities in an attempt to reduce the balance of payments deficit. Our experience with various closures is that, whatever the institutional background, some results are being systematically achieved when any particular closure is being adopted.

The important thing to bring out is that, there is not, in general, as Lance Taylor (2004a) has forcefully argued, an equilibrium towards which economies and exchange rates are moving. Any attempt to model econometrically the behaviour of exchange rates on the assumption that they are moving towards some underlying rate which conforms with 'fundamentals' is likely to be doomed to failure.

Appendix 12.1: A fundamental and useful open-economy flow-of-funds identity

Here we establish a link between our theoretical framework and its practical use that one of us has pursued over the years (Godley 1999c, Godley *et al.* 2005). Flow-of-funds accounts introduce a constraint on what can happen to external and government budget deficits, once we know what is the financial position of the private sector. This constraint can be very useful when assessing the reliability of predictions made by forecasting or government agencies, and in assessing the sustainability of possible scenarios. This crucial constraint is the following relationship, here calculated for the UK (£) country:

$$NAFA^£ = PSBR^£ + CAB^£ \qquad (B12.1)$$

which can also be written as:

$$\{NAFA^£ - PSBR^£\} - CAB^£ = 0 \qquad (B12.2)$$

where *NAFA* is the net accumulation of financial assets by the private sector, *PSBR* is the public sector borrowing requirement (as already noted elsewhere) and *CAB* is the current account balance.

The first two terms, inside the French brackets, account for domestic financial saving (the net financial saving of the private sector plus that of the public sector), while the third term accounts for funds lent abroad, since we know that $CAB + KABOSE = 0$, where *KABOSE* is the overall capital account balance, or the amount of funds lent *from* abroad. Therefore $-KABOSE = CAB$ represents funds lent abroad. By definition, domestic financial saving must equal funds lent abroad, or funds borrowed from abroad must equal domestic financial dissaving.[17]

We already know what two of these three terms stand for algebraically, since we know, in the case of the UK economy, that:

$$CAB^£ = X^£ - IM^£ + r^\$_{-1} \cdot B^\$_{£s-1} \cdot xr^\$ + r^£_{-1} \cdot B^\$_{cb£s-1} \cdot xr^\$ - r^£_{-1} \cdot B^£_{\$s-1} \qquad (12.15)$$

while *PSBR* is nothing else than the amount of new bills that must be issued by the (UK) government to finance its budget deficit:

$$PSBR^£ = \Delta B^£_s = G^£ - T^£ + r^£_{-1} \cdot B^£_{s-1} - F^£_{cb} \qquad (12.13)$$

As to *NAFA*, the 'net accumulation of financial assets' or *NAFA* for short, it stands here for the *net financial saving* of the household sector. In the real world, it also includes

---

[17] We find again the twin-deficit proposition that arises in a quasi stationary state. Assuming that households accumulate no new asset, that is with $NAFA = 0$, equation (B12.1) becomes: $PSBR^£ = -CAB^£$. The public budget deficit equals the current account deficit.

the net financial saving of the corporate sector (which itself in turn could be split into non-financial and financial firms). Financial saving has to be distinguished from saving as such, since investment in tangible capital has to be subtracted from overall saving to obtain *NAFA*. In addition, even in our simplified *OPEN* models without tangible investment, *NAFA* is different from the increase in the wealth of households, ΔV, since it does not incorporate capital gains. *NAFA* thus depends on the difference between regular disposable income and consumption:

$$NAFA^£ = \left(YD_r^£ - C^£\right) \tag{B12.3}$$

We can provide two proofs that derive the flow-of-funds identity, equation (B12.1). The first one is more heuristic, while the second one closely follows the definitions given above. The heuristic proof starts from the definition of GNP, Gross *National* Income by contrast to GDP. GNP is:

$$GNP = PX + G + X - IM + YF$$

where *PX* stands for private expenditures and *YF* is net foreign income. Subtract taxes and government transfers from both sides and rearrange to get:

$$(GNP - PX - T) = (G - T) + (X - IM + YF)$$

which is identity (B12.1), since the three terms in brackets are equivalent to:

$$NAFA = PSBR + CAB$$

If we wish to get a more formal proof, we start with our previously defined *NAFA* and regular disposable income (equation 12.1), obtaining:

$$NAFA^£ = \left\{Y^£ + r_{-1}^£ \cdot B_{£\,s-1}^£ + r_{-1}^\$ \cdot B_{£\,s-1}^\$ \cdot xr^\$ - T^£\right\} - C^£$$

From the definition of national income $Y^£$, given by equations (12.45) and (12.55), we obtain:

$$NAFA^£ = \left\{C^£ + G^£ + X^£ - IM^£\right\} + \left\{- T^£ + r_{-1}^£ \cdot B_{£\,s-1}^£ + r_{-1}^\$ \cdot B_{£\,s-1}^\$ \cdot xr^\$\right\} - C^£$$

Add and subtract $r_{-1}^£ \cdot B_s^£$, remembering the extended definition of $B_s^£$, as given by the redundant equation:

$$B_s^£ = B_{£\,s}^£ + B_{\$\,s}^£ + B_{cb\,£\,s}^£ \tag{12.82A}$$

and add and subtract as well the interest payments on foreign reserves $r_{-1}^\$ \cdot B_{cb\,£\,s-1}^\$ \cdot xr^\$$ to obtain:

$$NAFA^£ = \left\{G^£ + r_{-1}^£ \cdot B_{s-1}^£ - T^£ - \left(r_{-1}^£ \cdot B_{cb\,£\,s-1}^£ + r_{-1}^£ \cdot B_{cb\,£\,s-1}^\$ \cdot xr^\$\right)\right\}$$
$$+ \left\{\left(X^£ - IM^£\right) + \left(r_{-1}^\$ \cdot B_{£\,s-1}^\$ \cdot xr^\$ + r_{-1}^\$ \cdot B_{cb\,£\,s-1}^\$ \cdot xr^\$\right)\right.$$
$$+ \left.\left(r_{-1}^£ \cdot B_{£\,s-1}^£ - r_{-1}^£ \cdot \left(B_{£\,s}^£ + B_{\$\,s}^£\right)\right)\right\}$$

Rearranging, and taking note that the term in brackets inside the first French bracket represents central bank profits, as given by equation (12.11),

$$F_{cb}^£ = r_{-1}^£ \cdot B_{cb£s-1}^£ + r_{-1}^£ \cdot B_{cb£s-1}^\$ \cdot xr^\$ \tag{12.11}$$

we do get:

$$NAFA^£ = \{ G^£ + r_{-1}^£ \cdot B_{s-1}^£ - T^£ - F_{cb}^£ \}$$
$$+ \{ (X^£ + r_{-1}^\$ \cdot B_{£s-1}^\$ \cdot xr^\$ + r_{-1}^£ \cdot B_{cb£s-1}^\$ \cdot xr^\$) - (IM^£ + r_{-1}^£ \cdot B_{\$s-1}^£) \}$$

where the two terms in French brackets turn out to be $PSBR^£$ and $CAB^£$ as described in equations (12.13) and (12.15), and hence we have proved the flow-of-funds identity:

$$NAFA^£ = PSBR^£ + CAB^£ \tag{B12.1}$$

Appendix 12.2: An alternative flexible exchange rate closure

In view of the fact that the UK central bank holds part of its foreign reserves in the form of US bills that carry interest payments in dollars, it could be objected (as was done by Mathieu Lequain) that foreign reserves need not stay constant in a flexible exchange rate closure. The UK central bank could decide to retain the interest payments that it receives in US dollars from the US government, thus purchasing additional US Treasury bills in every period and making additions to its stock of foreign reserves. Such a closure will lead to a quasi stationary state, since some stocks of assets will be slowly changing through time, but the logic of the flexible exchange rate model will remain the same. Three equations need to be modified to complete this alternative closure. First, the stock of foreign reserves becomes endogenous instead of being constant, so that equation (12.91FL) becomes:

$$\Delta B_{cb£s}^\$ = r_{-1}^\$ \cdot B_{cb£s-1}^\$$$

Since the UK central bank is using its inflow of foreign interest payments to acquire foreign reserves, this interest flow is not used anymore to distribute profits to the UK government. As a result, the interest income paid out to the UK government, previously given by equation (12.11), gets reduced to the interest payments obtained from domestic sources:

$$F_{cb}^£ = r_{-1}^£ \cdot B_{cb£s-1}^£$$

Finally, we must incorporate the fact that the net wealth of the UK central bank increases whenever it declines to distribute all of its profits. The best way to take this into account is to revert once again to the constraint of the transactions-flow matrix (Table 12.2). Equation (12.84), under the new conditions, now becomes:

$$\Delta B_{cb£d}^£ = \Delta H_s^£ - \Delta B_{cb£s}^\$ \cdot xr^\$ - \Delta or^£ \cdot p_g^£ + r_{-1}^\$ \cdot B_{cb£s-1}^\$ \cdot xr^\$$$

so that, given the first of our three equations, this reverts back to equation (12.84FL).

13
General Conclusion

13.1 Unique features of the models presented here

We now wish to recapitulate the main features of our method and of our models. Since it was argued in Chapter 1 that our method shared many features with Tobin's New Haven approach, we shall emphasize here how and why our models are still distinct from those of Tobin. Indeed, we strongly believe that the *closure* of our models, as well as their *spirit*, make them indeed quite distinct. The reader having now gone through the various chapters and experiments that were conducted there should be able to appreciate the distinctions that we are about to claim. It should be understood that in several instances it is the features of the more sophisticated and realistic models, those presented in the later chapters, that are under consideration. We shall refer to the models enclosed in the present book as the G&L models.

13.1.1 General features

We first start with general considerations, which in fact transpire from the general statements regarding post-Keynesian theory that were made in the previous section.

G1. *The G&L models provide a fully explicit traverse towards the stationary state.* This point has already been made. In the works of Tobin, one-period models are still given an enormous amount of attention; the steady state solution is assessed, but how it is reached is usually left rather vague.[1]

G2. *The G&L models rely on procedural rationality, with agents reacting to past disequilibria relative to norms.* This point has also been made in the

---

[1] This is also the opinion of Randall Wray (1992: 86), who writes that in Tobin's approach, 'flow variables are exogenous, so that the model focus is solely on portfolio decisions'.

preceding subsection. Tobin's models usually assume profit maximization and access to an unlikely amount of information.

G3. *In the G&L models, institutions are not 'veils'.* Institutions have a life and
a rationality of their own. They are not intermediaries acting on behalf
of individuals. Several instances will be offered below, and contrasted to
the Tobinesque veils.

G4. *In the G&L models, market clearing through prices only occurs in some specific
financial markets.* Prices are generally administered, by business firms,
financial institutions or even the monetary authorities. In the goods
market, there is no market clearing at all: produced goods may be unsold,
and fluctuations of inventories are a key part of the analysis. This is in
clear contrast to the standard Tobinesque closure, where changes in asset
prices and changes in rates of return provide the main market-clearing
mechanism.

G5. *The G&L models are demand-led.* Supply constraints are conventionally modelled as fuelling inflation, at least when the rates of capacity
utilization or the rates of unemployment move out of a certain range.

G6. *G&L models provide inflation-accounted measures of the main variables.*
Besides real output measures, the real counterparts of disposable income,
assets and liabilities in periods of inflation are computed. The precise
conditions under which inflation is neutral are being assessed.

13.1.2 Features tied to households

We now move to some exemplars of the general statements made above.
We shall divide these examples along sector lines. We start with households,
and then move on to business firms and finally to banks and the monetary
system.

H1. *In G&L models, households make their consumption and portfolio decisions
sequentially.* The consumption decision is made on the basis of a
Modigliani-type consumption function, with disposable income or
expected disposable income and past accumulated wealth as the main
two arguments of the function. This generates an expected saving level
for the period, which, once added to past wealth, generates the expected
end-of-period wealth. Portfolio decisions – the relative proportions of the
different assets – are then taken on the basis of this expected wealth. This
framework allows us to keep a fairly standard consumption function, as
does Fair (1984: ch. 3), but in contrast to Fair it also allows us to keep a
large set of distinct financial assets. Broadly speaking, this was also the
framework advocated by Backus *et al.* (1980: 273) in the US empirical version of Tobin's model. In his theoretical work however, Tobin assumes
that consumption is a residual: it is the amount of income which is
left over once households have purchased all the additional financial

assets that they desire to acquire (their saving of the period). In that theoretical framework, everything seems to happen at once: time is condensed by the need for market clearing. One would achieve the steady state at once. To reintroduce some duration, Tobin is forced to introduce the hypothesis that households cannot achieve the desired asset ratios immediately, due to the existence of high transaction costs – a hypothesis that appears highly artificial and unlikely in today's computerized world.

H2. *In G&L models, households can make mistakes or make errors in expectations.* As pointed out above, households make consumption and asset purchase decisions on the basis of expectations. Adaptative expectations or random errors can be modelled. No such mistakes appear in Tobin's models.

H3. *In G&L models, cash money or money deposits act as a buffer for households.* Whenever there are mistaken expectations, something must give way. In our models, when revenues are overestimated for instance, household cash balances or deposit balances at the bank get reduced to absorb the unexpected shortfall, as would happen in real life. No such mechanism exists in Tobin's world, although this drawback is recognized by Backus *et al.* (1980: 288) when they mention that demand deposits and currency ought to serve as 'buffers or temporary abodes of purchasing power', pointing out that 'the partial adjustment assumption seems particularly inappropriate' in this case.

13.1.3   Features tied to producing firms

Let us now move to the description of business firms – non-financial firms to be explicit – to show that business firms in our models are institutions that have a life of their own, rather than simply being veils. Because producing firms are institutions, they must take a variety of decisions, which, we assume, are not based on standard profit-maximizing principles, and which may become intertwined nevertheless.

F1. *In G&L models, firms must take a production decision.* In the simplest models, firms simply produce what is demanded. In the more sophisticated models with inventories, firms must assess the demand of the period and they must also decide on the additional inventories that they would like to hold. The decision to produce is thus intertwined with the decision to accumulate circulating capital. Mistakes in expectations can also be introduced at this stage.

F2. *In G&L models, firms must decide on fixed capital investment and/or investment in inventories.* In Tobin's models, as well as in several other neo-classical models, fixed capital investment relies on q theory. In a non-growing world, it is claimed that net investment should be positive whenever the q ratio is above unity, that is, whenever the stock market values equities at more than the replacement cost of tangible capital. The logic of such an investment behaviour is that it would be conducive to the shareholders potentially maximizing the value of their equity. Clearly, in that instance, firms act as a veil, acting in the interest of households. By contrast, in G&L models, firms invest on the basis of stock-flow norms, assessed on the basis of expected sales. Investment behaviour is essentially demand-led, as is the rest of the model.

F3. *In G&L models, firms must make pricing decisions.* In the simplest G&L models and in some variants of Tobin's models, the price level is arbitrary and fixed. In the rest of Tobin's models, the price level is determined by a market-clearing mechanism, which clears the demand for and the supply of goods. In all these models, no pricing decision needs to be taken; the market does it or it is entirely arbitrary. In the more sophisticated G&L models, the pricing mechanism is essentially an income distribution mechanism, which distributes income between labour wages, entrepreneurial profits and creditors' interest receipts. Pricing arbitrates the income distribution conflicts between different categories of stakeholders. As pointed out earlier, pricing is based on cost-plus principles, whereby unit costs are assessed and a costing margin is calculated to yield a share of sales or a target profit level. In our ultimate closed-economy model, this target profit level is designed to provide a reasonable dividend yield as well as to provide internal funds to finance capital accumulation.

F4. *In G&L models, firms must make costing decisions.* These decisions are relatively simple when production takes no time and when wage rates remain constant. However, when wage inflation sets in, when there exists inventories, and hence when time must be taken into consideration, the computation of varying unit costs becomes a more complicated task. The more sophisticated G&L models provide what we believe to be fully coherent answers to this costing issue.

F5. *In G&L models, firms must take financial decisions.* In a Tobinesque world, firms are indifferent between finance by loans or finance by issuing equities. Only expected financing costs matter. In our models, there is a hierarchy of financing means, and decisions do have consequences. Firms can decide whether they wish to issue more shares or issue or retire corporate paper or simply draw on their banking line of credit. Producing firms also accumulate retained earnings, as do firms in Backus *et al.* (1980). The problem with the Backus *et al.* presentation, however, is that no sooner were retained earnings and financial decisions introduced as a highly realistic element of their model that another hypothesis cancelled the realism of their firms. Indeed, Backus *et al.* (1980: 266) assume that retained earnings are 'dividends paid matched by sales of shares'. In other words, 'business retained earnings ... are imputed to shareowners ... as if they were dividends ... . Retention of earnings is an issue of equity by business and a purchase of equity by households and other shareowners' (ibid: 268) – a view which can be attributed to Miller and Modigliani (1961). The water-tight accounting of our models, as well as the presence of institutions *qua* institutions, does not require such a strange hypothesis.

13.1.4 Features tied to banks and the monetary system

Dealing with financial decisions leads us to discuss the role of banks in G&L and in Tobin's models. We now move to the last set of key features that differentiate the revived New Cambridge school, as presented in this book, and the New Haven approach. Once again, the emphasis will reside in the fact that banks are institutions *qua* institutions, and not a veil.

B1. *In G&L models, banks are creators of credit-money, and they play an essential systemic role.* This must be contrasted to the role of banks in most of Tobin's models. Banks in his models are presented as a simple veil, that provide households with the opportunity to enhance their choice of assets. As is clear in Brainard and Tobin (1968), banks, like households, are assumed to make portfolio asset choices, based on rates of return, among free reserve assets, loans and government bills. Loans play no special role in this approach – they have no priority – and banks could as well be a non-banking financial institution.[2] This impression is reinforced by a reading of Tobin (1982a), where bank loans are omitted altogether from the formal model. When banks are mentioned, it is claimed that the 'traditional business of commercial banks is to accept deposits ... and to acquire assets of less liquidity and maturity ... . Other intermediaries likewise transform their assets into forms better tailored ... to the preferences and circumstances of their creditors' (1982: 193).[3] Backus *et al.* (1980: 265) also formally describe banks as pure intermediaries, but they do concede that, more realistically, bank loans play

---

[2] 'In the perception I at present have, and which may turn out to be quite misguided, Tobin never makes the final step – essential to my story here – where bank loans are required to enable industry to function at all; the raison d'être of Tobin's banks, *so far as I can see*, is to enlarge the asset choice of households and facilitate the agility with which it can be made' (Godley 1997: 49).

[3] Once again Wray (1992: 87) views Tobin's work in the same light as we do. Wray writes: 'Although Tobin argues that his model incorporates an endogenously determined money supply, money is not endogenous in any meaningful sense. Tobin allows for portfolio decisions of wealth holders to affect the ability of banks to lend by determining the size of the "deposit multiplier". However, because he has assumed that spending is exogenously determined, the money supply in his model is not endogenously increased as spending rises. Banks in his model passively accept the quantity of deposits, then allocate these deposits among excess reserves, bonds and loans

a special role in monetary production economy, admitting that 'banks regard business loans as a prior claim on their disposable funds, and meet these demands at the prevailing rate, only later adjusting this rate in the direction that brings loan demand closer to the bank's desired supply'. This 'more realistic' accommodating bank behaviour is more in line with the role of banks in G&L models, which to some extent resemble the banks described by Fair (1984: 72).

B2. *In G&L models, bank loans to firms act as a buffer for the fluctuations in inventories and are required for dividends to be distributed.* In our models, inventories or unsold production, must be financed by bank loans, otherwise the profits of producing firms, as assessed by accountants, just could not be distributed to shareholders. The money to be distributed would not be there. G&L models are consistent with the monetary circuit view of the economy, where production must be initially financed by bank loans to get the ball rolling (Graziani 1990). Under this view, the predominant role of banks is to create loans, providing credit to firms who carry on production in a world where goods take time to be produced and sold. In the simplest models, bank loans have to finance inventories of producing firms.

B3. *In G&L models, banks take pricing decisions: they set deposit and lending rates.* By contrast, in Tobinesque models, deposit and lending rates are market clearing prices, which adjust the demand for and supply of deposits and loans respectively. In the simplest G&L models, lending rates are set as a mark-up over deposit rates. In the more realistic model, lending rates are such that they allow banks to attain their target level of profits, as was the case with the prices set by producing firms. As to deposit rates, it is assumed, as in Godley (1999a), that deposit rates are hiked up or pushed down whenever the banks liquidity ratio goes outside its target range. There is thus some relationship with the Tobinesque assumption that banks target some loans to asset ratio, but the deposit rate is not market clearing in any sense.

B4. *In G&L models, various institutional features can be easily introduced.* It is possible to introduce compulsory reserve requirements, capital adequacy ratios, central bank advances, bank profits, bank retained earnings and bank equity issues. It is also possible to introduce consumer credit by banks to households or to assume that firms hold monetary or financial assets besides their fixed tangible capital. One could also trigger thresholds, whereby consumer credit or bank loans to firms would be cut off whenever some ratio is exceeded, as in Le Héron (2006) and Charpe

(Tobin [and Brainard 1969]). Thus Tobin's approach really does not deviate significantly from the exogenous approach, in which "deposits make loans". In contrast the post-Keynesian endogenous money approach insists that "loans make deposits" (Wray, 1990; Moore, 1988)'.

(2006). The simulation method is highly flexible as long as proper accounting is taken care of.

M1. *In G&L models, monetary authorities take pricing decisions.* In our models, just as in the real world, central banks set the bill rate.[4] To achieve this, the central bank must be prepared to purchase or sell any residual amount of Treasury bills. This is clearly consistent with the approach taken by central banks nowadays, since they now attach very little importance to monetary aggregates, while all of their announcements are concerned with interest rate setting (and inflation rate targets). We believe that it never was any different, even at the height of monetarism, since central banks tried to achieve the announced money targets by modifying short-term interest rates, on the basis of elusive money demand functions.

M2. *In G&L models, the entire monetary system is 'accommodative' or 'passive': financial liabilities are supplied on demand.* We believe this is a requirement of a well-functioning capitalist economy. It is a systemic requirement. To assume that high-powered money and the money supply are given is a serious mistake. Even though the system is accommodative, interest rates may still fluctuate provided the various financial actors, such as banks or the monetary authorities, entertain norms with regard to various liquidity ratios. In Tobin's models, although the money supply appears to be endogenous, ultimately it is not: the New Haven models, as in Tobin (1982a: 182) and Backus *et al.* (1980: 267), assume that a *given fixed* proportion of the government deficit is being monetized, which goes against the principle of a truly demand-led endogenous supply of money.

13.2 A summary

The sketch of what an alternative monetary theory ought to look like, as has been presented in this book, had been put forward by Godley (1992: 199–200). We reproduce below its ten main elements, without further comment, in the belief that they provide a fair summary of the content of the book and of our intentions when writing it.

1. Institutions, in particular industrial corporations and banks, have a distinct existence and motivation;
2. The production process must be seen as taking time, and hence requires credit and is tied to the monetary system;

---

[4] In reality, central banks set the target overnight rate (or target one-day repo rate), with the overnight rate closely tracking this target rate, leaving the bill rate adjust to the overnight rate. But the introduction of the overnight rate in a model such as ours would require at least two sets of banks, so that one set could borrow from the other.

3. A realistic model must start with a comprehensive system of national accounts, flows of funds and balance sheets, which are coherently related;
4. Hypothetical equilibrium conditions should be conceived in terms of real stock-flow ratios;
5. The entire system of accounts needs to be inflation accounted;
6. Both closed and open economies should be modelled, so as to highlight different features;
7. Firms operate under conditions of imperfect competition and non-decreasing returns;
8. Pricing decisions are inter-related with growth and adequate finance;
9. Government budgetary policy plays a key role;
10. Inflation may be generated out of a struggle for shares of the real national income.

References

Allen, P.R. and P.B. Kenen (1980) *Asset Markets and Exchange Rates: Modelling an Open Economy* (Cambridge: Cambridge University Press).

Amirault, D., C. Kwan and G. Wilkinson (2004–2005) 'A survey of the price-setting behaviour of Canadian companies', *Bank of Canada Review*, Winter, pp. 29–40.

Andrews, P.W.S. (1949) 'A reconsideration of the theory of the individual business', *Oxford Economic Papers*, 1 (1) (January), pp. 54–89.

Andrews, P.W.S. and E. Brunner (1975) *Studies in Pricing* (London: Macmillan).

Arestis, P. and A.S. Eichner (1988) 'The post-Keynesian and Institutionalist theory of money and credit', *Journal of Economic Issues*, 22 (4), pp. 1003–21.

Backus, D., W.C. Brainard, G. Smith and J. Tobin (1980) 'A model of U.S. financial and nonfinancial economic behavior', *Journal of Money, Credit, and Banking*, 12 (2) (May), pp. 259–93.

Bain, A.D. (1973) 'Survey in applied economics: Flow of funds analysis', *Economic Journal*, 322 (December), pp. 1055–93.

Baker, D. (1997) 'Conceptual and accounting issues in the analysis of saving, investment, and macroeconomic activity', in R. Pollin (ed.), *The Macroeconomics of Saving, Finance, and Investment* (Ann Harbor: Michigan University Press), pp. 35–82.

Bank of Canada (2004) 'Intervention in the foreign exchange market', http://www.bankofcanada.ca/en/backgrounders/bg-e2.htm

Barnes, M.L. and G.P. Olivei (2003) 'Inside and outside bounds: Estimates of the Phillips curve', *New England Economic Review*, pp. 3–18.

Basel Committee on Banking Supervision (1988) *International Convergence of Capital Measurement and Capital Standards* (Basel: Bank for International Settlements).

Basel Committee on Banking Supervision (2005) *Basel II: International Convergence of Capital Measurement and Capital Standards: A Revised Framework* (Basel: Bank for International Settlements) http://www.bis.org/

Bibow, J. (2000) 'On exogenous money and bank behaviour: The Pandora's box kept shut in Keynes's theory of liquidity preference?', *European Journal of History of Economic Thought*, 7 (4) (Winter), pp. 532–68.

Bispham, J. (1975) 'The "New Cambridge" and "Monetarist" criticisms of "Conventional" economic policy making', *National Institute Economic Review*, November, pp. 39–55.

Blinder, A.S. (1991) 'Why are prices sticky? Preliminary results from an interview study', *American Economic Review*, 81 (2) (May), pp. 89–96.

Blinder, A.S. and R.M. Solow (1973) 'Does fiscal policy matter?', *Journal of Public Economics*, 2 (4) (November), pp. 319–37.

Bloch, H. and M. Olive (1996) 'Can simple rules explain pricing behaviour in Australian manufacturing', *Australian Economic Papers*, 35 (June), pp. 1–19.

Bloomfield, A.I. (1959) *Monetary Policy under the International Gold Standard: 1880–1914* (New York: Federal Reserve Bank of New York).

Boulding, K.E. (1944) 'A liquidity preference theory of market prices', *Economica*, 11 (May), pp. 55–63.

Brainard, W.C. and J. Tobin (1968) 'Pitfalls in financial model building', *American Economic Review*, 58 (2) (May), pp. 99–122.

Branson, W.H. and D.W. Henderson (1985) 'The specification and influence of asset markets', in R. Jones and P.B. Kenen (eds), *Handbook of International Economics*, volume 2 (Amsterdam: North Holland), pp. 749–805.

Buiter, W.H. (2003) 'James Tobin: An appreciation of his contribution to economics', http://www.nber.org/%7Ewbuiter/tobin.pdf

Charpe, M. (2006) 'Credit rationing, debt deflation and non performing loans in a detailed banking system: A stock-flow consistent model', Working paper, Ecole des Hautes Etudes en Sciences Sociales, Paris.

Chiang, A.C. (1984) *Fundamental Methods of Mathematical Economics*, 3rd edition (London: McGraw-Hill).

Chiarella, C. and P. Flaschel (2000) *The Dynamics of Keynesian Monetary Growth: Macrofoundations* (Cambridge: Cambridge University Press).

Chick, V. (1992) 'Financial counterparts of saving and investment and inconsistency in a simple macro model', in P. Arestis and S.C. Dow (eds), *On Money, Method and Keynes: Selected Essays* (London: Macmillan), pp. 81–94 (first published in *Weltwirtschaftliches Archive*, 109 (4), 1973, pp. 621–43).

Chick, V. (1995) 'Is there a case for Post Keynesian economics?', *Scottish Journal of Political Economy*, 42 (1) (February), pp. 20–36.

Chick, V. and S.C. Dow (2002) 'Monetary policy with endogenous money and liquidity preference: a nondualistic treatment', *Journal of Post Keynesian Economics*, 24 (4) (Summer), pp. 587–608.

Christ, C.F. (1968) 'A simple macroeconomic model with a government budget restraint', *Journal of Political Economy*, 76 (1) (January–February), pp. 53–67.

Clévenot, M. and J. Mazier (2005) 'Investment and the rate of profit in a financial context: The French case', University of Paris-Nord.

Cohen, J. (1986) *Money and Finance: A Flow-of-Funds Approach* (Ames: Iowa State University Press).

Copeland, M.A. (1949) 'Social accounting for moneyflows', *The Accounting Review*, 24 (July), pp. 254–64, in J.C. Dawson (ed.) (1996), *Flow-of-Funds Analysis: A Handbook for Practioners* (Armonk, NY: M.E. Sharpe).

Coutts, K.J., W. Godley and G.D. Gudgin (1985) 'Inflation accounting of whole economic systems', *Studies in Banking and Finance* [Supplement to Journal of Banking and Finance] (Amsterdam: North Holland), pp. 93–111.

Coutts, K.J., W. Godley and W. Nordhaus (1978) *Industrial Pricing in the UK* (Cambridge: Cambridge University Press).

Creel, J. and H. Sterdyniak (1999) 'La politique monétaire sans monnaie', *Revue de l'OFCE*, 70 (July), pp. 111–53.

Cripps, F. and W. Godley (1976) 'A formal analysis of the Cambridge economic policy group model', *Economica*, 43 (November), pp. 335–48.

Cuthbertson, K. (1979) *Macroeconomic Policy: The New Cambridge, Keynesian and Monetarist Controversies* (London: Macmillan).

Dalziel, P. (2001) *Money, Credit and Price Stability* (London: Routledge).

Davidson, P. (1968a) 'Money, portfolio balance, capital accumulation, and economic growth', *Econometrica*, 36 (2) (April), pp. 291–321.

Davidson, P. (1968b) 'The demand and supply of securities and economic growth and its implications for the Kaldor-Pasinetti versus Samuelson-Modigliani controversy', *American Economic Association*, 58 (2) (May), pp. 252–69.

Davidson, P. (1982) *International Money and the Real World* (London: Macmillan).

Davidson, P. (1988) 'A technical definition of uncertainty and the long-run non-neutrality of money', *Cambridge Journal of Economics*, 12 (3) (September), pp. 329–37.

Davidson, P. (1994) *Post Keynesian Macroeconomic Theory* (Aldershot: Edward Elgar).

Davis, E.P. (1987) 'A stock-flow consistent macro-econometric model of the UK economy – Part I', *Journal of Applied Econometrics*, 2 (2) (April), pp. 111–32.

Dawson, J.C. (1991) 'The conceptual relation of flow-of-funds accounts to the SNA', in J.C. Dawson (ed.) (1996), *Flow-of-Funds Analysis: A Handbook for Practioners* (Armonk, NY: M.E. Sharpe), pp. 313–23.

Dawson, J.C. (ed.) (1996) *Flow-of-Funds Analysis: A Handbook for Practioners* (Armonk, NY: M.E. Sharpe).

Denizet, J. (1969) *Monnaie et financement: Essai de théorie dans un cadre de comptabilité économique* (Paris: Dunod).

Dixon, R. (1982-83) 'On the new Cambridge school', *Journal of Post Keynesian Economics*, 5 (2) (Winter), pp. 289–94.

Dobrev, D. (1999) 'The currency board in Bulgaria: Design, peculiarities and management of foreign exchange cover', Discussion Paper 9/1999 (August).

Docherty, P. (2005) *Money and Employment: A Study of the Theoretical Implications of Endogenous Money* (Cheltenham: Edward Elgar).

Dos Santos, C.H. (2002a) 'Notes on the stock-flow consistent approach to macroeconomic modelling', *Three Essays in Stock-Flow Consistent Macroeconomic Modeling*, PhD Dissertation, New School University (November).

Dos Santos, C.H. (2002b) 'Cambridge and Yale on stock-flow consistent macroeconomic modelling', *Three Essays in Stock-Flow Consistent Macroeconomic Modeling*, PhD Dissertation, New School University (November).

Dos Santos, C.H. (2005) 'A stock-flow consistent general framework for formal Minskyan analyses of closed economies', *Journal of Post Keynesian Economics* 27 (4) (Summer), pp. 711–36.

Dos Santos, C.H. (2006) 'Keynesian theorising during hard times: stock-flow consistent models as an unexplored "frontier" of Keynesian macroeconomics', *Cambridge Journal of Economics*, 30 (4) (July), pp. 541–65.

Dos Santos, C.H. and G. Zezza (2005) 'A simplified stock-flow consistent Post-Keynesian growth model', Working Paper No. 421, The Levy Economics Institute of Bard College, Annandale-on-Hudson.

Dow, S.C. (1997) 'Endogenous money', in G.C. Harcourt and P.A. Riach (eds), *A Second Edition of The General Theory*, volume 2 (London: Routledge), pp. 61–78.

Downward, P. and F. Lee (2001) 'Post Keynesian pricing theory "reconfirmed"? A critical review of *Asking About Prices*', *Journal of Post Keynesian Economics*, 23 (3) (Spring), pp. 465–84.

Duménil, G. and D. Lévy (1993) *The Economics of the Profit Rate: Competition, Crises and Historical Tendencies in Capitalism* (Aldershot: Edward Elgar).

Duménil, G. and D. Lévy (1995) 'Vrais et faux dilemmes', *Recherches économiques de Louvain*, 61 (3), pp. 359–94.

Dutt, A.K. (1992) 'Rentiers in Post-Keynesian models', in P. Arestis and V. Chick (eds), *Recent Developments in Post-Keynesian Economics* (Aldershot: Edward Elgar), pp. 95–122.

Dutt, A.K. (1997) 'Profit-rate equalization in the Kalecki-Steindl model and the over-determination problem', *The Manchester School*, 65 (4) (September), pp. 443–51.

Earley, J.S., R.J. Parsons and F.A. Thompson (1976) 'Source and use analytics', in J.C. Dawson (ed.) (1996), *Flow-of-Funds Analysis: A Handbook for Practioners* (Armonk, NY: M.E. Sharpe).

Eichner, A.S. (1976) *The Megacorp & Oligopoly: Micro Foundations of Macro Dynamics* (Cambridge: Cambridge University Press).

Eichner, A.S. (1986) 'The demand curve for money further considered', in A.S. Eichner (ed.), *Toward a New Economics: Essays in Post-Keynesian and Institutionalist Theory* (London: Macmillan), pp. 98–112.

Eichner, A.S. (1987) *The Macrodynamics of Advanced Market Economics* (Armonk, NY: M.E. Sharpe).

Eisner, R. (1996) 'The retreat from full employment', in P. Arestis (ed.), *Employment, Economic Growth and the Tyranny of the Market: Essays in Honour of Paul Davidson*, volume 2 (Cheltenham: Edward Elgar), pp. 106–30.

Fair, R. (1984) *Specification, Estimation and Analysis of Macroeconometric Models* (Cambridge: Harvard University Press).

Felipe, J. and J. McCombie (2006) 'The tyranny of identity: growth accounting revisited', *International Review of Applied Economics*, 20 (3) (July), pp. 283–99.

Filardo, A.J. (1998) 'New evidence on the output cost of fighting inflation', *Federal Reserve Bank of Kansas City Quarterly Review*, 83 (3), pp. 33–61.

Firmin, C. (2006) 'Financiarisation, accumulation et État social libéral: quelles perspectives pour les politiques keynésiennes', University of Paris-1, Paper presented at the Paris conference on *État et régulation sociale*.

Flaschel, P., R. Franke and W. Semmler (1997) *Dynamic Macroeconomics: Instability, Fluctuations and Growth in Monetary Economics* (Cambridge MA: MIT Press).

Flaschel, P., G. Gong and W. Semmler (2001) 'A Keynesian macroeconometric framework for the analysis of monetary policy rules', *Journal of Economic Behavior and Organization*, 46 (January), pp. 101–36.

Foley, D. and L. Taylor (2004) 'A heterodox growth model', Working Paper, CEPA, New School University (June).

Fontana, G. (2002) 'The making of monetary policy in endogenous money policy: An introduction', *Journal of Post Keynesian Economics*, 24 (2) (Summer), pp. 503–10.

Forman, L., M. Groves and A.S. Eichner (1985) 'The demand curve for money further reconsidered', in A.S. Eichner (ed.), *Toward a New Economics: Essays in Post-Keynesian and Institutionalist Theory* (Armonk, NY: M.E. Sharpe), pp. 98–112.

Franke, R. and W. Semmler (1991) 'A dynamical macroeconomic growth model with external financing of firms: A numerical stability analysis', in E.J. Nell and W. Semmler (eds), *Nicholas Kaldor and Mainstream Economics: Confrontation or Convergence?* (London: Macmillan), pp. 335–59.

Friedman, B. (1978) 'Crowding out or crowding in? Economic consequences of financing government deficits', *Brookings Papers on Economic Activity*, pp. 593–641.

Fullwiler, S.T. (2006) 'Setting interest rates in the modern money era', *Journal of Post Keynesian Economics*, 28 (3) (Spring), pp. 495–526.

Gandolfo, G. (1977) *Economic Dynamics: Methods and Models* (Amsterdam: North-Holland).

Garegnani, P. (1990) 'Quantity of capital', in J. Eatwell, M. Milgare and P. Newman (eds), *The New Palgrave: Capital Theory* (London: Macmillan), pp. 1–78.

Garratt, A., K. Lee, M.H. Pesaran and Y. Shin (2003) 'A long run structural macroeconomic model of the UK', *Economic Journal*, 82 (April), pp. 412–55.

Gigerenzer, G. and P.M. Todd (1999) *Simple Heuristics that Make Us Smart* (New York: Oxford University Press).

Godley, W. (1959) 'Costs, prices and demand in the short run', in M.J. Surrey (ed.), *Macroeconomic Themes* (Oxford: Oxford University Press), pp. 306–9.

Godley, W. (1983) 'Keynes and the management of real national income and expenditures', in D. Worswick and J. Trevithick (eds), *Money and the Modern World* (Cambridge: Cambridge University Press), pp. 135–78.

Godley, W. (1992) 'Wynne Godley (born 1926)', in P. Arestis and M. Sawyer (eds), *A Biographical Dictionary of Dissenting Economists* (Aldershot: Edward Elgar), pp. 193–201.

Godley, W. (1993) 'Time, increasing returns and institutions in macroeconomics', in S. Biasco, A. Roncaglia and M. Salvati (eds), *Market and Institutions in Economic Development: Essays in Honour of Paolo Sylos Labini* (New York: St Martin's Press), pp. 59–82.

Godley, W. (1996) 'Money, finance and national income determination: An integrated approach', Working Paper No. 167, The Levy Economics Institute of Bard College.

Godley, W. (1997) 'Macroeconomics without equilibrium or disequilibrium', Working Paper No. 205, The Levy Economics Institute of Bard College.

Godley, W. (1999a) 'Money and credit in a Keynesian model of income determination', *Cambridge Journal of Economics*, 23 (4) (July), pp. 393–411.

Godley, W. (1999b) 'Open economy macroeconomics using models of closed systems', Working Paper No. 285, The Levy Economics Institute of Bard College.

Godley, W. (1999c) *Seven Unsustainable Processes: Medium-Term Prospects and Policies for the United States and the World*, Strategic Analysis, The Levy Economics Institute of Bard College.

Godley, W. and F. Cripps (1974) 'Demand, inflation and economic policy', *London and Cambridge Economic Bulletin*, 84 (January).

Godley, W. and F. Cripps (1978) 'Control of Imports as a means to full employment and the expansion of world trade', *Cambridge Journal of Economics*, 2 (2), pp. 327–34.

Godley, W. and F. Cripps (1983) *Macroeconomics* (London: Fontana).

Godley, W. and C. Gillion (1965) 'Pricing behaviour in manufacturing industry', *National Institute Economic Review*, 33, pp. 43–7.

Godley, W. and A. Izurieta (2001) 'Strategic prospects and policies for the U.S. economy', Special report, The Levy Economics Institute of Bard College.

Godley, W. and M. Lavoie (2003) 'Two-country stock-flow consistent macroeconomics using a closed model within a dollar exchange regime', Cambridge Endowment for Research in Finance, Working Paper 10, University of Cambridge.

Godley, W. and M. Lavoie (2005–6) 'Comprehensive accounting in simple open economy macroeconomics with endogenous sterilization or flexible exchange rates', *Journal of Post Keynesian Economics*, 28 (2) (Winter), pp. 241–76.

Godley, W. and M. Lavoie (2006a) 'Prolegomena to realistic monetary macroeconomics: A theory of intelligible sequences', Working Paper No. 441, The Levy Economics Institute of Bard College.

Godley, W. and M. Lavoie (2006b) 'A simple model of three economies with two currencies: the *Eurozone* and the *USA*', *Cambridge Journal of Economics*, 10.1093/cje/bel 010.

Godley, W. and G. McCarthy (1998) 'Fiscal policy will matter', *Challenge*, 41 (1), pp. 38–54.

Godley, W. and W. Nordhaus (1972) 'Pricing in the trade cycle', *Economic Journal*, 82 (327) (September), pp. 853–82.

Godley, W., D.B. Papadimitriou, C.H. Dos Santos and G. Zezza (2005) *The United States and her Creditors: Can the Symbiosis Last?*, Strategic Analysis, The Levy Economics Institute of Bard College.

Godley, W. and A. Shaikh (2002) 'An important inconsistency at the heart of the standard macroeconomic model', *Journal of Post Keynesian Economics*, 24 (3) (Spring), pp. 423–42.

Godley, W. and J.R. Shepherd (1964) 'Long-term growth and short-term policy', *National Institute Economic Review*, 29, pp. 26–33.

Godley, W. and G. Zezza (2006) 'Debt and lending: a cri de coeur', Policy Note 2006/4, The Levy Economics Institute of Bard College.

Goodhart, C.A.E. (1984) *Monetary Theory and Practice: The UK Experience* (London: Macmillan).

Gray, H.P. and J.M. Gray (1988-89) 'International payments in a flow-of-funds format', *Journal of Post Keynesian Economics*, 11 (2) (Winter), pp. 241–60.

Graziani, A. (1990) 'The theory of the monetary circuit', *Économies et Sociétés*, 24 (6) (June), pp. 7–36.

Graziani, A. (2003) *The Monetary Theory of Production* (Cambridge: Cambridge University Press).

Gurley, J.G. and E.A. Shaw (1960) *Money in a Theory of Finance* (Washington, DC: Brookings Institution).

Haig, R.M. (1921) 'The concept of income – economic and legal aspects', in R.M. Haig (ed.), *The Federal Income Tax* (New York: Columbia University Press), pp. 1–21.

Hall, R.L. and C.L. Hitch (1939) 'Price theory and business behavior', *Oxford Economic Papers*, 1 (2) (May), pp. 12–45.

Hamouda, O.F. and G.C. Harcourt (1988) 'Post Keynesianism: From criticism to coherence?', *Bulletin of Economic Research*, 40 (1), pp. 1–33.

Harcourt, G.C. (1972) *Some Cambridge Controversies in the Theory of Capital* (Cambridge: Cambridge University Press).

Harcourt, G.C. (2001) *50 Years a Keynesian and Other Essays* (London: Palgrave).

Harcourt, G.C. (2006) *The Structure of Post-Keynesian Thought* (Cambridge: Cambridge University Press).

Harcourt, G.C. and P. Kenyon (1976) 'Pricing and the investment decision', *Kyklos*, 29 (3), pp. 449–77.

Harrod, R.F. (1933) *International Economics* (Cambridge: Cambridge University Press).

Hein, E. (2002) 'Monetary policy and wage bargaining in the EMU: Restrictive ECB policies, high unemployment, nominal wage restraint and inflation above the target'. *Banca del Lavoro Quarterly Review*, 222, pp. 299–337.

Henry, J. (1993) 'Post-Keynesian methods and the Post-Classical approach', *International Papers in Political Economy*, 1 (2), pp. 1–26.

Hetzel, R.L. and R.F. Leach (2001) 'The Treasury-Fed Accord: A new narrative account', *Federal Reserve Bank of Richmond Economic Quarterly*, 87 (1) (Winter), pp. 33–55.

Hicks, J.R. (1937) 'Mr Keynes and the "Classics": A suggested interpretation', *Econometrica*, 5 (April), pp. 147–59.

Hicks, J.R. (1965) *Capital and Growth* (Oxford: Oxford University Press).

Hicks, J.R. (1974) *The Crisis in Keynesian Economics* (Oxford: Basil Blackwell).

Hicks, J.R. (1989) *A Market Theory of Money* (Oxford: Clarendon Press).

Howard, D. (1998) 'A primer on the implementation of monetary policy in the LVTS environment', *Bank of Canada Review* (Fall), pp. 57–66.

Howells, P.G.A. (1999) 'The source of endogenous money', *Economic Issues*, 4 (1) (March), pp. 101–12.

Howells, P.G.A. and P. O'Hara (1999) 'Interest rates: Term structure', in P.A O'Hara (ed.), *The Encyclopedia of Political Economy* (London: Routledge), pp. 553–6.

Hubbard, R.G., K.N. Kuttner and D.N. Palia (2002) 'Are there bank effects in borrowers' costs of funds? Evidence from a matched sample of borrowers and banks', *Journal of Business*, 75 (4), pp. 559–81.

Isard, P. (1995) *Exchange Rate Economics* (Cambridge: Cambridge University Press).

Izurieta, A. (2003) 'Dollarization as a tight rein on the fiscal stance', in L.P. Rochon and M. Seccareccia (eds), *Dollarization: Lessons from Europe and the Americas* (London: Routledge), pp. 143–64.

Kahn, R.F. and M.V. Posner (1974) 'Cambridge economics and the balance of payments', *London and Cambridge Economic Bulletin*, 85 (July), pp. 19–32.

Kaldor, N. (1956) 'Alternative theories of distribution', *Review of Economic Studies*, 23 (92), pp. 83–100.

Kaldor, N. (1960) *Essays on Economic Stability and Growth* (London: Duckworth).

Kaldor, N. (1964) 'Monetary policy, economic stability and growth', in *Essays on Economic Policy*, volume 1 (London: Duckworth), pp. 128–53.

Kaldor, N. (1966) 'Marginal productivity and the macro-economic theories of distribution', *Review of Economic Studies*, 33 (October), pp. 309–19.

Kaldor, N. (1970a) 'The new monetarists', *Lloyds bank Review*, (July), pp. 1–27.

Kaldor, N. (1970b) 'The case for regional policies', *Scottish Journal of Political Economy*, 17 (3) (November), pp. 337–48.

Kaldor, N. (1980) 'Monetarism and UK monetary policy', *Cambridge Journal of Economics*, 4 (4), pp. 293–318.

Kaldor, N. (1982) *The Scourge of Monetarism* (Oxford: Oxford University Press).

Kaldor, N. (1983) 'Keynesian economics after fifty years', in D. Worswick and J. Trevithick (eds), *Money and the Modern World* (Cambridge: Cambridge University Press), pp. 1–48.

Kaldor, N. (1985) *Economics without Equilibrium* (Armonk, NY: M.E. Sharpe).

Kalecki, M. (1944) 'Professor Pigou on "The classical stationary state": A comment', *Economic Journal*, 54 (213) (April), pp. 131–2.

Kalecki, M. (1971) *Selected Essays on the Dynamics of the Capitalist Economy* (Cambridge: Cambridge University Press).

Karacaoglu, G. (1984) 'Absence of gross substitution in portfolios and demand for finance: some macroeconomic implications', *Journal of Post Keynesian Economics*, 6 (4) (Summer), pp. 576–89.

Kenen, P.B. (1985) 'Macroeconomics theory and policy: How the closed economy model was opened', in R. Jones and P.B. Kenen (eds), *Handbook of International Economics*, volume 2 (Amsterdam: North-Holland), pp. 625–77.

Keynes, J.M. (1936) *The General Theory of Employment, Interest and Money* (London: Macmillan).

Kim, J.-H. (2006a) 'A two-sector model with target-return pricing in a stock-flow consistent framework', Robinson Working Paper WP06–01, University of Ottawa.

Kim, J.-H. (2006b) 'Demand-led growth and long-run convergence in a two-sector model', Robinson Working Paper WP06–02, University of Ottawa.

King, J.E. (2003) *A History of Post Keynesian Economics since 1936* (Cheltenham: Edward Elgar).

Kirman, A. (1989) 'The intrinsic limits of modern economic theory: The emperor has no clothes', *Economic Journal*, 99 (395) (supplement), pp. 126–39.

Klein, L. (2003) 'Some potential linkages for input-output analysis with flow-of-funds', *Economic Systems Research*, 15 (3) (September), pp. 269–77.

Kregel, J. (1985) 'Hamlet without the Prince: Cambridge macroeconomics without money', *American Economic Review*, 75 (2) (May), pp. 133–39.

Lavoie, M. (1987) 'Monnaie et production: une synthèse de la théorie du circuit', *Économies et Sociétés*, 21 (9) (September), pp. 65–101.

Lavoie, M. (1992) *Foundations of Post-Keynesian Economic Analysis* (Aldershot: Edward Elgar).

Lavoie, M. (1995) 'Interest rates in post-Keynesian models of growth and distribution', *Metroeconomica*, 46 (2) (June), pp. 146–77.

Lavoie, M. (1998) 'The neo-Pasinetti theorem in Cambridge and Kaleckian models of growth and distribution', *Eastern Economic Journal*, 24 (4) (Fall), pp. 417–34.

Lavoie, M. (2000) 'A Post Keynesian view of interest parity theorems', *Journal of Post Keynesian Economics*, 23 (1) (Summer), pp. 163–79.

Lavoie, M. (2001a) 'Pricing', in R.P.F. Holt and S. Pressman (eds), *A New Guide to Post Keynesian Economics* (London: Routledge), pp. 21–31.

Lavoie, M. (2001b) 'The reflux mechanism in the open economy', in L.P. Rochon and M. Vernengo (eds), *Credit, Interest Rates and the Open Economy* (Cheltenham: Edward Elgar), pp. 215–42.

Lavoie, M. (2002–3) 'Interest parity, risk premia, and post Keynesian analysis', *Journal of Post Keynesian Economics*, 25 (2), pp. 237–50.

Lavoie, M. (2003) 'A fully coherent post Keynesian model of the euro zone', in P. Arestis, M. Baddeley and J. McCombie (eds), *Globalisation, Regionalism and Economic Activity* (Cheltenham: Edward Elgar), pp. 98–126.

Lavoie, M. (2005) 'Monetary base endogeneity and the new procedures of the asset-based Canadian and American monetary systems', *Journal of Post Keynesian Economics*, 27 (4), (Summer), pp. 689–710.

Lavoie, M. (2006a) 'Endogenous money: Accommodationist', in P. Arestis and M. Sawyer (eds), *A Handbook of Alternative Monetary Economics* (Cheltenham: Edward Elgar), pp. 17–34.

Lavoie, M. (2006b) 'Do heterodox theories have anything in common? A post-Keynesian point of view', *Intervention. Journal of Economics*, 3 (1), pp. 87–112.

Lavoie, M. (2006c) 'A fully coherent post-Keynesian model of currency boards', in C. Gnos and L.P. Rochon (eds), *Post Keynesian Principles of Economic Policy* (Cheltenham, UK and Northampton, USA: Edward Elgar), pp. 185–207.

Lavoie, M. (2006d) 'A post-Keynesian amendment to the New Consensus on monetary policy', *Metroeconomica*, 57 (2) (May), pp. 165–92.

Lavoie, M. and W. Godley (2001–2) 'Kaleckian Growth Models in a Stock and Flow Monetary Framework: A Kaldorian View', *Journal of Post Keynesian Economics*, 24 (2) (Winter), pp. 277–312.

Lavoie, M. and W. Godley (2006) 'Features of a realistic banking system within a post-Keynesian stock-flow consistent model', in M. Setterfield (ed.), *Complexity, Endogenous Money and Macroeconomic Theory: Essays in Honour of Basil Moore* (Cheltenham: Edward Elgar), pp. 251–68.

Lavoie, M. and M. Seccareccia (eds) (2004) *Central Banking in the Modern World: Alternative Perspectives* (Cheltenham: Edward Elgar).

Layard, R., S. Nickell and R. Jackman (1991) *Unemployment: Macroeconomic Performance and the Labour Market* (Oxford: Oxford University Press).

LeBourva, J. (1992) 'Money creation and credit multipliers', *Review of Political Economy*, 4 (4), pp. 447–66.

Lee, F.S. (1985) 'Full cost prices, classical price theory, and long period method analysis: A critical evaluation', *Metroeconomica*, 37 (2) (June), pp. 199–219.

Lee, F.S. (1998) *Post Keynesian Theory* (Cambridge: Cambridge University Press).

Le Héron, E. (2006) 'Liquidity preference and endogenous money: A reconciliation in a post-Keynesian stock-flow consistent model', Working paper, University of Bordeaux, paper presented at the 9th International Post Keynesian conference in Kansas City.

Lequain, M. (2003) 'A three-country study of the euro zone versus the rest of the world: The implications of a monetary union in an open environment', Working Paper, University of Ottawa, paper presented at the annual conference of the Eastern Economic Association, in New York (February).

Levy-Garboua, V. and G. Maarek (1978) 'Bank behavior and monetary policy', *Journal of Banking and Finance*, 2, pp. 15–46.

Lydall, H.F. (1958) 'Income, assets and the demand for money', *Review of Economics and Statistics*, 40 (February), pp. 1–14.

Malinvaud, E. (1982) *Théorie macroéconomique*, volume 1 (Paris: Dunod).

Malinvaud, E. (1983) 'Comment on Godley', in D. Worswick and J. Trevithick (eds), *Money and the Modern World* (Cambridge: Cambridge University Press), pp. 157–62.

McCallum, B.T. (1996) *International Monetary Economics* (Oxford: Oxford University Press).

McCombie, J.S.L. and A.P. Thirlwall (1994) *Economic Growth and the Balance-of-Payments Constraint* (New York: St Martin's Press).

Means, G. C. (1991) 'Corporate power in the marketplace', in F.S. Lee and W.J. Samuels (eds), *The Heterodox Economics of Gardiner C. Means: A Collection* (Armonk, NY: M.E. Sharpe), pp. 318–34.

Meyer, L.H. (2001) 'Does money matter?', *Federal Reserve Bank of St Louis Review*, 83 (5) (September–October), pp. 1–15.

Millar, J.R. (1996) 'Institutionalist Origins', in J.C. Dawson (ed.), *Flow-of-Funds Analysis: A Handbook for Practioners* (Armonk, NY: M.E. Sharpe), pp. 83–92.

Miller, M.H. and F. Modigliani (1961) 'Dividend policy, growth, and the valuation theorem', *Journal of Business*, 24 (October), pp. 411–33.

Minsky, H.P. (1975) *John Maynard Keynes* (New York: Columbia University Press).

Minsky, H.P. (1986) *Stabilizing an Unstable Economy* (New Haven: Yale University Press).

Minsky, H.P. (1996) 'The essential characteristics of Post Keynesian economics', in G. Deleplace and E.J. Nell (eds), *Money in Motion: The Circulation and Post-Keynesian Approaches* (London: Macmillan), pp. 532–45.

Modigliani, F. (1944) 'Liquidity preference and the theory of interest and money', *Econometrica*, 12 (January), pp. 45–88.

Modigliani, F. (1963) 'The monetary mechanism and its interaction with real phenomena', *Review of Economics and Statistics*, 45 (February), pp. 79–103.

Modigliani, F. (1986) 'Life cycle, individual thrift, and the Wealth of Nations', *American Economic Review*, 76 (3) (June), pp. 297–313.

Moore, B.J. (1988) *Horizontalists and Verticalists: The Macroeconomics of Credit Money* (Cambridge: Cambridge University Press).

Moore, B.J. (1997) 'Reconciliation of the supply and demand for endogenous money', *Journal of Post Keynesian Economics*, 19 (3) (Spring), pp. 423–8.

Moosa, I.A. (2004) 'An empirical examination of the Post Keynesian view of forward exchange rates', *Journal of Post Keynesian Economics*, 26 (3) (Spring), pp. 395–418.

Mosler, W. and M. Forstater (1999) 'A general framework for the analysis of currencies and commodities', in P. Davidson and J. Kregel (eds), *Full Employment and Price Stability in a Global Economy* (Cheltenham: Edward Elgar), pp. 166–77.

Mouakil, T. (2005) 'Les dysfonctionnements du système monétaire international: une approche post-keynésienne', University of Bordeaux.

Moudud, J.K. (1999) 'Finance in classical and Harrodian cyclical growth models', Working Paper No. 290, The Levy Economics Institute of Bard College.

Moudud, J.K. (2007) *Disequilibrium Dynamics, Stock-Flow Consistency, and Economic Policy* (Cheltenham: Edward Elgar).

Mundell, R. (1961) 'The international disequilibrium system', *Kyklos*, 14 (2), pp. 153–72.

Neild, R.R. (1963) *Pricing and Employment in the Trade Cycle* (Cambridge: Cambridge University Press).

Nurkse, R. (1944) *International Currency Experience: Lessons of the Inter-War Period* (Geneva: League of Nations).

Ott, D.J. and A.F. Ott (1965) 'Budget balance and equilibrium income', *Journal of Finance*, 20 (1), pp. 71–7.

Palacio-Vera, A. (2005) 'The "modern" view of macroeconomics: Some critical reflections', *Cambridge Journal of Economics*, 29 (5), pp. 747–67.

Palley, T. (1996) *Post Keynesian Economics: Debt, Distribution and the Macro Economy* (New York: St Martin's Press).

Papadimitriou, D.B., E. Chilcote and G. Zezza (2006) 'Are housing prices, household debt, and growth sustainable?', Strategic Analysis, Levy Economics Institute of Bard College, January.

Papadimitriou, D.B., A.M. Shaikh, C.H. Dos Santos and G. Zezza (2005) 'How fragile is the U.S. economy?', Strategic Analysis, Levy Economics Institute of Bard College, March.

Pasinetti, L.L. (1993) *Structural Economic Dynamics: A Theory of the Economic Consequences of Human Learning* (Cambridge: Cambridge University Press).

Pasinetti, L.L. (2005) 'The Cambridge school of Keynesian economics', *Cambridge Journal of Economics*, 29 (6) (November), pp. 837–48.

Patinkin, D. (1965) *Money, Interest and Prices*, 2nd edition (New York: Harper & Row).

Patterson, K.D. and M.J. Stephenson (1988) 'Stock-flow consistent accounting: A macroeconomic perspective', *Economic Journal*, 98 (September), pp. 787–800.

Peston, M. (1983) 'A failed attempt to reconstruct Keynes', *The Times*, 12 May 1983.

Pigou (1943) 'The classical stationary state', *Economic Journal*, 53 (212) (December), pp. 343–51.

Ponsot, J.-F. (2002) *Le Currency Board ou la négation de la banque centrale: Une perspective historique du régime des caisses d'émission*, PhD dissertation, Université de Bourgogne (November).

Prasad, E. and A.J. Wei (2005) 'The Chinese approach to capital inflows: Patterns and possible explanations', IMF Working Paper 05/79, IMF.

Ritter, L.S. (1963) 'A framework for financial analysis', in J.C. Dawson (ed.), (1996), *Flow-of-Funds Analysis: A Handbook for Practioners* (Armonk, NY: M.E. Sharpe), pp. 115–23.

Robinson, J. (1956) *The Accumulation of Capital* (London: Macmillan).

Robinson, J. (1982) 'Shedding darkness', *Cambridge Journal of Economics*, 6 (3) (September), pp. 295–6.

Roe, A.R. (1973) 'The case for flow of funds and national balance sheet accounts', *Economic Journal*, 83 (June), pp. 399–420.

Romer, D. (2000) 'Keynesian macroeconomics without the LM curve', *Journal of Economic Perspectives*, 14 (2) (Spring), pp. 149–69.

Rowthorn, R.E. (1977) 'Conflict, inflation and money', *Cambridge Journal of Economics*, 1 (3) (September), pp. 215–39.

Ruggles, N.D. (1987) 'Financial accounts and balance sheets: Issues for the revision of SNA', *Review of Income and Wealth*, 33 (1) (March), pp. 39–62.

Ruggles, N.D. and R. Ruggles (1992) 'A market transactions view of U.S. households', *The Review of Income and Wealth*, 38 (2) (June), pp. 119–27, in J.C. Dawson (ed.) (1996), *Flow-of-Funds Analysis: A Handbook for Practioners* (Armonk, NY: M.E. Sharpe).

Sawyer, M. (1982) *Macro-economics in Question: The Keynesian-Monetarist Orthodoxies and the Kaleckian Alternative* (Armonk, NY: M.E. Sharpe).

Seccareccia, M. (2005) 'Growing household indebtedness and the plummeting saving rate in Canada: An explanatory note', *Economic and Labour Relations Review*, 16 (1) (July), pp. 133–51.

Setterfield, M. (1993) 'Towards a long-run theory of effective demand: Modelling macroeconomic systems with hysteresis', *Journal of Post Keynesian Economics*, 15 (3) (Spring), pp. 347–64.

Setterfield, M. (2002) 'Introduction: A dissenter's view of the development of growth theory and the importance of demand-led growth', in M. Setterfield (ed.), *The Economics of Demand-led Growth: Challenging the Supply-side Vision of the Long Run* (Cheltenham: Edward Elgar), pp. 1–16.

Shaikh, A. (1974) 'Laws of algebra and laws of production: The humbug production function', *Review of Economics and Statistics*, 56 (1) (February), pp. 115–20

Shaikh, A. (1989) 'Accumulation, finance, and effective demand in Marx, Keynes, and Kalecki', in W. Semmler (ed.), *Financial Dynamics and Business Cycles: New Perspectives* (Armonk, NY: M.E. Sharpe), pp. 65–86.

Shaikh, A. (2005) 'Nonlinear dynamics and pseudo-production functions', *Eastern Economic Journal*, 31 (3) (Summer), pp. 447–66.

Simon, H.A. (1959) 'Theories of decision-making in economics and behavioral science', *American Economic Review*, 49 (3) (June), pp. 253–83.

Simons, H.C. (1938) *Personal Income Taxation: The Definition of Income as a Problem of Fiscal Policy* (Chicago, Il: Chicago University Press).

Skott, P. (1989) *Conflict and Effective Demand in Economic Growth* (Cambridge: Cambridge University Press).

Smithin, J. (1986) 'The length of the production period and effective stabilization policy', *Journal of Macroeconomics*, 8 (1) (Winter), pp. 55–62.

Solow, R.M. (1983) 'Comment on Godley', in D. Worswick and J. Trevithick (eds), *Money and the Modern World* (Cambridge: Cambridge University Press), pp. 162–68.

Sood, A. (1999) *The Economics of Government Deficits: Some Alternative Formulations with Time Series Evidence*, unpublished PhD dissertation, University of Ottawa.

Stone, R. (1947) 'Definition and measurement of the national income and related totals', appendix to *Measurement of National Income and the Construction of Social Accounts* (UN: United Nations Press).

Stone, R. (1966) 'The social accounts from a consumer's point of view', *Review of Income and Wealth*, 12 (1) (March), pp. 1–33.

Stone, R. (1973) 'Personal spending and saving in post war Britain' in H.C. Bos, H. Linneman and P. de Wolff (eds), *Economic Structure and Development: Essays in Honour of Jan Tinbergen* (Amsterdam: North Holland), pp. 75–98.

Stone, R. (1986) 'Nobel Memorial Lecture 1984: The accounts of society', *Journal of Applied Econometrics*, 1 (1) (January), pp. 5–28.

Taylor, J.B. (2000) 'Teaching modern macroeconomics at the principles level', *American Economic Review*, 90 (2) (May), pp. 90–4.

Taylor, J.B. (2004) *Principles of Macroeconomics*, 4th edition (Boston: Houghton Mifflin).

Taylor, L. (1991) *Income, Distribution, Inflation, and Growth: Lectures on Structuralist Macroeconomic Theory* (Cambridge, MA: MIT Press).

Taylor, L. (2004a) 'Exchange indeterminacy in portfolio balance, Mundell-Fleming, and uncovered interest rate parity models', *Cambridge Journal of Economics*, 28 (2), pp. 205–28.

Taylor, L. (2004b) *Reconstructing Macroeconomics: Structuralist Proposals and Critiques of the Mainstream* (Cambridge, MA: Harvard University Press).

Thirlwall, A.P. (1979) 'The balance of payments constraint as an explanation of international growth rate differences', *Banca Nazionale del Lavoro Quarterly Review*, 32 (March), pp. 45–53.

Tobin, J. (1969) 'A general equilibrium approach to monetary theory', *Journal of Money, Credit, and Banking*, 1 (1) (February), pp. 15–29.

Tobin, J. (1982a) 'Money and finance in the macroeconomic process', *Journal of Money, Credit, and Banking*, 14 (2) (May), pp. 171–204.

Tobin, J. (1982b) 'The state of exchange rate theory: Some skeptical observations', in R.N. Cooper (ed.), *The International Monetary System under Flexible Exchange Rate: Global, Regional and National. Essays in Honor of Robert Triffin* (Cambridge, MA: Ballinger), pp. 115–28.

Tobin, J. (1995) 'The natural rate as new classical macroeconomics', in R. Cross (ed.), *The Natural Rate of Unemployment: Reflections on 25 Years of the Hypothesis* (Cambridge: Cambridge University Press), pp. 32–42.

Tobin, J. and J.B. De Macedo (1980) 'The short-run macroeconomics of floating exchange rates: An exposition', in J. Chipman and C. Kindleberger (eds), *Flexible Exchange Rates and the Balance of Payments: Essays in the Memory of Egon Sohmen* (Amsterdam: North Holland), pp. 5–28.

Trivedi, P.K. (1970) 'Inventory behavior in U.K. manufacturing, 1956–1967', *Review of Economic Studies*, 37 (4) (October), pp. 517–36.

Turnovsky, S. (1977) *Macroeconomic Analysis and Stabilization Policy* (Cambridge: Cambridge University Press).

Tymoigne, É. (2006) 'System dynamics modeling of a stock-flow consistent Minskian model', paper presented at the ASSA meeting.

Vallageas, B. (2001) *Le circuit et le financement de l'économie*, Class notes for the course 'Analyse financière des entreprises et théorie économique', University of Paris-Sud.

Wood, A. (1975) *A Theory of Profits* (Cambridge: Cambridge University Press).

Wood, A. (1978) *A Theory of Pay* (Cambridge: Cambridge University Press).

Worswick D. and J. Trevithick (eds) (1983) *Money and the Modern World* (Cambridge: Cambridge University Press).

Wray, L.R. (1990) *Money and Credit in Capitalist Economies: The Endogenous Approach* (Aldershot: Edward Elgar).

Wray, L.R. (1992) 'Alternative theories of the rate of interest', *Cambridge Journal of Economics*, 16 (1) (March), pp. 69–91.

Wray, L.R. (1998) *Understanding Modern Money* (Cheltenham: Edward Elgar).

Zezza, G. and C.H. Dos Santos (2004) 'The role of monetary policy in post-Keynesian stock-flow consistent macroeconomic growth models', in M. Lavoie and

M. Seccareccia (eds), *Central Banking in the Modern World: Alternative Perspectives* (Cheltenham, UK, and Northampton, USA: Edward Elgar), pp. 183–208.

Zhao, J. (2006) 'A three-country model with fixed and flexible exchange rates under a stock-flow coherent approach', Working Paper No. 06-03, University of Ottawa.

Index

Note: Page numbers in bold refer to **tables** and **figures**

Printed and bound in the United States of America